WITHDRAWN
HARVARD LIBRARY
WITHDRAWN

The Spiritual Writings
of Pierre Favre

The Spiritual Writings
of Pierre Favre

Introduction

Edmond C. Murphy, S.J., and John W. Padberg, S.J.

The *Memoriale*

Translated by Edmond C. Murphy, S.J.

Selected Letters and Instructions

Translated by Martin E. Palmer, S.J.

The Institute of Jesuit Sources
Saint Louis 1996

Number 16 in Series I: Jesuit Primary Sources
in English Translation

BX
4705
.F23
A313
1996

© The Institute of Jesuit Sources
3700 West Pine Boulevard
Saint Louis, MO 63108
tel: [314] 977-7257
fax: [314] 977-7263

All rights reserved

Library of Congress Card Catalog Number: 96-80280
ISBN: hard cover: 1-880810-25-5
paperback: 1-880810-26-3

CONTENTS

FOREWORD vii

ABBREVIATIONS xi

INTRODUCTION

Spiritual Autobiography	1
Religion in Pre-Reformation Europe	5
Favre's Early Years in Savoy	8
The University of Paris in the Sixteenth Century	11
The First Three Companions	15
The Paris Theologian	19
Favre's Life of Ministry	24
Favre and the World of the Sixteenth Century	33
Devotion to the Angels, and the Discernment of Spirits	42
The Text of the *Memoriale*	48
The Letters and Instructions	51
At the Threshold of the Society of Jesus	53

THE *MEMORIALE*

Speyer	59
Mainz	153
Aschaffenburg	189
Mainz	203
Cologne-Louvain	273
Coimbra-Portugal	279
Évora	291
Valladolid	299
Madrid-Galapagar	309

v

Contents

Selected Letters and Instructions

To Ignatius of Loyola and Pietro Codazzo, Sept. 1, 1540	319
Rules for the Sodality of Parma, Sept. 7, 1540	321
To the First Jesuit Scholastics at Paris, May 12, 1541	323
Some Chapters on Faith and Morals, March-June 1541	326
To Alvaro Alfonso, Spring 1542	330
To Ignatius of Loyola, April 27, 1542	333
To Diego Laínez, August 30, 1542	336
To Ignatius of Loyola, Nov. 7, 1542	339
Instructions for Those Going on Pilgrimage, Spring 1543	340
To Gerhard Kalckbrenner, April 12, 1543	343
To Claude Périssin, May 28, 1543	347
To Gerhard Kalckbrenner, June 14, 1543	350
To Gerhard Kalckbrenner, July 10, 1543	351
To Cornelius Wischaven, Jan. 24, 1544	354
To Cornelius Wischaven, Jan. 1544	356
To Wendelina Van den Berg, Feb. 1544	261
To Francis Xavier, May 10, 1544	363
Aids to Self-Reformation, Spring 1544	365
To Guillaume Postel, Dec. 3, 1544	368
To the Jesuits of Coimbra, Dec. 1544	371
To the Jesuits of Coimbra, March 2, 1545	373
To King John III of Portugal, July 13, 1545	375
To Martín Santacruz, Jan. 13, 1546	378
To Diego Laínez, March 7, 1546	379
To Peter Canisius, March 10, 1546	381
To Diego Laínez, July 23, 1546	383
Teachings of Pierre Favre	385

Glossary of Names 391

Bibliography 399

Index to the *Memoriale* 407

Index to the Introduction, Letters, and Instructions 431

FOREWORD

The structure of this volume, *The Spiritual Writings of Pierre Favre,* is tripartite. First in order of appearance is the Introduction, which places the author's life and work in its historical setting. Following this is an English translation of the *Memoriale* or spiritual diary of Favre, the first companion of Ignatius of Loyola. Last of all is the first translation of certain letters and instructions, taken in all but two instances from the critical edition of Favre's writings included in the Monumenta Historica Societatis Iesu.

The greater part of the *Memoriale*, including the autobiographical introduction and the diary proper, was written in one year, from June 1542 to July 1543. Later Favre added a few further entries as occasions warranted, the last in January 1546. His purpose was spiritual clarification; he concentrated all his attention on his interior life. The *Memoriale* may be a work totally without literary grace; but it abounds in a more important quality: it reveals a power of introspective analysis unique for its age, and for this reason remains to this day probably unmatched in the literature of mysticism. Favre first recorded his life up to June 1542, so that he could recall in a spirit of thanksgiving the blessings he had received from God; the entries that then follow show him absorbed in the study of his inner experience, intent upon finding the will of God. The *Memoriale* is the kind of spiritual writing that demands the slow and meditative reading that Ludolph the Carthusian had in mind when he advised those who took up his *Life of Christ* not to read through it in a hurry but to relish a part each day, or that Ignatius of Loyola advised in his *Spiritual Exercises* when he asked the person making the Exercises to stay with or return to whatever brings relish and consolation.

The *Memoriale* itself has an unusual history: it led a hidden existence in manuscript form until the Latin text was printed privately in 1853 for use within the Society of Jesus. Then the first vernacular translation appeared, a French edition published in 1874. The Introduction to this volume goes into the history of the text in greater detail and serves as a guide to help the reader enter the world of the *Memoriale* and of the letters and instructions, of Favre's life and origins, and of sixteenth-century Europe.

The letters and instructions constitute the third part of this book. Almost immediately after the foundation of the Monumenta Historica Societatis Iesu, its editors wanted Favre's letters and other writings to be among its first publications. But, as those editors explained when the volume was finally published in 1914, over a period of twenty years the discovery of more and more source material on Favre kept delaying the completion of the volume. Finally they judged that they could no longer put off publication even if at a later date yet more material came to light. One hundred and forty-eight such documents appeared in that volume, *Fabri Monumenta*. Two other letters have been found since its publication. Almost all come under one of three headings: those meant to be of spiritual help to Catholics, those meant to assist in bringing adherents of sixteenth century Protestantism back to Catholicism, and those involved with the growth and spread of the Society of Jesus.

This volume presents in translation twenty-seven of Favre's letters and instructions. They have been chosen to exhibit the character, depth, and range of his spirituality and the methods by which he conveyed it to others.

Just as for several reasons it took the editors of the *Monumenta* many years to bring out the critically edited collection of Favre's writings, so for several reasons it has taken some years to produce this English translation of his spiritual writings. Pride of place and of thanks, of course, goes to Edmond C. Murphy, S.J. (1913–1994), of the Irish Province of the Society of Jesus for the translation of the *Memoriale* that he made more than a decade ago. That translation provided the impetus for the whole volume. Although Fr. Murphy's introduction provided information necessary if the reader was to understand and properly assimilate the *Memoriale* in its historical sixteenth-century religious context, it presented problems of source material and interpretation. Solving these problems entailed a regrettable delay in completing work on this project. Ultimately, the author of this Foreword undertook the revision of the introduction, after consulting with others who suggested further material that would aid the reader to understand more fully the sixteenth-century religious context. By far the greater part of the text of the introduction is the work of Fr. Murphy. A lesser part of that text and many of the sources to which the introduction refers are the work of the present writer. In addition, he and all the readers of this work owe a debt of gratitude to Peter J. Togni, S.J., of the University of San Francisco, who greatly assisted by clarifying, simplifying, and rearranging several parts of the Introduction.

In the course of editorial work on the *Memoriale*, it became clear that including in this volume a selection of Favre's letters and instructions would make possible an even deeper understanding both of the author's own spiritual life and experience and of his work and influence in the realm of spirituality. Martin E. Palmer, S.J., an associate editor at the Institute of Jesuit Sources, first proposed the inclusion of such documents, took on the exacting and very time-consuming task of choosing the ones that were to appear in this volume, and then translated

Favre's often very difficult text into an English both seriously faithful to the original and readily accessible to the present-day reader.

A good many from both sides of the Atlantic collaborated in the preparation of this volume. Father Murphy records his gratitude to those who assisted him in Europe, and the present writer will acknowledge those in the United States. On the Continent, Francisco Solís, S.J., of Madrid helped with the more difficult passages of Favre's Spanish; Giuseppe Mellinato, S.J., the translator of the first complete Italian version of the *Memoriale,* brought his scholarship to bear on some of the knotty points in the text. In Ireland several members of the Society of Jesus, Peadar Mac Seumais, Joseph Veale, Edward FitzGerald, Dermot Fleury, Brian Grogan, and Peter Troddyn, contributed to the quality of the translation of the *Memoriale.* Mary Purcell, author of *The Quiet Companion: Peter Favre,* provided books about Savoy and Favre's native valley; and Eilis Brennan prepared Father Murphy's typescript and encouraged him with her sustained interest as his work progressed. Finally, Father Murphy willingly acknowledged his grateful dependence on the article of Brian O'Leary, S.J., "The Discernment of Spirits in the *Memoriale* of Blessed Peter Favre." In the United States, at the Institute of Jesuit Sources, two of the present members also greatly contributed to this volume: Nicholas F. Pope, S.J., converted Father Murphy's typescript into computer format; John L. McCarthy, S.J., prepared both the *Memoriale* and the letters and instructions for final submission to the printer. A former member of the Institute, Philip C. Fischer, S.J., also gave generously of his time and expertise and in so doing contributed significantly to the editing of the *Memoriale.* E. Glenn Kerfoot, S.J., had the happy inspiration and, even better, the competence and patience to compile a glossary listing the myriad important names that appear in the texts and the Introduction.

Pierre Favre was destined to wait patiently for the recognition so much due to him. As the Introduction to this volume makes clear, more than three hundred years elapsed before he was beatified. Another forty years slipped by before his collected works were published. After another delay of more than sixty-five years was this present English translation done; finally, only after still more years could the Introduction be revised, the letters translated, and this volume be completed.

The *Memoriale* and the letters and instructions of Favre make clear how appropriate are the words of the second Scripture reading for the Eucharistic celebration of his feast day, August 2: "When I came to you, my brothers, proclaiming the mystery of God, I did not come with sublimity of words or of wisdom. For I resolved to know nothing while I was with you except Jesus Christ, and him crucified. I came to you in weakness and fear and much trembling, and my message and my proclamation were not with persuasive words of wisdom, but with a demonstration of spirit and power, so that your faith might rest not on human wisdom, but on the power of God" (1 Cor. 2:1–5). May their publication help to hasten his canonization and contribute to making him known more deeply by his fellow Jesuits and more widely in the Church and in the world.

John W. Padberg, S.J.
General Editor

August 1, 1996

The four-hundred-and-fiftieth anniversary
 of the entrance into eternal life
  of Blessed Pierre Favre
  of the Society of Jesus

ABBREVIATIONS

AHSI: Archivum Historicum Societatis Iesu
BS: Bibliotheca Sanctorum
ConsMHSI: Constitutiones et Regulæ Societatis Iesu, vols. 63–65 and 71 in MHSI. See MI below.
ConsSJComm: The Constitutions of the Society of Jesus, G. Ganss
Dbib: Dictionary of the Bible, J. McKenzie
DbibTheol: Dictionary of Biblical Theology, ed., X. Léon-Dufour
DeCertMem: De Certeau, *Mémorial*
DeGuiJes: De Guibert, *The Jesuits: Their Spiritual Doctrine and Practice*
DNTest: Dictionary of the New Testament, X. Léon-Dufour
Dspir: Dictionnaire de Spiritualité, 1932–1995
DV: The Catholic Douay English Version (1609–1610) of the Latin Vulgate
EppCan: Beati Petri Canisii Societatis Iesu epistulæ et acta, O. Braunsberger
EppMixt: Epistolæ mixtæ ex variis Europæ locis, 1537–1556, ed., V. Agusti, vols. 12, 14, 17, 18, 20 of MHSI
EppXav: Epistolæ S. Francisci Xaverii, ed., Schurhammer and Wicki, vols. 67–68 in MHSJ
FN: Fontes Narrativi de Sancto, vols. 66, 73, 85, 93 of MHSI
IntJesLife: An Introduction to Jesuit Life, T. Clancy
MellConfess: G. Mellinato, "Confessioni" di Pietro Favre, 1506-1567
MellStudPat: G. Mellinato, "Revisione Testuale delle *Confessioni* di Pietro Favre," *Studia Patavina*
MHSI: Monumenta Historica Societatis Iesu: The Historical Records or Sources of the Society of Jesus in critically edited texts, 100+ vols. (Madrid from 1894, Rome from 1929)
MI: Monumenta Ignatiana: The writings of St. Ignatius of Loyola, vols. 25, 56, 66, 73, 85, 93 of MHSI
MonFabri: Fabri Monumenta, vol. 48 of MHSI (Madrid, 1914); Favre's letters and *Memoriale*
MonLain: Lainii Monumenta, ed., E. Astudillo: letters of Ignatius's companion, Diego Laínez, vols. 44, 45, 47, 49, 50, 51, 53, 55 of MHSI
MonNad: Epistolæ et Monumenta P. Hieronymi Nadal, vols. 13, 15, 21, 27, 90 of MHSI
NcathEnc: New Catholic Encyclopedia, 15 vols.

PL: *Patrologia Latina,* ed., Migne
Ps.(ps.): The Vulgate number of a psalm is given in parentheses
RAM: "Le texte du Mémorial de Favre," M. de Certeau, *Revue d'ascétique et de mystique*
RSV: The Revised Standard Version (1965) of the Bible
SacMundi: *Sacramentum Mundi,* ed., K. Rahner
SpEx: *The Spiritual Exercises of St. Ignatius*
SpExMHSJ: *Exercitia Spiritualia S. Ignatii . . . et eorum Directoria,* ed., A. Codina, 1 vol. Madrid, 1919
ST: *Summa Theologiæ* of St. Thomas Aquinas
VatCouncII: Vatican Council II: *The Conciliar and post-Conciliar Documents,* ed., A. Flannery

n.: the number of a footnote. In some contexts the number preceding the *n.* indicates the page number in this volume and the number following it indicates the footnote number. In other contexts the number preceding the *n.* indicates the paragraph number (§) of the *Memoriale* and the number following it indicates the footnote number.
no.: a numbered section (comprising one or more paragraphs) of the text of the *Memoriale* (= §).
§: a numbered section (comprising one or more paragraphs) of the text of the *Memoriale* (= no.)

It is high time that I return to you the little book [the Memoriale] about the holy life of our Blessed Pierre Favre. I refrained from having a copy of it made, because when you sent it to me you referred to it as something reserved to your Society for the present. However, I should very much like to have a copy of that account of such a holy life—that of a saint to whom for many reasons I am and ought to be devoted. . . . I like to think that the Society will some day decide to honor this first companion of its founder as highly as it has honored the others. Although his life, because it was brief and lived in an age when events were not so accurately recorded, cannot offer as rich biographical material as the lives of others, it will nevertheless yield nothing but the sweet honey of devotion.

—St. Francis of Sales, bishop of Geneva, Doctor of the Church, in a letter addressed "To the Reverend Father in our Lord, Father Nicolas Polliens, of the Company of the Name of Jesus"

Introduction

INTRODUCTION

Spiritual Autobiography

Favre's *Memoriale* belongs to that form of writing sometimes classified as "spiritual diary," sometimes as "spiritual autobiography," a form much practiced by the early Jesuits.[1] They had taken it up for its general spiritual utility, but quickly came to realize its value in discernment. They knew that Ignatius used to write down every day whatever happened in his soul and that he constantly kept adding to the notes of his spiritual experiences. For him and for the early Jesuits, experience was of the greatest importance in the spiritual life. They looked on it as "given" them by God: it revealed God's will, expressed God's love. In it they read "signs" of God's "acceptance" of them.[2] Favre's introspective and scrupulous temperament, his continual dissatisfaction with his spiritual life and the results of his pastoral labors, made him pay close attention to what was happening in his soul, and led him to develop a habit of reflecting on it. Three main influences prompted him to record these reflections: the teaching and example of Ignatius, his philosophical and theological formation, and an impulse rooted in his temperament.

He began his *Memoriale* at Speyer in the Rhineland on June 15, 1542, little more than four years before his death. On that day he wrote a retrospective introduction—an account of his life up to that time—and the first entry in the diary proper. Writing day after day, he completed

---

[1] Such writing can be found as early as the two discourses of St. Paul, recounting his conversion on the way to Damascus (Acts 22:3-21; 26:9-20). It was added to over the centuries and in the Middle Ages popularized by the school of the *Devotio moderna* (the New Devotion). Early Jesuits took it over from them as an aid to religious development. The autobiography or memoirs of St. Ignatius of Loyola is, of course, the first of them. Jerónimo Nadal, Peter Canisius, Pedro Ribadeneira, and Juan de Vitoria also produced such accounts. See Brian O'Leary, S.J., "The Discernment of Spirits in the *Memoriale* of Blessed Pierre Favre," *The Way*, Supplement no. 35 (1979), pp. 29-32, and Jean-François Gilmont, *Les Écrits spirituels des premiers Jésuites* (Rome, 1961).

[2] These views were strongly influenced by the nominalism of their philosophical and theological formation; this stressed the importance of the individual as opposed to the universal and thus emphasized the value of experience, in which it sought evidence ("signs") that one is "accepted" by God. For more on Favre's emphasis on the primacy of experience, see John O'Malley, S.J., *The First Jesuits* (Cambridge, Mass., 1993), p. 247.

the bulk of the work in one year. In July 1543 he left for Cologne and gave up keeping the journal until January 1545, when he began the few final pages covering five months.[3]

After the introductory prayer he states the purpose of the *Memoriale:* "to begin writing down so as to remember them some of the spiritual graces given me by the hand of the Lord in prayer: whether by way of admonishments *(avisos)* about the course to take, or for the improvement of my prayer or my contemplations, or for discernment, or for action, or concerning any other way of making progress in spirit."[4] This fundamental aim, spiritual progress, gives unity to the whole work.

If a spiritual autobiography is a record of God's dealings with an individual and that person's acts of thanksgiving to God for graces received, Favre's *Memoriale* is fully in that tradition. God is at the center, the one who acts, who takes the initiative, who guides. The graces God gives are not simply to be admired or to be used for the instruction of others or as a help towards self-analysis. Favre looks on them as given to show him the path he must follow. God intervenes to make known the divine will, while also aiding in its accomplishment; the daily remembrance of favors received is a participation in the desire to know and do the will of God. Such remembrance enables Favre to discern the work he should undertake and reveals how he ought to pray. His prayer is always a dialogue, and this is its most fundamental characteristic.[5] During the dialogue he has the trinitarian God as his primary partner, and secondarily the angels, the saints, and the souls in purgatory. Favre conducts his side of the dialogue through desires and longings; the divine side causes him to experience spiritual motions which, when interpreted correctly, reveal themselves as signs, warnings, answers, favors, and so forth. But in order to interpret them correctly, Favre has to remember these motions, study and scrutinize them until they become unambiguous. Yet even at this stage the process is itself a dialogue, since he is aided by God and the good spirit to interpret, to understand, and to discuss.

Moreover, the literary structure of the entries themselves provides important insights. First, the fact is recorded in phrases such as "There

---

[3] Jotted down in a hurry because of his many activities, the entries seem to have been written in the morning after Mass, perhaps also in the evening, generally the day after and, on occasion, some time after the events reported. See §198. Note that hereafter § or §§ without any other indication refers to the numbered sections (one or more paragraphs) of the *Memoriale.* These numbers owe their origin to the editors of the *Fabri Monumenta,* vol. 36 of the Monumenta Historica Societatis Iesu (MHSI) (Madrid, 1914).

[4] *Memoriale,* entry for June 15, 1542.

[5] Michel de Certeau, *Mémorial* (Paris, 1960), pp. 80–81.

came to me," "I was given," "I experienced certain deeply felt longings," "I felt much devotion." Then comes the development of the initial grace: "methods of prayer," "ways of acting," decisions and resolutions. So there is, in the first place, a passive reception of the divine visitations; they are always unforeseen, set down just as they are, regarded merely as starting points. Favre's objective, however, is to follow where they lead, so he is less concerned with describing what they are than with examining them as starting points for a developing activity in which God and the person play a part.[6] This minute examination of his inner experience, carried out over many years, brings him a high degree of confidence in identifying what is going on within him at any particular time. Favre makes a careful distinction between three aspects of his inner experience: "*(a)* the object which is being experienced, felt, or understood; *(b)* the area of his being in which the feeling or experience takes place; *(c)* the spirit which is provoking the experience, feeling or understanding."[7]

The *Memoriale* is almost exclusively concerned with Favre's inner life. The entries vary in kind. Some describe God's dealings with him, or record apostolic experiences or the influence of spirits. Some reveal him in dialogue with his soul as he reproaches himself for past shortcomings and urges himself on to greater fidelity and generosity. Some are discursive—attempts to interpret the signs given him in experience. Some are prayers addressed directly to God. He writes much about prayer and methods of prayer, from high forms of contemplation to the litanies he loved. The influence of the Ignatian Spiritual Exercises is manifest. There are entries about his devotion to the Mass, about ways of improving his recital of the Breviary, about care in following the liturgical cycle, and about devotion to the saint of the day.

This record of his most intimate soul searchings—clearly not meant for other eyes—is always the dialogue. The "I" that predominates throughout is himself. There are two different partners in the dialogue, both of them addressed as "you." This may refer to God—most often in scriptural quotations, versicles from the psalms, and liturgical invocations. He uses the language of the Church as the authentic language of

---

[6] But in spite of the extreme care he takes in analyzing his experience, this problem arises: How can he be sure of preserving the same spirit all through the process that leads to action? He decides that he must pray for the spirit of continuity, asking "in what spirit" at each stage and making efforts to keep the original spirit to the very end. So it will greatly help him if his memory of the original experience is accurate, in order that he can compare each stage with the preceding one and thus check the development of the whole process.

[7] O'Leary, "Discernment," p. 78.

communication with God, and he is careful never to depart from it.[8] The other "you" in this dialogue, its use disconcerting at times, most often refers to Favre himself or, rather, to his soul: "Remember, O my soul . . ."[9] Speaking on behalf of God, as it were, he addresses his soul—reminding, entreating, reproaching. This is a reflection of the duality revealed in all interior spiritual experience. It arises from the close link that exists between the "I" and God's action in the depths of the being, the seat of the divine interventions. From that source come the impulses that should pervade every level of the being. The "center of the heart," the "hidden dwelling" of the Spirit, the secret "root" of a person's being—all these expressions refer alike to that center in which the divine operation, developing within and without, gradually forms the person in whom the Holy Spirit dwells. But such a gradual formation results in a tension between the divine initiative and its development in a soul, a tension that is expressed in a dialogue between the "I" that speaks for grace and the "I" that speaks for nature. It is a process of discernment initiated by the divine intervention, and it appears under the form of an interior debate.

As time goes on, this debate between "I" and "my soul" becomes more rare and ceases towards the end. The intimate reflections give way to notes on the apostolate or on matters connected with various ministries. From the evidence of his journal itself, we cannot know much about the growth in Favre's power of discernment, but there is no doubt about his growth in self-knowledge and in spiritual awareness. For instance, constantly scrutinizing his desires led him to classify them and so determine a hierarchy of desires, placing the desire for immediate union with God above *all* other desires no matter how good and holy. We find awareness of a new grace (§188): he records that he is drawn inward by a movement which has its origin within him. It is the first stage of infused prayer and of the mystical life, and from that point on it will be mentioned in the *Memoriale* in a form ever higher and deeper. God becomes more and more the center of his life. The influence of created spirits diminishes, gradually making way for the action of the Holy Spirit. The desire for more immediate union with God continues to increase and is fulfilled in the end. Favre's general spiritual progress, then, implies that he began to find the will of God with greater ease, and this is the purpose of discernment. For discernment forms one element in a person's spiritual life, and the more healthy the spiritual life, the clearer becomes the spiritual vision.

---

[8] §297. See also, De Certeau, *Mémorial,* p. 336 n. 3.
[9] §122 is a typical example of this dialogue.

Religion in Pre-Reformation Europe

Favre's life covered the period when the Reformation finally helped to destroy the unity of medieval Christendom and created a new Europe of sovereign states and separated churches. Because the hierarchical system of the medieval Church had broken down, disorders and abuses had accumulated, and even the Roman Curia had become notorious.[10] The main evils were well known: first, pluralism with its attendant nonresidence; second, simony or the purchase of ecclesiastical appointments and spiritual privileges; third, nonobservance of the canonical rules for episcopal visitations and diocesan synods; fourth, the low standard of clerical education and the laity's ignorance about religious matters. And with these went deplorable laxity in sexual morals even among the highest clergy. Drastic reforms were necessary; they were being called for on every side and by men utterly devoted to the Church. But a great many of the evils were built into the very structures by which the Church carried on its governance; and no one was strong or courageous enough to carry out a reform either of the particular disorders or, more importantly, of the structures that undergirded and fostered those very evils.[11]

It would be quite wrong, however, to represent the age as one of faith permanently weakened and of disbelief in God ever on the increase. Among the common people religious practices varied from country to country—in fact, the pattern in religious matters was more diverse in the early fifteenth century than it had been at any time during the previous four hundred years, and the diversity lasted to the end of the century and beyond it. So it would hardly be possible to make any general statement regarding religious practice and sentiment that would be true of all the countries of central and western Europe during the century before Luther's manifesto in 1517.

At one end of Europe lay Bohemia, already penetrated by Wycliff's radical teaching; at the other end, Spain—faithful to the Church and soon to become the citadel of the Counter-Reformation. Between these two extremes lay Italy—in some ways the least Christian of countries,

---

[10] For contemporary evidence of the need for Church reform, see the memorial of Giovan Batista Cassia in Ludwig von Pastor, *The History of the Popes* (London–St. Louis, 1891–1923), vol. 11, pp. 33ff.; see also vols. 5 and 6 on disorders in the Church. In 1497 Alexander VI, no less, appointed a commission of cardinals to draft a scheme of general reform; this scheme, worked out in detail during months of competent labor, was never carried into effect. It is a terrible indictment of the Roman Curia.

[11] See Barbara Hallman, *Italian Cardinals, Reform and the Church as Property* (Berkeley, 1985) for a good discussion of how the ecclesiastical fiscal system worked.

yet in other ways the most tenaciously Catholic. To the north were the Low Countries, radiating an immense spiritual influence, the home of the New Devotion *(Devotio moderna)*. In that land flourished all the popular religious manifestations of the day: the numerous beguinages of men and women whose convictions varied from strict orthodoxy to sheer heresy, the multitudinous processions, the extravagant devotions. Then came Germany, which, in spite of the endemic abuses of feudal and papal autocracy, was still in many districts and towns profoundly devout: recent research shows little change in the religious climate there during the fifteenth century. France, ruined by the Hundred Years' War, found a real religious revival at the heart of its national resurgence. And in England, Scotland, and elsewhere, the devout life of the Middle Ages continued, sustained by a stream of devotional books from the printing presses and by the multiplication, through foundations and legacies, of chantries, Masses, and prayers for the dead. In spite of widespread abuses and disorders, the spiritual level of the common people remained high, in many ways as high as that of the previous age. But unusual and disquieting characteristics began to manifest themselves, the symptoms of a deep spiritual malaise.

It is true that there had been a certain lack of balance about religion in the preceding century, a lack that a study of the symptoms shows had persisted and even worsened. For instance, superstition was just as widespread as it was at the end of the Middle Ages, and perhaps more so; and the cult of the saints tended to occupy such an enormous place in Christian piety that it bordered at times on the scandalous—if not on idolatry. Relic hunting took on the appearance of collective hysteria: no matter how spurious relics might appear, every kind of power was ascribed to them. Frightful havoc was caused by belief in witchcraft: trials multiplied; no one seemed safe from suspicion.

People no longer turned for spiritual nourishment to the depths of the Christian mysteries, but rather to the mysteries as they had been shown to the senses. The imagination and the emotions now began to play a greater part than before in the spiritual life, and this change came to be reflected in religious art. Periodic outbreaks of the Black Death, endemic in Europe since 1348, began to have a cumulative psychological effect that unsettled further the precarious balance that the devotional life had to maintain between reason, the new emotions, and the imagination. On the one hand new luxury and new lusts arose; on the other a deep melancholy began to invade the people's minds. Then came the Great Schism and the conflict between the popes and the councils to undermine further the certainties of men, to remind them that glory is short-lived, happiness all too brief, and that high ecclesiastical office is no guarantee of a virtuous life. A new obsession began to haunt the imagination of Europe, a new preoccupation with sin and its consequences and a morbid brooding on death and judgment as the moment when merited punishment would begin.[12] Man is born to die; the doleful message was repeated in a thousand different ways, but the world too is in the process of passing away.

For help and hope and in an effort to allay their fundamental insecurity, the unfortunate people took to exaggerated forms of devotion and to the practice of a mysticism that soon broke with tradition. Inevitably, the grossest superstitions took root, grew, and began to spread throughout Europe, insinuating themselves into even the most orthodox devotions. Belief in witches, warlocks, werewolves, vampires, and suchlike could be found everywhere; witchcraft, astrology, and magic flourished; the educated classes and even the clergy dabbled in the occult.[13]

So widespread did these weird rites become that the papal legate to Germany and the northern kingdoms, Cardinal Campeggio, felt constrained to include in his *Constitutio* of 1524 a clause stating that ecclesiastics who practiced sorcery, divination, or the casting of spells were to be branded with infamy.[14] Worship of the devil appeared even in Savoy; people were reported to have had carnal relations with demons; the old demonologies were resurrected and elaborated in bulky tomes that circulated widely and could be found even in remote villages. But these were merely symptoms. Horrifying visions, terrors that flew by night, haunted minds and filled imaginations; everyone had tales to tell of wonders that passed belief; prodigies and portentous natural phenomena abounded; comets frightened everyone. Europe experienced a thirst for the irrational and the mysterious that was impossible to slake.

And not one of the cultured minds that soaked itself in that seductive lore ever seemed to have realized the gullibility involved—an attitude surprising in a generation that subjected sacred texts and even the dogmas of religion to rigorous criticism. Such was the world into which Favre was born.

---

[12] The painter Hieronymus Bosch (ca. 1450–1516) illustrates the grotesque imagination of that age. His mature work is peopled with sinister figures who, from the background, gaze mockingly on religious scenes. To this day his iconography remains ambiguous.

[13] The famous scholar Reuchlin was addicted to the bizarre lore of cabalism; his grandnephew, the cultured Melanchthon, believed in horoscopes and auguries; the popes of the time employed their official papal astrologers to aid them in their own work.

[14] The *Constitutio* was a plan for the reform of the German clergy prepared by Cardinal Lorenzo Campeggio. See Pastor, *History*, vol. 10, pp.114–115; see also James Brodrick, *St. Peter Canisius* (London, 1935), p. 271 n. 2.

Early Years in Savoy

Favre's life spanned the first decades of the Reformation period. He was born on Easter Monday April 13, 1506, in Le Villaret, a village in a valley of the Savoy Alps called Le Grand Bornand, and baptized the same day in the parish church of Saint-Jean-de-Sixt. His native valley, in those days part of the Duchy of Savoy, belonged to the Diocese of Geneva.[15] Conditions in Savoy were thus similar to those obtaining in large areas of Europe that were still anchored in medieval spirituality:

> Records of the passing scene left by contemporary travelers show that there was little skepticism and no general revolt against Christian teaching and principles. Festivals, sacred as well as profane, might sometimes be marked by grossness, immorality, and brutality, but on the whole life was anchored in a profound if not always well-instructed faith. Denial of dogma, sacrilege, failure to receive the sacraments at Easter, prolonged absence from Mass were rare.[16]

Two influences ruled the soul of Savoy: Catholicism and the mountains. The mountains confront the Savoyards at every turn: summer and winter they impose a way of life on them. It is a pitiless struggle—a struggle that has bred in them the qualities that mark their character: courage, foresight, ingenuity, a tenacious effort that refuses to slacken until victory is assured. Catholicism too has marked the Savoyards: the example and inspiration of the saints, the spiritual blessings that flow from the shrines of our Lady dotting the land. It was a region of strong traditional piety—not just a matter of pious observances—that linked family to family. The Confraternity of the Holy Spirit, a branch of which had been established in nearly all parishes by Favre's day, included members from every family in a parish. From each person they collected offerings of crops, firewood, fleeces, meat, and other necessities of life for distribution among the needy, the sick, widows, orphans, and the aged. The poor were not neglected: there were special boxes for the collection of alms to be distributed to them.

Of such stock were Favre's parents. He describes them as "good and very pious Catholic parents" (§1) who brought him up well "in the fear of God our Lord" (§2). Indeed, fear of God was to play a not inconsiderable part in his spiritual life even from an early age.[17] His parents, like the other families in the valley, lived close to the land, sending their flocks to pasture on the slopes of the mountains during the summer

---

[15] Annexed by France in 1860, the area is now known as the *département* of Savoie and Haute-Savoie (Savoy and Upper Savoy).

[16] Mary Purcell, *The Quiet Companion* (Dublin, 1970), p. 13.

[17] §2, §9.

months. One member, usually a child, would accompany the flocks and remain with them. At the age of seven Favre carried out this task for the first time. But as time went on he began to realize that he had neither taste nor aptitude for the life his parents planned for him on the farm with his two younger brothers. He began to realize too that he wanted very much to go to school, and so intense did this desire become that he was unable to sleep at night for weeping. His tears were the tears of frustration shed by an intelligent child aware of his talent but without an opportunity to develop it. In the end his parents, though unwillingly, had to yield to his entreaties.

Favre's spiritual life up to his departure for Paris at the age of nineteen was nourished and formed by the liturgical year as celebrated by his parish. As a young child he had been an apt pupil; he had learned his prayers (including the rosary) at his mother's knee. A neighbor recalled that he was able to recite the little children's catechism from memory at the age of five. Contemporary accounts credit him with a quick and retentive memory, capable of repeating word for word the Sunday sermons and religious instructions of his parish priest. This he would do standing on a rock, his congregation a group of local children.

He was deeply attached to relics of all kinds and profoundly affected by crucifixes, statues, the decoration in churches and chapels, ceremonies with incense, music and chanting, and by liturgical gestures and sacramentals. They filled him with intense reverence and awe and brought him a sense of God's presence, for he held that God was in whatever had been blessed with the sign of the cross.[18] All these things kindled his devotion and led to affective prayer.

At first he went to school at Thônes, a town about six miles from Le Villaret. The year after, he went farther afield to the school at La Roche kept by the priest, Pierre Velliard, and remained there until he was about nineteen. He was strongly influenced by Velliard, who showed him how to read the authors of antiquity in the light of the Gospel.[19] So effectively did he teach both by word and example that Favre could not forget him and expressed his gratitude to him in more than one passage of the *Memoriale*.[20] The literary formation Velliard gave was humanistic and may have helped to direct Favre's thoughts to Paris and the Collège de Sainte-Barbe. The spiritual influence he exercised upon his charges

---

[18] §§130–133.

[19] Ignacio Iparraguirre, S.J., "Influjos en la espiritualidad del beato Pedro Fabro," in *Revista de Espiritualidad* 5 (1946): 438–452.

[20] §§3, 4, 28, 190.

was itself the fruit of his acquaintance with the ideas propagated by the Brethren of the Common Life, for instance, their approach to learning and their devotion to Christ's humanity.[21]

Another and perhaps decisive influence on the boy was his Carthusian relatives. He often visited them in the monastery of Le Reposoir about seven miles from his home: Dom Mamert Favre, his parental uncle, prior until 1522, who gave him and his parents constant guidance and advice; and his maternal cousin, Dom Claude Perissin, prior from 1522, who directed him to Paris for his further studies and put him in touch with his brethren at Vauvert, a monastery only a short kilometer from Sainte-Barbe, founded in 1460 in what is now the locale of the Luxembourg Palace and Gardens in Paris. The close link between himself and the Carthusians became closer when he joined the Society of Jesus, and wherever he worked in after years he always kept in touch with the nearest charterhouse.[22] Even more than Velliard, the monks of Le Reposoir and Vauvert brought him within the spiritual influence of the school of Gerhard Groote, Ludolph of Saxony, Hendrik Herp, and Ruysbroeck; for it was from the charterhouses of Trier, Mainz, Cologne, and Louvain, in addition to the Brothers of the Common Life, that the influence of the New Devotion spread over the Rhineland.

His studies in Sainte-Barbe were to last, with one break of seven months, from 1525 until 1536. He was in his twentieth year, older by four or five years than the average first-year students and much more advanced than they in Latin and Greek. Indeed, his competence in these languages and his passionate desire to continue his study of them may well have been the reason why his Carthusian relative in Le Reposoir, in close touch with his brethren of Vauvert in Paris, advised Pierre to enter Sainte-Barbe, in those days a humanist stronghold holding the doctrine of letters-for-letters' sake. Twelve years later Favre would accuse himself,

---

[21] So rapid was the spread of their spirituality—known as the New Devotion (*Devotio moderna*)—and so great the popularity of its classic *The Imitation of Christ* that Velliard must surely have absorbed some of its principal ideas. Ideas and books traveled fast in the region; the library of the Franciscan house at Cluses-Velliard, which had come from there to La Roche in 1517, was well stocked. The first book printed at Geneva in 1478 could be found in it the year after. Books printed at Geneva or at Chambéry before 1525 rapidly found their way into Savoy: theological works, commentaries on the Gospels, missals, devotional almanacs, collections of prayers, and lists of pilgrimages. Both Thônes and La Roche, where Favre would have had to stay while attending school, were towns rather than villages; new ideas, pious and not so pious, found attentive ears, and gossip spread rapidly. Thomas Clancy, S.J., in his *Introducion to Jesuit Life* (St. Louis, 1976), pp. 29–30, lists ten characteristics of this school of spirituality. See also R. R. Post, *The Modern Devotion: Confrontation with Reformation and Humanism* (London, 1968).

[22] De Certeau, *Mémorial*, pp. 28–37.

in a letter to the scholastics at Paris, of having looked on his university studies as ends rather than means.[23] His faith, his virtue, remained intact, but he had eyes only for his books. He was, in a sense that he came to understand before he left Paris for good, an unspiritual man. But in September 1525 success in literary studies was in the forefront of his mind as he made his way to Paris and its university. Still on fire for whatever further education was available—"a persistent and inordinate desire for the knowledge and study of letters," he would call it years later—he set off for Paris and in September 1525 enrolled in the Collège de Sainte-Barbe. There he quickly became friends with Francis Xavier, who had entered in the same month.

The University of Paris in the Sixteenth Century

Paris in the sixteenth century was a city of some three hundred thousand inhabitants, a Catholic city in which one could also experience a set of currents and crosscurrents inimical to that faith as traditionally taught and practiced. The university's faculty of theology was proud of the authoritative position it had enjoyed since the Middle Ages, a position that gave it great freedom to make theological pronouncements independent even of Rome. The university itself was divided into about fifty colleges that served as residences for intern students and professors. It concentrated on theology, philosophy, and letters; but by far the most numerous faculty was that of arts, dedicated almost entirely to the study of Aristotle. No student could proceed to the higher faculties before graduating in arts. On the average, the four thousand students were about fourteen or fifteen years old when they entered the university, though some were younger. All of them faced a regime of incredible harshness. One notable example of this regime was the Collège de Montaigu, founded in 1314, which had been reformed some years before under its rector, Jan Standonck. The reform worked such a change for the better that in spite of its strictness students flocked to its doors and wept if they failed to gain entry. It attracted students like Erasmus, who suffered so much there that by way of revenge he gave details of the trials he and others had to endure within its walls: scurvy, fleas, hard beds, and harder blows (all the masters carried canes and used them frequently and mercilessly), putrid herrings, rotten eggs, and wine so sour that it tasted like vinegar.[24] There was still worse: some first-year

---

[23] *Fabri Monumenta,* pp. 103–104 (abbreviated hereafter as *MonFabri*).

[24] A somewhat less dramatic account of life in Montaigu at that time can be found in Georg Schurhammer, *Francis Xavier: His Life, His Times* (Rome, 1973), vol. 1, pp. 95–107. Also see the recent popular work by Jean Lacouture, *The Jesuits: A Multibiography* (Washington, D.C., 1995), pp. 49–50. Lacouture's second chapter,

students died of hardship and hunger, went blind or mad, or became infected with leprosy. Erasmus may well have exaggerated; but the evidence indicates that the students, many of them mere children, were underfed, overworked, and mercilessly bullied.[25]

Daily life in all the colleges followed this pattern. Roused at 4 A.M., the students, carrying inkpots, candles, and notebooks, stumbled bleary-eyed to the first class at 5 A.M., followed by Mass at 6 A.M., after which the shivering youths broke their fast with a piece of dry bread and some water. The second class lasted from 8 A.M. until 10 A.M., followed by dialectical exercises for an hour. Next there was a frugal dinner with a Latin text being read in the background, after which the students were questioned about the matter dealt with in the morning. Then, by way of relaxation, came the reading of Latin authors until the third class, which lasted from 3 P.M. until 5 P.M.; next came another disputation, followed by a wretched supper at 6 P.M.; at 7 P.M. the students were again questioned, this time on the day's studies, and at 8 P.M. in winter and 9 P.M. in summer, after a visit to the Blessed Sacrament, they were sent hungry to bed.

There were some compensations for the rigors of life and the unremitting study: pageants, masquerades, fairs, dances at the crossroads, sports on the Ile aux Vaches, and numerous fights in which students vented their pent-up frustrations and resentments.[26]

Sainte-Barbe, where Favre lived, was a comparatively new college, founded in 1460, which had always enjoyed a high reputation for learning; under the generous patronage of the Portuguese kings, it had acquired amenities unknown in other colleges. The rector (or principal), Diogo de Gouveia, most of the regents, and the majority of its two hundred students were Portuguese. Favre and Xavier had enrolled at a

---

"The Scholars from Montmartre," also vividly portrays college life in Paris and the forming of the first companions around Ignatius.

[25] One young professor at Sainte-Barbe in Favre's day, the Scot George Buchanan (who later became tutor to Mary Queen of Scots and her son James, and then a Presbyterian leader) left for posterity his views on students. He complains bitterly about their inattention and slumbering during his lectures, that some kept staring at their feet or pretended to be ill or wrote letters to their parents, that latecomers drifted in with much noise or drifted out again just as noisily to cross the stinking Street of the Dogs and take refuge in the Montaigu. He winds up his tirade by sadly declaring that the rod was the only way to produce scholars.

[26] This island is the present Ile St. Louis. The variety of sports then available is quite surprising. See Abel Lefranc, *La Vie quotidienne au temps de la Renaissance* (Paris, 1958), pp. 172–182, as well as the recent volume by Lacouture, *Jesuits*, pp. 35–74.

period when the newly reformed Montaigu came close to surpassing it in scholarship. The resulting rivalry led at times to high feelings and, at least once, to a pitched battle between the two colleges.[27] Relations were all the more strained because most of the Montaigu students were French nationals, whereas Spaniards and Portuguese who supported the emperor, Charles V, made up the bulk of the student body in Sainte-Barbe. While Montaigu was traditionalist in its teaching, laying a good deal of stress on logic and dialectic in its arts course, Sainte-Barbe, encouraged by its rector, Gouveia, had gone over to humanism and was devoting itself to the Greek and Latin classics. It boasted some distinguished professors, most of whom were humanists and followers of Erasmus.

But following Erasmus meant much more than cultivating Latin and Greek. He advocated the reform of religion by a return to the sources, above all the New Testament in its original Greek and, secondly, the Greek and Latin Fathers. As the Italian humanists had looked on classical literature as the central and highest expression of human values, "so Erasmus and his friends and disciples set up the ideal of Christian Antiquity as its counterpart in the spiritual realm and made it the standard of moral and religious values."[28] But they related the two ideals by showing how classical antiquity was a preparation for the Gospel. They also concentrated on the moral wisdom of the Gospels—Erasmus called it *philosophia Christi*—and criticized the Church not only because it had substituted scholastic metaphysical systems and endless exercises in dialectics for the *philosophia Christi* but also because it had abandoned simple evangelical teaching for a multiplicity of pious practices.

As a moralist, Erasmus was the source of the humanitarian and liberal tradition that was to play such a great part in the history of modern Europe. He abhorred violence, especially against heretics, and understood, as few of his contemporaries did, that gentle persuasion, not torture and execution, was a better way to heal the divisions of Christendom. Favre, though never a follower of Erasmus, was inclined by nature and temperament to gentle persuasion, regarding it as far preferable to any kind of force or violence. Favre's idea of reform involved a more personal focus of the soul's humble and repentant turning to God, while Erasmus's could be viewed as more learned, based on the critical study of original texts of the Scripture and the Fathers.

---

[27] Mary Purcell gives a lively account of this fray in *Quiet Companion,* pp. 26–27.

[28] Christopher Dawson, *The Dividing of Christendom* (New York, 1965), pp. 52–62.

But there were other ideas in the air that by Favre's time had successfully challenged traditional scholastic philosophy and theology (the *Via antiqua*) and had led to dialectical exercises as an important part of the university curriculum. Collectively, the ideas were known as nominalism, a system of philosophy elaborated initially by the Franciscan scholar William of Ockham. By the time Favre arrived at Paris, nominalism in its various forms had superseded almost all other kinds of philosophy in the universities of Europe.

Nominalism influenced the scholasticism of the Middle Ages and in the fourteenth and fifteenth centuries gave rise to a broad current of philosophy and theology called the New Way *(Via moderna)*. In his biography of Martin Luther, Heiko Oberman thus describes the differences in theology:

> The representatives of the via antiqua, followers of Thomas Aquinas and Duns Scotus, were realists. They held that universal concepts *(universalia)* are more than just human tools to inventory the extramaterial world, but are the expression of reality itself, indeed that final, higher reality behind all individuality.
>
> In contrast the followers of the via moderna dared to tread a new, uncertain, and controversial path: sensory perception of reality does not lead to the cognition of universal realities but to abstract thought. Universals are the result of such abstractions and are devoid of independent reality. What is real is the individual, the human person as a unique entity perceived by the senses.[29]

Ockham thus recognized no universal truths at all—even the existence, unity, and infinity of God were made pure articles of faith. Metaphysical arguments gave only probable conclusions; revelation was the sole source of absolute certainty. For Ockham the divine will is the norm of morality: the moral law is founded on the free divine choice.[30]

---

[29] Heiko Oberman, *Luther: Man between God and the Devil* (New Haven, 1989), p. 117.

[30] The following comment by David Knowles, Regius Professor Emeritus of Modern History in the University of Cambridge, gives an idea of how nominalism influenced European history: "The epoch of open religious conflict that began with the emergence of Luther in 1517, was indeed momentous, but in many ways the revolution in *thought* [emphasis added] and theology had begun two centuries earlier, when Duns Scotus and William of Ockham departed from the tradition of philosophy as a body of accepted reasonings *(philosophia perennis)* and began the construction of personal systems that has continued ever since, while Marsilius of Padua and John Wycliff broke with the traditional views on the government of the Church and primitive Christianity." Quoted in Dawson, "Introduction," *Dividing of Christendom*, p. ix.

The University of Paris itself was the great center of nominalist thought as interpreted by Gabriel Biel[31] (regarded as the leading nominalist theologian of the fifteenth century) in his commentary on the *Sentences* of Peter Lombard.[32] It was Biel's teaching, as presented by various professors of theology in Paris, including Favre and Xavier's tutor, the Spanish master of arts Juan de la Peña, that formed the early Jesuits.[33]

The First Three Companions

Francis Xavier (1506–1552) had been assigned the same room as Favre in that September of 1525. Although the two quickly became close friends, they could not have been more different. Favre, a shepherd from Savoy, was pious, reserved, sensitive, and studious; his affable manner and tranquil exterior masked an inner turmoil that at times almost drove him to despair. Xavier, a Basque nobleman from Navarre, was exceedingly ambitious, proud of his athletic skill and his family pedigree, but less enthusiastic for study than Favre. The pair were alike in sharing a strong traditional Catholic faith, alike also in an immaturity that went with their age but showed itself differently in each. Xavier, anxious for a great name on earth, spent much time endeavoring to acquire it in the student milieu by demonstrating his athletic prowess and consorting

---

[31] Gabriel Biel (ca. 1410–1495), the leading theologian during the latter half of the fifteenth century and the last Catholic theologian of his school, the *Via moderna*. A thoroughgoing Ockhamist in philosophy and theology, his *Commentary on the Sentences of Peter Lombard* is the classical handbook of Ockham's theology, where it openly appears as a complete system. Biel's commentary was an epitome of Ockham's commentaries on the *Sentences*. Printed in 1501 for the first time, it became perhaps the most popular compendium of theology in the universities of Europe. It played a major part in the theological formation of Favre and the early Jesuits; Martin Luther found congenial ideas in its pages. Biel had a great name as a preacher of popular devotions and all his life kept in close contact with the Brothers of the Common Life. A fuller discussion of Biel can be found in Heiko Oberman's *The Harvest of Medieval Theology: Gabriel Biel and Late Medieval Nominalism* (Cambridge, MA, 1963).

[32] Peter Lombard (ca. 1095–1160), one of the most famous of all medieval theologians, taught in Paris for most of his life. He is renowned for his *Book of Sentences (Liber sententiarum)*, which presents the whole of Christian doctrine in one brief volume. Based on Scripture, the Fathers, and the Doctors, it contains relatively little theological speculation. A sound, brief, objective summary of doctrine, the *Book of Sentences* was quickly recognized as the best of its kind and came into use all over Europe. It continued to be used and commented on in all the schools of western Christendom until well into the seventeenth century.

[33] The two became friends and Favre always remembered Juan de la Peña with gratitude (*Memoriale*, §§6, 7, 8). See Lacouture, *Jesuits*, pp. 47–48.

with pleasant but questionable companions.[34] Favre lacked self-knowledge and wanted to do well in his studies, but he was unable to make up his mind about his future. This indecision, a form of diffidence and mistrust of self, would reveal itself in later years as exaggerated dependence on orders from above when faced on occasion with important decisions.[35]

By background and temperament Favre was ill fitted for the rather freethinking atmosphere he encountered in Sainte-Barbe. Velliard had prepared him well for his university studies and had trained him in a way that profoundly affected the religious formation given him by his parents (§3). Sainte-Barbe won Favre's praise years later when he was mature and experienced enough to pass judgment on its quality. But the university was quite different from his earlier sheltered and self-contained life, and his temperament subjected him to severe interior trials. Even before he left for Paris, he was already suffering greatly from remorse of conscience and was a prey to constant scruples—a burden he would carry for years until it was lightened by Iñigo de Loyola. There was no help for him in Sainte-Barbe. He had little understanding of his spiritual life and was increasingly tormented by scruples about past confessions, tempted to impurity, to vainglory, to gluttony, and to rash judgments. As the time for his final examinations drew near, he was unable to make up his mind about the future. Such inner turmoil must have left him in a pitiable condition.[36] The literature he loved was perhaps his only comfort. But, in spite of the anguish in his soul, he kept up his study, prepared for his examinations for the licentiate, and successfully completed them in February 1529. Then help came from the oddest source in the person of a limping, middle-aged former soldier who entered Sainte-Barbe in September of that same year.

Like Xavier, the new student, Iñigo de Loyola, was a Basque. He came from the Province of Guipuzcoa south of the Pyrenees, born there in the family castle at Loyola in 1491. His reputation had preceded him: a converted nobleman, a gentleman of Spain who had become a vagrant and a beggar, a Catholic who had been in trouble with the Inquisition. Moreover, he had acquired a bad name among the students and the university authorities for having turned the heads of some young men

---

[34] Thus Xavier admitted in a letter to his brother written about March 1535; see Georg Schurhammer, S.J., and Josef Wicki, S.J., *Epistolæ S. Francisci Xaverii*, MHSI (Rome, 1943) 1:9–10. He was saved from excess by a loathing for the ulcers that his companions had contracted.

[35] *MonFabri*, pp. 162–163; 228–229; §145.

[36] §§8, 9, 10, especially the passage from §9 where he describes the torments he suffered from scruples about past confessions. It was the anguish of a delicate conscience in dire need of help.

toward religious practices, thereby causing a minor riot.[37] Perhaps this was the reason why Xavier kept aloof from him—"in spiritual matters he was not much taken by him," writes Polanco. Reading between the lines, one senses that the relatively unspiritual Xavier must have disapproved of Ignatius's way of life. More than five years afterwards, though, Xavier, in a letter to his brother Juan, wrote that he would never be able to repay his debt to Iñigo for having helped him with money and friends and for having saved him from the ill-advised company which in his inexperience he had not recognized as such. He begs his brother to consult Ignatius and to trust his advice because his counsel and conversation will profit him greatly, "so much a man of God is he and of all virtue."

Shortly after Ignatius's arrival in September, Favre, who had become a bachelor of arts on January 10, 1529, a month before his licentiate examinations, began to coach the newcomer in Latin and Aristotle (§8).[38] Very soon they became such close friends that Favre gained enough confidence to unburden himself completely to this man who was already a master of the spiritual life. Since Ignatius himself had gone through the same ordeal in Manresa, he was just the one to help Favre.

In his *Memoriale* Favre briefly traces the stages of his spiritual training under Ignatius. He was given the self-knowledge he needed so desperately, not by an illumination that lit up his troubled conscience, but by a reasoned method, a systematic explanation, a set of tactics that would help him grow in knowledge of himself and teach him to identify the various "spirits" that tried him. This brought him peace of soul, though it would not free him entirely from interior trials. Now he knew how to understand his conscience, how to deal with temptations, how to recognize scruples, and how to take measures against his frequent bouts of depression. In addition, Ignatius showed him how to eradicate his recalcitrant faults, taking them one at a time beginning with the most deep rooted; then he showed him how to concentrate on building up positive virtues. The strategy worked, but it did not change Favre com-

---

[37] They were notably these three: Amador de Elduayen, a Basque, the most promising scholar in the whole Latin Quarter; Pedro de Peralta; and Juan de Castro. For the latter see §10. Purcell, *Companion,* pp. 34–36, gives an account of the event.

[38] §7; linking passages 6a and 7a. [The passages in question, prepared by the translator to furnish historical background, "link" (occur between) §6 and §7, and between §7 and §8. The same holds true of all subsequent references to linking passages.—ED.] There is a disagreement about the date; De Certeau, *Mémorial,* p. 110 n. 2; Giuseppe Mellinato, *"Confessioni" di Pietro Favre (1506–1547)* (Rome, 1980), p. 9 n. 15. Xavier and Favre received their bachelor of arts degrees on the same day.

pletely: his scrupulosity and his tendency to fits of depression remained, as did his diffidence and mistrust of self. But he was now in possession of planned tactics for the lifelong struggle he would have to wage, by no means the least important of which was the realization that his difficulties and shortcomings had a value all their own: "for the Lord had left in me those goads *[espuelas]*, which never allowed me to remain lukewarm."[39]

In the meantime Favre gave himself to the study of theology in an unmethodical way. For about six years he went from college to college, taking in whatever lecture or series of lectures seemed most suitable, hoping in that way to gain his doctorate of theology when the time came. These studies, however, were interrupted, first by paying a seven-month visit to his native village in Savoy, then, almost immediately after his return, by making the full thirty-day Exercises under Ignatius in January and February of 1534. He heroically devoted himself to them, living alone in a little room in the Faubourg Saint-Jacques. When Ignatius visited him after about a week, he found that Favre had eaten nothing for six days, had built no fire during weather reputedly the coldest within living memory, and had been sleeping in his shirt on the timber given him for a fire. He made his meditations out in a little snow-covered courtyard. Ignatius allowed him to fast for one day more, then told him he should eat and have a fire. These mortifications, of which the *Memoriale* mentions only the fast, are a measure of his devotion to the service of God and the sign of a self-offering that would never be withdrawn. His thirty-day retreat was a prelude to his ordination the following May. He briefly mentions it, adding only that he offered his first Mass on the feast of St. Mary Magdalene, describing her as "my advocate and the advocate of all sinners" (§14).

By 1534 Ignatius had attracted seven disciples to himself. They met frequently in the room he shared with Favre and Xavier to discuss their future. They were determined to follow Christ but did not yet know how. On Sundays they went to the Carthusians at Vauvert for prayer and meditation. There they found peace from the hubbub of Sainte-Barbe and were able to consult with their friends in the community. The charterhouse at Vauvert, half a mile outside Porte Saint-Jacques, was widely but discreetly influential. The monks there were well aware of what went on in the university; for many students and regents came seeking advice and spiritual direction and, especially, hoping to experience for themselves what it is to live with God. There is no doubt that the seven discussed their plans with their monastic friends and

---

[39] §12; §302 nn. 159, 160.

profited from their advice and prayers as they formulated the vow they pronounced on the Feast of the Assumption, 1534.

But Ignatius knew his friend well. He delayed giving the Exercises to Favre for four years, very likely because he judged him not yet ready for the full Exercises of thirty days.[40] When he left for Spain in 1535, he put Favre in charge of the companions not so much as superior but, as Diego Laínez put it, as their "elder brother." This meant that he took the place of Ignatius at the head of the little group at a most critical stage. He would have to foster unity and interpret the mind of Ignatius for others; he would have to guide Claude Jay, Jean Codure, and Paschase Broët through the Exercises, then take it on himself to admit them into the Society. He acted as superior for eighteen months all told. By choosing Favre at that juncture, Ignatius showed his knowledge and confidence in him. Early in 1537 he sent Favre to Rome as head of a delegation to outline to the Pope their plan to go on pilgrimage and to request permission for them to devote their lives to apostolic work in the Holy Land. They were also to request permission for those of their number who were not yet priests to receive ordination.[41] In a few entries of the *Memoriale* (§§15, 16, and 17), Favre recounts very briefly the events of August 15, the companions' departure from Paris, and their reception by the Pope. A few years later, when electing the first general of the Society, Xavier, Rodrigues, and Codure made Favre their second choice.

The Paris Theologian

Favre spent eleven years in Sainte-Barbe, his intellectual formation being more literary and philosophical than theological. His first five years were devoted to the arts, comprising grammar, dialectics, geometry, cosmology, literature, and philosophy. "This should have given him a well-nigh encyclopedic intellectual baggage, ranging from a Hebrew vocabulary to astral influences. It also called for incessant mental gymnastics, dialectical exercises of all kinds, attacks and defenses."[42] He studied the logic of

---

[40] De Certeau, *Mémorial*, p. 18, has an interesting theory about the delay.

[41] Ignatius felt it might be undiplomatic on his part to lead the delegation to Rome; he feared two influential men at the Vatican: Doctor Pedro Ortiz, who had delated him to the Inquisition in Paris for having turned the heads of some Montaigu students, and Cardinal Gian Pietro Carafa, cofounder of the Theatines, for whom Ignatius had written some well-meant advice (probably never sent) on how to improve the organization of his order. He saw all the more need, then, for a skillful negotiator in Rome. See William V. Bangert, *To the Other Towns: A Life of Blessed Peter Favre, First Companion of St. Ignatius* (Westminster, Md., 1959), pp. 47–50, for an account of the journey to Rome and the success of the delegation.

[42] De Certeau, *Mémorial*, p. 20.

Agricola, which stressed rhetoric, the art of convincing, rather than reasoning, and, significantly, put itself forward as a logic of the probable and more probable.[43]

> Little of all this appears in the *Memoriale:* a few definitions from Boethius and Aristotle, a taste—almost a mannerism—for distinctions and divisions, and a mania, widespread in those days, for emphasizing in Latin certain more technical expressions or for breaking up with *atquis* and *ergos* a text which did not require them at all. In short, it was a language more than a reasoning process.[44]

It would be impossible to gauge how much influence humanism had on him; it does not seem to have been permanent. There is little doubt that the arts' course Favre followed was the primary alternative proposed by the humanists to the scholastic curriculum. Peña consulted him when the interpretation of certain passages in Aristotle required that he have recourse to the original Greek. He was friendly with famous humanists; some of the most learned among them lectured in Sainte-Barbe. But there is no evidence that they ever taught Favre.

He would have read some of Erasmus's works and listened to discussions about the great humanist's ideas for reform of the Church, ideas much in the air during those years. Favre's own concern, however, was for a different kind of reform. He and his companions envisaged an interior reform much more in harmony with the ideas of the Circle of Meaux.[45] He would have known a good deal about Standonck's reform of the Collège de Montaigu—it was often talked about and criticized in university circles—but as it concerned itself with the disciplinary and curricular reorganization of an ecclesiastical establishment, it agreed neither with his taste nor his convictions. The spiritual aspect of the new movement for reform was more in conformity with the ideas and plans

---

[43] Rudolphus Agricola (1444–1485), the father of German humanism. The work in question is *De inventione dialectica,* which sought to demonstrate the true function of logic as a basic element of rhetoric.

[44] De Certeau, *Mémorial,* p. 20.

[45] This was a group of orthodox Catholics, humanists in the main and some of the finest minds of the age, who formed around Jacques Lefèvre d'Etaples about 1515, hoping to purify the Church in France. In practice Lefèvre and his group desired a reform carried out by the Church within the Church; it was to be an intellectual reform and would replace a degenerate scholasticism with a positive theology based on a study of the Scriptures and the Fathers, and with it would go a reform of morals and discipline. Unfortunately the group became suspect of heresy because their doctrine, though Catholic to the core, was so loosely formulated that it seemed to advocate a personal religion independent of the Church. Denounced by the Franciscans, they were condemned by a bull of Clement VII and dispersed in 1525.

The Paris Theologian

of Ignatius's little group, and it was that side of reform that attracted Favre.

Favre's studies were somewhat eclectic. In Paris he attended lectures in theology where they were offered: at the Convent of the Dominicans and the Convent of the Franciscans, both in the Rue Saint-Jacques; at the Sorbonne; and at the Collège de Navarre.[46] He also attended the lectures given in Sainte-Barbe by the Scot Robert Wauchope, archbishop of Armagh in absentia and a controversialist who later played an active part at the Council of Trent. So Favre went from one lecture hall to another, as did his companions, no doubt in search of the best lectures. He became a competent pastoral theologian, nothing more; he was intelligent but not an intellectual. In his mind theological speculation took second place to an exclusive concern with bringing men back to God.

We know the names of his professors—all of them adherents of nominalism to a greater or lesser extent.[47] He preferred the more devout among them, his favorite being the Franciscan Pierre de Cornibus, who was faithful to the Franciscan tradition and very much recommended by the first Jesuits. Then there was François Picart, a popular preacher, a keen opponent of the reformers, and a friend to the poor.[48] But it was Favre's tutor and friend, Juan de la Peña, who seemed to have exerted the greatest influence on him. He shared the same room in Sainte-Barbe with his tutor for eleven years, so they had plenty of time for discussion. Peña expounded with enthusiasm a rather eclectic doctrine, a mixture of Ockhamism, Scotism, and Thomism. Notable for his open mind, he relied heavily upon Gabriel Biel's *Commentary on the Sentences of Peter Lombard.*

Thus, eclecticism played an important part in Favre's intellectual formation, especially the fundamental philosophical and theological position held and taught by almost all professors at the time; and it was this philosophy that determined the validity of rational thought. The adherents of Ockham's nominalism distinguished between what God, free, all-powerful, and all-merciful, has in fact ordained *(potentia ordinata)* and what he could have decreed *(potentia absoluta)*. The latter,

---

[46] For a portrayal of theology at Paris before and during these years, see James K. Farge, *Orthodoxy and Reform in Early Reformation France: The Faculty of Theology of Paris, 1500–1543* (Leiden, 1985).

[47] He gives their names in a letter to Gouveia (*Sti. Ignatii epistolæ et instructiones,* Monumenta Ignatiana, MHSI [Rome, 1964]) 1:133–134: Jacques Barthélemy, professor at the Sorbonne; Pierre de Cornibus, Franciscan; François Picart and Jean Adam, who both taught in the Collège de Navarre; Robert Wauchope, from Sainte-Barbe; Thomas Laurent and Jean Benoit, Dominicans from Saint-Jacques.

[48] Lacouture, *Jesuits,* pp. 52–53.

implying absolute freedom, is alone certain; the former, God's declared way of acting in the universe, possessed no speculative significance either philosophical or theological. As a consequence, arguments depending on the de facto or historical order could only lead to probable conclusions—probable because God's freedom means that he can always intervene to transform the present order. Therefore, no matter how rigorously established a conclusion might be, it would be valid only within a given system that could always admit of change. Similarly, just as no general statement about the external universe could be called true, so no kind of act in itself could be called good. The true was what God had revealed; the good, what he had commanded. All things depend upon his will; however, the present order of nature and salvation is not necessary but has been freely established by God, who could have established a different order (and acted according to it) so long as it did not involve contradiction. The ultimate foundation of the moral order and of the distinction between good and evil is also the will of God, so that sin comes to be equated with prohibition and good is determined by the will of God rather than any intrinsic intelligibility. (The most radical of this school went so far as to say that God could command someone to hate him.) Revelation and faith became the criteria for conclusions formerly held as rationally demonstrable, and with this change went a corresponding skepticism about the intellect's capacity to arrive at certainty in natural science or in philosophy.[49]

To some extent this teaching formed Favre's vision of the universe and there are traces of it in the *Memoriale*—a universe that depends for its order upon God's goodness exclusively, one whose values are founded on his "favor" *(gratia)*, one in which everything can be hoped for from the always unforeseen "generosity" *(liberalitas)* of his love. This insistence on personal relationships could emphasize a contingent aspect in religious experience. Consequently, the successive instants of the interior life, like the unforeseen events of history, were looked on as signs of God's "favor" and intimations of his decisions. The will of God who is love makes itself known to the heart and imparts to many greater

---

[49] However, as Copleston says in commenting on nominalists in general, "[T]his critical attitude in regard to metaphysical speculation was practically always combined with a firm theological faith and a firm belief in revelation as a source of certain knowledge. . . . If one attempts to turn the nominalists into rationalists or even skeptics in the modern sense, one is taking them out of their historical setting and severing them from their mental background. In the course of time nominalism became one of the regular currents in Scholastic thought; and a theological chair of nominalism was erected even in the University of Salamanca." Frederick Copleston, S.J., *A History of Philosophy*, vol. 3, part 1, p. 60.

certainty than they could gain from an intellectual understanding of the faith.⁵⁰

The *Memoriale* reflects this theological background: time and again we meet the underlying principle and the characteristic terminology of nominalist theology. Implicit in Favre's pages, this point of view starts from the same voluntarist and extrinsecist presuppositions that Luther employs. Like Luther, Favre had been taught a will-based theology that stressed personal relationships with God, and so led him to seek in interior experience for the sign that he had been accepted by God. Luther, too conscious of his sinful state to believe in an inner transformation of his being, looked on the relationship as one of "trust" *(fiducia)*, a passive expectation of God's forgiving mercy, the sole transformation being in man's personal attitude to God. From the same presuppositions Favre reaches quite different conclusions: the relationship is founded on God's action in the depths of the being; the transformation is an ontological reality.⁵¹

Thus we find Favre recording his subjective experiences, mostly in prayer, aware that they must be set down in full and exactly as they happened, without any addition (§140). There is also a danger of distortion in any attempt to describe a nonconceptual *datum,* for by its nature such an experience cannot be expressed in words. This, of course, is the fundamental problem in the communication of subjective experience, and efforts to solve it have always proved inadequate. There is, too, the personal problem—indeed, it is one of the permanent anxieties of every devout Christian: how can a certainty of God's presence in the soul be made to prevail over a consciousness of one's own weakness? As we know from the *Memoriale,* Favre shared in the anguished quest for certainty common at the time, constantly bewailing his own shortcomings and spiritual backwardness. He had to struggle continually against temptations to pessimism. To shore up his inner conviction of salvation, he had need of external signs: faith in the Church in spite of its degeneracy and its seeming incapacity to reform itself, faith in the lives of men and women who had been transformed by the Spirit, the Eucharistic presence, sacramentals. For all these things bear witness to the inner reality of the faith, and they increase the hope of salvation.⁵²

---

⁵⁰ Nothing more vividly illustrates the complete separation between reason and faith, between philosophy and theology, between theological speculation and devotion, than the simple piety and geuine holiness of life observed in some of the nominalists. Good religious that they were in the main, they left their skepticism at the doors of their churches, chapels, and oratories before entering.

⁵¹ A fuller discussion of this point can be found in §289 n. 127.

⁵² §§129–130 nn. 262, 263.

But Favre does not seem to have clearly conceived how the divine "favor" *(gratia)*, which attests the truth of that inner reality, could at the same time be God's action in him and the communication of the Spirit as well. That they are two aspects of one and the same reality his own experience had taught him; but in his expression of them—really in his thinking about them—they do not appear to have been reconciled. For in describing them he has recourse to two sets of terms, one deriving from nominalist theology, the other reverting to themes found in mystical tradition. On the one hand, grace is synonymous with a benevolent attitude on God's part and made known to man through his "favors": there is a reward of glory for faithful souls (§§289–292). On the other hand, grace is the divine life poured out into the humanity of Christ as into a vessel, so that those who are linked with Christ may in their turn be filled from its overflow (§275). This double terminology betrays an uncertainty of thought that is still either unable to give an account of an experiential relationship with God or does not see the need for such an account.

So much for Favre's intellectual preparation. His theological studies, begun in 1530, had to be broken off six years later, on January 25, 1537, when Ignatius and the first companions honored their pledge to begin a pilgrimage to the Holy Land. Favre was never to receive his doctorate.

Favre's Life of Ministry

Once the first companions had arrived in Rome and placed themselves at the service of the Pope, they began a series of apostolic ministries that would eventually define the new order.[53] Mobility would prove to be paramount among the characteristics of this band, and the papal order that dispatched Favre and Laínez from Rome to Parma in May 1539 began the constant movement that would end only with Favre's death in August 1546. From that month of May on, pope or emperor, cardinal or nuncio, or his superior, Ignatius, would decide when and where Favre went, turning his life into a round of constant travel, endless pastoral activity, and charitable enterprises. It formed the background against which the drama of his inner life was to be played out. Circumstances made him a pilgrim, a perpetual traveler; and he willingly embraced

---

[53] O'Malley, *First Jesuits,* pp. 14–18, presents his three theses on the early companions: that the Society of Jesus underwent great change between 1540 and 1565; that efforts to counter Protestant reform also brought change in Roman Catholicism; and, especially, that the Jesuits could best be known by the apostolic works they undertook. "What the Jesuits did will tell us what they were."

that life with all its trials, mirroring a pilgrimage in the spiritual life as well as in physical reality.

He made his slow and toilsome way along the roads of the empire mostly on foot, sometimes on muleback. His baggage consisted of a few papers, including the notes of the *Memoriale,* some books, his Breviary, and a small bundle of personal effects. From 1543 on, he also carried the portable altar for which he had obtained permission.[54] What he brought with him was all he had on earth, and the road he trod was the only ground he could claim as his own. He stayed with friends, passed the night in inns or in hospitals, and sometimes he even slept under the stars. Though usually with a group, he was constantly at risk from the dangers that beset all travelers in those days. He traveled in any kind of weather, always overworked, frequently undernourished, a prey to the recurring fever that gradually undermined his health and eventually brought on his collapse. Sustained throughout those seven years by his faith in God, by a vocation growing ever more stable, and by an acceptance of trials, he began to see his wandering life as an image of that greater pilgrimage made by the human soul to its home in heaven.

But his endless journeying involved a psychological suffering that was even harder to bear than the physical difficulties. He arrived a stranger in a country, new to its customs and its ways of thinking. In Germany, for instance, he never learned German; instead he spoke Latin or faulty Spanish or made use of an interpreter when needed. Each new center meant a fresh adaptation, and each new posting took him away from friends and from pastoral work, the long-term results of which he was never to see.[55] And his sensitive temperament intensified his suffering. Yet so deeply convinced was he that this was the life God wanted him to lead that he wrote to Ignatius five months before his death, "For my part I should be glad never to be settled in a place but would rather set forth on a lifelong pilgrimage through one or other parts of the world." He then offers himself for further missions "without a settled place and without rest."

Favre and Laínez remained in Parma until September 1540, engaged in pastoral work with the aid of Jerónimo Doménech. In August Favre was ordered by Pope Paul III to accompany Dr. Pedro Ortiz on his return to Spain, in the hope of establishing a Jesuit community there. Ortiz was a learned theologian in his own right and had been serving as

---

[54] *MonFabri,* p. 214, a letter to the nuncio, Poggio.

[55] "Our Lord knows the reasons why I do not deserve to stay in one place for any length of time but am always being taken away at the moment when the harvest begins to peak." See document VIII below, p. 339. A remonstrance, gentle but pained.

Emperor Charles V's personal representative to the papal court.[56] Favre was doing so much good in Parma that prominent citizens began to use influence to keep him among them. Writing to Ignatius about his ministry, he mentions these efforts with some embarrassment, disclaiming any part in the matter: "You may be certain, no matter what happens, that I had no part in it."[57] Nothing in fact did come of it, and in a farewell letter to his "dearest children and brothers in Christ" entitled *Directions for Persevering in a Truly Christian and Spiritual Life,* Favre recommends frequent reception of the sacraments, especially the Holy Eucharist; gives instructions about night and morning prayer; and, as a preparation for sacramental Communion, recommends making an act of spiritual Communion at the consecration of the Mass. The "instruction" is worth study as an illustration of his pastoral practice.[58]

In the meantime, arrangements had been completed for holding a colloquy in the city of Worms between Catholic and Protestant divines. The emperor, Charles V, commanded Ortiz to attend this gathering as his representative rather than going to Spain, bringing along Master Pierre Favre, the Paris theologian, who was to accompany him to Worms as a member of his household. So Favre left Parma at the beginning of October, met Ortiz and his retinue at Piacenza, and rode on with them to Worms, reaching there on October 24, 1540, the feast of St. Raphael the Archangel.

They found the city of Worms a stronghold of Lutheranism. It is likely that experiencing there the growth and penetrating power of Lutheranism made Favre realize for the first time the challenge it posed to the Church. He began pastoral work, engaged in spiritual direction, and gave the Exercises to eminent churchmen and to the household of the imperial ambassador. In that way he undertook the inner reform of individuals, which for him was the only true reform.

Things went so badly in the assembly that the Emperor was forced to adjourn it to Ratisbon (Regensburg), where he could be present in person and make efforts to restore religious peace in Germany. On their way south to Ratisbon, Ortiz and his party stopped for about fifteen days in Speyer. There Favre found himself much in demand among

---

[56] Lacouture, *Jesuits,* pp. 66–67, gives an especially good description of the turnabout in Ortiz's estimation of Ignatius and the early companions.

[57] Document I below, p. 320.

[58] It had been written for a group who would a few months later be formed into a confraternity. The full text is included among the letters in this volume, document II, pp. 321–323. See also Christopher F. Black, *Italian Confraternities in the Sixteenth Century* (Cambridge, 1989) for a comprehensive study of such organizations of the laity.

priests, prelates, and those in high places. Even during the short time then available to him, he began giving the Exercises. At the beginning of February 1541, Ortiz and he left for Ratisbon, arriving there on February 23, just before the beginning of Lent. While Ortiz addressed the Emperor and his court twice daily, Favre heard confessions, engaged in spiritual direction, and again gave the Exercises, his most effective pastoral ministry.[59]

But Favre was losing hope. He wrote to Ignatius that words and arguments were no longer sufficient to convince heretics either in Ratisbon or in any other place.[60] The Catholic side was divided both politically and religiously, and had no idea how to communicate its position in the vernacular, a skill at which the Protestant side excelled. Catholics relied too much on the Fathers of the Church and too little on scriptural arguments. In July the Diet finally collapsed over questions concerning the sacraments, transubstantiation, and the authority of the pope. At the end of the month, Favre left Ratisbon for Spain with Ortiz, who was now free to resume his interrupted journey home. On their way they spent nine days in Savoy, but Favre merely mentions that the party passed through his native district. After leaving there, they entered the small town of Nantua near the Rhone River. There the French garrison imprisoned them for a week. Released at last, they traveled down the Rhone, then went west through Nîmes, Montpellier, Béziers, and Narbonne. Crossing the Spanish frontier, they made their way to Montserrat and progressed by slow stages to Madrid, arriving there at the end of October 1541. Their journey had taken about three months.

Once in Madrid, the indefatigable Ortiz saw to it that Favre did not lack for work. A few days after their arrival, he took Favre to Galapagar nearby, where he had a benefice with a right to the revenue of the parish. Though not a priest, Ortiz was conscientious enough to have appointed a priest, a licentiate in arts and in theology, to look after the spiritual needs of the parish. After three days he departed for Madrid leaving Favre to spend November and December in Galapagar. As soon as he could, Favre began to teach catechism to the children and gave the Exercises to some priests. So pleased was Ortiz with his success that he instructed Favre to remain in the parish until the work was finished.

In January 1542, however, a letter from the Pope summoned Favre to Germany. He was to join two other Jesuits, Nicolás Bobadilla and Claude Jay, as advisers to Cardinal Giovanni Morone in drawing up proposals for a council of the Church. After spending three days with the

---

[59] O'Malley, *First Jesuits,* 286–287.
[60] *MonFabri,* 98–99.

Infantas, children of the King, whose court was located in the city of Ocaña, he went to Toledo to bid farewell to Ortiz. The doctor was greatly distressed at his leaving, for he had entertained high hopes that Favre would have accomplished much good in Spain and for the Society there. He went so far as to protest Favre's recall in a letter to Cardinal Alessandro Farnese, but in vain. So Favre left Ocaña with one of the court chaplains, who had been sent by the Infantas, to accompany him to Toledo. Then the other court chaplain was dispatched to join him and to proceed beyond Toledo. The three traveled to Barcelona, left there in early March, reached the French border by way of Perpignan, and by March 26 were in Lyons. From Lyons they journeyed through Savoy, passed through Switzerland, and finally reached Speyer on April 14, 1542. In his *Memoriale,* Favre mentioned the dangers of the journey, and two days later he described them again in a letter to Ignatius.[61]

By the time they arrived in Speyer, the plan for the reform of Catholic life in Germany, drawn up in outline by Cardinal Contarini under the authority of Cardinal Morone, whom Favre and the others were advising, had already been put into effect.[62] It was the modest beginning of an activity that would one day spread across Europe. Claude Jay had been sent to work with Robert Wauchope, the primate of Armagh, in Bavaria and the area of the upper Danube. Bobadilla had left Speyer for Ratisbon a few days before Favre arrived, but left behind a letter containing Cardinal Morone's instructions for him, which gave him a good deal of freedom. Favre's regret at having missed the papal legate, Morone, and the fear that he might have been to blame caused him some worry. He would have been more at ease if Morone had given him precise directions. So, feeling unable to choose a course of action himself, he wrote to Ignatius for instructions.[63] The local bishop, whom he had known from his brief visit of the year before, advised him to remain in Speyer for the time being. There was plenty of priestly work to be done in the capital of the Bavarian Palatinate, which was in great need of reform. A cathedral canon he had met in Ratisbon, Otto Truchsess von Waldburg, at this time an imperial councilor and later bishop of Augsburg and cardinal, made him welcome and invited him to stay in the presbytery as a guest.

Favre must have been grateful for the kindly act, for he and his companions were being treated by some Catholics as if they were papal spies sent to report on the faith and morals of the priests and people of

---

[61] *MonFabri,* 159.

[62] For Contarini, see Elizabeth G. Gleason, *Gasparo Contarini: Venice, Rome, and Reform* (Berkeley, 1993).

[63] Document VI below, pp. 333–336.

the Rhineland. Known to be the nuncio's assistant, he was often received with great coldness and even open hostility. At the same time, he felt deeply depressed about the state of religion in the Rhineland.[64] But the inhabitants of Speyer soon realized that the reputed spy was a man of God, wholly selfless, whose only purpose was to serve God and with infinite gentleness persuade others to do the same. In only a month many, including a good number of priests, were coming to him to confess and make the Exercises.

With the exception of ten days spent in Mainz from September 15 to 28, he remained in Speyer until October. During that visit the cardinal-archbishop of Mainz, Albert of Brandenburg, was so impressed with Favre that he insisted that the Jesuit be transferred to Mainz. Though sorry to leave Speyer, Favre was glad to remain among the German people, for whom he felt a growing affection. He even admitted to Cardinal Contarini that he himself felt greater inspiration and deeper devotion in Germany than he had in Spain.[65]

The Pope was busy making arrangements for the opening of the Council of Trent early in 1543 and had invited prelates from all over Europe to attend. The cardinal-archbishop's first intention was to send Favre to Trent with Michael Helding, one of his auxiliary bishops; but as news came that the council had to be postponed because only a very few bishops had gone to Trent, Favre and the two chaplains, who were now novices of the Society of Jesus, began to hear confessions and give the Exercises to the clergy of Mainz. One of his retreatants, a priest of the cathedral, remarked that God had brought Favre into Germany solely for the salvation of the Germans. On November 7, Michael Helding, the suffragan bishop, and Julius Pflug, bishop of Naumburg, began the Exercises under his direction. Favre had great hopes that these men would do much good in Germany.[66]

---

[64] "God knows what I went through in Speyer, struggling against despair of any good for Germany." Document VIII below, p. 339. See Stephen E. Ozment, *The Reformation in the Cities: The Appeal of Protestantism to Sixteenth Century Germany and Switzerland* (New Haven, 1975).

[65] *MonFabri*, p. 171.

[66] Pflug (1499–1564) is an apt example of the religious complexity that Favre confronted in sixteenth-century Germany. He was undoubtedly Catholic, indeed the last Catholic bishop in sixteenth-century Saxony. Yet he was never consecrated a bishop and not even ordained a priest, and he never had an auxiliary bishop to carry out episcopal functions. He has been taxed as a "political" prelate; but he knew, and he was right about it, that the survival of Catholicism in the north of Germany depended in great part on politics. He championed two "Protestant" positions, clerical marriage and the Eucharist under both kinds for the laity; but even before Trent he also worked to set up his own diocesan seminary, something that took many German

At the bidding of the cardinal, he added to his work by giving a series of lectures on the Psalms to the theological faculty of the university of Mainz. He attracted three times more listeners than did the ordinary lecturers at the university. In addition to his ever increasing pastoral work, he induced the cardinal to open a hospice for pilgrims and needy travelers. He walked the city streets begging alms for the sick poor, brought them to hostels, and there visited, tended, and consoled them. By now his reputation for holiness had traveled down the Rhine as far as Cologne and brought Peter Canisius to meet him in Mainz.

Favre captivated Canisius and gave him the Spiritual Exercises. On his return to Cologne, Canisius described Favre to Gerhard Kalckbrenner in such glowing terms that the latter began to exert his influence to have him transferred to that city.[67] Favre was needed there to help the clergy, the university, and the civic dignitaries who together were fighting a strenuous campaign against the attempt by their archbishop, Hermann von Wied, to Lutheranize his enormous diocese. So to Cologne he went. Within a short time the Catholic party there had formed such a high opinion of his tact and persuasive powers that they appointed him the university's ambassador extraordinary to the Emperor at Bonn. On his return he began his customary pastoral work. After only a month his success was so great that the townspeople got up a petition to the nuncio to have him remain in Cologne, where his work, as he said himself, bore more fruit than it had in any other place in Germany. But a letter from Ignatius summoned him to Portugal, since King John III was strongly insisting on Jesuit foundations in his realm. He left Cologne for the port city of Antwerp at the end of September 1543. He could not find a ship bound for Portugal and so went to Louvain in October. There he fell ill for two months. Still, he persisted in exercising his apostolates from his sickbed, took care of the formation of the Jesuit novices there, and worked with the university students. In January 1544 he returned to Cologne at the request of the nuncio, preached and gave conferences, founded a Jesuit community there, and wrote his *Instructions on Confes-*

---

bishops almost two hundred years to do after Trent.

[67] Gerhard Kalckbrenner, born at Hammont in Limbourg ca. 1489, entered the Carthusians at Cologne in 1518. Professed in 1520 and elected prior in 1536, he retained that office until his death in 1566. In addition to translating Hendrik Herp, he wrote a number of works with the aim of making Rhenish mysticism accessible to all. He was a leading member of the Counter-Reformation. One of the brightest lights of his order, he was, after Xavier, Favre's greatest friend. For an overview of the remarkable persistance of the Carthusians in those tumultuous times and for remarks on Kalckbrenner, see Dennis P. Martin, "Carthusians during the Reformation Era: 'Cartusia Numquam Deformata, Reformari Resistens,'" *The Catholic Historical Review* 81, no. 1 (January 1995): 41–66.

sion. Finally, in July he was able to take ship at Antwerp and arrived in Portugal on August 24, 1544.

He remained five months with the court at Évora but was in poor health and in low spirits, suffering and unable to do much work. While in the Jesuit house at Coimbra for a few weeks, he advised about some problems in the community, heard confessions, and gave exhortations. From January 1545 he was with the court in Évora once again, but his health was clearly deteriorating. In March 1545, despite his weakened condition, he left Évora for Spain and devoted the next twelve months to a series of apostolic journeys. First he set out for Valladolid in March, then paid a brief visit to Galapagar in May; he returned to Valladolid from May to September, then traveled to Madrid and Alcalá, with side trips to neighboring towns. Then in Madrid he fell ill again for three weeks; scarcely recovered, he went off to Toledo and then returned to Madrid, departing from there in April 1546 bound for Rome and the Council of Trent by way of Gandía and Barcelona. Each of these journeys had an apostolic purpose: In Valladolid and Alcalá it was to found Jesuit communities, in Ocaña it was to console a bereaved family, in Toledo it was to give the Exercises. We can only guess what effect this incessant traveling had on him, with his constitution already undermined by years of overwork, mortification, and recurrent bouts of serious illness.

In mid-July 1546, just over seven years since he had set out for Parma with Laínez, he arrived back in Rome. Measuring his journeys straight as the crow is said to fly, we conclude that he had covered seven thousand miles during those seven years. To add unrecorded journeys to the twists and turns of the road would surely double that total. In a week of reasonable health in Rome, he wrote to Laínez, then at Trent, what was to be the last letter of his life, reminding him to write and console his mother in Spain on the recent death of his father, and assuring him that he himself had taken care to have many Masses said for the repose of his soul. His purpose in writing was to explain that the Roman dog days had delayed his departure for Trent and consequently prevented him from delivering the letters, entrusted to him in Spain, that had been addressed to persons, both important and unimportant, in Rome. Still, the letter was also a typical act of kindness, full of a tender concern for the members of the Laínez family, to whom he had already sent a letter of consolation while he was still in Spain.

Favre died, joyfully looking forward to heaven, on August 1, 1546, the feast of St. Peter in Chains, leaving his brethren in Rome and elsewhere and his multitude of friends everywhere, desolate at his passing. Polanco recorded the event as follows: "Since God in his goodness summoned his Favre to the Council of Heaven instead of the Council of

Trent *[ad coeleste concilium potius quam ad Tridentinum]*, he was, on the feast of St. Peter in Chains, set free from the chains of his earthly life and so took wing for the liberty of heavenly life."[68]

The news traveled fast and aroused sorrow wherever he had worked in Europe. Everywhere, with remarkable unanimity, people looked on him and referred to him as a saint. In Spain, he was held in such repute for sanctity that people even said that his death would spell the end of the Society, although it had by then spread to many places. And his reputation was no less high in those other countries where he had toiled so zealously. In a way, Favre was canonized by universal acclaim at his death, and since then no one in his native village or in the surrounding district has ever used his name without the prefix "blessed" or "saint."

No authentic portrait of Favre exists, and the description we have of him is vague. He is said to have been fair-haired, of good height, and soft-spoken.[69] All agree about his kindness and wonderfully attractive manner. Simão Rodrigues, one of the first companions of Ignatius, paid him this tribute two years before his own death in 1579: "In his dealings with others he revealed such a rare and delightful sweetness and charm as I have never to this day, I must admit, found in anyone else. In some way or other, he used to make friends with people, and by the kindness of his manner and speech so won his way into all hearts that he set them on fire with the love of God."[70]

That was the key to his apostolate: friendship leading to conversion. Wherever he went, his irresistible charm drew people to him for spiritual direction. They thronged his confessional, grew disconsolate and complained when he was transferred, and if they were in a position to do so, used influence to have him remain with them.[71] They never forgot him, nor he them, for he highly valued his friends and prayed for

---

[68] *MonFabri*, pp. 839–841.

[69] De Certeau, *Mémorial*, p. 9. n. 2; *MonFabri*, p. 776.

[70] *Epistolæ PP Paschasii Broëti . . . et Simonis Rodericii*, vol. 24 of MHSI (Madrid, 1903), p. 453.

[71] Consider, for instance, the efforts of the city council of Parma in 1540 to influence the Holy See to have either Favre or Laínez left in Parma, and those made by Giacoma Pallavacino to persuade Pope Paul III to cancel the order commanding Favre to go to Spain, as described in Bangert, *To the Other Towns*, pp. 79–80. Some years later she regularly signed herself "Jacoppa dela Compagnia dai Jesus" and argued with Ignatius for admittance to the Society because she had been called by God through the voices of Master Peter [Favre] and Master James [Laínez] of your holy Company" when they had been in Parma. Then too there is the letter of September 7, 1543, from the citizens of Cologne to the apostolic nuncio, Poggio, formally requesting him to allow Favre to remain in that city. *MonFabri*, pp. 451–452.

them constantly when they were dead. So all-embracing was his sense of gratitude that he remembered his relatives and even those who had administered the sacraments to him during his life. This gift for friendship with high and low, learned and unlearned, was the source of his greatest successes in the apostolate: personal contacts leading to spiritual conversation, then conversion; and the spiritual direction of those making the Exercises. They were, as he called them, his "spiritual sons and daughters," and they came from all walks in life.

He reveals himself in the *Memoriale* as simple, unaffected, sensitive, with a compassion universal in scope and a conscience delicate at times to the point of scrupulosity.[72] Unshakably confident in his vocation, he nonetheless worried on occasion about the best course to follow or felt irresolute when faced with a decision. This may well be linked with his constant recourse to discernment; indeed he may have experienced a certain compulsiveness in his manner of practicing it. He was prone to extremes of elation and depression. Such an emotional instability hindered his apostolate by making it difficult for him either to judge a situation objectively or initiate a course of action when in the throes of depression. A principal cause of this depression was the religious state of Germany: the dread that it would totally defect from the faith haunted him and brought him at times close to despair. Yet so great was his strength of purpose that he never asked to be relieved of this mission despite temptations to do so. His steadfastness and determination came from a level much deeper than his emotions.

Favre and the World of the Sixteenth Century

It was only during their journey from Paris to Venice (1536–1537), it seems, that the first companions grasped the reality of Protestantism and saw with their own eyes how widespread it had become. They realized then that it was no longer a doctrine held by a few but a religion lived by many. When considering the part that Favre played in those circumstances, we must remind ourselves that in Renaissance Europe both Catholics and Protestants recognized and upheld the medieval principle "One faith, one law, one king." Luther and Calvin consolidated it by encouraging rulers to enforce religious unity within their borders. Though he hesitated at first, Luther gave a prince the right to punish dissenters with death. To allow religious dissent and the form of worship

---

[72] The references are in §§6–14. Gonçalves da Câmara relates that in Paris Favre once could not make up his mind whether to tip the barber a *double* or a *liard*—coins of quite low value, the difference between them being exactly one-twelfth of a *sou*. The story is indicative. *Fontes narrativi de Sancto Ignatio,* vol. 66 of MHSI (Rome, 1951) 1:724–725.

it entailed was regarded all over Europe as tantamount to weakening the state.

The sixteenth century valued human life, but it valued the afterlife still more. The average person feared death, but did not attribute to it the absolute finality with which the unbeliever of today regards it. So both the Catholic and the Protestant facing execution in that century went to pyre or scaffold in the unshakable confidence that they were witnessing to Christ. At the beginning of the sixteenth century, all European Christians saw that reform was necessary, yet no one was strong or courageous enough to carry it out.

At the center of this disturbed and unsettled spiritual world was the uncertainty spawned by Ockham and his skepticism, a skepticism that discouraged any attempt by the human reason to attain to certain knowledge of God. It discarded as an unnecessary assumption any God-given habit or capacity in the human soul, the "sanctifying grace" of traditional Catholic theology. This form of nominalism, which had captured most of the universities of Europe by 1500, turned theology into an exercise in dialectical ingenuity with little reference to traditional teachings. Thus theology began to separate itself from philosophy and the devotional life from theology, though as yet devotional life had not parted company with the Church. Reason and faith were totally cut off from each other. Indeed, one of the most striking phenomena of the age was precisely this mixture of skepticism and credulity.[73]

Furthermore, this intellectual anxiety continued to affect the emotional and devotional lives of its victims. People did not dare to act without invoking the saints, but they were also very much afraid of the punishments those same saints could inflict, even for something as trivial as not showing them due respect. At the same time, the faithful were preoccupied with sin and its consequences, and morbidly brooded on death, judgment, and the merited punishment that they ushered in.[74]

In truth, death held a fascination for people. It became one of the most popular themes for sermons to the faithful. Together with providing a moving iconography of the Passion, at times of startling realism in accord with the devotional taste of the age, artists created a multitude of *Danses macabres* picturing a naked Death leading an unwilling yet submissive file of the dead in a wild and irresistible dance, the round dance of man's destiny. The human person is born to die: this doleful

---

[73] For a similar portrayal in the life of Martin Luther, see Oberman, *Luther*.

[74] See Jean Delumeau, *Sin and Fear: The Emergence of a Western Guilt Culture, 13th–18th Centuries,* trans. Eric Nicholson (New York, 1990). The author gives a thoughtful and extended treatment of these circumstances.

message was repeated in a thousand different ways, but the world too is in the process of passing away.[75] A mortal anguish, apocalyptic in its proportions—indeed, it possesses people of every age, but weighs more heavily on them in times of trial and misfortune—loomed over those decades.

But by far the worst affliction of the century was its all-pervasive fear of the devil; it was the age of the original Dr. Faustus.[76]

> A healthy belief in the devil can be a tonic part of religion without which Christianity would no longer be the religion of Christ, but the belief of those days had turned to a disease. Indeed, it was not so much a belief as a perpetual nightmare that lay heavy on Catholic as well as Protestant imaginations. Fear of the devil pressed like an icy hand on Luther's heart and inspired a good deal of his theology, while on the Catholic side it created a whole body of literature on the problems of possession. Often enough, ability to deal with cases of alleged possession was regarded as a touchstone of true religion, and in many places in Germany keen competition sprang up between ministers and priests to see which side could get a particular devil out first.[77]

And not one of the cultured minds that steeped themselves in that seductive lore ever seemed to have realized how necessary it was to guard against a state of universal gullibility, which, as we have seen, was a surprising attitude in so critical a generation.

Favre's contacts with Protestantism were for the most part indirect; aside from a debate with Bucer and some other Protestant leaders in Bonn, his dealings were with Catholics who had already left the Church or were contemplating that step. He could not but regard them as lost or straying sheep to be brought back to the fold, to the teaching and authority of the Catholic Church. He reveals no understanding of the strength of Protestant convictions. In the *Memoriale* his frequent

---

[75] The celebrated sequence written by Thomas de Celano in the previous century, the *Dies iræ*, was now a popular part of the liturgy of the dead. The reader acquainted with the original Latin might well read it again and note how the poem expresses the dread of the age as it contemplates death, judgment, and the end of the world. It matters little whether the equally celebrated melody was written expressly for the words or not; the marriage of text and music was surely an act of genius. Consider, for instance, how the first eight notes imitate the motion of a corpse swaying in time to the steps of its bearers.

[76] Georg (later Johann) Faust (ca. 1480–1540) was a historical figure around whose colorful and somewhat scandalous person a mass of legendary tales has accumulated. Their common theme was one of man's oldest dreams, to acquire boundless knowledge and happiness through a pact with preternatural powers. The development of these legends, reflecting the intellectual climate of sixteenth-century Germany, added to the traditional plot the ruin of man's soul by demons.

[77] Brodrick, *Canisius*, pp. 64–65.

references to the reformers and their doctrine show that for him their leaders were defectors, "teachers of division and secession." Yet we find not a single trace of a harsh or bigoted judgment: those "teachers of division and secession" become the objects of his pastoral solicitude as he prays for them and even for the scourge of western Europe in those days, the Grand Turk. At most, one senses a kind of incredulous scorn as he describes how the Protestants "put together their own faith—better called their opinions and their errors."

By temperament he was in favor of conciliation, gentle persuasion instead of constraint, moral reform rather than theological controversy. His humanist formation in Sainte-Barbe would have inclined him to abhor the use of violence against heretics, as would the many public executions he had witnessed; for all university students were required by rule to attend executions of heretics.[78] The *Memoriale* is silent about them, but we can form an idea of what he must have thought as a spectator. In a letter from Madrid on March 12, 1546, to Kalckbrenner, prior of the Cologne charterhouse, he deplores the use of violence in so many places against Lutherans, Zwinglians, and Calvinists. He does not mince words:

> It pains me to see that the authorities and rulers of the earth, and even the Cherubim and Seraphim, consider the public execution *[extirpatio]* of known heretics to be their only course of action in these our days. I mean—and I have often told them this to their faces—that the builders of the City of God are using both hands to brandish their swords in the presence of the enemy. Good Lord! Why do we not leave one hand free for the work of restoration? Why is nothing being done to bring about a reform of all Christian life and states?—I am not referring to doctrinal and moral teaching, for there is nothing wrong there.[79]

In a letter to Laínez, who had asked for advice on how to deal with those who left the Church, there is no compromise, for his purpose

---

[78] On October 18, 1534, Paris awoke to find that placards attacking the Mass in blasphemous terms had been posted throughout the city. The same had been done in other French towns such Orléans, Rouen, Tours, and Blois. A placard was attached even to the door of the King's bedchamber in his château at Amboise. The King, sincerely shocked at the blasphemy, became furious at what he considered a threat to his authority and a danger to the realm. Many arrests were made. During the winter of 1534–1535, Favre and his fellow students were constrained as a matter of university discipline to attend about forty torturings and burnings in the grim Place Maubert. Among them were a draper from Noyon, a printer, a weaver, a mason, a schoolmistress, a well-off merchant, even a half-paralyzed shoemaker, and a fifteen-year-old schoolboy said to be a Lutheran. Most piteous of all was the young chorister from the royal chapel, scarcely fourteen years old, who had affixed the poster to the door of the King's apartment.

[79] *MonFabri*, pp. 412–416.

remains to bring them back to the Church and have them submit again to its discipline.[80] Not, however, by way of controversy; he is convinced that in the long run this approach is sterile. Rather, he counsels a friendly, compassionate, and loving approach to them as persons who need spiritual help. Before entering into detail, he lays down two basic principles for the apostolate among Protestants:

> 1. Anyone wanting to help the heretics of this age must be careful to have great charity for them and to love them in truth, banishing from his soul all considerations which would tend to chill his esteem for them.
>
> 2. We need to win their goodwill, so that they will love us and accord us a good place in their hearts. This can be done by speaking familiarly with them about matters we both share in common and avoiding any debate in which one side tries to put down the other. We must establish communion in what unites us before doing so in what might evince differences of opinion.[81]

Favre's development of these "rules" *(reglas)* reveals his conviction that appeal to anyone must be made primarily through the affections, without however neglecting debate. Though he set down what first came to mind as he wrote, it is clear that his advice was the fruit of long and prayerful meditation.

Because of his presence at the Colloquies of Worms and Ratisbon (1540–1541) he found himself in the center of the polemical arena; around him were the contestants. The Protestant position had been immensely strengthened by the Schmalkalden Articles of 1537, the second part of which, agreed to by the Protestant princes, asserted justification by faith alone. These articles rejected the Mass, purgatory, pilgrimages, relics, indulgences, and the invocation of saints. Monasteries and convents were to be suppressed, and the institution of the papacy itself was deemed to be of human origin. Sharing in the conciliatory mood and policy of Contarini, Favre had hoped for some result from Worms and Ratisbon. He was willing to debate with the Protestant leaders, but after his own manner. He would not provoke them nor would he treat with them in a spirit of contradiction nor would he consider compromise even for a moment.[82] He would agree with what his friend and superior, Contarini, wrote to Johann Eck: "Even in a desperate cause, the Christian must not abandon all hope; he should hope against all hope."

The cause was truly desperate. Favre, who missed little of what went on, was astonished to learn the weakness of the Catholic side and

---

[80] Document XXIV below, pp. 379–381.
[81] Ibid., p. 379.
[82] *MonFabri*, p. 49. The whole letter (pp. 44–51) is worth reading.

its tendency to compromise; no such tendency manifested itself among their opponents. In his letters to Ignatius, he makes shrewd comments on the various groups congregated in the Rhineland town and on the mixed motives, often more political than religious, that had brought them there. The eight Catholic theologians chosen to dispute with eight Protestant divines were at loggerheads with each other, forming a wavering and irresolute group even on the eve of the disputation. And because of their nominalist theological formation, they were hopelessly confused about the doctrine of justification. Moreover, they relied too little on scriptural arguments and too much on the Fathers and ecclesiastical authors; they were overly credulous about historical matters, too ready to accept as genuine what were really apocryphal documents.

In a letter to Ignatius from Worms on December 27, 1540, Favre mentioned that he was giving the Exercises to a dean who had for a long time been vicar general of Worms and who no longer saw how he could shepherd a flock "so enamored of the wolves that they no longer feel their bites, being already dead."[83] He lamented that in Worms there was little hope of converting a single Lutheran. In fact the Lutherans were winning adherents even among those who went there as Catholics.

Events forced Favre to make the same judgments in Speyer and in Ratisbon: Germany is sliding unchecked into Protestantism; the sole efficacious remedy is the spiritual renewal of the Church; violence, the remedy commonly resorted to, is useless. He thanks his Roman correspondents for edifying news about the spiritual vitality of the Church, for it will serve to show Germans that the Church lives in the Spirit if she can still boast of sons and daughters whose lives and teachings are of such high quality. Holiness of life will save the Church. A month later, writing from Ratisbon on May 12, 1541, to the scholastics in Paris, he comments that "mere learning is so ineffective against the heretics. With the world having reached such a state of unbelief, what are needed are arguments of deeds and of blood; otherwise things will only get worse and error will increase."[84]

Eventually, in a letter dated March 12, 1546, a few months before his death, and addressed to Kalckbrenner, prior of the Cologne charterhouse, he wrote that colloquies (assemblies of theologians from both sides with the hope of hammering out agreed statements) offered no solution to the religious crises of the time, as had been demonstrated on more than one occasion. Theological discussion tended only to harden attitudes, and any attempts at conciliation turned out, at most, to be wishful thinking and became positively dangerous at times. In the same

---

[83] Ibid., pp. 44–51.

[84] Document III below, p. 326.

letter he offers comfort in St. Paul's words: "Trust in Christ Jesus, who does not suffer his own to be tempted above their strength," and, "You know well, dearest brothers, that there must be heresies in order that men really tried by fire may appear to strengthen us."[85] Though it would not have occurred to him, he himself was one of those men "tried by fire."

As we have seen, Favre had rejected violence as a way of stamping out heresy. His own way was that of interior reform: Catholics should be guided to live more fervent lives, and there should be incessant prayer for all men without exception. In a way, he was undertaking the formation of a Catholic spiritual elite to fill that need. The Marian congregations that were later founded as a part of Jesuit ministry, both those attached to Jesuit schools and colleges and those that enrolled adults of all occupations and classes, would eventually constitute such an elite.[86] Reformation was his goal, one that had at its center a desire to return to the life of the early Church. It was a popular contemporary idea that became an ideal for many, including Favre himself. "Why do we not return, by means of teaching which is both old and new, to practices which were once those of the early Christians and the holy Fathers?"[87] His longing for reform became a kind of fever as he contemplated what he so often called the "ruins" of the Catholic Church.[88] In fact this contemplation colored his view of Protestantism, as he beheld Catholics lapsing into heresy. And the changing field of his ministry convincingly brought home to him how much the Protestants were gaining as the spiritual life of Catholics progressively weakened. He does not appear ever to have studied the works of the reformers—in Germany Catholics were forbidden to read them—and he was so immersed in pastoral work that he could spare little time for such study.[89] In and through that pastoral work, he came to know Protestantism, especially through his ever increasing spiritual direction of priests.

---

[85] *MonFabri*, p. 415.

[86] They later came to be called sodalities and are now called Christian Life Communities. See Louis Chatellier, *The Europe of the Devout: The Catholic Reformation and the Formation of a New Society* (Cambridge, 1989) for an illuminating and scholarly account of such congregations and of their accomplishments in the restoration of Christian life and practice in the seventeenth and eighteenth centuries.

[87] *MonFabri*, p. 414.

[88] *MonFabri*, pp. 44–51, pp. 54–58, and his only letter in French written to his cousin Claude Perissin, then prior of Le Reposoir. In a kind of summing up he writes, "[I] begin to recognize that these heresies of our day are nothing but a lack of devotion, a lack of humility, of patience, chastity, and charity." See document XI below, p. 347.

[89] *MonFabri*, p. 50. In this letter to Ignatius he noted that those in Rome had "permission to read the books of heretics." See also Brodrick, *Canisius*, pp. 462 ff., and n. 15 of chapter 1 about this prohibition.

What he saw must have filled him with pessimism. While Luther's reform was preached openly in the Dominican church at Worms, Favre himself was forbidden to teach catechism to some boys in that city lest Protestants be offended and cause riots *(seditiones)*.[90] Many parishes were without priests, and the few priests who remained were non-residents. For the most part the clergy were unworthy; many were living in concubinage.[91] Monks were deserting their monasteries and discarding their habits—"our Lord permitting the desertion and the ruins you see before your eyes," he wrote to his cousin, Claude Perissin, prior of Le Reposoir. Towards the end of the *Memoriale,* he refers to many abuses in ecclesiastical and civil administration: so bad are things that one should rather "wonder that Lutherans are not more numerous."[92]

In a passage of the *Memoriale* dated January 7, 1543, he enumerated the stages through which a Catholic passes on his way to leaving the Church.[93] When faith begins to weaken, practice declines; then come moral lapses and attempts to justify them by a selective appeal to tradition. This leads to skepticism about belief and so to a complete loss of faith. Then an endeavor is made to fill the lacuna by searching the Scriptures for a faith based on private judgment. All this begins when the heart ceases to be Catholic—in other words, when faith ceases to be lived interiorly. Three years after, in a letter to Laínez suggesting means to bring Protestants back to the Catholic faith, Favre proposes an alternative course.[94] In a word, if they can be persuaded to amend their lives, then they will give up their new faith. That was his own way with them, and he could point to successes. In the same letter, he mentions the priest who challenged him to prove that his convictions were erroneous, especially the conviction that it was entirely proper for priests to marry. Favre refused to dispute with him on such matters, but talked to him in such an irresistibly kind and understanding way that he admitted his scandalous life and was brought to amend it. Moral rehabilitation has to precede, not follow, the recovery of a lost faith; and it begins in the will, not in the intellect, just as defection begins not in the mind but in the heart, not in the intellect but in the will.

Some saw the problem purely in moral or intellectual terms; Favre went deeper, to the heart where faith begins to weaken and defection has its origin and where also reconciliation and conversion stir to life.

---

[90] *MonFabri*, p. 57. It was the Emperor's representative, Granvelle, who issued the interdict for the sake of peace. The Protestant side appears to have been allowed more freedom.

[91] *MonFabri*, pp. 189–190.

[92] *MonFabri*, p. 160.

[93] From §§217 to 222.

[94] Document XXIV below, pp. 379–381.

He saw the problem and its solution in existential terms. We should remember that the field of his apostolic experience, the Rhineland in 1543, was restricted. He had only limited contact with Protestant adherents: he dealt only with Catholics newly converted to Protestantism, and it was for them that he had to plan his campaign.

As his references to his campaign of reformation indicate, he looked on it rather as a kind of rebuilding or restoration. He aimed at the reform of monasteries and convents, the spiritual renewal of the clergy, and the formation of a Catholic laity well grounded in their faith. But this interior reformation begins with the action of the Holy Spirit in the soul, so his first step would be to conduct people through the Exercises—"our way of proceeding"—a procedure that was common to all the first Jesuits.[95] Favre excelled at it, for he had a charismatic gift for spiritual direction. All through the *Memoriale* we find him working at analyzing and refining his understanding of the individual soul and its spiritual struggles. He believed that reforming individuals interiorly would reform the Church, and the means he employed to achieve this reform was the Spiritual Exercises.

Beginning in Parma with Laínez in 1549, he continued to use the Exercises in Worms, Speyer, Mainz, and Cologne.[96] He regarded it as his most urgent and most necessary task. In Spain and Portugal, too, the work of the Exercises went on wherever and as often as he found the opportunity and the time. Among his retreatants were cardinals, bishops, nuncios, doctors of theology, priests (in the majority), religious men and women, students, and many others. His choice of retreatants indicates the main thrust of his pastoral campaign: Reform the pastors, and they will reform their flocks. These retreats were mostly private and therefore time consuming. But once a priest had been formed by the Exercises, he gave them to others.

Even those who were so taken up with administrative and other duties that they could spare only a short time each day were persuaded to undertake them. Favre always distinguished between the full Exercises of several meditations a day lasting for a month, and shorter, more flexible forms, consisting essentially of the First Week and a general confession. But he gave much time each day—an hour or more—to private interviews with each of his retreatants, for such conversation is

---

[95] *Nuestro modo de proceder*: this phrase recurs many times: *MonFabri*, pp. 50, 69, 111, 114, 115, 137, and so forth. It always had the meaning of giving the Exercises. It may have been used to put the officials of the Inquisition off the scent; they had examined the *Spiritual Exercises* more than once.

[96] In Parma their retreatants guided others through the Exercises in groups of ten to fourteen, and soon the city was on its way to conversion. The same procedure was followed in other places too.

an essential element in spiritual formation. It was the way he himself had been formed by Ignatius, and the disciple eventually outdid the master. Ignatius afterwards acknowledged that of those he himself had trained to give the Exercises, no one gave them better than Favre.

The results were such that Favre, humble and self-effacing though he was, could say: "Of all those who made the Exercises or who after making them became my spiritual sons, not one, so far as I know, has ever turned back."[97] The effects were near miraculous: doctors of theology began to preach—like Cochlaeus, who had never preached in his life nor had ever dreamed of doing so; bishops and abbots undertook to reform their dioceses or their monasteries; crowds of students became Carthusians, Franciscans, or Jesuits; noblemen changed their way of life. This was the kind of reform that he sought to bring about. So highly did he esteem the Exercises that there was nothing he would not do, "even to risk being accused of heresy," in order to defend them. His pastoral strategy consisted of "confessions, conversations, and Exercises"—his customary description of his ministry.[98] For him conversations and confessions became a form of spiritual direction leading up to and invariably ending with the Exercises. They became in time one of the most widely used and effective pastoral instruments of the Catholic Reformation.

Devotion to the Angels, and the Discernment of Spirits

Favre believed in an invisible world of spirits both good and bad, a belief common to everyone in the sixteenth century.[99] It was a time when angelology had attained its greatest development, when belief in the beneficent activity of angels had never before been so prevalent, and Favre shared that belief to the full. Speculation about their nature and functions was widespread and went hand in hand with fears and forebodings—only too well justified by contemporary events—and with an awareness more sensitive than ever before to the presence of awesome invisible forces. The irrational is a close neighbor to the spiritual.

For Favre, spirits had a part in the running of the universe, so that the most trivial and circumscribed event took on a universal extension. The world lay open to the intervention of the saints and to those always unforeseen interventions that depended entirely upon God's goodwill—so he had been taught by Peña. But the universe was ruled by still more

---

[97] *MonFabri*, p. 112.

[98] *MonFabri*, pp. 96, 138, and 221.

[99] See the text of the *Memoriale*, §§309–314, and the accompanying footnotes for the multiple ways in which the word "spirit" is used and understood by Favre.

mysterious beings, those angels who were present within it and moved its huge machinery from on high. There were other spirits too who dwelt in the hearts of men and, all unknown to them, guided their lives and activity. All took it for granted that spirits entered not only into their lives but into their very beings, and thus were a force to be reckoned with in the conduct of their lives and affairs. And as has been well said, "As a result, the borderline was vague and ill-defined between orthodox Christian devotion to the angels, combined with vigilance in face of the devils, and a wide variety of superstitious attitudes and practices."[100]

Devotion to the angels had spread widely during the fifteenth and sixteenth centuries, so it is not surprising that it played a part in the spirituality of Ignatius and an even greater part in that of Favre. According to the received theology, angels are members of the heavenly court, the spiritual universe that surrounds God and carries out his designs. They are God's messengers, collaborators with divine providence. They transmit God's orders, communicate his lights and his graces, and sometimes carry out his judgments. Both men also were convinced that angels took part in liturgical worship and aided them in their apostolate; they looked on them as perfect contemplative and active beings—ideal models therefore for the members of the Society of Jesus.

A noteworthy feature is Favre's special devotion to the guardian angels. Like many of the Fathers of the Church, he believed that not only individuals but also nations had guardian angels, as did cities and Christian communities. These "good angels" or "good spirits"—he employs both expressions interchangeably—protect himself and all the faithful with an impregnable rampart.[101] He prays constantly to his own angel; he invokes the dean of Speyer's angel, those of Esteban Carolo (one of his novices) and of St. Jerome, and "all the angel guardians of the saints mentioned in the Roman calendar or in any other one."[102] He notes that he discovered many new methods of prayer while on a journey from Worms to Ratisbon: "As you drew near to some place and looked at it or heard it talked about, you received a method of asking grace from our Lord that the archangel of the region with all the angel guardians of its inhabitants might be well disposed to us."[103] He was conscious of a special spiritual link between himself and his guardian angel, the being who prepared his heart for the divine inspirations and defended it against the suggestions of the wicked one. Angels, as real to

---

[100] O'Leary, "Discernment," p. 72. See also the article by Karl Rahner, "Angel" in *Sacramentum Mundi* (New York, 1968), vol. 1, pp. 27–35.
[101] §260.
[102] §118.
[103] §21.

him as material reality, accompanied him on his journeys along the roads of Europe, ever faithful friends to humankind everywhere. Immersed in their invisible presence, Favre felt himself together with the whole Church, joining in the worship offered by the heavenly host and constantly supported and strengthened in his apostolic mission. And through the good angels he was enabled to share in the spiritual combat of Christian tradition between the good and the bad angels, described dramatically in the abundant apocalyptic literature of the age.[104] In that literature the imagination runs riot, exaggerations and even absurdities are common; but the doctrinal core of the tradition is orthodox.

Favre, heir to the sixteenth-century convictions regarding spirits, did not remain unaffected by its preoccupation also with bad spirits and their influence on people. His beliefs about them caused him a good deal of worried reflection on their activities and their baneful effects on his soul and the souls of others. He prayed frequently for help against them and their power to disturb souls, and especially for help against the spirit of fornication. When moving into new lodgings at Mainz in April 1543, he invoked the guardian angels of the neighborhood and then prayed "that the wicked spirits in the neighborhood might be powerless to harm either myself or those coming to live with me in the house—above all the spirit of fornication which is sure to haunt the prostitutes, the adulterers, and those others whose presence in the vicinity I had been told about" (§283). On February 12, 1543, he resolved to invoke Blessed Martina every Monday "for grace and assistance against the wicked spirits who trouble and deceive us in manifold ways and thus bring us to ruin" (§250). Two days later he regretted not having assisted as much as he could his novice Stephen's guardian angel, who had kept the youth obedient and humble to him. He concluded this prayer with these puzzling words: "without allowing his evil spirit to trouble me as much as I might have deserved" (§252). In December 1542 he prayed to be delivered from a coldness in his manner which he attributed to the evil spirits and to "diabolical influences . . . that cause men to close their hearts to each other" (§199).

Not only do spirits act on a person from outside, they also enter a person's body. Favre begged that the power of the spirit of fornication might no longer dwell in his loins but be cast out from every place occupied by the vital or animal spirits of his body. He understood how necessary it was that evil spirits should lose their great power to trouble his flesh or his spirits (§35). The following significant passage appears during the course of reflections on the nature of angels:

---

[104] Favre refers to this spiritual conflict in §§35, 175, 199, 250, 251, 252, 283, 311, 316.

> For myself, as long as I remain so inclined to evil and surrounded by so much defilement from the flesh, the world, and bad spirits, I greatly rejoice that I do not yet possess a nature which is simple. For if it were so, my whole soul would be all too speedily permeated by some evil spirit and thus become completely corrupted. At present, however, though some evil spirit may penetrate my flesh, for example, or my understanding or my affectivity, it does not happen that I become at once totally evil, for it is in my power to withhold consent to these evils and reject them by an act of will. (§311)

There is in this passage no trace of the superstitious belief that people are at the mercy of demons and have no power at all against them. On the contrary, Favre asserts the freedom of his will to withhold consent to sin. And in spite of what modern minds view as a morbid concern with the influence of demons in the lives of men, he preserved a sturdy common sense and independence of judgment in these matters. For instance, he refused to be impressed by Canisius's enthusiastic account of Cornelius Wischaven's exorcisms. The credulous Wischaven had written Canisius a glowing account of his feats; deeply impressed, Canisius reported the news in a letter to Favre. The latter, not in the least impressed, sent back a stern admonition: "I do not in any way approve of Master Cornelius's activities in banishing demons from the possessed; rather would I have him know that there is much fraud in the matter. Let him cast out demons from souls, which is work proper to a priest, and leave exorcists to their own business. Has not Master Cornelius already fallen a victim more than once to the illusions of demons? Indeed he has, and not without danger to himself."[105]

Though influenced by mysticism, Favre remained alive to the dangers of illuminism and took critical note of some ideas that clashed with his faith, such as the following: Everything is permitted to a spiritual man (§§107–108); everything comes from God, therefore austerity of life is in vain (§174); once converted to God a person has no further need of expiation (§202); there is neither reward for good works nor punishment for sin (§290).

Finally, his belief in good and bad spirits led him to practice discernment of spirits with the additional object of discovering how to take part in the struggle between the forces of good and evil. "Discernment, therefore, had a marked apostolic dimension, as Favre tried to range himself on the side of the angels, God's ministers, who were protecting, supporting, strengthening and guiding men in their journey through life, in their battles with the evil powers."[106]

---

[105] *MonFabri*, pp. 331, 332.
[106] O'Leary, "Discernment," p. 75.

Favre's basic knowledge of discernment was gained, of course, from Ignatius and can be found in the latter's *Spiritual Exercises*.[107] Favre added to it from his own personal experience and practice of discernment, and also from the observations he made when guiding others through the Exercises and acting as spiritual director in the broad sense. The *Memoriale,* however, does not contain any systematic theory of discernment; its nature precludes that kind of writing. But a study of certain passages reveals aspects of discernment that he considered of greater importance, and in them we can find the outline of a theory.

In the first rule for discernment in the *Exercises* ([314]), we are brought face to face with the "enemy" who tempts habitual sinners to go from sin to sin by causing them to imagine "sensual gratifications and pleasures," while "the good spirit acts in the contrary way in such persons, causing them to feel the stings and the remorse of conscience by the reproaches of reason." The seat of this conflict is within a man, and there the good and the bad angels strive for possession of his soul, the conflict being an image of the greater conflict in the world between good and evil, between truth and falsehood, both moral and religious.

The "enemy," as the Church has always taught, is a personal evil spirit: "Your adversary the devil prowls around like a roaring lion, seeking someone to devour" (1 Peter 5:8). Ignatius's rules take for granted the traditional teaching of the Church about the devil and provide a strategy for outwitting him with the grace of God. As has been said,

> Favre's understanding and interpretation of "spirits" and their effects is the foundation of his theory of discernment. If spirits did not really exist, or if they played no part in human lives, or if it were impossible to experience their activity and influence, then investigation into Favre's teaching on discernment would be otiose. It may be possible to find psychological categories to fit the various kinds of spirits, God himself excepted; and it may well be that one could thus put together a valid theory of discernment. But such a process would have to ignore com-

---

[107] *SpEx,* [313–336]. For a good historical survey of discernment of spirits, see the *Dictionnaire de Spiritualité* (Paris, 1932–1995) 3:1222–1291, with its valuable bibliographies. See also George E. Ganss, S.J., "Endnotes on the Exercises" in his translation and commentary, *The Spiritual Exercises of Saint Ignatius* (St. Louis, 1992), pp. 189–195; see also *Ignatius of Loyola: His Personality and Spiritual Heritage,* ed. F. Wulf (St. Louis, 1977). Also of value are Jules J. Toner, S.J., *A Commentary on Saint Ignatius' Rules for the Discernment of Spirits* (St. Louis, 1982); and Michael J. O'Sullivan, S.J., "Trust Your Feelings but Use Your Head," *Studies in the Spirituality of Jesuits* (22/4 [September 1990]), and Michael J. Buckley, S.J., "The Structure of the Rules for Discernment," in *The Way of Ignatius Loyola: Contemporary Approaches to the Spiritual Exercises,* ed. Philip Sheldrake, S.J. (London and St. Louis, 1991), pp. 219–237.

pletely Favre's intellectual and imaginative world. To understand his theory it is necessary to accept his world, as a working hypothesis, and therefore those personal spirits, good and evil, who form an integral part of it.[108]

While concluding, as we have seen, that the *Memoriale* does not contain any worked-out theory of discernment, we can at least "move towards a theory of discernment" by considering certain passages where Favre "records rules or principles for discernment." From these passages the following generalizations can be made:

1. Priority must be given to the affective over the intellectual element.
2. The spirits make their presence felt through affective movements over which the person has no control—this is the experience, essentially passive.
3. Ideas and reflections are less important; they require further discernment.
4. But the evil spirit can insinuate false meanings into the intellectual element, unsuspected by the person enjoying consolation from the presence of the good spirit, and those reasonings require further discernment.

Pessimism, depression, desolation—all are due to the presence of the evil spirit. Yet the reasonings that accompany such a spirit are not all necessarily false, so we can learn from them. As has been said, the primary principle is a return to the basic affective experience so as to identify the spirit at work. That done, one can proceed to further discernment. And in the discernment of desires, faith and charity will guarantee that they are from God.

A last word on Favre's tactic of stirring up spiritual conflict in exercitants who cannot otherwise be brought to detect a diversity of spirits. He does so by proposing to them a higher state of perfection. He suggests the same tactic with devout folk who live blameless lives; the results, a spiritual struggle, will be the same. For he has grasped that a person must experience real internal conflict; if there is none, Favre will set about provoking it. This, as O'Leary remarks, "says a great deal about his theory: not perhaps about the subtleties or the connections with other areas of spirituality or theology, but the simple core, the *sine qua*

---

[108] O'Leary, "Discernment," p. 111 and n. 15 of chap. 1; see also Toner, *Commentary*, pp. 260–270; and Adolf Durlap, "Demons"; and Karl Rahner, "The Devil," in "Devil," in *Sacramentum Mundi*, vol. 2, pp. 70–75.

non, without which the very term 'discernment of spirits' would be meaningless for him."[109]

The Text of the *Memoriale*

Favre's *Memoriale* was known in the early days of the Society. In 1567 Leonhard Kessel, writing to Nadal, it would seem, indicates the dispatch to him of Pierre Favre's writings "left with me by Your Reverence"; he is most likely referring to the *Memoriale*.[110] In the same year Ribadeneira refers to what he calls Favre's "book."[111] In 1583, Peter Canisius quotes a number of passages from it.[112] Orlandini made use of it for his *Historia Societatis Iesu* (History of the Society of Jesus), which came out in Rome in 1594, and for his *Vita Petri Fabri* (Life of Pierre Favre), published at Lyons in 1617. In 1615 Luis de la Puente mentions it in his life of Balthasar Álvarez.[113] Much later, in his history of the Society in the lower Rhineland, Reiffenberg mentions what he calls an "autograph" (which can only have been a manuscript copy then [1764]) at Cologne, and quotes six lines from §33.[114] Favre's own autograph appears to have disappeared long before that date.

To this list Mellinato adds a reference to the *Memoriale* given in the *Directories of the Spiritual Exercises,* which he found very useful in his work on the text.[115] He judges that when Favre, in bad health at the time, was leaving Spain in July 1546, he left behind most of his manuscripts. He left behind, too, such vivid memories of himself that very shortly after his death a shorter text of the *Memoriale,* with the first part in Spanish, began to circulate. A longer text, known as B, with the first part already translated into Latin, soon followed. It was advantageous to have the complete text in Latin, especially in the humanistic circles of

---

[109] O'Leary, "Discernment," p. 123; for Favre's use of the word "Spirit," see pp. 76–81.

[110] Otto Braunsberger, *Beati Petri Canisii Societatis Iesu epistulæ et acta* (Freiburg-im-Breisgau, 1896–1923), vol. 6, p. 23.

[111] See *Fontes narrativi de Sancto Ignatio*, vol. 73 of MHSI (Rome, 1951) 2:379.

[112] Parts of §§21, 28, 34, 283, 433, 434, 435; text in *EppCan*, vol. 8, pp. 119–121.

[113] P. Abad, *Vida y escritos de V. P. Luis de la Puente* (Comillas, 1957), p. 388.

[114] F. Reiffenberg, *Historia Societatis Jesu ad Rhenum inferiorem* (Cologne, 1764).

[115] *Directoria Exercitiorum Spiritualium* (1540–1599), ed. Ignacio Iparraguirre, S.J., vol. 2 of Monumenta Ignatiana, 2nd series, vol. 76 of MHSI (Rome, 1955), pp. 193, 203. For an English translation of this work, see *On Giving the Spiritual Exercises: The Early Jesuit Manuscript Directories and the Official Directory of 1599,* trans. and ed. Martin E. Palmer, S.J. (St. Louis, 1996).

northern Europe. This translation, according to de Certeau, was either made by Nadal or inspired by him.[116] The notes written by Favre at Valladolid (§§420–439) and the final pages (§§440–443), which he must have carried around with him on his last journey, were added to the existing text to form the definitive and longest copy, designated as R.

Research undertaken by de Certeau and Mellinato leads to the firm conclusion that sixteen manuscript copies of the *Memoriale* are extant. They differ in length and in language, as well as in their degree of accuracy. They are the work of many scribes, some of whom either did not understand Latin or had to transcribe from dictation—perhaps in a foreign accent; and the copies, even the best, contain many errors, especially in the Spanish text of the first part. From a study of the manuscripts, scholars have concluded that the following five are of primary importance in the reconstruction of a critical edition of the text:

- *B:* A manuscript belonging to the Bollandist library in Brussels, dating from the end of the sixteenth century.
- *H:* A manuscript belonging to the Roman Archives of the Society of Jesus, dating from the second half of the sixteenth century. Though abounding in errors, it is judged to be the closest to the lost autograph.
- *L:* A manuscript belonging to the Archives of the Ministry of Foreign Affairs, Lisbon. It probably dates from about the end of the sixteenth century.
- *R:* A manuscript belonging to the Archives of the Society of Jesus in the section relating to the Postulation of Causes, dating from the sixteenth century.
- *S:* A manuscript belonging to the library of the University of Salamanca, dating from the middle of the sixteenth century.

Manuscripts *H* and *R*, together with variant readings from others, were the ones mainly used in the preparation of the French and Italian translations.[117]

---

[116] Michel de Certeau, "Le texte du *Mémorial* de Favre," *Revue d'ascétique et de mystique* 36 (1960), 101, and *EppCan*, vol. 6, p. 23.

[117] De Certeau, *Memoriale*, p. 96; also Giuseppe Mellinato, *"Confessioni" di Pietro Favre (1506–1547)* (Rome, 1980), p. 5. In 1853 and 1858, Sébastien Fouillot, who had during the 1830 revolution saved an ancient copy of the *Memoriale* and who almost uninterruptedly for thirty-four years was tertian director in France, brought out a lithographed edition for use only within the Society. It was followed in 1873–1874 by Marcel Bouix's very defective editions in Latin and in French, inspired probably by Favre's beatification in 1872. The edition, probably based on the copy that Fouillot had saved, in accordance with the taste of the time, more literary than critical, had to be purged of the supposedly "barbarous expressions" that disfigured it; in addition, other supposed corrections were made. An Italian version was made by

After Favre's beatification an intensive but fruitless search began (lasting until nearly 1900) in all the principal archives of Europe for the autograph of the *Memoriale*. In 1914 an edition of the Latin text based on a study of twelve manuscripts appeared as volume 48 in the series Monumenta Historica Societatis Iesu.[118] But in spite of the greater care devoted to this edition, it became unsatisfactory when taken alone if judged by the increasingly strict standards of modern critical scholarship. It was, nevertheless, used as the basis for the first Spanish version, done by J. M. Vélez and J. M. March and published by Casulleras, Barcelona, in 1922. The result was equally unsatisfactory. What was needed was a text based on a comparative study of all the surviving manuscripts with their variant readings.

However, apart from a few efforts at a restoration of passages from the text, nothing was done until Michel de Certeau undertook a critical examination of the sixteen extant manuscripts in preparation for his French translation. Some years later Giuseppe Mellinato subjected the same manuscripts to a thorough reexamination for his Italian version, the first to be made of the complete text into that language. His research has confirmed the accuracy of de Certeau's conclusions and differs from them only in a few minor points. These two versions, though the efforts of individuals, go very far towards supplying for the lack of a critically established text.

At the beginning of 1983, J. Amadeo and M. A. Fiorito published in Buenos Aires a new Spanish version with commentary, a revision of the Vélez-March edition. The editors thought it better not to make a new translation. They corrected the errors in the Vélez-March edition, at times retranslating complete sentences and having recourse to de Certeau's French version for help in clarifying obscurities in the Latin.

This present English translation of the *Memoriale* has been made from the Latin text known as manuscript *R* and published in *Fabri Monumenta*, pp. 489–696, volume 48 of the Monumenta Historica Societatis Iesu. The first part, consisting of nos. 1–120, was translated from the Spanish version in *Fabri Monumenta*, pp. 856–886. This Spanish original was preferred to the Latin version because, in the view of scholars, it was the original language of that part. The latter, however,

---

Giuseppe Boero and published in 1873, the first part of the volume containing an account of Favre's life. In 1878 there appeared an English translation by H. J. Coleridge, S.J., of Boero's Italian version, forming the eighth volume of the *Quarterly Series*. None of these editions was based on a critical study of the manuscripts, nor was there overmuch care taken with fidelity to the text—in fact, Boero took liberties with the Latin text, curtailing and simplifying wherever it presented difficulties.

[118] *MonFabri*, pp. xix–xxi.

because of its authority, was used pari passu with the Spanish. In addition, the French and Italian versions by Michel de Certeau and Giuseppe Mellinato respectively were consulted during the work, and the translator here acknowledges his debt to them.

Translators of older texts are required to provide versions as faithful as possible to the originals; this was the chief aim in the present work. Should the readers find anything more in it here and there, they are welcome to look on such additions as by-products of the translation process.

The Letters and Instructions

This volume presents for the first time in English a selection of Pierre Favre's letters and instructions. Arranged in chronological order, each document is preceded by a very brief introduction along with a reference to where the original-language version can be found. The persons to whom Favre at one time or another wrote the one hundred and fifty letters and instructions that are still extant range from Pope Paul III and Cardinal Contarini to some of the first Jesuits, such as Simâo Rodrigues and Nicolás Bobadilla. From that total collection the translator chose twenty-seven documents which exhibit and illustrate the various facets of Favre's apostolic activities and of his personal spirituality as he communicated it to others. In this correspondence Favre displays many of the same personal characteristics that are reflected in the pages of the *Memoriale*.

Many of his letters went to some of those who had been his first companions in Paris, foremost among them Ignatius of Loyola. The first letter we have from him, penned in September 1540, was to Ignatius and Pietro Codazzo, one of the first Italian recruits to the Society; Favre wrote this just a few months before leaving Italy to begin his life of apostolic journeying. It is also the first letter in this present collection (I).[119] Ignatius had made the request of all his brethren who were to go on such journeys that they write back to Rome and keep him and the other companions informed of their work. This request for regular and frequent correspondence later came to be incorporated into the Jesuit Constitutions as one of the aids to union of minds and hearts in the Society of Jesus. Two other letters to Ignatius in this collection provide examples of Favre's apostolic activities in Speyer and Mainz in Germany (VII, VIII). To Francis Xavier, now in distant India, he wrote about his spiritual activities in Cologne in 1544 and about the various people he

---

[119] A capital Roman numeral in parentheses refers to the documents to be found below, in the third part of this volume. In this case, it refers to document I, the first letter included.

dealt with in the course of those activities (XVII). Three letters to Diego Laínez in this collection illustrate again Favre's apostolates and the ways in which he carried them on, for instance, in his dealings with heretics (VII, XXIV, XXVI). Favre's last surviving letter, written a week before his death, reveals his affection and personal concern not only for Laínez but also for the latter's recently deceased father and for his own many brethren and friends dispersed throughout Europe.

Among other Jesuit recipients of Favre's letters in this selection were a Spanish royal chaplain and novice-to-be, Alvaro Alfonso, and Cornelius Wischaven, later an outstanding Jesuit. In Alfonso's letter he dealt with charity (V); in the first of Wischaven's two letters he discussed a choice to be made between hearing confessions and singing the Gospel at successive Masses (XIV), and in the second, a very important letter, he set forth his views on hearing confessions, witnessing to how he conceived of that ministry (XV). He also wrote to Guillaume Postel, the famous French humanist who was for a short time a Jesuit novice (XIX), treating the subject of humility and using examples that ranged from zero and its value in arithmetic to turnips and onions that rooted themselves solidly. The young Jesuit who was to prove the greatest of those whom Favre helped toward a Jesuit vocation was Peter Canisius; in the letter to him, written before he left Madrid on his last journey to Rome, Favre included a "tract," as he designated it, on persevering in a religious vocation (XXV).

Canisius figures once again in Favre's correspondence, this time in a letter to Peter's stepmother, Wendelina Van den Berg, who was quite wroth at her stepson's joining the Jesuits (XVI). Favre attempted to calm and console her now that Peter, "who has hitherto always been the dearest of sons to you, has now turned altogether unnatural—and wholly, as you believe, through my doing." The other lay recipient of a letter among those presented here is a generous benefactor of the Society, King John III of Portugal (XX). His daughter, Maria, wife of the future King Philip II of Spain, had died after giving birth to their son, Don Carlos; and Favre wrote a touching letter to console the King in his grief. Only one letter survives written by Favre to a relative, and this same letter is also the only one extant written in French, his native language (XI). It is addressed to Dom Claude Perissin, a cousin and prior of a Carthusian house in Savoy and deals with activities that help toward spiritual growth.

The most frequent non-Jesuit recipient of Favre's letters was Gerhard Kalckbrenner, also a Carthusian and prior of the charterhouse at Cologne. Three letters here make evident how he shared with the prior a lasting friendship, a deep concern for the reform and renewal of the Church, and a realistic appreciation of what, in addition to the grace of the Spirit, is required in the way of human endeavor to make progress in the spiritual life (X, XII, XIII). Kalckbrenner, in turn, in the last document in this collection, bears witness to that friendship and to Favre's spiritual teachings (XXVII).

Favre wrote letters not only to individuals but also to several groups. A very early letter went to the group of young Jesuit recruits who, following in the footsteps of the first companions, were sent by Ignatius to Paris to study (III). Studies, the spiritual life, the apostolate, and the interrelation of all these were for them then, as for others now, an urgent topic. Two later letters were dispatched to the Jesuit community at Coimbra in Portugal, one treating obedience and some of the realities of life in community (XX) and the other expressing a loving farewell to the young Jesuits there (XXI). But Favre was realistic enough, too, to recognize that not all is always peace and light in a community, so some months later he wrote a brief ten-line note to the rector of the house at Coimbra, of whom he "had an image and a picture of the great load you bear," encouraging him to carry his burdens bravely (XXIII).

Finally, there is a series of instructions. They range from rules for a confraternity of laypersons at Parma that he had helped to set up, even before the Society of Jesus was officially recognized by the Church (II), to a program for Christian life to be presented at the end of retreats in Germany early in his apostolate there (IV); they include instructions for those (probably several early novices) going on pilgrimage (IX) and a set of guidelines, probably to the Cologne Carthusians to help them in their work of spiritual reform (XVIII).

These letters and instructions together with the *Memoriale* and the history of Favre's unceasing travels demonstrate how apt, except for one phrase, are the words of the opening antiphon from the Song of Songs for the Mass of his feast day: "I have searched for the one who is the love of my heart; I have searched for him but have not found him. I will rise and go round the city; in streets and squares I will search for him, the one who is the love of my heart" (3:1b–2a, 5). In the case of Favre, he surely did find that love of his heart, Jesus Christ, and helped to give him to so many other men and women in the streets and squares of so many cities.

At the Threshold of the Society of Jesus

Some years after Pierre Favre's death in August 1546, his memory began to fade among the second generation of his brethren in Rome. Early Jesuit writers always linked him with Ignatius and Xavier, and they looked on Favre and Xavier as the foundation stones upon which Ignatius had built his Society. The founder's fame is secure, and Xavier's brilliant odyssey has caught and held the imagination of the world; but we look in vain for a comparable appreciation of Favre's importance and achievements in the order he helped to found. Such reticence about a well-beloved and famous son is not characteristic of the Society; it is due in part to its troubled history—a history that wonderfully concentrated the minds of Jesuits on the business of surviving crisis after crisis. Then came the double canonization of Ignatius and Xavier in 1662, an eagerly sought-after official seal of the Church's approval, one necessary for the Society at that time.

The canonization of Borgia in 1677 had the effect of further diverting attention from Favre. Gradually and imperceptibly he became little more than a name lingering in the memories of the majority of Jesuits. A modern biographer of Ignatius could write that "the early history of the Society of Jesus is very largely the history of two Basque gentlemen—Ignatius Loyola and Francis Xavier."[120] It expressed, perhaps, what the average Jesuit would have said until very recently, the result of a neglect that obscured the significant part played by Favre during the formative years of the Society and did scant justice to his greatness.

Very early on, in 1575, and as a result, apparently, of a decree issued by the fourth general of the Society of Jesus, Everard Mercurian, discouraging the indiscriminate reading of certain spiritual books in the Society, superiors were ordered to keep the manuscript copies of the *Memoriale* out of general circulation, allowing them to be read only by those with special permission. It appears too, that the manuscript was subjected to censorship at the time, so that for many years there was no hope of proceeding with Favre's cause for beatification.[121] If it is too strong to say that his name came under a cloud, it does not seem an exaggeration to characterize the Society's attitude to the *Memoriale* in those days as one of reserve. Thus, a certain measure of prejudice grew up; the journal remained in manuscript until 1853, and no official steps were taken to bring out a critical edition. The inevitable result was that Jesuits never came to know it well enough to realize its importance or to be in a position to evaluate its rich spiritual teaching.

---

[120] James Brodrick, *The Origin of the Jesuits* (Chicago, 1986), p. 1. That view, of course, has been radically changed by the work, among others, of O'Malley, *First Jesuits,* and of André Ravier, S.J., *St. Ignatius of Loyola and the Founding of the Society of Jesus,* trans. Maura Daly (San Francisco, 1987). For the life of Borgia, see Cándido de Dalmases, S.J., *Francis Borgia: Grandee of Spain, Jesuit, Saint* (St. Louis, 1991).

[121] Mellinato, "Revisione testuale delle *Confessioni* de Pietro Favre," *Studia Patavina* (Padua, 1980), p. 576 n. 27. His article presents the results of the latest research on the manuscripts of the *Memoriale.*

To be fair to Mercurian, however, we must take into account the controversies about contemplative prayer that troubled the Society during the last thirty years of the sixteenth century. The General judged that there was a "danger of turning Jesuits away from their vocation of apostolic service by leading them to seek inordinately for that union with God which is found in the depths of the soul and in detachment from all that is corporeal and external."[122] The matter was rightly regarded as serious, especially since the Inquisition was on the lookout for certain mystical or illuministic tendencies; even the slightest suspicion of such deviations was quite likely to bring its watchdogs snuffing at the doors of Jesuit houses. The Society had good reason to be wary of those watchdogs. Mercurian, of course, would have had no idea that his decree would affect Favre's standing in the order, but it did; and those who are interested in coincidences, portents, and similar things may like to reflect that the circumstances surrounding the transfer of his remains to the Church of the Gesù proved in their own way to be prophetic.

Favre had been buried in the chapel of our Lady of the Wayside on August 2, 1546. Twenty years later in 1568, when the Roman Jesuits decided to build the Gesù over their founder's tomb, the little chapel had to be pulled down to make way for the new church. Care was taken to identify and translate the remains of Ignatius; but as it was impossible to distinguish Favre's bones from others exhumed at the same time, the remains were all gathered together and reburied under the main door of the Gesù. Ever since, pilgrims have been coming to the great church to venerate Ignatius and Xavier, but without a thought for Favre, on whose unmarked grave at the threshold they tread as they enter and leave. It was a fate, surely not displeasing to the man who prayed that he might become Christ's broom and be known as such even in heaven.[123]

But he was never forgotten in his native Savoy. About fifty years after his death, three members of the secular clergy collected testimony about him, noting that in the district he was already and commonly referred to as "saint" and "blessed"; four years later a priest, Jean Favre, hearing that people called Pierre "blessed," put up a chapel to him on the site of his original home. In 1607 the altar of this chapel was consecrated by St. Francis de Sales, who paid a splendid tribute to his memory the year after, when he published his *Introduction to the Devout Life*.[124] In 1626, at the request of the general of the Society, Mutius

---

[122] Joseph de Guibert, S.J., *The Jesuits: Their Spiritual Doctrine and Practice*, trans. William J. Young, S.J. (St. Louis: The Institute of Jesuit Sources, 1986), p. 219.

[123] §441.

[124] St. Francis de Sales, *Introduction to the Devout Life*, trans. Allan Ross

Vitelleschi, the bishop of Geneva set up an official and authoritative inquiry into the life of Pierre Favre. It provided striking evidence of the devotion to him that flourished among the Savoyards. He continued to be openly referred to as "blessed" and even "saint"; there were processions in his honor; cures were reported. But for some reason or other the authorities in Rome did not act on the results of the inquiry. Then, in 1773, came the long-threatened suppression of the Society and its restoration in 1814 in the midst of the post-Revolutionary turmoil. When the work of reconsolidation was nearing an end, the time came to reopen Favre's cause. The bishop of Annecy was requested to start an official process with a view to obtaining pontifical approval of the public cult that had been rendered to Favre for nearly three hundred years. The result was that both the cult and the use of the title "blessed" were officially approved. Three years later, on September 5, 1872, Pope Pius IX gave solemn approval of the public devotion to Blessed Pierre Favre.

So, tardily, the Society made amends to the first founding companion to join Ignatius, the first priest in its ranks. So, too, this English translation of his spiritual writings, published in 1996, the 450th anniversary year of Favre's death, pays homage and tribute to a Jesuit companion who in friendship, journeyings, and labor as a servant of Christ's mission so clearly embodied the Ignatian ideals of love of Christ and service of others.

(London, 1934), p. 84.

The Memoriale

of Pierre Favre

Here follows a record of some of the good desires and good thoughts of the Reverend Father Master Pierre Favre.

—Title borne by some of the manuscripts of the *Memoriale*

SPEYER

In January 1542, Favre was ordered by Pope Paul III "under holy obedience" to leave Spain and go to Speyer as assistant to Cardinal Morone, the nuncio of Germany. But by the time he arrived in Speyer on April 13, 1542, the nuncio had already departed to visit other German towns, leaving instructions that Favre was to consider himself free to undertake whatever work God might inspire him to do until further orders from either Ignatius, the pope, or the nuncio himself. So he remained in Speyer and at once began the pastoral work at which he excelled and which had first place in his heart. There on June 15, 1542, in his thirty-sixth year, he set about writing the Memoriale. *Little more than a year later, in July of 1543, he had completed the bulk of the work.*

BLESS THE LORD, O MY SOUL, and forget not all his benefits. He redeems your life from death and crowns you with his mercy and his kindness. He pardons you and satisfies your desires with his good gifts. No day passes but he forgives all your iniquities and heals all your diseases, giving you good hope that your youth will be renewed like the eagle's.[1]

Cry it aloud ceaselessly, O my soul, and never forget the favors which our Lord Jesus Christ has done for you and goes on doing for you from moment to moment through the intercession of his Blessed Mother, our Lady, of all the holy men and women in heaven, and also of all the living and the dead who pray for you in the Catholic Church.

Adore the heavenly Father, O my soul, honoring him always and serving with all your strength, wisdom, and will him who with his blessed love so mercifully helps and goes on strengthening you.

Adore your Redeemer, our Lord Jesus Christ, who as true way, truth, and life[2] goes on instructing and enlightening you with his grace alone.

The chronological headings that divide the text by month and year as well as the boldfaced numbers that appear at the beginning of a paragraph or of several paragraphs are taken from the critical edition of the *Memoriale,* published in *Fabri Monumenta,* volume 48 of the Monumenta Historica Societatis Iesu. The editors of that edition provided these headings and numbers as aids to reading and citing the text.

[1] Ps. 103 (102): 2–5, a song of thanksgiving for the Lord's blessings. Favre begins his record of the graces he has received from God in the same spirit as the Christian community offers the Eucharistic Sacrifice in thanksgiving to the Father through Jesus Christ.

[2] John 14:6.

Adore the person of your glorifier, the Holy Spirit, the Paraclete, who with his gentle communication goes on preparing your body, your soul, and your spirit to be pure, upright, and good in all things.[3]

▸ *June 15, 1542*

In the year 1542, on the octave day of the Body of Christ our Lord,[4] there came to me a notable desire to do from that time on something I had left undone until then through sheer negligence and laziness.[5] It was to begin writing down so as to remember them some of the spiritual things which the Lord had given me from his hand in prayer: whether as counsel [*avisos*] about the course to take, or for contemplation or understanding, or for action, or for some other spiritual benefit.

But before going ahead into the future, I thought it good to note down some things from my past life up to now according as I remember experiencing them in the past, with a special awareness of thanksgiving, contrition, compassion, or some other spiritual feeling from the Lord, or by way of counsel [*aviso*] from my good angel.[6]

The Early Years: Autobiographical Account (1506–1542)

1   The first benefit which I noted with gratitude was that, in 1506 during Eastertide, our Lord brought me into the world[7] and gave me the grace to be baptized and to be brought up by good and very pious Catholic parents.[8] They were farming folk and had enough of the world's goods to be able to help me to have the proper means of saving my soul in conformity with the end for which I was created.

---

[3] The whole of this passage seems to have been inspired by the last section of the Second Epistle to the Corinthians. "The grace of the Lord Jesus Christ and the love of God and the fellowship of the Holy Spirit be with you all" (2 Cor. 13:13). Note that emphasis on the Trinity and on the intercessory power of the communion of saints is rarely absent from Favre's prayer.

[4] June 15 of that year.

[5] Favre writes that this desire "entered into me" (*me entró*). His spiritual attitude to these interior movements is one of passivity throughout the *Memoriale* and can be seen in the very frequent use of the phrase "given to me" (*datum est mihi*). Care has been taken to show in translation this attitude of passivity with regard to spiritual movements.

[6] It looks as if this review of the principal events in Favre's past life was written very quickly, either on the same day or in a few days, for the *Memoriale* properly so called begins with §34, which can be dated June 15.

[7] Easter Monday, April 13, 1506. *MonFabri*, p. 810.

[8] Louis Favre and Marie Perissin. *MonFabri*, p. 761.

2   My parents brought me up in the fear of God our Lord in such a way that I began, while yet quite young, to be conscious of myself.[9] Even about the age of seven, and this is a sign of an additional grace from God, I felt some especial movements of devotion. So from that time on, the Lord and spouse of my soul willed to take possession of the depths of my soul. Would that I had known enough, would that I had then been canny enough, to bring him in and to follow him so as never to be separated from him![10]

▸ **1516**

3   At the age of about ten, I felt a desire to study, but being a shepherd and destined for the world by my parents, I could not get any rest but used to weep with longing to go to school. And so my parents were compelled, against their plans, to agree to send me to school.[11] And when they saw the notable progress I was making in understanding and memory, they could not prevent me from continuing my studies, what with our Lord, moreover, permitting me to have not the slightest aptitude or taste for secular concerns.

The school I attended was conducted by Master Pierre Velliard, a person whose instruction was not only Catholic but holy as well. His life was one of ardent sanctity. Thus all the poets and authors he read with us seemed to be like gospels because all of it had pertinence for cultivating in youth the holy and chaste fear of the Lord.[12]

---

[9] *Mihi esse conscius* in a Spanish context: to be conscious to myself of wrongdoing or of my actions. Favre means that he was fearful of transgressing the law of God as taught him by his parents. In this they showed their wisdom: fear of God is the heart of any genuine religious disposition (*DBibTheol*, p. 174). At an early age he had begun to take stock of his behavior, to examine his conscience; this is surely the beginning of a lifelong habit of introspection.

[10] See *MonFabri*, pp. 697–756.

[11] He went to the little town of Thônes about six miles from Le Villaret to be taught reading, writing, and grammar, probably by the hospital chaplain who ran a little school there. In only seven months Favre had outdistanced all the other scholars (*MonFabri*, pp. 762, 774, 802). He says nothing about the part played in this decision by his Carthusian uncle, Dom Mamert Favre, forty-fifth prior of the charterhouse of Le Reposoir from 1508 to 1522. Dom Mamert, himself a native of the Grand Bornand and a brother of Louis Favre, was prior of Val-Sainte from 1495 to 1497 and of Dijon from 1501 to 1508. He was very interested in his young nephew, and it is likely that he would have invited him to Le Reposoir on occasion. From his monastery he watched over the youngster's progress and helped to guide his formation. J. Falconnet, *La Chartreuse du Reposoir* (Montreuil-sur-Mer, 1895), pp. 593–594.

[12] Not much is known about this holy Swiss priest. In 1517, while at Cluses, he published a book *Modus componendi epistolas* (How to Write Letters). He seems to have begun his Latin school at La Roche in 1517 or 1518, about the time Favre

The place where he lived and now lies buried is called La Roche.[13] It is three leagues distant from the soil and village where I was born, called Le Villaret, in the Grand Bornand, in the diocese of Geneva, all of which was then very Catholic.[14]

4 With the instruction and the example of life given by this master, we all, his pupils, went on growing in the fear of God our Lord.[15] So, when I was about twelve years of age, I had certain impulses from the Holy Spirit to offer myself for the service of God our Lord. And one day during the holiday time, I went into a field where from time to time I helped to guard the flocks, and there, full of joy and with a great desire for purity, I vowed perpetual chastity to God our Lord.

O mercy of God, you walked at my side and longed for me! Ah, Lord, why did I not recognize you clearly from that time on? O Holy Spirit, why from that time on was I not able to separate myself from all things so as to seek you and enter into your school, seeing that you kept on inviting me and preparing my way with such blessings?[16] Nevertheless, you took possession of me; you signed me with the indelible seal of your fear. If you had allowed it to be destroyed like other gifts of your grace, should I not have become like Sodom and Gomorrah?[17]

▸ *1517–1525*

5 I was nine years in that school, growing in age and in knowledge though not, up to the end of my time there, in the wisdom of goodness and chastity of the eyes. There is enough in this to be grateful and give thanks for; there is also much matter for sorrow and repentance of heart because of the sins I used to commit against my Lord—each day being born to some of them and growing in them. And I should have committed many more if his divine goodness had not permitted in my soul, with a persistent fear of him, an immoderate desire for the knowledge and study of letters. And through that inclina-

---

became a pupil there. Velliard taught him Latin literature, some Greek, a little theology, and by word and example the fear of God. Favre never forgot this good man and in afteryears revered him as a saint. He was buried at La Roche, in Favre's opinion, but Pochat-Baron thinks Clets more probable. See Pochat-Baron, *A propos du bienheureux Pierre Favre* (Chambéry, 1906), p. 28.

[13] La Roche is about six miles from Le Villaret, a village in the parish of St. Jean-le-Sixt.

[14] *MonFabri,* pp. 115–116.

[15] One of Favre's schoolmates at La Roche was Claude Jay (or Le Jay), ordained a secular priest in 1528. He later became, with Ignatius and Favre, one of the founding fathers of the Society of Jesus.

[16] Ps. 21 (20): 4.

[17] Isa. 1:9; Rom. 9:29.

tion our Lord took me away from my country, where there was no way that I could entirely and effectively serve him in the future.

Be eternally blessed, Lord, for having granted me then such a great favor as when you willed to draw me away from my flesh and from my nature—a nature so corruptive of my spirit and so slow to rise to the knowledge and awareness of your Majesty and of my so numerous fellowmen.

▶ *1525*

> *5a: For advice about his further education, Favre turned to his maternal cousin Dom Claude Perissin, who had succeeded Dom Mamert Favre, his paternal uncle, as prior of Le Reposoir in 1522, and from him he received encouragement, advice, and material support (MonFabri, pp. 762, 774). Favre, then in his twentieth year, began his journey to Paris in September 1525, traveling with others for greater safety. In the same month he entered the Collège Sainte-Barbe as a paying boarder. That college was then at the height of its fame and was known for the humanistic tendencies of its professors. It had about two hundred students, mostly Spaniards and Portuguese, many of whom lodged in the college. Favre shared a room with Francis Xavier, who had entered at the same time. Both were under the direction of a regent (an assistant lecturer or tutor), Juan de la Peña, not much older than themselves and a roommate of theirs.*

6   In the year 1525, at the age of nineteen, I left my native place and went to Paris.

Remember, my soul, the spiritual goads *[espuelas]* that your Lord had already planted in your conscience through your fear of him. They were some scruples and remorse of conscience by which the demon began to drive you to seek your Creator, if you yourself had not been so dull-witted. Without those scruples Iñigo perchance might not have been able to get through to you, nor you to desire his help as happened later on.

▶ *1529*

> *6a: Favre became a bachelor of arts on January 10, 1529. The course for this degree was a long one. First came a year's preparatory study of the first elements of logic; then three and a half years of logic properly so called. The examination for the degree was mostly on logic. The preparation was done under the direction of a regent (perhaps corresponding to a tutor in a modern university), often very young—one could become a regent at the age of twenty-one (Charles Thurot, De l'organisation de l'enseignment dans l'Université de Paris, au moyen âge [Paris and Basançon, 1850], pp. 37- 39). A successful candidate was called a bachelor of arts. Then came his course of philosophy. It consisted of ethics, mathematics, cosmology, and metaphysics, all out of Aristotle's treatises on these subjects. After Easter of*

the following year, Favre received his philosophy degree, the licentiate; his studies were directed by Juan de la Peña, who became a friend of his. This man, a native of Sigüenza in New Castile, matriculated in the University of Paris in 1522, becoming a master of arts in 1525. He gave his first series of philosophy lectures during the years 1526-1530. This was the course followed by Favre and his friend Francis Xavier (1506-1552), a Basque from Navarre who entered Sainte-Barbe in 1525 with Favre; he also had Peña as regent. The master's degree followed almost immediately if one could meet the seemingly endless expenses involved; there was no strict examination. Xavier had the means and in the same spring became Master Francis. Favre had to postpone taking the master's degree until the spring of 1536.

7   On January 10, 1529, at the age of twenty-three, I became a bachelor of arts and after Easter was awarded the licentiate under Master Juan de la Peña, now a doctor of medicine.

May it please the divine goodness to grant that I may remember with gratitude the corporal and spiritual benefits conferred on me in various ways during those three and a half years: such a master for myself and such companions as I met in his room, especially Master Francis Xavier, a member of the Society of Jesus Christ.

7a: Iñigo de Loyola (Favre changes to Ignatius at a certain point), a Basque from Guipúzcoa, arrived in Paris in 1528 to begin the study of Latin grammar at the Collège de Montaigu. Too poor to pay his expenses as a student, he spent the summer of 1529 begging in Flanders. Then, with enough money for his keep, he entered the Collège Sainte-Barbe in September 1529 and was assigned lodgings with Favre and Francis Xavier. He intended to follow Peña's philosophy lectures but being backward needed coaching, which was given him by Favre in their lodging.

8   That year Iñigo entered the same Collège Sainte-Barbe and lodged in the same room as ourselves, intending to begin the course in arts on the coming feast of St. Remy;[18] our master (mentioned above) was to give this course.

Eternally blessed be all this that divine providence arranged for my good and for my salvation. For after providence decreed that I was to be the instructor of that holy man, we conversed at first about secular matters, then about spiritual things. Then followed a life in common in which we two shared the same room, the same table, and the same purse. As time passed he became my master in spiritual things and gave me a method of raising myself to a knowledge of the divine will and of myself. In the end we became one in desire and will and one in a firm

---

[18] October 1. See Schurhammer, *Francis Xavier: His Life and Times*, trans. M. Joseph Costelloe, S.J. (Rome, 1973) 1:141, n. 257, where he amends the Latin text to suggest that it was Juan de la Peña who arranged that Favre should tutor Ignatius.

resolve to take up that life we lead today—we, the present or future members of this Society of which I am unworthy.

9 May it please the divine clemency to give me the grace of clearly remembering and pondering the benefits which the Lord conferred on me in those days through that man. Firstly, he gave me an understanding of my conscience and of the temptations and scruples I had had for so long without either understanding them or seeing the way by which I would be able to get peace.

The scruples were over the fear that over a long period I had not properly confessed my sins, which gave me so much anxiety that to get a remedy I would gladly have gone to a desert to eat herbs and roots forever.

The temptations that I experienced at that time were over evil and foul carnal images suggested by the spirit of fornication, which spirit I knew at the time only from reading and not from spiritual experience.

10 Secondly, Iñigo advised me to make a general confession to Dr. Castro[19] and to go to confession and Communion once a week for the future. To help me in this, he gave me the daily examination of conscience, unwilling to put me through other exercises for the time being, though our Lord was giving me a great longing for them.

In that way we passed about four years together and had the same kind of relationship with others. I myself made daily spiritual progress as regards others as well as myself, while my soul (for some years and almost up to the time of my departure from Paris) was passing through many fires of temptation and waters of vainglory.[20] Through these our Lord gave me much knowledge of myself and of my faults, allowing me to fathom them and to be distressed as a remedy for my vainglory. In this way he granted me, through his grace alone, great peace in this matter.

11 With regard to gluttony also I had many struggles, and I was unable to find peace until the time of the Exercises. Then I spent

---

[19] Dr. Juan de Castro (1485-1556), born in Burgos, entered the Collège de Coqueret in 1526. While still a student he made the Spiritual Exercises under Ignatius in 1529. They completely transformed him. In 1532 he gained his doctorate in theology, returned to Spain some time after, and became a Carthusian. He died as prior of the charterhouse of Porta Coeli (Valencia) in 1556. Favre came to know him through Ignatius, whose close friend he was. See Villoslada, *La Universidad de Paris durante los estudios de Francisco de Vitoria, O.P. (1507-1533)* (Rome, 1938), pp. 247, 341; *FN* 1:33, n. 15.

[20] Ps. 66 (65): 12. His temptations to vainglory came from his victories over himself. Ignatius himself had a fierce struggle against that subtle enemy. See Brodrick, *Loyola,* pp. 87-91; also Hughes, *History* 3:369, on fame with its consequent vainglory as the main purpose in life of public men of all kinds up to about 1500 or so.

six days without food or drink except once at Communion, where there is always a little wine with the sacrament.[21] I was also greatly troubled by other temptations to contemplate the defects of others, to suspect them, and to pass judgment on them. But in this matter too the grace of my Consoler and my Teacher did not fail me, who set me on my first steps in charity toward my neighbor. At that time also and until I left Paris, I had scruples over every single one of countless imperfections that nobody knew about.

12 Our Lord, then, instructed me in so many ways, giving me remedies against so many bouts of depression which came that way to me that I would never be able to remember them. However, I can say that no distress or worry, scruple, hesitation, fear, or any other kind of evil spirit that I was able to feel to a notable degree ever came to me without my finding, at the same time or a few days after, its true remedy in God our Lord. He would grant me grace to ask, to seek, and to knock for that grace. And that remedy included countless graces to recognize and to experience the different spirits, with which I was getting more acquainted from day to day, for the Lord had left in me those goads *[espuelas],* which never let me remain lukewarm.

And so, knowing or judging or feeling something of these many bad spirits as regards myself or God our Lord or my neighbor, I say that never did our Lord let me remain tied up or deceived in anything, as I think; but in everything, with inspirations and enlightenment from his holy angels and from the Holy Spirit, he would always free me at a time that seemed good to him and was opportune for me.[22]

13 At the end of those four years or about then, the following happened; namely, finding myself already much strengthened in God our Lord alone with regard to the resolution I had already made and persevered in for more than two years, that is, to try to follow Iñigo in a life of poverty; and not waiting for anything but the end of my studies and his and those of Master Francis and of the others who were of the

---

[21] The custom of taking a little wine after Communion was observed at Louvain in 1553. See *FN* 1:34, n. 17.

[22] These passages show Ignatius, with great delicacy, at work on the mind and heart of Favre. Antonio Araoz, one of the early Jesuits, who spent a long time in Spain with Favre and knew him very well, recounts that Ignatius kept Favre for two years like a novice, getting him to examine his conscience daily on his thoughts, words, and actions. Then he made him work hard to root out his bad habits, taking them one by one, beginning with those which gave scandal to others or hampered his own spiritual progress and giving special attention to the ones most deeply rooted in him. See N. Orlandini, *La Vie du R. Pierre Favre* (Bordeaux, 1618), p. 163, a French translation of the Latin original published in Lyons in 1617 as *Vita Petri Fabri.* Orlandini had this account from Araoz himself. Purcell, *Companion,* p. 40.

same mind and resolve, I set off to visit my relatives. I stayed about seven months; my earthly father was still living and my mother was already dead.

▶ *1534*

> *13a: Favre never finished the course of theology based on Peter Lombard that he had begun during his last year or two with Velliard in La Roche and continued in a somewhat haphazard way in Paris. His formation, like that of his companions, was more literary and philosophical than theological. He made the Exercises for a month under Ignatius, the first of the companions to do so, was ordained subdeacon on February 28, deacon on April 4, and priest on May 30, 1534, in Paris. He mentions that the documents giving proof of his title had not arrived from his own diocese by the day of his ordination, so he was ordained titulo sui patrimonii, a proof that he must have possessed some little property. The scruple was typical. He waited two months before saying his first Mass on July 22, 1534.*

14   In 1534, at the age of twenty-eight, I returned to Paris to finish my theological studies. I made the Exercises and received all the Holy Orders, though the certificate of my title had not arrived. I said my first Mass on the feast of St. Mary Magdalene, my advocate and the advocate of all sinners, men and women. In this part are included the countless favors that God granted to my soul by calling it to so high a state and by granting it the grace of directing all things to him alone without any worldly desire of acquiring temporal honors or advantages.

Before that—I mean before having settled upon the course of my life through the help given me by God through Iñigo—I was always very unsure of myself and blown about by many winds: sometimes wishing to be married, sometimes to be a doctor, sometimes a lawyer, sometimes a lecturer, sometimes a professor of theology, sometimes a cleric without a degree—at times wishing to be a monk. I was being borne about previously by these winds, according as the greater or the lesser heavenly body was dominant, that is, according as one or other attraction reigned.[23] Delivering me, as I have said, from these attractions by the consolations of his Spirit, our Lord led me to make a firm decision to become a priest completely dedicated to his service.[24] So high and

---

[23] Favre describes attitudes, fleeting ideas, momentary attractions—characteristics of immaturity and adolescence. They were by no means firm resolutions—indeed, how can his promise of chastity at the age of twelve be reconciled with his desire to get married? His inner turmoil and the suffering it caused him were psychological in origin.

[24] To become a good priest devoted entirely to the service of God was central to his vocation just as it was the reason that brought the little group together and

perfect a service is it that I shall never be worthy to serve him in it, nor shall I be worthy of his choice of me, for it is a vocation so great that I should respond to it at all times with the utmost endeavors of this body and soul of mine.

▶ August 15, 1534

> **14a:** *Favre now comes to the events of August 15, 1534. Ignatius and his six companions, five of whom had made the Exercises (Xavier's retreat had been postponed because he was lecturing in the Beauvais College as regent in order to support himself), climbed to the little chapel that stood halfway up the hill of Montmartre. There, at the Communion of a Mass said by Favre, the only priest among them, each in turn pronounced a vow of chastity, of evangelical poverty as soon as their studies at the university were completed, and of making a pilgrimage to Palestine if transport could be found within a year of their leaving Paris. The vows, though private, bound them strictly in conscience as engagements to God. There was an implied vow of obedience to the pope if they were unable to labor in Palestine for life. Besides Xavier and Favre there were also present Nicolás Bobadilla (1509-1590), Diego Laínez (1512-1565), Alonso Salmerón (1515-1585), and Simão Rodrigues (1510-1579). None of them had any idea of founding a new religious order, but they had made history, for from their action that morning would spring the Society of Jesus.*

15 On the day of our Lady in August of that same year, all of us who were already united in the same determination and formed by the Exercises (except Master Francis, who had not yet made them though he was one with us in the enterprise) went to Our Lady of Montmartre near Paris. There each took a vow to set out for Jerusalem at the time decided[25] and, on his return, to place himself under obedience to the Roman pontiff. Each vowed too to make arrangements for leaving his "parents and his nets,"[26] retaining only provision for the journey. There were present at the first meeting Iñigo, Master Francis, myself (Favre), Master Bobadilla, Master Laínez, Master Salmerón, and Master Simão. Jay had not yet arrived in Paris; Master Jean and Paschase had not yet been won over.[27] Likewise the following two years, on the same day of

---

united them. Later on, in 1541, Favre was to call them "The Company of the Priests of Jesus" (*la Compañia de los sacerdotes de Jésus*). See *MonFabri*, p. 119. For a note on *Compañia de Jésus*, see George E. Ganss, S.J., *The Constitutions of the Society of Jesus*, p. 76, n. 3 (abbreviated hereafter as *ConsSJComm*).

[25] The day was to be decided by circumstances which would indicate the will of God.

[26] Matt. 4:18–22, an allusion to the calling of the apostles.

[27] Claude Jay, born at Mieussy in Savoy about 1500, was with Favre at La Roche under Velliard, whom he succeeded as principal of that school. Favre, who met him in Le Villaret in 1533, persuaded him to come to Paris and finish his theological

our Lady in August, we all returned to the same place to reaffirm our aforesaid resolutions, and for this we received each time a great spiritual increase.[28] And in those years, or rather in the last one, the other three joined us: Master Jay, Master Jean Codure, and Master Paschase.

▶ 1536–1538

15a: At the beginning of April 1535, Ignatius left Paris for his native Spain at the entreaties of his companions, who were greatly worried about his health; he had appointed Favre to take his place as head of the little group while he was absent. (During the summer of 1535, Favre may have given the Exercises to the young English humanist John Helyar, who wrote them down. His copy is the earliest known; but Venice and 1536–1537 are suggested in DeGuiJes, pp. 115–116, n. 16.) Before he left, Ignatius had arranged to meet the companions in Venice some time in the spring of 1537 so that the group could take ship together for Palestine. Because of war between Emperor Charles V and Francis I of France, Favre and the others concluded that it would be better to cut short their theological studies and leave for Venice earlier than the date agreed upon with Ignatius.

They began their journey in two groups, one leaving on November 11, the other on November 15, 1536, traveling on foot. Each wore his threadbare student's gown and furred cap as a protection against the appalling cold and the incessant rain that changed into snow in northern Italy. Each had on his back a knapsack containing a change of linen and a Bible; the three priests had each, in addition, a breviary. They wore their rosaries around their necks quite openly. The long and exhausting journey of about eight hundred miles ended on January 8, 1537 (Brodrick, Origin, pp. 52–54).

They had six months to wait in Venice for a ship to Palestine, so they went to live and work in the two hospitals for the incurables. These were by no means hospitals in the modern sense: they were rather hostels, and the

---

studies there. He entered Sainte-Barbe in September 1534, gained his licentiate on March 6, 1536, and became master of arts the same year. Then, under Favre's direction, he went through the Exercises and made up his mind to join the little group. He took vows with them on August 15, 1535. Master Jean Codure, born on June 24, 1508, at Seyne in the diocese of Embrun, betook himself to Paris at the age of twenty-seven and entered the college of either Torcy or Lisieux. Tormented by a desire for holiness, he came to Favre for direction. He made the Exercises, extending them to forty days, then joined the little community and took vows with them on August 15, 1536. Master Paschase Broët, born at Bertrancourt in Picardy around 1500, studied at Amiens and was ordained priest, most probably in 1524. He settled in Paris around 1534 to complete his theology. Worries about orthodoxy haunted him. Through Claude Jay he got to know Favre, who advised him to make the Exercises. He took vows with the other companions. So, as a result of Favre's winning personality, the nascent Society found itself with ten members.

[28] Their certainty of doing the will of God increased with the graces given them at each renewal of their vows.

work in them was unpaid, voluntary, exhausting, and revolting. The companions made beds, swept out the wards, washed whatever needed washing, including the patients, emptied and cleaned chamber pots, brought meals, laid out the dead, dug graves for them, and then buried them. Favre, who could make himself understood in Spanish and Italian, heard the confessions of the patients with Diego de Hozes.

In mid-March Ignatius sent his companions to Rome to obtain from the pope a permit to travel to Palestine and permission for the ordination of the nonpriests. On April 3, 1537, they were received in audience by Pope Paul III and given that permission. Cardinal Pucci, the pope's penitentiary, empowered them by decree to seek ordination from any bishop they chose in the Patriarchate of Venice or elsewhere under the "title of poverty." On June 24 of that year, Ignatius, Xavier, Laínez, Codure, Bobadilla, and Rodrigues were ordained priests in Venice; Salmerón, not yet twenty-three, could only be ordained deacon with the others. Favre, Laínez, and Ignatius then spent a month in solitude and prayer, followed by several months of pastoral work. They came to Rome in November 1537. The Pope then assigned Favre to lecture on Scripture and positive theology and Laínez on scholastic theology in the University of Rome, the Sapienza. Favre began his lectures in November 1537 and continued them until May 1539. By April 1538 all the companions had arrived in Rome. On May 5 they were given faculties by Cardinal Vincenzo Carafa to preach everywhere, to hear the confessions of both sexes, to absolve from certain reserved cases, to distribute Communion, and to administer the other sacraments. The Romans were thunderstruck to hear them preaching: only in Advent and in Lent was preaching done in Rome.

Trouble came, however, in the shape of false charges which were spread throughout Rome, and so critical did the situation become that Ignatius felt it necessary to have their good names cleared by an official inquiry. On November 18, 1538, Benedetto Conversini, the governor of Rome, put his name to a document vindicating the life and teaching of Ignatius and his companions.

Late in November 1538, when all hope of going to Jerusalem had gone forever, the companions offered themselves unreservedly to Pope Paul, who gladly accepted the offer. Favre interpreted the event as the quasi foundation of the Society. Circumstances then led them to begin deliberations whether they should, in addition to their vows of poverty and chastity, take a vow of obedience to one of their number. This vow would mean the assumption of the obligations of formal religious life. The long-drawn-out prayerful deliberations on the matter lasted from mid-March to June 24, 1539, Favre, it seems, acting as secretary. Ignatius then drew up a summary of their decisions and had it formally presented to the pope. One year and a week later, on September 27, 1540, Pope Paul III gave formal approval of the Society of Jesus as a canonical religious order by the bull Regimini militantis Ecclesiæ (Ganss, ConsSJComm, pp. 64–66, [1]; Brodrick, Origin, pp. 80–81).

▶ *1536*

16 On November 15, 1536, we set out from Paris together. There were nine of us: all those mentioned above except Master Iñigo, who eighteen months before had gone ahead to Venice, where he awaited us. We reached that city after Christmas. During the journey our Lord granted us so many favors that it would be impossible to write them down. We traveled on foot, passing through Lorraine and Germany where there were already many Lutheran or Zwinglian towns, such as Basle, Constance, and so forth. It was a very cold and deep winter; besides, France and Spain were at war, but the Lord preserved and delivered us from all these dangers.

We all arrived at Venice in good health and joyful in spirit. There we went to live in the hospitals, four in the Hospital of SS. John and Paul and five in the Hospital of the Incurables, waiting until Lent before going to Rome to get the permission of Pope Paul III to set out for Jerusalem.

▶ *1537*

17 In the year 1537, after Easter, having received the above-mentioned permission, we were for going to Jerusalem. But not being able to make the journey at that time, we dispersed to various places, intending to spend three months in solitude without being involved with others. Our purpose was, besides, that those who were not priests might thus prepare themselves better and render themselves more fit for so great a ministry. Iñigo and I and Master Laínez were in Vicenza; Master Francis with Salmerón, some twelve miles from Padua; Master Jean and the Bachelor,[29] in Trieste; Master Jay and Master Simão, in Bassano; Bobadilla and Paschase, in Verona. The three months over, we were summoned to Rome, and the three of us who were in Vicenza set out. By then it was October.

▶ *1538*

18 By the year 1538, when all of us companions had gathered in Rome and seen that there was no way of traveling to Jerusalem that year either, we got permission as "apostolic preachers" to preach

---

[29] Diego de Hozes, a native of Malaga, was friendly with Ignatius in Alcalá and in 1537 joined him in Venice. He accompanied Codure to Trieste, then to Padua. At the end of 1538 he died in that town, having worked himself to death. De Guibert suggests that this period of solitude and prayer gave Ignatius the idea of an extra year devoted to spiritual formation, to come after ordination and the completion of theological studies. It came to be called the tertianship. *DeGuiJes*, p. 37, n. 40.

and hear confessions everywhere. The cardinal of Naples, then legate at Rome, granted us the apostolic brief; the date of the brief was sometime in May.

Pray our Lord that I learn to acknowledge what falls to my share from the favors which our Lord did for us in common all year. Our worthy designs came up against many obstacles; we were tried as if by fire,[30] especially by the inquiry we took care to have made into our Society. This, in spite of opposition in high places, did take place in the end. That same year, after the verdict which cleared us, we were favored with a very special grace which is, as it were, the foundation stone of our whole Society. We offered ourselves as a holocaust to the sovereign pontiff Paul III so that he himself could determine what way we might be able to serve Christ and do good to all those who are under the authority of the Apostolic See, while we ourselves led a life of perpetual poverty, holding ourselves ready to set off at his order for the uttermost point of the Indies. The Lord willed that he should receive us and show himself pleased with what we proposed.

On account of that, I shall always, as will each of the others, feel the need of thanking the Lord of the universal harvest of the Catholic Church, Christ Jesus our Lord. For through the voice of his vicar on earth, which gives the clearest of calls, Christ thought it good to show us that he was pleased with our offer to serve him and that it was his will to make use of us forever.[31]

▸ *1539*

18a: On April 21, 1539, the pope appointed Cardinal Ennio Filonardo as legate in Parma to administer that part of the Papal States known as the Legation which stretched across northern Italy from Genoa to Venice. It was a disturbed and contentious district, rapidly going over to heresy. The cardinal, dedicated to Church reform, asked the pope for "two priests of reformed life" who by their preaching would defend the Catholic faith. For this task Favre and Laínez were chosen by their companions and left for Parma in May; the cardinal delayed his departure until June 20. The two priests preached and gave the Exercises to individuals and to small groups. Those who had made the Exercises gave them in their turn to others so that after nine months' work the city was "converted to religious fidelity," as its

---

[30] Ps. 66 (65): 12.

[31] The grace of their vocation had been given to each by the same Lord, but the judgment on and confirmation of that vocation came from the Church in the person of the pope. It was a witness to its universality and its unity in Christ. At a time when the Church and the pope were under criticism for delaying reform, this offering of themselves by the companions was remarkable. Equally remarkable at that time was Favre's statement that the voice of Christ's vicar on earth gives "the clearest of calls." See O'Leary, "Discernment," pp. 128–131.

council testified in a letter of March 1540 to Constanza Farnese, daughter of Pope Paul III (MonLain 1:4; Tacchi Venturi, Storia della Compagnia di Gesù in Italia, *vol. 2, pt. 1, 223–224).*

19   In May 1539 Master Laínez and I, at the bidding of the Roman Pontiff, left Rome for Parma with the cardinal of Sant'Angelo and remained there until September 1540.

Remember, O my soul, the graces you there received and which bore so much fruit in that place through the labors of Jerónimo Doménech[32] and ourselves in preaching, hearing confessions, and giving the Exercises; remember too what took place at Sissa.[33] Remember also that illness of yours which began on April 25, 1540, and lasted almost three months. You know, nor can you forget, the great spiritual profit you were able to derive from it according to the knowledge given you by our Lord for the purpose of causing you to bear fruit in spirit.

Remember your debt to the entire households of Laurencio and Maximo, who received you into their houses.[34] Remember in a special way the opportunity you took advantage of there so as never to lose your devotion to the feast of SS. Peter and Paul and principally to the feasts of St. John the Baptist and of our Lady of the Visitation, for your debt to them is so great that you must never forget it.

▸ *1540*

19a: *Dr. Pedro Ortiz (c. 1500–1548), a Spanish layman, a member of the Theological Faculty of Paris, had been appointed one of the papal theologians to the colloquies to be held in Germany. But Cardinal Contarini,*

---

[32] Jerónimo Doménech (1516–1593) had known Ignatius and the others at the University of Paris. He had been ordained in his native Spain about 1537. Wishing to do further theological studies in Paris, he first went to Rome and, armed with a letter of recommendation from Francis Xavier to Favre and Laínez, betook himself to Parma. There he made the Exercises under Favre and remained to work with the two Jesuits. In 1540 he returned to Rome and joined the Society.

[33] A small market town of some five thousand inhabitants nearly fourteen miles from Parma. Favre moved about a good deal among the neighboring villages, preaching, hearing confessions, and giving the Exercises. He refers no doubt to the efforts made by Doménech's influential uncle to prevent his nephew from entering the Society. Hearing that the fuming uncle was on his way to Parma from Rome, Favre sent the nephew to give the Exercises at Sissa. In Parma the uncle had Laínez and Favre summoned before the cardinal legate and complained that his nephew had been induced to give up a promising career and enter the Society. But the cardinal approved of the young man's decision and suggested that the uncle himself should make the Exercises. He did so and in time became a good friend of the Jesuits.

[34] Nothing at all is known about these charitable families. *MonFabri,* pp. 15–20; Schurhammer, *Francis Xavier,* pp. 525–535.

papal legate to the Diet of Ratisbon, judged him to be too unbending in his opinions to treat with the reformers. So, at the bidding of the pope, he began preparations for his return to Spain. Favre, who had left Parma at the beginning of October, was to join him in Piacenza and accompany him to Spain. Ortiz set out for Piacenza at the end of August, but was intercepted about sixty leagues north of Rome by a messenger from the emperor informing him that he was to travel to Germany as the representative of Charles V at the Colloquy of Worms and that Master Pierre Favre, the Paris theologian, was to accompany him to Worms as a member of his household (MonFabri, p. 36, n. 6; on Ortiz, see Purcell, Companion, pp. 73-77).

20 This same year, 1540, I was ordered by His Holiness to accompany Dr. Ortiz to Spain. On the way there Dr. Ortiz was recalled by a message from the emperor and brought me with him here to Germany to attend the Colloquy of Worms.[35] We arrived there on October 25.

Remember, O my soul, how on that same day our Lord gave you a very special and notable devotion that you were to take up and practice until your death. This has to do with the life of Christ and of our Lady; you were to commemorate in a special way from that day on during the canonical hours each of our Lord's days from his incarnation to his ascension and similarly the days of our Lady's life from her conception to her death. You must remember as well that great hope you received of being able to complete it all before your death.[36]

Remember how our Lord gave you such very special consolations in your prayers at Worms and gave you too such great knowledge of how to find methods of prayer, methods of thanking God our Lord, and methods of petitioning various graces for yourself, for the living, and for the dead. Be particularly mindful of the prayers for the Germans suggested to you by the Holy Spirit.[37]

---

[35] The emperor hoped that the Colloquy of Worms, which opened on November 25, 1540, and dragged on until January 18, 1541, might lead to doctrinal agreement between the Catholics and the Protestants. The Protestant side was united, the Catholic quite divided, so the colloquy came to nothing. At Worms Favre quickly realized that conferences, colloquies, and diets could not bring religious peace— among other things, they were too open to power politics and to manipulation for purely secular aims. Contarini's objections to Ortiz become understandable when we remember that Ortiz was one of the two men Ignatius really feared, the other being Gian Pietro Carafa, then a cardinal and later to become Pope Paul IV. Ortiz had a short and perpetually glowing fuse. So explosive was he in debate that Contarini feared he would wreck any chance of agreement at Worms the moment he opened his mouth. See Pastor, *History* 11:399–419.

[36] This devotional practice was based on the liturgical prayer of the breviary: Favre meditated on the lives of Christ and of Mary, linking his prayer to each canonical hour.

[37] Favre thanks God for methods of prayer, not for consolation; he is aware of

This year there was drawn up and confirmed the bull establishing our Society of Jesus Christ our Lord.[38]

▶ *1541*

20a: After the collapse of the Colloquy of Worms on January 14, 1541, Favre journeyed south to Speyer on the same day. He arrived there on January 20 and was straightaway invited to dine with the bishop of Speyer, Philip II of Flersheim, and distinguished guests, such as the duke of Bavaria (William II), the bishop of Worms (Henry IV) who was brother of the Count Palatine, and John IV of Hagen, archbishop of Trier (MonFabri, p. 63). Favre also had an interview with the duke of Savoy and with Cochlaeus (he and John Eck were the foremost Catholic theologians). He left Speyer on February 6 and reached Ratisbon (Regensburg) on the day of the emperor's arrival there on February 23. The Diet began in early April. Favre played no part in its deliberations but found plenty of pastoral work in the city. His six months in Ratisbon taught him a good deal about the state of Catholicism in Germany.

21 In January 1541 we left for Ratisbon, where the imperial diet was in session. On the journey you received great consolations in different prayers and contemplations, and you were given many new methods and subjects of prayer as you traveled along. For example, as you drew near to some place and looked at it or heard it talked about, you received a method of asking grace from our Lord that the archangel of that region with all the angel guardians of its inhabitants might be well disposed to us.[39] You asked also that Jesus Christ, the true guardian and shepherd present in the church of that region, might come to our aid and take special care of the needs and necessary-seeming benefits of all the people there: sinners, people at the point of death, the souls of the dead, those in distress, and those passing through some trial or other.

And when I passed through mountains, fields, or vineyards, many methods of prayer occurred to me. I prayed for an increase of the plenty

---

the constant influence of the Holy Spirit.

[38] See end of linking passage 14a. On December 27, 1540, Favre sent to Rome from Worms his vote for Ignatius or, in his stead, Francis Xavier as general of the newly confirmed Society of Jesus. MI, *Constitutiones et Regulæ Societatis Iesu*, 4 vols. (abbreviated hereafter as Cons*MHSJ*), vol. 1, *Monumenta Constitutionum prævia*, ed. A. Codina (Rome, 1934), pp. 32–33.

[39] Liturgical devotion to the angel guardians of persons, cities, and countries dated from the beginning of the century. It spread rapidly and seemed to answer a religious need of the age. *DBibTheol*, pp. 14–6; Xavier Léon-Dufour, ed., *Dictionary of the New Testament* (London, 1980), pp. 92–93 (abbreviated hereafter as *DNTest*); *NCathEn* 1:506–516; *DSpir*, vol. 1, art. "Anges."

I saw around me; I gave thanks for it on behalf of its owners or sought pardon for them because spiritually they are unable to recognize those blessings nor the hand they come from.

Similarly I made invocations through the saints who take care of these places, asking that they might desire to accomplish what the inhabitants of the places do not know how to do, begging pardon for them, giving thanks on their behalf, asking for what they need.[40]

22 That same year in Ratisbon I was given other favors. In the first place, our Lord granted me grace to accomplish some remarkable things in his service, especially in the confessions of many noblemen of the imperial court or at the court of my prince, the duke of Savoy,[41] who had chosen me as his personal confessor. Much good was done in these confessions, and much seed was sown for the still greater good which resulted from them.[42] And the same is true of the Exercises made by important persons, Spaniards and Italians as well as Germans, all very influential. From these Exercises there resulted almost all the good that has been done since then in Germany.

For my own spiritual progress, I received from the hand of the Holy Spirit other very notable graces: receiving new methods of prayer and contemplation for the future or being strengthened through more knowledge and feeling in my ordinary ones; for example, taking the litanies, or the mysteries of Christ, or Christian doctrine[43] with a view to

---

[40] Always on the move, Favre found that his long and slow journeys fed his apostolic and profoundly religious soul with subjects for prayer: people, good and evil, the temporal and spiritual welfare of all those in the countries he passed through. As he went along he called on the intercession of saints and angels, turning his prayer into a kind of continuous litany.

[41] Charles III of Savoy had just lost most of his territory to the Swiss and to his nephew, Francis I. He had come to the Diet of Ratisbon to appeal for help; promises were made but not kept, and he died in 1553 without having recovered his territory. Favre always had a soft spot for him. *MonFabri*, pp. 65, 78, 86, 100, and so forth.

[42] The image of the seed which develops into fruit through an inner and invisible agency expresses the idea of spiritual growth from its invisible origin to its visible manifestation in the world. It is constantly used by Favre.

[43] This *Christian Doctrine* (Favre refers to it also as a Children's Catechism) was a manual for the Christian recommended by Favre. It contained "the twelve articles of the Creed, the ten commandments of God, the four commandments of the Church, . . . [list of the] mortal sins, the five senses of the body, the spiritual and corporal works of mercy, the three powers of the soul, . . . the seven gifts of the Holy Spirit, the three theological virtues, the seven virtues opposed to the capital sins, as well as the duties proper to one's state, profession, dignity, and responsibilities" (*MonFabri*, p. 122). All these points, expressed in a way to aid the memory, were reproduced in countless manuals of piety at the time. They supplied Favre with

asking for various graces in conformity with each point; or seeking forgiveness or thanking our Lord, making use of the three ways.

Another method was to do the same thing, going through the three powers of the soul, or the five senses, or the principal parts of the body, or the temporal favors I have received.[44] And just as I can use that method for myself, so also can I use it for any other person living or dead, offering then a Mass for the greater efficacy of those prayers.

I also happened to find in Ratisbon a book by the blessed virgin St. Gertrude, which contains some special devotions by which, during her lifetime, she had felt herself making daily progress. I found in it many ways of praying and many helpful items.[45]

▸ *July 9, 1541*

23 In that same year, on the octave of the Visitation of our Lady, our Lord conferred on me a signal favor. In Ratisbon, at the main altar of that church called Our Lady of the Old Chapel, I took the solemn vows of my religious profession and sent them to Master Iñigo, who had been elected superior general.[46] As I made them I felt much spiritual consolation together with a great fortifying of my soul in the renunciation of the possessions I had already given up and the pleasures of the flesh I had already forsaken, and in humility, which consists in submission and in the denial of one's entire will. For all this, I say, I received fortitude anew and knowledge anew and deep feelings of goodwill. My vows were of chastity, poverty, and obedience to the general of the Society, together with another vow of obedience, in which we all promise obedience to the Supreme Pontiff with regard to missions.

---

matter for his meditations and for a continuous and litany-like prayer or *discursus*. See §30 n. 61 below. Favre called these practices exercises "of the third order" (*MonFabri*, p. 85). See also *SpEx,* [18–20], about adapting the Exercises to the exercitant.

[44] Favre derived these methods of prayer substantially from the Exercises. They correspond to a great variety of spiritual awareness and depth as well as to different stages of spiritual growth. *Epistolae P. Hieronymi Nadal* 4:677 (abbreviated hereafter as *MonNad*).

[45] This was entitled *Insinuationum divinæ pietatis libri iii* followed by Gertrude's *Exercitia* (spiritual practices), edited by Dirk Loer and Lanspergius (who wrote the preface). It had been published in Cologne five years previously. Favre learned methods of prayer from it; he was nothing if not serious about learning to pray. Jean Dagens, *Bibliographie chronologique de la littérature de spiritualité et de ses sources (1501–1610)* (Paris, 1952), p. 83.

[46] He had, in fact, sent three copies for safety's sake: in December 1540; on January 10, 1541, from Worms; and on January 22, from Speyer. *MonFabri*, pp. 51–53.

I made my profession before the Blessed Sacrament at the time of Communion, using the following formula:

> I, Pierre Favre, promise and vow to God our Lord, to our Lady, and to all the saints of heaven to observe with their aid perpetual chastity, perpetual poverty, and perpetual obedience to the superior of the Society of Jesus Christ. Likewise, perpetual obedience to the Supreme Pontiff with regard to the missions. And I promise to observe all this in conformity with the constitutions and rule of the said Society.

That is the way I made my profession. And because it is true and because I make it once again to God our Lord and to our Lady and to you, Master Iñigo of Loyola, who as its superior take the place of Jesus Christ in this Society, I sign it with my hand this day, July 9, 1541.[47]

▸ *Summer 1541*

24   On July 27 of that year, Dr. Ortiz and I left Ratisbon,[48] he with his whole household. We passed through my native district,[49] then through France where we were arrested and imprisoned for some seven days.[50] The great favor conferred on us there by our Lord should never

---

[47] Favre gives here the text of the letter in which he sent to Ignatius on July 9, 1541, the formula of his solemn profession. It is the same, with a few slight differences, as the one used on April 22, 1541, by the first fathers in Rome in the Chapel of the Crucifix in the Basilica of St. Paul Outside the Walls. *MonFabri*, pp. 117–118.

[48] They were on their way to Spain, their original destination. Ortiz, who had completed his mission in Germany, wanted to give some time to his benefice in Galapagar, north of Madrid, and take up lecturing again. Favre had to abandon much pastoral work: the giving of the Exercises and private spiritual conversations with people of all kinds who had come to Worms for the colloquy. They included bishops, parish priests, professors, princes and noblemen of the court, and others. He cooperated with other theologians in this work and moved round the neighborhood even as far as Nuremberg. During his stay in Ratisbon, he put together a written "instruction" for those who had done the Exercises or were about to give them. *MonFabri*, pp. 119–125. It deals with the examination of conscience (chap. 2), confession and frequent Communion (chaps. 1, 3), prayer (chaps. 4, 5, 7), self-denial (chap. 6), the apostolate (chap. 8), and interior reform (chap. 9).

[49] They went up the Danube, traversed Switzerland by following the banks of the Aar, and made a short stay in Savoy. Favre traveled on foot accompanied by another Jesuit(?) and Ortiz, whom he called "brother." *MonFabri*, pp. 770, 777. He spent three days with the Sieur d'Arenthon (*MonFabri*, pp. 762, 763, 768) and six days with his relatives at Le Villaret (*MonFabri*, pp. 764, 769). He preached there and taught the people how to say the rosary (*MonFabri*, p. 777).

[50] On their way to Lyons they were arrested near Nantua. The district was then occupied by the French, so the little group would naturally have been suspect since most of them were Spaniards. Even in these trying circumstances, Favre was true to his apostolic vocation and succeeded in winning the friendship and respect of their captors.

be forgotten. In his goodness he delivered us from our captors and granted us so much grace for conversing with them and benefiting their souls that their captain sought confession and confessed to me. Thus it happened that the feelings of warm friendship for everyone inspired in us by our Lord were not taken captive, nor did relations between ourselves and our captors become cool or even strained.

Nevertheless, I had some temptations to discouragement from time to time, fearing that we might not be freed soon or without causing much cost to the doctor. But at the same time—as their contrary and cure—I received consolation in the form of a total and good hope of almost all that, in the event, came about in our release.[51]

▸ *November 19, 1541*

25   On the day of St. Elizabeth, queen of Hungary, I felt great fervor as eight persons became present to me along with the desire to remember them vividly in order to pray for them without taking notice of their faults. They were the sovereign pontiff, the emperor, the king of France, the king of England, Luther, the Grand Turk, Bucer, and Philip Melanchthon.[52] That came about through experiencing in my soul how severely these men were judged by many; as a result I felt for them a certain kind of holy compassion accompanied by a good spirit.

26   On that same day of St. Elizabeth, I promised Christ our Lord and made a vow never to accept anything for confessions, for Masses, or for preaching[53] and never to live on a fixed income, even if offered to

---

[51] Traveling by way of Montserrat, Saragossa, Medinaceli, and Alcalá, the group reached Madrid on October 27, 1541. With the Galapagar presbytery as a base, Favre began another apostolate in the surrounding district. Ortiz renewed his friendships with the notables of Madrid, Ocaña, and Toledo and introduced his companion to them. This time Favre had more time for teaching. At Galapagar he was seen every afternoon at about two o'clock teaching nearly a hundred little boys and girls, to whom on occasion adults, even priests, added themselves. Favre met again many from his Paris days and many he had known in Germany. *MonFabri*, pp. 126–129, 130, 135.

[52] These were Pope Paul III, Charles V, Francis I, Henry VIII, Luther, Suleiman I, Martin Bucer, and Philip Melanchthon. Their salvation was one of Favre's constant preoccupations, as we know from his friend Kalckbrenner (§390–§391). The kind of criticism they were subjected to in Spain can easily be imagined: the treacherous alliance of Francis I with Suleiman I, the policy of appeasement adopted by Charles V, the persistent procrastination of Pope Paul III, the repudiation of Catherine of Aragón by Henry VIII. Favre's judgment of these men and his prayers for them reveal an ecumenical outlook and a desire for unity unusual in those days. It was quite in keeping with Cardinal Contarini's conciliatory policy at Ratisbon and with the general spirit of the colloquies. For an account of this period see Pastor, *History*, vol. 11.

[53] The refusal of priests to administer the sacraments or to celebrate marriages

me in such a way that I could not in good conscience refuse it. I must keep the memory of that vow ever present to my mind, recognizing it as a very special favor from Christ our Lord, who in this way keeps helping me in the better observance of my vow of poverty.

▸ November 21, 1541

27 On the day of the Presentation, with the help of the Spirit of all holiness and of perfect chastity and for guarding my vow of chastity better, the Lord gave me an experience of special reverence for that most pure girl, our Lady. As an attestation and reminder of that reverence, I resolved to abstain forever from putting my face close to any young boy or girl for any reason at all, even lawful, let alone doing so to older people.

▸ Autumn 1541

28 This same year, as I journeyed into Spain, I had many noteworthy devotions and spiritual feelings concerning the invocation of the principalities, the archangels, the angel guardians, and the saints of Spain. I conceived, in particular, great devotion to St. Narcissus in Gerona, St. Eulalia in Barcelona, our Lady of Montserrat, our Lady of the Pillar, St. James, St. Isidore, St. Ildefonsus, the holy martyrs Justus and Pastor, our Lady of Guadalupe, St. Engratia of Saragossa, and others. I asked them all to be willing to look favorably on my travels in Spain and help me by their prayers to produce some good fruit; and so I did, thanks more to their intercession than to my own efforts.

I decided to do the same in each kingdom and principality, that is, commend myself to the angelic principalities, the archangels, the guardian angels, and the saints whom I was able to know to be specially honored in that province or domain.

This practice confirmed in me the devotion I had to other saints who are venerated in Italy and who are mentioned more at length in my Roman breviary. I felt the same devotion to other saints I have seen venerated in Germany, especially the Three Kings, the eleven thousand virgins, in particular, St. Ursula and St. Pinosa (whose head and the very arrow I saw with my own eyes in a certain Benedictine monastery). Likewise, St. Sebald at Nuremberg, and St. Maximinus at Trier.

---

and funerals without a fee was a constant theme of the reformers. The generosity of Favre's many rich and noble friends must have been the occasion of his feeling that a solemn promise to God in the matter was a necessary precaution. A. Renaudet, *Préréforme et humanisme à Paris pendant les premières guerres d'Italie (1494–1517)* (Paris, 1916), p. 179.

In France I retain my devotion to St. Genevieve and to St. Marcellus, bishop of Paris, whose bodies rest in the city for its great protection; to St. Denis the Areopagite, whose body is kept at St. Denis in France; to St. Paul Sergius at Narbonne; at Marseille to St. Mary Magdalene, her sister Martha, and their brother St. Lazarus.

In Savoy I have devotion (and I have no desire to abandon it) to St. Bruno, the founder of the Carthusians; to St. Amandus, who is in Nantua near where we were imprisoned; to Fray Juan of Spain, Frère Jean Bourgeois, and my master Pierre Velliard—to me these men are saints though not canonized. Likewise, to St. Claude, who is a canonized saint.[54] I took note of many other saints at that time; and taking them as advocates I proposed to never forget them, calling upon them for myself and for the living and the dead, especially for those who live or died in the place where those saints died, were born, or lived, whether in Europe, in Africa, or in Asia, or somewhere in the islands.[55] In these spiritual practices I felt much devotion along with much spirit to continue them and give myself freely to them, calling upon by turns the apostles and the other saints who labored fruitfully in various parts of the world to have a special care of our Society and of all the souls in the countries or provinces where they once exercised their charity.

Whenever I wish to pray in a special way for the living or the dead of some district or some kingdom, I invoke the aid of those angels and saints who had or have special care of those souls living or dead.

29 At that time, or before it, I took up a devotion which our Lord gave me to improve my recitation of the canonical hours. It consisted in reciting between psalms, for the renewal of my spirit, this short prayer which I had taken from the Gospel: "Heavenly Father, give me your good spirit"[56]—in which I have experienced many different benefits.

I likewise received another devotion as an introduction to each of the seven canonical hours, with the idea of applying them to some

---

[54] Favre's many long journeys throughout Europe left him much time for prayer. No better way was there of keeping distractions at bay and of widening his prayer as much as possible than to invoke the saints of each place and town he visited, as well as the angels especially honored there. The information he collected about local saints and local devotions nourished his prayer and inspired in him desires for the success of whatever mission he was engaged in at the time. This long passage gives a very good idea of the universality of his intercessory prayer and of his vivid realization of the Communion of Saints.

[55] On the sixteenth-century map these "islands" represented whatever inhabited lands, already discovered or still unknown, remained after the naming of the three continents.

[56] Luke 11:13.

things especially worthy of attention.[57] It is to say "Jesus, Mary" ten times at the beginning of each hour, so that I may have an opportunity of remembering the following ten intentions:

1. The honor of God our Lord
2. The glory of his saints
3. Good people, for their growth in whatever good intention they may have at the time
4. People at that hour in mortal sin that they may profit from that office, give up sinning, and be converted
5. The advancement of matters concerning the Catholic faith
6. Universal peace between the Catholic and Christian princes
7. Those at that time in some bodily affliction
8. Those in spiritual affliction or distress
9. Those at the point of death
10. The souls in purgatory, so that at that hour and at the corresponding hour of the office I am then saying[58] they may find some alleviation of their pains and sufferings

30 Note here, O my soul, how our Lord drew you out of great spiritual tribulations and distress caused by the severe temptations you endured because of your defects and also because of the turmoil stirred up by the spirit of fornication and because of your negligence in bearing fruit.

Remember the very clear understanding you received about the causes of those temptations. Remember that you almost never had grievous temptation without finding consolation not only through clear knowledge but also through a spirit contrary to the melancholy moods, the fears, the fits of discouragement, or the dejection that succeeds illusory hopes.[59] For our Lord gave you very clear knowledge and genu-

---

[57] The canonical hours were matins, lauds, prime, terce, sext, none, vespers, and compline. Since Vatican II some of these have been suppressed, and the rubrics governing the time of day when they are to be said have been modified.

[58] In Favre's day the daily recitation of the seven canonical hours was a grave obligation in conscience. But religious not bound to office in choir (such as Jesuits) and diocesan priests were not obliged to say each canonical hour at the time of day laid down for its recitation.

[59] This passage is a record of a campaign waged and won. Favre distinguishes two aspects of consolation: one, light in the intellect to detect the temptations that lie under discouragement; the other, a matter of the feelings and the will. It encourages and emboldens, bearing the heart in quite the opposite direction to the preceding temptations. The light or knowledge that Favre possesses is clear because it arises from discernment; his feelings are trustworthy because they are in conformity with

ine feelings to serve you as remedies against the spirit of fornication and as means of purifying the flesh and the spirit. These he gave you as remedies and as means to resist the world and its spirit and others as a defense against evil spirits. You had and received also from the Lord great desires with the hope of becoming the abode of the Holy Spirit and the hope that bad spirits might not lodge in the vital or animal spirits of my body.[60]

To obtain that grace I used to make various meditations [*discursos*] by means of the powers, the senses, the principal members of the entire body, and so forth, asking that it might be our Lord's will to purify me thoroughly.[61] With regard to the virtues of temperance, chastity, and diligence and also those of humility, patience, and charity, I received many gifts of knowledge and feelings, our Lord himself granting me to pray often for them with deep feelings of faith and hope. May he be blessed for ever and ever! Amen.

31 About Catholic doctrine in conformity with the Roman Church, I had innumerable [interior] visitations, and likewise about constitutions, states of life and orders, ceremonies, good works, pilgrimages,

---

faith, hope, and charity.

[60] These vital or animal spirits are imperceptible forces existing in man, giving entry to external influences whether from matter (the stars) or from demons. The corporeal spirits are defined by St. Thomas as vital movements and impulses (*Summa Theologiæ*, I, q. 27. a. 4; q. 36, a. 1. [abbreviated hereafter as *ST*]), mysterious entities akin to the humors. Towards the end of the Middle Ages, these corporeal spirits were divided into two or three categories according to their functions: the vital spirit affecting the heart, the animal spirit the brain, the natural spirit the liver (*Patrologia Latina*, Migne, ed., 40, 789, 793 [abbreviated hereafter as *PL*]). The expression "the influence of the stars" (*influenza delle stelle*) was used in medieval Italy to describe and state the supposed causes of the many diseases that struck down town dwellers in the summer season. Medieval men were not so simple as they may appear; they sought the causes of observed effects and looked to authority in the person of Aristotle, Galen, and others to supply the answers. Not until about the middle of the nineteenth century were the answers found and variously named as germs, bacteria, bacilli, viruses, and so on. See O'Leary, "Discernment," pp. 72–75, on Favre's belief in the spirit world.

[61] See *SpEx*, [238–243] on the First Method of Prayer; [246] on the powers of the soul; and [247–248] on the five senses. They are ways of putting a person in touch with God but are based on the reality of grace and on man's nature composed of body and soul. The form of prayer Favre calls the *discursus* is a meditative review of the mysteries of Christ's life in order during the same period of prayer. See §42, §43, §47, §68, §72, §86, §114, §175, §342, and so forth. Favre will gradually abandon this form of prayer for one more simple (§35), one in which there is a perception of the spiritual sense of the Scriptures and of the theological texts—that is, an immediate contact with the reality of the Word and of the divine action. On Favre's *discursus (discursos)* see *DeCertMem*, p. 92, n.6.

vows, fasts, and the honoring of the saints, the angels, our Lady, the souls in purgatory, and so forth[62]—in all this feeling my spirit deeply moved with much devotion and approval of them.

32 In January 1542 I left Spain, returning to Germany at the order of His Holiness.[63] During the journey God our Lord granted me innumerable favors, especially by fulfilling the greatest earthly desire I have experienced, that is, to be given companions for his service. They were Juan and Alvaro Alfonso.[64]

Another favor during that long and perilous journey was our preservation, contrary to all expectations, from all temporal misfortunes, such as brigands in Catalonia, imprisonment in France, soldiers on our crossing from Savoy into Switzerland, and heretics in Germany; we were preserved from sickness too, though some of us were delicate enough. And what is worth more than anything else, he preserved us from temptations that divide, I mean from the spirit of division.

33 During that journey our Lord gave me many feelings of love and hope for heretics and for the whole world. He had done so in the past as well, in particular granting me a devotion to take up and practice until death with faith, hope, and charity regarding the welfare of these seven cities: Wittenberg in Saxony, the capital of Sarmatia (though I do not know its name), Geneva in the dukedom of Savoy, Constantinople in Greece, Antioch (also in Greece), Jerusalem, and Alexandria in Africa.[65] I

---

[62] All the points mentioned here by Favre are those which constantly came up in discussions about Protestantism and Erasmianism. They were mentioned by Pedro Ortiz in his deposition of 1529 at Toledo against the errors of Erasmus. M. Bataillon, *Erasme et l'Espagne* (Paris, 1937), pp. 477–479. Perhaps some of the "Rules for Thinking with the Church" in the *Spiritual Exercises* were derived from Favre's wide and varied experience in Germany. *SpEx*, [353–359], [362], [357–370].

[63] Favre was recalled to Germany by a letter of Cardinal Farnese from Rome, dated December 22, 1541. *MonFabri*, pp. 140–141. He parted from Ortiz in February 1542, reached Barcelona on March 15, and entered Speyer on April 14, having traveled by way of Perpignan, Lyon, and Soleure.

[64] Juan de Aragón (or João Aragonese), a Portuguese, and Alvaro Alfonso, a Spaniard, were court chaplains to the infantas Maria and Juana, daughters of Charles V. Favre had gone to the court at Ocaña to see his friend Ferdinand de Silva, count of Cifuentes, who was house steward or majordomo to the infantas. As an act of courtesy they sent the two chaplains to accompany him on his journey out of Spain. They fell so much under his spell that they got permission from the infantas to join him. Juan de Aragón became a Jesuit and died in Portugal about 1565. For Alvaro Alfonso see §179 n. 69 below. See *MonFabri*, p. 151, for Favre's account of the incident.

[65] The towns that Favre intends to pray for are the ones in which the Church was most under threat in those days: Wittenburg, the Lutheran capital; Moscow or Kiev, the capital of the new Orthodox empire (Sarmatia was an ancient name for Poland and Russia); Geneva, the Calvinist capital; Constantinople, the captured

resolved to keep them always in mind, hoping that I or some other priest of the Society of Jesus Christ may eventually say Mass in all of them.

▸ *June 15*

34 On the octave day of Corpus Christi, wanting to make contact with the dean of Speyer[66] so that I might help him by means of the Spiritual Exercises, but being unable to achieve my purpose in any way except through prayer, a certain devotion came to me which I had not thought of before. This consisted in praying first to the dean's heavenly Father, who was the first to gain him; secondly, to his Mother and Lady, the mother of Jesus; thirdly, to his guardian angel, his master and his instructor, so to speak; fourthly, to the men and women saints, who, like brothers and sisters, have a special spiritual affection for him. This practice seemed to me a good way of gaining a person's friendship. So I came to recite for the first-named person the Our Father, for the second a Hail Mary, for the third the prayer *Deus, qui miro ordine angelorum . . .* , and the fourth by saying the prayer *Omnes sancti tui, quaesumus, Domine. . . .*[67]

There occurred to me also something very necessary for retaining a person's goodwill, apart from what other things can be done for him: to have great devotion to all the guardian angels, for they can predispose people toward us in many ways and curb the violence and temptations of our enemies.[68]

---

capital of Byzantium which, with the Patriarchates of Jerusalem, Antioch, and Alexandria, had fallen under Moslem rule. The geography of his prayer is that of the Church's spiritual conflict; it refers directly to the frontiers of the faith and is more concerned with the Near East than with the Far East. During his time in Paris, the Moslem problem was very much in the air. It is clear that the Society was already looking far afield, planning to bring the faith into all regions on earth. This passage is evidence of Favre's ecumenical preoccupations. F. de Dainville, *La Géographie des humanistes* (Paris, 1940), p. 15.

[66] Most likely George Mussbach, the vicar general of Speyer. *MonFabri*, p. 67. Under Favre's direction he made the First Week of the Exercises with great generosity.

[67] The first prayer is the opening one of the Mass for the feast of SS. Michael, Gabriel, and Raphael, archangels, said on September 29. It invokes the intercession of the saints for peace, for the good of the Church, for all men, for benefactors, and for the souls of the faithful departed. This universal preoccupation must have appealed to Favre.

[68] Favre was deeply devoted to the guardian angels. This devotion had been spreading rapidly since the beginning of the fifteenth century. *NCathEnc* 1:516–519; K. Rahner, ed., with C. Ernst and K. Smith, *Sacramentum Mundi* (New York and London, 1968) 1:27–35 (abbreviated hereafter as *SacMundi*).

35 Note here, my soul, and remember that our Lord gave you in the past great understanding of the temptations and the troubles caused by the demons. That led you at certain times to pray and meditate [*hiziste discursos*] on the saints, on the mysteries of Christ, on Christian doctrine, or on the members of your body, and so on.[69] Similarly, you were led to seek grace against your enemies and especially against the spirit of fornication, that his power might no longer dwell in your loins but be cast out from every place occupied by the vital or animal spirit of your body. Likewise, from your intellect, your memory, and your will. Likewise, from the places where you were.[70] You begged that grace with great fervor of spirit and with much hope that it might be given to you before your death. For this the Holy Spirit suggested that you pray earnestly to his divine goodness and purity that he might dwell in your body as in his temple and in your spirit. Likewise, that the angels might drive out your enemies and find a corporal abode in the spirits of your body. You found great hope of that purification, resolving to practice (as I had already been doing for a long time) much moderation in food and drink and much moderation, with modesty, in all your external behavior. For you saw how necessary it is that evil spirits not retain that great power of theirs to inhabit and move your flesh or spirit, but find instead a heart not weighed down by food and drink.

Bless the Lord, therefore, my soul, for his great gift to you of so efficacious a desire for holiness of body and purity of spirit and for the gift of time to feel those spurs which, along with the hope of obtaining it, were necessary for the virtue of chastity of body and of spirit and to preserve a hope of obtaining it. Likewise, in my having special devotion to my own angel, I experienced many helps, asking him to protect me from my bad spirit and especially from the spirit of fornication.[71]

---

[69] This method of prayer was well suited to Favre's wandering, busy, and distracting life. It helped to reconcile that life with his need for prayer and his deep concern with the great issues of the time. Taking in order a list of related points served to anchor his mind and nourish his affective prayer. See §30 n. 61 above.

[70] The loins ("reins" was the older term) were looked on as the parts of the body under the immediate influence of corporeal spirits whether good or bad, and those which had to do with chastity were ranked first. Places were also considered as subject to the influence of the occult, at times malign, power of spirits. *NCathEnc* 4:752–757; *DBibTheol*, pp. 149–151.

[71] Favre was much preoccupied by chastity: at twelve he had, however unwisely, made a vow of chastity (§3); at school under Velliard he hints at faults against chastity (§5); as a student in Paris he suffered persistent and violent temptations to impurity (§9); he places the vow of chastity first among the three he took as a Jesuit (§23); the anguish he suffered on account of this virtue can be read over and over again in the *Memoriale*—even in the last passage (§443) he mentions the revival of his defects and among them this kind of temptation.

The Later Years: Introspection (1542–1546)

▸ *June 24*

36   On the day of St. John the Baptist[72] I had and experienced in my spirit a notable feeling of a certain grandeur and awesome majesty in St. John, and I felt great spiritual sorrow that here in Germany his feast was not made as much of in the way of solemnity as it was in other countries. I desired therefore, with much feeling, to be able someday to have a share in moving those who have a bishop's authority to have this feast celebrated with greater solemnity.

▸ *June 26*

37   On the day of SS. John and Paul, I was given knowledge and an indication of a means to improve my recitation of the office. It was to note four things as limits and bounds beyond which I should determine not to pass during the time of the office. First, the place where it is recited; second, the persons or saints mentioned in the prayer; third, the words; and, fourth, the gestures which belong in the office. These are useful also to beginners for driving away any memories, thoughts, impressions, or desires connected with other places, persons, conversations, or activities that suggest themselves. And likewise regarding the time.

I took note also of another help which I had often before experienced to be of great use for the same purpose. It consisted in looking ahead, long before saying the office, to each of its principal parts or each hour by itself with a great desire to concentrate on it—as if a person were to say to himself, "You have to say this psalm first, then this one, then that other, and so forth"—and beginning the office with that consideration.

Likewise, after ending the recitation, taking care (at least in desire) that the spirit does not depart from it and that you prolong your reflection as much as possible so as to avoid becoming completely distracted by external matters.

Similarly, it is a great benefit to a busy man (before reciting the office as well as after) to make frequent efforts to withdraw as far as possible from what he is doing by turning his thoughts and desires to

---

This long entry, §35, ends the retrospective section of the *Memoriale*. From this point on the entries will concern what he is "given" from day to day.

[72] The feast of St. John the Baptist, celebrated on June 25, was the titular feast of the parish church where Favre had been baptized, the saint being the patron of his parish, Saint-Jean-de-Sixt; hence Favre's devotion to him (§104).

the subject matter of the next office or of the one he has said. For it is clear that the person who never desires to pray well except when the designated time comes cannot (short of a miracle) possess solid devotion.[73] Hence, it is very necessary to lay down for oneself definite times for prayer, to call them to mind often and with longing and with an ever present fear of not praying well; and afterwards, if there has been some defect, to have a sense of regret that lasts until the time comes for the next exercise. And let your sorrow be not only because of the distractions, which displease you, but ultimately let it proceed from love and affection for the words of God and the matter of your prayer.

Many are distressed at not having fervor in prayer—though not out of love for prayer itself (that is, for God and his saints and the words of the prayer)—but out of hatred and fear of distracting thoughts and desires arising from other temporal concerns—even necessary ones. They also dislike and fear harmful and idle things and even good but irrelevant things. This is, however, a way that leads to love; but, when that love has been attained, one gives attention to those very things—attention not merely mental but even heartfelt[74]—on account of God himself and his words and the works of his that are dealt with in the office, even though one may feel not in the least distracted by extraneous things.[75]

38   At the same time, during the octave of St. John the Baptist, I noted something very necessary for setting in order one's personal concerns, one's desires and preoccupations—in short, for the right ordering of one's interior life so as to attain tranquility in one's spiritual and corporal occupations. That was in connection with the saying of our Lord "Do not take thought about the morrow."[76] This means that even in

---

[73] Because of his busy and distracting life, Favre felt it necessary to arrange a definite place and time for the recital of his office. This would not smother the spontaneity of his prayer nor would careful preparation do so; it would rather strengthen his resolve to banish distractions and help him to pray with more concentration. But desire for prayer as a means of getting in contact with God *(attingere Deum)* and not as a means of avoiding distractions must always be present—an echo of the ever attentive spouse in the Canticle of Canticles who sighs for the Beloved. So concern about prayer and constant efforts to improve it can lead to a desire for greater union with God.

[74] Favre distinguishes between the attention of the mind *(attentio mentis)* as it recollects itself in God and the affective inclination *(intentio affectus)*, an interior movement which has its origin in the depths of the heart and bears the whole man to God.

[75] It is a matter of finding God, not of avoiding distractions. See §54 n. 108 below.

[76] "Be not therefore solicitous for tomorrow; for the morrow will be solicitous for itself. Sufficient for the day is the evil thereof" (Matt. 6:34 [Douay Version]). Favre was constantly on the move at the behest of superiors, temporal and ecclesiastical.

spiritual desires and anxieties it is good for us not to take thought, as far as possible, about the morrow. One should rather arrange the hours and the time available during the day so as not to allow one's attention to stray or one's thoughts to dwell either joyfully or sadly on what might happen afterwards.

If one's soul is divided among many things so far off, it is impossible to do well what is at hand and devote yourself to it with that degree of attention you would have with a spirit that wandered less.

Another time there came to me a petition to be made to the Most Holy Trinity, namely, that it might give me the grace that in every good desire, work, or contemplation of mine my three faculties might always concur so that one might not impede the other and, on the contrary, if one of them should happen to wander off in pursuit of some evil end, that the others might never concur but instead prevent it.

▸ *July 2*

39   On the day of the Visitation of our Lady, apropos of the humility we owe to our elders (and which it is good to have with regard to all creatures for the love of God our Lord), I was given a deep sense of our Lady's humility, which was to serve her relative St. Elizabeth[77] and humble herself, seeing in her the mother of the Precursor of Christ our Lord. At this point I had a very great desire in my spirit that all those who live in some way under obedience might exercise themselves in it so as to obtain perfect humility, patience, and charity in bearing with and honoring their elders whether good or bad, having eyes and affections only for what is good in them without attending to what is evil. And the less good the superior appears in his position, the more perfect will the subject make himself in his own, which is that of an obedient, diligent, and faithful servant in the fear and the love of God our Lord.

In this way, when they had become pleasing to God, these servants would then deserve ultimately to have good masters, and in the other way, namely, when they themselves had quit being servants. For

---

[77] Favre uses the word *cuñada* (sister-in-law) in reference to St. Elizabeth; the word seems to have had that meaning even in the sixteenth century. It is an error on his part unless the word, in current usage, retained the more general meaning of relative by marriage in any degree. He was reflecting on the problems involved in obedience to unworthy ecclesiastical superiors—Germany having its share of them, as his travels had taught him. Mary's "humility" in visiting her cousin Elizabeth and in serving her leads him to the idea that we owe humility (here synonymous with obedience) to our superiors and indeed to all creatures. So begins a series of reflections on obedience to superiors (§39–§45). Pastor, *History* 11:133ff.

disloyal subjects no more deserve to have good masters than the bad master deserves from the Lord better servants and subjects.[78]

40 One day within the octave of the Visitation of the Blessed Virgin Mary, I experienced certain deeply felt longings in which I asked God the Father to be a father to me in a special way (unworthy though I am) and that he might make of me his son to obey and acknowledge him. I asked the Son of God our Lord that he might deign to be my Lord and that by his grace I might serve him in all fear for the future. I begged the Holy Spirit to be my master and to teach me to be his disciple.

To obtain these gifts I implored with great devotion the help and the intercession of her who was the chosen daughter of God the Father, the servant and mother of Jesus Christ, and the disciple of the Holy Spirit—I mean the Blessed Virgin Mary, who can with ease obtain all these graces from God.

I desired also that she might teach me the true way to be a son, and to be a servant, and to be a disciple according to his example, because she knows how Jesus Christ lived as her son and servant and disciple, and thus will know how humble he was and how he fitted into each of those three states of life.

41 Similarly, dwelling more at length on this matter, I recognized the great need of preaching about it, because when subjects have been brought to that degree of true obedience, humility, respect, and reverence they should have for their superiors, our Lord might be pleased with them and consequently give them superiors after his own heart. On the other hand, it can be said that a person who is not disposed to acknowledge goodness does not deserve to possess it himself and that he who has not yet become a servant does not deserve to have a master whose goodness he knows and rejoices in. Hence one can expect that when subjects (at least the better ones) shall have attained such a degree of humility, patience, and charity as to enable them to honor, serve, obey, and bear with any superior however unsuitable without losing their goodwill but, on the contrary, always growing in it

---

[78] To those who refuse to obey unworthy bishops and ecclesiastical superiors, Favre proposes interior reform and religious submission as the only way to deserve good superiors. This inner reform or conversion, a slow interior transformation of a person, leads ultimately to a transformation of institutions. Vatican Council II (abbreviated hereafter as VatCouncII), *Dogmatic Constitution on the Church*, ed. Austin Flannery, O.P. (Dublin, 1975), "Religious", no. 46. Ignatius had the same idea: True reform does not come from without, from those who leave the Church, but rather from those within it. As history teaches us, corruption had unfortunately gone too far for this interior reform to be effective against it everywhere. See §8 n. 18 above on obedience to the pope, and O'Leary, "Discernment," pp. 128–131.

with a resolve to persevere in that way until death—in that case, I say, there is good reason for greater hope that our Lord may be moved to give them better superiors, but not in the opposite case, that is, when the unworthy are observed to be going from bad to worse in regard to obedience.

On a day within the octave of the Visitation of the blessed Mary, I felt great desires for certain graces for which I had already been asking in some way within the preceding Pentecostal season. These desires were that God the Father, my Guardian, might deign by a spiritual grace to be a father to me by making me his son; that Jesus Christ, the Redeemer, might make me his servant and be to me a master; and that the Holy Spirit might be my master in all things, instructing me and forming me into a true disciple of his. I felt a desire, too, regarding the Virgin Mother, my Lady and my Advocate, to be so good as to teach me how I could be a son of the Father, a servant of Jesus Christ, how I should be a disciple of the Holy Spirit; for she herself is the daughter of God most high, the servant but also the mother of Jesus Christ, and a true disciple of the Holy Spirit, who has sanctified, instructed, and directed her always and in all things.[79]

42 Another day also within this time of the Visitation, when I started to go through the mysteries of Christ, as was my custom, and while I was reflecting on the Annunciation, at the Blessed Virgin's total offering of herself as the handmaid of the Redeemer, there came to me great and surpassing desires to have, whatever I was on the point of doing, a right intention beforehand through the grace of a kind of "annunciation."

Likewise, I desired that all women, before giving birth, should direct their thoughts to all the good works that the Lord is going to require of their sons and daughters. And in like manner I desired that fathers according to the flesh and spiritual fathers who have spiritual sons or disciples who obey them should have similar thoughts. And whatever I now see myself to have gained from my good works or labors or studies in the past, I wished that it might all have been directed from the beginning of my life to the good of these Germans.

43 Reflecting on the Visitation and on the grace of the Virgin, so pleasing to the Most High as to be able to bring about the sancti-

---

[79] Reflecting further on obedience, Favre links it with the Trinity— obedience is essentially to the Triune God. The words he uses—son, servant, disciple—each express a different aspect of obedience, and this obedience can be achieved at every moment and in every action. But for it there is need of a right intention. So he desires to experience, before doing anything, an "annunciation" analogous to that of our Lady (§42).

fication of John the Baptist, I wished that the Virgin would see fit to visit me so that my body and whatever goodness was there might be sanctified, and, if anything was impure, that God might be pleased that it would be purified.

At the passage about the shepherds who came to Jesus at his birth, I sought this grace, that the Lord deign to reform my entire self and raise me to higher things as he reformed the shepherds, who desired the lowest things and understood things accordingly. But with the Magi I then felt an eager longing to become lowly and humble in heart and desires as well as to have my mind lifted up with the shepherds.[80]

44   At Mass the same day, as I was reflecting that God is merciful and compassionate, that he is mindful of toil and anguish, and that all things are present to him,[81] I asked him to deign to have mercy on this German nation and to have compassion on it as if it were already suffering all those evils which are in store for it if is not drawn back to the Catholic faith and allegiance to the religion of Rome.[82]

▸ *July 9*

45   On the octave day of the Visitation, at the thought that it was the first anniversary of my profession, I felt much devotion about my vows. I petitioned the grace of perseverance from God the Father as well as a continual increase of chastity. This increase should restore the flesh that has been subdued and strengthen it against its weaknesses which reveal themselves above all in carnal desires. I committed my obedience to the care of the Son, who himself was made obedient unto death. I commended my vow of poverty to the Holy Spirit, praying that he would always will to preserve in me such a love of poverty that I would never fail to feel its effects.

I prayed also that my three faculties might make continuous progress in the knowledge, memory, and inclinations which are in conformity with these vows; and to that end I asked that the Father might pour his power into each of my faculties, with special care for my

---

[80] *Sicut mente elevari cum pastoribus. Mens* can mean mind, soul, heart. The Annunciation, the Visitation, and other mysteries are, at the same time, events in the life of Christ on earth, liturgical celebrations of the Church, and also times of personal grace for Favre. In addition, the mysteries prolong, in a certain sense, their efficacy by enabling the faithful to participate not only in the liturgical celebrations but also in the grace given to each according to his personal dispositions.

[81] Ps. 111 (110): 4; Ps. 103 (102): 8; Exod. 34:6.

[82] The term religion *(religio)* as used today to designate a cult, a body of teaching, and a society was not used in that threefold sense in Favre's time. For him the Catholic and revealed faith recognizes its identity and its universal character in the pope of Rome. *SacMundi* 5:246ff.; *NCathEnc* 12:240ff.

memory. I asked the Son to pour into them his wisdom and his light, watching especially over my understanding, and that the Holy Spirit might breathe his gifts into each of them, watching especially over my will. I prayed to the Most Holy Trinity, one in essence, to receive my heart into its unity and to pour its personal attributes into my three faculties.[83]

I prayed to our Lady to be my advocate in all things since she is the true model of virginity, obedience, and poverty—she whose flesh is most chaste, whose soul is most pure, and whose spirit is most holy. In her each of these graces acts with so much power from the divine virtue, such great wisdom and goodness, that each of itself would be enough to preserve for the other two their own sinlessness; for the flesh would become so perfectly chaste that it would be enough to preserve the soul and the spirit from even the approach, not to speak of the least taint, of defilement. For its part, the spirit would be so loaded with gifts that it could prevent the entry into the soul or the flesh of anything not perfectly pure. Likewise, the perfection of the soul would be so great that it could, of itself, enlighten the spirit and the flesh.[84]

▸ *July 15*

46 On the day of the Dispersion of the Apostles[85] I had a great desire to have that feast held in much veneration everywhere in the world. There came to me also in prayer some great thoughts, and I desired that all the apostles might follow Jesus Christ into my dwelling, for they would be better able to honor and minister to him, to understand his will and his discourses and his words as well; and they would make excuses for me because I am incapable of doing such things. There occurred to me also many prayers of commendation for my scattered brothers.

---

[83] The reality of the mutual coexistence of the three faculties of memory, understanding, and will within the unity of the human person is looked on as an image of the Trinity: the mutual indwelling of the three divine persons who possess one and the same divine nature. The heart *(cor)* is the seat and image of the unity. Once again Favre considers obedience, poverty, and chastity in relation to the Trinity, committing his obedience to the care of the Son.

[84] The intercommunication of the faculties, in Mary active in a more perfect way, is imperfect in man because of sin, wicked habits, and the influence of evil spirits. Here Favre regards each faculty as capable of exercising some influence on the other two if they fail in any way. See §38.

[85] This feast, called *Divisio seu Dispersio Apostolorum,* commemorates the dispersal of the apostles after the Ascension. It was of recent origin and inspired the first Jesuits, apostolic wanderers themselves, with much devotion. MI, *ConsMHSJ* 1:90–91; *MonNad* 4:682.

▶ *July 17*

47   On the day of St. Alexis, as I was meditating on the mysteries of Christ in sequence, I had, with regard to the Three Kings, a great desire that the Reverend Juan might make his pilgrimage in memory of the journey of the Three Kings who came to adore Christ,[86] for they so highly honored our Lord that it would be fitting to go and visit their relics. The journeys of St. Alexis, St. James, St. Roch, of Jesus Christ, of the apostles, and of others came to my mind,[87] and in them I found the hope that pilgrimages like these might be very acceptable to our Lord and to all the saints, especially at this time and in these lands where so few pilgrimages now take place because of heretics who take from them that value and esteem which are so important for works of that kind.

48   One day as I was thinking over the Annunciation, there came to me a desire to hear good news about my companions announced at once.[88] I understood how greatly it would please our Lord if all my sorrows and afflictions were caused by these things alone, or some of them: the first, the recognition (though without fear) that one is offensive and displeasing to God our Lord and to his saints because of personal imperfections and failings; the second, the thought that one is far from God; the third, the fear of producing no fruit at all, considering the little that one does produce.

Hence I had a great desire that our Lady, who is "full of grace," might favor me and make me pleasing to God; that, through her, the Lord might become my near neighbor since he was ever "with her"; that

---

[86] Juan de Aragón, §32 n. 64 above. On August 25 Favre dispatched him on a pilgrimage to Cologne "with a stick in his hand and without a penny in his pocket" (*MonFabri*, pp. 175–176) so as to follow Christ more closely. A pilgrimage was one of the "experiments" or tests laid down by Ignatius as part of the formation of a Jesuit novice. It was a kind of apprenticeship or preparation for the wandering apostolic life many of them would live in imitation of Christ and of the founding fathers, Ignatius, Francis Xavier, and others. Those experiments included pilgrimages. See *ConsSJComm*, Index 1, "Experiences," p. 381.

[87] Pilgrimages multiplied in the sixteenth century, and ever increasing crowds flocked to the ancient places: Jerusalem, Rome, Santiago de Compostella, as well as to the new shrines of the Holy Shroud at Chambéry and of our Lady of Loreto. *NCathEnc* 2:362–374; *SacMundi* 5:26–28.

[88] The first companions of Ignatius, once they had left Italy, were required by Ignatius to send news to Rome every fortnight. Ignatius, writing to Favre on December 10, 1542 (*EppIgn* 1:238), gives details of what he thinks should be mentioned and then curtly takes him to task for the incoherence of his writing. Favre never succeeded in correcting this fault (*MonFabri*, pp. 80–83). Each companion looked forward eagerly to news of the others, not so much because it was a practical necessity in the government of the nascent Society but out of their great affection for each other.

I might not deserve to be accursed among men since she was "blessed among all women"; and, since "the fruit of her womb is blessed," that she might grant me the grace of producing some good fruit in the service of Christ our Lord.[89]

49 On the day that Father Juan intended to begin his pilgrimage to Cologne, I had keen desires that his pilgrimage would be very acceptable to God our Lord, to his mother, to all the angels and saints, and especially to the Three Kings[90] and to St. Ursula and her companions. All these wishes were for Juan's welfare, for a peaceful end to war's tumults,[91] for the coming of fine weather, for the rewarding of the Germans for the good that resulted from their many great pilgrimages[92] to Spain in former days, pilgrimages that were so acceptable to God. They used to visit St. James of Compostella, our Lady of Montserrat, our Lady of Guadalupe, and other shrines. I prayed for the protection of the road from brigands and all other dangers; that our Lord and his saints might condone the offenses being committed against them in these lands for some years past by those who belittle pilgrimages and other pious and holy works of penitence, devotions in honor of God and his saints, and other kinds of pious practices. Similarly, I felt greatly moved in spirit to esteem highly any good work done solely for God our Lord and the glory of his saints.

50 There came to me also a feeling of keen sorrow because I saw that no one now meditates on the works of God or even reflects deeply on the mysteries of the life and the holy passion of Jesus Christ. I felt especially afflicted that the sufferings and the torments of the saints were no longer given close attention, considering that they were so precious and so pleasing to God our Lord Almighty.

Then I noted four points, among others, which allow us to judge the value of a work. The first, to consider what is being done: whether it tends to the honor of God, to the glory of the saints, or to penance for the good of the soul, or to the benefit of the neighbor, and so forth. The second, the person for whom the work is being done, looking to the aim

---

[89] A meditation in four points on the Hail Mary according to the Second Method of Prayer (*SpEx,* [252–253]).

[90] See §216.

[91] Since 1537 a state of war had existed between Charles V and Duke William of Cleves, which ended in the Treaty of Venlo, September 1543, by which Charles took over Gelderland. Then Francis made an alliance with Suleiman I, and another campaign began, this time with Charles and Francis on opposing sides. See §391 n. 43 below.

[92] Pilgrimages were an expression of the international character of the Middle Ages; to Favre they were a sign and a promise of the spiritual solidarity and unity of Europe.

and intention of its author. The third, the spirit in which it is being done: whether through fear of God either servile or filial, or out of love for God or one's neighbor, or from some holy and worthy attraction that moves the will, or even from a lawful demand of conscience[93] to which the will submits itself. The fourth, its acceptance by God, who is so generous, good, and merciful and who takes labor and hardship into account,[94] for it is of him that it is said: He will honor those who have served his Son, Jesus Christ our Lord, and it is by his will that Christ himself is that great angel, the bearer of the golden thurible, for he alone can best give value to our good works.[95]

▸ *July 21*

51   On the day of St. Praxedes, as I was going through the mysteries of Christ's life, it occurred to me to ask for certain graces, making petitions to God himself for them through the merits of the Annunciation, the Incarnation, the Visitation, and other mysteries.[96]

I asked that he might teach us how to praise and honor him, to think about and know him; how to remember him, long for him, love, desire, and serve him; how to seek to see and hear him, to perceive his fragrance, to delight in him and touch him.[97] I sought all this through

---

[93] Word for word *dictamen rationis*: the judgment of the practical reason about the morality of an act (*ST,* I–II, q. 19, a. 5, ob. 2); *NCathEnc,* 196–197, art. "Conscience."

[94] Ps. 10 (9): 14.

[95] Apoc. 8:3. Many medieval commentators interpreted this passage in the light of Isa. 9:5. They held that the angel was Christ himself receiving the offerings of men and laying them on the altar of heaven. This fourth criterion then differs from the others; the divine acceptance must be sought and awaited. It is a confirmation of the decision made; it reveals God's acceptance of the choice, and this will happen through consolation which is mainly affective. For Favre, however, this divine acceptance is more than a confirmation, because he is depending upon a theology of acceptance (*acceptatio*) derived from the nominalist tradition—almost certainly from Gabriel Biel. According to this theory any value or goodness possessed by a human act comes from a decision of God's will to accept it as good. Favre attributes the power of acceptance to Christ, "the great angel, the bearer of the golden thurible." "A full explanation of Favre's fourth criterion would include both the fact of the divine *acceptatio* through Christ, that is, the giving of value to the proposed action (or to the decision to abstain from the action), and the communication of that *acceptatio* which we call the confirmation" (O'Leary, "Discernment," p. 118). See §289 n. 127 below.

[96] Favre may be referring here to the short ejaculatory prayers accompanying his meditation on the mysteries of Christ's life or the announcing of each mystery of the rosary, or he may have in mind the petitions that in the Litany of the Saints follow the invocations of the principal mysteries of Christ.

[97] The five senses begin to play an increasing part in Favre's prayer; here his desire is for greater union with Christ.

the mediation of Christ in conformity with the practice and decrees of his holy Church: in Catholic doctrine, in the holy sacraments, in prayers and invocations made to the saints, and in good works done for the souls in purgatory.

At Mass I felt another desire: that whatever good I might accomplish in any way might be done through the good spirit and not through the bad one. Hence the thought came to me that God does not approve of the way in which heretics wish to reform certain things in the Church. For though they say (as do the demons) many things that are true, they do not say them with the spirit of truth which is the Holy Spirit.[98]

After Mass, as I did not experience that spiritual delight which I had been seeking, another good desire came to me that our Lord Jesus Christ might be pleased to visit me in secret in order to set right the deeply hidden defects of my understanding, memory, will, and senses and that he might grant me the hidden virtues and gifts on which I never reflect, though perhaps they are more necessary for me than the ones I feel that I lack.[99]

52 Before that I had another desire: that the Lord might teach me by his grace how to speak about things I have experienced (for myself or for others) under the influence of the good spirit. For I am accustomed to say, write, and do many things without remaining faithful to that spirit in which I had first experienced them. For example, I sometimes express myself in a familiar way, lightheartedly and with a merry exterior, when speaking about something I had previously experienced in a spirit of compunction, or of compassion or admiration, and with some spiritual tears. Hence this benefits the hearer less because it has not been expressed to him in such a good spirit as that in which I had received it.[100]

---

[98] The point is an important one; even with an honest desire to reform the Church and an accurate understanding of existing abuses—the heretics have as much—there is need of the Spirit of Truth. True reform begins gently and gradually from within the Church and under the influence of the Holy Spirit, from whom it will derive its efficacy.

[99] Favre is aware that even in desolation God's work goes on in the depths of the soul, secretly and unperceived; it is the essential part of spiritual progress, the root from which will grow the fruit yet to come. O'Leary, "Discernment," p. 109.

[100] The problem that Favre states here in a general way has to do with the interior life and the apostolate. What is the relationship between the grace that inspires some work or other and the development of that work? If God inspires a work, how can it be carried on with the same spirit that originally inspired it? (*SpEx,* [333]). It is a complex matter; the longer the time that elapses from the original impulse, the more danger there is that both internal and external influences may modify or even corrupt the original inspiration. For Favre the problem is one of

So I asked the Lord to grant me in the birth and in the growth of my labor and in what I say and write the same spirit as in their conception. That will come about when the first movement, then the reflection, the expression, and lastly the execution have all been influenced by the same spirit.[101] From this I concluded that our Teacher and Master was to be imitated even to his manner of speaking so that, if the Holy Spirit caused us to experience or know something with tears, we should try to express it also with tears when we speak or write about it. And we should desire to edify the hearer in the way the Holy Spirit has edified us when he gave us a knowledge or an awareness of it.[102]

From this I gained a special understanding of this text, "Jesus was led by the Spirit into the desert,"[103] and of this, "He came by the Spirit into the temple."[104] In them one perceives a special awareness of the Spirit which takes hold of a person and moves him to act or to speak without leaving him to himself and to his own personal experience alone.[105]

▶ *July 25*

53 One day, the feast of St. James, as I went to the altar and began Mass, I felt myself in bondage to all my imperfections. And when I began the third versicle, "Why do I walk in sorrow while my enemy afflicts me?"[106] there came to me a thought in the form of a question as if the good spirit were speaking to me thus: "Why be downcast because

---

action. It is not enough just to do good; it must be done in the spirit in which God wills it to be done. Here good people can be very quickly deceived by the bad spirit. But it does not draw them into serious evil; it seeks to diminish the effects of God's grace and the influence of the Gospel by urging them to become judges of the good they do, they themselves deciding their mode of action. See §140; O'Leary, "Discernment," pp. 51–52, nn. 29, 30.

[101] Discernment is necessary for the apostolate, for its continuity and especially for its motivation. So the original spirit, when preserved, guarantees the authenticity of each stage in the process leading to action. See VatCouncII, *The Decree on the Ministry and Life of Priests*, "Unity and Harmony of Priests," no. 14.

[102] Favre is deeply sensitive to the working of the Holy Spirit and is anxious to remain loyal to that Spirit who communicates spiritual truths.

[103] Matt. 4:1.

[104] Luke 2:27.

[105] This entry shows Favre developing his understanding of the third point he mentions in §50 for judging an apostolic work: "In what spirit?" This question has to be put not once but over and over again at each stage from the initial inspiration to the carrying out of the work itself. He comments, as an example, on his own preaching or teaching. O'Leary, "Discernment," pp. 119–120.

[106] Ps. 43 (42): 2. This psalm was recited at the foot of the altar by the priest at the beginning of the pre–Vatican II liturgy.

the enemy afflicts you? If he troubles you, it is because you do not comply with his will. Were our Lord Jesus Christ to afflict you, you would surely have a reason for being sad, judging that he acted so because you did not follow his divine will."[107]

54   That same day there returned to my mind something I had experienced before at other times:[108] How necessary it is that a person, the better to prepare himself to find the Spirit and spiritual things, should direct his primary intention to the resolve to experience, desire, or love divine things because God is in them and because he benefits from them himself. Nor should his chief aim be, as mine was most times up to now, to find a remedy for his troubles, his moods of depression, or his temptations. For he who in seeking after God our Lord and his gifts has as his main, indeed, his sole, purpose the finding of a remedy for his temptations and moods of depression while not seeking immediate devotion for its own sake—that person is fully prepared and disposed to give no further thought to devotion once he is no longer afflicted. This is a quest for love through fear of imperfections and trials, a search for good and spiritual sentiments so as to avoid the experience of bad ones.

In his justice and mercy, therefore, God sends you such trials for a time or permits them because you were so indifferent to his good gifts; then, to prevent your becoming lukewarm and apathetic, he leaves you with stings and goads to drive you ceaselessly forward until at last you find rest in God our Lord. Nor are you going to feel satisfied even though you experience neither trials, temptations, evil or vainglorious feelings, nor imperfections, as the lukewarm do and all those who look only to avoid a fall and care nothing about ascending. For them the certainty of not falling is sufficient spiritual happiness, even though many can see the way that leads upward.

Do not be content, therefore, that you do not descend, that you neither decrease nor go back; but "dispose your heart to ascend,"[109] to increase and to make interior progress, not through fear of descending or going back or falling but through love of holiness and not merely because such reflections could protect you against evil thoughts.

---

[107] A particular application of the rules for the discernment of spirits: Favre, in desolation, questions his state in the words of the psalmist. The answer assures him that since he is serving God he himself cannot be the source of his desolate state; it is rather the enemy. *SpEx,* [329], [331].

[108] §37, §295, §296. Favre makes a distinction between devotion which leads directly to God and that which has some other result or at least is sought for some other purpose. The distinction appears in other passages. O'Leary, "Discernment," pp. 66, 67.

[109] Ps. 84 (83): 6, one of the songs of ascent sung by pilgrims on their way to Jerusalem. Favre addresses himself.

Desire and thirst to experience spiritual realities for what they contain in themselves and not as remedies for evil or vain tendencies. In that way you will in the end attain the love of God for his sake alone. Get rid, then, of all that is vain or idle—though not yet sins—as so many obstacles which impede access to God and sight of him, rest in him, and living in his presence.

▸ July 29

55 On the day of St. Martha, the virgin who received Jesus Christ into her house, I prayed for the soul of Donna Tullia, whose death I had learned about at the same time as that of Donna Antonia, who had been in the service of the Marchioness of Pescara.[110] I found much devotion and had many spiritual reflections about them [*discursos*]. And while reading some of the prayers that according to custom are said in church for the dead and for commending to God the bodies of those buried, I felt my spirit strongly moved to make these holy commendations of the bodies of the dead. There came to my mind also, with a holy sentiment of faith, some great and good reflections which I desired might occur more than ever before at the burial of the Catholic faithful, even granted a certainty that their souls are in heaven. For I felt that prayers for the resurrection of those bodies are pleasing to God.

Later on, happening to see a funeral, I again reflected on the sovereign wisdom which would one day bring about that marvelous resurrection, thinking that the dust we now behold is destined to become a body radiant with the glory proper to each one of us. When we see what remains of these bodies, we can thank God for all the good he has done through these instruments which now are nothing in their tombs.

By means of these thoughts and others like them, Christians are not only encouraged to remember the souls of the dead, to give thanks if they are already in heaven, and to implore pardon for them if they are

---

[110] The marchioness of Pescara was the celebrated Vittoria Colonna (1492–1547), poetess and friend of Michelangelo. In 1525 she married Don Ferrante de Avales, marquis of Pescara. The marchioness, passionately concerned with Church reform, became friendly with Alfonso de Valdés, the emperor's secretary, who was suspected of being a Lutheran. She was on friendly terms too with Bernardino Ochino, the general of the Capuchin Order, who apostatized. Consequently, she came under suspicion of heresy, but the suspicion was without foundation. Pastor, *History* 11:600, see index of names under Colonna, Vittoria. She came to know Jay and Simão Rodrigues at Ferrara and recommended them to Duke Ercole II. From the end of 1537 on, she had dealings with Ignatius and helped him in the work he had begun for the reclamation of fallen women.

in purgatory, but also to let their own belief in that article [of faith] concerning the resurrection of the body increase and develop.

▸ August 2

56 On the day of the dedication of St. Mary of the Portiuncula, the solemnity of Our Lady of the Angels, I was given many spiritual favors and felt much fervor at the thought that my soul and body were already consecrated as a living temple to the Lord for the reception and the preservation of God's spiritual gifts.[111] In addition, I felt an intense desire that I and all others should note with great attention and care all the events, the words, or the holy inspirations which have had God as their source and dispenser up to now; likewise, that we should reflect with gratitude on whatever things have been established in the Church by our holy and devout predecessors, fearful lest we be deprived of them as unworthy.

57 I also thanked God during Mass, as I had resolved beforehand,[112] for all the general chastisements that he has up to now inflicted or permitted for the purpose of bringing peoples, provinces, cities, and individuals to amend their lives. I grieved that no notice was taken of such things as, for example, plagues, earthquakes, wars, floods, droughts, and other temporal evils of that kind; for in them we ought to have recognized our sovereign and fearful Judge reminding us in these ways of our last end and desiring our return to the way of repentance so as to receive the gifts of his goodness and mercy. He puts before our eyes his second coming when he sees that the memory of his first coming in lowliness has already faded. Seeing that we despise and no longer accept the Gospel of his kingdom, he wills to strike us with the fear of his judgment and of his coming in the kingdom of his majesty.

---

[111] This consecration must be understood of baptism. Its reception dedicates or consecrates a person as a temple destined to receive the gifts of the Spirit in confirmation and through spiritual movements.

[112] The special Portiuncula indulgence which could be gained on that day had been obtained by St. Francis from the pope for the benefit of all the faithful both living and dead. The epistle of the Mass he was about to say for the anniversary of the Dedication of a Church (Apoc. 21:2-5) describing the New Jerusalem where there will no longer be sorrow or mourning or death, together with his reflections on the indulgence, may well have inspired Favre to meditate on God's providence in relation to natural catastrophes. In addition, he was well aware of the ravages caused by the plague in his day; towns and cities often lost a quarter or even half of their population in the course of a summer. Knowing nothing of hygiene, sanitary precautions, or germs, Europe was helpless against infection. F. Braudel, *La Méditerranée et le monde méditerranéen à l'époque de Philippe II* (Paris, 1960), p. 273; §285 n. 115 below; DeCertMem, p. 158, n. 2. Braudel's work is published in English under the title *The Mediterranean and the Mediterranean World in the Age of Philip II*.

58   That day I wished to note and bear in mind the great care I should take when making the sign of the cross each night, as the Lord had given me to understand how to make it long before, and that I should also say these versicles: *Dignare me laudare te, virgo sacrata* and *Da mihi virtutem contra hostes tuos.*[113] These enemies are the enemies of faith and humility, chastity and purity, meekness and charity. Likewise I should say: *Procul recedant somnia,*[114] *Noctem quietam et finem perfectam,*[115] and *Hostem repellas longius, pacemque dones protinus.*[116] Nor should I omit an Our Father, a Hail Mary, and the Creed, continuing to seek the inspiration which was so often given me for that purpose. I shall do this after my customary litanies and my examination of conscience, and after arranging what I have to do on the following day. Also in the morning after washing and getting ready for the day, I must not omit saying these versicles after the sign of the cross, or some others according to the need of the moment, together with the Our Father, the Hail Mary, and the Creed.[117]

59   The same day, with regard to this text, "Every place on which the sole of your foot treads shall be yours,"[118] I reflected that the holy fathers[119] had first lived as aliens in the land which afterwards was their own. Hence I conceived in a good spirit a great hope of possessing one day the spiritual reality and the patrimony of the Lord where now we are aliens, living there only in thought and desire.

60   On the day of the Finding of St. Stephen, the protomartyr,[120] while I was reflecting on those bodies discovered together, I began with fervent longing to ask Christ the Lord to be willing at last to

---

[113] "Let me praise you, most holy Virgin" and "Give me strength against your enemies" are the antiphons for first and second vespers in the post-Tridentine office of the Blessed Virgin.

[114] From the hymn in the old office of compline: "Keep wicked dreams far from us."

[115] Part of the blessing from the same office: "May the all-powerful Lord grant us a peaceful night and a perfect end."

[116] Two lines from the hymn to the Holy Spirit for the vespers of Pentecost: "Drive our enemy far from us and give us always the gift of peace."

[117] Favre gives a brief account of his evening and morning prayer. In the evening, he plans for the day after; in the morning, prayer gives a spiritual direction to the day.

[118] Deut. 11:24.

[119] Those of the Old Testament (abbr. OT).

[120] August 1 is the feast of the Finding of the Body of St. Stephen, the first martyr, and those of his companions, Gamaliel, Nicodemus, and Abiba. There were three churches in Paris dedicated to St. Stephen, and devotion to him was widespread. Favre would certainly have seen relics of the saint during his student days in that city. P. Perdrizet, *Le Calendrier Parisien de la fin du moyen âge* (Paris, 1933), p. 279.

let me see with my own eyes the glorified bodies of those whose relics I have hitherto seen and in general of all the blessed.

61 Saying my office once, I had some distractions and wished to be rid of them. I then received a response which had been given me frequently on other occasions: that I should have striven to discover outside the time of prayer the causes of my distractions with the desire of taking my repose when the time for it should come, so that at the time of prayer I might deserve to find joy in the reading of the word of God.

At Mass on the same day, having a desire to adore the body of Christ with fervor, I realized I am at fault when I am not accustomed to cherish similar desires at other times outside of Mass itself. For then it happens that I do not merit another grace, not even the one that I might wish to understand and then might desire to feel what I am doing. It is as if a person, having taken no care to preserve and work up an appetite for food before a meal, should then at table begin to complain of not having an appetite. Or as might happen if a person, invited to receive choice liquors which were to be distributed at a fixed hour in some house to those who brought along clean vessels, were to neglect to clean out his receptacle until the time of distribution had come and by doing his cleaning at that moment were to lose his share and be obliged to wait for the next distribution. He would have to keep his own vessel clean in the meantime and prepare it better to receive the liquor when the time should come.[121]

62 I felt great sorrow once because I was unable to adore Jesus Christ as the Three Kings had done or weep like the Magdalene and because I did not deserve to hear the many consoling words spoken by Jesus Christ to so many in this world. In a reply I was told that I had not acted as the Three Kings had acted nor prepared my soul as they had done. For they had left behind rich estates, their native land, and their property in order to come and make an offering of themselves, and so forth. In the same way there came to me some understanding of the dispositions of those on whom Jesus Christ had conferred similar graces. I saw very clearly how glad I should have been to hear these words, "Your sins are forgiven you,"[122] and still more, "Today you will be with me in paradise."[123] But I did not realize how far I myself was from the dispositions of those persons, nor did I ever have a true desire of finding

---

[121] Ignatius laid great stress on immediate preparation for prayer, looking on it as a sign of respect for the Lord to do the utmost to dispose oneself for the making of the colloquy. Eastern religions regard such preparation as essential. See *SpEx*, [45–54].

[122] Matt. 9:2.

[123] Luke 23:43. See §71.

myself on a cross in the same state as the good thief or of acting like the Magdalene, who came to the banquet to weep. When I, because of my spiritual blindness, shall have experienced as many trials as the blind man because of his lack of physical sight, I may perhaps, if my faith does not fail, obtain the grace of spiritual vision. I went on to consider in the same way the other bodily infirmities, comparing them with the physical afflictions that Christ the Lord used to heal—and goes on healing day by day—for he takes into account the sufferings and labors as well as the faith of the afflicted and those who pity them. And out of the depths of his charity he looks down upon the needs of all with those devoted eyes of his.[124]

▶ *August 5*

63   On the day of our Lady of the Snows, I understood how our Lord had kept me for some days past in a state of continual dissatisfaction because I was unable to find devotion in my prayers and meditations, and that he had done so to preserve in me, above all other desires in the world, the desire of finding devotion. It seemed to me that he had granted me a great blessing in not allowing either my habitual state of discontent or those desires of mine to possess me, for they would take away from me the aforesaid desire of finding in God our Lord devotion for my soul. I saw in this a sign, therefore, that he was beginning to give me grace to set my soul in such order that the first desires of my heart might be for what is essential and comes first. This means that the first place should be occupied once and for all by an exclusive concern for finding God our Lord in my own soul through the principal exercises at everyone's disposal for seeking and finding him. They are prayer and contemplation and, above all, the Mass.[125]

---

[124] Ps. 10 (9): 14. Favre reproaches himself for his spiritual blindness. He has not understood the value of a suffering that rewards the sufferer with spiritual vision. He too may attain to that vision if his faith remains firm.

[125] §63–§67, but especially §63–§65, show that Favre believed in a qualitative hierarchy of desires, specified by their objects. Desire expresses the attraction felt for God as the supreme good, worthy of all love, but desire also leads one to seek a more and more intimate union with God. Favre, discontented because he could not find devotion in his prayers, realized that God was the source of his desire. Here the distinction is between the desire for immediate union with God and all other desires (no matter how good and holy) whose direct object is other than God—Favre calls them "temporal desires." So it is a question of finding God in his soul through prayer and through the eucharistic sacrifice by reason of Christ's special presence in it, offering himself with his people to the Father. O'Leary, "Discernment," p. 59.

▸ *August 6*

64   I felt a great sadness because I did not find devotion on the day of the Holy Transfiguration. However, I was much consoled by the recognition that my sadness had already lasted many days and that no other desire or mood of sadness had been able to banish it from the depths of my heart. Up to now it had been quite otherwise with me, for whenever I found myself afflicted or desirous of directly finding God our Lord, I straightaway allowed myself to be possessed by some other desire or by a mood of sadness: a desire to edify others or to have some good news or signs of a growing service of God as regards our neighbor, or a mood of sadness due to temptations arising from my sins and imperfections.[126] So it happened that such sorrowful moods used to deprive me of that better kind of sorrow which tends directly towards God. I saw it clearly therefore that day: The more the Lord abandons me to that sadness and to that desire of finding him and the more he causes the desire to grow and increase in breadth, in length, and in depth (without allowing it to be superseded by other and less elevated ones), the greater the favor he confers on me.[127]

65   I then took note of another grace of much consequence for my soul: how I had never before found my heart so free from those other troubled longings which usually came to me in connection with the progress of souls in grace or their resistance to it—I refer to that progress which should have been brought about through my efforts. Whenever I had some success in this matter, I felt consoled accordingly,

---

[126] Among Favre's desires, that for direct union with God is preeminent. It has its source in the heart *(cor)*, ever since Augustine's day considered the very center of a person where God comes to fix his abode and unite himself to the soul in a union of love. Accordingly, sorrow that he has not experienced that desire should take precedence over other kinds of sorrow which, since they do not directly concern God, rank lower than the desire that tends directly towards God. Favre looks on the persistence of this desire, though it may remain unfulfilled, as a kind of consolation. If God grants him to desire direct union with himself, that desire must not be allowed to give place to desires regarding lesser concerns, no matter how good or how apostolic. In the past he had often allowed worries about his pastoral and apostolic activities to crowd out this fundamental sorrow that came from his unfulfilled desire to find God. O'Leary, "Discernment," pp. 59, 68. For a latter-day treatment of *cor*, see F. J. Sheed, *The Instructed Heart* (London, 1979); also M. D'Arcy, *The Mind and Heart of Love* (London, 1945).

[127] Eph. 3:18. See §241 about the double cross. Here consolation does not mean passing from a mood of sadness; it is the recognition that it had not been replaced by other moods of sadness which do not directly refer to God. See §69 and §173, where desolation appears also in faith as a more interior form of consolation. There is a sorrow that leads straight to God, as well as an ever present longing for him and a sorrow at not possessing it is a favor that he grants.

just as I used to feel saddened by failure. Now it seemed to me that no success in this could console me unless our Lord had given me an abundance of that devotion which is directed to him and to his saints. Neither can I, at the moment, become possessed by sadness because of the little that I accomplish and that I have the opportunity to do.[128]

66 Blessed be the Lord, who has countless ways of leading us to perfect knowledge and love of himself but only little by little because we do not deserve to attain them at a single bound. For there must first come so many kinds of fear, so many kinds of disgust, repugnance, and aversion concerning those lowest things in which peace cannot be found, even though they are means to ascend to the love of the Lord and to enter fully into it. But once a person has arrived there, he "goes in and comes out" with joy and "finds pasture" both inside and outside.[129] So, when he has found that new way which begins with love, he can also "return to his own country"[130] from which he had journeyed by a fearful path full of many dangers and come to acquire the love for God most high. Before having that love, he could but mount up and gaze towards the heights. But once he has entered loving intimacy with God, he will be able to go on increasing in that love while daily getting to the heart of many things in God himself, and he will be able with more assurance to go down among his neighbors, seeing them and listening to them, and so on.[131]

---

[128] This grace is perhaps mystical: a higher stage of detachment, the soul becoming more and more fixed on God himself, less attached to consolation arising from success in apostolic work and less affected by depression on account of the little he does accomplish. True consolation is to be sought only in God himself—not in spiritual or apostolic labors as such—for God is above success and failure. *SpEx*, [316].

[129] John 10:6. Once God has been found, with him is found all that comes from him, that is, internal and external realities, but in a better and more profound way. And those to whom he has granted the grace of finding him he bids enter, as it were, into his dwelling. So these internal and external realities become indistinguishable from each other as the "pasture" of one and the same Master. Here it is that permanent intimacy with God takes place and ceaseless working together—the work of finding God in all things.

[130] Matt. 2:12. An allusion to the return of the Three Kings to their own country and to the disciples returning with Christ from the Mount of the Transfiguration to go out into daily life. (Matt. 17:9).

[131] Once Christians have entered the world of divine love, they are more certain of never straying far from God when they move among others. They remain with God, fearing neither success nor failure, for both come to them from their master. This is the confidence that St. Paul possessed all during his missionary life. 1 Thess. 1:5; Col. 2:2; Heb. 6:11. On leaving that solitude where they have found God in prayer, apostles find again those to whom they have been sent. They remain united to them, but in a new way.

67   May God grant charity of that kind to me,[132] to all my brothers, and to all living men and women. For I confess that I am still far from it: I mean, from such—that is, so great a—charity. For I am not conscious of being a stranger to all forms of charity or to the grace of Christ the Lord. But Christ can be considered differently inasmuch as he is the Way, the Truth, or the Life.[133] What are called the purgative way, the illuminative way, and the way of perfection differ from each other just as beginners, those making progress, and the perfect differ from each other. Although all these can be in charity, it is not the same thing, so to speak, to be in charity, to live in charity, and to move in charity.[134]

Beginners have charity insofar as they acknowledge and detest their sins. Those who are advancing have charity insofar as they meditate on and long for divine things, that is, Christian virtues, in which they desire to grow and increase from day to day.

But it is the perfect who have and experience charity properly so called, that is, insofar as they are already being impelled by love to seek the knowledge of God and of his will so as to carry it out in all ways possible to them. In the first group, therefore, charity works by making them struggle against their personal sins in order to drive them out. In the second group, it works by making them strive eagerly to acquire virtues. In the last, it makes them devote themselves, because of immediate knowledge of God, to growing also in the love of God himself and, whatever they do or say or think, makes them proceed from love as from a first principle, in the same way as the first principle of all their good deeds is, for beginners, hatred of sin and, for the advancing, the desire of the virtues with which they can be adorned. The first ones, that is, the beginners, strive earnestly to put off the old man; the advancing wish to get, so to speak, decently dressed for daily living; perfect men seek to appear in wedding attire.

It should be noted, however, that in each of these three categories of people there are three degrees, so that we can even say that among the perfect are beginners, the advancing, and the perfect. The same can be said in a way of the other two categories, for a beginning, a middle, and an end are in each of them.[135]

---

[132] This charity comes from God to humankind and through them is spread throughout the world.

[133] John 14:6.

[134] Acts 17:28; Rom. 8:14; Gal. 5:18–25.

[135] The triple imagery of ways, of degrees of perfection, and of wearing apparel introduced here in an analysis of love is common in the literature of the late Middle Ages. Favre's division of the spiritual life is somewhat theoretical and not strictly applicable to the realities it attempts to describe.

▸ *August 7*

68   On the day I was celebrating the feast of our saintly Father Dominic,[136] I had at the communion of the Mass a great longing in roughly these words: Would that my whole inner being, especially my heart, were so yielding to Christ coming in as to open up and leave to him the place in my heart's center. Would that all my vices and imperfections were being driven from before his face as wax melts away in the face of fire.

Before Mass, as I was making my customary review of the mysteries of Christ, I felt myself much inclined to ask mystery by mystery, through the intercession of St. Dominic, for graces corresponding both to the feelings he had about each mystery during his life and to the understanding he gained from contemplating them. I prayed that he might intercede with Christ in the Annunciation, with Christ in the Visitation, with Christ Born, and so forth.

69   Going through the streets the same day, I found no joy in what met my eyes but rather distractions and temptations to idle and wicked thoughts; the result was a mood of sadness.[137] I then received this reply: You should not be sad at not finding peace in idle things; be glad rather and give thanks. Instead, feel sad because you do not find peace and all kinds of consolation in prayer, in holy exercises, and in the citizenship that is in heaven. No doubt many of those you consort with would have little taste for citizenship in heaven if they found peace in citizenship as seen in the world. Direct the eyes and ears of your soul, therefore, and the attention of all your senses to the things of heaven, where your sight can see nothing that does not strengthen and console, and likewise with your ears and their hearing, and so forth.

Here below, on the contrary, if you wished to gaze without restraint at everything that goes on, you would at once see evil things such as people's actions and postures; you would at once hear idle or wounding words. Here below you see nothing but frivolity, pleasantry, mockery

---

[136] The Dominic mentioned here is not Dominic de Guzmán, whose feast was celebrated on August 5 in those days, but most likely Dominic Hélion, one of the Carthusians of Trier. He appears to have been the first to suggest meditation on the mysteries of Christ's life. His two books, *Libri experientiarum duo cum libello humilis confessionis*, which appeared in 1458, contained a method for meditating on the rosary which became widespread. Favre had known the Carthusian well since childhood, hence his reference to "our (my?) saintly Father Dominic."

[137] Returning from saying Mass in a church or in some convent chapel, Favre has to pass through busy streets (§72). After his meditation at home, he writes the notes in which he records the fruit of the day before, as was his custom.

and obscenity, nothing earnest and weighty, giving praise to God. Instead, jesting, laughter, and sport accompany the most wicked behavior.

If, therefore, a person is kept away from these various temptations and is in some way driven to meditate on and desire heavenly things, let him thank God that he does not will to abandon him to harmful or even useless reflections, to sloth, or to wasting his time.

▸ **August 8**

70 On the feast of the holy martyrs Cyriacus, Largus, and Smaragdus, I desired greatly that our Lord through the merits of his life, passion, and glory might grant that the Mass I was saying for the souls in purgatory would have for them the same value as if I had offered it in union with all the holy desires, the sighs and prayers, the anguish and gratitude of those souls who are unable to profit by them for their own relief. The desire of mine I refer to was that our Lord might grant me to feel for each of them, so far as I can, what they themselves experience at the thought of their sins and of the benefits given them by God, and so forth; and being myself incapable and unworthy of such a grace, that it might be supplied for by this sacrifice and by the intercession of the saints and the blessed in heaven, especially of those whose feast was being celebrated that day.

71 That day there came back to my mind the memory of something I had often felt at other times: how very efficacious and beneficial a practice it is for the souls in purgatory during your prayers to Jesus Christ for them that you should represent him to yourself and see him with that charity and compassion from which came the words "This day you will be with me in paradise."[138] For the faithful souls in purgatory can be, at least very often, in a state of incomparably greater necessity than the good thief on the cross to whom these words were addressed. It is good to keep before one's mind in a general way those seven words spoken by Christ on the cross, seeing that the souls endlessly repeat words like them. They pray for the enemies they left behind in the world; they pray for their friends and for those who have sinned against them so that they may be provided for and have all their needs supplied. They complain of their own unbelievable woes and torments. They are continually animated by charitable desires to perform, if only they could, some work of mercy for the welfare of all the souls in this world and especially for the welfare of all their former companions. Their constant wish is to be able to say "It is consummated"[139] and in the end to be

---

[138] Luke 23:43, a text often quoted by Favre. See §62 and §229.
[139] John 19:30.

delivered from the power of those infernal torturers so as to pass under the authority of God the Father, all-powerful, glorious, and eternal.

▸ *August 9*

72 On the vigil of St. Lawrence (it was the day of the martyr St. Romanus) before Mass, a desire came to me to ask for graces against all my distractions, in particular to seek from the Lord grace to enable me to master and control my thoughts and my desires, for I was a prey to distractions at the time.[140] I found, accordingly, enough grace by making my customary review [of the mysteries of Christ] and especially by seeking this grace through Christ the Lord's sufferings when his soul was sorrowful and when he was in agony and when on the cross he said, "My God, my God, why have you forsaken me?"[141] To obtain more grace, I often had the thought of asking for it through the most holy grace of Christ's hypostatic union.

When I was about to receive Communion at Mass, with great fervor I asked the Lord to be so good as to call me and welcome me, sinner though I am, to pay me a visit, to forgive my sins, and to sit at table with me.[142] When I had finished Mass and the things after it and was returning home through the neighborhood, I felt a rather large grace in that I recalled that Mass in rather great detail and reflected on it by pondering over each of its parts.[143] I was also given the urge to refresh my memory about my practices in spiritual matters. Now as I was often forgetful at that time and could not concentrate on my other activities and business or on my actions or my conversations about or reflections on certain matters only indirectly connected with God, I asked the Lord to grant me in prayer and in spiritual contemplation the

---

[140] Favre looks on desires regarding the apostolate or his own spiritual and moral progress as secondary and as lesser gifts from God. Here he considers these desires as "distractions," though they are good, because they hold him back from the fundamental longing which is for God in himself. He insists on preserving his hierarchy of desires: "A desire came to me to ask for graces against all my distractions . . . to enable me to master and control my thoughts and my desires" (O'Leary, "Discernment," p. 60).

[141] Mark 15:34, one of the mysteries of Christ's life so often meditated on by Favre.

[142] Apoc. 3:20; Favre often quotes this text. Also Luke 19:7.

[143] The memory in act is traditionally looked on as a species of "rumination." This rumination (chewing of the spiritual cud, so to speak, or turning things over in one's mind) helps in the assimilation and the interiorization of the word or the mystery by causing them to penetrate into the heart, to the center where what comes from God becomes man's life and the source of his renewal.

power of applying myself to these things with the greatest possible intensity.

That is what will happen, I hope, when there will be as much order in my inclinations and actions as there is now disorder. That disorder arises from an excessive attachment to things that are not to be loved with one's whole heart, one's whole soul, one's whole mind, and one's whole strength, at all times and in every place. But when that love which is true charity shall have taken possession of our entire will and spirit everywhere and always, then all other things will attain the order of tranquility, namely, peace. Nothing will further trouble the intellect, the memory, the will, or any other thing. But this will be in the homeland of the blessed, towards which day by day we are ascending.

73   On the same vigil of St. Lawrence, after compline, Father Juan returned from his pilgrimage to Cologne,[144] and our Lord made his return an occasion for giving me the greatest spiritual consolation I had ever experienced on hearing news of that kind. And my consolation was all the greater because our Lord preserved me from becoming agitated in spirit out of joy at his arrival and out of longing to talk to him and hear some news—I mean news of spiritual things. Before this I used to feel these longings so deeply that I was deprived of that fervor whose immediate object in mental prayer or in contemplation is the Lord our God. But at that moment I felt my soul entering further into the Lord our God with most fervent prayers of thanksgiving, finding in them contentment and the deepest peace without yielding to that agitated desire of having a conversation with the returned pilgrim. So it seemed to me that our Lord himself and his saints celebrated that homecoming with me in a way incomparably greater and more festive than any human consolation I might have received from the pilgrim's presence and from conversation with him about the spiritual success of his journey from start to finish.

Our Lord gave me a series of thanksgiving prayers [*discursos*] in the form of litanies: I asked the Father to bless the Son and the Holy Spirit, the Son to bless the Father and the Holy Spirit, and the Holy Spirit to bless the Father and the Son. In the same way I asked the Virgin Mary to thank the Holy and Undivided Trinity for these gifts,[145]

---

[144] Juan de Aragón had been sent to Cologne on a pilgrimage, some episodes of which are related in the letter of August 24, 1542 (*MonFabri*, pp. 175–177). He returned "after compline," that is, during what was known in religious houses as the "great silence," which lasted from compline at nightfall to a fixed time next morning. This silence no longer exists except perhaps in strict contemplative orders. Hence Favre, though overjoyed at the pilgrim's return, put off speaking to him until the next morning.

[145] The safe return of the pilgrim and the blessings he received during his pilgrimage.

and the Trinity to bless the Virgin Mary for all the favors conferred on us through her intercession. I followed the same method for the other invocations as the Spirit guided me. I prayed also for all those who in one way or other had been kind to Don Juan, for those who had done him wrong in any way; and I made a special thanksgiving to the Three Kings, to SS. Ursula and Pinosa, and to all the other saints.

▸ August 10

74 On the day of St. Lawrence, in the morning, I went through the mysteries in order *[discurso]* in the same way, giving thanks as seemed appropriate to the subject matter of each. I had a great desire that the application and efficacy of the Mass might supply and make up for all the labor I should have to undertake in searching through all the diocesan calendars for the purpose of honoring in a special way and by name all the saints mentioned in them, each of whom is a masterpiece of sanctity fashioned by the hand of God.

I also felt great confidence in all the help our Lord will never fail to give both to myself and to our whole Society through these saints. I chose suitable examples of this help as if I had been told that one single individual aided by a St. Lawrence can do more to convert the world to good than he could with the support of an emperor.

I felt myself also much moved spiritually when reading the versicle "Come to my aid, and I shall be saved, I shall meditate on your just precepts."[146]

While I was saying the following words from the Our Father during Mass, "Give us this day our daily bread," I had a heartfelt desire that the heavenly Father might grant me an understanding of how he gives me bread both for my soul and my body. I said, "Lord, grant me to experience in faith how you give me this bread which is your Son."

On the same day there came to me likewise a holy desire of being always able to remember, each time I commend myself to God our Lord and make my prayers of petition and thanksgiving to him, to have our Lady, my good angel, and the saint of the day as mediators and the favor of the Holy Spirit to support me in my approach to Christ our Lord and Redeemer.[147]

---

[146] Ps. 119 (118): 117.

[147] Favre seems to mean that the intercession of the angels and saints possesses a twofold meaning—a movement, so to speak, of ascent and descent: Through the angels and especially the saints one ascends to Christ; through them the Spirit descends on us to pour out charity; through them we ascend to God, for God descends to us through them. This twofold function of the angels and saints corresponds, in Favre's mind, to the two characteristic aspects of the spiritual life: one, our

▸ **August 11**

75   On the day of SS. Tiburtius and Susanna,[148] I considered how St. Tiburtius, with such great spirit, upbraided a certain Torquatus[149] for giving himself up to carnal pleasures and glorying in them and for seeking to please others by these habits of his, especially women. Thus there came to me the desire to ask St. Tiburtius time and again to obtain for me by his prayers the perfect grace of never seeking my own satisfaction or my own glory, of never wanting to find favor with others or of wishing others to find favor with me, but ever of seeking to find favor with God alone. For we should appear before his face in such a manner as to please only him along with his saints who are in glory.

76   Before going to say Mass, there came to my mind for the *Memento*[150] those persons who had shown greater kindness to Father Juan during his pilgrimage. I felt great devotion as I begged our Lord to reward them not only according to their works but with his customary generosity and mercy. I pondered over their actions, their words, and their kindly feelings. Some had shown goodness by giving him alms; others had guided him along his way; others still had spoken to him courteously as they gave him information; and finally, others had congratulated him on his happy arrival. So there came to me many good desires for all of them.[151]

77   Nor did I omit to pray for those in whom nothing but rudeness and harshness had been found. It seemed to be our Lord's will that persons like them should reveal themselves on occasion and show themselves for what they are—above all to the charitable so that they might then pray for them and give an edifying example of humility and

---

personal and perceptible efforts; the other, in which the guidance of the Holy Spirit is evident together with a more perceptible passivity on our part. *DeCertMem,* p. 95.

[148] This Susanna was reputed to be a saint in early Christian Rome, but history is silent about her. *Bibliotheca Sanctorum* 12:78–80 (abbreviated hereafter as *BS*).

[149] See the *Acta S. Sebastiani,* chap. 21; *PL* 17:1053–1054. In the legendary account of the martyrdom of St. Sebastian, we find that a St. Tiburtius, son of the prefect of Rome, Chromatius, and converted with him, was betrayed by Torquatus to the prefect, Fabianus, who had him arrested. Tiburtius had reproached Torquatus for his scandalous life (*BS* 12:465). The phrase *con tanto spirito,* rendered in the text as "with such great spirit," has been translated by de Certeau as *mû par l'Esprit* (moved by the Spirit). This may well be correct.

[150] During his preparation for Mass, Favre calls to mind those he intends to pray for as he commemorates the living. This commemoration was called the *Memento* (from the first word of the Latin prayer) in the pre–Vatican II liturgy.

[151] Juan de Aragón had, no doubt, given Favre a detailed account of his pilgrimage, and Favre recalls the details in the form of a thanksgiving prayer.

patience to those very ones who brought them to realize how a person's holiness is tested by suffering.

So our Lord Jesus Christ willed for himself the greatest sufferings ever known, for he was best able to bear them and to pray with efficacy for his tormentors. He judged that they needed to be given an example of the greatest humility, patience, and charity ever seen. Therefore it would always be better to have the worst of men find themselves in the company of the best because in that way they could better help each other to make more progress—provided that the good man observes his rule, which is this: The more he is aware of the strictness of justice in his own regard, the more he will stretch his generosity to the limits of goodness and mercy.[152]

78 At prayer in a chapel of St. John, where I had just finished Mass, and remembering that house in my prayer, there came to me a great longing that whatever prosperity I wished for that house and its inhabitants might be extended also through the mercy of God our Lord to all the houses and inhabitants of this city.[153] I wished too that our Lord in his goodness might approve my request as if I had made it while living in each of these houses.[154]

79 There came to me likewise a prayer of thanksgiving in these terms as I called to mind the benefits of God our Lord: I thanked him for all the works, words, and spiritual gifts that are manifested in our creation. I thanked him likewise for all the words and spiritual gifts manifested in our redemption; and finally for all the works, words, and spiritual gifts of glorification—especially for all those things I have already noted and experienced to my profit and consolation.[155]

80 On that same day, how I cannot tell, whenever I petitioned God for myself, for the living, or for the dead, I often felt great devo-

---

[152] The development of this doctrine concerning Christian forbearance and forgiveness of personal offenses for the sake of the common good may appear very strict but is quite in the gospel tradition. Favre had been brought up in these sentiments. *MellConfess,* n. 182.

[153] Favre had just said Mass in a chapel dedicated to St. John, perhaps in a convent or hospice or in some private house in Speyer. He is making his thanksgiving.

[154] Physical presence in a place gives a special efficacy to prayer for that place. On the other hand, prayer is free from ties of time and place, so it can extend itself to the whole world. Prayer then is a reflection, at one and the same time, of particular human circumstances and of the divine omnipresence.

[155] The *spiritus* (the communication and the movement of the spirit) signifies, in each of the three spiritual orders distinguished here by Favre, the grace which in us is the effect of the divine words and works. It is a characteristic of the interior life proper to each of the three great spiritual stages: creation, redemption, glorification. It designates one's experience of *gratia;* it designates too what God works in humankind.

tion at the thought that the Lord our God in his goodness would accept that prayer and make it as efficacious as if it had been made by Jesus Christ himself our Redeemer, or by the Virgin Mary, or by some saint, or the suffering souls in purgatory. This consideration gave me fervor during Mass; for Mass possesses in itself by reason of the victim and the sacrifice offered in it such great value that nothing we could with justice ask is impossible to obtain if we make our request through that sacrifice which was accomplished on the cross, especially if our Lord grants us appropriate faith in it and a very special confidence.

▸ August 12

81 During Mass on the day of St. Clare, I felt myself somewhat distracted by my desires; one was to edify those present, the other to obtain devotion for that purpose. In the past I had often experienced the same, at first without being aware that it was a temptation. But when I realized that it was one, I did not know how to banish it,[156] for it was then more deeply rooted in me than it is at present, now that I put up a greater resistance to such imperfections.

Thinking over the matter that day, I found grace from the Lord not to consent to feelings such as these; they were imperfections in which I was not conscious of sin. And I learned from him to take care that devotion, which is the immediate knowledge of and feeling for the things of God our Lord (especially for his person and those free gifts of his through which man is made more pleasing to his Creator), should be desired only for the glory of God and for personal perfection and edification, because, unlike other graces given gratuitously, these are not intended for the neighbor.[157]

---

[156] Both desires, to edify the congregation and to find devotion for that purpose, seemed good. But further thought raised the question: Should devotion be sought for that purpose? Favre had often done so in the past, at first unaware that it was a temptation, and then found himself unable to banish it when he realized that it was one. Knowledge alone did not suffice.

[157] God teaches him a lesson about devotion. It should be desired "only for the glory of God and for personal perfection and edification." To desire it for any other reason is to misuse it. Favre makes the traditional scholastic distinction between *gratia gratum faciens* (a divine gift which unites a person with God) and *gratia gratis data* (given to enable a person to cooperate with God for the sanctification of others (*ST*, I-II, q. 111, a. 1.). He identifies the former with devotion *(devotio)*. This must not be sought or used as a means to anything outside itself, for it brings with it immediate contact with God. Favre was already aware of the distinction that lay at the heart of the discernment, but this intellectual awareness became affective knowledge by God's intervention. See O'Leary, "Discernment," pp. 66, 105, 106.

> *August 13*

82   On the Sunday within the octave of St. Lawrence, I had some notable spiritual feelings[158] while I was saying the Sunday matins. With deep emotion I asked the Most Holy Trinity (on a day devoted to the Trinity) through the glory of our Lord's Resurrection to grant me a special grace for all the Sunday offices. I asked also that I might find something in the Sunday offices to help me in the offices of the coming week, whether ferial or of the saints. I made the same petition at the beginning, the middle, and the end of my Mass.[159]

83   That same day also, I recalled some points which had affected me on other occasions but had then been forgotten, but which are to be noted. For example, this: to ask and desire with great hope that our Lord, in his goodness and forbearance, might make allowances for all my shortcomings so that the humiliations I often deserve to have inflicted on me because of my many negligences should if they come tend only to the glory of God and the salvation of my neighbor. I desired too that bad spirits should not gain through my fault the power to induce those who know of or witness my failings to dwell on them, especially if they feel that they greatly diminish the glory of God our Lord and harm the neighbor.

Mark now, O my soul, that those defects and imperfections of yours that you revealed in so many places and to so many persons, good and evil, were neither taken account of nor examined in accordance with strict justice. For that reason you are the more in debt to the Lord your God, the God who, of himself and by virtue of the intercessory prayers of his saints and through the ministry of his angels, does not permit your conduct to be looked upon unfavorably or judged according to strict justice. Above all, despite his very clear understanding of your words and actions up to now and that they could or should be judged unfavorably, he has not yet taken account of them or retained a memory of them.

84   On the same day there came to me a spiritual desire that our Lord might give me an interior awareness of the *Gloria in excelsis Deo* of the Sunday and of the *Kyrie eleison* and other prayers and that he might give me a spirit in conformity with Sunday, the day of the Lord.

---

[158] These spiritual feelings (in Latin, *sensus spiritus;* in Spanish, *sentimientos de espiritu*) denote a sensitivity of the soul reacting affectively to an awareness of God's presence. The difficulty of translating *sentire* and its derivatives should be borne in mind here.

[159] Sunday is a renewal of the Paschal mysteries, a commemoration of the Resurrection in honor of the Trinity.

▸ *August 14*

85 On August's vigil of our Lady, while I was saying the office of St. Hippolytus and his companions, I came to the reading about St. Concordia, whose body, flung into a sewer, was drawn out by the holy sewerman Irenaeus to the great consolation of the priest St. Justin.[160] This caused me a feeling of deep remorse[161] as I considered how that man, in the course of his duty, had performed a deed so holy and so pleasing to God our Lord. At this consideration there came to me another deep feeling at the sight of my uselessness. So, in great anguish, I prayed to the Mother of our Lord (who is her very perfect fruit) to obtain for me the grace of being able to serve her Son and of knowing how to do so in my priestly office with a will perfectly devoted to him, just as that man at his humble and lowly work found an opportunity of doing something great in the service of our Lord. I asked the same grace for all those who have authority, whatever their station in life, that our Lord might give them the grace to find an occasion for doing something of immediate profit for their souls or something to benefit or truly console or relieve the needs of others whether living or dead.[162]

86 Likewise in connection with the psalms *Benedicite* and *Laudate*,[163] I felt a keen remorse which led me to understand and realize that all creatures serve man by bringing him efficacious aid, consolation, and relief in his needs. The sun sheds its light on him, water refreshes him, fire warms him, and so forth. But I, because my spirit is so lacking in

---

[160] We read in the *Gesta S. Laurentii* that at Rome, under the emperor Decius, the subprefect Hippolytus and his household, lately converted to Christianity, were all condemned to death. Hippolytus's nurse, Concordia, and nineteen others were beheaded outside the Porta Tiburtina. He himself was torn to pieces by wild horses. The bodies, left near the Campo Verano on August 15, were gathered together by the priest, Justin, and buried in the same place. With them he buried the body of Concordia, which had been recovered from a sewer by Irenaeus, a sewerman, and Abundius. These two men, condemned in their turn, were thrown into a sewer. Their bodies were taken out by Justin and buried near the body of Laurentius, a member of Hippolytus's household. There is some confusion about the identity and the history of St. Hippolytus. BS 7:868–875; A. Dufourcq, *Etude sur les Gesta Martyrum romains* (Paris, 1900), pp. 199–209.

[161] *Habui magnum spiritum compunctionis* in Latin.

[162] This reflection on the value of good works continues to §88. It was suggested to Favre by the contrast between an outstanding deed done by a man in a humble station and his own comparative uselessness, even though a priest. The reflection brings him to realize that work is always a gift of God, just as the holiest of all works, the birth of her divine son, was in Mary the gift and the fruit of the Holy Spirit.

[163] The Canticle of the Three Young Men. Dan. 3:57–58; Ps. 148–150.

devotion, do nothing worthwhile for his glory or for his service, yet this is the duty of men.[164]

So reflecting, I meditated on the mysteries in turn, thinking of the notable fruit that our Lady saw our Lord bear at the Annunciation, at the Visitation, and at the Nativity. She saw the shepherds raised to higher knowledge; she understood the meaning of the mystery of the Circumcision; she saw the kings bow down so low.[165] Lastly I begged her to obtain for me the grace of bearing some modest fruit as the servant of her Son and inspired by faith, hope, and charity.

And while I experienced that desire, it seemed to me that there arose in me a hope like that of a man who, wishing to enter the service of some great master, remains for years a servant to that man's servants, thus proving himself trustworthy in their eyes. His hope is that when at last his master appears he will judge him worthy to be taken into his service and will indicate to him his intention of doing so. At this thought I paused and submitted myself to our Lord's will, for he alone knows the order of our needs and what conduces to our salvation.

87   At first vespers of the Assumption I found great spiritual devotion when I was in the cathedral of our Lady of Speyer. This was because the ceremonies, the lights, the organ, the chanting, the splendor of the relics and the decorations—all these gave me such a great feeling of devotion that I could not explain it. I blessed the person who had placed the votive lights there, lit them, and arranged them in order, and also the person who had left an income for that purpose. Likewise I blessed the organ, the organist, the benefactors,[166] and others, as well as all the priestly vestments that I saw had been laid ready there for the worship of God. So too the choir and the sacred music sung by the boy choristers, and I blessed in the same way the reliquaries and those who sought out relics[167] and adorned them fittingly when found.

In short, I was led by that spirit to esteem the least of these devotional activities, performed with a simple Catholic faith, more highly than a thousand degrees of that idle faith[168] made so much of by those

---

[164] *SpEx,* [60].

[165] To recognize God's action in that of man is the kind of contemplation practiced by Mary.

[166] *Fundadores* (founders) in Spanish: those who left money for the support of an organist and the upkeep of the organ.

[167] These quests for relics, very common in medieval times, meant journeys all over Europe; perhaps Favre refers to a special collection got together from the town for the feast day.

[168] *Fee ociosa* (Sp.) or faith without works. The whole anti-Lutheran polemic centers on this point. Luther however denied that his "faith alone" *(sola fides)* meant a denial of works. See *DeCertMem,* p. 182, n. 4.

who ill agree with the hierarchical Church. Similarly I realized the great goodness and mercy that God our Lord shows to all and to every one of those who give something of their own for the public *cultus* of God and of his saints, whether the work of their hands, a gift of money, the offer of advice, or some other thing.[169]

▸ August 15

88 On the day of our Lady, while I was reciting matins without attending to the office being said in the church and also while I was saying Mass, I was almost completely left to myself without being moved by any spirit either good or bad. That brought me to realize how halfhearted and sluggish I was in prayer and in my efforts to remain attentive to it. Some time later, however, though still left to my own resources, it seemed to me that I was no longer so downcast and dispirited in myself, so uncontrolled and disordered as at other times when our Lord left me thus, deprived of any spiritual motion from the outside, on my own but with a sufficiency of his grace.[170]

May it please God our Lord to grant me the grace of increasing each day so as to become a larger vessel,[171] one of greater capacity and interior cleanliness, made ready to deny entrance to the bad spirits and to admit the good ones.[172]

Then I remembered and took note that on the principal feast days for nearly a year I found myself without any devotion—I mean without that devotion which comes from an interior motion of the Spirit which is wont to change our own nature into another and better one and whose presence overshadows and hides what is in us.[173] And it is a great gift from God, it seems to me, that a person should often have to live relying

---

[169] Favre was always in favor of popular manifestations of piety.

[170] A somewhat rare experience for Favre: the complete absence of spiritual motions either from the good or from the bad spirit. He seems to look on it as a form of desolation as his description of previous experiences suggests: "I was no longer so downcast and dispirited in myself, so uncontrolled and disordered as at other times. . . ." The experience must have been quite disconcerting. See O'Leary, "Discernment," pp. 92–93; *SpEx,* [320], on God's help in desolation.

[171] The image of the vessel *(vas)* is often used by Favre to express the reception of grace by the creature. It is common enough in devotional literature, for example, the invocation "Singular Vessel of Devotion" *(vas insigne devotionis)* from the Litany of Loreto.

[172] Grace is needed to prepare for the reception of the spirits, and also to discern between the good and the bad spirits.

[173] A further examination of his lack of devotion—that form of it which comes from the Holy Spirit, whose presence in us guides, protects, envelops, and transforms us.

on himself with essential grace; for in that way he better recognizes his own spirit, common to each one in his ordinary state, and knows how to distinguish it from the state which is due to a spirit, whether good or bad, that visits him only on occasion [el spirito adventitio].[174] Similarly, in order to distinguish clearly the good spirit from the bad, it is very important to be able to understand and experience in oneself the heights and the depths of each state, as also the increase or diminution likely to come about in each of these three ways of life that we happen to experience in ourselves. In the first, we could somehow accurately say—not excluding God's grace—"I live, it is indeed I who live"; in the second, "I live, not I, but Christ lives in me";[175] in the third, "I live, no longer I, but sin or the bad spirit who rules over the wicked lives in me."[176]

---

[174] This passage deals with discernment of spirits. The process begins with an experience of interior states—the word *cor* having a phenomenological sense—the diversity of which allows them to be distinguished from each other in such a way that their origins can be identified: either one's personal spirit or an occasional spirit, whether good or bad. This occasional spirit *(spirito adventitio)*, which Favre in another context calls a contingent spirit *(spiritus contingens)*, must be distinguished from the more interior essential spirit (§89) and from the spirit proper to each one (his personal spirit) which describes at one and the same time the ordinary state of a person and the weakness that is natural to him. Being left to oneself does not mean that one is deprived of essential grace. That experience of abandonment, however, helps a person to distinguish between "his own spirit" and the one "which visits him only on occasion."

With regard to the clause beginning "for in that way he better recognizes" and ending, "on occasion," there is a discrepancy between the Spanish original and the Latin version in *MonFabri*, p. 538. Our translation follows the Spanish and agrees with the French of de Certeau. But the Latin of the second half of the sentence runs as follows: "ut melius cognoscat et sciat distinguere inter proprium spiritum, quem habet a suo communi, et etiam quod habet in spiritu a necessario modo, bonus vel malus sit." The Spanish version shows some differences: "porque mijor conosca y sepa distinguir el proprio spirito que tiene en su commún ser, y el ser que tiene en el spirito adventitio, sea bueno ó malo." Note the absence of "a necessario modo" and the substitution of "que tiene en el spirito adventitio" for "quod habet in spiritu." Mellinato accepts the Latin version and turns the passage as follows: "Così impara a meglio cognoscere e distinguere lo spirito proprio, che è caratteristico di ciascuno nella sua condizione ordinaria, da ciò che gli viene da una mozione come vincolante, sia essa buona o cattiva" (In that way he learns the better to recognize and to distinguish his own spirit, which is common to everyone in his ordinary state, from that which comes to him from a motion, whether good or evil, that all but constrains him). See *MellConfess*, p. 162.

[175] Gal. 2:20.

[176] Discernment consists in observing what is manifested in internal experiences not simply as good or bad but according to the varying intensity of each experience. However, the significance of each experience is revealed in its development; that is to say, whether it leads one in the right or wrong direction, to this or that way

89 After Mass I thanked the Lord God and then our Lady for her intercession; I reflected on the perfection that she had always possessed in her own nature, that she was under the unceasing and effective influence of the Holy Spirit, though not always, as I think, in the same way. For though she was at all times full of grace and though the Lord was with her and though she was blessed above all women, she was probably not affected at all times and to the same degree by the fervor and consolation which comes from the Holy Spirit. There was still room left in her for the most perfect humility, for a hunger and thirst to please the Almighty more and more, room too for a fear lest she might not serve God in accordance with his will.

Then I asked God's Mother to obtain for me the grace of being fortified, refashioned, and reformed interiorly, so that when later on it might be very just and necessary to withdraw from me the actual motion and sensible operation of the Holy Spirit, I should not then be so ready to squander, dissipate, and thus lose the gifts of God that filled me, nor should I be so slack, negligent, and carnal, so heedless in spirit with regard to spiritual things.[177]

May it please the divine goodness to confirm thus in me his essential grace so that, when passing graces have been withdrawn from me, I may become daily stronger, wiser, and better able to labor. And may these dispositions be in my body, in my soul, and in my spirit so that by their means I could take advantage of his grace when I act no longer under the influence of spiritual fervor.[178]

▶ *August 16*

90 On the day after the Assumption, as I was commemorating St. Roch[179] (I had resolved to do so each year on the same date as the Carmelites in their house in Paris), I felt these words deeply: *Mariam sanctificans, Mariam gubernans, Mariam coronans* in the *Gloria in excelsis*.[180] So with great devotion, faith, and hope I begged that our

---

of life. O'Leary, "Discernment," pp. 92–93.

[177] The image is that of the receptacle, implying the idea of passivity with regard to the prevalent operation of grace.

[178] See *SpEx,* [318–321]. To the teaching of Ignatius, Favre adds the distinction between accidental and essential. Once the accidental disappears, it is necessary to have recourse to the essential. He is led from what he *feels* to what *is,* from what he experiences to what he believes; from now he finds greater stability in his faith, that is, in God.

[179] The cult of St. Roch was of recent date.

[180] "Sanctifying Mary, governing Mary, and crowning Mary." These phrases were added to the Gloria of an old Mass of the Blessed Virgin. About 1570 the Mass was reprinted at Antwerp by Plantin as part of a volume entitled *Horæ beatissimæ*

Lady would obtain for me, firstly, holiness and the purification that results from chastity, self-control, and total purity of body and spirit. Secondly, I asked for the grace to be guided to rule myself and direct my life according to the service of Christ her Son. Thirdly, that she would obtain for me peace in this world by the practice of all the virtues and glory in the next.[181]

91 Desiring also to adore with fervor the body of Christ our Lord there on the altar before me, I remembered how the Blessed Virgin Mary enthroned above all the choirs of angels was of all creatures that came from the hand of the Almighty the one who most worthily honors and serves the divine Majesty. So her aid for mankind is far greater and higher than that of any angel or seraphim. For not only does she reign over all creatures in a state of happiness, but she also (and better than any of them) magnifies, praises, and serves her Son and the most holy Trinity as Lady and Queen, our Mother and our Advocate. She asks for and obtains the renewal of all those who have not yet reached their full essential and accidental perfection.[182] Daily she procures for mortal men new gifts of grace and peace, ending in glory, and for the blessed new gifts of accidental glory.[183]

> *91a: Paragraph 94, dated August 19, comes before paragraph 92 and 93, as they are dated August 20.*

▸ *August 19*

94 On the day of St. Louis, bishop and confessor,[184] I experienced great fervor at this thought among others: to offer Mass in order to atone for all my negligences in pondering over and noting with open and attentive eyes the benefits offered to me every day and every moment through the works of God our Lord, through his internal and external words, and through his body and his person, which I daily hold in my hands and have before my eyes. Hence there came to me a very clear understanding with a great desire to keep these thoughts always in

---

Virginis Mariæ.

[181] Favre may well have been meditating on the Gloria of the Mass according to the Second Method of Prayer in *SpEx*, [247–257].

[182] Essential perfection is complete union with God, but it may be accidentally incomplete insofar as some conditions necessary for a full enjoyment of God are not yet present—for example, when the body is still separated from the soul (§138). See *NCathEnc* 11:123–127, arts. "Ontological Perfection" and "Spiritual Perfection."

[183] A reference to the Blessed Virgin's part in the work of redemption.

[184] This St. Louis was bishop of Toulouse, a member of the Order of Friars Minor and grandson of the St. Louis who was king of France. See *BS* 8:300–307.

my soul, according to this versicle: "Open my eyes and I shall be attentive to the marvels of your law."[185]

Having been wondering daily at the changing states of my soul from despondency to rapture as it considered at one time the reality of its defects and at another the mercy and forgiveness of God our Lord, I had at the offertory an understanding of this text: "My truth and my mercy are with him."[186] This consoled me as much as if someone had told me that our Lord has recourse to his truth at times when revealing his justice, that at other times he gives tokens of his mercy, and that in these two ways he tests his servants.

▸ *August 20*

92   On St. Bernard's day I found very great devotion at Mass and shed many tears as I reflected on the lessening of honor for the Blessed Sacrament as a consequence of the tepid lives of many Christians, and ultimately because those who separate themselves completely from the Church influence others to leave. I felt similarly affected as I thought over the harm done to the souls in purgatory by these erroneous ideas. I saw as well how there followed so many acts of impiety committed against sacred objects and against superiors, and also mutual recriminations; and I saw how there is no longer any tolerance for what is not to one's own liking.[187]

93   The same day I had a feeling of great devotion as I offered myself to St. Bernard. I asked him to be so kind as to accept me as his disciple, he who had given himself up so completely to the service of the Mother of Jesus Christ our Lord.

▸ *August 21*

95   On the vigil of the octave of our Lady of the Assumption, in the afternoon, I had a clear recollection of some aspects of Christ's passion. They were effective ways of finding devotion in my office and in my customary prayers and meditations. I refer to these texts particularly:

---

[185] Ps. 119 (118): 18.

[186] This versicle from Ps. 89 (88): 25 formed part of the offertory antiphon of the Mass for a confessor not a pontiff in the Missal of St. Pius V.

[187] Favre analyzes some elements of religious individualism gained from his own observations and those of others. His predominant feeling is sorrow at the damage done to the Church, but there is a trace of bitterness in the last sentence. These thoughts are scarcely distractions, for they can pass through the mind in a flash; they may well have been touched off by a word or a phrase in the Mass of St. Bernard.

"My soul is sorrowful . . . ," "Let this chalice pass . . . ,"[188] "My God, my God, why have you forsaken me?"[189] "Woman, behold your son . . . ,"[190] "Father, into your hands. . . ."[191]

I understood, also with reference to the Assumption, that our Lady was raised above all the angelic choirs by reason of her compassion with the suffering of her Son—his passion being the perfect road that mounts straight to heaven. So it seemed to me then that a fitting way to raise oneself to the contemplation of her glorious Assumption was to reflect deeply on the passion of our Lady's Son and on the compassion of Mary.

▸ *August 26*

96 At Mass the thought came to me to meditate on what takes place before the consecration, then on what takes place up to the communion, and lastly on what follows up to the end of Mass; this makes three points. Profoundly moved by the good spirit, I thought it good to recall Christ's existence in three stages: the first, before his incarnation; the second, during his life on earth; the third, after his ascension. Similarly for our Lady: first, the time that elapsed up to the conception of her Son; second, the time up to the death and the ascension of her Son; third, the time after his ascension until her own death. In this way there were indicated to me some good desires that new graces might be communicated to me for the purpose of knowing and loving Christ better through the intercession of his Mother. They came to me in connection with that meditation of mine on the Mass and consisted first in desiring gifts in keeping with the time before the incarnation, and these I should recall during that part of the Mass up to the consecration; second, the gifts in keeping with the time from the incarnation to the passion of Christ; third, whatever is in keeping with the time from the passion to the day of judgment.[192]

---

[188] Matt. 26:38–39.

[189] Mark 15:34.

[190] John 19:26.

[191] Luke 23:46. Christ's passion and his seven words on the cross were two of Favre's favorite subjects for meditation (§71).

[192] Since the Latin Mass was not understood by the people during the Middle Ages, it became a pastoral necessity to explain by means of commentaries the Mass as a symbolic representation of sacred history and especially of our Lord's life. The action of the Mass and the words and gestures of the priest were said to correspond to the words and gestures of Christ. Favre's approach to the Mass was, of course, medieval: it was the priest's business, and the congregation assisted much as spectators. See J. A. Jungmann, *The Mass of the Roman Rite* (New York, 1959), pp. 66–100; O'Leary, "Discernment," pp. 54–55.

97 It is in conformity with my devotion to our Lady to desire during the year, within the time that elapses from one of Mary's feasts to another, that our Lord give me graces similar to those she was given in profusion. I took first the time from the conception to the annunciation of God's Son. This should be a time of continuous preparation, so that I may be able to say with truth one day, "Behold the handmaid of the Lord,"[193] already become the tabernacle of the Almighty[194] and prepared to serve him. Then I took another time, from that moment to the death of her Son, during which she suffered with him, and lastly the time from then to the Assumption—a third time, after which one returns to the beginning.[195] During the first two times I asked that our Lord might give me the grace of experiencing his presence, of suffering with him, and of imitating him, and then the grace of being conscious of his absence with holy desires of following him into glory after completing my task on earth of fulfilling his holy will.

98 On that same octave day of the Assumption, reflecting that the passion of Christ and the compassion of our Lady were like the steps of a ladder mounting straight up to the Ascension and the Assumption, I was moved to great devotion in offering up the heights and the depths of these mysteries with gratitude for my own heights and depths. And I desired that our Lord might grant me in time to come the grace of having no joys or sorrows except in conformity with, or depending on, or as a means to the above-mentioned sorrows and joys of Christ and his Mother.[196]

---

[193] Luke 1:38.

[194] Ps. 46 (45): 5.

[195] The liturgy endlessly repeats the life of Christ in an annual cycle, each mystery bringing with it a corresponding renewal of grace. Favre's prayer repeats the liturgical prayer of the Church and interiorizes it.

[196] The full acceptance of life with its joys, sorrows, and pains in conformity with Christ and Mary is a principal element in the spiritual life. As Favre noted in §95, the passion is the direct and perfect road that leads to heaven. This road begins low down in suffering with Christ suffering, thence mounts up with him to where he has ascended. The imitation of Christ implied here by the context together with the word ladder *(scala)* gives evidence of Favre's contact with Rheno-Flemish spirituality and with the circles of the Common Life *(vita communis)*, no doubt through Ludolph the Carthusian *(Vita Christi,* pars I, caput 61). The latter sets side by side reflections on the spiritual life and reflections on the Assumption: ascent through contemplation, descent to the active life. After the event Favre realizes that the ups and downs of his spiritual states are graces which enable him to participate in the mystery of Christ's humiliation and of his elevation. Thus his life reproduces what is essential in Christ's life. So what is passing takes on significance; it is through spiritual experience that the law of every religious life becomes known.

▸ *August 24*

99   On St. Bartholomew's day I offered Mass, among other intentions, for all the hardships and labors that some of my brothers,[197] friends, or relatives might have to suffer. I refer not only to present hardships but also to those in the past and in the future. I wished that this sacrifice might help them to fulfill their duty of thanksgiving, of asking forgiveness, and of finding the graces that are to be sought through these trials.

100   I had devotion also thinking about something which could well happen. It was that I might one day find myself in the presence of all the martyrs and say to each of them with David: "May the Lord hear you in the day of your tribulation," "May he grant you according to your heart and confirm all your designs," "May he grant all your requests, and may your holocaust be acceptable to him."[198] All this came to me with an experience of the good spirit.

101   That same day, wishing to say compline, I found my soul very downcast and in bitterness because, all that day and even from the evening before, I had been in a state of great turmoil and also because some of my old infirmities and weaknesses were reasserting themselves on that very day, during the course of which I would not have wished to experience any other movement except that of the good spirit. In addition, I had distractions during my office.

There came to me then a certain consoling thought that perchance it pleased God on such days to humble me and bring me back to my old wounds so that the saints of the day might see them and be especially earnest in asking God our Lord to draw me away from these imperfections. It is certain that, on almost every one of the major feasts for more than a year past, I found myself farther from that spirit in which are devotion, peace, tears, and so forth.[199]

So then these thoughts filled me with great hope and I prayed earnestly to our Lord to have things happen in this way that not only his Majesty but also his Mother, the apostles, St. John the Baptist, St. Anne, the Magdalene, and the other saints might all by these means be made aware of my great spiritual needs.[200]

---

[197] His fellow Jesuits.

[198] Ps. 20 (19): 2, 4, 5, 6.

[199] This definition of the good spirit given in Latin in the Spanish text corresponds to the definition of consolation given in *SpEx*, [316]. With regard to the absence of consolation on great feast days, see §88. The absence of tears surprises Favre more than does their presence and forces him to seek for the reason. O'Leary, "Discernment," p. 64.

[200] Alvaro Alfonso left on pilgrimage that day, August 24, as Favre wrote to

▶ **August 25**

102 On the day of St. Louis, king of France, I felt much devotion as I offered for the intentions of the cardinal the Mass I had to say for him.[201] I wished to fulfill in his name all his duties; the honor due to that saint and the welfare of the entire kingdom of France which has received so many benefits and in which so many sins have been forgiven, where too there are so many needs both spiritual and corporal.[202] Then I said the Mass for his person and for the whole of France, past, present, and to come with all its kings, dukes, counts, and other noblemen with their lands, for its archiepiscopal and episcopal sees, its abbeys, parishes, and universities, its commercial and other towns however administered.[203] I felt much devotion in this series of prayers, desiring that our Lord might grant them all. And I made known to him that I wished those same desires to come true in each of the other kingdoms.

103 Saying my office one Sunday, I was much affected by some words from the psalms, these especially: "I shall love thee, Lord, my strength"; "The Lord is my stronghold, my refuge, and my deliverer"; "My God, my helper, my protector, my power of salvation, and my defender."[204] I felt these words deeply; I pondered over them with faith and hope in the Lord, desirous of loving him.

Then I considered that in man the flesh is weaker and of a nature more easily corrupted, the dissolution of his body more rapid than in all the other bodies;[205] and, on the other hand, that his soul is so blind, his spirit so wicked and perverted in judging his own needs and the remedies he seeks for body and soul—that is, for the soul and for the flesh of the body in which he lives.[206] These considerations brought me much devotion, and I thought of asking the Father Almighty to have compas-

---

Ignatius. *MonFabri*, p. 177.

[201] Most likely Louis de Bourbon-Vendôme, cardinal in 1507 and archbishop of Sens from 1533 to 1557.

[202] He refers to the ravages of war in France and the progress of the Reformation, which he knew from the Jesuit scholastics in Paris.

[203] This is a form of the prayer Favre calls *discursus*—a *dilatatio* or amplifying of prayer by following through space and time the subject which gave rise to it.

[204] Ps. 18 (17): 2–3.

[205] A reflection on some of the traditional teaching about original sin. K. Rahner, ed., *The Teaching of the Catholic Church* (Cork, 1967), pp. 131–141; *SacMundi* 4:328–334, art. "Original Sin."

[206] Favre designates the soul *(anima)* as the animating principle of the body, while the flesh *(caro)* is that by means of which the soul, the form *(forma)* of the body, experiences as through a medium the material world. See *ConsSJComm*, p. 77, n. 10, for a comment on the use of the word *anima* (Sp.) in the spiritual writing of the time.

sion on my flesh and on my body and to strengthen and sanctify them. I commended my soul to the Son that he might enlighten and sanctify it. I commended my spirit to the Holy Spirit that he might inspire it and bestow on it goodness enough never to neglect the duty it owes to the soul—by "soul" I understand the sensitive part taken together with the inferior part of the reason, by means of which the intelligence reasons about what is received through the senses. By "spirit" I understand that superior part which occupies itself with divine things, receiving its reasonings, desires, and affections[207] through the Holy Spirit and through the angels and also through the faith that comes from hearing.

I then asked the Son to grant those requests of mine in my reception of his most precious Body, soul, and divinity which are present in this sacrament.

▸ August 29

104 On the day of the Beheading of St. John [the Baptist],[208] finding myself somewhat distracted and seeing how difficult it was to recollect myself,[209] I found much devotion in the thought that it is properly in the most holy Sacrament that the grace to attain recollection is found. Our Lord wishes to enter into us and lead us to conversion of heart so that by following him we may daily enter more and more into the deepest depths of ourselves.[210] I prayed to St. John the Baptist, the

---

[207] Scholastic philosophy speaks of man in terms of body and soul; Favre, using here the language of the Bible and of spiritual tradition, refers to man in terms of body, soul, and spirit (1 Thess. 5:23). The soul is the principle of natural, experimental knowledge; the spirit is the principle of supernatural, interior knowledge. Favre considers this distinction from the point of view of knowledge. For him "spiritual" knowledge is the result of a direct intervention of the Spirit and of the angels; only in a subsequent reflection does he purge this idea of its overly spiritualized or illuminist (?) tendencies by adding the expression "from the teaching of the faith" *(fides ex auditu)*. See O'Leary, "Discernment," p. 77; *DBibTheol*, pp. 565–568; *SacMundi* 6:138, art. "Soul"; *NCathEnc* 13:447–471, a comprehensive treatment of the soul, and especially 471–473 on "Soul-Body Relationships."

[208] Still celebrated on this date; "beheading" *(decollatio)*, however, has been changed to "martyrdom" *(passio)* in the Roman calendar. See §36 n. 73 above.

[209] The expression "to recollect myself" (in Latin, *redeundi ad me;* in Spanish, *volver en si*, literally, to return to oneself) is the same as "to return to the heart" *(redeundi ad cor)* in §188 above; Luke 15:17.

[210] Favre's sacramental theology, especially that which arises from experience of the purifying effects of the sacraments, is based on an intuition that predates the discoveries of Freud about the "depths" of our interior being. Here this intimate union with God at the center of his being *(cor)* has a sacramental dimension which he links, in this entry, with the Eucharist. The eucharistic presence of Christ in us is superior to any felt, personal awareness of it; Christ has entered into our heart *(cor)*, bringing

voice crying in the wilderness "Prepare you the way of the Lord,"[211] to teach me how to prepare that way for the Lord.

105 These two things does Christ desire from us above all: that, on the one hand, we continue making ever more progress in raising our spirit heavenward and, on the other, we enter and penetrate deeper and deeper into ourselves until we find God present within us. The kingdom of God should be sought nowhere else but within us and in heaven.[212]

Christ was raised up on the cross, then he ascended to heaven in order to draw us all to himself.[213] He gave himself in the Sacrament as food for our souls that we might have a way to draw him into us, according to this text, "We shall come to him and make our abode with him,"[214] and this, "If anyone opens to me I shall sup with him."[215]

106 While I was saying the office of St. Sabina, martyr, I thought of this devotion: that I should commemorate also at each hour of the breviary[216] the virgin and martyr St. Seraphia, who had converted St. Sabina while living in her house.

107 The same day I considered how men commit not only carnal sins but almost all other kinds with close application of soul and spirit. They brood over the matter of these sins; they make it a subject of conversation; they devote their eyes and ears to it. Then a series of prayers [*discurso*] came to me in which I asked our Lord to restrain evil spirits from tempting men so much. For at present there is so much talk and discussion and still more reflection and craving devoted both to the pleasures of the table (now become, so to speak, nourishment for the spirit) and to other, even lawful, bodily satisfactions that as a result men give themselves to these pleasures with all their souls. It is as if they

---

with him the power (grace) to draw us after him. This movement of interiorization (a going inward) is the essence of the spiritual life. It is symbolized here by the Eucharist. The "return to the heart" is an entering into the interior, following Christ who enters the depths of the soul, there to plant the seed, his own life, from which will spring up apostolic fruit. This concept of the spiritual life is central to Favre's thought. It is based on the sacramental life; only the personal aspect, however, receives emphasis here. See §124 above.

[211] Luke 3:4.

[212] The two movements, one of ascent, the other towards the interior, are both present in Favre. The second, interiorization, is symbolized by the Eucharist, an allusion to Luke 16:21.

[213] John 12:32. The Johannine idea of "elevation": Christ's elevation on the cross is both a sign of glory and the revelation of the divine mystery of Christ. See Eph. 4:8–10.

[214] John 14:23, one of the great mystical texts to be found in St. John.

[215] Apoc. 3 and 20.

[216] The canonical hours of the breviary.

wished, in nourishing their bodies and satisfying their needs, to nourish and provide for the soul, which requires to be fed with another food and be satisfied with other delights than those of the body.

So it happens in our day that libertines worsen their sins by making their spirits participate to excess in them and by involving their souls in the defilement of their bodies. It happens too that even married folk dishonor the marriage bed by getting their spiritual life too much mixed up in their conjugal relations and by seeking to satisfy the longings of the soul at the same time as they satisfy the longings of the flesh,[217] and in the end there is an excessive indifference to and estrangement from the things of God.[218]

108 Hence it happens that the spirit is unable to find for itself proper food, and soon it desires to satisfy its hunger with the pods that the body feeds on as if it were a pig.

It would, however, have been better to lead the body to relish the spiritual food enjoyed by its soul and its spirit so that, when we gazed on some work of God or listened to his words or implemented them with our own hands, our spirit would enter so fully into all those things as to draw with it our entire sensitive soul to the perception of them. This is indeed to go out and find pasture.[219]

In truth, we cannot succeed in this before we have drawn everything into our deepest depths, that is, before we have achieved complete interior recollection and are prepared to live in that state. This happens when we first make efforts to free ourselves completely from being affected by sensual impressions. And so we should petition God to raise us up to the world above and to the contemplation of matters altogether spiritual so that in the end all else becomes in some way spiritual and is

---

[217] An idea of marriage which goes back to Augustine, that it is a concession to the weakness of the flesh: lawful conjugal pleasures can have nothing to do with the spiritual life.

[218] Here Favre takes to task those who, when they sin, though recognizing that they do wrong yet want to lower their spiritual life to the level of their sins. He is concerned with the lack of spiritual discernment they reveal in their state and perhaps also with a sin against the spirit. Does he allude as well to certain forms of illuminism and certain tendencies in Protestantism with regard to spiritual "liberty" in moral matters? Mellinato, referring to this attitude (*MellConfess*, p. 176, n. 248), suggests that it is one of the commonest sources of anticlericalism: a secularist mentality which, by a refusal to accept man as he is and by not understanding him, refuses also to accept God and the Church.

[219] John 10:9. The phrase occurs several times in the *Memoriale* and each time refers to that moment when the Christian, detached from all things and transformed from within, sees that his interior life is being renewed by grace and recognizes God's presence and action in all things. And when it is time for him to leave his place of retirement with God, he finds himself still in the divine realms.

apprehended in a spiritual manner. This is far superior to receiving a grace of the Holy Spirit by means of which we would experience the things of this world in a holy but yet in some way sensible manner.[220]

109 So raise up your mind[221] now to those realities in which nothing is perceptible to any of the senses, realities such as the divinity of Christ, which is identical with that of the Father and the Holy Spirit. Seek God where nothing else can be found but God, that is, in himself.

Then, having reflected on God in his divine nature and persons, seek Christ in his humanity in heaven rather than on earth; after that, the Blessed Virgin, seeking in both the soul before the body. After the Virgin, soul and body, come the angelic spirits and the other blessed souls who dwell in heaven.

It is through these, and in the order given, that our heavenly Father is to be sought and invoked, since we can neither find nor imagine him in himself. But on earth, since you wish to live in close friendship with the Lord but do not know how to raise yourself to heavenly things, there is first Christ and his words and all the sacred words.[222] Contemplate him nailed to the cross, if you look to the past, and if to the future, imagine him as descending for the judgment.[223]

---

[220] Between the apprehension of things in a spiritual manner and the experience of them in a holy but in some way sensible manner, there is a difference of spiritual degree. In the first, things are grasped as coming from God through a kind of interior participation: a person experiences the world as coming from God, "to know or grasp [apprehendere] God in the creature" (§305–§306 below). In the second, there is an experience, holy both in its origin and in its intentions, which seeks to find God in the sensible (material) world without yet perceiving that world as the very presence of the being who is sought. In this a person strives to ascend to God without understanding that every ascent to God is, at the same time, a descent from him. These are inner experiences which defy accurate description.

[221] *Erige igitur iam mentem tuam:* Favre addresses himself. In accordance with the universal medieval practice which was influenced by Augustine, he uses as synonyms with the greatest freedom the terms *mens, animus, anima,* and *cor* to designate the very center of a man, the preeminent seat of his moral, spiritual, and religious life. This center is a very complex reality; time and time again it requires in its activity the intervention of the intelligence, the will, the memory, the imagination, the sentiments, and the emotions. See *DSpir,* art. "*Cor.*"

[222] The "sacred words" are those found in the Bible and the liturgy.

[223] The two great revelations of God in Christ were his "glory" (that is, his coming), appearing first in his state of humility on the cross, then in the splendor of the judgment. Beginnings and ends are always present to Favre's mind in that way as a kind of synthesis; he finds the meaning of a beginning in a knowledge of its end—for instance, in the birth and death of Christ.

110 Later on, then, go through Christ's life again if you seek from more perfect realities a progression in conformity with our spirit. After Christ, there is nothing more profitable than familiarity with the life and actions of the Blessed Virgin, for nowhere else will you find such an effective example of suffering with Christ and of following and serving him. After the Virgin there come the other saints: the martyrs, the hermits, and the rest who have renounced the world and held its rewards in contempt. In these persons too God himself is found, and all the more insofar as they led holier and more spiritual lives. After them come God's other works of creation and redemption and whatever else provides some profitable matter for reflection.[224]

In times of trial there are two ways of making progress: either by meditating on the sufferings of Christ and on eternal torments or by meditating on the resurrection and on glory. But in flourishing times one makes more progress by reflecting on the passion and on what conduces to humility.[225]

111 On that same day of St. Sabina, as I gazed on Christ under the species of bread and wine, there came to me a certain very good awareness of how his infinite Majesty willed to take on the function and the appearance of material bread and wine in order to nourish our souls and refashion our bodies for an existence surpassing that which material bread and wine could provide.

▸ September 1

112 On the day of St. Giles, abbot, after giving a short exhortation to some who were about to communicate and after finishing Mass, I was greatly moved in spirit by a desire to preach, as had often happened in the past. For that reason I then resolved more firmly than before to

---

[224] §107–§110 contain a long reflection on the spiritualization of the senses and the ascent of the spirit. Favre seems to recognize that he is unable to arrive at the term he has fixed for that ascent—the unfathomable reality of the Father—for he addresses himself at the end of §109 as being incapable of raising himself to heavenly things. Must he then content himself with contemplating God as he manifests himself in the world? Is this form of contemplation a stage to be left behind when one becomes capable of contemplating the mystery of the Trinity? Does a mystical knowledge of God in himself and in his Trinity of Persons exclude once and for all that other contemplation of God as he reveals himself in the world and in Jesus Christ? The question was once hotly debated by the classical authors of mystical theology, for instance, Ruysbroeck and Herp (Harphius), and it was still alive in Favre's day. He answers it from his own experience (§134) thus: Knowledge of God implies knowledge of his love and therefore knowledge of his coming into the world and into history, where he fully reveals himself. But it is also a knowledge in which the mystery of God himself is made manifest (§305–§306).

[225] *SpEx,* [331, 324].

make every effort so as to be able to preach or lecture in Germany, for otherwise a serious trouble would be born of so much prolonged silence.[226]

Also at that time I felt that I should be more careful about obedience to that spirit which moves me to fervor for the work of the word of the Lord, whether in personal exhortation or in public preaching not only to crowds in church but also to other gatherings of people in private houses or in neighborhoods (even if few there understand me); likewise at table in the presence of princes or notables.[227]

▸ *September 3*

113 On the first Sunday of September, I applied my series of meditations and especially the series on the mysteries of the life, death, and resurrection of Christ for the soul of a deceased man whose death had just been reported to me. This was Dr. de Cornibus, the Paris theologian.[228] I felt much devotion when I was about to say Mass for him. I begged pardon for him, clearly recognizing that he had not followed the example either of Christ himself or of those who served and obeyed him, adoring and thanking him, listening to him, sharing his sufferings, and begging from him grace and everything necessary.

There came to my mind also those ways in which the deceased could have sinned and fallen short of the perfection he might have attained [if he had made use of the manifold means available to him]. For example, I asked pardon for all the faults he could have committed against his vows of obedience, poverty, and chastity (he was a monk of the Order of St. Francis). I asked pardon too for any deficiency in his teaching as a doctor and preacher, for any excessive intellectual curiosi-

---

[226] Ignorance of the local language seriously impeded the apostolate of almost all the early fathers of the Society. Favre was no exception. He never learned German, so he used Latin, understood and spoken by educated people, or Spanish because it was the language of the imperial court. But he was reluctant to deprive his possible hearers of the Gospel by remaining silent, and so becoming like one of the prelates and priests who had completely abandoned preaching.

[227] He was present at these meals with princes and notables without participating in them because he had been invited, as was the custom, to clarify some doctrinal point for the company. See *MonFabri*, p. 221.

[228] Pierre de Cornibus, one of the reformed Friars Minor, a doctor (1524) and a professor in the University of Paris, had attached himself to the reforming school of Crockaert while Ignatius and his companions were doing their university studies. They had a high opinion of him. He was one of the theologians with Favre at the Colloquy of Ratisbon in 1541 (*MonFabri*, p. 99). He died on May 22, 1542, but the news did not reach Favre until September 1 of that year.

ty,[229] and for any vainglory—which usually attaches itself to men so important.[230]

And at that place in the Mass where one commemorates the dead, as I was led to pause at the *Memento* by a rather great lifting up of my soul, it came to me to ask the Father to deign to be glorified in that soul. I asked the same of the Son, the Holy Spirit, and the Blessed Virgin Mary. I asked also that his soul might be admitted to the ranks of the doctors crowned in glory according to this promise: "And those who are wise shall shine like the brightness of the firmament; and those who turn many to righteousness like the stars for ever and ever."[231]

> *113a: Favre wrote no entries from September 4 to 27 because of a ten days' absence in Mainz. On his return he wrote to Ignatius from Speyer on September 28, giving an account of his long conversations with Cardinal Albert of Brandenburg, who had asked for his opinion about certain doubtful doctrines and writings (MonFabri, pp. 183–184).*

▸ September 27

114 On the feast of SS. Cosmas and Damian, I experienced great and heartfelt desires regarding the veneration of the most holy Sacrament and the saints in heaven and about the honor to be paid to the images and relics of the saints. And I would have wished I could be always in the presence of the most holy Sacrament wherever it is reserved in Germany and likewise in the presence of every image of Christ, of the Virgin Mother of God, and of any man or woman saint. Since this desire must remain unfulfilled, I asked the Lord that our guardian angels might supply for my shortcomings and those of others concerning such veneration so that the duty people have may be carried out by their guardian angels.

115 While I was reflecting, with some elevation of mind, that Christ, seated in power at the right hand of God the Father,[232] sees even with the eyes of his humanity all the evil that is committed under the sun—so many acts of ingratitude and malice, so many blasphemies against God, and so forth—I felt a kind of amazement at Christ's great

---

[229] Religious engaged in intellectual work were frequently blamed for this fault.

[230] The intellectual pride of theologians was for some centuries a recurrent theme in the New Devotion—characteristic of the divorce between theology and spirituality. *The Imitation of Christ* 1, chap. 5; *SacMundi* 6:147 ff., art. "Spirituality"; *Nouvelle Revue Théologique* (1950) 72:372–389, art. "Le divorce entre théologie et mystique."

[231] Dan. 12:3 (DV).

[232] Mark 14:62; *SpEx,* [102].

forbearance and goodness when he is so powerful in heaven and on earth. And I reflected that it is something ironically similar to crucify the mortal Lamb and think nothing of it or neglect him now reigning triumphantly in heaven. And so the forbearance of the living and indeed reigning one can be seen to be good in the measure of the relation between those evils.

▸ *September 29*

116 On the day of St. Michael, the archangel, I felt great devotion to him, making many devout contemplations which moved me to a holy affection for him and for all the angels. While saying my office, I had a great desire that the angels might praise the Lord each time these words are recited, for they have a better awareness and understanding of them. I desired also that the saints might do the same, not only the ones named in the prayers and hymns[233] but all the saints, and that the recital of the office by myself and others, our words and our thoughts, might give them a never-failing opportunity of praising our Lord, of thanking him, or of asking graces for ourselves. I wished too, in spite of my remissness, that they might remain attentive to the holy words pronounced by my tongue and to the gestures and signs made in God's honor, even if they are often made only in the faith of the Church through a personal and anterior gift of faith which is no more than implicit or habitual.[234]

117 At the offertory of Mass this reflection moved me to desire that the Mass might be offered to the glory of St. Michael and all his host and add to that glory as if the angels in bodily form had been perfect imitators of Jesus Christ in this world. I desired, on the other hand, that the Mass might be a source of merit for myself and for all the living, as if we had angelic power and knowledge with which to praise Christ here on earth (as we are bound to) and afterwards in glory. I rejoiced at the thought that I might be enabled, through God's grace, to take the place of the angels in the labors and afflictions of this life and that they, for their part, might offer in my name to God the honor I owe to the divine Majesty, for "a thousand thousands serve him and ten thousand times ten thousand stand before him."[235]

---

[233] *Alabanças* (praises): the word here means hymns in honor of the saints.

[234] ". . . in sola fide ecclesiæ, aut in propria, licet tantum virtuali aut habituali, . . ." a Latin addition to the Spanish text. The meaning is that gestures can be made during prayer without in each case an accompanying and explicit act of faith because faith is already present by reason of a habit *(habitus)* of faith; so the gestures are made in union with the Mystical Body. See *ST*, I–II, q. 55, a. 1, ad 1.

[235] Dan. 7:10 (DV).

But I well realized that it was enough for me to recognize, serve, honor, praise, and imitate Christ insofar as I could from reflecting on his way of life on earth. He was content with so little; he left behind on earth his successors and his representatives: "Who hears them hears him, and who despises them despises him."[236] Besides, he left behind his poor of whom he said: "As you did it to one of these the least of my brethren, you did it to me."[237]

▸ September 30

118 On the day of the blessed doctor St. Jerome,[238] it was made known to me in a special way how to gain his favor and that of the other saints whose memory may remain alive among men. This is of great value in obtaining their aid for men. I was to do so by cultivating great devotion to that angel who had been appointed his guardian on earth and to all the angel guardians of the saints mentioned in the Roman calendar or in any other one. We may also petition these angels or communicate with them in spirit by faith as we may with the saints.

As I was saying my office before daybreak, I felt great devotion at the thought that the angels and saints can avail of the opportunity afforded by those words of mine in order to praise God and aid us in obtaining what we seek. I perceived then how very profitable it is to ask them with great devotion, faith, and hope to sustain with their presence our contemplation and praise of God, because they contemplate and praise God and see him as he is in all things, in every good work, and in every word that comes from the mouth of God.[239] It is good also that man should desire that they play their wonted part in all situations and with their voices and glorified natures excuse the shortcomings of our minds, of our acts and words, and especially of the powers of our souls.

119 I had a great desire (and felt joy in thinking that it might come true) that the saints in heaven might now have the means, the power, the knowledge, and the will to accomplish and compensate for whatever they had left undone on earth by reason of their lack of will, their ignorance, and their powerlessness in working for God's interests and those of Christ our Lord and of their neighbors both living and dead.

---

[236] Luke 10:16.

[237] Matt. 25:40.

[238] St. Jerome is one of the saints most often invoked, painted, and sung about during the fifteenth and sixteenth centuries. He was also regarded as the patron of priests.

[239] Matt. 4:4; Isa. 34:16; Job 37:2; 41:10.

Then there returned to me a certain desire to have the joy of being able to express in act or in word or in any other way that might be plain to every saint and angel all that our Lord has done and all the words he has spoken in this world. In that way each saint might be enabled to recognize all of them and see in them him who glorifies them and so acquire for themselves a greater degree of accidental glory through us, for we can become for them a cause of that increase.[240]

120 I noted also the devotion I found through the crucifix and the other images kept in the church of the Holy Cross at Mainz, especially the crucifix; they bled when that abandoned fellow hacked off the head of the crucifix and seriously damaged the others. That penetrated me with this all-but-continual reflection: the great goodness of God, who gives and sheds his blood for the sinner as often as he offends him. After his death he gave it also for the poor blind Longinus, who through it recovered his sight.[241]

So it often seems to me that, while I go on committing so many senseless deeds and so many acts of ingratitude and of ill will against my Lord, he makes no return for my blows but goes on giving me grace to profit from the blood he has shed for me.

So it is in this world, where so many offenses and blasphemies are committed against the honor of Christ our Lord, of his saints, and of his Church: God in his goodness continues to pour out his blood, the token of his love, on all those who wound him. He allows them to strike such heavy blows that at length, when they have dealt him some fearful blow (for many there is now no other remedy), we enter into ourselves and become aware of our hardheartedness and find that most pure and innocent blood which can cure it.[242]

121 While I was meditating thus on the blood of Jesus Christ, the spotless Lamb, I experienced the great power of the Christian

---

[240] Here, Favre's reasoning seems to be the following: The glory of the saints, which essentially consists in the vision of God, would receive an accidental increase through Favre's desire to praise God in all his works. The blessed would then recognize in that praise, as in the mirror of their souls, the image of him who glorifies them by finding his glory in them. His reasoning seems oversubtle and farfetched, but these qualities come from a zeal to analyze as clearly as possible the nature of the relations that exist between the different members of the Mystical Body. For the idea of accidental glory, see §91 above and §393 n. 46 below.

[241] According to Ludolph the Carthusian (*Vita Christi Domini,* pars II, caput 64), the blind Longinus recovered his sight when he pierced the heart of Christ with his lance. Converted on the spot, he spent thirty-eight years living a kind of monastic life at Caesarea in Cappadocia. In mentioning this latter point, Favre shows that he is following Ludolph rather than the Pseudo Bonaventure.

[242] See §77 and §115 above.

meekness that Christ taught us by word and deed. There is no more effective way to overcome harshness, anger, and whatever is contrary to charity than if you are so meek that you do not return blow for blow but, welcoming everyone with kindness and meekness of heart, leave your attacker free to do what he pleases. At long last, otherwise never, his heart will yield and soften at the sight of your patience and the depth of your goodness.[243]

O how harsh I am, so excessively hardhearted, slow to believe and listen to Christ the Lord, who has so often shed his tears and his blood for me in vain!

122 O my soul, wretched and exceedingly hardhearted, why is it that those tears of Christ, shed for you at his entrance into this world and at his first impressions of this mortal life of yours, did not move you to pity when first you came to understand their significance? For you he came forth from his heavenly Father into this world and marks with his tears the first pitiable evils of this life. But you gazed at them unmoved; you waited until he shed his blood. And this he did; at his circumcision he shed both blood and tears, a child only eight days old, but even then you were not moved to pity. Why? Might it have been because he was still but a child, appearing to you in the condition of mere flesh and bodiness,[244] and so you wait for signs of your God's inner awareness? But then, seeing that he wept over the death of Lazarus and that those tears were shed for you and over you, why then did you remain unmoved? What are you waiting for? I await, you will say, and have awaited signs of greater suffering from my God so that being moved to pity by them I may feel them more deeply.

Oh, how wretched you are and lamentable for such hardheartedness! See, then, and understand the tears the Lord sheds over the coming destruction of Jerusalem and its exceedingly great ingratitude; likewise, those tears he shed on the cross as he breathed forth his

---

[243] This is a meditation on Christ's shedding of blood on the cross (§120–§122) considered first from an apostolic, then from a personal, point of view. It describes Favre's conception of the apostolate: The great spiritual need of the world can be met only by recourse to the heart of Christ, the fount of love and healing. In §121 he considers the proper attitude for the Christian to adopt in face of opposition and criticism; he himself experienced them both and found them particularly trying and painful.

[244] During the fifteenth and sixteenth centuries the child, especially the child Jesus, took on an importance wholly lacking in previous ages. Children began to be considered as subjects worthy of artistic representation and of study in themselves as full human beings. Favre, sensitive to all that has to do with the infancy of Christ, is at the same time a man of his age—an age which saw in the suffering of children something "at the level of flesh and bodiliness," not yet fully human. See Philippe Aries, *Centuries of Childhood: A Social History of Family Life* (New York, 1965).

spirit.[245] If they do not suffice or if you find yourself needing the shedding of the Lord's blood more than his tears, gaze on his bloody sweat in which the two are mingled together.[246] Besides this, gaze on the flow of blood from all parts of his body as a result of his bonds, the blows, the scourging, and the crowning with thorns—all this for your sake as if you alone existed.

But if these signs still do not move you, go within to his veins[247] and consider how on the cross all of them are emptied of the pure blood of the immolated Lamb.[248]

If all this is not enough, receive the blood most pure in itself and receive separately the water that flowed from the Lord's side—and with Longinus heal your soul, and do not try to find any greater signs of the divine goodness in sufferings borne by his humanity, because, rising from the dead after this, Christ suffers no longer.[249]

▸ October 3

123 On the vigil of the feast of St. Francis, as I was saying the office (postponed) of a martyr to whom I have had great devotion for a long time, I offered Mass for my relatives both living and dead and for all those who left our family home, and then for all the families of my brethren in the Society of Jesus Christ. While I was doing so, the memory of our debt to our natural parents came back to me with intense emotion. Hence it seemed to me an excellent practice to invoke the guardian angels of those families: those now alive, those passed away, and those yet to come. In addition I should invoke, after the Blessed Mary, the holy men and women who watch over those families of ours, have done so in the past, and will do so in the future. Under God, it is

---

[245] The Gospels do not mention tears, but this text from Heb. 5:7 was so interpreted: "Who, in the days of his flesh, with a strong cry and tears, offering up prayers and supplications to him that was able to save him from death, was heard for his reverence" (DV).

[246] Luke 22:44.

[247] Literally, come to the veins *(veni usque ad venas)* through which the blood circulates—the interior life. About the blood which purifies, see §270.

[248] The emptying of Christ's veins signifies the giving up of his interior life, the supreme sign of his love. John 19:31–37.

[249] Rom. 6:9. St. Gertrude (1256–1301), a Cistercian of the monastery of Helfta, belonged to the mystical school of the thirteenth-century spiritual renaissance of the Cistercians which centered on a loving union with Christ. Her three Latin works were influential: *Exercitia spiritualia sanctæ Gertrudis* (Paris, 1875), pp. 688, 694, 696—a set of seven affective meditations. There is an English translation, *The Exercises of St. Gertrude,* edited and translated by a Benedictine of Regina Laudis (Westminster, Md. 1960).

to these holy people that we should give thanks; through them should we seek pardon for the many sins committed by those families up to the present time, without limiting ourselves to the countless benefits they have received; through them must we hope for the various graces and blessings they now need and will have need of in time to come.

From the bottom of my heart, I wished also that through this special sacrifice I might obtain pardon for all the sins I have ever committed by neglecting to plead on behalf of my brethren whenever I found it possible or was given the opportunity—in prayer, by petition and thanksgiving, or by requests in their favor or in favor of those for whom they themselves are bound to do the same.[250]

124 After communion I felt a great desire—such as I had felt on the previous day at the same moment—that Christ, whom I had received, might enclose me with him altogether within myself so that I might dwell with him and work with him at the refashioning and the restoration of myself.[251] I begged too that he who possesses in himself infinite modes of being,[252] at least accidentally, might have the goodness to renew in me my own being itself, my life and its operations. This would ensure the renewal of my relationship with him and with all others, give me a new mode of life and a new way of setting about all my activities. So, day by day, he would go on changing me for the better —he who alone possesses existence, life, and act. These are in themselves immutable.

▸ *October 4*

125 On the day of St. Francis, among the other holy desires experienced in my prayers and meditations, I had this wish above all and asked, feeling an attraction both filial and spiritual, that the blessed Francis and the other saints might remember me through the virtue of the Mass from that time on and do so with the same efficacy as if I had, with great distress of heart, sought the same from each one of them at

---

[250] Favre was acquainted with the families of a number of Jesuits: Laínez's father and sister and Peter Canisius's mother (*MonFabri*, pp. 127, 152, 435 and 253–255).

[251] See §104 above.

[252] In himself unique, Christ possesses by his presence and his operation in the world—and therefore through the relation of all beings to him—infinite modes of being which are accidental links with all things. This multiplicity, which depends on the multiplicity of beings, is contained in Christ's simplicity; it is, as it were, the riches of his "divine humanity" so often referred to in the *Memoriale*. Favre wishes for a renewal based on a participation in that wealth which will renew all his relations with others.

the moment of his death in these words: "Remember me when you come into the kingdom of Christ."[253]

126 Reflecting the same day on how to pray well and on different ways of doing good,[254] I wondered how holy desires in prayer are, as it were, ways of disposing us to perform good works and, on the other hand, how good works lead us to good desires. I then noted, indeed clearly perceived, that, by seeking God in good works through the spirit, one will more readily find him afterwards in prayer than if one had sought him first in prayer so as to find him subsequently in good works, as is often done.

For he who seeks and finds the spirit of Christ in good works makes much more solid progress than the person whose activity is limited to prayer alone. So then, to possess Christ in our actions or to possess him in our prayer often amounts to either an "effective" or an "affective" possession.[255]

You must therefore strive hard to subdue yourself, to mortify and conquer yourself, making every effort to become capable of undertaking all kinds of good works. That is the best preparation for mental prayer, as you will often experience. Your life should have something of Martha and Mary in it. It should apply itself both to prayer and to holy works. In short, it should unite the active and contemplative lives.[256] But if you practice one for the sake of the other and not for itself, as often happens —that is, if you intend your prayer to be a means of improving your pastoral efforts or if your efforts are for the sake of your prayer (I mean if you have the idea that you must make each exist for the sake of the other)—then you will do better, as a general rule, to direct all your prayers to the storing up of good works rather than vice versa, which is to have as the purpose of your activity the gaining of the treasure of prayer.

It would be otherwise with a person leading a purely contemplative life. His purpose is to work at laying up the treasure of divine

---

[253] Luke 23:42.

[254] §126–§129 are a series of reflections on prayer and action.

[255] This *affective* spirituality was taught by Ignatius to his followers, for his own experience had shown him that pastoral work nourished his affective prayer and this in its turn aroused pastoral zeal. Favre's restatement of this conclusion is worth noting: "By seeking God *in good works through the Spirit,* one will more readily find him afterwards in prayer than if one had sought him first in prayer so as to find him subsequently in good works" (italics ours).

[256] The Society of Jesus was destined for the mixed life: a union of contemplation and action. The mixed life was much reflected on and discussed in the early days of the Society. Nadal looked on it as "a superior kind of active life" *(vita activa superior)*. See *ConsSJComm,* Index II, p. 407, under Contemplative life and active life.

knowledge and love, for he has not such a great need of asking for himself at all times those graces which are necessary for those in the active life.

127 These latter, indeed, have manifold functions and manifold duties to others. There are a thousand things below them, above them, near at hand, within them, before and behind them, to their right and to their left, and in other places—all of which require different virtues in the person engaged in the active apostolate. Hence, they should be gifted with many talents, for without these they will turn out failures. They need a particular kind of patience, humility, and charity, accompanied by other virtues, for work with the poor and the sick, with sinners, or their persecutors or others. They need another kind of virtue for dealing with inferiors or even superiors and still other kinds of these same virtues or others for dealing with this or that situation. Their labor soon brings them face to face with the multitude of needs that exist, including their own, which require the power of God, his unction, and the outpouring of his various gifts,[257] not alone for themselves but for those others whose welfare is their concern. To bring efficacious aid to our fellow men, we need many spiritual lights; we need our eyes, our ears, and our other senses; and to add to these we need physical vigor, devotedness, generosity, zeal, and other qualities of soul and body. And when we find ourselves destitute of these, we can soon see the double disadvantage: to ourselves because of our failings; to our fellow men because the care and support they receive, instead of being constant, become indifferent or worse, or even bad in many ways.

128 To this end, therefore, will our prayers be directed more frequently than to its contrary, which is having prayer as the end of our activity. I should state this as a general rule, having regard to the ideal aimed at in this kind of mixed life.[258] Considering the matter more closely, however, and taking particular cases, things could turn out otherwise; for we often pray for the success of this or that good work while, on the other hand, we devote considerable effort to attain what we have sought in prayer. But we should not only devote ourselves to seeking Christ's aid for purely spiritual practices such as contemplation and prayer, both mental and affective, for the purpose of performing them well and even very well, but also put forth our best efforts to find

---

[257] The expressions "power of God," "unction," and "gifts" indicate the active presence of the Holy Spirit.

[258] The "mixed life" was attacked again and again in the early days of the Society and had to be defended often and vigorously. A recurring and practical problem was how much prayer, how much pastoral work?

the same grace in our external labors, in our vocal prayers, and even in private conversations or in sermons to the people.[259]

But it is true that many things can easily be said and done without any spiritual movement, especially if they are not things that must be done or said against one's own inclination, whether innate or acquired, or against one's custom or one's will. For at these times our need of the spirit appears more clearly evident, and without it we too often quit.[260] In all situations, however, the spirit must be sought for the understanding and the more prompt willing of the good that lies in these labors, especially in those I referred to as being more difficult and more opposed to the old man.[261] These, since they have their source in a greater spirit, obtain in their execution a spirit greater than that acquired in less irksome labors. They will lead you to perceive what is in man and why you need the spirit of God, and they will do this better than those things which are done easily and without opposition. This happens in both mental and affective prayer, which requires a special actual spirit; otherwise the mind goes completely astray and does not pursue the aim proposed in prayer.

129 With regard to works, we must note three kinds to which we should especially apply ourselves: those concerned with ourselves, those concerned with our neighbor, and those concerned with God himself.

The following concern ourselves: penitential works done for our own mortification or self-renunciation, for our chastisement, or for the sake of atonement. These are fasts, pilgrimages, the discipline, vigils, the giving up of certain material comforts or even wealth, and whatever tires out the body and prevails over the self-interest of the will.

The following concern the neighbor: whatever helps, consoles, and comforts him, such as almsgiving and all the other spiritual and corporal works of mercy. Although all the works mentioned tend as well to God, those refer directly to him which have to do with the honor and worship of God and the veneration of his saints and of divine things: offerings, the adornment of churches, beautiful ceremonies, costly lights, and so forth.

In the exercise of the first of these three kinds of works, you become in some way your own enemy in order to conquer yourself. In the second kind you become in the end useful to your neighbor. In the third you manifest your devotion to God himself and to holy and sacred

---

[259] See reference to VatCouncil on §52 n. 102 above.

[260] Ignatius understood clearly what was to be done in these situations. *SpEx*, [6], [16], [13], [83–87], [317–322].

[261] Luke 14:12–14; Eph. 5:15–21; 6:5–9.

things. It is also possible to qualify the first kind as having to do with penitential works, the second with works of charity, the third with works of piety; yet all these can be in a true sense termed penitential, charitable, and pious works.[262]

▸ October

130 As I was about to say Mass one day in the Church of the Holy Cross for its deceased benefactors and founders, my general intention being the entire city of Speyer, I decided to say the Mass of the Holy Cross. My reason was the presence in that church of a certain crucifix which, once held in great veneration, had by the power of God rekindled faith and aroused devotion. It had even worked many miracles because the same faith was living in many at the time. The Lord then gave me a very good spirit and a feeling of great devotion to that cross which led me to venerate it and, together with it, every standard and every sign of the cross. I perceived too with trustful faith the wonderful power of the cross against the demons, and therefore I desired it to be possible that I might always bear that cross (I mean that material cross) in my soul, in a real but spiritual way through faith and hope.[263] With faith I had the same wish about holy water and about everything sanctified by the word of God or marked with the sign of the cross; also about representations of the crucified Savior, the Blessed Virgin, and the saints, about the relics of their holy bodies, and about other things of that kind.

131 I went as far as desiring that the whole material fabric of a church, with all the visible signs in it that awaken piety, might enter spiritually into my soul and remain always in me as realities. I wished to dwell in a spiritual manner in a church, gazing with faith and devotion on all the sacred objects about me and especially on the very body of the Lord there reserved with all the fullness of his divine attributes—for Christ is there present in his body, and that body is the corpo-

---

[262] Favre makes distinctions here for the sake of accuracy. Is there a hint of anti-Protestant polemic? See §67.

[263] This long entry (§130–§133) deals with two further aspects of devotion *(devotio)* as Favre understands them. Can sacred though material things be objects of devotion? What is the link between devotion and faith? The celebrated crucifix aroused so much devotion in himself that he desired to possess it always in his soul "in a real but spiritual way through faith and hope"—not only that crucifix but also all other sacred objects. In Favre there is not the slightest trace of magic or superstition in the use of the sacraments, sacramentals, sacred images, and other sacred objects. All of them serve to stir up religious feelings; above all, they serve to strengthen the theological virtues. They are means, not ends. O'Leary, "Discernment," p. 65; see also §308.

real dwelling place, the veritable temple, of the divine power in its totality and of all the fullness of the Godhead.

I saw it clearly, and I felt it too in spirit: Christ wills not only that we possess him through faith, confident of his protection, but also that we grasp with our minds and handle with our hands, as it were, all that derives its virtue from him and which, in accordance with our faith and piety, has been prepared for us by the benevolence of God in order to lead us to him. He urges us along that way, bestowing devotion on the lowly and simple, a holy attachment to these things, and faith in them. And this faith he would by no means grant did it not tend to his honor and our benefit.[264]

132 It happens now and then that God causes us to experience something of his power through holy things, though at the moment we do not advert to it with faith, so that only afterwards do we say: "This place, this object, is holy, and I was unaware of it."[265] Faith and devotion awaken after the event when we have seen what God has worked in the first instance without us and without an act of faith on our part. So it is evident that God of his own accord wills to honor these things and that he is not content with communicating his power to us directly; it is evident too that everything does not find its source in our faith.[266]

O my soul, what steadfast joy would be yours (seeing that of ourselves we are powerless to introduce these things into our souls) could you but grasp and possess not only the name of Jesus Christ our Lord, in whom is the fullness of salvation,[267] but also the name of that very real person the Virgin Mary, the Mother of God! If you could but delight in the name and in the sign of the cross! If you could but keep in your mind St. Peter's name and above your heart his person itself in a spiritual manner, no doubt then but that you would experience the

---

[264] Favre's desire for union with God is so intense that he wishes to possess spiritually in his soul "the material fabric of a church with all the visible signs in it that awaken piety." This unusual desire will seem less so in the light of the whole paragraph. Sacred objects, in some way signs of what they represent, make their way into the soul and there awaken faith. So the use and contemplation of these objects is particularly suited to "lowly and simple folk." The paragraph sheds some light on Favre's understanding of *sentire*.

[265] Gen. 28:16; Exod. 3:5; art. "Holy," *DBibTheol,* pp. 236–239, and John L. McKenzie, *Dictionary of the Bible* (London-Dublin, 1965), pp. 365–367 (abbreviated hereafter as *DBib*).

[266] The Protestant position was that man's salvation began with his faith and his trust *(fiducia)*. Favre limits himself to reflecting that, at least sometimes, this does not correspond to the truth. See §289 n. 127 below.

[267] Acts 4:12.

power of the divinity that dwells in these things and in these names![268] If indeed you loved them and bore their likeness in your heart, your influence with God and with his holy angels and saints would be quite different. Quite otherwise would you appear to the demons and the other wicked spirits who strive relentlessly, and not without reason, to have all holy and hallowed things and all symbols of the truth blotted out from the memory of men. For they hope that, once all else has been forgotten, the memory and the very name of Christ may fade in their turn.

133 Grow therefore, O my soul, in devoted veneration of all the holy and blessed objects that have been marked by the sign of the cross. Each day exercise yourself more and more in contemplation of them. With faith and confidence in the divine power present in them, impress them, engrave them, paint them on your heart until there opens before you the way that leads to the wellsprings whence stream forth the waters of sanctification. And if it is given to you to draw somewhat from that fountainhead which is the Savior himself,[269] beware lest you disdain or do not value as highly as you should those streams that flow from it through the Mother of God, through his saints, or through all the virtues that flow from other creatures, as I said.

If the water given to you is from the fountainhead, it does not mean that its streams cease to be abundant, for they are more abundant than you deserve or are able to absorb. The water is given so that you may the better praise the fountainhead, not only for what it is in itself, but also for the many different streams that gush forth in profusion from the divine waters and have their source in them, as your own spiritual experience has taught you.[270]

134 One day as I was reflecting on these words of Christ which had come to my mind, "The bridegroom will be taken from them," and these, "Can the wedding guests mourn as long as the bridegroom is with

---

[268] A name possesses a mysterious identity with its bearer; it can be considered as a substitute for the person; it can express his activity or his destiny. Accepted with faith, it becomes a means of grace from God. See art. "Name," *DBibTheol*, p. 377; *DBib*, p. 603; and *DNTest*, p. 300.

[269] Isa. 12:3. This is the kind of devotion that Favre found useful, the one that appealed to simple folk. By his origin he was one of them himself.

[270] This passage answers a difficulty which has to do with every form of spiritual life. The difficulty had become particularly acute in Favre's day when men were in search of a spiritual religion. What is the connection between devotional practices and the knowledge of God in himself? Between the knowledge through which God gives himself and what he is in himself? For Favre, God is present in the whole sacramental order. Union with him gives rise to a familiarity which extends to the most diverse situations in life.

them?"[271] there came to me a very great sense of wonder with a spirit of tender devotion to Christ. I expressed it to him in a cry: "Lord, what is this? You call yourself a bridegroom in relation to your disciples so that they may rejoice in you as the wedding guests rejoice while the bridegroom is with them. Yet you yourself, insofar as it concerns you, do not take delight in being a bridegroom; you rather prefer to be a servant to all and the least in comparison with all, looked down on as the last and the lowliest of all. You labor; you are covered in sweat; you are reviled and despised up to the time of your passion and your condemnation to death on the cross. Yours the labors, O my Lord, that your followers may have rest; yours the afflictions that they may rejoice; and you long for death in the end that they may rise again.

"In truth, it is as the poet says: 'Sheep, you do not bear your fleeces for yourselves; bees, you do not make your honey for yourselves; birds, you do not build your nests for yourselves.'[272] For others you became the bridegroom, while for you life was a constant cross. For others you became the bridegroom; for you those others became a burden, crosses, and torments.

"May your name, which is Jesus, be blessed. Amen! And praised and exalted forever. Amen!"

135 Another day, a Sunday morning, I was distracted while saying my office, so I sought the help of God and the Blessed Virgin. I then received not a few moments of pure devotion with various interior intimations *[responsa]* which encouraged me to desire that the sustaining presence of the good spirit might be prolonged, above all in order to bring about a greater interiorization[273] of my spirit the more I read on to the end of the office. This interiorization is a kind of attraction towards the interior which is brought about by God if we ask for it and if we strive for it with all our might. By its means we gain a deeper understanding of the holy words; it causes them to strike root in us and penetrate us with their life-giving power.[274] For every word that comes

---

[271] Matt. 9:15.

[272] These lines, though missing from Virgil's works, are traditionally ascribed to him. C. Brummer, *Vitæ Vergilianæ* (Leipzig, 1912), pp. 30–31. Favre's quotation is incomplete.

[273] *Intractus:* Favre uses this word in the sense of a movement inward, a seeking of the center—the heart. It is properly a spiritual impetus or force, the source of which is God. The word is used in mystical theology, especially by the Rheno-Flemish mystics. See Maximilianus Sandaeus, *Pro theologia mystica clavis . . .* (Cologne, 1640), p. 257.

[274] A description of the ordinary conditions in which the word of God takes effect. Matt. 13:16–23 (the parable of the sower).

from the mouth of God is God's true seed; it produces and engenders within us in some way God himself, according to its power.[275]

With regard to the canonical hours, in order to make greater progress as I read on to the end, I reflected that Christ's sufferings increased and that ever greater torments were inflicted on him the nearer he approached the end of his life. For that reason I felt I should have an increasing devotion to the canonical hours so that, having reached None, I might be enabled to realize the innate power of Christ's last breath and of his death on the cross, which took place at that time of the day.

▸ *October 9*

136 On the day of St. Denis the Areopagite and his companions,[276] I found much devotion as I begged them to obtain for me a grace to come from the heavenly Father, another from the Son, another from the Holy Spirit, yet another from the Blessed Virgin, and so on from the other saints and especially from those saints I thought of as I mentioned their names in turn during my litanies.

From St. Denis himself I sought special help: to obtain for me grace that I might begin truly to sense, for my heart's good, the meaning of the words I spoke to the Lord, whether out of fear or love or out of an impulse to any other virtue I might have most need of. I sought something similar also for my eyes and for my senses of hearing, touching, tasting, and smell. Then I experienced this new desire, that at its entry into my body the most Holy Sacrament might feed and nourish the soul of my body in the way that material bread and wine feed and nourish my flesh and the body animated by my soul.[277]

▸ *October 10*

137 On the day of St. Cerbonius, bishop and confessor, as I was thinking over in turn the life and death of Jesus Christ our Lord, the words of some prayers came into my mind. So, using those words, I

---

[275] Isa. 55:10–11; 1 Pet. 1:23; John 3:9.

[276] This was one of the principal feast days in Paris, a day of great popular devotion. Favre and his companions had taken their first vows for three successive years in the crypt of the chapel at Montmartre, the spot where St. Denis was said to have been martyred. He may also have had in mind the legend according to which our Lord visited St. Denis in prison and brought him Communion (Perdrizet, *Le Calendrier*, pp. 236–239).

[277] "Soul" is taken here in its Aristotelian sense as the unifying and animating principle of the body; it explains the unity proper to the vegetative life. But that too must be transformed by the divine life. See §174.

addressed the Lord in a spirit of some tenderness: "O Jesus Christ, may your death be my life; may I learn to find life in your death. May your labors be my rest, your human weakness my strength. May your humiliation be my source of glory, your passion my delight, your sadness my joy.[278] May your abasement be my uplifting[279]—in short, may your sufferings be all I possess. For you, O my Lord, have renewed a life drifting helplessly towards death and you destroyed death, which seemed destined to remain forever, never to be dissolved."

▸ *October 11*

138 On the day I said the office of St. Mark, pope and confessor, I experienced numerous good desires. Among them was this: that whatever desires blessed Mark himself had during his lifetime for the salvation not only of the Germans but also of all the faithful might see fulfillment in our day. I asked that the same might happen with regard to all the desires of the other saints, so that someday this saying might be more universally fulfilled, "You have granted him the desire of his soul."[280] Then we shall see fulfilled not only what each saint in glory now desires[281] but also whatever pious and holy longings that saint felt during his lifetime for the honor of God and the salvation of souls.

139 The same day another desire came to me as I was about to say Mass. It was that God would deign to accept that sacrifice so that this city of Speyer might gain from it as great a degree of fruit as I and my companions could produce for it were I to remain there until my death. This desire and others like it, although it may not be fulfilled according to my mind or my will, is not without worth in the sight of God, who is its source and in whose spirit it is suggested.

140 After Mass, as I recalled how I had said it, I thought it very much worth noting that I should pray earnestly to God for a memory retentive enough to recall every spiritual exercise I have made in the past. I was to pray for this through the merits of the Lord's passion, which is our greatest memorial; secondly, for a mind attentive to the exercises I was making at the time; thirdly, for a will eagerly desiring the exercises yet to be made. Not that these three faculties work sepa-

---

[278] Phil. 2:5–9.

[279] 2 Cor. 11:7.

[280] Ps. 21 (20): 3.

[281] In Thomistic theology all the desires of the blessed soul are fully satisfied in heaven. But separated as it is from its body, it still desires to have the body share in its state of glory. Favre's extension of this idea to include the fulfillment of all holy longings "each saint felt during his lifetime" seems somewhat fanciful.

rately in such acts as these, but the memory, as I understand the matter, looks to the past, the intellect to the present, while desire reaches forward to the future.[282]

▸ October 12

141   The next day, as I was saying the office of St. Stephen, pope and martyr,[283] whose head is preserved and venerated in the church of Speyer, I felt great desires accompanied by deep faith and confidence in their fulfillment. One was, for example, that Pope St. Stephen himself might deign to be the first to open before us some door leading to spiritual things. I put my request in these words as they were given to me: "O most blessed father, most sanctified in the truth, grant through your prayers that the work I ought to be engaged in may open up," as if I had said: "It is not enough that I myself be disposed and prepared for tasks in the harvest fields of Jesus Christ. It is necessary too that these tasks be made ready and prepared for me by the grace of God."[284]

142   At the communion of my Mass, I had another desire: I wished and besought with great fervor that the most holy Sacrament might make of me an instrument obedient to him, to his Mother, to each one of the angels and saints, to all the souls in purgatory, and to all the living—an instrument that each might use according to his will. In this way I offered myself to all of them on that day.

May Christ grant that I may give what I have offered and that I may belong to all—not only belong but live and work for all, on behalf of all, in the name and place of all for the praise of God and the salvation of all, both living and dead.

---

[282] Memory, understanding, and will have each a part to play in prayer. The memory recalls the subject matter of prayer, the understanding reasons about it so as to penetrate more deeply into it and thus move the will to affective prayer. See §79. Favre's reflections on his experiences in prayer constitute the greater part of the *Memoriale*. Now since the recording of these experiences takes place after their occurrence, there is danger of either omission or distortion or even of additions because of a defective memory. This entry shows an awareness of these hazards. See O'Leary, "Discernment," pp. 51–52, nn. 29, 30.

[283] This feast was usually celebrated on August 2. Favre had put it off until October 22.

[284] 1 Cor. 16:9; Col. 4:3. God inspires interior dispositions, but they are not enough; he must also clear the ground for his laborers by removing external obstacles to the successful outcome of the work, and by so doing he confirms the interior vocation.

▸ **October 13**

143 While I was saying Mass on the day of the Seven Brothers of the Order of Minors, I felt some uneasiness lest the charity of my heart become dimmed and restricted instead of opening itself to certain persons whose defects would keep on coming to my mind. I then received this answer which spoke to me interiorly: "Be afraid rather lest the Lord whom you see before you close your heart to his joy or lest your heart narrow itself to him and to his concerns. If in your generosity you remain open to God and he to you, all other things will, as a result, quickly appear open to you and you to them. Seek therefore genuine devotion to God and his saints, and you will easily discover how to deal with your neighbor, be he friend or enemy. But if there is anything to be said or done at the time in order to reconcile yourself with your neighbor, it is by carrying out this duty in the first place that you will be reconciled with God according to these words: 'If your brother has anything against you . . .'"[285]

But we are referring here to feelings that have their source solely in fancies of the mind or in affective states, in which case there is need of a change of interior attitude alone. The reconciliation necessary is, however, of a spiritual kind, as in the case of those bitter feelings we must eradicate from our heart in order that our charity may be accompanied by feelings of kindness, forbearance, patience, and resignation, so that it does not grow angry, does not cease to trust others,[286] does not lose that hope deeply inspired in it by the principal spirit, holy, upright, and good.[287] That spirit brings devotion at once and with it all the gifts I have mentioned and, above all, a generosity of heart towards all men and to all things. In that way illusions arising from wicked thoughts or

---

[285] It is God who "opens the mind" to instruct Favre as to what he *ought* to do; it is a practical instruction, not a speculative understanding. Here he feels uneasy about his attitude to "certain persons"—we do not know who they were—and the "answer" he receives is from the Gospel: first, reconciliation with the neighbor, then with God. See Matt. 5:23.

[286] External charity is not enough; it must be internal too; it must approach the Pauline ideal (1 Cor. 13:4–7).

[287] The expression "principal spirit" derives from the Vulgate version of Ps. 50:14 *(spiritu principali confirma me);* compare "Strengthen me with a perfect spirit" (DV) and "Uphold me with a willing spirit" (RSV, Ps. 51:12). In the psalm this spirit is looked on as a spirit of conversion. Favre uses the expression here to indicate a divine influence that operates at a deeper level than superficial feeling or accidental devotion; it stirs up both genuine devotion and a desire for apostolic work. Through it we participate in God's love for men. It is the spirit to be identified in discernment (O'Leary, "Discernment," pp. 87–89; *DeCertMem,* p. 85).

even from thoughts which may be true according to human reasoning but suggested by the bad spirit vanish from the mind. And there is an end, too, of that illusion in the will caused by unwholesome or at least defective tendencies which have installed themselves in it and lead to a loss of peace.[288]

144 Beware of seeking to come victoriously out of this kind of trial by flight, that is, avoiding those things and persons which give rise to such a sudden change of heart and spirit. Rather should one draw near to them in imitation of Christ, who drew so close to his tormentors that, when pierced by a lance thrust after his death, he even poured out his blood on Longinus, that blood which is the clearest evidence of his never failing love for his enemies. The greater the hatred they showed to Christ and the more they sought to drive him away and destroy his power, the more he gave proof of his love. In a desire for close companionship and union with the one who set himself up against him and caused him suffering, he delivered himself up to him without reserve, instead of shunning him and banishing him from his presence and from his mind. He offered his body to the one who dealt him blows, and to heal him he shed his blood during his lifetime and even after his death. In this way did Christ will to make himself wholly accessible to all his enemies.

---

[288] *SpEx,* [316], [317], [332], [333].

MAINZ

144a: *In September 1542 Favre was instructed by the nuncio, Morone, to visit Mainz at the request of its cardinal archbishop, Albert of Brandenburg, who wanted him to examine some writings of doubtful theological orthodoxy. He remained in Mainz from September 15 to 28, then returned to Speyer. But he had made such a deep impression on the cardinal that he was ordered to transfer to Mainz with his two priest-novices. He arrived there about October 20. Since the journey took about two days, it would explain the absence of entries in the* Memoriale *from October 12 to 22. With his departure from Speyer, Favre's work there came to an end. He wrote to a friend, "We left with sorrow and in spirit shall remain always in Speyer" (*MonFabri, *p. 186).*

▸ *October 22*

145 On a Sunday, October 22 of this year 1542, the day before being the feast of St. Ursula and her companions,[1] having found resolution in God's presence, I made up my mind to obey the command of the very reverend archbishop-elector of Mainz.[2] He had expressed the desire that in his name, I should go with his other delegates to Trent for the council to be held there and which was due to open on the first of the coming November. With regard to this matter, I had experienced different spiritual motions and moods of despondency before I could make up my mind. But the Lord delivered me from all of them by virtue of a holy and blind obedience which does not take into account either my personal insufficiency or the magnitude and gravity of what has been imposed on me.[3] Therefore, whatever good will result from this deliberation of mine (or rather obedience) will have to be attributed—after the

---

[1] The feast of St. Ursula and her companions, the eleven thousand virgins whose bodies were venerated at Cologne, was celebrated on October 21 or 22. See *NCathEnc* 14:490.

[2] The reference is to Cardinal Albert of Brandenburg, archbishop-elector of Mainz. See §204; also *NCathEnc* 1:264–265, art. "Albrecht of Brandenburg."

[3] A typical example of how Favre set about coming to a decision. The cardinal's request had plunged him into an experience of contradictory spiritual movements; he could not decide what he should do. God then gave him grace to make an act of total abandonment in blind obedience. God's intervention here was at a deeper level than his previous spiritual experiences. For a penetrating analysis of this, see O'Leary, "Discernment," pp. 94–96.

most Holy Trinity, the resurrected Christ, and Mary the blessed Virgin of virgins—to the eleven thousand holy virgins.

146 As I was saying my breviary the same morning, I had distractions about that matter and about the answer I would have to give to the suffragan bishop.[4] I was then given a clear intimation that in order to devote myself fully to the holy prayers uttered by my tongue I should not give access during the office to other inspirations alien to the words and to the letter of the office or to the ideas suggested by quite different words or things or matters. During the recitation God may allow us to fall under the influence of a variety of spirits, a variety of ideas about many matters, a variety of apprehensions. For our part, however, we should seek after the principal spirit[5] so as to abide in it in peace. We should attach ourselves to the words, to the ideas, to the decisions, and to the desires which tend directly to God in conformity with the matter of our prayer at the time. By doing this we show whether we love and fear God alone or at least place him before all things by the fundamental inclination of our heart.

It is above all when the manifold winds of our desires and preoccupations are rising that the object of our love or of any other devout attraction for God manifests itself. If, therefore, during the office you find yourself in spirit or in mind well disposed to preach or to have this or that conversation, remember at once that you are no longer in the state required for the recitation of the office or for the fulfillment of your duties to God.

May Jesus, in his almighty goodness, grant us inspirations and preoccupations in conformity with the requirements of our varied succession of labors in preaching and in prayer. Since we have to devote our bodily energies to these in different ways and at different times, may we be given the necessary spirits and the goodwill of our friends in arranging all things in such a way that we avoid disorder in our work, our words, our thoughts, and our desires.

147 In this month of October, having business one day in a little fortified market town and lodging there in the house of a gentleman of Speyer, I arose in the middle of the night to pray and was led to converse with God, the Blessed Virgin, and the saints on behalf of these people both living and dead. I made that prayer with much fervor and with many tears. It was then granted me to recall in turn all the benefits

---

[4] This was Michael Helding, the auxiliary bishop of Mainz, who had made the Exercises under Favre at his own request (*MonFabri,* p. 187).

[5] Favre is concerned with the harmful effects of distractions on his prayer. He sees the need of personal effort, but again the aid of the "principal spirit" must be sought (§143).

I perceived these people to have received. On behalf of all I begged for forgiveness, I gave thanks, I sought various graces, I grieved at their shortcomings. I wished that whatever God by his own action or through his saints had done and was still doing in that land might be acknowledged.

I prayed, therefore: "O Lord Jesus Christ, has anyone acknowledged that goodness of yours which has conferred such plenty and prosperity on this land, which has preserved here for such a long time the sacrament of the Eucharist and the other sacraments and the words and the rites of Christian traditions? Spare these people, Lord, for they are heedless of these things; they do not seek after them; they have no knowledge of them. Spare them, for they no longer remember, according to their needs, the souls who must undergo purification. Preserve for these people, Lord, all these benefits. Do not look upon their ignorance, their negligence, their ingratitude, but rather upon Christ the Redeemer, the holy angels, and all the holy souls who on our behalf acknowledge all these blessings."

I recalled the benefits conferred on this land and the sins committed in it up to now. I included the fruits of the earth, temporal peace, the Catholic faith, churches, images, the ministers of the sacraments, and the sacraments themselves, holy water, the relics of the saints, and cemeteries. I included too the peace and the prosperity secured for the inhabitants by a long succession of temporal rulers, and the priests, bishops, and preachers they have had.

I wished them even more excellent blessings: that they might come to know all these gifts; that they might learn to recognize the good they possess in their God, and in Jesus Christ incarnate, born, circumcised, dead, and so forth, in the Virgin Mary, in the angels and saints, in sacred things, in the souls who are in purgatory, and in the Scriptures.

▸ October 25

148 On the day of SS. Chrysanthus and Daria, before I began the day's office in the morning, I found myself in a mood of great devotion as I offered myself together with what good I may ever do and whatever I am destined to endure until the day of my death. In return I wished to receive each and every degree and particle of those virtues which may be necessary or useful for myself and for everyone else at any moment and anywhere in the world for the glory of God and of his saints, for the salvation of my own soul and the souls of my fellowmen.

149 In the light of much clear knowledge about the merits of Jesus Christ, I asked earnestly for his grace. For through it he has merited for each and every one and even for all who have but a possible existence,[6] with an abundance beyond words, all the gifts together and each of those which are necessary or merely useful for the attainment of salvation in the state of grace and the state of glory in the heavenly kingdom.[7] But his absolute and signified will[8] is that all these gifts should not be distributed directly to all men by himself and the Holy Spirit alone but also by the mediators he has appointed. These differ from each other and are divided according to the differences that exist among men. So I asked the Lord that through his merits he might accept me entirely as I am, as one born of Christ, and each of my companions[9] as well. I asked that through his grace he might also accept all my good actions insofar as all of them have been already directed and preordained according to the future or possible needs of myself or of others anywhere in the world. Similarly I asked for all the virtues and all the gifts of God proper to each one. It was given me to draw down on the world the merits of the life and the passion of Christ, whose actions, even during his lifetime, reached out to all men and by reason of his infinite power assured the salvation of each to the full.

I also felt moderately keen remorse because from the beginning of my life I had neither sought nor made efforts to prepare myself, at least in those days, for the spiritual gifts I am now receiving. I thanked the Son of God, who in his eternal love prepared for me the gifts that he destined for me and which I now receive. He willed too that whatever labor and pain he suffered in his humanity should be endured for me and for my welfare. May he be eternally blessed for it!

150 I then remembered a desire which came to me on other occasions in the form of this wish: Would that I had been for the sake of Christ a servant to Adam, to Abraham, to David and to others, and lastly to the Virgin Mary, who conceived, bore, and nourished him; then a servant to the successors of the apostles, and to every pope who succeeded Peter up to the reigning pope, Paul III, whose subjects we are, and so on. In this desire of mine to have been a servant to so many for

---

[6] Everything that is possible is included in redemption. For a consideration of "contingent futures," see §156.

[7] *Patria* was used for the heavenly kingdom and *status patriae* for the state of heavenly glory, the end of exile on earth.

[8] The distinction here is between God's eternal will in himself *(voluntas absoluta)* and God's manifestation of his will through what he commands, forbids, or counsels *(voluntas signi)*. There is a trace of nominalist influence here.

[9] In the Society of Jesus. The passage is somewhat obscure. Were efforts made to amend its voluntaristic tendency? See §50 n. 95 above and §289 n. 127 below; *MellStudPat,* n. 27.

the sake of Christ my Lord, there was, on the one hand and considering his humanity alone, the desire to have been able to serve in bodily tasks and duties all the patriarchs of whom he is born according to the flesh and, on the other hand, the wish that I had been able to offer spiritual services of all kinds to the fathers of the New Testament,[10] those servants of Christ who in a certain manner have begotten him in us by their spiritual ministry.[11]

▸ October 26

151 On the day of St. Evaristus, pope and martyr, having risen from bed at about the third hour after midnight, I found great devotion in a well-disposed will and in many holy desires which inspired me to pray for the needs of others. I made a general commemoration of Christians, Jews, Turks, pagans and heretics, and also of the dead.

There came to my mind the manifold afflictions of men: their diseases, their sins and their obduracy, their moods of despair and their tears, disasters, famines, plagues, woes, and other trials; and on the other hand, as a remedy for all these, I called to mind Christ the Redeemer, Christ the Consoler, Christ the Giver of Life who enlightens and succors, the merciful and compassionate one[12] who is our Lord and our God. Calling on all the power in those titles of his, I prayed that he might come to all men and relieve their needs.

Then, with great fervor and a totally new awareness, I wished and petitioned that I might at last be allowed to become the servant and the minister of Christ, who consoles, helps, delivers, heals, liberates, saves, enriches, and strengthens. I asked that I also, through him, might be enabled to come to the aid of many, to console them and free them from many ills, to deliver and strengthen them, to bring them light not in spiritual matters alone but also (if I may be allowed the boldness of presuming it in God) in a material way, together with whatever charity can do for the soul and body of any of my fellowmen.

---

[10] The Fathers *(patres)* are the patriarchs and the prophets of the Old Testament. St. Paul called them "our fathers" (Rom. 9:5).

[11] The idea of service, and wholehearted service at that, dear to the Society, finds its original expression in the Exercises *(SpEx,* [114]). It is service through love in imitation of Jesus Christ *(DeGuiJes,* pp. 83–85).

[12] Ps. 111 (110): 4.

152 Take note:[13] on that day as often at other times, by relying on Christ rather than on yourself and on your merits, you were led to anticipate many events which cannot be brought about naturally or without a miracle, events such as healing the sick, giving sight to the blind, curing lepers, casting out demons, comforting the bereaved, and so on. Your desire extended to all these things but without vanity of spirit because the Holy Spirit visited your soul and prompted you to desire these and other things and even to hope for them, though this hope was, on other occasions, accompanied by a livelier interior motion and a greater faith. For I happen at other times to have frequently found greater faith with regard to such impossibilities, but never without my being granted to feel interiorly by charity how these holy works allow one to relieve the needs of one's neighbor, to comfort him, or to perform some work of mercy for the glory of God. It is from this faith, be it but a grain,[14] and from charity that there springs a confidence neither imprudent nor presumptuous. Otherwise it would be difficult to find a faith which might be a help to the salvation of the doer himself of such works: "For if I shall have faith enough to move mountains, but have not charity, it shall avail me nothing,"[15] even though it benefits my neighbor.

Faith, therefore, which is destined to accomplish great things for our fellowmen should be engendered and sustained in some way by charity towards them—a charity in which we grasp and, as it were, understand without any other sentiment but that of pure charity the needs of others, what can be of service to them, and how to console them. All this can be seen when our neighbor is in extreme need because on account of human imperfection we do not understand or realize the troubles and trifling needs of others as readily as we consider our own little comforts. The lover of God's glory, on the other hand, who with the aid of the Holy Spirit reflects deeply on divine realities will attain more readily through the gift of that same spirit a degree of faith which will enable him to accomplish in due time great things for the glory of God.[16]

---

[13] In §152–§158 Favre begins a series of reflections on the relation between the real and the possible. Convinced that good desires come from God, he regards his desires to be able to perform miracles as favors from God. He then proceeds to examine the connection between the virtue of faith and his desires for what is naturally impossible. He recalls Christ's words about the grain of mustard seed and Paul's warning that everything must be motivated by charity. The three theological virtues are central to these reflections on desires (O'Leary, "Discernment," pp. 58, 80, 116).

[14] Matt. 17:20.

[15] 1 Cor. 13:2–3.

[16] In this passage, unintentionally, Favre sketches himself. In a few years he exercised an apostolate of the highest quality, recognized as such by many eminent

When you yourself experience need, especially if it is extreme or casts you into a state of great or pressing affliction of heart, you have within easy reach a faith by means of which against all human hope you can obtain grace for your soul or even for your body—grace such as delivery from some misfortune or the acquisition of some necessary good which would otherwise remain unobtainable.

153 In this matter it is very necessary that a man's love for himself should not be an end in itself but that he should be totally ordered to the glory of God, to the welfare of his own spirit, and to the good of his neighbor.[17] Seek, therefore, in all things the higher gift which is charity,[18] put it into practice, grow continually in it, and do not be satisfied with that degree of it necessary for your own or your neighbor's salvation. So acting and so tending to perfection, you will acquire with ease an abundance of other graces (beyond necessary ones) for your own good and that of your fellowmen—graces such as faith and hope in regard to great things.

Seek grace for the smallest things, and you will also find grace to accomplish, to believe in, and to hope for the greatest things. Attend to the smallest things, examine them, think about putting them into effect, and the Lord will grant you greater. Extend yourself and give yourself up fully to doing what you can with a little grace from God, and the Lord will grant you a great grace that will enable you to perform even what is beyond your capabilities.

Many seek anxiously (you often did so yourself) for grace to perform good works of a more general kind while neglecting in the meantime particular tasks for which it would have been easy to find grace.[19]

154 Many dream of almost impossible undertakings and in the meantime do not give any thought to the work they have in hand.[20]

---

contemporaries.

[17] *SpEx*, [23].

[18] 1 Cor. 12:31. Charity should have the highest ideals, and whatever desires it engenders should have ideals as high. Favre always examines his desires in the light of the theological virtues, thus providing himself with a criterion which saved him from the danger of relying on purely personal inner experience (O'Leary, "Discernment," pp. 59, 117).

[19] The devil tempts holy people under the aspect of good (*SpEx*, [332]). But desires, whether for great or little things, are good if their source is seen with certitude to be God (Matt. 25:21). For Favre faith is "objective" insofar as it is closely linked with the teaching authority of the Church. So it becomes a norm against which personal experience must be measured. And the need for such a norm was never more pressing than in the age of the Reformation.

[20] Ps. 90 (89): 17.

Faith is proposed to you as a grain of mustard seed and charity as the first and greatest commandment,[21] so that, with what little knowledge and faith you possess in your intellect, you must grow more courageous in undertaking work instead of seeking always to add to your learning and develop your intelligence while you neglect the progress which comes from a will that is active.

If you have but a single talent's worth of knowledge and faith, trade with it and make it yield two.[22] Take care not to bury it in the ground, and do not say that you need two talents' worth of knowledge before you will set to work. As I said above, you must, by trading and working with that one talent, gain another one, and so forth. Do not neglect those everyday duties of yours and those that lie ready to hand, to engage instead in idle contemplation of future undertakings and of others finished long ago.

155 Desires in themselves are good, provided they come from God, through him, in him, and for him.[23] So it happens that we often desire in prayer things that will not take place, things beyond our power, and even what is naturally impossible. These desires do not displease God, for it is he who communicates them; to him are they ordered, and in his Spirit are they experienced. What is more, he rouses us to faith and hope in that way and to a charity not merely interior but which extends itself also to the good works it undertakes. God often causes us to desire and envisage the most exalted things, to place our hope in them in order that we may accomplish readily and without diffidence at least quite ordinary things.[24]

> *155a: The continuation of this paragraph is omitted in the best manuscripts. It will be found in its correct place at paragraph 409 below.*

156 You frequently judge, looking only to yourself and to outward appearances, that you are capable of nothing, that you know nothing and have no hope of helping others. But the Lord, in his Spirit, is leading you along a path entirely the opposite. He shows you countless things which with him appear easy of execution; he gives you confi-

---

[21] Matt. 22:38.

[22] Matt. 25:14–30.

[23] *SpEx*, [333].

[24] O'Leary comments as follows on this paragraph: "This pragmatic observation expresses an acute psychological insight. It also reveals something of the degree of self-knowledge attained by Favre, and of the manner in which he uses desire as motivation to spur himself on to more and greater activity. That this motivation is not always effective he admits, when he wryly comments that all too often he fails in external works, though full of interior desires and sentiments" (O'Leary, "Discernment," pp. 58, 59).

dence and much courage for many undertakings which surpass the powers of even all men. In that way you are roused up to labor instead of giving way to discouragement about everything.

But there is a great difference between the manner in which we learn from the Spirit that certain things are possible and the manner in which we are induced by a contrary spirit (whether your own or the spirit of the wicked angel) to believe they will come true in the future. Something like it happens as a rule, but to the opposite effect, when we envisage the likelihood of certain misfortunes and trials which in the event will not come about. Others are represented as imminent which never do take place, and there it is that we soon find the evil spirit, who is not only evil but a liar as well.[25] On the other hand, whatever the Spirit of the Lord foretells is sure to happen and at all times (with the exception of events relating to the contingent future and depending on causes capable of modification by the free will).[26]

157 We must be on our guard, however, against accepting as certain to happen on earth in our day what God reveals as possible without assigning a definite time. Inspired by the Lord, you will often look upon some person, city, or undertaking in a good and favorable light and will straightaway hope for much fruit from it and abundant success while, in reality, the situation is almost hopeless. (And on the other hand, troubled by the contrary spirit—the wicked one—you will be in complete despair about the matter and believe in the likely collapse of that undertaking.) In that good spirit, then, you believe that God has decided on a change for the better, though there is a chance it may never come about for want of the instruments willed by God to carry out and accomplish, regarding the undertaking, whatever your good spirit leads you to foresee and believe, hope and desire.

158 Do not put your trust therefore in those wicked spirits who represent all things in an unfavorable light as bound to have an unsuccessful outcome and who exaggerate the evil in what is turning out badly. Being evil themselves, they portray in their own likeness a situation they want and wish to make hopeless.[27] Strive rather to become an

---

[25] John 8:44. Behind this reasoning lie some of Favre's doubts about the efficacy of his apostolate. But he never loses his assurance of being guided by the Spirit of God. "For all who are led by the Spirit of God are sons of God" (Rom. 8:14).

[26] The different philosophical positions adopted in the debate on "future contingents" are irrelevant here. Favre was concerned about the freedom of the human will; some reformers tended to deny it. In this paragraph he poses the problem of how to judge his desires for what sometimes lies beyond the power of human nature (O'Leary, "Discernment," p. 115).

[27] These "wicked spirits" may be not only demons who suggest depressing and despairing thoughts about everything but also those critics of the Church, both

instrument of the good spirit, for he it is who shows you what he wishes to bring about in a situation and in the circumstances and how he is ready, with your help, to change it. And if it happens, which is likely, that a genuine inspiration from the Lord arouses a desire in you or a hope or gives you some knowledge of the spiritual ruin of a given town, people, or individual, and if you believe you see in it the will of God, you should then seek yet another motion of the spirit—I call it "another" according to its effect in you. This will enable you to pray for mercy and to believe that the will of God there manifested was not absolute but conditioned. Nor should you refrain from doing all in your power, nor should you yield to despair—even if you heard the voice of God himself telling you "This person will be damned." In us, and also in the Scriptures, God's words are often absolute, but his will is not so, by reason of circumstances which can change.[28]

▸ **October 27**

159 On the vigil of the apostles Simon and Jude, having arisen in the quiet of the night to pray, I felt strongly inspired to do my very utmost to provide for the needy and the homeless sick wandering about the city of Mainz, a hospice where they could be gathered together and given shelter so as to receive treatment there and recover their health.

I had a clear perception of my many acts of negligence and forgetfulness and my want of concern for a number of beggars whom I saw not so long ago covered with sores. I had helped them sometimes but in an offhand and reluctant manner. For although I was then without resources, I could have seen to it that others came to their aid. I could have begged from door to door some additional relief for them. I could have made known their plight to the religious authorities of the locality, to the doctors and the surgeons, the noblemen and magistrates of the

---

Protestants and Catholics, who delighted in spreading unfavorable gossip about the pope and the Roman curia and in exaggerating the defects of the Church. By so acting they did much harm to believers (*MonFabri,* p. 114).

[28] Favre describes here the tactics used by the spirits. For a commentary see O'Leary, "Discernment," p. 116. The problem touched on in the last sentence of the paragraph is classical: the reconciliation of certain events in the Bible (for instance the prophecy of Jonas about the destruction of Nineveh) with God's absolute will, immutable, and identical with his essence. This absolute will was distinguished from the *voluntas signi,* later called the conditioned will. So the statement of the divine will implies (but need not mention) the free response that will be given to it and therefore the contingency of the event which it announces. A prediction then need not come about, and what is forbidden may be committed without being in any way excluded from God's will or "unforeseen" in his decree of permission.

towns in which these sick people and others like them were living in misery.

I was strongly moved to pray to the spirits of these sick people and in a general way to the spirits of all the wretched in this world that they might become at that very time the advocates of the sick poor who still survive in this city of Mainz and elsewhere, and that they might obtain for me from God some new grace that might enable me to succor them.

▸ *October 28*

160 After Mass on the day of the apostles Simon and Jude, I found much consolation in some meditations and prayers addressed directly to God himself: now to the Father, now to the Son, now to the Holy Spirit, and also to the humanity of our Lord Jesus Christ. That series of reflections, prayers, petitions, and acts of thanksgiving[29] brought me much more solid consolation than prayers which have as their object the salvation of others or the invocation of the saints. Up to now I was more often visited by the Lord in this latter kind of prayer than in those which are directed to the immediate love and knowledge of God himself. But it is more than enough for me that so great a Lord and God should communicate himself to me through and in his saints for my own progress and the salvation of my neighbor.[30]

As for loving my neighbor the more slothful I am in my deeds, the more profuse become my feelings. In other words, the less effort I put into the work I do, the more I am worked upon and tormented by various desires and feelings of attraction for the salvation and progress of others. So it happens that I am too frequently remiss in the performance of my external tasks while inwardly I overflow with desires and affections.

161 May the infinitely good and great God[31] direct, set right, order, and purify all things according to the gracious purpose of his will and make me seek not only who he is in himself but also what he wants of me.

He is infinite in every way: infinitely above the comprehension and understanding of a created being, infinitely prior to every created capacity, infinitely beyond every created intellect, infinitely before all

---

[29] Phil. 4:6; 1 Tim. 2:1.

[30] For the relation between the wellspring and the streams that flow from it, see §133.

[31] *Deus optimus maximus,* one of the ritual references to Jupiter in pagan antiquity and dear to the humanists of the 16th century.

created beings, infinitely future to all created beings, and infinitely deep-seated in every creature, and so on.[32] This he is in his substance.

But when he wills to give orders, he is so humble and sets such limits and bounds to his commandments that not one of his obligatory precepts is beyond the powers of any man however weak, aided as a man is by the grace available to him and which he can more easily draw upon than upon his own powers.[33] God commands and makes obligatory nothing that is not within or even inferior to man's powers, nothing that is beyond the limits of man's capability with regard to what is beneath him, behind him, and ahead of him.

For this reason alone God is highly to be praised, who, though having nothing in him but what is infinite and without limit, is yet content with what our efforts can accomplish; for, though limited and circumscribed on all sides, our efforts are aided by the grace and gifts he grants us. He does not even require us to exert ourselves to the limit of our capabilities, our knowledge, and our willpower. May he be blessed for ever and ever!

▸ *October 29*

162 On the Sunday after the feast of SS. Simon and Jude, my spirit was seized with a sudden dread from which I was then gradually delivered and restored to the serenity that comes from the good spirit. I then became aware of these consoling words: "He who knows how to take away the fear of evil knows too, and has power enough for it, how to ward off the evils which give rise to these states of fearfulness and anxiety in souls. He whose nature it is to give good hope in time of misfortune[34] knows also how to grant the selfsame reality which is the object of that hope. May he therefore be blessed, who is able to mitigate equally the hardships of life itself and the afflictions of our souls and who has no more difficulty in granting complete success than he has in giving merely a hope of such success."

---

[32] In height, in depth, before and behind (in the future and in the past), God has no limits. He transcends all, is immanent in all things; he totally eludes our grasp. This symbolic terminology (height, depth, before, behind) to express the divine immensity is very old. It is found in St. Augustine (*Confessions* 1:3, 4).

[33] God always yields to great faith in him; either he grants what is asked of him or he gives grace to overcome difficulties.

[34] Good hope *(bona spes)* is a biblical expression (Wisd. 12:19; 2 Thess. 2:16). It designates not only the quality of a hope which is founded on faith but also the blessings it allows us to hope for.

▸ *November 1*

163   On the Feast of All Saints I felt a great desire that this feast and solemn celebration on earth in memory of all the heavenly host might have on that day a corresponding celebration in heaven, with mercy and compassion, in memory of all the inhabitants of this world and especially of those who are sinners. I desired the celebration to be such that not a being on earth, not a soul in purgatory would go unremembered in heaven by the saints and that all the souls in purgatory would do the same. My desire was all the greater because each saint can see mirrored in the divinity[35] and so call to mind every single one of those on earth.

▸ *November 2*

164   On the day of the Souls,[36] as I was saying Mass and already during my preparation for it, I felt a great devotion to the dead from the beginning to the end of my Mass such as I had never experienced before on that day. It was all due to a spiritual motion which moved me to compassion for the dead with a great shedding of tears. I thought of my father, my mother, and my relatives, my deceased brethren in the Society, our benefactors, and the relatives of all my brothers.[37] All those who had been commended to the Blessed Virgin Mary came to my mind,[38] as well as many saints who are particularly dear to me, and the angels, who themselves wish for special friends in this life, which is for acquiring merit.

165   Being strongly moved in spirit to genuine humility, I was to some extent consoled by a feeling which was a kind of answer to my

---

[35] The image of the mirror designates God himself inasmuch as he is the source of all beings. They can be known in him by an act of contemplation that is totally absorbed in him.

[36] *Dies animarum,* the Day of the Souls or All Souls' Day in English. In those days it was the official title of the feast of the Commemoration of All the Faithful Departed, celebrated on November 2.

[37] By July 1533 his mother was already dead; his father was still living (§13). On his return to Savoy in 1541, his father too seems to have been dead, because none of the witnesses to his brief stay make any mention of him (*MonFabri,* pp. 706–802). The passage is one of Favre's very rare comments on his family, a tender and loving remembrance of his dead relatives and of his dead companions in the Society: Master Jean Codure (§15 n. 27 above), who died on August 29, 1541, and the bachelor Diego de Hozes (§17 n. 29 above), who had laughed all night long from joy as he lay chained in prison at Padua. He died in that town from overwork towards the end of 1538.

[38] The dead and the dying were entrusted to the special care of the Blessed Virgin, as we know from the prayers of the rosary.

perpetual hunger and thirst to serve Christ and to imitate him in the salvation of souls. The words which accompanied the said feeling were these: "If you are not worthy to serve Christ himself, the Lord of Lords,[39] or do not deserve to work in the harvest field of souls,[40] take comfort at least in seeking out what you could do for Christ in the service of some master who is inferior to him—for instance, by venerating a saint who has no official cult[41] or by helping the suffering souls in purgatory." This last is a great work, and it was the sole duty of some in days gone by.[42]

166 On that same day of the Souls, having said None immediately after my midday meal, I experienced great devotion. I was given to know in various ways through a holy enlightenment how men could be divided into five classes.[43] The first comprises those in heaven; they are absolutely perfect and possess total happiness. The second comprises the souls in purgatory, detained there for a time in the severest of torments and suffering the keenest remorse. The third is made up of the souls of those children who died in a state of original sin and are in limbo, where they suffer the loss of all the benefits that Christians can acquire through Christ, though they do not in any sense undergo torments either within or without, either now or ever. The fourth comprises those who are condemned to the pains of hell, undergoing extreme sufferings in every possible way now and for eternity. The fifth comprises those who walk midway between the hope of heaven and the fear of hell, having in their own hands the power of saving or damning themselves. This latter they can cause of themselves alone; the former

---

[39] See Deut. 10:17; Apoc. 17:14; 19:16; 1 Tim. 6:15.

[40] This phrase seems to refer to Favre's state of mind as he thought of what he was unable to accomplish in Speyer because of his departure from there and in Mainz because he was due to leave for Trent. He makes a sorrowful comment on these leave takings in a letter to Ignatius: "Our Lord knows why I do not deserve to be left long in the same place. They always summon me away at the coming of the fine weather and of harvest time" (*MonFabri,* p. 187).

[41] *Sanctus privatus*: the term refers to persons venerated for their holy lives and whose names do not appear in any official calendar of saints but who are prayed to and looked upon as such by Favre. One of these was his master, Pierre Velliard (§28).

[42] This was the main, perhaps exclusive, work of some religious orders in the tenth century. It quickly developed with the extension to the whole Church of the Commemoration of the Dead. Prayer for the dead is founded on the doctrine of the Communion of Saints (See *NCathEnc* 4:671, art. "Prayers for the Dead").

[43] Men are divided here according to their spiritual state, the division having something in common with *SpEx,* [71].

comes from the grace of God which is in us as our own, or better, more our own than our free will.[44]

Thinking over these five classes, I felt various interior movements, above all with regard to the souls in purgatory and those who are still living in this world.[45]

167 Also I felt great desires that the saints might pray for us—they who have so much power in their state of glory—that the souls in purgatory might offer prayers for us amidst those remorseful lamentations of theirs which can benefit them no more but which, did they come from mortal hearts, could not but merit for them in the briefest of moments all the happiness of heaven. These souls then can do much for us (more than we can tell) if we retain our faith and if, instead of treading underfoot what is holy,[46] we value it highly in the light of a faith which is the conviction of things not yet visible.[47] May Jesus grant that these lamentations of theirs be admitted into his presence on our behalf.

I felt also that it was an excellent thing to invoke the souls in purgatory in the presence of God to this end, that we might be given a true knowledge and awareness of our sins, diligence in doing good, concern to bring forth fruit that befits repentance and, in a general way, all those graces the lack of which now causes those souls so much suffering.

▸ *November 3*

168 The morning after All Souls' Day, I noted that many things came to me about the way I understood a certain bareness[48] of my soul and my spirit. For this reason I begged the Lord, my whole heart and mind in a state of some fervor, that through the intercession of all the saints he might be so good as to clothe me in the garment of purity, innocence, chastity, and spotlessness as a protection against all the ardors that lead to the stains and defilement of an unchaste life. I asked also to be clothed in the garment of burning love for him and for my

---

[44] Lack of self-confidence increases confidence in God, who dwells within us and whose grace is more efficacious than our will. See §161 above.

[45] Those who are in need of Favre's aid.

[46] Heb. 10:29 (DV). The text refers to apostasy. See also Matt. 7:6. A clear reference to the reformers' rejection of purgatory and of prayers for the dead. To Favre this is tantamount to contempt for sacred things.

[47] Heb. 11:1.

[48] "Bareness" *(nuditas)* here means the absence of virtues *(DeCertMem,* p. 38 n. 2). See Ps. 79 (78):11. This versicle was the introit of the Mass of many martyrs in pre-Vatican II liturgy.

neighbor as a protection against all those evil chills threatening from outside, from human perversity and opposition of every kind.[49]

169 I had a clear enough understanding of the nakedness of the souls in purgatory. From it I learned that I should reflect on their sufferings more than I had done up to this so as to have compassion on them. More than anything else it can be said of them that they are utterly naked, because they undergo all their sufferings in a spirit and in a soul divested of a body. Just as a soul feels true consolation more when it is separated from its body than when it is united to it (if the body is not yet glorified), so the sufferings of the separated soul are more bitter than if it were in its mortal body (if the body is not yet in the most wretched state).[50]

Suffering which penetrates directly into the soul and the spirit is keener and pierces far more deeply than that which affects it through the medium of the body. This mortal body with its senses reduces and blunts the physical and even the spiritual pains received through organs or through the soul's faculties when they are inserted in the body. So the pains do not affect the soul with the same intensity as if everything took place independently of the body and outside it.

170 I noted as well that a person should be very much on his guard against allowing himself to be penetrated by those chilling winds that come from overcareful observation of the defects of others. That often causes us to lose hope of their salvation, or it destroys our esteem for them and our trust in them as well as the love and the charity we once had for them. Through warmth of spirit we must rise not only above our perception of these faults but also, as far as possible, above those faults themselves as they are in others so as to vanquish evil by good.[51] In spite of their defects, we should remain on good terms with others and continue devoting our attention to them.

For this reason it is very necessary to consider the details of each particular case not as they are in themselves but as they are in God,

---

[49] These "ardors" are impure passions whose source is within. They lure a person into external relationships in which charity plays no part. The "states of coldness" designate a cooling of charity caused by external opposition. This coldness turns a person in on himself and puts an end to all love for God and for the neighbor.

[50] What effect in a soul does separation from its body have? Favre is aware that the feelings of the soul are limited by the body, whether that body be glorified or damned. "For a perishable body weighs down the soul, and this earthy tent burdens the thoughtful mind" (Wisd. 9:15). His point is that the soul in a state of separation from the body as it is before the Last Judgment finds its joy or its pain increased or intensified by the absence of the body.

[51] Rom. 12:21.

indications of his good pleasure.⁵² For he who prefers to contemplate these things as they are in themselves, with a growing awareness of their defective and troublesome nature, such a one will soon become disturbed and cold in manner. He despairs of success and is driven, full of disgust and sadness, to take refuge in flight. Further, he is easily deceived, is ready to judge whatever happens as for the worst, and quickly becomes filled with suspicion.⁵³

▸ November 4

171 On another day during the octave of All Saints, I began to feel a new and somewhat lively desire to press forward⁵⁴ to whatever lies ahead, forgetful of what lies behind. For example, after doing or saying anything, thinking over or reflecting on anything, I should compel my understanding and my will to continue applying themselves to and reaching out towards what remains to be done, towards what is better, higher, more useful, and more acceptable to God.

172 While I was saying the office of that day and then during my Mass, I was granted in part to strive at all times for a closer interior attention to the words I was pronouncing and to penetrate more deeply into them, fearful lest my soul and my spirit might be drawn to other things instead of trying to make more and better progress.

173 I noted also that it is often an advantage to us not to experience great devotion. We must learn to labor on with a little grace or, in other words, to cooperate with a little grace from God so as to make the best of what is in us and depends on our efforts. Quite often it is God's will that, with the help of a small grace, you try to preserve at least some keen desire or some generous impulse to accomplish such and such a work or to bear such and such a spiritual fruit. On occasion he inspires in you a wholesome fear which, if it persists, is often better for you than a fervor that is the result of great devotion, for we should prize highly not devotion alone but also the longing quest for it and even our sorrow at not possessing any of it. All these must grow in us just as good seeds once planted must grow and develop until the fruit is harvested.⁵⁵

---

⁵² *Signa beneplaciti* are the signs through which God manifests his will. See §158.

⁵³ This disgust and sadness *(acedia)* are spiritual maladies which were given much attention during the whole monastic tradition. Mellinato looks on the passage as an excellent example of introspective analysis and a help in the development of certain aspects of discernment. *MellConfess,* n. 393; *NCathEnc* 1:83–84.

⁵⁴ Phil. 3:13. The idea of "pressing forward" *(se extendere)* in doing good occurs often in Favre.

⁵⁵ The "little grace" *(parva gratia)* is sensible devotion, which is an "accidental" grace, and Favre distinguishes it more carefully here from "essential" grace—that

It is good for the spirit to seek, to ask, to knock at the door—even without feeling much devotion. So "we make our way," we sow in hardship and in tears;[56] I mean we make our way to God himself, and when at last the sheaf of devotion or consolation is ready to hand, "we return"; and it is as if we came from God the Consoler whom we have found at the end of our search.[57]

174 That saying of St. Paul according to which we are not sufficient even to think anything of ourselves as of ourselves[58] does not mean that we can do nothing of ourselves as of ourselves, but that we are not sufficient for a certain good. God therefore must anticipate, accompany, and follow whatever comes from ourselves as of ourselves (insufficient though it is), so that even in the smallest things we should attribute the sufficiency to him. Our own activity is indeed necessary, cooperating with the grace of God and from it receiving its sufficiency even in the first perception of the good under consideration.[59] Let no one therefore say that he cannot do the good always and everywhere, for our sufficiency comes from God—only that we do not have to wait for it as if it did not exist in us.[60] On the contrary, it is in us, though it does not come from us; grace stands at the door ceaselessly knocking; always and everywhere it forestalls us, awaiting our working with it with what does come from us (though given to us, of course, in our very creation) and by other means.[61]

---

which maintains us in a state of union with God. We must value devotion enough to desire and search for it when it is absent, and we must value too our sorrow at not possessing it. This is in accordance with Ignatius's advice, "ever intent on what I desire" (*SpEx*, [76]). And these desires, fears, and sorrows—all concerned with devotion—must grow in us like seeds in the ground (Matt. 7:7). Although sensible devotion played a large part in Favre's interior life, his attitude to it was one of caution. O'Leary, "Discernment," p. 66; *DeCertMem*, p. 85; §153, §154.

[56] Ps. 126 (125): 5–6.

[57] The image of growth from seed to harvest is extended; the end of this passage is an interpretation in mystical terms of the psalm referred to in §173 n. 56 above.

[58] 2 Cor. 3:5, Latin Vulgate.

[59] John 15:5; 1 Cor. 12:3. Revelation and salvation are completely gratuitous. Rahner, *Teaching*, p. 382 ff., art. "Justification"; Denzinger, *Enchiridion Symbolorum* (Barcelona, 1951), p. 799.

[60] Luke 17:21.

[61] Here Favre defends the necessity of working with grace, one of the characteristic marks of Ignatian spirituality. He considers the Pauline text from the standpoint of a personal spiritual problem: the effort necessary in the quest for God when the quest is no longer stimulated by devotional feelings. His comments are directed more against certain popular forms of illuminism than against Protestantism properly so called. Illuminism, however, could tend in that direction by proposing to add in

▸ *November 5*

175 On the fifth day within the octave of that same feast of All Saints, in the morning time after my prayer and the contemplation I make each day by going through the life of Christ, I felt great devotion to the holy angels, the saints, and the souls in purgatory. I prayed to the angels who were once the guardians of all the saints and the souls in purgatory to be propitious to me through the merits of Christ. I prayed also to be delivered from the ill will of those evil spirits who were permitted to put these holy ones to the test, for I began to have some awareness of the dire fate awaiting those who fall into the power of those wicked angels.[62]

176 I also prayed very fervently to Christ himself, reflecting that he submitted himself to the external power of the bad angel of Herod, Archelaus, Annas, Caiaphas, Pilate, Herod, and those others who afflicted him exteriorly.[63] I reflected too how he had submitted to the tempter Satan, who with all the power he could bring to bear externally tempted him in the desert, on the pinnacle of the temple, and on the mountain. His purpose was to lure him into sensuous desire and into pride and ambition. I wished that the demons and the wicked angels through the grace of such great humility might no longer have any power within me but rather external power (if it cannot be otherwise).

I recalled how the demons, by means of men's hands and by scourges, nails, and other external objects, were able to torture Christ, but in no way could affect him by means of thoughts or other harmful influences capable of inciting the flesh and the spirit to evil.[64]

---

some way to God what it takes from man. To this basing of God's greatness on man's abasement must be opposed God's greatness as revealed in creation and in the interior transformation of man. For Favre, then, there are two kinds of grace. By creation God gives man being and power *(quod ex nobis est)* and by the grace of Christ God comes to dwell in us, adding a deeper dimension *(spiritus)* to those who receive him; in that way he permits them to enter into an active relationship with him of knowledge and of love. See *DeCertMem,* p. 248, n. 2.

[62] The tradition that demons molest holy people goes back to the first centuries of the Church.

[63] The first Herod was Herod the Great (Matt. 2:3), father of the second, Herod Antipas, tetrarch of Galilee, who played some part in Christ's passion. Luke 23:6–9.

[64] Favre sees in every evil deed, besides the guilt of the perpetrator, a malign influence working on men to commit evil—this would be true at least of those who tortured Christ. Devotion to the instruments of the passion developed very much towards the end of the fourteenth century and the beginning of the fifteenth, as is shown in the art of the age.

An idea akin to this occurred to me: The Blessed Virgin Mary and many, indeed all, saints suffered external afflictions but were not all tried interiorly in the same way. Some of them, both men and women, were tempted interiorly on occasion, even often, by the seductions of the world (this never happened to the Virgin Mary) or by pangs and anxieties (I refer here to the afflictions and sensual feelings that come through the agency of bad spirits). The Blessed Virgin Mary experienced great sorrows, as here expressed: "And your own soul a sword shall pierce."[65]

▸ November 13

177 On November 10, the burial day of Bartholomeo Monsono in the town of Lower Ingelheim, two leagues from Mainz,[66] I had some remorseful feelings at my neglect of him; it seemed to me that I had done nothing at all to help him. I then received this answer: It is better to forge ahead, resolved to do some good, rather than to weary and wear out the will under the burden of the past.

I became aware of another instruction as I reflected on the feelings of aversion commonly experienced by those who do charitable work with the sick, especially the sick poor. These feelings are aroused by the dangers of infection, the poisonous odors, or other harmful things likely to cause a person to contract the same or other illnesses. This taught me that a person engaged in that kind of service or in any other kind of good work solely for the sake of Christ should be ready to lay down his life gladly at that work in whatever place he may find himself.[67]

178 Canon Bartholomeo died during the night of Sunday to Monday at about two o'clock in the morning, and I sought in that event matter for devotion and thanksgiving. The following reflection gave me good hope: From the manner of his death and the testimony of his

---

[65] Luke 2:35.

[66] Canon Bartholomeo Monsono seems to have been a Spaniard, which perhaps explains why Favre began his note on him in Spanish. He was buried in Nieder-Ingelheim, on the Rhine, over twelve miles to the west of Mainz. The gap of eight days between §176 and §177 can be explained by the journey Favre had to make.

[67] Care of the sick was one of the constant preoccupations of the first Jesuits. It was a crying need everywhere at the time, a true corporal work of mercy since there were no hospitals in the modern sense of the word. But it needed a strong stomach. See linking passage 15a above. Favre laments that he had not helped the canon who died in the hospital at Nieder-Ingelheim. For an analysis of Favre's discernment in the matter, see O'Leary, "Discernment," pp. 100–101. Care of the sick in one of these hostels was one of the "experiences" or tests *(pruebas)* imposed on Jesuit novices. See *ConsSJComm,* Index I, p. 381, under "Experiences."

companion, I learned that for many years the canon had practiced a very deep and constant devotion to Michael the Archangel. Now, as it happens, many churches consecrate Monday to him and the other angels by making a special commemoration of them. The canon's death on that very day was a source of joy and consolation to me.[68]

179 Another day I celebrated Mass, first intention, for our Alvaro Alfonso,[69] who had left for Louvain the previous day. As I was holding in my hands, though unworthy, the most worthy sacrament of the Eucharist,[70] I recognized the greatness of God's generosity to me—gone unrecognized until that moment—in leaving for the service of my soul a body to help me to honor Christ and his Father in many ways.[71]

Without my body it would be easy for me to commit many faults from which I am preserved because the body does not obey the first nod from the soul, nor does it submit itself all at once to the impulses and influences that flow from it. I prayed, therefore, that Christ himself might be so good as to grant to all my friends and to others as well as to myself the grace of not breathing forth my spirit from my body before my soul is well prepared to be received into the hands of Almighty God. For in what way could it resist evil spirits if it lay open and accessible to them, free from the body which shelters it? And who would prevent it

---

[68] It was customary to say the Mass of the Angels on Mondays; on this day too Favre used to make a special commemoration of the angels; in addition the cult of the Archangel Michael was widespread in Germany. Favre saw signs of a divine intervention in these coincidences; the relation between the practice of a lifelong devotion and the circumstances of the canon's death gave him hope of the dead man's salvation.

[69] Don Alvaro Alfonso and Juan d'Aragón (§32 n. 64 above) were chaplains at the court of the Infantas. Alfonso got permission to absent himself from the court in order to make the Exercises under Favre. He overtook Favre in Almunia on February 12, 1542, as he was on the point of leaving Spain for Germany. Having made the Exercises (*MonFabri*, p. 174), Alfonso attached himself to Favre and began to work with him. On August 25, 1542, Favre sent him on pilgrimage to Trier and to Cologne. He returned to Speyer towards the end of September. Sent off again, this time to Louvain, he joined the community of Jesuit students there who, forced to leave Paris, had arrived in Louvain about mid-August: Jerónimo Doménech, Andrés de Oviedo, Emiliano Loyola, Pedro de Ribadeneira, Jacobus Spech, Antonio and Francesco Strada, and Laurentius Dels. *MonFabri*, pp. 151, 174, 185, and so forth; A. Poncelet, *Histoire de la Compagnie de Jésus dans les Anciens Pays-Bas* (Brussels, 1927) 1:41.

[70] The moment before the priest's communion, when he said "Lord, I am not worthy . . ." (*Domine, non sum dignus*). Favre would have said it three times but without striking his breast at each repetition. This gesture dated from the beginning of the sixteenth century and was by no means widespread.

[71] Rom. 12:1. ". . . to present your bodies as a living sacrifice, holy and acceptable to God, which is your spiritual worship" (RSV). As usual in Paul, "bodies" means "selves." The body too has its part to play in the worship of God.

from wandering about unchecked if its own body or some other spirit did not hinder it from putting all its resolves into execution? Now it would be in Rome, now in Spain, now again in my native district with my parents and relatives, now in some other place.[72] Fortunate it is for the soul that its need is to be detained in a body, unable to act but through the medium of that body. May he be blessed, the God who orders all things sweetly![73]

▸ November 25

180 On the day of St. Catherine of Alexandria, I had a spiritual light on how to improve my saying of the divine office: that it would help me greatly, as long as I gave close attention to the divine words, to have confidence that the Lord would take upon himself the care of my duties and my labors. For that reason you should not allow yourself to be distracted by any other matters however pious, lest you prevent God from giving careful attention to them himself.

181 I noted also how very fitting it was during your recital of the office for you to consider, on the one hand, that God is present to you with his holy angel who observes and estimates most accurately each advance you make and the effort you put into your recitation. I reflected, on the other hand, that the enemy, the bad spirit, observes all the faults you commit so as to have something to accuse you of in time to come.[74]

▸ November 28

182 On the vigil of St. Saturninus's day, as I was saying the office of St. Caesarius[75] (the celebration of whose feast I had put off till later),[76] I had a deep feeling of devotion to that martyr Caesarius though I lack information about his life and his martyrdom. For the first time I was given to understand in spirit how fruitful it would be on the feast of each saint of the day to make a contemplation on that saint. This would comprise, after three customary preludes, these five points.[77]

---

[72] These are the places where his heart is.

[73] Wisd. 8:1.

[74] The enemy (Matt. 13:28) is the "accuser of the saints" according to Jewish religious tradition (Rom. 8:33; Job 1:9–11), as the Holy Spirit is their defender.

[75] Most likely St. Caesarius the deacon, martyred for having buried in the cemetery of Domitilla the bodies of SS. Nereus and Achilleus, who were commemorated on November 1. See Perdrizet, *Le Calendrier,* p. 250.

[76] An office or a Mass not said on the day appointed for it in the liturgical calendar but put off until later is said to be deferred *(relictus).*

[77] This contemplation with its three preludes (preparatory acts) and five points

First, to thank God the Father, the Son, and the Holy Spirit for having predestined that saint from eternity, for having then chosen, called, justified, exalted, and finally glorified him.[78]

Second, to thank the Blessed Virgin Mary, blessed Michael, and the good angel of that saint, and all the holy men and women who had helped him to gain salvation by their prayers in the presence of God or in any other way.

Third, to pray to God and the saint himself on behalf of all the souls of the dead and for all the living who were and still are devoted to that saint.

Fourth, to consider how advantageous it is to pray to the Lord for the preservation of those traditions and writings which might enable us to keep alive the memory of some of the edifying sayings or even actions of that saint during his lifetime.[79]

Fifth, to consider how good and profitable it is or might be to preserve with the greatest veneration either all or some of the relics of his body.

Let the person not able to find in these points matter to exercise his mind stir up "the purpose of his heart"[80] to desire all these things with more and more intensity.

▸ *November 29*

183 On the day of St. Saturninus, the vigil of the apostle St. Andrew, at a time when I intended to say Mass, it was given to me to ask the heavenly Father with fervor for his grace and for whatever is wanting to my memory, to ask the Son for whatever is wanting to my mind, and the Holy Spirit for whatever is wanting to my will. In that way I commended my three faculties to the Holy Trinity; in addition I commended my soul to the soul of Christ our Lord and Savior—in short, my whole being composed of body and soul and called "man"—to Christ made man for our sake.[81]

---

is typically Ignatian. But its hierarchy of Trinity, Virgin, saints, and sacred things cast in the form of a litany is characteristic of Favre.

[78] Rom. 8:30.

[79] That age was deeply interested in the lives of the saints, and it abounded in books and works of art about them. "Artists were never more familiar with the saints than in the time of Louis XII and François I" (Mâle, *L'art,* p. 158).

[80] 1 Chron. 29:18.

[81] Devotion to the Trinity and to the Incarnation of Christ forms a solid foundation for every kind of spiritual life and is of great effect in promoting an increase of faith, hope, and charity. See *DeCertMem,* pp. 93–94.

184 Feeling a keen spiritual desire and with a heightened consciousness of what I might call the cringing and despondent state of my spirit, I begged for an elevation of my mind through grace so that, instead of being habitually stooped and drawn downward in its abjection towards that "spirit which causes its infirmity," it might through the grace of Christ devote itself rather to growing in that life which consists in "looking ever upwards."[82]

To this end a thought came to me which I often had before: that it would be good for me to have devotion to that holy woman freed by Christ from the spirit that caused her infirmity and prevented her from looking up; once freed, she was able to do so at once. That day I resolved more firmly than before to retain the memory in time to come of Christ working that miracle and of the woman who received such a great grace. It sustains us greatly to consider Christ, in answer to our most urgent needs, continuing to distribute his graces as he did during his life on earth.

185 And with no little benefit do we call upon the recipients of such graces to beg and obtain for us from the same Lord the same and similar graces. Far from contradicting the true faith, it is in conformity with it to teach that it is a holy thing to invoke the saints, particularly for certain graces either for the spirit or the body. God can do all things by his own power, to be sure, and equally well through a saint or anyone else, but he does not will to do all things in just one single way.[83]

▸ December 1

186 On the day of St. Eligius, bishop and confessor, I found holy fervor in repeating several invocations to have him obtain for me some graces from God our Lord[84] and particularly those described in two

---

[82] Favre must have been unusually depressed to have used the word *reptilitas* (the quality of creeping or crawling like a snake) in a description of his interior state. But his prayer is for grace to devote himself to growth in hope and to raise himself up in spirit, as the woman who was bowed down was cured in body and so could look up once again. The passage is a meditation on Luke 13:10–17, which Favre uses to console and encourage himself. Once again his tactic is to avert his gaze from the wretched state of his soul and lift it up to heaven.

[83] The unity of the divine action and the multiplicity of its instruments are not mutually exclusive. The different functions and the special activity attributed to each do not in the least take from God's liberty and omnipresence. Favre's target here is the Lutherans ("Far from contradicting the true faith . . .") who criticized devotion to the saints as superstition because it limited God's power and the efficacy of his action.

[84] St Eligius (Eloi) of Noyon (ca. 588–660) was originally apprenticed to a goldsmith, then entered the service of kings Chlotar II and Dagobert I as an official of the Royal Treasury at Paris. In A.D. 641 he became bishop of Noyon. His cult existed in the eighth century, and he was adopted as the patron saint of metal workers. In

words from the collect of the common of confessors, in which we seek an increase of devotion and salvation. During the Mass of St. Eligius, I relished these two words.

After Mass I felt still more devotion in addressing this kind of petition to God: "Deign to look neither to my merits or demerits nor to my spiritual desires, so cold are they, but rather to my needs, my shortcomings, my wretchedness, and to my good."[85]

187 During Mass I was given this prayer: Lord Jesus Christ, take from me any wretchedness and imperfection that might cause the eyes of your humanity to turn away from the sight of me, your ears from the sound of my voice. Take from me any filth that is in me lest its stench offend you, any insipidity lest your palate be displeased. Take from me my coldness, my feverish ardors, my excessive dryness or overflowing sentiment.[86]

In short, O my Lord, I beg you to take from me whatever divides, separates, and distances me from you and you from me. Take from me whatever makes me unclean, dries me up, makes me inflexible, sends me astray, and enfeebles me.[87] Take from me all that makes me unworthy of your visitation, of your chastisement and your reproofs, unworthy of your consoling words and your communications, and lastly of your love and your benevolence.

Have mercy on me, O Lord, have mercy on me always; drive far from me all the evil in me which hinders me from beholding you; from hearing you and delighting in you; from perceiving your fragrance; from touching, fearing, and ever remembering you; from understanding you and hoping in you; from loving and possessing you; from abiding in your presence and beginning to find delight in you.[88]

---

the thirteenth century he enjoyed great popularity; power against all ills of the stomach was attributed to him, and he was also invoked against fires. A host of legends accumulated about his person. Prayers and even litanies were composed to him. It is perhaps to these litanies that Favre refers (NCathEnc 5:274).

[85] *Devotio et salus:* the first tends towards God; the second comes from him: ascent and descent. The two terms occur in the collect, or opening prayer, of the Mass *Statuit* in the pre-Vatican II liturgy.

[86] *Humiditas:* moisture. The translation "overflowing sentiment" is an interpretation. Favre was always on his guard against emotional feelings. See §160.

[87] An obvious reference to the liturgical hymn to the Holy Spirit *Veni, Sancte Spiritus,* the sequence for Pentecost Sunday.

[88] To help him to meditate on Christ's attitude to him and his to Christ's, Favre employs the five senses, adding on his own account the three powers of the soul. This form of prayer corresponds to the First Method of Prayer in the Exercises (*SpEx,* [247]).

And what I say of you, O Lord, of your divinity and of your humanity, I keenly desire—or at least beg—that it may be granted me through every word that comes from your mouth;[89] for it would be enough for me to have the words of Jesus Christ my Lord abiding in me and that I should perceive them with all my senses.[90]

▸ **December 3**

188   On the day of St. Andrew the Apostle (the first Sunday of Advent), on the day of St. Barbara and St. Eligius the confessor (the first of December), and until the day of the abbot St. Sabbas,[91] I began to experience a certain grace which I had never before noted in myself.

It was this: Up to then, distractions in prayer drew me away, not from good thoughts and holy feelings (rarely indeed from these), but rather from emptiness of spirit and in that way prevented me from remaining without fruit. With regard to this point, I noticed a difference between what began in those days and what I was previously accustomed to.[92] In the past, as a rule, I used to be recalled from my distractions to an interiorization[93] by a more extrinsic power (by extrinsic I mean violent temptations caused by bad thoughts). Without their blows I should neither have returned nor sought the grace of returning to the heart.[94] The same thing used to result from remorse of conscience, from fear, and lastly from the manifold reproaches I was wont to address to myself. These were a source of anguish in my distractions, and all of them caused me a suffering which of itself drove me to seek devotion and a remedy against my distractions.

---

[89] Isa. 55:10–11; Matt. 4:4; 1 Pet. 1:23; §135.

[90] The words of Scripture and the liturgy affect us through our senses and awaken a spiritual relish which pervades our whole sensibility. Later in the *Memoriale* we find many examples of this Second Method of Prayer (*SpEx*, [249–257]). This lovely prayer, inspired by a tender personal love of Christ, breathes an intense desire for union with him through the removal of all imperfections.

[91] November 30 and December 3, 4, and 5.

[92] Favre's distractions, by the agitation they caused him, tended to rouse his dormant attention and so turned his mind to prayer again.

[93] *Intractio:* a movement towards the interior. The word *intractus* is used for the same movement in §35. It would seem to mean here a deeper kind of recollection. *Intractio* is found in the "Directorium" of Hendrik Herp (Harphius), O.F.M. (a fifteenth-century spiritual theologian), *Spieghel der Volcomenheit,* ed. L. Verschueren, 2 vols. (Antwerp, 1931) III, 53, 56, 57. See *DeCertMem,* p. 38, n. 2.

[94] To return to God by a conversion of heart (Isa. 46:8) has here the special, though quite traditional, meaning of a return to that inner Presence which is nurtured by meditative prayer.

These were the more common states of my soul and were the ones I more often detected. However, I did not fail to desire and petition from the Lord that grace which I am now beginning to feel is being granted to me in part. It is that my soul, if ever she strays from her peace, may be recalled to herself by what is inmost in her and that this drawing back may begin from the deepest depths and from the heart.[95]

Consequently, I noted the following more than ever before during these days: Whenever I was drawn away from the peace of my spirit into a contrary state of soul, I was often aware that the movement of interiorization and drawing back had proceeded from the interior. So I found great devotion in applying my series of meditations on Christ's life for the purpose of seeking this grace. For he himself, when he came among us, began from the interior by preserving his Mother from even the least taint of original sin in her conception,[96] by becoming man in her womb, and by visiting John, who was in the womb of his mother. Only afterwards did Christ leave his mother's womb and begin to grow in the outside world.[97]

189 Then I noted how Christ, during the thirty years of his life before beginning to teach the world by his words, had taught us by his actions that a person must carefully watch over himself in order to make progress within himself.[98] So he teaches us before anything else to

---

[95] Favre feels that he is drawn inward by a movement which has its origin within him; he judges that it is a new grace. This experience of the divine action which originates in the interior is characteristic of a new and higher mode of the spiritual life, the first stage of infused prayer and of the mystical life. Often before sought (§135), this grace will be mentioned from now on in the *Memoriale* in a form ever higher and deeper. See O'Leary, "Discernment," pp. 68–69. Note the term *retractio* which Favre uses of this movement that originates within him.

[96] Since 1497, when they had to take an oath to teach the doctrine of the Immaculate Conception, the Paris theologians defended it with the utmost vigor in spite of opposition from some quarters. The same oath was imposed on the teachers in the faculties of theology at Cologne (1499) and at Mainz (1501). So Favre's masters would have instilled in him their conviction, so much in accord with his own thinking. See Renaudet, *Préréforme*, pp. 106–107.

[97] Here Favre expresses a spiritual law which is central to his thinking: Movement in the Spirit begins in the interior and then manifests itself in exterior works. "Birth" then is the external appearance of what was first "conceived" in the interior. External manifestations are only a sign of something much more noteworthy in the Spirit itself. So it was with Jesus and Mary.

[98] *In seipso perficiatur:* Christ's hidden life teaches us to look first to our own personal spiritual perfection. Everything must begin from that central point of contact with God where he acts on the soul and where we must constantly seek him. Favre's own experience makes him insist on this initiation into the mystical life. Purity of heart prepares a person for docility to the Spirit, that is, to God's action experienced and studied in the depths of the soul. Lallemant and Grou were later to follow Favre

imitate him as he was when hidden in the womb and lacking those experiences which allow men to understand, to remember, to desire, to see, to hear, to taste, to smell, and to touch. To imitate him in this, we must observe that he willed to see and perceive with his external senses before making use of his human reason; he willed to listen before being able to speak; he willed to submit before commanding; to be a disciple —to be one in reality and not just be called one—before becoming a master; and to be directed before directing.

▶ **December 5**

190 On this day of the abbot St. Sabbas as I was about to say Mass for the intention of my confessor, I remembered vividly and with the grace of a deep and unusual feeling of gratitude all the confessors I ever had in my life.[99]

I similarly remembered the priest who had baptized me, the one who had confirmed me, those who had conferred sacred orders on me, and in general all those who had administered any of the sacraments to me. My memory included my masters and, in short, all those who by word or example or in any other way had become for me the ministers of some grace of God.[100]

I did the same in the name of all my brethren, desiring to represent them in this respect through our common faith in Jesus Christ[101] as they represent me in so many things and plead for me before God as members of the same body.

It may be that God communicates to me certain gifts in order to excite me to gratitude and thanksgiving—gifts which he does not communicate to all; but, on the other hand, there are countless things known to others about which I have never known anything at all.

---

along the same road. O'Leary, "Discernment," pp. 68–69; see §68, §307, and §355.

[99] Especially Dr. Castro (§10 n. 19 above).

[100] He had been baptized by Antoine Agnillet, parish priest of Saint-Jean-de-Sixt, and confirmed by Jean-François of Geneva, bishop from 1513 to 1522. It is possible, however, that he was confirmed by Pierre Farféni, titular bishop of Beyrouth and vicar general to the bishop of Geneva, a Franciscan. This bishop made the pastoral visitation of Saint-Jean-de-Sixt on October 4, 1517. Favre was ordained subdeacon on February 28, 1534, by Monsignor Milo d'Illiers, bishop of Luçon; deacon on April 4, 1534, by Monsignor Laurent de Saint Marcel d'Avançon, bishop of Grenoble (1518-1561); and priest on May 20, 1534, by Jean Cardinal du Bellay, archbishop of Paris. See *MonFabri*, pp. 2–4. The masters he remembered include Pierre Velliard, Juan de la Peña, and Pierre de Cornibus. See §3, §4, §7, and §14, and their footnotes.

[101] By the faith that unites his religious brethren in Jesus Christ and constitutes them members of one and the same body (1 Cor. 12:27).

I greatly desired the salvation of all those who had ever administered the sacraments to me (as I mentioned already) or any other gifts and blessings of God, for I wished that God might deign to grant me, as dispensers of his glory and of heavenly blessings, those very ones he appointed as ministers to me of grace and temporal benefits. I was also given to make with a feeling of deep humility this other request: that I might be granted through the grace and mercy of Jesus Christ to have as benefactors in glory all those who were my generous benefactors in this life, and then that I, through a kind of glorious servitude in the realm of grace, would submit myself to all those I ever had to obey in this life. Amen.[102]

▸ *December 8*

191 During the days on which the conception of the most Blessed Virgin Mary is celebrated, I perceived quite a new stability and steadfastness in my heart and in the depths of my being. As a result it seemed to me that I was becoming less accessible to temptations from the outside. Not that I experienced moods of great fervor with regard to impressions which moved me to deep emotions and ardent feelings of devotion, nor did I feel, as I usually did, an invasion of thoughts from the evil spirit of impurity. The foundation of my being had, through the grace of God and in some new way unknown to me, become solid and unshakable,[103] as one could say of a house that it was to some extent solidly built with regard to its foundations, its walls and columns, and the remainder of its structure even though its facing remained unadorned.[104]

On other occasions I frequently experienced within me fervor from good and holy inclinations and inspirations; at the same time, however, I felt the utter weakness and unreliability of my foundation itself.

May Jesus, infinitely good and holy among the holy ones, through the intercession of his Mother, of all the angels, and of the heavenly

---

[102] The ecclesiastical hierarchy has to be obeyed, so also its counterpart in heaven; this is a "glorious servitude."

[103] *Subjectum* (subject), translated here as "foundation," does not belong to the spiritual vocabulary; it is a technical term of scholastic philosophy. Favre uses it here in the broader sense of "foundation"—the interior foundation of being, in opposition to the accidental (*ornatus:* decoration), the superficial, the ornamental—what is fundamentally inessential. To express his spiritual experience, he has to borrow the term from metaphysics, the vocabulary of the Rheno-Flemish mystics proving inadequate here for the expression of his mystical experiences.

[104] A reference to Renaissance buildings, which were often built with columns. Their inside and outside walls were covered with a decorated facing of a more costly material.

host, grant me the daily renewal of my foundation and of my facing as well as the lessening of my imperfections. May this renewal affect my existence itself, my life, my sensibility, and lastly my human capabilities. May it then affect whatever qualities and holy additions are necessary to perfect the foundation for eternal life in heaven, according to God's good pleasure.[105]

192   During this time around the feast of the Conception, I noted this particular feature of my lectures: I was becoming somewhat clearer and was to some degree getting rid of that incoherence and confusion which was natural to me; my memory too and my powers of retention were improving, and I was beginning to feel less troubled than at other times.[106]

If only these things were the beginning of that happy state in which I could at long last leave my body for that inaccessible light[107]— leave the depths of my own confusion, my powerlessness, and my enfeeblement for that very different kind of life which is the fullness of power and permanence! The Lord knows the measure and the nature of what I am and of what I can do when left to myself. He knows my unsightliness, the defilement of my person, and all the wickedness and shamefulness that have come upon me. But the Blessed Virgin Mary, our mother and our advocate, all beautiful and immaculate within and without, she who is our Lady, has power with the Father, the Son, and the Holy Spirit. She will obtain for me by her prayers grace that the very foundation of my life may be reformed interiorly and decked with all the outward adornments[108] of sanctity. *Fiat. Fiat!* And whatever will come about on that day will proceed from the power of the Father, will be

---

[105] Favre uses a metaphysical vocabulary to describe the degrees of being of the subject, all of which need to be penetrated and transformed by grace: existence, vegetative life, animal or sensitive life, and lastly the specifically human level of life *(ipsum posse)*. He calls the latter his "human capabilities." The transformation of the exterior in glory constitutes a necessary condition for the full enjoyment of God (§138 n. 281 above). The renewal begins in the very root of the being and pervades the whole person so that all his "exterior" (the body and its qualities) is transformed in heaven. The seed, at work in secret, will at last produce its fruit of glory (§280–§281).

[106] By command of the cardinal of Mainz, Favre was giving a course of lectures on the Scriptures which were more successful than those being given by the university lecturers *(MonFabri,* pp. 189, 485). He attributes this to the effect of the mystical grace he had received. Before that he lacked coherence; his memory was faulty; he found it difficult to memorize and suffered from nervousness. He also mentions the faults he finds in his letter writing *(MonFabri,* p. 81).

[107] 1 Tim. 6:16.

[108] Literally, "with holy accidents" *(sanctis accidentalibus),* a scholastic term not used here in its strict meaning.

dispensed by the wisdom of the Son, and administered in the goodness of the Holy Spirit. *Fiat! Fiat!*

▸ *December 25*

193 On the most holy night on which Jesus Christ our Lord was born, I was in the cathedral for matins and, while reciting the office before the relics there,[109] experienced great fervor with many tears from the beginning to the end. The words of Isaiah[110] the prophet especially, which were read there in the first nocturn, penetrated me deeply. I was given great desires for sincerity in my wishes to be born of God, not of blood, nor of the will of the flesh, nor of the will of man.[111]

194 I also wished with full knowledge and heartfelt emotion that this night might bring forth good and sure remedies against the evils of our age. I felt too a deep longing to be born myself from then on to all manner of good works that might advance my salvation, the honor of God, or the welfare of others. This would come about if the Lord granted me an inspiration[112] as an interior source and as a means to dedicate and direct myself entirely to each one of these good works in imitation of him who was conceived and born and who died for each one of us.

It is in the Spirit[113] that we ought to live out the remainder of our lives and to work in all things for the service of our neighbor and for the praise of God. In the past we have lived enough—indeed overmuch—for ourselves and for our comfort in this world as if we had been born for ourselves alone.

195 Three elements worked together in our physical birth: the first, the material reality of the blood from which we have issued; the second, the will and the carnal desire of those who begot us; the third,

---

[109] Manuscript H gives the reading *reliquiæ Dei*, literally "relics of God," which is curious but may perhaps refer to relics of the Child Jesus exposed for veneration in many churches during the Middle Ages, relics such as the dress of the Child Jesus at Cologne or the umbilical cord at Châlons-sur-Mer.

[110] The text gives Jeremiah instead of Isaiah, and it is found in all the manuscripts. But Favre was quoting from memory.

[111] John 1:13. On Favre's tears see O'Leary, "Discernment," p. 91.

[112] *Spiritus* designates at once the Holy Spirit, the action of the Spirit in the soul, and the experience a person has of that divine action. Favre emphasizes the last but keeps in mind that *spiritus,* the divine action, is the source in him of his resolution and pastoral fortitude. He makes it clear that *spiritus* is both the gift of that fortitude *(in quo)* and a means of discerning the divine will *(per quam)*—at once a principle and a guide of action.

[113] Like St. Paul's expression *en pneumati,* its Latin equivalent *in spiritu* can be turned by either "in the Spirit" or "spiritually" (John 3:3–5). To be born "from above" or to be "born again" is to receive the life of Christ.

that other will and desire of our parents, who longed for children because they wanted their sons to become wealthy in the world.

Likewise, he who is to be born again from on high must issue from God himself, whose nature is all-perfect and whose purposes are always most upright and most holy. He must live in such a manner that he no longer gets carried away by the tendencies of that corrupt nature of his which he has from his blood, nor should he be guided either by his carnal appetites or by human and worldly motives. By fruits such as these do we recognize the true birth which is brought about by God.

196 I said the first Mass, the one at midnight, in the cathedral with the intention of applying it for the whole of our Society. With all my heart I wished for the birth in it of all kinds of goodness and the fullness of sanctity and justice before God,[114] and I wished that each of its members might be born for the whole world.[115]

I said the second Mass in the Carmelite monastery for the birth of all kinds of spiritual good in the lord bishop of Mainz, and in all that part of the Rhineland entrusted to me.

I said the third Mass in the Church of the Virgin of the Stairs,[116] where I had an opportunity of meditating on the feast of the most Blessed Virgin Mary "giving birth." I said this Mass for the birth of those remedies so sorely needed in these calamitous times of ours: for peace among Christian princes,[117] for the rooting out of heresies, and for all the great universal intentions.

197 At the first Mass, when I was feeling cold before Communion and was grieved that my dwelling was not better prepared, there came to me a somewhat lively spiritual movement. In it I received this answer accompanied by an interior feeling of devotion that moved me to tears:

---

[114] Luke 1:75.

[115] The idea of a worldwide apostolate was one of the characteristics that made up the vocation of the early Jesuits. See *ConsSJComm*, Index II, under "Apostolic," p. 403, and John W. O'Malley, S.J., *The First Jesuits* (Cambridge: Harvard University Press, 1993), 68, 300–301.

[116] This church in Mainz, called the Virgin of the Stairs *(Maria ad Gradus)* from the great flight of steps leading up to it, was built in the tenth century not far from the cathedral. Favre's celebration of the third Christmas Mass in a chapel dedicated to the Blessed Virgin Mary led him to consider the mystery of the Nativity as a feast of the Virgin giving birth *(puerpera)*.

[117] In this first half of the sixteenth century, peace between "princes" both Catholic and Protestant was one of the great questions that troubled Germany. De Certeau describes Favre's intentions in prayer during his Christmas Masses as a typical example of *dilatatio* or amplification of his prayer; first, the Society, then the bishop of Mainz, the Rhineland, and finally the world become one by one the matter of his prayer.

"This is what the coming of Christ into a stable means. If you were already very fervent, you would not see here the humanity of your Lord because spiritually you would correspond less to what is called a stable."

So I felt consoled in the Lord, since he condescended to enter such a cheerless habitation. For myself I wished it could have been better adorned so that I might find consolation in that, but I saw how the Lord was housed, and that consoled me. If then, for just reasons, I have not been permitted to see in myself the manner, appearance, and disposition I should like to have in the presence of my God, of Jesus, of his Mother, and of the saints, may I be given grace to see and perceive the disposition, appearance, and manner that he adopts towards me.[118]

▸ *December 26*

198   So far I have always cared more about seeking how to adorn myself in order to draw near to God and his saints than I have about my quest for that knowledge in which I might perceive the adornment of the saints, those of them who look on me and love me or show themselves patient or helpful towards me. I have always sought to clothe myself somehow in devotion or to deck myself out in those other ornaments in order to draw them to me and attract their love and their favorable regard.

But I have not sought how to draw near to them myself, which would have been easier for me since I could contemplate in them those good qualities which make them so lovable and attractive.[119] May the Almighty Father, the Son, and the Holy Spirit grant me grace to possess the understanding, fortitude, and willpower to seek and petition these

---

[118] Favre was consoled at seeing in himself a reflection of the wretched conditions in which Christ was born, but it was not the sensible consolation he desired. This month of December 1542 marks an important stage in his spiritual growth. The new grace granted him since the beginning of the month was one of passivity; from now on he will concern himself more with God and less with himself (O'Leary, "Discernment," p. 107).

[119] Favre's desire to captivate by a holy exterior the saints whom he admires and the fear of losing their love betray in him a somewhat vain characteristic. But he quickly discerns the superficiality and the ambiguous nature of this desire, just as Ignatius at Manresa came to realize that his desire to do heroic deeds before the heavenly court was suspect. So Favre will allow himself to be captivated by those others instead of making efforts on his side to attract them, in the same way that Ignatius gave up seeking God's favor by doing heroic deeds for his sake, devoting himself instead to doing what was great in the eyes of God.

two graces:[120] to be loved by God and his saints and to love them in my turn.

For the future I must take more care to do what is better and more generous and what I have done less of: to will to love rather than to will to be loved. I shall have to seek signs of my love for them with more diligence than I await signs of their love for me,[121] and I shall undertake these labors for Christ and for my neighbor according to the words of Christ to Peter: "Do you love me more than these? Feed my sheep."[122]

Take care to be Peter first so as then to become John, who was loved more and in greater favor. So far I have wanted to be John, and then Peter.

I wrote this on St. Stephen's day, having said the vespers of blessed John the Evangelist.[123]

▸ *December 27*

199 On St. John the Evangelist's day I offered Mass for a number of spiritual needs and against a certain coldness in my manner (its source being the evil spirits) which frequently turns me so much against some and them against me that we find each other intolerable and cannot engage in mutual correction.

I found moderate devotion in praying for that intention with much hope of being delivered from diabolical influences—I mean those influences that cause men to close their hearts to each other and habitually prevent one from tolerating the other in such a way that, if there is something that needs correction, they do not know how to set about it or have no will to do so, preferring rather to sever relations completely because of the trouble stirred up by that spirit of division.[124]

---

[120] To ask for what I want *(petere id quod volo)*. This is the Ignatian formula. A keen desire for something is itself the result or fruit of grace and proceeds from the whole being. It is not the result of any influence from without.

[121] Favre realizes that he must not be self-centered, must not be preoccupied with himself, but rather must make God his center. In §198–§203 he develops this insight which he gained on Christmas Eve. See O'Leary, "Discernment," pp. 107–108.

[122] John 21:15–17. Since love ought to be shown in deeds rather than in words, Favre looks for signs of his love in the work he undertakes for Christ and his neighbor. Peter showed his love for Christ through his apostolic labors, while John received signs of Christ's love for him. Favre wished to be John before being Peter—the wrong order and an indication that he put self first (§203).

[123] This note must have been written in the evening on December 26; Favre's custom was to write in the morning after Mass.

[124] This spirit of division bothered Favre on at least one other occasion (§32). It was at work here. Who were those he found intolerable and who, in their turn,

200   Then I went on to pray fervently to the guardian angels of men and to all the other angels that they might be born for us with Christ, and I made the same prayer to the saints of God both men and women or the souls who reign in heaven. I desired the same for those in this life: that each might be born for his own salvation and that of all his neighbors. This means to begin at once a complete and earnest dedication of himself, directed to the welfare of all his brothers—the welfare first of their souls and then of their bodies.

201   During Mass, as I read what is said about the love of Jesus for John, I felt a great desire to love and honor John himself.

I understood that my desire was pleasing to the Lord, for he who wishes to love the Lord should love whatever he loves: salvation above all and the spiritual life, the consoling and sustaining of souls—his sheep and his lambs whom he himself commended to Peter after asking him three times, "Do you love me?"[125]

202   I think that whatever benefit I have received during these days of the Nativity can be summed up as a spiritual birth, a new earnestness in my desire to give witness of my love for God, for Christ, and for the things that concern him.[126] This means that from now on I should, to a greater degree, reflect on and desire, preach on and carry out with more generosity the designs of God. Until now I have been overmuch concerned about those feelings that can be taken as a sign that one is beloved of God and of his saints—for I greatly desired to know how they looked upon me.

To be sure, there is nothing wrong in that; it is even the first stage for those on their way to God or, more precisely, for those seeking reconciliation with God. From the first moment of our conversion and with much more reason before it, we must not think or even hold "as of certain faith" (according to an erroneous opinion)[127] that God, his Christ, and all the heavenly court look on us with a benevolence that is free from the least trace of displeasure. Not even if God forbears to inflict on us the eternal punishment he threatens us with should we conclude that

---

found him intolerable? Regular or secular clergy? Laymen did not engage in "mutual correction."

[125] John 21:15ff.

[126] Favre's expression *(hoc unum bonum . . . consecutus . . .)* indicates a summing-up of what he experienced during these days: the interior events he noted form one and the same grace.

[127] It is difficult to know exactly what Favre is alluding to here—perhaps a form of illuminism which looked on faith as both a certainty of salvation and an exemption from all penitential works in the apostolate; perhaps a popular form of Protestantism according to which any work of expiation meant a lack of faith in God's saving power and, for that reason, was opposed to penitential works and to purgatory.

we will be required to undergo no further expiatory sufferings. Remember what he said to Paul, chosen as a vessel of election: "I will show him how much he must suffer for the sake of my name."[128]

203 When we first begin to lead a better life, it is as a rule, and rightly so, our principal concern to make ourselves pleasing to God by preparing for him in our bodies and in our spirits a spiritual and corporal dwelling. But there comes a time (and the Holy Spirit himself with his unction teaches it to each of those who walk in righteousness)[129] when we are inspired—and are indeed bidden—to seek and to tend not so much to be loved by God but to love him. This means that we should seek him not so much as he is in us but rather as he is in himself and in other created things, and we should seek to know what greatly pleases and displeases him in his creatures. The first attitude of mind, then, is to draw God to us; the second, however, is to draw ourselves to God.[130]

In the first we seek to have him remember us and assume complete care of us; in the second we seek to remember him and to be fully engaged only in what pleases him. In the first we find the way that brings to perfection in us true fear and filial reverence; in the second, the way that leads to charity in its perfection.

May the Lord grant that I and all others may walk along the way that mounts up to God on these two feet of true fear and true charity.[131]

So far it seems to me that fear has been my right foot and charity my left; my wish for the future is that love be my good right foot, fear my left and weaker one. May I be born today for this grace and grow into a perfect man![132] Amen.

---

[128] Acts 9:15–16.

[129] John 2:27. The Holy Spirit is the master of the spiritual life; he determines the stages of its development and reveals them to the heart.

[130] The time for changing from the first attitude to the second is made known by the unction of the Holy Spirit.

[131] One goes to God through fear and love. The classical text, 1 John 1:18, is developed by the Fathers to show both the opposition between fear and love and their integration into the development of the Christian life. See *MellConfess*, n. 472.

[132] Favre's wish for the future is that love be the stronger influence and fear the weaker. But fear is not excluded; it becomes subordinate—so far has Favre's thought traveled from his original feeling of spiritual coldness during his first Christmas Mass. His development has a spiritual logic about it (O'Leary, "Discernment," pp. 108–109). The imagery of the two feet is biblical but was extended by mystical writers such as Herp (Harphius) to include the intellect and the affective faculty of man (Herp [Harphius], *Theologia mystica* 3, Sermo 9). The concluding prayer is based on Eph. 4:13 (DV).

ASCHAFFENBURG

203a: *Favre was absent from Mainz from December 28/29 to January 13/14 on a visit to Cardinal Albert at his residence in Aschaffenburg, about forty miles east of Mainz on the river Main. He made the journey on foot accompanied by Stephen, a young man who was shortly to enter the Society. While there he stayed with the dean. The cardinal received him with the utmost friendliness and ordered his collection of relics to be laid out for him in his private chapel. Favre, who accepted without question the authenticity of all relics, was greatly impressed.*

It may be of interest to note that the cardinal, who had become archbishop of Magdeburg and administrator of the diocese of Halberstadt in 1514, had attained to these three high and lucrative offices by the payment of ten thousand ducats to the Roman Curia. To recoup himself he engaged Tetzel, a Dominican, to preach on indulgences. Language used by the preacher, for example, "No sooner have the coins jingled in the collection box than the soul is freed from purgatory," led directly to Luther's Wittenburg theses on indulgences (November 1517), the first Protestant manifesto.

But in spite of his wealth, his worldliness, and his pluralism, the archbishop was well aware of the need for reform and had a sincere desire to bring it about. He ordered Favre not to leave for Trent, thus countermanding a previous order (no. 145 above); he was to continue his lectures on Scripture and preach in Latin every Sunday. The cardinal also succeeded in persuading Favre to participate in his plan of reform. It was with some reluctance that he agreed to do so, finding that "teaching about approved customs was reduced to a minimum" (MonFabri, p. 192). There seems little doubt that one of these "approved customs" was the veneration of relics, and it was proposed to jettison this and other practices of popular piety in favor of a hoped-for reconciliation around the fundamental doctrines of Catholic faith. It was a compromise, and Favre accepted it as such in that conciliatory spirit characteristic of him. We find echoes of these contemporary debates in a long passage of the Memoriale *(nos. 217–222 below).*

▶ January 1, 1543

204 On the day of the Circumcision of our Lord Jesus Christ and on the evening before, I found great devotion as I listened to the chanting of vespers in the cathedral of Aschaffenburg and gazed at the decoration of that church. There came to me many desires about the year just beginning, particularly concerning myself, with various other intentions which concerned the whole world: peace, the upholding and the restoration of the Catholic faith and of divine worship.

At Mass in the morning I felt, in a lively spiritual motion, how good and how conducive to peace it is to have God alone as judge and witness whenever people do good to us.[1]

205 I also noted that Christ before he shed his blood was unwilling to be known to the Jewish community under his name Jesus Christ. So it seemed to me that we should above all ask God for grace to enable us to prune away whatever in us does not bear perfect fruit[2] so that we might deserve to have some worthy name that derives from that of Christ. Let us seek for ourselves in this life no other name but one linked with that of Jesus, which means Savior.

For it is wrong to desire the name of father without looking to the welfare of one's children. Similarly, this is true of the name of doctor, pastor, master, bishop, administrator, king, duke, and emperor, and true of other names also, which gain all their meaning from their relationship to the meaning of the name Jesus.[3]

206 A holy desire led me to wish that my soul might have four spiritual seasons during this coming year: a winter, so that the seeds sown in the soil of my soul by God might be tended and so be enabled to put down roots; a spring, so that my piece of earth might germinate and grow its crop; a summer, so that the fruit might ripen into an abundant harvest; and an autumn, so that the ripe fruit might be picked and gathered into the divine barns for safekeeping lest any of it be lost.[4]

207 I also wished that our Lord Jesus Christ, whose body was circumcised, then delivered to death in order to seal his compact of obedience with God the Father, might grant me through the Holy Spirit

---

[1] The upholding and the restoration of the Catholic faith and of divine worship were two of the subjects Favre had been discussing with the cardinal. So many marks of favor had he been shown that he sought solace in the thought that God alone was his judge, and so he need pay no attention to the praise of men.

[2] John 15:2.

[3] The name of a thing represents in some way the reality of what it designates; it is a kind of sacramental (*DBibTheol,* pp. 377–380). Favre enumerates here some of the titles which gain their glory from their relation to Christ and to his salvific mission as expressed in the name Jesus (Savior). Those unfaithful to that mission are unworthy of the name they bear. The passage is a veiled criticism of the archbishop. See §132 and §229.

[4] Favre uses the images of sowing, ripening, harvesting, and gathering into barns in a commentary on his spiritual life. Nothing must be lost of what God has planted (John 6:12; Matt. 13:20). But he also refers to apostolic endeavors. See his letter in French of June 14, 1543, to his cousin in the charterhouse of Le Reposoir (*MonFabri,* pp. 201–205).

the grace of a true spiritual circumcision as a token and pledge of my steadfast love for him and of his for me.[5]

208 During vespers I remained gazing at a picture of the Virgin Mary, drawn by her look of modesty. I realized then to some degree the great value of that grace from God through which a person's sole concern is to please God alone,[6] to preserve all his grace and retain it in his heart like a person unwilling to attract to himself the love or the attention of others by an open and unrestrained communication of himself.

So all the beauty of Mary was within and remained hidden in God.

▸ January 2–3

209 On the octave day of St. Stephen, I said Mass in the chapel of the lord archbishop of Mainz, which for my sake had been splendidly adorned with all his relics and treasures.[7] The day after (the octave of St. John the Evangelist), I said Mass in the cathedral in another chapel reserved for the lord archbishop; it too was splendidly adorned.

Going towards the altar in these richly embellished places, I found very little fervor in myself—indeed, as I was going up the altar steps and even at the altar itself, I was in a state of almost total aridity, and this state lasted until the end of Mass. Then it happened that a grace from Christ crucified deprived me completely of any longing I had to seek in these outward shows a means either of increasing interior devotion or of finding Christ crucified with more success.[8] For it often happens as it did

---

[5] Circumcision was both a sign of membership in a community and a sign of the covenant. But, as Jeremiah pointed out, only circumcision of the heart really mattered. This spiritual circumcision is the only form admitted in the New Testament; it is the sign of the New Covenant whose author is Christ, who died and was raised from the dead. By virtue of his obedience to his Father unto death, he consecrated the eternal pact of love. Acts 7:8; Rom. 4:11; Col. 2:11–12; Phil. 3:3. For the rite consult *DBibTheol*, pp. 78–80.

[6] A reference to Luke 2:51, "Mary kept all these things in her heart," and perhaps also to Col. 3:3, "Your life is hidden with Christ in God."

[7] Some bishops had collections of relics which became so famous that they attracted visitors from all parts. See *MonFabri*, p. 191.

[8] Doubts about the authenticity of relics never seemed to have crossed Favre's mind; for him they were objects which excited devotion, signs of God's beneficent presence, external aids to devotion. But he detected illusion somewhere in the brilliant display he saw in the cardinal's chapel. Should interior devotion depend on such outward shows? See *SacMundi* 5:244–246, art. "Relics," and 375–398, art. "Sacramentals"; *NCathEnc* 12:234–240, art. "Relics," and 790–792, art. "Sacramentals"; VatCouncilII, *The Constitution on the Sacred Liturgy*, "The Other Sacraments and the Sacramentals," §59–§82.

to me that the man who is most favored among men is the one left more forsaken interiorly in the presence of Christ and his Spirit.

210 I experienced then in my soul a certain shrinking from the favor of men and the patronage to be obtained from the great. I saw that there was no more efficacious way of retaining God's goodwill than to be forsaken by men and so draw very near to the state of the crucified one. The esteem of men should never be sought or, if offered, accepted unless it is intended for the benefit of one's fellowmen and not for itself. For it is when there is complete absence of esteem that the Jesus of our souls can more readily be found.

211 The inclination of our heart should always urge us along the direction that leads to the cross. For Christ crucified is the sure way that brings our souls and bodies to their glorification—not only the way but also the truth and life.[9] If, therefore, you are in earnest about yourself, if you seek to build up in yourself a spiritual man, to receive genuine consolation and to advance, see that you preserve yourself at all times against the favor and esteem of men by pressing on to what is interior and related to the cross.

Others, before attaining a certain degree, will do better to give thanks through the beauty, the power, and the goodness they see being offered to them; and, it may be, they will be more strongly impelled to glorify God, who is omnipotent and infinite in all respects. But one day we shall have to come—if we have not done so from the beginning—to that cross on which hung our Savior. For it is in Christ crucified that we find our salvation, our life, and our resurrection;[10] and these three gifts, received in order, precede the glory which awaits us in heaven and which itself comes to us through Jesus Christ glorified, from him, and in him.

212 Let us first seek the power of Christ crucified, then the power of Christ glorified, not the other way round. That power of his lay in his willing acceptance of death and of whatever sufferings his enemies willed to inflict on him. By that power he destroyed our death—a death that had taken up abode in us,[11] that still abides and is in a way becoming even stronger by our fear of suffering and death.

He alone it was who truly destroyed death and, in a sense, reduced it to nothing; for he alone, of his own accord, took upon himself a body for our sake so as to deliver it up to all kinds of sufferings and to death. So should we arm ourselves with the same mind and the same

---

[9] John 14:6.

[10] The introit, corresponding to the opening antiphon, of the Mass of the Cross in the pre-Tridentine liturgy.

[11] Heb. 2:14–15.

resolve and offer ourselves up of our own accord for his sake to suffer and die, in order to destroy this sinful body of ours[12] and find in the end a body born of the grace and glory of God,[13] in Christ Jesus our Lord, in whom our spirit should find its being, its life, and its movement.

▸ *January 6*

213 On the day of the Lord's Epiphany, the feast of the Kings,[14] I experienced great spiritual consolations. The first was during my customary litanies, in which I asked that all the saints might adore in my name Almighty God and his Christ, Jesus our Lord.

Then, under a holy impulse, I wished for myself and for others that all gestures and movements made for God might always be acceptable to him even when the heart or the spirit itself, more free of the flesh, is at times incapable of rising up.

I felt then a sense of compassion as I considered the outrages suffered by our Lord Jesus Christ all during his life up to his death, so great a contrast did they make with the gifts he received from the Magi.

214 I then had a desire to be granted the grace of finding no joy but in God or in my neighbor and of never feeling depressed on account of my own temporal misfortunes but solely on account of those suffered by others and of those which have to do with God himself. Then I felt full of admiration and high esteem for the good works done by those who occupy themselves in working for me, for others, or for God in any way at all.

215 During the Mass sung at the altar of the Three Kings, I felt a deep desire that I might be given the grace to leave after me some remembrance, even material, of God and his saints and that I myself should fade from the memory of those living in the world before this remembrance of God should disappear from these regions. What should I possess on earth, I reflected, without some remembrance of God and of his saints?

---

[12] Rom. 6:6.

[13] Our glorified bodies will show forth God's goodness *(gratia)* and kindness but, at the same time, will be a participation in and a revelation of Christ's glory. He it was who first glorified the human body he had assumed for our sake (Phil. 3:21). Acts 17:28; §67. Favre looks on this participation rather as a gift of God. See *DeCert-Mem,* p. 279, n. 3.

[14] The Magi, or the Three Kings, were greatly venerated in Germany, especially in Cologne, where their bodies were said to be preserved. §28, §43, §49, §62, §73, §215, §216, §227, and so forth; *NCathEnc* 9:61–65.

These considerations were suggested to me by images of the saints and by some external paintings which represented different mysteries of Christ. They always helped me, on that day and at other times, to call to mind and understand various holy things.[15] Because of them, I loved and respected all the more his most reverend lordship, Albert, prince-archbishop of Mainz, who has shown a great and lifelong concern (and still does so) for the conservation of the relics of saints, bequeathing both them and their memory to posterity.[16]

The more these external testimonies are despised and treated with indifference, the more they are needed. For if images and whatever else represents the likeness and form of divine things and persons were not adorned with the greatest splendor, men would speedily come to disdain them all. Seeing that sacred things, even when displayed in the greatest splendor, are in almost universal disfavor, how could they escape contempt if they were treated without due honor and respect?

216 During Mass I had a great desire that Alvaro Alfonso,[17] then in Cologne, might make a special remembrance of me before the Three Kings whose bodies are preserved there[18] and that he might do so not only in my name but in that of all my companions.[19] And I felt and desired that all the rest living in places where there is a cult of saints whom we hold in great veneration were doing the same.

▸ *January 7*

217 On the Sunday within the octave of the Epiphany, I intended (among other things) that my Mass be a sacrifice and offering in gratitude—which I owe and never felt enough and could not express sufficiently—for the various gifts of faith and spiritual humility infused in me and in all Catholics, not only at the request of each but also at the petitions of the Church and because of her faith.

---

[15] The paintings were probably the decorated panels or retable above the altar. Favre was saddened at the thought that Germany might one day lose all these traditional aids to devotion, the heritage bestowed by centuries of loving artistry and craftsmanship.

[16] This judgment on the cardinal archbishop is overgenerous; in reality he was a worldly ecclesiastic.

[17] Alvaro Alfonso had been sent on pilgrimage to Louvain by Favre about mid-November (§179 n. 69 above). On the return journey, and probably without passing through Mainz, he stopped at Cologne about the end of 1542. In the spring of 1543, he began to attend lectures at the Montanum with Canisius. See *EppCan* 8:309.

[18] The supposed bodies of the Magi were carefully preserved in the Metropolitan Cathedral of Cologne (§213 n. 14 above).

[19] His companions in the Society of Jesus.

218 Then I noted and began to realize how those who abandon the Church begin by becoming more and more lukewarm in the performance of the works and practices which correspond to the graces and different gifts of God.[20] As a consequence, they regard as negligible and worthless anything they do not recognize as having been acquired by their own judgment. The result is that they begin to seek reasons for their faith and hope, casting doubt on everything; and in that way they squander the gifts infused by the Spirit and lose that true faith which is founded on Catholic belief and on the communion of saints. Once they have cast away all this, they begin to cherish a will to seek after and found a faith based on their own personal judgment. They look for reasons and examine them, each on its own account. They search both the Scriptures and interpretations of them, deciding themselves what meaning to adopt. Thus they put together their own faith—better called their opinions and their errors.[21]

219 When they wish to win someone over to their errors, the first thing they require as a principle and presupposition of everything else is that he should rid himself of every "passion."[22] By this word they mean a firm adhesion to what the true Catholic Church teaches through her judgments and decisions and the authority of her doctors.

For to rid oneself of this "passion" according to their way, what else is it but to cast away and so lose of one's own accord the Catholic faith and the simplicity and humility of a mind which is subject to the obedience of the faith?[23] Then when they have led a person away from that holy and necessary subjection, they require him to seek out a faith for himself with means at the disposal of all:[24] by the Scriptures and by

---

[20] With §218 Favre begins to examine how the reformers set about reaching their own position and persuading others to follow them. This will continue until the end of §222. He considers first the gifts that come from the one Spirit: There is diversity but there is also a unity of origin—all come from God—and a unity of end, for all are destined to strengthen the bond of unity that exists between the members of the one Mystical Body. There is here perhaps a reference to Rom. 12:6; 1 Cor. 12:4–11; Eph. 4:11.

[21] The psychological state of many who leave the Church. For Favre the process of abandoning the Church begins with tepidity, which gives rise subsequently to intellectual aberrations. For him faith is not a cold intellectual assent; it "is always God's gift molded by love" *(fides caritate formata)*. O'Leary, "Discernment," pp. 109–110, n. 37.

[22] A term used by Protestants in discussions.

[23] 2 Cor. 10:5; Rom. 1:5. Favre would have known these passages by heart and quoted them to Catholics attracted to Protestantism.

[24] *Communiter:* as given to all. The Scriptures and reason are at the disposal of all men, who therefore do not need to have their faith dictated to them. The word, used here in a special sense, does not appear to have come from any Protestant

reasoning, having recourse to no other arbiter than his own private judgment.

If, while remaining faithful to that method in his quest, he perceives that he has already lost his faith or is imperceptibly losing it, they then tell him that he must seek faith from God together with the discernment necessary for him to make correct judgments about the Scriptures and about what is to be believed. Faith is a gift of God which is not granted to all, they tell him, and other things of that kind which are very true in themselves but are of no spiritual benefit in this case. For it would have been a greater benefit to know that these gifts can be wasted and lost by anyone at all of his own free will.

That person, therefore, who has of set purpose lost the faith which was his as long as he adhered to the teachings and the mind of the Catholic Church and did not repudiate her doctors should not feel astonished at no longer being able to find the faith he now seeks in other ways according to his own judgment. Nor should he accuse God of being unwilling to grant it to him, for God wills to give it to all men but not to him who wants to live outside the Church, where there is neither salvation, nor life, nor true resurrection.[25]

The countless senses of Scripture and the variety of interior gifts are the possession of any faithful Christian who is a Catholic. But if he begins to examine for himself their validity, the proofs for each, and the arguments drawn from Scripture (or the sacred words[26] which support them), relying on his private judgment in his search, he may come to no little harm.

220 Eve had received the gift of a great grace to enable her to believe in the commandment given her by God through the words of Adam. But the moment she gave heed to the serpent's question, asking why God had given that commandment (that moment, I mean, when she sought reasons to justify her belief in it to a being incapable of giving or receiving spiritual help—as are most heretics), she herself lost her gift of faith. This lost, it became easy to deceive her and persuade her to act as she did. Not through reasoning but by the infusion of grace had she been led to believe on Adam's word that she would die the very moment she ate of that fruit. But it was her own reasoning and judg-

---

source.

[25] These words once formed part of the introit of the pre-Vatican II votive Mass of the Exaltation of the Holy Cross (September 14); now they are part of the entrance antiphon of the Mass of the Triumph of the Cross to be said on the same date.

[26] The "sacred words" are the words of the liturgy, the Fathers, and conciliar canons.

ment that led her into the error of thinking that by eating the apple she would acquire the attributes of the immortal gods and the knowledge of good and evil.[27]

221   Let us therefore, with many prayers of thanksgiving, acknowledge the gifts we have received by God's favor without having to judge them, without even having asked for them or understood them. So when we were baptized into the faith of the Catholic Church and of our parents, the seeds of the true and Catholic faith, of hope, of charity, and of the other virtues were implanted in us. In the other sacraments too, the graces given are not in proportion to our capacity, our understanding, or our inner perception of the matter and form of the sacraments,[28] for those graces surpass our thoughts and even our desires.[29]

222   If someone, unable or unprepared to help you or unwilling to be helped by you, should question you, do not start a discussion with him. Avoid him rather; fly far from him as from a serpent or a scorpion; make no reply to his questions. If your replies are good, they will be of no advantage to him; if they are weak, he is not the person either to teach or instruct you.[30]

223   The same day at Mass, while I was holding in my hands the most precious Body of the Lord, I had an intense awareness of what it is to be in the presence of the sacrament of truth, the sacred sign containing in itself all truth and all goodness.

Only after careful purification and examination of himself should a man approach it, for he who comes to it without having first been reconciled to God before the representative of Christ in the tribunal of penance will find condemnation in the eating and drinking of the food of salvation.[31]

224   Let us take as an example a man who has been ordered by his prince to go into exile because he has incurred his wrath on

---

[27] An example of faulty discernment analogous to that of the reformers.

[28] The classical and traditional distinction between the "matter" (the things used: water, oil) and the "form" (the words employed to indicate the meaning of the sacrament and the intention of the Church).

[29] Eph. 3:20.

[30] This kind of heretic is to be avoided. In general, Favre looked upon Protestants as lapsed Catholics to be won back to the faith; he had no understanding of the convinced Protestant or of the strength of his position. But he did not hate them and deplored attempts to coerce them into the Church by force of arms; above all he prayed for their leaders. *DeCertMem,* pp. 63–72.

[31] 1 Cor. 11:12. Because of many and widespread abuses, both Mass and the Blessed Sacrament had fallen into disrepute. Favre must have often preached what he writes here, and there was dire need of preaching. He is referring, of course, to those who are conscious of the guilt of serious sin.

account of some offense. If he treats that order with contempt, if he refuses to take flight while awaiting pardon, if he carries his audacity to the point of entering the presence of his prince, it is clear he will be accused of appearing before him without being summoned and without having previously asked pardon for his offense.

But his crime is so offensive and in so many ways insupportable that the prince cannot bear to have its perpetrator in his presence but must have him banished from his sight. What then does that brazen fellow do but make greater and greater efforts to approach nearer so that his intolerable transgression is there before the very eyes of his prince![32]

Such is the person burdened with the stench of his sins, which have made him an exile from the grace of God, who yet enters the presence of Jesus Christ and receives him without having been pardoned by him. It is as if the person to whom these words were addressed, "Remove that loathsome object from my sight, I do not wish to see it," were, on the contrary, to come closer not only to be seen but to be greeted with a kiss. This man says in effect, "I know you cannot bear the sight of me, but, even so, I want to be greeted with a kiss; I know, my Lord, that you cannot tolerate either my presence or my appearance, but I want you to enter into my interior, the abode of filth, impurity, and other things of that kind."[33]

▸ *January 9*

225   On the third day within the octave of the Lord's Epiphany, I remembered a series of prayers from a previous occasion which had given me long ago an understanding of how the graces to be sought and asked for were linked with each other and corresponded to the order of my litanies.[34] I thought of this through a comparison. I took the

---

[32] Favre's prince is medieval, regarded as having been "invested" with authority from God. Since he participates in that authority, his person is regarded as sacred, and his actions have in them something of that sacred quality. The modern concept of authority as service for the common good according to the prescriptions of a constitution has separated the person from the source of his juridical power. So Favre's comparison has lost its original force. *DBibTheol*, pp. 36–39, art. "Authority"; *SacMundi* 1:129–138; *NCathEnc* 1:1111–1115.

[33] Favre's treatment of the wretched exile can only be understood, and excused, as a reflection of the ideas of his age. The person of the prince is invested with a power and privilege analogous to God's. Favre's examples of this kind are couched in an outmoded language which describes a society and a way of life that has long passed away.

[34] This meditation is closely linked with the reflections in §224 on the attitude

case of a man who was engaged to serve in the court of some great prince and whose good qualities could be stated in the following order:

1. Above all, he should have the ability, the will, and the knowledge to serve. Similarly we ask the Trinity of divine Persons for these gifts: ability, knowledge, and will to serve Jesus Christ our Lord.

2. The servant-to-be is in need of his prince's favor, otherwise he will be dismissed as unsuitable; that favor is recognized and expressed by his virtue of humility. Accordingly, we pray to the Blessed Virgin Mary, who is and always was altogether favored, that she may obtain for us the grace to serve God and his saints in a way acceptable to them.

3. That servant must be hardworking and fitted for his tasks. So we too shall desire that the angels, those spirits who serve,[35] may obtain for us that fitness and readiness to serve.

4. That servant must love to appear in a decent and properly trimmed uniform, so that there is nothing to offend the eye of his master as he passes by. He should always be in a state of anxious desire to have everything in proper order and well prepared. In like manner we too ask through the intercession of the patriarchs and the prophets that we may be enabled to prepare all the ways of the Lord as worthy forerunners of Christ.

5. That servant should be ready to follow the court wherever it goes. We therefore, like the apostles, must seek grace to follow the Lord wherever it pleases him.

6. His duty as a court servant is to pay close attention to every word of his master. We likewise shall ask the disciples to intercede for us so that we may become true disciples of Christ and attentive hearers of his words and those of all the saints.

7. Because of his position this servant should always be careful not to offend anyone in the court; he should rather strive to make himself useful in all ways and to do nothing wrong, so that no one may have cause to complain about him to his master.[36] We shall accordingly beg grace from the Holy Innocents never to wound, scandalize, or dishearten anyone.[37]

---

of the wicked servant.

[35] Heb 1:14. "Are they not all ministering spirits sent forth to serve, for the sake of those who are to obtain salvation?" (RSV).

[36] In the last resort the servant's worth is determined by the judgment of his prince. See §224 with its footnotes 32 and 33 above. An echo of nominalist teaching about God's will?

[37] Etymologically, the "Innocents" are those who have harmed no one.

8. His position as a servant requires that he should be ready to suffer even unto death for the honor, the property, the lawful defense, and the safety of his master. We likewise shall invoke the martyrs to obtain for us the virtue of patience, which is the ability to endure all trials for our Lord Jesus Christ, for his honor and the fulfillment of his will.

9. That servant, as befits his position, will always and everywhere speak favorably about his master with the intention of adding to his glory and his reputation. We shall accordingly invoke the confessors of Christ so that through their prayers we may be enabled to praise and exalt Jesus Christ our Lord in all places, at all times, and in all ways.

10. His position as servant may require him to be diligent in avoiding pleasures and diversions of all kinds as well as those places or conversations that might hinder him from faithfully carrying out the will of his master. We shall, in the same sense, invoke the holy monks and hermits who renounced all comforts so as to be able to carry out the manifest will of the Lord.

11. That servant should take care to be always clean and properly attired so as to gain the affection of his master; with this intention we shall invoke the aid of the holy virgins who did their utmost in every way to please Christ alone, their spouse.

12. If he is accepted as a friend and becomes a member of his master's household, he will strive to remain faithful to him, nor will he impose upon his master's kindness but rather respond to it. We shall to the same effect invoke those holy women who remained faithful to their marriage vows.

13. During his generous master's absence, even during a temporary separation from him, that servant will not become estranged from his master, nor will he turn to other sources of consolation which would soon hinder him from preparing for the certain return of his master. From this we form our last petition as we seek the aid of widows and of those who led chaste lives: May they obtain for us grace to seek consolation from no other source than from God and, if we are denied for a time the enjoyment of God, to prefer always and everywhere to mourn and lament its absence rather than turn to other kinds of delight which do not come from him and do not end in him.[38] Amen! Amen!

---

[38] Every detail of this comparison has been carefully worked out. The good servant mirrors Favre's ideal of the service he owes to God. It is a close analysis of single-minded service, and each of the thirteen qualities mentioned is accompanied by the outline of a prayer for the quality in question. The invocations are linked with Favre's customary litanies; they follow the order and the content of the Litany of the Saints, in those days frequently recited. There is however a closer link with the

▸ *January 10*

226 Another day during this octave of the Lord's Epiphany, I became aware of a certain good spirit which led me to marvel at the grace of God which had already allowed me to see the feasts of the Nativity and the Epiphany thirty-seven times. So I went through the other feasts whose light had shone on me during the past years of my life.

But I have gained but little fruit from them, nor has my gratitude to God ever been great enough for me even to acknowledge his goodness to me. For it was that goodness which so many times during the thirty-seven years I have lived multiplied those feast days and others like them and set them before my eyes as their dates came round each year. From these repeated graces God wants me to draw salvation and make reparation for my past negligences on these feast days.

I thanked him for them; I acknowledged my ingratitude, my lack of concern, my negligence, and my thoughtlessness. Blessed be the God who opened my eyes to these things![39] May he grant me to grow from now on in the holy knowledge of the Christ revealed to us, announced in manifold ways and at so many different times.[40]

So, for this clemency of God towards me, for his overflowing mercies towards the entire human race, for my ingratitude and that of all men, I offered the sacrifice of praise and reparation as a holocaust and an offering for the remission of our sins. May God the Father deign to accept it!

227 On my way to say Mass after the morning office, I had a clear light about the Child born for us and given to us.[41] For I realized that he had then acted as God for the first time because, being but a helpless infant, he was unable to act as a man.[42] I realized also how, through his divinity, he then drew the shepherds to him—the shepherds

---

meditation on the Kingdom of Christ (*SpEx*, [91–98]). But Favre views service as attachment to a master who commands his wholehearted loyalty, while Ignatius looks rather to service as something undertaken side by side with the master. For both men the idea of service with and for a prince powerfully stirs up the soul to serve God (O'Leary, "Discernment," pp. 53–54).

[39] Ps. 16 (15): 7. Life expectancy in those ages was low.

[40] The main liturgical theme of the Epiphany is the revelation of Christ to the human race.

[41] Isa. 9:6, words from the introit (now the entrance antiphon) of the Mass for Christmas Day.

[42] Favre seems to note that God's more direct action is reserved for those who are in the state of spiritual infancy. On the other hand, this action reveals itself as all the more divine in that it is more hidden, exercising a more interior attraction and making use of humbler instruments.

who were very far from recognizing a divinity so great and hidden so deeply in mortal flesh. He then drew the Magi who were of no mean spiritual and natural capacity—they too, measured by the standards of the flesh and because of their grandeur, were far above the little infant Christ. Then I realized how he had summoned the innocent children to martyrdom without any effort on their part.

Therefore I prayed to Jesus Christ, who appeared in these ways and manifested himself to these persons who were very far away from him so that they might be enabled to seek him by themselves. I prayed that he would condescend to accept the prayers and good works performed in the name of those who are ignorant of their salvation in him or are unable to seek it.

Here I was inspired to pray fervently for all little children—even for those still in the womb—for they have not the knowledge or ability to pray, or to act, or to recognize the good gifts already given or to be given in the future through our Lord Jesus Christ.[43]

228 After Mass I considered how Christ had given himself to us and had been given to us by his Father so that we might avail of him in various ways for our salvation. He was given to us as a remedy, as food and drink, as an offering—to be our physician and our priest, to make reparation for us, to become the life, death, and resurrection of the body and the soul; and, what is of more consequence, he gave himself up in the end to be slain by us and to allow wicked men to work their will on him.

Hereupon I felt deeply grieved because I had in no way offered myself up in earnest for him to do with me what he might will, either through my life or my death.

So I asked him to make use of me and of what I possessed in any way that might seem good to him from that moment on for his glory, for the welfare of others, and for the salvation of my soul. I asked too that he might grant us to accomplish before our death and at the times laid down by him in his wisdom whatever he might have given to me and to all others to will, to think, and to perceive.[44]

---

[43] Unable to exercise an apostolate directly affecting all men, Favre turns his desires for their salvation into prayers for all those who are in any way incapable of working out their own salvation.

[44] A reflection on the following of Christ: By baptism all become members of the Mystical Body of Christ; all therefore have a duty to others and can fulfill it by imitating what Christ did for all. Favre concludes by an offering of himself in the spirit of the offering to be made in the Exercises (*SpEx*, [234]).

MAINZ

228a: The beginning of this entry indicates that Favre had taken up the Memoriale *again; he must then have arrived in Mainz from Aschaffenburg shortly before January 15.*

▸ *January 15*

229 After the feast of the Epiphany, on January 15, the day on which I celebrated the feast of the most Holy Name of Jesus, I found a moderately great degree of fervor, being moved in various ways to affection for that sweetest of names.[1]

I then said Mass for our whole Society because it bears the name of the Society of Jesus Christ our Lord. During these days I began to discover a special way of recalling my heart to the right path at the times assigned to prayer. It was to remember the presence of Christ hanging on the cross and saying these words: "Woman, behold your son," "Forgive them," "My God, my God, why have you forsaken me?" "Today you will be with me in Paradise," "Father, into your hands I commend my spirit," "I thirst," and others.[2]

While I was turning over these words in my mind and considering Christ hanging on his cross, I experienced a quieting of my heart that proceeded from a certain interior attraction[3] which led it into a state of more profound repose and even to raise itself to become attentive to the words of my office.

230 The bull of the jubilee granted by the pope reached us during these days.[4] In accordance with its terms, I prepared myself for the reception of the grace which it announced, and the Lord too disposed me to receive it by imparting to me in varying degrees faith and

---

[1] The traditional devotion to the Name of Jesus was given new popularity by the preaching of St. Bernardino of Siena (1443). The feast was instituted in 1528 and fixed for June 1. Favre seems to have celebrated it out of devotion because of the link between the feast and his order. *Nomen mellifluum:* the honey-sweet name—the adjective is traditional ever since St. Bernard.

[2] Texts in order: John 19:26; Luke 23:34; Matt. 27:46; Luke 23:43; Luke 23:46; John 19:28.

[3] *Attractu:* according to manuscript R "by a kind of movement of the heart"; manuscript H gives *affectu. Attractus* is found in the *Directorium* of Herp (Harphius). See *DeCertMem,* p. 38, n. 2.

[4] The Jubilee granted by Paul III was mentioned by Favre in a letter dated April 24, 1541 (*MonFabri,* p. 94).

hope in those spiritual blessings. I prayed him to grant me grace to enable me to enter again into possession of whatever spiritual gifts I have alienated, sold, or lost. This desire was inspired in me by the symbolic jubilee of the Israelites during which each one was allowed to repossess his property, no matter how it might have been alienated.[5]

I felt variously moved in soul about my reconciliation with God. I wished to have all my faults blotted out, whatever their cause: ignorance, weakness, ill will, impurity, ingratitude, or any other defects of the soul, the spirit, or the body—so that there might no longer be anything in me to offend God, his Mother, or the saints. Concerning the temporal punishment I have incurred, I wished, being variously moved, to be granted perfect reconciliation with the Lord and with his saints.

I wished too that there might be no more universal calamities in the world because of my sins; for it often—indeed almost always—happens that widespread calamities such as plagues, wars, famine, and so forth come about as a result of the accumulated sins of many men, each bearing his own share of the responsibility.[6]

▸ January 20

231 On the Saturday before Septuagesima Sunday,[7] at nightfall, while praying that all my sins be forgiven me and above all that my past failings might never cause me to fall into fresh sins,[8] I began to feel great consolation. This came from realizing somehow the joy of a man to whom God, his Mother, and his saints were favorably disposed and would show signs of their favor, no matter how trifling. I seemed then to hear within me certain words of Christ, the Virgin, and some saints dear to me; but I perceived them as possible rather than actual, as if I heard

---

[5] Lev. 25; *DeCertMem,* p. 292, n. 8; *DBib,* p. 460.

[6] See §49, §57, §285. A reference to contemporary calamities: the frequent plagues against which there was no remedy; the long-drawn-out war was between Francis I and Charles V; famines which decimated whole countries. Preachers linked personal sin with public disasters. It is an Old Testament idea; the theology of sin reaches its culmination in the prophets who interpret the fall of Israel as the necessary consequence of national guilt. There is no affliction in the personal or social life of man or in nature which cannot be attributed to the sin of man; whatever suffering he has to endure is no more than the just reward of his misdeeds. *DBib,* art. "Sin," pp. 817–821; *DBibTheol,* art. "Punishments," pp. 475–477; O'Leary, "Discernment," pp. 50–51.

[7] In the old liturgy, this Sunday (the third before Lent) was the beginning of a liturgical season which had its center at Easter. In the Roman rite this period before Lent was observed as a time of preparation for the strict penitential rigor of Lent.

[8] For Favre the worst punishment for personal sins was to be permitted to fall into them again.

someone saying, "If you could only hear the words of such a saint, your friend!" and so on.

▸ *January 21*

232 On the day of St. Agnes, the glorious virgin and martyr, I was inwardly moved by my reflections on those human miseries for which there is often no relief except in God, through Christ and his saints. Then I felt a great desire that each of the saints now in heaven might pray particularly for his afflicted fellow countrymen and for the dead[9] of his native land, and that he might plead on our behalf. I offered Mass for this intention. In addition, I asked the heavenly Father to look down upon all those in need of salvation anywhere (either in this world or in purgatory) whenever we invoke the name of his Son, Jesus. I asked too that he might bear constantly in mind all that Jesus merited and desired for the salvation of men during his life on earth.

233 The same day, at the thought that a time was approaching when we might lack the necessities of life,[10] I experienced a keen and holy desire to possess nothing at that moment. So from the depths of my heart I asked Christ there on the altar before me (provided it was according to his will and good pleasure) that not a single year of my life should pass without seeing that desire of mine realized at least once, that is, without my being stripped of all I have and reduced to a state which in reality is nothing else but to lack the bare necessities of life on that day either for myself or for others.[11] And if this grace which I value highly cannot come to me from external circumstances, may I be granted to know if it please God that I make a vow to fulfill it insofar as I can by divesting myself once a year of all that I possess at the time so as to practice in that way true actual poverty. By the grace of God, I have had a resolve to do this for a long time now. May God grant me, therefore, to know in all things what tends to his glory, so that his will, good, beneficent, and perfect, may be done in all things.[12]

234 I did not restrict this desire to my own person; I included others in the supposition that there might be a number of us living in the same community or in the same house.[13] As to myself, the Lord gave me

---

[9] Favre uses the word souls (*animae*). See §164.

[10] Favre appears to have been in financial difficulties. He was responsible for the support of Juan de Aragón, Alvaro Alfonso, and Esteban Carolo; in addition, he had started a hostel in Mainz for needy pilgrims and travelers and a house for the sick poor.

[11] His desire extended to the other members of the community.

[12] Rom. 12:2.

[13] Should he impose poverty on the whole community? It is a problem of

a long time ago the resolve to beg from door to door for whatever food I might need wherever I lived in the world.

May that resolve of mine, and all those concerning renouncement, self-deprivation, the practice of virtues and of obedience to grace keep on growing in me as fully as if I had been devoting myself effectively at this moment to what has not been granted me to put into practice.[14] For there are many people who, once they have become strangers to actual poverty, to begging their bread, and to the holy actions inspired by the cross of Christ, soon begin to lose their liking for such practices. So let us ask Christ crucified that no form of activity either turn us aside or withdraw us from, or even slow us down in, that race which should ever bear us along to the cross and to the death of Jesus Christ our Lord. The person who journeys thus far is on his way to salvation, to the true life, and to the true resurrection. But those who love this temporal life walk along difficult and dangerous paths.

▸ *January 23*

235 On the feast of St. Emerentiana, I understood why my soul should bless Jesus Christ, its Lord, who on this day took to himself that virgin-martyr while she was still a catechumen. I think it was through her prayers that I felt a great and profound devotion while reciting my office and during Mass. In addition, I was given abundant consolation at Mass and shed many tears. At that moment particularly, I wished that the Lord might remember—along with our sacrifice—that sacrifice which had been offered on that day by Jesus Christ in the blessed Emerentiana.

After Mass I prayed that God might not remember the sins committed by those who had stoned the saint to death. So I came to perceive that in the sight of God it was good, while celebrating through Christ the memory of the martyrs and the other saints, to present to him daily their good works and their merits so that God by contemplating them might look on us with favor—us who have done nothing of the kind. I felt at the same time that we should pray that he might not remember the wicked and unjust acts committed against these saints.

236 That day, in a moment of true spiritual consolation and desiring to have that consolation communicated to a certain person and to all others as well, there suddenly came another desire in answer:

---

discernment. Ignatius faced the same problem the following year. Both men sought light in the same way, and it led them in the same direction. *The Spiritual Journal of St. Ignatius Loyola,* trans. W. Young (Woodstock, Maryland, 1958), pp. 1 ff.; pp. 61–63.

[14] Only the practice of poverty strengthens the resolution; otherwise it weakens and dies away. For a discussion of this entry (§233–§234) as an example of discernment of spirits, see O'Leary, "Discernment," pp. 96–97.

"Would that you yourself could delight and share in the consolation that Jesus wills to communicate to you or in the consolation that the blessed virgin and martyr Emerentiana would be pleased to have you profit by." I then had an intense feeling, new to me, which could be expressed in these words: "O my God, would that I could clearly distinguish your will in all my actions! For it would mean for me a most agreeable life."[15]

▸ *February 2*

237 On the day of the Purification of our Lady, I received much light about the Gospel as well as great devotion during the blessing of the candles. I had a keen desire not to die before learning to know Jesus Christ well and before seeing him establish a peace in my soul inaccessible to all assaults, delivering it from all dangers, giving it interior enlightenment in all ways about his service, and conferring on it a glory which will free it from all its troubles, sorrows, and turmoil.

238 That same day I became conscious in many ways of that misery of mine which comes from my imperfections and my deficiencies, above all in the conduct of my affairs.

In these moods of depression, this single consideration brought me some spiritual comfort: I saw that God was favorable to me. If I retain the certainty and the awareness of God's presence in me, he will make of me what I can and should be. On the same day I rejoiced somewhat at seeing myself so naked and destitute in spirit that the Blessed Virgin Mary might well have pity and compassion on me at the sight of my miserable state.[16]

239 I resolved then in my heart to say this prayer often: "Lord God Almighty, give me at my death the grace of that peace which comes from the vision of your salvation, a light to all the nations and the glory of your Christian people."[17] That will come true on the day Christ will be perfectly known as savior and as the giver of light and glory.

240 One day shortly after the Purification of the Virgin Mary, I felt in the depths of my being the words of this saying of Christ: "And

---

[15] The Son's consolation is to do the will of the Father (John 4:32). Favre wishes to share in that consolation by doing God's will. But he must know it first, and that knowledge would save him from the torment of uncertainty and irresolution that was a mark of his temperament.

[16] Favre's realization of his wretchedness and spiritual poverty hardly ever left him, but it leads him to put all his trust in God, to become as a little child (Matt. 18:3).

[17] §103, §228, §303. A repetition of some phrases from the Canticle of Simeon (Luke 2:29 ff.).

everyone who has left . . . father or mother . . . will inherit eternal life."[18] Dwelling on the words,[19] I came to realize what it is to possess eternal life.

On the same day, as I was examining myself interiorly on the use of my time, I saw clearly how exact an account God will demand of it, for he alone has power to grant it to us. Another person can demand of me an account of what he has entrusted to me, but God will demand an account not only of time (which no one at all can bestow or prolong) but also of all the other gifts he has given us.

▸ *February 4 or 5*

241   Around Shrovetide[20] I felt a somewhat heavy weight of depression. It came to me from my imperfections—or more accurately, not so much from the imperfections themselves as from the reflections on them which were suggested to me, in a way I am long familiar with, by that spirit which is not the "principal spirit"[21] but rather that human spirit proper to me, or else by that which has been given me in order to try me by blows. So I became very slack in doing good at this time, distracted and drawn away from a vivid and penetrating perception and consciousness of things on high.[22]

I had but this slight consolation, that these things, it seemed, made up that cross of mine familiar to me for a long time. It is almost always made up of these three parts: the first concerns my inmost self, when I observe in my flesh such great inconstancy in the pursuit of sanctity; the second lies all about me, to the right and to the left, when I

---

[18] Matt. 19:29.

[19] The Second Method of Prayer (*SpEx,* [250–257]).

[20] *Circa dies carnis-privii:* literally, around the days of flesh-privation. The expression was used to describe a custom of the clergy—it did not last long—which anticipated the Lenten fast by beginning it on the Sunday before Ash Wednesday. This Sunday was known as Quinquagesima Sunday in the pre-Vatican II liturgy. Favre refers to the Sunday, Monday, and Tuesday before Ash Wednesday—called Shrovetide in English—by the name common among the clergy.

The English expression "Shrovetide" meant the three days before Ash Wednesday when the faithful had to confess their sins (to shrive themselves) in preparation for Lent.

[21] §143 n. 287 and §146 n. 5 above; O'Leary, "Discernment," p. 88.

[22] From long experience of this kind of depression, Favre knows it well. It comes from his inability to accept his limitations and failings, to forget the past and look with hope to the future. The result is slackness in doing good and indifference to the things of God. This experience cannot come from the *spiritus principalis* (§143 n. 287 above), for through that spirit God communicates directly with man, and man with God.

see all the works of charity towards my neighbor that I leave undone; the third concerns what is above me, when I recognize my lack of devotion and my remoteness from what directly has to do with God and his saints. The consideration of these three torments of mine from a human standpoint has long since laid upon my shoulders a cross with three arms, the weight of which frequently overwhelms me.

May I learn to bear this other cross which is one more acceptable to God: great and continuous labors for the love and the glory of God, for my personal sanctification, and for the salvation of my brothers; for God, by ascending ever higher; for myself, by descending ever lower; for my neighbor, by daily extending myself more to right and to left and stretching out to him my toil-worn hands. But because I do not bear wholeheartedly this cross of mine, the other one becomes for me a source of suffering and a trial for my spirit.[23]

▶ *February 6*

242 On the feast of St. Dorothy, virgin and martyr, I experienced a great desire concerning the salvation of those who are afflicted or in any kind of need. From the bottom of my heart, I begged God to open the understanding of all sufferers so that they could invoke his mercy in their wretched state. I was grieved to see that many who suffered in so many ways were unable to make known their afflictions to God and to his saints but would keep on always having recourse to human and natural remedies in which there is no true salvation.[24]

Let us always pour out before him our troubled hearts because he is mindful of sorrow and pain; he weighs them up and can appreciate perfectly their nature and their magnitude.

▶ *February 9*

243 On the feast of St. Apollonia, I found moderate devotion in applying Mass for that person (whoever it might be) who most of all in this world wished to be helped by the prayers of the Church. I wished also for the deliverance from the pains of purgatory of that soul (who-

---

[23] He finds some slight consolation in seeing all this as a cross with three arms: his failure in personal sanctification, in charity towards others, and in his worship of God. But there is another cross which is more acceptable to God: laboring for God's glory at his personal sanctification and for the salvation of his neighbor. There is a difference; he averts his gaze from himself and fixes it on God. The cross is heavy, but he desires to bear it by leaving himself and going to God and his neighbor. For an analysis of this important entry, see O'Leary, "Discernment," pp. 101–102; *DeCertMem,* pp. 299–300, n. 3.

[24] See Acts 4:12.

244 On the same day I recalled that as a child I was accustomed to read a prayer to this most holy virgin, a practice I had begun because of a toothache, and I never suffered from it afterwards.[25] So I thanked this virgin, who had so readily obtained for me the preservation of my teeth, and I asked through her intercession and her merits with Christ that I and my companions might be preserved for the future from these and from all other ills.

I also asked the saint to pray to the other saints for us, according to the part allotted to each by Christ in ministering to souls, to obtain for us not only virtues and salvation for our spirits but in particular whatever can strengthen, heal, and preserve the body and each of its parts. I wished, for example, that one saint might obtain for me humility by a constant watch over me in that matter; another, patience; another still, health of body for this purpose or that. In this way I extended my prayer to include all my religious brethren[26] down to the least detail with a spirit of holy piety, with a simple faith and a good hope.

245 May the God who has created us and all things give us grace to recognize through his Spirit all gifts that come to us from him and to thank him for them as soon as we become aware of them. If only we were conscious of what he works in us, in our bodies or in our spirits, through his own immediate action or through that of his ministers! If only we could someday see him, who is and who works all things in us, through whom all beings have existence and movement and in whom all beings subsist![27]

But the approach to this cause needs to be made through its branches:[28] to the supreme Principle and Cause of all things through mediate causes; to the supreme and first Mediator and Intermediary,

---

[25] St. Apollonia of Alexandria, virgin and martyr, was invoked against toothache because her executioner began by breaking her teeth (*Analecta Bollandiana* 40 [1922]: 13). The fifteenth-century Geneva Missal has a special prayer for that intention—surely the one Favre said. Could it have been taught him by Velliard?

[26] *Sanitatem* in manuscript R; the variant *societatem* has been suggested (*MonFabri*, n. h, p. 614), and de Certeau translates it as *communauté* (community); Mellinato gives *compagnia* (Society [of Jesus]).

[27] Acts 17:28.

[28] Those branches, or offshoots, are the multitude of secondary causes through which the power of the first cause makes itself felt and is recognized. See §133 on the water from the spring which of itself flows out into streams. Scholastic treatises used the term to express multiplicity in unity.

through mediate intermediaries; to the first End, the term and form of all things,[29] through the other mediate ends and mediate forms.

The first in the hierarchy of origins is the Father; the first in the hierarchy of mediation is the Son; the first in the hierarchy of forms is the Holy Spirit.[30] From the Father every created thing derives existence; from the Son all things derive their being; in the Spirit all things are accomplished.

These are to be understood as attributes because, for all beings which are created, made, and brought to completion, the Father, the Son, and the Holy Spirit are the sole principle from which all proceeds, through which all is ordered, and in which all subsist. May he be blessed for ever![31] Amen.

▸ February 10

246 On the feast of the blessed Scholastica, virgin, I offered her Mass for my own intention. I noted and realized also that it was something very necessary and fitting on these feasts of the holy virgins that the graces to be sought should be for our own perfection. For these holy virgins labored with the greatest earnestness to build up in themselves a temple sanctified by the Holy Spirit. It was their wish to become vessels of holiness acceptable to their spouse, Jesus Christ, to whom they had consecrated themselves. They are the souls whose greatest desire is to have us all arrayed in that interior adornment so that, in the fullness of sanctity and justice[32] and freed from all blemishes offensive to the eyes of God, we may please him. That is why these virgins will watch over us, if we have sought these graces through their intercession.

247 Other saints also may be fittingly invoked according to the function assigned to each[33] and according to the graces and merits

---

[29] Since the end of a being is defined by its essence or its form, the Spirit as the formal cause of all beings is also their end.

[30] Word for word: The first "from whom" *(a quo)* is the Father; the first "through whom" *(per quem)* is the Son; the first "in which" *(in quo)* is the Holy Spirit. See §192.

[31] These "attributes" are traditional and serve to indicate the real distinction of Persons in the Trinity. They are found in Peter Lombard. St. Bernard deduces the simplicity of God and the Trinity of Persons from an analysis of God's being, based on a consideration of his creative activity. He uses the same vocabulary. These elaborations are based on Rom. 11:36. See §317, §318; Augustine, *De Trinitate* 6, chap. 10, no. 12; *Petri Lombardi Libri IV Sententiarum* (Florence, 1916), 1, dist. 36, 4; O'Leary, "Discernment," p. 79.

[32] Luke 1:75.

[33] Favre recognizes that the saints all have their place in the hierarchy of heaven *(ordo suus),* that saints differ from each other in merit *(via meritorum),* and

God honored them with in this life and by means of which they attained eternal life in Christ Jesus, their Lord and ours. For God does not deprive his saints of their function, which is that each desires to see God communicated to all in the way each possesses him. Their lives followed different paths on earth; not all received the same graces, nor did God will to form them all by the same labors and the same spiritual exercises.

Why then should it not be fitting for each saint to wish to have God praised and made known in the same manner as he was given to honor and acknowledge him? And why should he not wish that others, at least those who invoke him in this life, might find God through the practice of the same good works?

▸ *February 11*

248 On the first Sunday of Lent, as I asked God with longing to drive all enemies far from me, I received this answer: "It is for you to see to it that God draws you away from those places that are the haunts of your enemies, for here you are in their dwelling, not in your own."[34]

249 The same day, while saying my office I began to regulate my clock without need. It came to my mind then to ask God for the grace of being "regulated" by him and set in order so as to pray well; for he can do that more easily than I, with my hands, can regulate or put right some material object.

This consideration led me to find fault with myself in that I had too frequently up to then allowed myself to engage in needlessly handling, gazing at, or fixing this or that object at a time when I should have been in the right mood for attending to the painstaking performance of my prayers and meditations. All my efforts should have been directed to preparing and disposing myself for the proper accomplishment of the work I have to do, whether with my hands, my mouth, or my mind. Such exercises are carried out well only when a person gives himself up completely to them, working in union with all the required faculties. If a person is fully engaged in them, I can readily believe that the good angel will not fail him; and when he is present, the Holy Spirit, who is God, will not delay in bringing our activity to completion.[35]

---

that there is also a difference based on the vocation of each on earth.

[34] Most likely a reference to Ps. 91 (90) which formed part of the Mass for this Sunday (the tract) to be said or sung before the Gospel.

[35] It is the Spirit who "brings to completion" *(perficere)*. See §245.

▸ *February 12*

250 On the day I was allowed to say the postponed office of the blessed Martina, virgin and martyr, the lessons in which she is mentioned inspired great confidence in me. She enjoys great power with the holy angels and also against the wicked ones seeing that their temples—and even their statues of the demons—tumbled down before her.

At Mass I conceived the great resolve of invoking her against evil spirits and proposed to put that purpose into effect every Monday, the day on which I have the custom of making a spiritual remembrance of the good angels. For, just as it is helpful to invoke them and devote oneself to them, it will also be helpful on that day to make a special invocation to God and to the angels as well for grace and assistance against the wicked spirits who trouble and deceive us in manifold ways and thus bring us to ruin.

251 May I always enjoy the patronage of that most blessed virgin (whose feast I celebrated on the first Monday of Lent) so that I may remember every Monday not only the good angels—my practice for a long time—but also the bad angels for their destruction. Never before have I been so deeply conscious of this. Blessed be he from whom, through whom, and in whom we have received such feelings and such knowledge![36]

▸ *February 14*

252 On the day of St. Valentine the martyr, which was February 14, Stephen[37] left us for Rome. At his departure I felt great devotion in invoking both his good angel and the other angels on his behalf.

I was aware also of another good spirit as I considered how his good angel had spent so long in our community, unknown to me, and had then departed from our midst. I regretted not having done all I could to assist his efforts with the young man given into his keeping and whom he had kept humble and obedient to me without allowing his evil spirit to trouble me as much as I deserved.[38]

---

[36] Rom. 11:36; §245.

[37] Stephen was a young man from Speyer whom Favre had taken into his little community and who frequently accompanied him on his journeys—to Aschaffenburg, for instance. See linking passage 203a above. The young man's health became so bad in Rome that in September 1555 he had to be sent back to Speyer to recuperate. He then went to Cologne, where he died on October 15, 1557, shortly after his arrival.

[38] A somewhat cryptic comment. Evil in others is contagious, but its workings are deep-seated and mysterious. Favre seems to hold that with the good (guardian) angel there is also a bad angel assigned to each.

253 Then, making a long reflection on the part played by the angels in the affairs of men, I clearly realized how necessary it is for us that the Spirit who contains all things most perfectly[39] should make ready our souls from their inmost depths and guide them by the infusion of his gifts.

Let us pray then to Christ to preserve his Spirit for us, for without the operation of the Spirit even our good angels would not suffice to guide our spirits. Without God's touch, all else seems but words incapable of penetrating to the depths of our souls.

But the word of God is living and active; sharper than any two-edged sword, it discerns the spirits[40] and the intentions of the heart. It pierces to the division of soul and spirit, right in to the marrow. These are the effects of the divine word if taught and imparted by the Holy Spirit.[41]

To maintain myself in better hope in spite of all the perils of the journey,[42] I felt a great desire that all along those roads there might be found many people whose patience and prayers would obtain from God grace for all those destined to travel and go on pilgrimage after them.

254 The same day after Mass I reflected on the different kinds of spirits which often agitated me, causing me to change my mind about the likelihood of bearing fruit in Germany. I often became aware that in no single instance should we give assent to the words of that spirit who insinuates that everything is impossible and keeps on bringing up difficulties. We should rather attend to the words and the effects of the spirit who suggests possibilities and inspires courage.[43] But let us be on our guard against veering too far to the right as we run. We must make use of discernment so that, by keeping midway between right and left, we may avoid mingling our hopes with illusions that feed on abun-

---

[39] Wisd. 1:7.

[40] Favre quotes Heb. 4:12 from memory and somewhat inaccurately: "For the word of God is living and effectual and more piercing than any two-edged sword and reaching unto the division of the soul and spirit, of the joints also and the marrow: and is a discerner of the thoughts and intents of the heart" (DV). His main change is to put "spirits" instead of "thoughts"; it may be an indication of his preoccupation at the time.

[41] The understanding of the Scripture and spiritual understanding in general is given by the Spirit who acts interiorly. Both spirit and word are needed in order to reach any true spiritual understanding. Favre looks to find the Holy Spirit emerging as the ruler of all other spirits in us. O'Leary, "Discernment," pp. 121–122.

[42] Stephen's journey to Rome.

[43] A Christian should be optimistic no matter what difficulties present themselves, his optimism being founded on a firm belief that God will be faithful to his promises. This is the virtue of hope and needs to be renewed each day in prayer.

dance or adding to our fears through a discouragement induced by penury.

But if we cannot prevent ourselves from veering to one side or the other, it is safer and less perilous to forge ahead with confidence as in a time of abundance rather than yield to that depression in which lie a thousand errors and deceits together with the seeds and shoots of a thousand moods of bitterness and bewilderment.

When one has learned to recognize the spirit of abundance and his words and also the spirit that tempts and disturbs, one can draw a lesson from both experiences. We will have to preserve joy and consolation, comfort and tranquility, and all the feelings which spring from a good interior disposition, and to these we shall have to return so that eventually they may become more deeply rooted in us. But the same welcome should not be given to all the words which present themselves. Some may have an admixture of falsehood because the evil spirit can transform himself into an angel of light.[44]

But in dealing with the contrary spirit and his words, we must act in the opposite way. That spirit and all the feelings that proceed from him are to be driven out and put to flight. Not so with all his words, for you can accept many of them as warnings about being more cautious, and so you will be brought to act with more prudence in your affairs. Many of these words are true and useful, provided they are interpreted afterwards in the sense suggested by the other spirit.[45]

---

[44] 2 Cor. 11:14; *SpEx*, [332].

[45] This passage is an important reflection on Favre's own discernment of spirits. He analyzes his moods with regard to his apostolate in Germany. They go from one extreme to another, from optimism to pessimism and back again. As O'Leary suggests ("Discernment," n. 5, p. 112), these words "optimism" and "pessimism" give a better sense than literal translations of *abundantia* and *penuria*, both used here and elsewhere by Favre in a spiritual sense. For the sake of fidelity, the translator has retained "abundance" and "poverty" in the body of the text, the context making it clear that both are being used in a spiritual sense. The passage may be taken as an example of the general theory of discernment discussed in the following important quotation: "The priority to be given in our experience to the affective element over the intellectual element is one of the cornerstones of Favre's theory of discernment. The spirits make their presence felt through affective movements over which the person has no control: This is the *basic* experience, and it is essentially passive. Ideas and reflections, whether accompanying or following, are less important even when they come from the same spirit as the basic experience, or even when there is no guarantee that they have come from the same spirit at all. It is the basic experience alone which is self-authenticating; the intellectual component requires further discernment" (O'Leary, "Discernment," p. 112). To summarize Favre's comments on the spirits: The good spirit of optimism *(abundantia)* is to be accepted because it is apostolically fruitful, but the bad spirit of pessimism *(penuria)* is to be banished because it is apostolically sterile. Both spirits operate on the affective level. Into the

255 As I was about to say Mass for the intention of the supreme pontiff, Paul III (on that day I celebrated the postponed office of St. Hyginus,[46] pope and martyr), there came to my mind thoughts of admiration about the goodness of Jesus Christ. So great was his generosity that he gave himself up fully in ways so different, not only to the good who are grateful to him but also to the wicked—for he delivered himself up entirely to the traitor at the Last Supper.[47]

That was a lesson for me: If Christ communicates himself to me each day when I celebrate and if he is ready to communicate himself in all other ways in prayer and in the works done for his sake, then I too should communicate myself and abandon myself to him in all ways, not only to him but also to all my fellowmen, whether good or evil, for his sake. I could do this by speaking kindly to them, preaching to them, doing them good, working and suffering for them, laying myself open to them to the utmost extent in order to console them as far as I can be of help to them, and, to end, by giving to all my entire self and whatever I possess. *Fiat! Fiat!*[48]

256 The day on which I was able to celebrate the feast of the blessed Bridget, virgin,[49] I had many thoughts about the pastoral care of souls. My thoughts made me sad at heart when I remembered the numerous Catholic parish churches in this province which lack a priest of their own—or indeed any priest at all, worthy or unworthy.[50]

I felt greatly afflicted in spirit at the thought that St. Bridget had been a woman of holy desires for the salvation of souls, as attested by the writings and prayers she left us.[51] Then I was given the grace to thank God from the bottom of my heart for all the benefits he has

---

intellectual element, the words *(verba)*, the bad spirit may introduce falsehood. For a long and careful analysis of this passage (§254), see O'Leary, "Discernment," pp. 112–114.

[46] St. Hyginus (A.D. 138–142) was pope but not a martyr though he is reported as such in the Roman Martyrology. See *NCathEnc* 7:282. His liturgical feast is January 11 according to all the martyrologies.

[47] The Eucharistic context here extends the meaning of the word "to communicate" *(communicare)*.

[48] The motive of the apostolic vocation of the Society was the surrender of oneself and all one's possessions; this was derived from the *Spiritual Exercises*.

[49] Her feast day was transferred from February 1.

[50] Parishes without priests and parishes neglected by their clergy plunge him into depression *(MonFabri*, p. 159).

[51] According to de Certeau *(Mémorial*, p. 309, n. 4), Favre confuses St. Brigid, abbess of Kildare in Ireland (d. 523), with St. Bridget of Sweden (ca. 1302–1373). The latter left written accounts of her prophecies and revelations. *NCathEnc* 2:799, art. "Bridget of Sweden"; 803, art. "Brigid of Ireland."

conferred—and continues to confer—on his Church through the mediation of that virgin.

257 The day on which I said the postponed office of St. Gilbert, the confessor,[52] I found such great devotion during Mass in regard to the souls of the dead and such great feelings of compassion for them that I shed tears during the whole of Mass.

Before Mass I wished for communion with Christ as far as was possible for me and attained it then to a moderate degree. So during Mass I had a feeling that in this communion with him the better part is to share in what he experienced during his passion, not only in his body but also in his soul.[53] For his soul was sorrowful at the thought of the dangers that threatened souls: eternal suffering, temporal punishment—especially the pains of purgatory.

The above was not imparted to my understanding or recalled to my memory by means of words new in themselves, but my awareness of them was something new and unusual.[54]

▸ February 22

258 On the feast of the Chair of St. Peter, I experienced during Mass some of the bitter feelings that usually arise from my imperfections. I then received this good thought as an answer: I was not to make so much of these imperfections, nor was I to pay so much attention to them as I used to, for they soon disappear if treated with contempt. It often happens that the mere brooding over them causes me to fall into them anew.[55]

259 On the day I celebrated the feast of St. Genevieve, virgin and patroness of Paris,[56] there came into my mind certain obstacles to the conversion of souls, obstacles that did not depend on me. I became disheartened and disturbed at this, losing that confidence I retain as a rule. To banish that mood of depression, it was given me to reflect on and become conscious of the following:

---

[52] Usually celebrated on February 4.

[53] Phil. 2:5

[54] Here again we find the distinction between the intellectual *(verba)* element and the affective *(sensus)* element. See, among others, §254, §287, §288, and §300. There is no new knowledge but a deeper interior perception and spiritual awareness due to the action of the Spirit (O'Leary, "Discernment," pp. 64, 114).

[55] Favre's introverted and sensitive temperament reveals itself here. Experience teaches him that it is better not to yield to the spirit of perfectionism.

[56] Her feast was usually celebrated on January 3; Favre may have postponed it to the end of February.

1. I ought not to allow myself to be so easily distracted from business which concerns me and in which I am already engaged.
2. I ought not to allow my human and personal preoccupations to extend themselves so widely.
3. I ought to devote all my efforts to the work I have in hand.
4. In charitable work I am to act as one would who wishes to make his way only through what he is engaged in. I must therefore get rid of those obstacles and defects which could be put down to me or to what depends on me. Then the hope of bearing fruit will increase.[57]

▸ **March 1**

260 On the day I celebrated the feast of our Guardian Angels, which is on the first of March, I found great devotion especially during Mass, which I said for our Society, asking the Lord to surround and fortify it with a guard of holy angelic spirits as a protective enclosure.

261 On the day when I celebrated the office and the Mass of St. Bruno,[58] the father of the Carthusians, I felt deep and intense desires about the restoration of that order and of all the other monastic and eremitical orders. So I said Mass for our Society, greatly desiring, according to the will of God and of Jesus Christ and with the goodwill of the fathers of all the holy orders, that it might someday work for and make some contribution to the reformation of that and all other institutes which have been established, approved, and authorized by the Roman Church.[59]

262 Then I felt a deep desire that many persons might be found willing to stoop to even the most menial tasks for Christ's sake;[60] for

---

[57] Again Favre is depressed at his lack of progress in converting souls and feels powerless. He analyzes the reasons for his disheartened state and, in order to combat it, comes to four practical conclusions. They can be summed up as a resolution to concentrate on the present moment and to get rid of the obstacles that he himself places in the way of conversions.

[58] His feast was October 6. Favre must have had some reason for transferring it to March: perhaps the reformation of monasteries, which he had on his mind at the time, or perhaps certain relaxations of the Carthusian rule condemned by the Carthusians themselves. He would have known about these through his relatives in the order. *MonFabri*, pp. 199, 204; *DeCertMem*, p. 312, n. 1.

[59] The early Jesuits were entrusted with the apostolate of reforming monasteries of both men and women. It was one of their most important ministries (*DeCertMem*, p. 312, n. 2).

[60] The early Society did, in fact, perform the most menial tasks all over Europe and by so doing strongly influenced the refined and fastidious society of the cinquecento.

example, that there might be many sufficiently advanced in the spiritual life to be ready in spirit to carry out the duties of a cook in order to atone for the numerous faults that are being committed and to prevent many sins by priests who do not have menservants prepared to undertake any household tasks.[61]

I wished also that many might be found who would look upon it as an honor and reward to serve Mass and answer the responses with fervor. *Fiat! Fiat!*[62]

263 That day I observed how profitable it was for every man to be present to the memory of the just man who prays to God in charity and in the light of the spirit. Further, I wished very much that the saints who stand always in the presence of God might in their state of glory remember me in their desires.[63]

264 I also had some lights about the quality of all that is created in Christ. If whatever is in God is God himself, it cannot be that whatever is in Christ insofar as he is man is not endowed with perfect beauty.

Let us then, with an ardent desire, beg him to be so good as to admit us into his memory so that, living in him, we may please God and that thus a love may be born in us which will enable us to contemplate and in our turn love God himself and Jesus Christ our Lord forever.[64]

265 With regard to our Society (concern for which never leaves me, by a grace from God), I felt a desire which had aroused great devotion in me at other times. It was that the Society might one day grow sufficiently in numbers and in virtue to be capable, through the quantity and quality of its members, of restoring at some time the ruins of all religious orders, the present ruins and those soon to come[65]—unless God intervenes.

To bring this about I wished that a multitude of persons both lay and ecclesiastical, having left all behind, might resolve to offer them-

---

[61] Having no male servants, priests engaged young women as servants and sinned with them. It was a widespread scandal especially in Germany.

[62] The serving of Mass had been given up, partly as a result of Protestant attacks on the Mass and on the sacraments, partly as a result of popular Catholic ignorance of what the Mass and the sacraments meant. Attendance at Mass had been largely abandoned.

[63] Luke 1:19; Tob. 12:15. In a letter to Kalckbrenner (document X below, pp. 343–346), Favre recalls his joy at knowing that he is remembered by a "saint" while he is in this life (*MonFabri*, p. 194).

[64] We can please God only when we are united with Christ.

[65] Another comment on the disastrous state of religious life in Germany (§261 n. 59 above).

selves for any kind of life under obedience[66] which has been instituted by the Roman Church. From these some might be chosen and found suitable for our order and some for other orders.[67]

May it be God's will that these desires come true. May he also send us persons able to test the spirits,[68] to discern not only which ones are of God but also, among those persons who are from God, which ones are called to one order and state of life and which ones to other states.[69]

May Jesus send us persons of a faith, hope, and charity so universally Catholic and of a spirit so universal and so open as to concern itself with the restoration of all the ancient orders of the Church. May all monasteries and all monastic sites be once again thronged;[70] and lastly (this is first in the order of ends) may the understanding, the memory, and the will of all men, their hearts, and their bodies, be sanctified and made perfect in Christ Jesus. Amen.

266 Another day, while reciting the office of St. Roch, confessor,[71] I became aware of the usefulness, the truth, and the necessity of the external worship rendered to Christ and to his saints. Then I felt deep sorrow that in our day public rites and ceremonies were so much despised, seeing that they are so necessary to keep men in a state of humility, union, charity, and, finally, every virtue of religion.

In the Old Testament there existed a great diversity of animal sacrifices and other kinds of rites, carried out according to the flesh, which were to find their fulfillment in the true and mystical body of Jesus Christ.[72] Why then should our liturgy and the external worship of

---

[66] The vow of obedience to a superior establishes a person as a religious and must be in conformity with the Church, which is the rule of all obedience.

[67] Favre retraces here the stages of a vocation as found in the *Spiritual Exercises:* first the offering of oneself and the choice of a life of poverty; then the "election" under the impulse of the Spirit; lastly the confirmation of a vocation by the reception of a candidate into the religious institute.

[68] The reference is to spiritual directors who are skilled enough to discern spirits and to distinguish genuine from false vocations. Favre was much preoccupied with this problem. See §333.

[69] There is a double criterion: the spiritual movements inspired by God on the one hand and the personal qualities and gifts of a candidate on the other. They too come from God and are an indication of his will.

[70] On March 10, 1546, Favre wrote in the same sense: "By this do we recognize the true doctor and preacher Christ, that he brings man to the naked Christ and that through him monasteries are filled" (*MonFabri*, p. 406).

[71] St. Roch was born in Montpellier, France, about 1350 and died in Angera, Lombardy, about 1378. His feast was celebrated on August 16, 17, or 18. *NCathEnc* 12:540, 541; §90.

[72] Around the ninth century the expression "the Body of Christ," in a Eucharistic context, referred to the Church. Then, undergoing a long and slow transformation,

the New Testament, which are an extension of the body of our Lord and his saints, be considered as contrary to the will of God?

The ceremonies of the Old Testament—to speak in general terms—were symbols of others which were to appear with the New Testament, but these latter contain spiritual realities alone.

The Old Testament not only foretold the spirit of Christ but also his holy body.[73] Thus, through the corporal rites of the New Testament, we fulfill what had been promised: the worship of the holiness of Christ incarnate and the imitation of Christ not only in spirit but also in body because our bodies are the temples of the Holy Spirit.[74] In Old Testament days they offered up the flesh of animals; now we offer up the Body of Christ. They purified their bodies with natural water to give us to understand that we should wash away that old man of ours with spiritual water.[75] In these outward gestures we possess an external worship, the purpose of which is the fulfillment of the Old Law and its symbols and not the foreshadowing of something else to be looked for in this life.[76]

We possess an interior worship also in the words of God, of Christ, and of the Church, and at the same time in the Holy Spirit. Those who care nothing for external worship do not understand what the humanity of Christ means, and they neglect, in addition, the duty of sanctifying our bodies and our flesh. For some rites of the New Law are, in a way, shadows that foretell the heavenly worship to be given to God in his glory.[77]

---

it came to mean the Eucharistic Body of Christ in opposition to the expression "Mystical Body," which was applied to the Church. This latter was the meaning Favre was taught as a student in Paris. H. de Lubac, *Corpus Mysticum* (Paris, 1944), pp. 125–135; *NCathEnc* 10:166–170.

[73] Col. 2:17.

[74] 1 Cor. 6:19.

[75] Heb. 10:22.

[76] The worship of the New Testament is not only the fulfillment of the Old Testament rites and the reality of what they foreshadowed but has in itself its own validity and worth. It is not just a preparation for a purely spiritual worship in this life that transcends all external rites.

[77] The earlier reformers, Luther and Calvin, maintained a purely spiritual and interior worship as a reaction to the abuses they noted in the external worship of the Catholic Church, in this way hoping to eliminate these abuses. Instead, they brought into being something quite the opposite. In heaven man's soul and spiritualized body will worship God, but as one being. There is an echo of anti-Protestant polemic in this passage.

▸ March 12

267 On St. Gregory's day (the Gregory who was bishop and confessor, pontiff, and doctor of the Church), I experienced a holy and deep-felt gratitude for the teaching which that great doctor and pontiff, more than any other doctor, left us about the souls in purgatory.[78] If he had not spoken so clearly and at such length about purgatory and about the means of bringing relief to the suffering souls, there would be much more disbelief in our day concerning that great and charitable duty.

May God be blessed, then, for having divinely instructed the great doctor in this devotion to the souls and for having given a great advocate so conformed to Jesus Christ to those who have to undergo purification. I then resolved in the future to be more mindful of this holy pope than I have been up to now when commemorating the dead. Not only would I observe but I would also preach this practice so that the friends of the saint might become the friends of the dead and, conversely, that those who pray for the dead might then remember to invoke the help of that pontiff in their prayers.

▸ March 23

268 On the day of the holy Passion of the Lord,[79] I noted and became aware of the following. First of all, I observed that during the whole of Lent I had been disturbed in different ways by thoughts and interior motions, a sign that the wounds of my miseries and imperfections were beginning to reopen. In spite of myself I was unable to do anything else but "weep over myself and over my children,"[80] I mean over my personal defects and those to be found in my labors either for Christ, for my fellowmen, or for my own self. My spirit was entirely drawn away from those things which, as it recognized a long time ago, were the places of its peace; and my flesh was totally immersed in those things in which, ever since my childhood, it had discovered only death for itself and disquiet.[81] Disorder in my actions, sluggishness, and want of spiritual perception seemed to have come again to life. In short, all those wicked feelings of mine I believed almost dead appeared to have

---

[78] St. Gregory the Great, doctor of the Church, born at Rome (ca. 540), was pope from 590 to 604. Favre alludes to the pious practice of saying thirty consecutive Masses for the souls in purgatory; they were known as Gregorian Masses.

[79] Good Friday. At Christmas Favre had received the grace of rebirth. During Passiontide and the Easter season (§268–§281), he comes to a new understanding of the Cross at the end of a slow process of deprivation (§238).

[80] Luke 23:28.

[81] Sexual temptations which would last all his life.

been reborn during that Lent. With justice was I afflicted; with justice did I walk in sadness, downcast in the midst of that turmoil that sorely tried my spirit, my soul, and my body.[82]

269   But when Passion Sunday came and I began to go over again in my mind those states of my soul, I became aware, and not without spiritual comfort, that they had all been of advantage to me.[83] That day and that season consecrated to the passion of our Lord is the time for remembering the wounds of Christ's body, his torments, his death, the insults and ignominies and mockery he suffered. It must then have been good for me that my spiritual wounds and the scars left by my infirmities (not fully healed at the time) opened, as it were, into fresh wounds from then on during that season in which we celebrate once again the sufferings and the merits of Christ.

270   God then granted me the favor of seeking with my whole heart, through the crucifixion and death of Jesus Christ, a remedy from those many great infirmities of mine. I prayed to the Lord that the virtue of his blood which was poured out on earth might purify the unwholesome humors[84] in my blood—the ones I desire to be freed from when I say "Deliver me from blood, O God, God of my salvation."[85] I prayed that the power of his body of flesh laid in the tomb might remedy the weakness of my flesh and my body. I asked that his soul, which became separated from his body and descended into the lower regions, might sanctify my spirit and my soul by driving out from it all those powers and forces that have up to now made it seem that I was given life for the sole purpose of committing sin—I mean that of my own self I am inclined to evil sentiments.[86]

That Friday, then, I resolved to offer the Mass I intended to celebrate on the coming Saturday to obtain from God the grace of a rebuilding and refashioning of myself in some worthy way. I hoped to obtain that grace through the merits acquired by Christ in permitting the destruction of his holy temple—a destruction of such a kind that all the

---

[82] A common state of soul with Favre; he sums it up in words from Ps. 42 (41): 2.

[83] The only change that St. Ignatius advises in desolation is to oppose the desolation by more prayer and penance (*SpEx,* [318–319]).

[84] *Sanguines* (which is distinct from *sanguis*) designates all the obscure influences or powers in the blood, unwholesome and dangerous humors (see §30 and §95 with regard to the *spiritus vitalis*), while *sanguis* represents life and in pouring itself out represents the gift of one's self. See §121, §122.

[85] The Douay Version (Ps. 50:26) is given here. The RSV seems to give a better sense: "Deliver me from blood-guiltiness (or from death)" (Ps. 51 [50]: 14).

[86] A reference to Rom. 7.

blood he shed remained in one place by itself, his body in another, and his soul in another still, awaiting the resurrection.[87]

271 There came to me then a desire inspired by special devotion and reflection to become more attached to this prayer: "Soul of Christ, sanctify me; Body of Christ, save me; Blood of Christ, inebriate me; Water from the side of Christ, wash me."[88]

I was very deeply touched by a singular understanding of the beatitude and power possessed by the soul of Christ separated from his body and united to the divinity as he was seen descending to the lower regions by the holy fathers in limbo[89] and by the souls undergoing purification.

While I was contemplating the body of Christ in the tomb, lifeless yet united to the divinity,[90] a great desire led me to ask that all the power of sin in me, of vanity and of illusion, might be brought to nothing; and I asked as well the grace of possessing life in God through Jesus Christ our Lord, risen from the dead.

▸ March 24

272 On Saturday, the vigil of Easter Sunday, there came to me some very worthwhile reflections on these two articles of faith: "He suffered under Pontius Pilate, was crucified, died, and was buried; he descended into hell, on the third day he rose from the dead." In accordance with them I was given a wish to suffer something for Christ, to bear my cross daily, to die to sin and to the world, to be buried by losing all awareness of this passing life, and to rise in newness of spirit and of flesh[91] so as to be led in all things by the Spirit of Jesus Christ our Lord. He died for our sins and was raised from the dead for our justification;[92] for it was his will that, dead to sin, we live to the justice of Christ[93] and that we live so as to die no longer, without ever falling back into sin, so that we never again allow that death which is sin to

---

[87] A reference to John 2:19 which recalls the liturgy of the Passion; Christ's death and resurrection are symbolized by the destruction and the rebuilding of the temple.

[88] This prayer, called the *Anima Christi*, was frequently found in the medieval books of hours. Its frequent recitation is recommended in the *Spiritual Exercises*. St. Ignatius, however, is not its author.

[89] The souls of the just detained in limbo. See §59, §288.

[90] A theological opinion defended by Peter Lombard (Lombard, *Sententiarum*, III, dist. 21, 1) and by St. Thomas (*ST*, III, 52, 3).

[91] Rom. 7:6.

[92] Rom. 4:25.

[93] 1 Pet. 2:24.

have power over us: "Christ being raised from the dead will never die again; death no longer has dominion over him."[94]

▸ March 25

273 On the holy day of the Lord's Resurrection, I felt unusual consolation during Mass but without that sensible devotion I too frequently desired to possess, either for my own satisfaction or for the edification of others. My desire for it was a kind of passion in which there was some self-seeking—or at least I was moved to desire it by an inordinate impulse—inordinate, I say, as regards the intensity of the desire that rose up in me all of a sudden.

274 I felt moved and as if enlightened by the admiration, the reflections, and the praises aroused in me by the humanity of Christ wholly united to his divinity. In truth, a human body united to the divinity is a wonderful means of acting on the world of material bodies. More wonderful still is the body's principle, the rational soul united immediately to the divinity.

How define, how measure sensible and rational activity when the act of the physical, organic body is conjoined to the omnipotent Godhead?[95] But the human spirit—that is, the soul insofar as it is in the act of abstract reflection[96] on eternal and spiritual realities—can appear far greater still when it is seen united to Almighty God and moved and guided by him in all ways.

275 I was then given a heartfelt prayer to God, through Jesus Christ risen from the dead, that my body, soul, and spirit might one day be glorified by his grace to the praise of him from whom, through whom, and in whom are all grace and glory and whatever natural goodness I possess.[97]

I wished too that the bodies of men, their souls, and their spirits, whose God-given nature is to be vessels of great capacity, could all be filled with graces and with glory from the overflow of that noblest

---

[94] Rom. 6:9.

[95] The expression *actus corporis physici organici* (the act of a physical, organic body) is the Aristotelian and Thomistic definition of a human soul; it is the "form" of the body and the principle of sensible life and of intellectual activity. See §136 n. 277 above.

[96] *Abstracte versatur* means the act of "abstraction" (nothing to do with absentmindedness), a technical expression used in scholastic language to describe the activity proper to the intellect through which it grasps the essence of an individual material thing by prescinding from what constitutes its individuality.

[97] Favre held that existence, insofar as it is good, comes from the Father, grace from the Son, and glory from the Holy Spirit.

vessel, the humanity of Christ, which contains all the fullness of the deity.[98] May we, in our turn, be filled from his abundance.[99]

276 By applying to myself the four properties of the glorified body of Christ, I sought, for the purpose of doing good and bearing with evil, these corresponding properties for my spirit. I wished that I might become through grace more ready, more acute, more receptive to enlightenment, and less sensitive to evil influences—this is a kind of impassibility.[100]

277 On Easter Monday, after saying matins I fell back again on to my long-familiar cross, that depression with its triple cause: first, my not being conscious of any signs of God's love for me in proportion to my desires; second, my feeling within me, more than I would wish, traces of the old Adam; third, my inability to bring forth all the fruit I desire for the salvation of my neighbor. Almost all the afflictions of my spirit are summed up in these three points, so that I am led to believe that they constitute my cross.[101]

278 On the same day, as I was thus distinguishing these three elements, I experienced within me something like an answer which said, You desired to be taken down from the cross before death,[102] but Christ died on his cross. Why then are you still unwilling even to begin dying on your own cross? But your sole desire is to be chastened and corrected so as to be capable of renewal even in this life. But the vivifying of your spirit, insofar as it depended on those accidental consolations[103] which were the only ones you perceived and became aware of up to the present, lay in the joy you received from feeling yourself devoted to God and in finding yourself less attracted by the tendencies natural to the old Adam. It lay too in the recognition that the labor of your hands has borne some fruit[104] which both you and the witnesses of

---

[98] John 1:16.

[99] The images of the spring (§133), the tree (§280), and the vessel (recipient) are used to express the "descent" of life from Christ.

[100] Traditionally, theologians have distinguished four qualities of the glorified body of Christ: immortality, impassibility, agility, and subtility. These were derived from an exegesis of 1 Cor. 15. See *NCathEnc* 6:512–513. Favre's description of the qualities he desires for his spirit gives a negative portrait of himself.

[101] See §241 on the three arms of the cross.

[102] The historical, liturgical, and spiritual order of these two mysteries of Christ cannot be inverted.

[103] Compared with eternal happiness (substantial consolation), these can be called accidental consolations. But to possess eternal happiness means the total transformation of human nature in imitation of the paschal mystery of Christ.

[104] Ps. 128 (127): 2.

✢ March 25 227

your good works could partake of. Even now, desire to die to this life of yours because it is unstable and changeable beyond measure.[105]

279 And you will be able to die in earnest to this life only through the death of the cross. It is the opposite to this life and comprises these three elements:

1. You should seek out that sleep[106] which is the renouncement of your attraction for deeply felt accidental fervor.
2. Be in no way disturbed even if all the old Adam in you grows up again stronger than ever with his roots and his concupiscence; they are neither venially nor mortally sinful.[107]
3. Do not be troubled if you find no fruit at all from your external labors in your hands, nor do others, who observe you closely so as to imitate you or delight in the good you are doing, or those again who watch in order to calumniate you or those who look on you with contempt.

Once you undergo that death of the cross (and in public, insofar as you desire it), when you will be like someone buried, gone from the memory of all men, safe from their admiration, their suspicions, and their scorn, no longer looked to with expectation, then you will be given at least to desire if not to lay the foundation[108] of a new kind of consolation for your spirit. In that way, through a resurrection of your body, your soul, and your spirit, you will experience a new kind of life—another life of which the root, trunk, branches, leaves, and fruit will not be like those of your present state. They will be more enduring, and each will have its own unchanging quality.[109]

280 Up to the present you found more consolation in the splendor of the tree, which proceeds from divine grace, than in its root, where abides its vigor and its power. You had eyes only for the branches and

---

[105] Favre realizes that he must die to himself; this is a passive death which purifies. It is in no way "the labor of his hands," for it is something that must be undergone—a radical transformation of his being so that he becomes completely renewed. See *DeCertMem*, p. 322, n. 4.

[106] "To seek sleep" *(ex animo in hoc obdormias)* is a literal translation of an expression from Scripture. Here it means to seek peace. "Sleep" in Scripture may mean death (Ps. 13 (12): 3; John 11:11) or the mystical sleep of the spouse in the Canticle of Canticles, 2:7 *(DBibTheol,* pp. 558–560).

[107] Concupiscence is not a sin, though it may be one of its roots, a point made against the Protestants.

[108] §191, §328. These new desires are for Favre the beginning and the foundation of a new kind of spiritual life.

[109] The imagery here forms a poetic description in mystical terms of the new interior life that is in store for Favre. It will come to full flower and fruit in heaven.

the flowers, for the leaves and the fruit—all very changeable things inasmuch as they tend to their own perfection. From them no constant and stable consolation can be derived.

Do not seek the root of this tree for the sake of its fruit, but rather the fruit and the other things for the sake of the root. Seek to tarry ever longer as days go by and to strike deeper roots where this tree has its roots, but do not seek to have its fruit remain in you. By its root and not by its fruit will you be led to the glory of this tree.

Put whatever you can close to the root, for one day it will appear in its glory as it first appeared in its glory in the bosom of the earth when the soul of Christ descended into the lower regions, that soul which is the true created root and which has become, of all rational creatures, the fruit which is the highest in glory. This tree is then inverted so that the root attains the highest point, dropping beneath it all its fruit and sending its power out in streams from the heights to the depths.[110]

281 The blessings to come from God's glory, the heavenly blessings, will show that the fruit, which is the glorification of the true root, will itself appear better than all the rest of the tree; for that life of beatitude is a state in which the better fruit and the greater accidental perfections find their place in what is better by its essence.

But things are not the same in this wretched life. It requires that what is better must be more deeply plunged in affliction and be more hidden. This is the way with the root, for though in its essence it is superior, its accidents do not possess a higher degree of perfection but rather one that is lower. If then you seek for fruit, seek those of the other life without wanting to taste what is accidental in these fruits before you have experienced whatever is accidental in these holy roots, destined one day to be glorified and changed into fruit.[111]

281a: Up to the beginning of April, Favre had been lodging with the parish priest of St. Christopher's in Mainz. (See no. 289 below, where Favre mentions his return to the church to say Mass.) This man, the Reverend Conrad, whom he had converted from a life of concubinage, was shortly to enter the charterhouse in Cologne. Favre rented a house and went to live in it on the first of April, which that year was the octave of Easter. He would stay there until his final departure from Mainz. The neighborhood was unsavory, as Peter Canisius notes (Braunsberger, EppCan *8:416). Settling into this new lodging awakened a train of reflections in Favre (nos. 282–287 below).*

---

[110] The symbolism here with its development is Favre's own.
[111] The condition of mystical death (*DeCertMem*, pp. 88–90).

▸ April 1543

282 On another day during the octave of that Easter, as I was settling into a house which I had rented, my mind and spirit were moved in various ways to desire that my entrance into that new dwelling place might be a happy one. So in every room and passage of the house I knelt down and said this prayer: "Visit, we pray you, O Lord, this dwelling and drive far from it all the wiles of the enemy; may your holy angels dwell in it and keep us in peace, and may your blessing be always upon us, through Christ our Lord."[112]

I felt that I had said it with holy fervor and that it was a fitting and praiseworthy act for someone going to live in a place for the first time.

283 I then invoked the angel guardians of the neighborhood, and I felt that this too was a fitting and praiseworthy thing to do when changing to a new locality. I wished also in a prayer that the wicked spirits in the neighborhood might be powerless to harm either myself or those coming to live with me in the house—above all that spirit of fornication[113] which is sure to haunt the prostitutes, the adulterers, and those other abandoned people whose presence in the vicinity I had been told about.

284 I also invoked SS. Ottilia, Jodocus, and Lucy, to whom the chapel beside my rented house was dedicated. I felt my spirit touched by grief in various ways as I looked at the ruins of that chapel,[114] defiled in a sense by the acts of fornication committed by people who pass through it.

This inspired in me great longings to restore it and to revive the divine worship once offered up by these saints. Their feasts were no longer celebrated with fervor in their chapel, nor was their devotion remembered in that very place where once there was such great and devoted trust in their patronage.

I said Mass and applied it as a remedy against the sins committed in the abandonment of that worship and at the same time for its revival and reestablishment. May God grant me through the intercession of these and of all the other saints grace to share someday in that restora-

---

[112] The concluding prayer of compline, now known as Night Prayer. In the modern breviary this prayer has been retained without a change.

[113] Favre, deeply influenced by the demonology of his time, seems to hold that a bad angel attends each person to do him harm (§175 n. 62 and §252 n. 38 above). The petition is from the Litany of the Saints: "From the spirit of fornication, set us free, O Lord." §9, §30, §35, §410; O'Leary, "Discernment," pp. 72–75.

[114] For Favre the ruins of this chapel are a symbol not only of material but also of spiritual ruin. The idea occurs frequently in the *Memoriale,* accompanied by desires of rebuilding and restoration.

tion, whether by a visible and material contribution or in some spiritual way.

285 The same day around nightfall, as I was to be the first and only one to stay overnight in that house, I felt some kind of physical upset and discomfort in my body which gave rise to a mood of depression in my spirit. I began to beg the Lord that he would grant me to have wholesome air in that dwelling or, if he so preferred, to contract some infection that might be for my good. On behalf of my neighbors, however (I mean my landlord and all those in the vicinity), I earnestly besought that the air of the entire locality might be beneficial to them, that they might be preserved from plagues and other ills, and lastly that my arrival among them might bring them all kinds of prosperity and good fortune. I wished too for the preservation of the house from fire and from all other accidents, which are never sent or permitted by God without a just reason.[115]

286 In this connection I was enabled to recall with a feeling of gratitude the many different lodgings in which I had stayed during my lifetime. As a life, it was wandering and restless[116] to a degree—as I believe God intended it to be, because it was for his sake alone that I have put up in so many lodgings ever since I came to know myself. Thinking over all these changes of dwelling, made neither for the sake of greater ease nor to avoid inconvenience, I thanked God that up to then I had not met death in any of them or fallen ill or become weakened in health.

I could not, however, avoid finding myself frequently in places either infected or threatened by all kinds of diseases. I very often spent the night in filthy hospitals,[117] often again in wretched lodgings, at times in bitter cold and in places destitute of everything except a roof, hay, and straw. And on occasion I even had to sleep in the open air.

---

[115] Favre, as superior, would most likely be the first to take up residence. His fears and anxieties resulted not only from his temperament but also from his deteriorating physical state; he was within three years of his death. In addition, his fears of infection were only too well founded; in those days plagues were frequent and struck suddenly with terrible effect. Fire, too, was a constant hazard in houses built of wood. Favre's reactions to his depression, the surprising prayer for some infection that might be for his spiritual good, was an act of generosity in accordance with the teaching of the *Exercises* (*SpEx*, [319]).

[116] He was a pilgrim like all the early fathers of the Society. See §47.

[117] In the Middle Ages and even well into the sixteenth century, these "hospitals" were rather night shelters or refuges for the poor and for wayfarers. They did not provide any treatment for the sick. The first Jesuits often stayed in them overnight or for a few days. Any nonspiritual work they did in them was of the most menial and repugnant kind. See linking passage 15a above.

✥   *April 1543–April 1*   231

May he be blessed forever who protected us in all these situations—myself and all those in the same or different conditions! For all this I thanked God, hoping for his protection in this new abode of mine as well.

And when he will come to meet me in death, he will not wish me less well, he who is God of life and death, and I shall not be any the less indebted to him for my bodily health and for all the other blessings I have received from his hand up to now.

287 Then I prayed for all those who have had or will have occasion to stay awhile or live in one of the places where I myself put up, or was made welcome for rest and refreshment, or was given accommodation, or was allowed to stay for a time.

May my God, who gave me these feeling, thoughts, and desires with others like them, deign to fulfill them according to the voice of his holy word and the mind of the Holy Spirit and not according to the literal content of my own reasonings[118] or of my spiritual perceptions.

▸ *April 1*

288 The same day, as I was writing to the Countess de Montfort[119] and to the vicar general *in spiritualibus* of the most reverend bishop of Speyer,[120] I began to understand for the first time with an inner perception[121] certain things about the Resurrection which I had not observed up to then. They were some conclusions I had drawn from the reflection that the beatification of our souls will first take place while they are separated from our bodies, just as Christ manifested the blessed state of his spirit before his body was glorified. The consideration that our souls can be, and in fact will be, beatified apart from their bodies, that is, outside them, leads us more readily to despise those bodies of ours,[122] to

---

[118] For the distinction between *spiritus* and *verba*, see §254, §300; O'Leary, "Discernment," p. 114.

[119] This letter has disappeared. The recipient was the wife of Count Jean de Montfort, supreme judge of the Imperial Court of Justice and a relative of Monsignor Truchsess, soon to be a cardinal. The countess was a staunch defender of the faith. Favre had met her in April 1542 as he was returning to Speyer from Spain, and they began and kept up a correspondence (*MonFabri*, pp. 160–161).

[120] This was George Mussbach, vicar general to the bishop of Speyer, Philip of Flersheim. The expression *in spiritualibus* means "auxiliary in pastoral affairs." He had made the Exercises under Favre, but his bishop could not spare the time for them. Both men sought and gladly received spiritual aid from Favre (*MonFabri*, pp. 67–69).

[121] Favre returns to a light he had been given before (§257) and finds a deeper interior understanding of it.

[122] Harsh conditions of life in the Middle Ages explain to some extent the rigid

realize that we should not attach ourselves to the flesh to the extent of having to live according to its will, and to recognize clearly that we should not become absorbed (as does happen) in the needs of the body.

For the body is not as indispensable as we seem to believe, seeing that we labor for it as if our happiness and unhappiness alike depended on it. In reality, some possess happiness already in their souls and not because of the body or in it or with it, whereas others not yet reunited to their bodies exist in misery and in wretchedness.[123]

May Jesus, who died first, then confirmed the holy fathers[124] in the state of beatitude before their resurrection from the dead, teach us to live with the life of a spirit separated from its body—not with that wretched life which consists in brooding over evil, calling it ever to mind, and desiring it. May he teach us rather to live with that life which is its opposite—a life which is experienced through the three powers of the soul itself, memory, intelligence, and will.[125]

288a: The gap of three weeks between the above entry and no. 289 does not necessarily indicate an absence. We know that Favre was still in Mainz on April 12 (MonFabri, p. 194). He must have been more than usually busy and, in addition, was taken up with Peter Canisius, who had arrived in Mainz about this time and was going through the Exercises.

▸ *April 23*

289 On the day of St. George the martyr, while I was saying Mass in the church of St. Christopher[126] and commemorating the soul of someone not long dead (the Mass was on the first day after the burial), I felt greatly consoled by a vivid awareness of the glory to be conferred on souls by Christ. In a special way I perceived the generosity shown by

---

asceticism then practiced. To despise the body was to express a preference for what was spiritual.

[123] Those who, before the resurrection of the body, already possess the happiness of heaven or are condemned to the pains of hell.

[124] The just of the Old Testament awaiting in limbo the coming of the Savior, who would lead them into the state of glory.

[125] Memory, understanding, and will, so often turned to evil in this life by the body's appetites, are destined, once separated from that body, to be the reflection of the Trinity, which created them in its image. To the extent that someone renounces a life of slavery to the body will such a person experience that divine life mirrored by the three powers of his soul.

[126] A church in Mainz. Favre had been lodging with the parish priest for some time. See linking passage 281a above.

him to his own with regard to their labors, for he rewards each one according to the works done out of faith in him.

The reward for each act done in the state of grace must needs be great (in the place and on the day of judgment God will take no account of acts not done in the state of Christ's grace). Must not the Almighty himself weigh up and evaluate those acts according to the charity and the generosity of his human nature and reward them through the infinite power of his divinity?

Because Christ's humility is infinite, he cannot forget the least acts done in the state of grace, and because at the same time his riches are infinite, he cannot but reward most bountifully.[127]

---

[127] In this passage Favre begins a reflection on justification (§289–§292), subjecting the Protestant position to some criticism. Gabriel Biel (see page 14 n. 31 above) held that no act can be meritorious without grace—understanding grace, not as a supernatural habit dwelling in the soul, but as the divine favor *(gratia):* God in his mercy freely accepting an act as meritorious. For Biel—and this is his fundamental position as it was that of all nominalist theologians—God can of his absolute power *(de potentia sua absoluta)* make an act meritorious which has been performed without the supernatural habit of grace, since in itself such a divine act does not involve any contradiction. The theology that underlies these critical reflections of Favre displays a tendency both voluntaristic and extrinsecist; it was the theology he had been taught by Peña out of Biel's *Commentary on the Sentences of Peter Lombard.* Its presuppositions are the same as those of Protestant theology: Salvation is not founded on a communication of sanctifying grace but on the divine favor *(gratia)* and on the trust that should accompany it. From these presuppositions Luther concluded that man's part in his justification is faith—faith being understood as a confident expectation of God's forgiving mercy. This view is a statement of psychological fact, a theology of religious experience in which man's awareness of his sinfulness remains despite his trust in God's forgiveness; it is his personal attitude to God, not his ontological reality, that undergoes change. In the Catholic position man freely cooperates with divine grace in repentance, faith, hope, and charity—yet it is God's grace that works the *whole* of a sinner's justification, including his free cooperation with grace. The changing of a sinner into a just man is something real and objective, whatever the accompanying experience; it is an ontological, not a merely psychological, happening. It is now possible to see that the conclusions Favre draws from the same presuppositions are different from Luther's: Because Christ became man and because he is compassionate and humble of heart, his will is to be satisfied with human actions which are of little worth; he condescends to accept as something of value and merit the least action performed in a state of grace. For these reasons the Christian ought not to lose trust in his master (§292) but should keep on acting out of faith in him *(in fide ipsius)* or, as Favre expresses it analogically, in the grace of Christ *(in gratia Christi)*—*gratia* here being an indication of the divine favor (§291). Favre therefore views the Redemption much more from the standpoint of a personal relationship, one of mercy and of trust, than from the standpoint of a relationship based on a communication of grace. But he does not, of course, exclude the latter. For the Nominalist origin of this position, see §50 n. 95 above, and for the theological objections against

290 Then I felt truly grieved that in these times good works are so much underrated and that people hardly ever talk of rewards for them.

It follows that there is no longer any fear of retribution for wrongdoing.[128] So the hope of finding what was sown in tears[129] is destroyed, and the fear of committing actual sin disappears because there seems to be no punishment for that sin.[130]

291 In short, to give up taking into account the physical acts of men whether good or bad is to give up taking the divine humanity into account. It made its appearance in the Incarnation precisely so that our salvation might be accomplished in a manner becoming human nature through Christ, God and man, who is destined to judge the living and the dead and to examine the deeds done by each man in his mortal life.[131] He will come in that same humanity in which he was seen ascending into heaven, according to this text: "He will come in the same way as you saw him going into heaven."[132] And all the gratitude, all the generosity and liberality towards servants and subordinates that can be thought of in men—all of it, we must assume, exists in Christ to a surpassing degree.[133]

292 It is plain that a mortal prince can fill one of his lowliest servants with joy simply by showing interest in his work. The delighted servant then marvels at the degree of attention paid to a kind of work which, in other respects, he judges of little value.[134] Why, therefore, do they wrong us by preaching that Christ's human state is divine but omit to say that it is similar to ours? Why do away with these comparisons

---

it, see O'Leary, "Discernment," n. 16, p. 118; see also *NCathEnc* 8:77–92, art. "Justification," and 10:483–486, art. "Nominalism."

[128] §202.

[129] Ps. 126 (125): 5; §173.

[130] Protestant theology recognized only two kinds of sin: original sin, which is common to all men and only death delivers them from it, and the sin against faith, which is a refusal to trust oneself wholly to the divine mercy and to the hope of future salvation. Although Luther always held that faith required good works, he nonetheless maintained that works as such had no meaning and that, as a result, personal (actual) sins could not be pardoned, nor did they deserve special punishment.

[131] 2 Cor. 5:10.

[132] Acts 1:11.

[133] If men are grateful for physical labor which is done for their sake, all the more will Christ in his body be grateful for physical labor (good works) done for him. The expression "physical labors" refers to works, in opposition to the purely spiritual faith of Protestants.

[134] Here again the value of labor comes solely from the esteem in which it is held by the master. See §224.

and likenesses between God and men while leaving in him that flesh of ours which he took to himself?

It was his will to have a body like ours and become a servant to him whose equal he was so that we in our lowly state might more readily believe in the promise of a likeness to God and reflect more deeply on the meaning of the signs.[135] Having a God who is man, we worship him as our God, and we should serve him not only spiritually as a Spirit[136] but serve him also in body as our incarnate Lord, a man like us in that nature in which he suffered for us and in which he now reigns, seated at the right hand of God the Father Almighty.

Our nature, therefore, exalted in that way by God, should be reverenced by us in holiness and in justice[137] because we see in it God's perfect instrument for our redemption, our election, our justification, our sanctification, and our glorification[138]—it is indeed the temple of the fullness of the divinity.[139]

293 The first angel refused to descend below that nature, to descend below himself through humility and, further, to submit to the Almighty. He wanted through his own efforts to enter into the joy and the glory of the Lord his God. The mystery decreed from all eternity[140] had been communicated to him: the humility of the Son of God which led him from all eternity to will and determine to become man and thus lower himself below him who had begotten him from eternity as equal to himself.

But Lucifer raised himself above himself because he would not lower himself below God made man, who is Christ, and so from the highest he descended to the lowest. Refusing to act in accordance with the faith and grace in which he had been created and unwilling to descend below that nature which had been assumed by God, he lost the grace of faith and ascended above himself saying, "I will ascend and be

---

[135] Here signs *(signa)* are the sacraments, sacramentals, and whatever shows forth the action of Christ. See §190, §223, and others.

[136] §291.

[137] Luke. 1:75.

[138] Rom. 8:30.

[139] Col. 2:9.

[140] The word "mystery" is taken here in its Pauline sense of "a design of God," hidden in the Old Testament and revealed in Christ. Favre uses the phrase *humilitas Christi* (the humility of Christ) to describe the mystery of Christ's lowering himself to become man (§289).

like the Almighty."[141] And that ascension brought about his ruin and his fall.

▸ April 25

294 On the day of St. Mark the Evangelist, in the morning before saying Mass, I became aware of a spirit drawing me downward. Then a mood of dejection stole into my heart because of that feeling, and I was grieved to tears to note that there existed still in my flesh something that gave entry to these disturbances, something that could be taken advantage of by that spirit whose nature it is to lead our spirit backwards and our flesh downward.[142]

My heart full of remorse,[143] I sought therefore from the Lord what I had at other times recognized as a true remedy against such temptations: that he might grant me grace to be always directed towards that good which still lies before me and above me and, if I have some just cause for regret, that I should feel more remorse because of the virtues I still lack than on account of the fault I committed by my cooperation in such sinful feelings; lastly, I petitioned that my desires for perfection should occupy me so fully in my quest for its attainment that no room would be left for the memory of those things that lead me downward or backward.[144]

295 Then I clearly understood, as I frequently did in the past, how a desire to know and experience the things of God brought us by a certain necessity to recognize different degrees of knowing and willing them—degrees that we had not previously possessed or attained. I understood too, in the light of all this, that we should keep on pressing forward to find these gifts and possess them in peace—not that we should intend to dwell there, but it is in this way that we seek to establish stages in our ascent.

This should be a threefold progress corresponding to the three kinds of virtue. The first looks to divine knowledge and to interior motions which guide the spirit directly to God; the second has to do

---

[141] Isa. 14:14. Grace is lost following a refusal to believe in a God who reveals himself through men. Favre notes the same process at work in Eve, who lost the grace of faith by refusing to believe the command that came to her through Adam (§220); it is the same with the Catholic who loses his faith because he refuses to accept the revelations that come through God's Church (§219).

[142] There is a dead weight in the flesh which presses it down so that it cannot raise itself up; in the spirit there are repugnances and fears which hold it back and hinder it from advancing and from growth. For Favre these are the two main tendencies of the spiritual life. See §241.

[143] *In spiritu compunctionis:* literally, in a spirit of compunction.

[144] See §54.

with whatever directly concerns our perfection; the third, with whatever concerns our neighbor.

It is evident that we need new knowledge every day, new and renewed interior movements for the benefit and the pressing needs, both spiritual and corporal, of our brothers. And our perfection results from all this, though our purpose should not be to make all serve the attainment of our own perfection; we should rather desire it and order it to God himself and to our neighbor for his sake.[145]

296 But as far as our perfection is concerned, as it necessarily includes the putting off of the old man as well as the putting on of the new,[146] we have to undergo, whether we like it or not, temptations of the spirit and of the flesh because they are good for us. In particular, we shall have to face not only those temptations which, like spurs, rouse us and urge us on to the practice of virtue and the attainment of peace,[147] but also those which lead to death and sin. Otherwise we would fail to recognize that we are but sand and would start building on that,[148] for Christ our rock is still incomplete in us and will have no solid foundation until we have first cast out the old man.

We must bear this, therefore, with patience. But we must also make every effort to form solidly in us what has been mentioned above, that is, to press forward with all our strength towards that which abides.[149] And we shall have to endure those incitements to sin that God permits in us.

297 . . . But because these distinctions of vocabulary[150] have not been respected, there is no reason to concern ourselves with them; they are new and not in use among the positive or even the scholastic doctors.[151]

---

[145] The relation between personal perfection, charity towards the neighbor, and the love of God has more than once given rise to notes about the ends to be pursued. See §126–§129 for the relation between prayer and apostolic activities.

[146] 2 Cor. 5:4.

[147] 2 Cor. 12:7; §63, §188. External temptations have a part to play in the deepening of the spiritual life.

[148] Matt. 7:24–27.

[149] Phil. 3:13. The life we lead as Christians, through which God works in us, must be infused with a degree of trust and optimism.

[150] There is here the conclusion only of some reflections; the first part of the manuscript is missing. Favre appears to have examined some doctrine expressed in novel terminology.

[151] Patristic theology, sometimes also called positive theology, is based on the writings of the Fathers, those writers of Christian antiquity who are invoked as witnesses to the doctrine of the Church; scholastic theology is the systematic elaboration of Christian doctrine taught in the schools. Favre's point is that the works of scholastic theologians are free from misuse of terminology.

We ought to be much on our guard against departing from the terminology in common use among Catholic doctors; and especially in treating of sacred matters we ought not to multiply expressions according to the multiplication of spiritual movements,[152] since we know that the same expression can correspond to different spiritual movements. Indeed, if everyone sets about writing and composing books using a terminology suited to his own ideas, there will arise (indeed, there has already arisen) a multiplicity of sects, of doctrines, a multiplicity of definitions and distinctions—even in sacred matters.

We should, therefore, bring our terminology into conformity with the approved writings and not try to wrest them to suit our terminology. And nothing must be admitted which in its spiritual sentiments and movements will be incapable of expression in the terminology approved by the teaching of the Catholic Church.[153]

▸ *April 26*

298 On the day of the holy martyrs and pontiffs Cletus and Marcellinus, having said the office of matins, I found great devotion in reflecting on the mercy of Christ. For through it the holy pontiff Marcellinus, who had once turned to the worship of idols through fear of death, rediscovered the heart of a most Christian martyr and so was rewarded with a martyr's crown.[154]

299 Then I was given a certain good spirit that led me to lament my numerous setbacks, backward glances, and returns to the past—these I shall never sufficiently lament. I began also to wonder that God, whether through an exercise of his mercy or his justice, had so acted towards me that rarely or ever had I experienced his Holy Spirit reproach me or threaten me with richly deserved punishment or blame me for my sins and my defects. On the contrary, he acted in such a way that the accusing voice I had been used to hearing and experiencing inwardly

---

[152] Favre refers here not only to the meaning of the terms used but also to the interior experiences they describe. Inner experiences are to be expressed in the traditional terminology of the Church. The decadent nominalism of the age lent itself to a superficial theology, the multiplication of useless questions, and to a corroding skepticism. Favre will not take part in that futile activity; for him reform must be initiated elsewhere.

[153] Not only theological teachings based on Scripture and on a tradition of revealed truth but also interior experiences have need of a terminology free as far as possible from ambiguity.

[154] Although manuscripts H, R, and S give Cletus, the reference is certainly to St. Marcellinus, pope (*NCathEnc* 9:188).

up to the present moment was that of my own conscience or of a spirit sent to try me.[155]

Hence I was given to make a wholehearted petition to the Almighty for this grace with a will to go on seeking it, that from then on I might have an inward awareness of his words and those feelings of sorrow for my sins that have been granted me by his Spirit. So I said:

"O Lord my God, up to now you seem to have been silent about the sins of my past life and even about my present failings and imperfections. You seem never yet to have spoken a word through the mouth of your Spirit about my sins, either to my soul or to my heart, at a time when you taught me in so many ways to do good and to follow your counsels.

"Begin, therefore, and in some new way—I mean through the direct action of your Spirit—impart to me the words and feelings of a true and perfect contrition. Move my soul to deplore my sins in your Spirit, as you have granted me to deplore them up to now by means of other spirits."

I experienced that desire, not because my sins had become more burdensome or because I felt the sting of a conscience not yet sufficiently untroubled and at peace. It was rather that I felt within me God's higher Spirit, in which I longed once again for a thorough renewal that would give me a new and interior awareness of my sins and a new understanding of my offenses against God.

299a: Peter Canisius (1521–1597), from Gelderland in Holland, was studying theology in Cologne when, sometime during the spring of 1543, he met and became friends with Alvaro Alfonso. From him he heard about the new order of priests and about Pierre Favre, the first companion of its founder. Learning that Favre was then in Mainz, he set off on the three days' journey up the Rhine to find him and arrived at Mainz about the tenth of April. Favre made him welcome in the presbytery of the parish priest of St. Christopher, where he himself had been lodging until April 1, and soon had him making the Exercises. On May 8, 1543, in Favre's presence, Canisius took a vow to enter the Society.

---

[155] Favre has a way of expressing his spiritual experiences as being through or in a certain spirit—always a good spirit. Here he goes on to pray explicitly for the grace of a true and perfect contrition through the direct action of the Holy Spirit. It is a sign of his spiritual growth. But some temperaments mature slowly; Ignatius waited for four years before judging Favre ready to make the full Exercises. Every spiritual director must learn to imitate the patience of the Holy Spirit. See O'Leary, "Discernment," pp. 80–81.

▸ *April 28*

300 Another day, during a visit to Master Peter from Gelderland, who at the time was going through the Exercises, I understood more clearly than ever from some very convincing indications how very important it is for the discernment of spirits whether we direct our attention to thoughts and interior locutions or to the spirit itself. For the spirit is wont to betray its presence through desires, feelings, strength or weakness of soul, tranquillity or disquiet, joy or sadness, and suchlike spiritual feelings. It is surely through these rather than through the thoughts themselves that one can more easily pass judgment on the soul and its visitants.[156]

301 But there are those who, despite the many different prayers and contemplations they make during their various spiritual exercises, cannot detect the changing spirits but always seem to be moved by one and the same spirit—though to a greater or lesser degree.[157] But the most effective way of bringing out the distinction between the spirits is to propose the choice of a state of life and then, in that particular state, the different stages along the road to perfection. And, in general, the higher the end you will have proposed for a person's activity, hope, faith, and love (in order that he may apply himself to it both affectively and effectively) the more likely will it be that you will have provided him with the means to bring out the difference between the good and the bad spirit.[158]

302 There are other people also (particularly those who are pious, long-practiced in devotion, and free from sin) in whom the bad

---

[156] The visit was most likely on April 28, and Canisius would have been on the point of making his Election (*SpEx*, [169–187]). Favre reflects on his efforts to help Canisius in the making of his own discernment. From this entry (§300, §301, §302), it can be concluded that Canisius did not yield without a struggle. Note that Favre, as always, gives priority to the affective elements in this experience; the intellectual elements, thoughts, and interior locutions (utterances) are of less importance. The spirits make their presence felt through affective movements over which a person has no control—and this latter point brings up the question of their origin. Hagiography often gives evidence of seeming demonic interference with and infestation of holy people—even those whose work for God and his Church lay yet in the future. See O'Leary, "Discernment," pp. 111–112.

[157] This group may be laboring under some spiritual illusion, or they lack self-knowledge. They are at a standstill in some stage of their spiritual life and so, for the time being, are not open to real spiritual growth. They need a skillful director.

[158] Favre answers the problem he poses: Propose to the exercitant the choice of a state of life and then the different degrees of tending to perfection in the state chosen. The greater the demand made on a person, the more clearly will he reveal himself: a stiff challenge brings out the best or the worst in a person. It is a sound psychological principle. See O'Leary, "Discernment," pp. 122–123.

spirit is not recognized because they have no thoughts which stray beyond the bounds of truth and goodness and no obviously inordinate affections.[159] However, no matter how holy they may be, if you bring these persons to examine themselves in regard to some stage of perfection in their lives and conduct either in their own state (if it cannot be changed) or in some more perfect state of life, then you will easily detect both spirits: the spirit which strengthens and the spirit which weakens, the spirit which enlightens and the spirit which darkens and defiles—I mean the good spirit and the one which opposes it.[160]

▸ April 29

303 On the fifth Sunday after Easter, I noted some points the sequence and meaning of which had been made fairly clear to me on the preceding Friday. They had to do with the petitions which are usually or appropriately made in the colloquies of the four Weeks of the Exercises and according to their respective subjects.

In the First Week, three graces are asked for which are well suited to its subject, which is sin: first, true knowledge of and sorrow for all the sins of the past; second, knowledge of the disorder in one's life; third, knowledge and intention of a true amendment and ordering of life in the future.[161]

In the Second Week, according to the aim proposed for the contemplations on the life of Christ, which is to know him in order to imitate him,[162] these three graces are mentioned with good reason in the colloquies (I always refer to the three principal colloquies with the Virgin, with Christ, and with the Father):[163] first, self-renunciation; second, perfect contempt of the world; third, perfect love of the service of Christ our Lord.[164]

---

[159] Favre considers those who are devout and have lived for a long time without sinning. They must be shaken out of themselves, provoked into a spiritual struggle. Both he and Ignatius (*SpEx*, [6]) hold that the absence of spiritual motions indicates the presence of the bad spirit.

[160] As before, the proposal of a higher state of perfection causes inner turmoil that leads to the identification of both the good and the bad spirit. See O'Leary, "Discernment," p. 123, and *SpEx*, [176].

[161] See *SpEx*, [63], where the third request is different.

[162] *SpEx*, [104]; "Textus B. Fabri," *Exercitia Spiritualia S. Ignatii . . . et eorum Directoria*, A. Codina, ed. (Madrid, 1919), p. 590 (abbreviated hereafter as *SpEx*-MHSJ); §113.

[163] *SpEx*, [63], [109], [147]; *SpEx*MHSJ, pp. 585–586, 591, 595; §117, §148, §156, §199.

[164] *SpEx*, [146–147]; *SpEx*MHSJ, p. 595. Favre is faithful to the spirit rather than to the letter of the Second Week of the *Exercises*.

Many show themselves well disposed to Christ and display love for his person but do not take kindly to the labors which make up the service of Christ. They often think a good deal about him, about his virtues and perfections—not without consolation—but they think but little or not at all about the labor he wishes his servants to engage in and thus follow him in order to be where he was until such time as they will be in the place where he is now.[165]

In the Third Week, its subject being the Passion, these three graces appear to suit that subject reasonably well: the first, compassion with Christ in his bodily sufferings; the second, compassion with Christ in poverty and despoiled of all he has; the third, compassion with Christ mocked and put to shame.[166] Far too many people do not know what it is to experience such a diversity of sufferings in a spiritual manner and are less disposed to experience them with compassion in their bodies.

In the Fourth Week, its subject being the Resurrection and its purpose the knowledge of the glorified Christ in his glory, it is fitting to ask for these three graces which include as a rule many surpassing blessings: the first concerns the reward which is the love of God and of Christ; the second, perfect happiness in Christ alone; the third, that true peace which is to be found only in him.[167]

▸ May 2

304 On the vigil of the Lord's Ascension, I felt, as I commonly did, troubled and in desolation as I thought over certain widespread evils[168] which seemed to cast a shadow over the service of Christ not only in a general way but also over the work that I myself am engaged in. Then I felt somewhat comforted in spirit[169] by considerations of the opposite kind, and at once I began to experience consolation.

I was then given to understand that consolations of this kind, arising from purely nonessential things or even from imaginary spiritual abundance, are just as much to be shunned as the desolation which is their contrary. I say this because of their tendency to end frequently in excess and because true stability of heart[170] is disturbed alike by superfi-

---

[165] John 12:26; 14:3.

[166] *SpEx*, [203], [193]; *SpEx*MHSJ, p. 602; *DeCertMem*, p. 341, n. 4

[167] This triple grace of love, happiness, and peace is not found so clearly stated in Ignatius's text (*SpEx*, [221]; *SpEx*MHSJ, p. 605).

[168] Evils independent of man's will and beyond his power to remedy (§259).

[169] The expression *confortatio spiritualis* has rather its original sense of a spiritual strengthening without any feeling of tenderness.

[170] *Stabilitas cordis* is at a deeper level than superficial moods of consolation or desolation.

cial joy or sadness—at times to a greater extent by joy. Yet that joy, in spite of an element of spiritual illusion, can help us more in our work for souls than the melancholy we find mingled with groundless disquiet.[171] This disquiet usually has its origin in the evil spirit, though it is wont to end in the good one, just as the joy (its contrary) which commonly has its origin in the good spirit often ends in the evil one. This is because the good spirit makes use of our moods of dejection to attract us to lasting good[172] and to bring us true consolation once that counterfeit and misleading joy has been brought to nothing. In the same way the enemy[173] is wont to take advantage of our joyful moods to draw us on to a superficial happiness from which sadness eventually results.

Let us be on our guard, then, and attend to the beginnings and the ends, both extremes, of these excessive tendencies so that we may be able to recognize which are the spirits that initiate, develop, and terminate these movements of the soul and these spiritual impulses.[174]

▸ *May 3*

305 On the day of the Ascension, there came to me a clear understanding of what it means to seek God and Christ outside and above every creature, with a will to know him as he is in himself. And I was also given to understand and to experience in spirit the ways in which the following differ from each other: knowing the creature without knowing God or knowing the creature in God, God in the creature and God without the creature.[175]

This is a true uplifting of the mind and the spirit, for it is from a knowledge of creatures and the attraction they hold for us[176] that we

---

[171] The Christian must be vigilant (Matt. 24:42; 2 Tim. 4:5; Apoc. 3:2), but his vigilance must be rooted in hope in spite of the changing states of his soul from joy to sadness and melancholy; in this latter state he lies open to the assaults of the enemy. See §158; *DeCertMem,* p. 342. n. 5.

[172] §185.

[173] The bad spirit (*SpEx,* [333–334]).

[174] This entry is a development of Favre's third criterion for judging the value of a work: "In what spirit is it being done?" (§50). It is based on his own experience of what he calls "steadfastness of heart" *(stabilitas cordis).* See §191. Other spiritual motions must be measured against this experience, not against each other, for in that way he feels himself more open to error. This new experience marks an advance in spiritual maturity, in greater self-knowledge, and in a deeper understanding of God at work within him. See O'Leary, "Discernment," pp. 120–121.

[175] §108 nn. 219, 220 above. Favre develops here these four spiritual stages.

[176] First stage: Our knowledge of things is not according to faith, for our faith remains, as it were, abstracted from and isolated in man's experience of the world, knowing the creature without God.

should ascend to a knowledge and love of their Creator, without in any way dwelling on them alone.[177]

306 Next we should come to the Creator, at least insofar as he himself exists, lives, and operates in creatures.[178] But neither should we delay there but keep on seeking God in himself and apart from, above, and outside every creature (but not excluded from any of them), and sustaining them.[179] Then we will come to know all creatures in him far more perfectly than they were known in themselves and even more perfectly than they in themselves are.[180]

Oh, that the time may soon come when I contemplate and love no creature without God and, rather, contemplate and love God in all things or at least fear him! That would raise me to the knowledge of God in himself and, in the end, all things in him, so that he would be for me all in all for eternity.[181]

307 To ascend by these degrees, I must strive to find Christ, who is the way, the truth, and the life, first in the center of my heart and below, that is, within me;[182] then above me, by means of my mind;[183] and outside me, by means of my senses.[184] I shall have to beg power

---

[177] Second stage: From now on the creature is seen in relation to God, knowing the creature in God (§108).

[178] Third stage: Not only do we ascend to God through creatures, but they reveal God to us, knowing God in the creature (§108).

[179] Fourth stage: Nothing is known but God, God without the creature.

[180] This kind of knowledge surpasses not only what man can know of things in themselves but also the knowledge he might have if, *per impossibile,* his understanding of them were identical with what they are.

[181] This prayer concludes with a text from 1 Cor. 15:28: "And when all things shall be subdued unto him, then the Son also himself shall be subject unto him that put all things under him, that God may be all in all" (DV). This text describes the taking up of the whole world into God through Christ's Ascension and his final triumph.

[182] See §161, §313. Christ acts through the Holy Spirit, who is the source of the life that comes from above and, issuing from the depths of the heart, gives rise to an attraction from within (*intractio:* §188, §135). This interior impulse initiates the ascent to the Father. See the continuation of this passage for the "return to the heart" which begins the quest for the Father.

[183] To find Christ "above oneself" is to be led upward by him to where he is seated at the right hand of the Father (§280). Favre has described the stages of this ascent in §305 and §306.

[184] To find Christ "outside of oneself" through the senses is to recognize that God enters into all aspects of the humanity of Jesus (§290, §291, §292). But this "outside," perceptible through the senses, is grasped from now on within the movement of the Incarnation and of God's bestowal of grace on man. This knowledge of God through Christ is that which was termed above (§305) a more perfect knowledge

from the Father to do this, for he is said to be "above"; wisdom from the Son, who on account of his humanity is said to be "outside" in a certain way; and goodness from the Holy Spirit, who in some way can be said to be "below," that is, within us. Otherwise, our interior cannot be laid open so that God may be inwardly beheld by a purified heart, nor can our superior part be elevated to the invisible mysteries of God which are above all things, nor can our members be mortified[185] so as to experience him who is outside all things and who moves through all things.

▸ May 4

308 On the day after the Ascension, the feast of the most Holy Cross, I said Mass in the church called the Church of the Holy Cross, outside the city of Mainz. In that church there are some objects which keep alive the memory of those celebrated miracles which took place there in former times. One of these objects, a crucifix, was found floating on the Rhine and moving upstream against the current; another crucifix —still kept there—after having its head knocked off by a blow from some mocker, began to bleed. To this day the blood can clearly be seen to have flowed down the statue.

When saying Mass there, I found most noteworthy fervor, and I felt deep sorrow that men have already forgotten such miracles. So I begged the Lord to give me a spirit in which in the name of all I might be enabled to acknowledge these gifts of his. I begged him to accept my own feelings as if they were those of all the members of our Society and those of all the holy people I have known until now and as if this sacrifice of praise, thanksgiving, and propitiation were offered by all men for these and for all similar immense benefits of God.

I also made a resolution to return once or twice to the same church before leaving Germany so that I could say Mass at the altar of that crucifix, the one which of itself floated on the water.

▸ May 8

309 On the feast of the Apparition of the blessed Michael the Archangel,[186] I was moved to make some special acts of thanksgiving to God for the benefits conferred on the angels. In particular, I recognized how great a privilege it was for them never to have been surrounded by the infirmities of our mortal bodies as our souls are—buried and en-

---

of things in God or, in other words, "to find pasture" (§66, §108).

[185] Col. 3:5. To practice interiority is not easy; there is need of purification through suffering. O'Leary, "Discernment," pp. 69–70.

[186] On that day, his own birthday, Peter Canisius made in Favre's presence a vow to enter the Society.

closed in our bodies as if imprisoned within them.[187] For our souls are subject to a great diversity of feelings—even contradictory ones—which provoke inner conflict and temptations to wrongdoing, while angelic natures, being simple, are unable to experience them. This absence of duality and multiplicity in action impels angels so very powerfully towards good that they never suffered interior conflict, even before they were confirmed in good; for if one of them is good in any respect, he is good in an absolute way.

310 We, on the contrary, are so changeable that even though we may appear good in one respect, in many other respects we show a tendency to evil. Our understanding is not straightaway attended by our will nor, on the other hand, our will by our understanding, while our senses for their part too often go in a direction contrary to our reason and its preferences. Therefore, a person does not at once become totally good and upright for the single reason that he is good in part. But I was often given to understand that a great benefit was conferred on man in that he is so divided, so fitful, and so changeable in his activity. It follows from this that if some part of him was affected or corrupted by evil, his whole being would not thereby suffer total loss. In addition, even if he did suffer total loss for a time, that loss would not be an eternal one because of his wavering and inconstant nature. Often too the sensual part of him appears completely corrupted, though his reason itself and his spirit may withhold consent and so remain untouched by evil.[188]

311 Nothing like this could have happened to the angels even before their confirmation, so there was a much greater danger of their falling with the other apostate angels. For once they consented to evil, they would have become completely corrupted by it on account of the simplicity of their nature, nor would there have been room in them for both refusal and consent at one and the same time. So it had to be that their whole nature should be straightaway permeated with good or filled with evil and thus totally corrupted.

For myself, as long as I remain so inclined to evil and surrounded by so much defilement from the flesh, the world, and bad spirits, I greatly rejoice that I do not yet possess a nature which is simple.[189] For

---

[187] *SpEx*, [47].

[188] A being acts according to its nature. The angels, who unlike human beings are wholly spiritual, of necessity know and will something with all the potentiality of their nature. Hence their actions whether good or evil are irreversible.

[189] Simple *(simplex)* is not quite accurate. The human soul, even separated from its body, cannot be called "simple" because it always retains a certain relation to the matter of its body.

if it were so, my whole soul would be all too speedily permeated by some evil spirit and thus become completely corrupted.

At present, however, though some evil spirit may penetrate my flesh, for example, or my understanding, or my affectivity, it does not happen that I become at once totally evil, for it is in my power to withhold consent to these evils and to reject them by an act of the will.

I should indeed wish to be penetrated entirely, totally, and in every way by the good spirit and to be profoundly affected by him in order to become through him a being altogether simple, steadfast, and unchangeable. But as long as wicked powers[190] assail me, as long as I am in danger of being affected by the sins that surround me on all sides—in that situation, I repeat, I prefer not to possess either that state of simplicity or a nature so permanent and unchangeable. For I should then be in too much danger of immediate and total corruption, and were I to fall, my fall would be an irreparable loss.

312 Blessed be our Lord Jesus Christ, therefore, who became man and who died; through him we have been created with a nature of manifold and varying possibilities of evildoing, such acts being accidents in us. Through his grace we shall in time attain to a state of complete simplicity and immutability: the just in heavenly bliss, the damned in a state of torment. This means that the saints will be penetrated through and through by that sovereign Good to which they will be eternally united, and the wicked by that suffering which is the wages of iniquity and will be their lot for eternity.

▶ May 13

313 On the holy day of Pentecost, I was borne towards God by keen longings that he might grant me through his Spirit to understand and will in a spiritual manner the things of the spirit. I asked him to make spiritual my being, my life, my feelings, and my thoughts. And I had a deeply felt understanding of my words.

I also began to recognize a very great difference between divine impulses in man according to whether they are related to his vital, his animal, or his rational spirit.[191] I went on to consider the great difference

---

[190] *Spiritualia nequitiæ* (Eph. 6:12) is translated as "spiritual hosts of wickedness" in the Revised Standard Version. A sound theology of sin and free will preserves Favre from the belief that we are at the mercy of demons and are powerless against them. But he did believe firmly in the existence of good and evil spirits; it was the accepted belief of his age. O'Leary. "Discernment," p. 75; *DeCertMem,* pp. 50–54; *DSpir* 3:189–212, art. "Démon."

[191] Medieval anthropology held that the "vital spirit" *(spiritus vitalis)* diffuses itself through the body by means of the blood and so organizes life in man; the

there is between an experience of something according to the flesh or according to the spirit, between existing in the flesh or existing in the spirit, between living in the flesh or living in the spirit.[192]

I was then given to seek grace from the Holy Spirit in prayer after prayer that my being, my life, and my inner awareness of things might be carried away into that Spirit so that the work of the salvation of my soul might be accomplished in those depths that lie open to the Holy Spirit.[193] I begged also to be delivered from my state of corporeal awareness of carnal and corporeal realities, I mean my awareness of them through corporeal and carnal thoughts and motions in the flesh or in the body. For our perception of things is not true unless we attain them through the rational spirit—above all if they happen to be spiritual realities and suggested by the Holy Spirit.[194]

314 I then turned my attention to the way in which I had so often experienced carnally and at the level of the flesh those carnal realities. Various examples came to my mind: at times they are experienced by the flesh and at its level,[195] sometimes at the level of the flesh but through the motion of an evil spirit,[196] and at other times through the same evil spirit but at the level of our vital or animal spirits[197] or

---

"animal spirit" *(spiritus animalis)* acts as the link between sensation and perception, while the "rational spirit" *(spiritus rationalis)* is the principle of knowing and willing.

[192] To experience something according to the flesh is to experience evil inclinations (with or without consent is not stated); to experience according to the spirit is to rejoice in consolation; existing in the flesh or existing in the spirit refers to an objective state which is spiritually harmful or spiritually beneficial; finally, to live in the flesh or to live in the spirit means the tendency to evil or to good of the whole man, with or without grace.

[193] Favre asks for grace that the Holy Spirit may penetrate not only his rational spirit but also his vital and animal spirits, in other words, his whole self beginning with his existence. See §191.

[194] The "rational spirit" is necessary in order that material realities may be grasped spiritually and by degrees at the level of perception. This is still more true of those special movements, of "spirits"—inspirations which come from the heart and are intended as guides to actions. If they come from the sensibility, they lead a person astray; they have, therefore, to be purified or "spiritualized," so that through an affectivity of the reason they create an affectivity of the soul.

[195] In this context "flesh" means human nature, weak and often inclined to evil. "Carnal realities" are instinctive impulses, sensations, appetites, needs, and so forth where the activity of the senses is not spiritually directed. There is disorder here without doubt.

[196] Sensation becomes concupiscence and an unwholesome attraction. See the end of §316 or §35.

[197] The bad spirit sometimes makes use of the more fundamental tendencies of human life and sensation for his own purpose.

even of man's rational spirit.[198] It is also possible to grasp at times spiritual realities with some degree of carnality through the activity of a spirit which is to some extent carnal,[199] just as it happens that corporeal realities can be understood and experienced in a spiritual manner.[200]

Therefore, we must earnestly ask the Holy Spirit to bring under control all the spirits that dwell in us, not only that spirit through which life is organized in us and that spirit in which sensation finds its origin, but also that spirit through which thoughts and affections are engendered. And may the action of the Spirit be prolonged until that time of happiness comes when God will be all things to all and will be seen thus.[201]

315 Another day during the octave of Pentecost, I experienced great devotion as I made a series of prayers to petition the gifts of the Holy Spirit. I reflected on the great importance of the gift of the spirit of understanding, of wisdom, and of fear.[202]

There came to me also a certain way of praying to the Holy Spirit inasmuch as he proceeds from the Father, and inasmuch as he proceeds from the Son, and inasmuch as he is the guide and sanctifier of Christ's soul—and still more, the one through whom Christ was conceived. I prayed to him inasmuch as he enriches with his gifts the Virgin Mary, the angels, the prophets, the apostles, the martyrs, the confessors, the monks, the virgins, the chaste, the widows, and others. I prayed to him inasmuch as he destroys the influence of the demons—in short, I prayed to him inasmuch as he is the being who fills all things and in whom all things have existence, life, and all their movement.[203] I felt that it was a great thing and the greatest of graces to possess his favor who in so powerful and intimate a way is for all things the beginning, the middle, and the end.[204]

---

[198] Through the "rational spirit" carnal and corporeal realities are consented to or reflected on with attention.

[199] This is often the case when the initial dispositions are good but then do not last or else give way more to good, comfortable habits than to the inspirations of the Lord.

[200] See §305, §306. This happens to very holy and spiritual persons for whom nothing exists beyond their own spiritual horizons.

[201] 1 Cor. 15:28. In all this Favre seeks that the Holy Spirit may take lasting possession of him. For the use of the word "spirit" here, see O'Leary, "Discernment," pp. 76–81.

[202] Manuscripts R and S add here: "of knowledge, counsel, piety, and fortitude."

[203] Acts 17:28.

[204] Because the Spirit dwells in the depths of the heart, he is for all beings their commencement; because that life whose source is within "completes" the work of the Trinity (§245) and brings to perfection the image of the Trinity in man, it is also the end. By that very fact, it is in the Spirit that the spiritual life unfolds itself,

316 There came to me yet again some very fervent prayers to the Holy Spirit. I desired to have him forever as my protector and defender (even more, as my being, my life, my senses, and my reasoning powers) against wicked spirits or rather against any kind of evil influences they are able and willing to bring to bear on us—influences such as evil thoughts and inclinations, occult powers, ill will, and disquiet[205]—with the object of leading us into greater wrongdoing and into a deeper experience of evil. These spirits have extensive power over bodies, but the Holy Spirit strengthens us against them through his own action and that of the holy angels.

▸ May 20

317 On the day of the most excellent and most holy Trinity, I felt a deep longing to have that feast celebrated with greater solemnity,[206] since it encompasses the three divine Persons and there can be no more worthy object of our reason and of our faith.

I made some petitions also that whatever strength and power I possess may be increased by the Father; that all light and lucidity in me, the right ordering of myself, my disposition, and my practical reason may be guided by the Son once their contraries have been driven out; and that all my affectivity, desires, tendencies, inclinations, and accidental qualities may be purified by the Holy Spirit once he has expelled all the evil influences that come from the flesh and from the spirit.[207]

318 As I began to apprehend well enough by faith, in the course of a meditation, how it is that God (Father, Son, and Holy Spirit) is absolutely outside all things; within, that is, below and throughout all things; and in all of us,[208] I felt deep devotion in begging him to give me the grace of seeking and finding him in all these ways.

I then noted and grasped the sense in which God is said to be almighty: He is so great that he has the power of creating[209] whatever

---

that is to say, life in the Spirit.

[205] See §22, §30, §34, §35, §156, §157, §176, §181, §252, §254, §259, §273, §283, §304, §310, §328.

[206] The feast of the Holy Trinity was approved by Pope John XXII for the universal Church only in 1334. It was a popular feast especially in France and in Germany.

[207] Favre's petitions to the Persons of the Trinity express his desires for a renewal that would penetrate into every nook and cranny of his being. The accidental forms (*formæ accidentales*) distinguish in a being not the fact that it exists but its further determinations. Favre is probably thinking of his personal characteristics.

[208] On these aspects of the relations between God and man, see §161 and §307.

[209] *Facere esse* in medieval philosophy and theology means "to create."

can exist per se or in any other mode of possibility, and, in general terms, whatever can exist as substance or accident or in a way simple or composite.[210]

Then I had a succession of prayers about the order in which one ascends from more imperfect beings to more perfect ones: first come all accidents, whose perfection can be comprehended and ordered according to the subjects they inhere in by their nature; second, the matter of corporeal beings; third, the substantial forms of corruptible inanimate beings; fourth, the heavenly forms; fifth, the corruptible forms of animate beings[211] such as plants and living things not endowed with reason; sixth, inanimate beings which are composite and which are corruptible, like vegetables; seventh, heavenly beings which are composite, that is, the heavenly bodies; eighth, animate beings not endowed with reason; ninth, the rational soul; tenth, man himself; eleventh, the angel.[212]

After all these comes God, who is above all and blessed above all: Father, Son, and Holy Spirit, a Trinity of Persons but one in substance and possessing the fullness of all perfection.

▸ *May 22*

319 On the Tuesday after the feast of the most holy Trinity, I became aware during my morning office of a certain grace which I had never before experienced so evidently, although the desire for it had frequently been given to me. It was this: My mind began to be raised up with a steady impetus that was stronger than usual to the sight of God who is in heaven.

I had often felt more devotion at other times in understanding his words or in some inspiration which either touched my soul with sorrow or moved it to fervor in some way. But on this occasion it was a raising up of the apex of the soul in which I was given to attain the presence of

---

[210] Beings can exist either as subsistent or possible; then come the classical distinctions of scholastic metaphysics between substance and accident, simple and composite beings.

[211] These "corruptible forms" correspond to the "accidental forms" mentioned above (§317) and have only a limited degree of being. They depend on the subjects in which they inhere.

[212] In his classification of creatures according to their order in the hierarchy of being, Favre takes accidents first, then matter, then the forms (of corruptible bodies, of incorruptible or heavenly bodies, and of living beings). After these come the subsistent principles: inanimate beings, heavenly beings, animate beings, the rational soul; and lastly persons—man, angels. So, after the category of accidents, this hierarchy is ordered by three ontological principles: matter, form, composition *(materia, forma, compositio).*

God as he dwells in his heavenly temple.[213] I then began to desire and will with all my power that such a grace might from that moment on be extended to all my prayers whether vocal or mental.

This straining of the mind after the Godhead[214] seemed not a little difficult, but I had good hopes that my mind might be fortified by grace.

320 During prayer it seemed to be easier to keep my mind fixed on Christ crucified as if he were there before my eyes, or on the Virgin Mother, or on some saint[215] rather than on God as he is in heaven.

I noted that it was extremely necessary for a person engaged in mental or vocal prayer to have in mind, first, the person addressed, as if to recall him to memory; second, the meaning of the words used in the prayer; third, the spirit in which all is felt in the heart. For perfect prayer the memory should be occupied by the throne of the majesty of God the Father and be raised up to it; the understanding should be enlightened by the wisdom of the Son, through whom all things are understood; the purpose of the heart should be dwelt in by the Holy Spirit, without whom nothing can be experienced in our deepest depths. May God and Jesus Christ give us the grace of attaining to these things by a daily growth. But in the meantime we must advance by degrees, aspiring to the highest and greatest so as to be more capable of moderate progress.[216] Such is what appeared advisable to me in this matter.

It also appeared to me that up to now I had never really employed the highest part of my soul (I mean the apex or topmost point of it) in that straining upward towards the heights. Instead I had until now kept it turned in the opposite direction, borne down to and wholly intent on what is basest in me—I mean huddled down and brooding over the wretched state of my flesh and of my spirit.

---

[213] Favre expresses himself through analogy and symbol, the language of mystical terminology, to describe this exceptional grace, the fruit of the interior renewal he had noted since December 1542 and which would lead to a higher form of prayer, simpler and more Trinitarian.

[214] *Tensio mentis* in the text: a mystical grace—not any kind of mental activity or natural striving in the mind. Favre seems to imply that he needs a special grace to sustain him in prolonging the experience. Note that *mens, animus, anima,* and *cor* are synonyms (§109 n. 221 above).

[215] This "easier" kind of prayer addressed to Christ on the cross, to the Blessed Virgin, or to some saint seems to indicate both the activity and the passivity of the powers of the soul: memory, understanding, and will. These naturally play a part in all kinds of prayer; here however they initiate a higher form of it, simpler and more Trinitarian. From now on, all activity in prayer tends to become passivity. Favre entered into this new form of prayer in December 1542.

[216] See §155, where the same spiritual principle is applied to the apostolate.

321 As for the understanding I received about these matters on the Tuesday after the feast of the Trinity, I shall have to recognize it as a gift which comes down from the most holy Trinity itself, and I must respond to it in the highest part of my soul as if it were a relic of that feast.

It is very fitting, then, that you should for the future refer all the progress you make each year to the feast of the most holy Trinity. For you it will be the starting point from which you will estimate all the fruit of the year; it will as well be the term of all your progress in the building of the temple—that temple you wish to turn into a holy dwelling, an eternal habitation for this most holy Trinity. For the celebrations of all the mysteries of Christ decreed by the Church, together with all the feast days and the Sundays that are observed throughout the year, find their achievement in the Trinity.

▸ *May 24*

322 On the feast of the most holy sacrament of the Body of Jesus Christ our Lord, I became conscious of understanding different ways of celebrating the feast and of adoring and receiving his Body. While the Blessed Sacrament was being carried in procession, I was touched in various ways and moved to devotion[217] at the sight of the variety of things used to embellish the procession and add to the solemnity of the occasion. I rejoiced that such a great crowd had flocked together to cooperate in praising Christ in so many ways. In short, I felt greatly moved by that act of external worship to which all can contribute by their work, their offerings, their heartfelt devotion, or their gestures of reverence.

In that act of worship, all the senses have a part to play; every kind of craftsmanship can be of use, and all the parts of a human body can find something useful to do. There is a place for choirs of human voices and for the different instruments made by men. For that act of worship, country folk bring along branches, greenery, and woven wreaths, and craftsmen too add their efforts in different ways. So it happens that all men in all ways, even physically, have a means of serving Christ and submitting their whole bodies to him from whom they have received them.[218]

---

[217] *Tactus et commotus:* The words indicate two aspects of the same grace, one passive, the other a spiritual impulse. Favre's affective understanding of the celebration of the feast led him, as always, to experience consolation (devotion). O'Leary, "Discernment," p. 86.

[218] Here Favre may have a polemical purpose: the justification of external rites as an element in worship as against the Protestants who maintained a purely spiritual

323 The same day I experienced great fervor with a good spirit which led me to offer myself entirely for the worship of Christ. I offered my understanding, my memory, and my will, my five senses, and whatever else is in me. I offered all these up to him in order to glorify and honor him; then, in order to serve and obey him for my own sanctification; and third, that I might resolve for his sake to devote myself to the welfare of my brothers and spend myself entirely out of love for them.[219]

324 I was also given a desire, according to all the parts of my body and my soul, to imitate Christ in his body in these two ways: first, by being enabled to spend and consume myself entirely in doing good for his sake; then, by undergoing suffering throughout my whole body and in each part of it as he suffered in all his members for me and for all men even unto the death of the cross.[220]

▸ *May 31*

325 On the octave day of that same feast, I was given to seek, with intense devotion and a keen awareness of my defects, grace for the remission from then on of all the punishment due on account of the sins I have committed because of evil personal habits or inclinations or other temptations arising from my own evil desires.[221]

326 I somehow became aware of the marvelous way in which Christ wills the Church, his spouse, to be quickened to life thanks to the great and admirable sacrament of his Body and Blood.

When we believe that under those sensible appearances there is present the Body and Blood of the Lord, it means that we state our faith in unseen realities:[222] We believe that the Body of Christ is really and truly present under the species of bread, that Christ is present there with all that he is,[223] and that transubstantiation of the bread has taken place,

---

or interior worship. Since man is composed of body and soul, the body rightly has a part to play in worship; the whole man should adore God, his bodily actions and gestures signifying the inner reality of adoration. Acts of public and external worship, such as this Corpus Christi procession, were much criticized by Protestants.

[219] The word "cult," here translated "worship," was first applied to the liturgy; Favre changes its meaning here to include the service of Christ through apostolic work. Rom. 6:13; 12:1; 1 Pet. 2:5; *SpEx*, [234].

[220] To receive Christ in the Eucharist is to participate in his sacrifice, to share in his labors and sufferings for the salvation of all. See §124, §142.

[221] Favre looks on his defects as the results of sin. The evil act gives rise to habits and desires which are at once the consequence of sin and its punishment. He prays for the remission of this punishment. *DBibTheol*, pp. 475–477, art. "Punishments."

[222] Heb. 11:1.

[223] The term concomitance *(concomitantia)* is a technical theological term which designates the necessary connection between realities which are such that the

that his blood is really present under the species of wine, that his soul and his body are really present there simultaneously with all the fullness of the divinity, and likewise that transubstantiation [of the wine] has taken place.[224]

Besides, we actively express ourselves in venerating that great sacrament not only in spirit and through interior movements of faith and hope but also in outward acts of adoration as if the Lord were visibly present in that place.[225]

Lastly, we work actively in that way at our own sanctification, making use of that food for the sustenance of our souls, for their comfort, enlightenment, and consolation, and for all manner of receiving the heavenly treasures.

327 Pitiable beyond measure are they who refuse to honor this sacrament as highly as they would honor the bodily presence of Christ himself. What has been bequeathed to us is in no way less than what was given to the apostles during the Last Supper. For they were given that body soon to be delivered up to crucifixion—not a dead body, for it was the living not the dead Christ who was delivered up, and when he had been crucified, he was not dead but living.[226]

327a: The absence of entries from May 10 to June 10 may indicate a journey.

▸ June 10

328 On the fourth Sunday after Pentecost, on my way to Mass I was given to ask that my soul and spirit might have protection against the evil spirits of demons and men. I then noted that up to that time I

---

existence of one implies the existence of the others. Such realities are the body and blood, soul and divinity of Christ; they are present in the Eucharist, as they are in heaven. In that state Christ's body and blood are not separated. The separate consecration of bread and wine in the Mass is a sensible sign and representation of the separation through death of Christ's body and blood on Calvary; this separation constitutes the sacrifice of the cross. *ST,* III, q. 76, a. 3 and 4; *NCathEnc* 4:44–46, art. "Communion under Both Species."

[224] Transubstantiation: All the substance of the bread is transformed into the body of Christ and all the substance of the wine into his blood (*SacMundi* 6:292–295).

[225] Inner faith and devotion animate and give meaning to external gestures of worship; the latter, when so animated, are of great value and importance. Favre is content neither with a purely ritualistic type of religion nor with a purely spiritual one (O'Leary, "Discernment," p. 65).

[226] Christ's sacrificial act is continued in his sacramental body. His sacramental presence makes permanent in the Church, under the form of his living body, the voluntary offering of himself at the Supper and on the cross. So it is the living Christ who remains present in the sacrament of his Body and Blood.

was frequently troubled in mind and deeply depressed. This would happen whenever I reflected on the evil spirits of men—I mean, when I considered those unworthy dispositions of theirs which caused me to suspect in one way or other that they, moved by some evil spirit, were about to assail my soul and my spirit and that they were observing and censuring my spiritual poverty and human weaknesses.[227] To be sure, I was well aware of my utter powerlessness to combat that ill will I imagined in others. It even seemed to me far less trying to have all men use their combined strength in a physical attack on me than to have one single man under the influence of an evil spirit endeavor to assail my soul in its weakness.

So I invoked the protector of my soul, and I came to understand better at the same time the nature of those persecutions we suffer in spirit from the wicked spirits of demons and of men.[228]

329 Then I adverted to and pondered on that torment which has never left my mind since I first came to know Germany: the dread of its total defection from the faith. May God prevent the realization of that thought, which has so often come to my mind, not from a good spirit, but rather from that spirit of diffidence that has harassed me in so many ways up to now. It strives particularly to bring me to outright despair of bearing any fruit, first by leading me to contemplate flight and then by provoking in me the desire to leave the Rhineland and so abandon the position entrusted to me there.

Oh, that the tepidity, the coldness, the malice, or the unfaithfulness, real or imagined, of evil men might cease invading my soul and my spirit—already poor, tepid, cold, and incapable in itself! Would that there were an immediate end to that instability of mine which has so often brought me to imagine at one time that everything looked successful and flourishing and at another that a situation was desperate or that all had been lost![229]

---

[227] Favre's temperament and his keen awareness of his shortcomings both natural and spiritual bring home to him how greatly these defects harm God's work. But this acute awareness together with his introverted character cause him to exaggerate the situation; he feels that others see him as he sees himself.

[228] Favre feels powerless against this inner turmoil. He realizes that his state of mind is a temptation which does harm to his apostolate. He himself may be responsible; he only "imagines" ill will in others. Then he invokes his guardian angel and comes to understand better the meaning of these persecutions and the part played in them by the bad spirits. See O'Leary, "Discernment," p. 102.

[229] The spiritual renewal of the German nation within the fold of the Catholic Church was at the heart of Favre's apostolic concern. But the difficulty of the task, his personal shortcomings, and the desperate state of the Church in Germany threw him into such despair that he was tempted to leave the country altogether. He judges that

330 That would not have happened to me if I were less well informed about the causes and situations which beget and increase evil.[230] For I had too great a desire for information about them and was excessively addicted to hearing about them and brooding over them. Besides, I was too much given to considering the power of sin and the methods used in spreading error and promoting defections. Hence, I came to the point of often overlooking whatever seeds of goodness and virtue God had planted in men. For if one looked on their virtues with a favorable eye—I mean prescinding from the evil present in them—that would bring greater peace; and if the virtues discovered were used as something to begin working on, the result would be more abundant fruit.

▶ *June 21*

331 On the feast of St. Alban, solemnized at Mainz on June 21, I celebrated Mass at the high altar of the Church of St. Alban. On it had been exposed the relics of various saints as well as the casket containing the body of that blessed martyr. I felt much fervor there as I reflected on the long journeys made by the martyr and on his coming to Mainz in the time of the Arians to die for its people.[231]

332 These thoughts heartened me, and I began to have good hope of bringing forth fruit in these days of the Lutheran heresies, which have subverted almost all of Germany. For these heresies are nothing other than a withdrawal from the Catholic Church so that the individual, having abandoned the teaching of his Mother, may now act, believe, and say with impunity whatever he wishes.[232]

---

the spirit behind this state of his soul cannot be good; he identifies it as the spirit of diffidence. It must be driven out or at least ignored. But he realizes that this will not be easy, given his faults and his tendency to be excessively influenced by the opinions of others. See O'Leary, "Discernment," pp. 23, 19, 49, 102, and 103 with its n. 22 on that page.

[230] By reason of his connections with the upper clergy, the university, and the court, Favre was well acquainted with the general and particular causes of the religious situation in Germany. What could an individual do? In addition, there were political differences, the attitude of the emperor and the princes, widespread ignorance on the part of the people, intrigue and compromise—the besetting sin of the Catholic side. All this bred in him a mood of utter pessimism. See O'Leary, "Discernment," pp. 104, 13–46; §412, §413, §421, §422, §429.

[231] St. Alban (Albanus), priest, was beheaded at Mainz during the reign of the emperor Theodosius and buried there. He had come to Mainz with St. T(h)eonesto about A.D. 404 and helped its bishop Aureus in his struggle with the Arians. *BS* 1:659–661.

[232] Some weeks before this, Favre had written on May 28 to his cousin the Carthusian Claude Perissin, prior of Le Reposoir: "I am beginning to realize that these heresies of our time are nothing else but a lack of devotion, humility, patience, chastity, and charity" (*MonFabri*, p. 202). Favre always held that moral and affective

It follows that the heretics of our time can justly be called teachers of division and secession.[233]

May God give us men of the opposite mind, men who will teach by word and deed true union, the acceptance of received teaching, and progress in all the Christian virtues.

▸ *June 24*

333 On the day of St. John the Baptist, before Mass I experienced deep devotion which led me to seek grace to set myself and all my undertakings in order, as well as my exercises and what concerns my spirit. I wished, above all, that my God through the grace of Jesus Christ our Lord may find me pleasing and acceptable to him; second, that I may fulfill conscientiously my priestly duties such as praying, offering the sacrifice, meditating, and so forth; third, that I may carry out in accordance with God's will whatever services I owe to others, whether my companions or anyone else; fourth, I sought a special grace for the direction of all those I may ever have to instruct.[234]

334 Then while I was reflecting on John the Baptist as an example of penance and that he was the one who had pointed out Christ, I became aware of thoughts which help greatly in understanding the teaching of the Exercises about sins,[235] for example, that one must find out what it is to do penance and that one ought not to desire tears of compunction first. Instead one should desire first the means of seeking

---

causes lay at the roots of the Reformation. But his knowledge was that of an outsider; he never shared the same religious experience as those he was trying to understand. See O'Leary, "Discernment," pp. 109–110, and Favre's letter to Laínez, the eighth and final point, in *MonFabri,* p. 402.

[233] Teachers *(doctores)* were authorized to teach only when approved by some center of learning such as a university; their authority was ultimately guaranteed by the papacy. The use of the word "teachers" is ironic; it implies such a question as: How could a person be authorized to teach secession (heresy)?

[234] There is no doubt but that Favre had a special gift for spiritual direction. He exercised it when giving the Exercises, during confession—"genuine spiritual direction," he called this in his *Monita circa confessiones* written at Cologne in January 1544 (*MonFabri,* pp. 245–252)—and in long spiritual conversations with individuals or groups. These conversations were one of the chief apostolic ministries exercised by Ignatius and his first companions. Again and again Favre recommends his "spiritual children" to the prayers of Ignatius (*MonFabri,* pp. 45, 68, 78, 83, 90, 108, 112, 115, 138), referring to them sometimes as "sons and daughters of the confessional" (*MonFabri,* pp. 89, 130, 433). See *IntJesLife,* n. 34, on "Spiritual Conversation," p. 363; Clancy, *The Conversational Word of God* (St. Louis, 1978) deals with spiritual conversation as a ministry.

[235] The First Week of the Spiritual Exercises.

them by trying the various ways of practicing exterior penance,[236] even though the ultimate aim must be that compunction of heart which leads to bitter tears.

Many are wont to lament because they have no compunction of heart; nevertheless, they have not yet endurance enough to experience the nature of compunction in the flesh. They would wish to experience torment in their souls but are unwilling to afflict the flesh in any way.

335 God often delays bestowing the more perfect gifts and the fruits of the final stage so that, in the meantime, we may learn to discover the lesser gifts and the means that bring us to the final stage. Some desire nothing so much as spiritual feelings—I mean sentiments of soul—which they would wish to experience sensibly in their hearts.[237] But more than anything they need patience[238] or some other virtue, and they neither know nor feel that they are destitute of it. It is, of course, God's will above all that we possess our souls, but it is only through patience that we can possess them, according to this text: "In your patience you shall possess your souls." For how can he who does not possess his own soul in patience deserve to possess God through sensible consolation?

▶ *June 26*

336 On the day of the holy martyrs John and Paul, after rising in the morning I experienced a notable enough grace which prepared my heart for the saying of the office and for the rejection of all impressions, either disheartening or encouraging, from exterior sources. While dressing and finishing what I have to do before saying my office, I was concentrated on the single desire of praying well, attentively and with devotion. Because of it I felt in my heart that a kind of salutary disquiet was possessing me, the fear of being unable to maintain myself in that disposition. That interior state lasted until after Mass, accompanied by a desire that I might always be able to follow the same way.

337 I then noted that it would be good for us to have always in our hearts either a certain sadness arising from the loss of God's sustaining presence and of that special enlightenment that is usually

---

[236] See *SpEx,* [89].

[237] *In carne cordis sui:* literally, in the flesh of their heart, that is, at a purely sensible level.

[238] Favre's text, Luke 21:19, gives "patience" *(patientia),* but the meaning is rather "perseverance" or "endurance" as the RSV translates it here: "By your endurance you will gain your lives," and in Heb. 10:36, "For you have need of endurance, so that you may do the will of God and receive what is promised." The Douay Version gives "In your patience you shall possess your souls."

received in a state of devotion or else the strengthening that comes from the felt presence of God.[239] Indeed, this seems to be a kind of continuous experience, making it possible for us to realize what it will ultimately mean to be deprived of or to possess the vision and enjoyment of God—the one being the reality of damnation, the other the plenitude of glory.

338   I said Mass that day for the soul of the very devout and learned man Landsberg[240] of the Carthusian order, and I had a holy desire to have him well disposed to me. At the Commemoration of the Dead[241] during Mass, I felt that the deliverance of a single soul from the pains of purgatory must mean very great glory for God and for his saints.

339   I understood too that such a deliverance gives great support to the living. For in purgatory the soul appears to be bound in some way so that it is unable to do anything about our salvation or for the glory of God. But the blessed, on the other hand, from the moment of their arrival in heaven all work together and with all their energy so that God and his Christ may be glorified ever more and more in heaven itself. At the same time they ensure that the glory of God may be manifested on earth through Jesus Christ and bring peace to the souls of the living. These two points are expressed in the angelic hymn: "Glory to God in the highest and on earth peace to men of goodwill."[242]

340   Another day within the octave of St. John,[243] while I was hearing someone's general confession, I was given a deep understanding of the value of works of mercy done for the sake of the living and the dead. This thought moved me to tears even while I was attending to my penitent's confession. Thinking over the matter again, I understood how the exercise of mercy was a sure way of obtaining God's mercy for ourselves and how easy it would be for us to have in God a generous giver if we ourselves were to give freely what we have and what we are.[244] If we show mercy by attending to the corporal needs of others,

---

[239] *Illustratio:* the brightness that indicates the presence of God (2 Thess. 2:8); it is a consoling presence. *DBibTheol,* pp. 316–319, art. "Light and Dark."

[240] Johann Justus Landsberg (1489–1539), born at Landsberg in Bavaria, entered the Cologne charterhouse in 1509. In 1530 he became prior of the charterhouse at Vogelsang but returned to Cologne in 1534 and died there five years later. He wrote many books which stressed, above all, the importance of prayer and the "return to the heart." Favre would certainly have read his preface to St. Gertrude's *Insinuationum divinæ pietatis libri II,* published in Cologne in 1536 (§22). Around this time he had many contacts with the Carthusians (*DeCertMem,* pp. 31 ff.).

[241] See §76 n. 150 above.

[242] Luke 2:14 (DV). The first words of the Gloria in the Mass.

[243] Either June 27 or 28 since §336 and §337 are dated June 26 and §342, June 29.

[244] The corporal works of mercy are helping the poor, visiting the sick, and

God in his mercy will repay us with not only material but also spiritual assistance.[245]

341 A more efficacious way, however, of meriting God's spiritual mercy is to devote ourselves to the spiritual works of mercy. There are some who are much given to prayer yet cannot find the spiritual consolation they seek, because they have no time for the spiritual needs of their neighbors. But some, by devoting themselves to the salvation of others solely for the sake of God, though without making much effort to seek it, find the greatness of the divine clemency shown them not only in the remission and pardon of their sins but also in their acquisition of God's manifold gifts.

So I felt myself strongly impelled to arouse all men to concern themselves more about the works of mercy. And if a person wants God to be truly merciful to him and not to limit himself to the demands of strict justice, he should on his part show kindness and leniency to everyone without being either overstrict or oversevere.

342 On the day of the apostles Peter and Paul, I said Mass for a friend and was given to hope that through the intercession of the Blessed Virgin and those apostles he might obtain certain graces which, to my mind, he needed greatly.

Likewise, in my series of meditations on the mysteries of the life of Christ, after I had reflected at greater length on the blood he had shed so often and on the multitude of his other sufferings and deeds, I prayed in this way: "Lord God Almighty, I beg, through the merits of that blood poured out on the earth, that it may be your will to grant me the grace I petition for that person so as not to waste such an abundance of blessings as yet, so to speak, unavailed of." For I pictured to myself some drops of Christ's blood, or some particular pains in certain members of his body, some words or actions or miracles of his, his sufferings and his drops of sweat, his hunger and his thirst, or lastly his human desires;[246] and I then spoke to God the Father much in these

---

other such deeds inspired by love of one's neighbor. These works must be considered in the light of the social conditions of the time. State-sponsored social welfare was nonexistent, so that engaging in corporal works of mercy meant relieving the most essential needs.

[245] One of Favre's rare references to the intermingling of his prayer and his pastoral activity. By becoming an instrument of God's mercy in action, he realizes what that mercy is and learns to put it into practice.

[246] Devotion to the Blood of Christ as a symbol of his love, as a sign of the new covenant, and as the price of our salvation was then at its height. It was one of the commonest themes in the art of the age: the blood shed during Christ's agony in the garden, during the scourging, on the way to Golgotha, and on the cross. The devotion was intensified by the influence of mystics such as SS. Bernard, Francis,

words: O my God, no one ever asked to have these applied to himself personally as salvific remedies. May they then serve as such for what I ask, so that there will be less reason to look on them as wasted after they have done such great good.

343 Many were the words of Christ that went unheard by the ears of the spirit and perhaps by the ears of the body; many more were heard but not understood; more still were understood but not grasped in the depths of the heart; and lastly, so many others were grasped by an intuition of the heart[247] but never carried into act. From this consideration comes the part played by the apostles and disciples of Christ and by their successors: whatever is of Christ; whatever comes from him, through him, in him; whatever is his and concerns him; whatever is ordained to his glory by the Father; and so forth—they have to go to great pains in searching for it, in meditating on it, in their affective grasp of it, in imitating and praising it, in spreading it abroad, and so on in order that none of the deeds done for our salvation may be wasted.

▸ *June 30*

344 On the day of the commemoration of St. Paul, a useful thought came to me which made me realize how the ugliness of the soul offends the eyes of its Creator, its stench his sense of smell, its bitterness his sense of taste, its excess of cold or of heat his sense of touch.[248]

This ugliness and foulness can be detected above all in lewd behavior and in the filthy sins of the flesh, sins provoked by lustful desires for one's own body or another's. The stench and the foul odor are to be found in an evil reputation and ill renown—indeed they say of a man leading a scandalous life that he smells rank not only to good men but also to God. And God is affected long before others are, for he sees in advance more than men see and more clearly than they do. The

---

Gertrude, Bonaventure, Angela of Foligno, and Catherine of Siena. It inspired hymns, prayers, sequences, and a host of legends—the "Holy Grail," for instance. Devotional books of the time were much preoccupied with the instruments of the passion and the details of Christ's sufferings. The devotion led to exaggerations, but fundamentally it was sound (Mâle, *L'art,* pp. 89–93).

[247] This "intuition of the heart" *(sensus cordis)* is the outcome of meditation on the divine words. They must first be listened to (the act of memory), then assimilated by reflection (the work of the understanding); in the end they penetrate to the depths of the heart and there stir up affective motions which influence the will. From this inner process there can and should arise actions which are the fruit of the Word. Favre has in mind the parable of the sower.

[248] The Christian should experience, even in the body, spiritual likes and dislikes. One might then, as a kind of reflex, come to realize God's "feelings" with regard to sin—his hatred of it, for instance.

bitterness and tastelessness so unpleasant to God's palate are perceptible in anger, pride, envy, and perverse hatred. The divine touch is offended by that lethargy which makes men cold in doing good and also by the passion for possessing that is avarice.

345   Let a man examine himself[249] then as to his own interior feelings, and he will soon come to see that the eyes of his soul[250] are offended by the ugliness of his impurity and bodily defilements, of his lewdness and gluttony. If he considers his evil reputation, he will come to perceive his own foul odor so that he will smell rank even to himself. If he goes on then to contemplate his fits of rage, his bad temper, his envy, and his pride, he will suddenly find that he has become bitter to himself: I mean he will become aware of his bitter and nauseating state—nauseating because of his pride, bitter because of his moods of anger and of envy.

Finally, if he realizes his spiritual sloth and his avarice, he will at once perceive the harm done to his spirit by contact with that excessive coldness which makes it incapable of being attracted by the good or with that excessive ardor which brings him to realize his inability to give up his attachment to the things of this world or his love for them.

He will also recognize these other two qualities of his sense of touch: an excessive indolence which keeps him in a state of idleness and an excessive degree of obduracy which makes him impervious to divine realities.

Let a man, then, examine himself, especially if he wishes to eat the Bread of Heaven, which is both nourishment and life for the whole body and the whole soul, a renewal and glorification for all the senses. For our part, we should strive to become a nourishing food for Christ to assimilate and so change us into his mystical body and into perfect men, strong and useful members of that body.[251]

Let us take care then that none of Christ's senses can find fault with us.

---

[249] Here Favre begins a series of reflections on the spiritualization of the senses and on apostolic life in the Church in union with Christ in the Eucharist (§344, §345). See also §326, §327.

[250] *Mens* (the mind). See §109 n. 221 and §332 n. 232 above.

[251] Eucharistic Communion brings about likeness to Christ; it renews the whole being and therefore the senses; it sustains a person so that one can arrive at that stage of perfection which consists in being of use to others by becoming the instrument and the continuation of Christ's body. The Eucharist is the center of Favre's spiritual and apostolic life.

▶ *July 3*

346 Once, during the time following the celebration of the feast of the Visitation, I found myself greatly desiring that grace which would enable me to know clearly in all my actions the will of God, good, acceptable, and perfect. And I was much consoled to have had my mind clarified about what course to adopt in a certain matter.[252]

▶ *July 4*

347 On the day of the dedication of the cathedral of Mainz, I found great devotion. It led me to consider myself—in everything I asked for, inwardly experienced, or reflected upon—as acting in the name and person of those whom I specially remember. As an example, I venerated Christ in my own name and also as representing my brothers,[253] my friends, my relatives, and others. I likewise venerated the relics of saints exposed on altars, doing this on behalf of others and especially on behalf of those who would be glad, as I know, to stand before those relics. I fervently wished also that the saints in heaven might adore, honor, and glorify God in my name and in the name of all of us on earth and that they might thank him too in that Spirit they now possess.

▶ *July 5*

348 On the vigil of the octave of the apostles Peter and Paul, at nightfall I became inwardly aware of many holy desires for myself, for my companions, for my parents, and in a general way for many others who came into my mind. I felt as well a great and keen longing to ask the Lord to be so good as to accept these desires of mine as if those very persons on whose behalf I experienced them were themselves experiencing and expressing such desires and petitions. I asked him too to make me Christ's representative *[vicarius]* especially in the Mass I intended to say.

▶ *July 6*

349 Entering the church on the octave day, I had great devotion as I took holy water. I asked God the Father that whatever power lay in that holy water to bless, sanctify, and fortify might be applied to me

---

[252] Favre's great desire was to know God's will for him—in all his actions. The desire was fulfilled here through enlightenment about a particular decision he had to make, and the knowledge brought him much consolation. God commands his servants, but he also guides them interiorly during their labors. He "opens" to them a knowledge of his will. Favre desires a mutual "opening" of God and man to each other—an opening of the whole person. See O'Leary, "Discernment," pp. 87–88.

[253] The members of the first group of Jesuits.

as a cleansing ablution for my soul and that its sprinkling might bring a blessing on me and protect me against my invisible enemies.[254]

350 As I turned to a crucifix to pray to Christ, I was aware at the same time of a clear understanding about the usefulness of images; namely, as I realized then for the first time that they represent persons in order to make them present to us anew.[255] So I begged God the Father with great fervor to grant that I might profit from this grace of Christ's presence and also that he might make Christ present to my mind through the vivid representational power possessed by the images of saints in the eyes of the devoutly believing Catholic faithful.

I found these thoughts confirmed when I turned to a picture of the Virgin, because the sight of it led me to wish that the Blessed Virgin might be present as much as possible to my mind.

351 There in that church I began with true devotion to wish for the gift of more abundant prayer, for it is in such places, according to his promise,[256] that God lends a more willing ear to the faithful.

In short, I realized on that day the great efficacy of these objects[257] among believers, not only by reason of the faith inspired by piety but also, and in the first place, because of God's words and the sense of our holy Mother the Church.

352 On my knees, humbly in the presence of the Blessed Sacrament, I experienced great devotion at the thought that Christ was really present there in body and that, as a consequence, the whole Trinity was present there in a wonderful way that is not found in other things and places. Other things such as images, holy water, and churches bring us in a spiritual manner the presence of Christ, of the saints, and of spiri-

---

[254] The Father is the origin of every act of purification and sanctification. The sacramentals, such as holy water here, signify effects particularly of a spiritual kind which are obtained through the Church's intercession. In this lies their value. They are a help in the process of spiritual purification. Holy water is traditionally used as a protection against the power of the devil. *NCathEnc* 12:790-792, art, "Sacramentals."

[255] Favre's understanding of the religious function of images was confirmed when he found himself thinking about the Blessed Virgin as a result of seeing a picture of her. On the crucifix which fixes attention upon itself and distracts from what it represents, see C. S. Lewis, *Christian Reflections* (Fount Paperback, 1981), p. 16, n. 1.

[256] Examples: 2 Chron. 7:11-16; Luke 19:46; *DBibTheol,* p. 237, art. "Holy," Section II.

[257] These are images and representations of Christ or of the saints, holy water, the Church itself—it was the octave of the dedication of the cathedral of Mainz (§347). Favre reflects at length (§349, §350, §351, §352) on the sacred nature of God's creation, especially on those things in which God more clearly manifests his activity: the sacraments, the word of God, the apostolic activity of the Church.

tual powers; but the Blessed Sacrament brings us in a real manner under these appearances[258] the presence of Christ with all the power of God. May his name be blessed!

353 On the same day during the octave of the apostles, at the memory of God's graces and blessings, there arose in my soul something like a lamentation such as I had never experienced before. It appeared to me that in many ways God was granting me through his grace interior abundance and peace, while I, in my external works of charity, was making but an ill response to his grace.

There was once a time when I was not conscious of my defects whether interior or exterior any more than I was then conscious of having experienced God's grace whether within or without—I mean either in my interior life or in my external activity.[259]

Then there came a time when I was given grace and a longing to seek the peace it brings. In those days I was distressed solely by my interior life, deprived as it was of comfort at a time when in body and in soul I had to endure great trials.[260]

Finally, to crown God's mercies, it has now been given me to see that I am too quiescent in my God and in love for my neighbor and that I am seriously remiss in making use of and in expending so many great talents.

God grant that I may not too easily find interior peace with regard to my evil inclinations, my spiritual coldness, and so forth—too easily, that is, before having gained all kinds of victories over myself both in

---

[258] From the middle of the eleventh century on, the words accident, appearances, species, and quality were used interchangeably when dealing with the Eucharistic transformation of bread and wine into the body and blood of Christ. The Fathers of the Church all taught that after the consecration Christ is truly present and that bread and wine are no longer present. Since the species (appearances) of bread and wine are the proper objects of the senses and declare to the reason the presence of bread and wine, the species serve as a sacramental sign—they require an act of faith in the physical presence of Christ under the appearances of bread and wine. See Denzinger, 884; *SacMundi* 6:292–295; *NCathEnc* 1:78–79, art. "Accident."

[259] Favre considers his spiritual life in retrospect, dividing it into three stages and noting how it had all been directed to the apostolic service of others. His comments are brief and so vague that the limits of each stage remain undefined. Here he describes in quite general terms the first period of spiritual childhood, a period when he was unconscious of either his defects or of God's graces. It is a judgment of the spiritually mature Favre on those far-off days.

[260] We do not know whether he alludes here to his pre-university days in Velliard's school or to his studies in Paris and the difficult first years of apostolic work prior to December 1542, when he received the grace of interior "stability." He may refer to both.

the bodily struggle against the demons and in doing away with evil suggestions.[261]

354 Another day, during the octave of the Visitation,[262] as the various necessities, privations, trials, disorders, misfortunes, or calamities that are the lot of mankind presented themselves to my mind, I felt myself possessed by a great desire. I wished that my reflections on the miseries of the living and the dead might never leave me and that I might always be able to pray for them, holding up my hands like Moses[263] while they struggle on and suffer, striving to attain some good for which they need the help of others. To obtain this grace I offered up to God the holy sacrifice of the Mass, the most sacred divine service. When I came to the words "Pray for me, brethren,"[264] I had an intense desire that those present might pray for me with attentive minds. Now since many pray with some negligence, I was given to desire, in a mood of holy fervor, that the guardian angels of those present might pray for me so as to make up in that way for the shortcomings of those committed to their care.

355 On the same day I had a clear enough inner perception and recognition that those who want to be enlarged, elevated, extended, consoled, and increased in God must first be well tried and tested in what they are; in body and in spirit they must suffer restrictions, curbs, humiliations, restraints, grief, diminishment, and so on.[265] For it is through the mortification of one's own flesh and the abnegation of one's own spirit that one is led on to the possession of God. Through the narrow gate must entry be made; and that narrow gate, if considered as it is in each person, is the way that leads on to the heart, and those who have returned to the heart enter into truth and life.

For in man the heart is the first organ to be animated by the soul and the last to be relinquished. Little by little, then, our whole sensible and rational life must be guided back to our hearts so that, gathered together there and united at last, we may pass on thence to that indivisible and spiritual life which is hidden with Christ in God.[266]

---

[261] Eph. 6:12; *SpEx,* [136–147].

[262] July 7 or 8.

[263] Ex. 17:11.

[264] *Orate pro me, fratres* (pray for me, brothers), the opening words of the prayer addressed in the early ages of the Church by the celebrant to the concelebrating priests.

[265] Here Favre deals with the practice of interiority and the necessity of purification through suffering.

[266] Favre held with Augustine that the human person was made in the image of the Trinity: memory being the image of the Father, understanding the image of the Son, and will the image of the Holy Spirit. The heart is an image of the unity. A

▶ July 9

356 On the octave of the Visitation of Blessed Mary, I recalled anew the grace which had been given me on that day—when I made profession of following the manner of life laid down according to the institute of the Society of Jesus.[267] By an inspiration I asked for the grace of increasing in all ways in conformity with the vows of that institute: that through my vow of chastity I may one day be found purified and have my body washed in cleansing water;[268] that through my vow of poverty I may be freed of all worldly desires, primarily the desire of possessing; that through my vow of obedience I may become a fit instrument for accomplishing every good work with diligence.

May Jesus see to it that I become cleansed and purified and faithful in the management of everything that has been or will be entrusted to me, cleansed, I repeat, in my body and in my exterior, purified in my innermost spiritual movements, and faithful in my labors.[269]

▶ July 13

357 On the day of St. Anacletus, pope and martyr, as I was about to leave for the monastery of the Brothers of St. Augustine where I was to say Mass, a thought occurred to me which strengthened me in my intention of saying it for the intention of the prior of that convent. The thought was to consider what I was about to do for the prior as done for a follower of St. Augustine. This reflection gave me the thought and the desire of envisaging all I could ever do for the prior of any convent as done for a follower of the founder of that order, for example, St. Augustine, St. Francis, St. Dominic, St. Benedict, St. Bernard, and likewise for the orders of nuns. And if I did anything for one of the other brothers, I wished that God might accept it in the same way as if I did it for a follower of the follower or for a colleague of a disciple of that saint. With regard to the generals of these orders, my desire was to act

---

return to the heart, therefore, a recalling of the different parts of the soul to the unity of the heart, is a mirror of the unity within the Trinity. Furthermore, the unifying cause within the Trinity and within the human person is the same God. God, one in essence, dwelling in man's heart *(cor)*, draws into himself *(intractio)* all a man's faculties and gives them a share in his unity (O'Leary, "Discernment," pp. 69–70).

[267] This was the profession of solemn vows made by the companions in the Basilica of St. Paul Outside the Walls at Rome in 1541. Favre, in Ratisbon, made his profession there (§23). The Institute of the Society existed only in outline at the time; the Constitutions would be formally adopted in 1558 by the First General Congregation of the Society of Jesus (*IntJesLife*, ch. 3).

[268] See Ezech. 36:25.

[269] The following day Favre wrote a long letter to Gerhard Kalckbrenner about spiritual progress and interior reform. See document XIII below, pp. 351–354.

as if they represented—and in fact they do—those saints and as if they themselves were saints.[270]

358   A similar thought came to me about bishops: I wished to look upon the bishop of Rome, who is the Sovereign Pontiff, as the vicar of Christ, his successor and the one who takes the place of Peter;[271] the other bishops as the vicars of the other apostles of Christ and as if they themselves were Christ's apostles; the priests as if they were the disciples of Christ because they are the vicars of those disciples;[272] deacons and other ministers of the Church as the disciples of the apostles and disciples of Christ; for in our day deacons are, as it were, the successors and the vicars of the disciples of the apostles.

So then the sovereign pontiff should be respected by myself and all Christians as if he were the person of Christ incarnate inasmuch as Christ is the Head of the Church,[273] Priest, and Chief Pastor[274] of whose fullness we have all received,[275] and the Dispenser of graces, gifts, virtues, and all the blessings of the New Covenant.[276]

359   As the minister of God Most High as far as justice is concerned[277] and as the arm of the power possessed by Christ inasmuch as he is Lord of Lords,[278] the head of the Christian empire[279] should also be respected and feared.

But since all things have been put in subjection under the feet of Christ[280]—though many have not yet effectively submitted—and since all power in heaven and on earth has been given to him,[281] it follows that without the authority of the vicar of Christ who is the Supreme Pontiff there can be no Christian emperor.

---

[270] Wherever he went Favre aroused those feelings of religious brotherliness which lie at the root of spiritual friendship.

[271] Manuscript H gives *Petri* instead of *Christi*; this seems correct in view of the mention of the other apostles of Christ *(reliquorum Christi apostolorum)*, which implies a previous reference to Peter. In the Middle Ages the pope was first called the vicar of Peter *(vicarius Petri)* and only later the vicar of Christ *(vicarius Christi)*.

[272] A reference to the theory which looked on priests as the successors of the seventy-two disciples.

[273] Col. 1:18.

[274] 1 Pet. 5:4.

[275] John 1:16.

[276] All the functions that the pope exercises in the name of Christ and through him.

[277] Rom. 13:4.

[278] Apoc. 19:16.

[279] The Holy Roman Empire of the German nation ruled at the time by Charles V (*NCathEnc* 7:92–95).

[280] 1 Cor. 15:27.

[281] Matt. 28:18.

Christ, therefore, is represented today in some manner by two persons: the Sovereign Pontiff and the sovereign king—I mean the Holy Roman Emperor. The former represents Christ, priest, prophet, pontiff, pastor, and minister of all his sacred dispensation.[282] The latter represents Christ as king and sovereign who possesses the power of ruling with a rod of iron.[283]

But since (though it was his by right) Christ gained this power for himself through his passion and his obedience, it is, therefore, subject to his own pontificate. It can also be said and, much more, can be understood that the Sovereign Pontiff dispenses in the place of Christ the mercy and grace of God and secret judgments on consciences,[284] while the emperor administers the justice of God. The former represents in a certain way the lowly Christ who lived in the flesh and died; the latter, the all-powerful Christ who rose from the dead and reigns in heaven and who will come to judge the living and the dead by fire.[285]

360 Finding myself drawn away [*distractus,* distracted] from prayer on another day, I thought of asking for the help of divine grace. To obtain it more readily, I found this thought a help: Jesus Christ our Lord had always lived during his mortal life withdrawn[286] from heavenly glory—at least in his body. From the first moment of his conception, that body was capable of glory, because in him no obstacle, no stain, no degree of unpreparedness obliged him to undergo death first. He could have been glorified; he could have received the corporeal attributes he received later on, those he revealed at the Transfiguration.

---

[282] The patristic term is economy *(economia),* which denotes all the means God makes use of for man's salvation.

[283] Apoc. 19:15; Ps. 2:9.

[284] Judgments pertaining to the internal forum, including sacramental confession.

[285] Favre upholds here the theory of the direct power, commonly defended at the time in Roman circles: The pope, as the vicar of Christ, possesses universal power, which he delegates to the Holy Roman Emperor insofar as temporal matters are concerned. Favre goes on to reflect that if the pope, the vicar of a suffering Christ, possesses *in radice* the authority he delegates to the emperor, who represents Christ in glory, it is because Christ acquired his glory only through his passion. So he explains that the power of the Church is in fact limited to spiritual matters and is a continuation of the lowly, compassionate, suffering life of Jesus. Favre's reasoning is eclectic and somewhat incoherent. On the one hand, he holds that the pope has the right of nominating the emperor and perhaps also of limiting the exercise of his power; on the other, he holds that the Church's work is that of spiritual service and of charity. The latter position is quite modern.

[286] *Distractus* (distracted) is usually applied to a person who cannot or will not apply his mind to prayer though it is his business to do so. Here it refers to the state in which Christ and the Blessed Virgin found themselves: "remote" or "withdrawn" from glory by the will of the Father.

Then I prayed through the merits and the grace of Christ, thus withdrawn from his glory, that I might be given healing for the distractions of my spirit. I found great comfort in that prayer.

Then many thoughts came to me about the Blessed Virgin Mary, withdrawn as she was, not from grace, for she always enjoyed the fullness of grace, but from glory of body and soul, although in her there was no original or actual sin to hinder it. She likewise lived withdrawn from the sight of that Salvation whom she afterwards conceived, brought forth, and nourished. Many other blessings, too, were "withdrawn" from her—though "withdrawn" is not the precise word, for it supposes the loss of what was once possessed.[287] "Deferred" is accurate, for the attainment of perfect glory in God was put off and delayed for Christ's body and for the body and the soul of the Virgin.

And the Virgin herself and many or nearly all saints endured deferral of the various desires towards which they were hastening; as a result those desires remained unsatisfied, nor could they be satisfied, until God appeared to them in glory.[288]

361 Another time, the day I was celebrating the office of the holy martyrs Processus and Martinianus, I began to reflect with some profit on the five wounds of Christ. This happened as a result of gazing on a crucifix. As I contemplated the wounds in his hands and feet, they seemed to urge me to lay great stress on progress in doing good and in desiring it so that we may labor on with effect and with fervor and that we may possess a zeal that does not fear the hardships inseparable from traveling and journeying on foot. Rather, may we live in such a way that our hands and feet may one day bear the marks of our labors, as St. Paul said of his whole body, "I bear the marks of the Lord in my body."[289]

---

[287] The idea of privation here is taken from a decadent scholasticism. The classical, scholastic notion of a privation refers not only to the loss of what was once possessed but also to what should have been possessed through a natural condition.

[288] §335; Ps. 17 (16): 15.

[289] Gal. 6:17. The supernatural motivation of Favre's apostolate, which sustained him to the end of his short life, was the imitation of Christ in his sufferings. And he would imitate Christ by accepting the hardships of his wandering life and the moral sufferings that came to him from sources both within and without himself. But his apostolate would not be simply a matter of fulfilling duty; it must engage his whole person, that is, his physical and mental powers and with them his affectivity. His contemplation of Christ's wounds arouses a desire to serve him not only in faithful service but also in love: "As I contemplated the wounds in his hands and feet, they seemed to urge me to lay great stress on progress in doing good and in desiring it so that we may labor on with effect and with fervor. . . ." The last clause (*sic ut operibus et affectibus laboremus*) is somewhat difficult to translate, but it clearly implies loving service, the devotion of a person to a person (O'Leary, "Discernment," pp. 37–38, 62).

362 I noted also that the wound in his side had been inflicted after death. Once all had been accomplished and all Christ's merits had been accumulated, that blood of his mixed with water flowed out for us at last,[290] bearing with it the ransom paid in full by his merits.

It taught us too that unless we die we shall be unable to savor those interior gifts which bring to perfection the salvation of hearts.[291] It was before his death, then, that the treasures of his hands and feet, like fountains, were opened for us and, after death, the treasures of his right side and of his heart.

---

[290] John 19:34.

[291] Only in the end, when all the fullness of grace has been accumulated within, will it overflow to the exterior in gifts for men and in glory for Christ. See §280.

COLOGNE-LOUVAIN

362a: *During August 1543, Favre left Mainz for Cologne. More than a year before, Gerhard Kalckbrenner, prior of the charterhouse, had invited him there for the first time. As the position of the Church in Cologne grew more and more critical, Kalckbrenner wrote again and again, Canisius adding his entreaties. But not until a special messenger arrived from clergy, university, and civic leaders of Cologne did Favre obtain from the cardinal archbishop of Mainz, Albert of Brandenburg, permission to leave that town for Cologne.*

That there is not a single reference in the Memoriale *to the month he spent there may be explained by the ceaseless pastoral activity that occupied him from the time of his arrival about the middle of August. In general, his task was to sustain the Catholics of Cologne and their leaders in a campaign of resistance to the Lutheranizing efforts of their cardinal archbishop, Hermann von Wied.*

Von Wied had been planning reform for years. But a more unlikely reformer could not be imagined. As a man he was an enigma; as a theologian, an ignoramus. Shifty, unreliable, and gullible to a degree, he was an obvious target for the manipulative abilities of clever Lutherans. It is difficult to detect in him a single quality that might have made him a spiritual leader. "Neither a Protestant nor a Catholic but a proper heathen," growled the emperor, Charles V; "how could the good man set about doing any reforming?"

The "good man" turned to the Lutherans for advice about reform and invited two of them, Bruckner and Medmann, to his court. They soon persuaded him that only Bucer and Melanchthon were fit to plan and carry out the reformation of his huge diocese. Bucer began to preach in Cologne in December 1542; Melanchthon arrived in May 1543, attended by a flock of itinerant preachers who at once set to work on the ill-instructed peasantry of the district around Cologne.

Shortly before Melanchthon's arrival, the archbishop said Mass in German at Bonn on Easter Sunday 1543 and afterwards distributed Holy Communion under both species. It was a sign of secession, and the pope looked on it as such. In a long letter to von Wied, he expressed his deep sorrow that he should be the first bishop to secede from the Church; he implored him to remember his duty to God, his solemn oath of fealty, the constancy of his brother bishops, and the unhappy harvest of blood and bitterness that the new doctrines had borne in Germany. His pleas were of no avail. The versatile and plausible Bucer, "that great architect of subtleties," as Bossuet described him, had become von Wied's guiding star in his quest for reform. The Book of Reformation *composed for von Wied by Bucer and Melanchthon appeared in the same year. It was a mixture of pietism, heterodoxy, and cleverly distorted pictures of Catholic teaching and practice. The issues had now become clear; the Catholic resistance under the*

273

archbishop's chancellor, Gropper, formed ranks, and the battle for the faith of Cologne was joined. At this critical juncture Favre arrived in the city.

What could he do there? The Catholic leaders were excellent and zealous men and skilled in polemics. For instance, in three weeks they put together and had printed an able refutation of von Wied's Book of Reformation. And once the danger of apostasy became clear, they began to organize their resistance around the university professors and certain notables of the city: Doctor Johann Gropper, the archbishop's chancellor; the Carmelite provincial, Eberhard Billick; the Dominican Stempel; Jörgen Skodberg, the exiled archbishop of Lund; Gerard Kalckbrenner, the prior of the Charterhouse of St. Barbara; and perhaps also the two consuls of that year, Arnold von Browiller and Peter von Heimbach. But they felt that something more than polemics was needed: a strengthening of religion through a revival of devotion and of Catholic practice. And Favre's presence in Cologne proved just such a stimulus.

Since the leaders knew Favre, they begged him to make representations to the nuncio and to the imperial court on behalf of the university. So on August 27 he left for Bonn, where the emperor had made a temporary stay. He delivered the appeal from the university to the nuncio, Poggio, and was able to describe the critical state of the Cologne Catholics to de Soto, the emperor's confessor, and to his minister Granvelle. The results were at first favorable: the archbishop, present in person at Bonn, promised to dismiss all Lutheran preachers from his diocese, to suppress Bucer's plan of reformation, and to make no innovations in matters of faith unless they had been decided by Rome. Favre's delight at this change of heart was short-lived, for the archbishop soon resumed his campaign of reformation as if he had made no promises at all.

Favre returned to Cologne at the request of the nuncio and took up his ministry again. This lasted for nearly a month. He wrote on September 3, 1543, to Cardinal Morone to excuse himself for not having returned straightaway to Mainz (MonFabri, p. 220). As it happened, he was never again to visit that city. A few days later a Jesuit scholastic who had been waylaid by robbers and beaten because he had no money stumbled into the city. He brought with him a letter from Ignatius in Rome ordering Favre to set out for Portugal.

King John III of Portugal, who had heard about Favre through Diogo de Gouveia, had asked for him by name. He wanted him to travel with the retinue which was to escort his daughter, the infanta Maria, to Spain; the infanta had become engaged to Prince Philip, the future king of Spain. Ignatius judged this an excellent opportunity to ease the way for a foundation in Spain. Favre journeyed to Antwerp only to be told there that the next sailing would not be until after Christmas. Back in Louvain on October 8, he fell seriously ill and was forced to remain in bed until the beginning of December. The following passage from the Memoriale (no. 363) sums up the events of four months from September to December 1543. It is missing from the best manuscript (H). A dry and precise summary, it is quite unlike Favre's style, spirit, and vocabulary. In addition, it implies that the illness mentioned below (no. 364) is over. The passage is almost certainly from another hand and must have been added to make up for the lacunae in the text.

▸ September–December 1543

363 About that time, I was ordered in the name of obedience to leave Cologne for Portugal, and I made my preparations for the journey in September. Having arrived at Antwerp and being unable to find a ship, I returned to Louvain, where I caught the tertian ague, which delayed me there for nearly two months.[1]

363a: The following brief entries appear to have been written during Favre's illness of September to December 1543. The opening words: "The day following . . ." and "The next day . . ." point to the existence of previously written notes which seem to have vanished.

364 Prostrated by illness one day, I found myself in a state of aridity and believed myself far from God. Then there came to me some consolation in an understanding of these words: "I am with him in his tribulations."[2]

The day following, wanting to sleep—for I had slept but little for seven days on account of my illness—I thought of this text, turning it over in my mind: "In peace, in the selfsame, shall I sleep and take my rest."[3]

The next day, my head aching and being exceedingly worn out from my illness, I began to think of Christ's head crowned with thorns. I was so greatly touched by that thought that I shed tears, and I was given a desire to have my head laid beside the thorn-covered head of Christ, there to be pierced.[4]

364a: As soon as he had sufficiently recovered from his illness, Favre took up his apostolic activity again; he gave the Exercises, visited convents, preached to the clergy, and had spiritual conversations with professors and students from the university, which at the time counted some six thousand students. He lodged in the house of Cornelius Wischaven (1509–1559), who had been ordained in 1533 and was carrying out the duties of a deacon in

---

[1] Favre was in Antwerp on October 13, 1543, and was back in Louvain by October 15. The ague, a type of malaria, was called "tertian" because it caused a crisis every third day.

[2] Ps. 91 (90): 15.

[3] Ps. 4:9.

[4] One of Favre's very rare comments on his physical state. He must have been suffering a good deal, and his health was rapidly deteriorating.

the Church of St. Peter of Louvain. Favre got to know him, won him over, and towards the end of 1543 accepted him as a novice. Wischaven began his noviceship in his own house. He was a good priest, both pious and zealous, but addicted to passionate and passing enthusiasms which had constantly to be kept in check, for example, liturgical singing (MonFabri, pp. 236–243), exorcisms (MonFabri, pp 331–332, 471–472). It was Favre's task, at a time when he was anything but well, to knock this temperamental and changeable character into shape.

▸ *January 1, 1544*

365   On the day of the Lord's Circumcision, the first day of the year 1544, I recognized with great devotion that Christ had received the sign of circumcision for us and that he had willed to do so in order to be looked upon as a member of the Jewish race. It was for us, too, that he had willed to be given a name among men. These thoughts aroused in me a great desire which led me to seek from God this twofold grace: first, that I might receive in my soul on that day by God's grace a sign of the circumcision and become at last a member of the people of God; second, I sought the grace of having my name inscribed in the book of life from that moment.

365a: Entries 366 and 367 below refer to Favre's return to Cologne after his stay in Louvain. It is perhaps necessary to accept them with the same qualifications as for entry number 363, but they help to make up for the long silence of the Memoriale *from January 1544 to January 1545.*

366   After the feast of the Kings this year, the journey I had already begun to Portugal was canceled, so I returned to Cologne, having sent on into Portugal Francesco de Strada, Master Andrés de Oviedo,[5] Father Juan de Aragón, and nine others we had gained for the Lord at Louvain through Jesus Christ. They were Master Peter Faber of Hall, Master Hermes, Master John, Master Maximilian, Father Leonhard, Master Jacques, Master Daniel, Thomas,[6] and the youth Cornelius.[7]

---

[5] Andrés de Oviedo (ca. 1517–1577), a member of the Society since June 1541 (*FN* 1:601, n. 35).

[6] Peter de Smet *(Faber)*, born at Hall near Brussels in 1518, (*EppCan* 1:104, n. 2); a student with whom Favre had spiritual conversations; a bachelor of theology, he had preached in 1543 on all the Sundays of Advent—a rare happening in those days (*MonFabri*, pp. 233–234); Hermes Poen of Renaix, a canon of the church of St. Peter and a professor in the Collège de Lys (Poncelet, *Histoire de la Compagnie* 1:94); Jean Cuvillon, a native of Lille, had come to see Favre in Mainz in June 1543 (*MonFabri*, p. 207), and was received into the Society by him on January 6, 1544 (Poncelet, *Histoire de la Compagnie* 1:44, n. 3); Maximilian a Capello (or de la Chapelle), also from Lille, then a student at Louvain; Leonhard Kessel from Louvain, a student; John

367 On my return to Cologne,[8] I brought with me Master Lambert and Emiliano.[9] There I rented a house, where I stayed until July. I preached in Latin in the College of Arts every Sunday and on some holy days, without counting sermons on special occasions. I left Alvaro there with some scholastics of our Society. May Jesus make of them a solid foundation for his Society.

367a: The Cologne community, not counting Canisius, who was staying with Andreas Herll, numbered seven at the time. They were supported by alms from the Carthusians and from two noble ladies (MonFabri, pp. 257). In May the community increased to eight, as Favre notes, and was being provided by kindly people with furniture and other needful things. Canisius, who had come into an inheritance, was looking for a house in which to start a school (MonFabri, p. 256).

Favre began to preach on all Sundays and important feast days, beginning on the Sunday before Lent and continuing until the end of Easter week. His congregations were made up of university students, priests, canons, the bishop of Lund, Skodberg, and others who understood Latin (MonFabri, pp. 257, 262). The special sermons were preached in convents and to the chapter of canons. He also heard the confessions of the students and began to give them spiritual direction. In addition, he had to give attention to Archbishop von Wied's plans for reform, as the emperor was showing himself favorable to them at the time. And with all this, he was preoccupied

---

Faber from Douai, a student; Daniel Paeybroeck from Termonde (*MonFabri*, pp. 207–208); Thomas Poghius from Tournai.

[7] Cornelius Wischaven, a nephew of the other Cornelius Wischaven (linking passage 364a above) was fifteen or sixteen years of age at the time. The day before the party was due to leave, he begged Favre on his knees and weeping, to admit him into the Society and send him to Portugal with the others. Favre refused on the grounds that the youth needed to test his vocation under the guidance of his uncle. Saying nothing to anyone, Cornelius hid himself on board the boat that was to take the party and in that way vanquished Favre's resistance (*MonFabri*, p. 235). By February 2 they had all arrived at Compostella (*MonFabri*, p. 260), but five of them were almost immediately sent back to Cologne by Simão Rodrigues: Daniel Paeybroeck, John Faber, Thomas Poghius, Peter de Smet, and Leonhard Kessel. They enrolled in the university on June 25, and at the end of July the young Leonhard Kessel was appointed their rector (Poncelet, *Histoire de la Compagnie* 1:45, n. 1). Daniel Paeybroeck soon left them for Louvain where, more mature and better endowed, he assumed charge of the first Jesuit community there after Favre's departure (Poncelet, *Histoire* 1:46).

[8] January 24 (*MonFabri*, pp. 232 ff.).

[9] Lambert du Château, born at Liège in 1520, a bachelor of theology, had attached himself to Favre. He died shortly afterwards at Cologne on September 29, 1544, and was buried there in the charterhouse. Emiliano of Loyola had been received into the Society by his uncle, Ignatius, towards the end of 1542 (*FN* 1:190).

during these months with plans for making Jesuit foundations in Germany (MonFabri, pp. 256, 259).

368 Having received a new command to set out for Portugal at the king's will, I left the city on July 12 with seven heads from the holy bodies of the eleven thousand virgins, together with many other sacred relics which had been given to me in Cologne.[10]

One of these heads had been given to me by the Cologne charterhouse, another by the nuns of the convent of St. Maximinus in the same town, and a smaller one by the convent of the "White Ladies." Two others had been presented to me by the convent of St. Michael. The sixth had come to me from the parish church of St. Columba. Alvaro Alfonso gave the seventh into my keeping for Doña Leonora Mascarenhas; he had himself received it as a gift from a holy woman of Cologne.[11] On the day of the apostle St. Bartholomew, I landed at Lisbon.[12]

---

[10] Gelenius, describing the collection of relics in Cologne, mentions that every one of the innumerable churches of the city possessed several of these heads.

[11] Among these "many other sacred relics" were those of the Four Martyrs, of St. Catherine, of St. Susanna (MonFabri, p. 309), with some other relics of St. Ursula's companions. See §404. Favre had to show authority from the Holy See before being allowed to transfer these relics. Such transfers were common. The charterhouse of Cologne, founded in 1334, numbered about thirty monks before 1645 (A. Gelenius, *De admiranda sacra et civili magnitudine Coloniæ Claudiæ Agrippinensis Augustæ Urbium Urbis* [Cologne, 1645], pp. 454–457). In their church of St. Maximinus, the nuns of the Order of St. Augustine had preserved up to 1645 the bodies of the companions of St. Ursula. It is likely that Favre preached in Latin to this community of about sixty nuns towards the end of the summer of 1543 (MonFabri, p. 221), and in the spring of 1544 (MonFabri, p. 262). The convent of the "White Ladies" were Augustinian religious. Reformed in 1446, they possessed many heads and other relics of St. Ursula's companions. The convent of St. Michael was another convent of Augustinians. Among their "treasures" they had many heads of the companions of SS. Gregory and Ursula. Of the nineteen parish churches in Cologne, the church of St. Columba was the most venerable of the five most ancient (Gelenius, *De admiranda,* pp. 390–392). These gifts give an idea of Favre's ministry in Cologne. Religious, both men and women, had a special place in it. As he left Cologne with these grisly objects in his baggage, Favre unwittingly helped to spread one of the greatest frauds ever perpetrated in the history of relics. The not very well authenticated story about a martyrdom in the fourth century, that of Ursula and a very few companions, grew into one of the most extravagant stories ever told about early Christianity. So when countless human remains, doubtless those of plague victims, were discovered at Cologne in 1255, they were accepted as those of the martyrs. Thus were born the legends of St. Ursula and her 11,000 companions. On the matter of credulity in general, see Brodrick, *Canisius,* p. 113, n. 1).

[12] August 24, 1544. His arrival was eagerly awaited by the scholastics he had sent from Louvain to Coimbra.

COIMBRA–PORTUGAL

The Final Months (1545-1546): Pastoral Activities

368a: In August Favre reached the court of King John III of Portugal at Évora. He spent three months there mostly in very indifferent health and in low spirits. He felt useless, doing and suffering nothing of consequence, as he wrote in a letter to Ignatius from Évora on November 30, 1544 (MonFabri, p. 280). In December he went with the king's leave to Coimbra, where the scholastics whom he had sent from Louvain awaited him with anticipation. All was not well at Coimbra: the community of sixty was in excess of the number permitted by the papal bull; the rector, Simão Rodrigues, who was also acting as novice master, had admitted twenty-three Portuguese with little regard for their suitability. They were receiving inadequate training because of the rector's frequent absences at court. During these absences he left all the scholastics in the charge of Martín de Santa Cruz, a young priest who was himself a student and a novice. Santa Cruz felt quite unequal to this task. He had a frank interview with Favre about the state of the community and the difficulty of his position—unable as he was to consult his absent superior. Favre heard the novices' confessions (no. 397) and gave them instructions and exhortations. The students and professors of the university town of Coimbra came to him in crowds for confession; some made the Exercises. By the end of January he was again with the court at Évora.

▶ *January 6, 1545*

369 On the day of the Three Kings in the year 1545, I thought of the following subject to preach on:[1] If Jesus Christ wished, among other things, to be hidden behind the veil of his flesh, it was to teach men to reveal their dispositions towards him. For the same reason he willed to conceal under his flesh all the treasures of divine knowledge so as to give us an opportunity of dispensing the treasures we have received from his Majesty. And he acted in such a way that the three Magi and all their servants opened up their treasures when they saw the poverty of their Lord. In short, while concealing his greatness, he brings his angels down on earth to proclaim it; while concealing his sinlessness and wishing to be baptized by John, he moves the Father to make it

---

[1] From this point on, the entries cease to be records of intimate reflections and become jottings about his apostolate or his ministries: preaching (§369, §370, §379, §380, §381, §382); confessions (§373, §391, §397, and so forth); the distribution of the Eucharist (§389).

known in these words: "This is my beloved Son . . ."[2] Again, while not wishing to manifest his charity at the wedding feast, he opens up the treasures of his mother when she says to him, "They have no wine,"[3] thus constraining him to manifest his glory before the time.

Today the Church celebrates these three manifestations.

370 The Magi offered gold to the Christ Child as if seeking to relieve him in his state of poverty and need, confessing as they did so that they held all their power from him. They offered him incense in an odor of sweetness,[4] as if seeking to comfort his spirit and his soul, believing and testifying as they did so that from him alone were holy desires and knowledge of good to be obtained. Lastly, they offered myrrh in the desire that the body formed for that Child might not know corruption[5]—the child whose sufferings would gain glory and incorruption for the bodies of all.

By passing through Jerusalem the Magi appeared to have exposed themselves and Christ to great danger, but that danger cannot be attributed to the star, for it had not guided them there.[6] And although that visit to Jerusalem resulted in the greatest good for themselves and all the world, they were given a warning, as we are told, and departed to their own country by another way.

371 Then I experienced some kind of obstinate resistance in my soul which prevented me from delighting in the joy and fervor attached to a feast so sacred and sublime. I received this interior reply about it: "This is the day of the Three Kings, the day the true King is adored. Therefore, bear the burden of that resistance in the knowledge that thereby you will more clearly see whether you are king over yourself or not. It is a small thing to master and conquer ourselves when we find ourselves near to Christ by devotion. But the true victory, the true mastery and control of oneself, can be better recognized when our King seems no longer present—he who wages our wars for us until he makes kings of us in the end."[7]

372 "All those from Sheba shall come, all the kings will adore him, and all nations will serve him."[8] This text should be understood as

---

[2] Matt. 3:17.

[3] John 2:3.

[4] Exod. 29:18; Eph. 5:2; Phil. 4:18.

[5] Ps. 16 (15): 10.

[6] Matt. 2:9.

[7] 1 Sam. 8:20. In the days of Samuel, the people wanted a king "to go out before us and fight our battles." Trials borne in desolation are more fruitful.

[8] Isa. 60:6; Ps. 72 (71): 11.

an upsurge of hope in the prophets through the Spirit who spoke in them, who wills all men to be saved[9] and who gave to all a Mediator and means in sufficiency.

One can also conclude from this text that the submission of such great kings to Christ allows the hope of as much again from their equals, even from those greater than they, and with much more reason from those who are less.

▸ January 10

373   On the vigil of the Sunday within the octave of the Epiphany, while hearing confessions, I considered that a confessor should not only take care of the soul that submits itself to him to be instructed, admonished, corrected, and led to perfection,[10] but should also see to it that his penitents bring help and comfort to all those—the dead, sinners, or others— who may be in material or spiritual need. For it is easy to help them through the prayers, pious works, and almsgiving of penitents. The confessor should, then, be a good and faithful steward,[11] an administrator who values highly, as treasures capable of answering many needs, the many precious wills submitted to him by his penitents.

▸ January 11

374   Sunday within the octave of the Epiphany: Christ's parents are bereft of his presence; then they seek him anxiously among their kinsfolk and acquaintances but without finding him; then in Jerusalem, where he had remained behind. Third, they find him in the Temple, sitting among the doctors, listening to them and asking them questions.[12] Fourth, they bring him back to their home and under their authority.

375   In what he teaches us at the age of twelve, Christ follows this order:[13] first, he wills to separate himself from his earthly parents so as to do the will of his Father in heaven; second, he wills to have his parents look for him; third, he wills to be found, and found in the temple in the midst of the doctors; fourth, he wills to return to submissiveness; fifth, he wills to share their lowly state; sixth, he wills to

---

[9] 1 Tim. 2:4.
[10] *MonFabri,* pp. 245–252; §333 n. 233 above.
[11] Matt. 25:23; Luke 12:42.
[12] Luke 2:46.
[13] These appear to be points for a meditation or a sermon.

live in Nazareth, which means "flower";[14] seventh, he wills to be subject to them.[15]

376 Once the festival days have been observed and completed, his parents return in accord with custom and their social status. But Christ has business in the temple more important than what could be conducted in the ordinary way.

So we should take care not to overly concern ourselves with common custom in the matter of physically leaving divine services. If the services have satisfied us, they have perhaps not satisfied God. And so we should not leave before we have made sure whether Christ is ready to go with us or not. And if he desires our worshipful attention there for a longer time, let us remain for his Father's sake and for his own sake who still desires to remain. We prefer to be left behind by our relatives and acquaintances rather than desert Christ.

377 Let the learned and the wise keep before their eyes in all circumstances this boy of twelve sitting in the midst of the doctors, listening to them, and asking them questions.[16] Let them, I repeat, keep him before their eyes at all times lest they desire to possess more wisdom than is proper for them.[17] Let heretics consider his lowly appearance and his youthfulness so that they listen to the doctors of the Church and ask them questions while sitting quietly in their midst.[18]

378 Christ our Lord dwelt for nine months in the womb of the Virgin as if in the root of a tree.[19] From his birth until the age of twelve, he dwelt as if in the trunk of the tree. From his twelfth to his thirtieth year he dwelt in flower, having himself become a flower. Then in his maturity, as we may piously believe, he remained in fruit so as to bring forth in us the fruits of salvation.

If you bring the Child Jesus with you to the temple and into the place of the vision of peace,[20] if you then seek him diligently wherever

---

[14] St. Jerome's interpretation of the name.

[15] Luke 2:51.

[16] See Luke 2:46.

[17] See Rom. 12:3; also §113, where Favre comments on the spiritual pride of theologians, a theme dear to the New Devotion.

[18] Favre, in Coimbra, cannot banish Germany and its Lutherans from his mind; news would have come to him from the Jesuits left in Cologne.

[19] The biblical image of the tree of Jesse was traditionally applied to Christ (Isa. 11:1–2; Matt. 2:23). For Favre, Christ is the tree (§279, §280) whose development (beginning, growth, end) starts from the root where it lies hidden under his suffering humanity and ends in the revelation of his glory.

[20] This traditional interpretation of the Hebrew word "Jerusalem" finds no confirmation in modern exegesis. But the word has a profound theological signifi-

he left you or where he remained unknown to you—if you do these things, he will readily go down with you to your own self and live among the flowers of the spiritual childhood of your spirit. And there, in the end, he will be completely amenable to your desires, ready to obey your will, which you once forced to serve you in your wicked desires.[21]

▸ **January 13**

379 On the octave of the Epiphany, I had taken this text as the subject of a sermon: "John saw Jesus coming to him";[22] I was just about to offer the sacrifice when I was touched by a deep desire that I might be able to see, and to feel in my heart, Jesus coming to me in the Sacrament. I knew well that he had very often come to me without my having seen him come. So I petitioned God, the Virgin, and certain saints that I, all my brethren, and all those about to receive Communion might be allowed to see him coming, to venerate him fittingly, and so to be properly prepared for his coming. While I was putting on the sacred vestments, I began to reflect on, and encourage in myself, the dispositions proper to the person who sees Jesus coming to him.

380 John caught sight of him; raising his eyes he saw Jesus coming towards him. So too Peter saw him somewhere when he said "Depart from me for I am a sinful man." And Elizabeth saw to some extent the same sight when she said "Whence is this to me that the Mother of my Lord should come to me?" But above all the Mother of God saw Jesus coming to her when she said "Behold the handmaid of the Lord."[23]

381 Jesus' Mother kept him subject to her obedience for a long time, until his thirtieth year. And those who keep their eyes on him with great solicitude and fear can in a way do the same—much as the bride keeps the bridegroom in view out of a love too great to let him out of her sight for any length of time.

382 By withdrawing from obedience to his parents and setting out for John's baptism, Jesus teaches that those who relinquish one kind

---

cance (*DBibTheol*, pp. 260–263).

[21] After the ascent to the temple, corresponding to the "return to the heart," after the time of "appearances and disappearances" (times of consolation and desolation), comes the time of "dwelling together" (interior stability). From that time on, the Lord follows those desires which come from him into the soul he has made his own. This union with the will of God produces the fruits of salvation. See §353 for these three stages as part of Favre's own experience.

[22] John 1:29.

[23] Texts in order: Luke 5:8; Luke 1:38; 1:43; 1:38. This "seeing" is with the eye of faith.

of duty should not seek freedom of the flesh, like those who exchange a more strict obedience for one less strict, but rather should ascend to something more difficult. Christ leaves the service of his parents in order to become a sort of disciple of his servant John. He does not seek teachers more highly regarded than his parents nor release from all obedience; he wishes instead to become the servant of all.[24]

383 He comes forth into the light in order to offer himself to all who desire to be saved. Let every mortal take notice and welcome him at his coming. Let him go out to meet him[25] and so receive the grace of the spotless Lamb of God[26] given as a ransom for him, the grace of him who bears the sins of the world and takes them away. Also let him already begin to open his eyes and see Jesus coming towards him, not as he once did to justify him but to judge him. At present he comes after us with great patience, he who sought us out before we existed and was waiting at the door. He has stood there knocking for a long time, our Savior, unknown to us. Let us go therefore to meet him; let him not find us sleeping,[27] for we have gone too long without knowing him.

384 Then I was moved by this great desire, that, wherever the sacrament of the Eucharist is being distributed to the laity, the priest, facing the communicants and showing the host to them, should say in an intelligible manner, "John saw Jesus coming to him and said, "Behold the Lamb of God, behold him who takes away the sins of the world.'"[28]

▸ *January 14*

385 The day after the octave of the Epiphany, while thoughts about Jesus drawing ever nearer to us as judge still occupied my mind, I recalled those signs that foretold the general judgment: wars, civil discord, earthquakes, plagues, and famines,[29] which occur and are experienced in various places every day. I thought too about those more universal signs which have not yet been witnessed: upon the earth distress of nations in perplexity at the roaring of the sea and the waves; the darkening of the sun and the moon; the shaking of the powers of

---

[24] Matt. 20:28. At the time Favre was giving talks on obedience at Coimbra. The notes which survive were most likely taken by some of those present (*MonFabri*, pp. 284–287).

[25] Matt. 25:6. The whole of the last part of the *Memoriale* is studded with references to chapters 24 and 25 of Matthew (and parallel passages), which deal with the last days, with death, and the last meeting with the Lord.

[26] 1 Pet. 1:19; John 1:29.

[27] Rev 3:20; Matt. 25:6.

[28] John 1:29.

[29] Matt. 24:7; Luke 21:6, 11.

heaven accompanied by other terrors in the heavens and by the appearance of the fearful sign of the Son of man. All this will come to pass in such a way that men will wither away through fear and foreboding.

When I reflected on the violence and the terrible consequences of all these signs, I could not help tearfully wishing, for both myself and all others—Christians and all the rest of the inhabitants of the earth, present and to come—wishing, I say, for everyone a soul that is vigilant and fearful of God the judge.[30]

386 When the fury of war takes over a city, it shakes hearts violently; when a disastrous famine rages to the point of destroying a whole population, it throws the souls of all into great agitation; similarly, earthquakes and epidemics have always struck terror in souls.[31] But far more widespread and serious would be the effects on mortals of those more universal calamities—were they to experience them—calamities such as the distress of nations, the roaring of the waves of seas in tumult, and terrors in the sky.

Since all these things terrify even those whose hearts are open and are not weighed down with the cares of this life or with dissipation and drunkenness, it follows that men must be exceedingly watchful[32] and concerned about that last day of Christ our Lord, which will be preceded and heralded by so many calamities.

387 Then there came to my mind these words from the twenty-first chapter of Luke: "Watch, therefore, praying at all times that you may be accounted worthy to escape all these things that will take place, and to stand before the Son of man." For this it seemed good to wish that all Christians would say the following prayer daily both in private and in public: "Lord Jesus Christ, Son of the living God, you have commanded us to watch and pray at all times that we may escape all those calamities that precede your fearful judgment and stand worthily before the Son of Man. We pray you, give ear to the supplications we make in fear and in confidence; grant that that day may not catch any of us unprepared. You who live and reign with the same Father in the unity of the Holy Spirit, God, for ever and ever. Amen."

▸ *January 15*

388 Another time, as I was saying Mass for my brethren and my spiritual sons,[33] these words of St. Paul came to my mind: "Parents

---

[30] Matt. 25:5–6. See §57; O'Leary, "Discernment," p. 91.

[31] §57 n. 110 above.

[32] See Luke 21:34, 36, §385; O'Leary, "Discernment," p. 50.

[33] His brothers are the members of the Society of Jesus; his spiritual sons are

ought to lay up treasure for their children."[34] At that I experienced a great desire to be able to put aside something in the way of spiritual treasure for others, to be handed over to them someday for their consolation. This would be in imitation of him who was made the receptacle of all the treasures of the wisdom and knowledge of God.[35]

I conceived good hope in the reflection that the holy fathers[36] (if only we are their true sons) had stored up for us a great treasure not only in heaven, in gifts of glory, but also on earth, in gifts of grace. This should console those who, living according to the teaching of one or other of these fathers, exercise any ministry whatever in uprightness and obedience. Even if in that ministry they may not have every kind of opportunity to lay up for themselves spiritual treasure, they know, however, that there is a great treasure stored up for them in the keeping of their fathers, whose place their own superiors take, and in the keeping of their superiors themselves when they are worthy ones.[37]

389 Those superiors, of course, whatever kind of house they direct, should pay most careful attention to laying up treasure for their sons and for all those whom Christ has placed under them, after first of all becoming spiritual treasuries themselves.

Generally, too, those who gather in material things which were in one way or another collected and stored up for them by others should sow and lay aside spiritual things for their sake. Those who accumulate material treasures for spiritual persons would be cheated if someday they were not to find a spiritual treasure stored up and laid aside for them by those persons.[38] And I would say the same about all those who serve Christ in lesser or more humble duties compared with those who serve him in higher and more honorable ministries. Having shared in labor and sufferings, they should also have their share of ease and consolation. What Christ will say to all the saints is relevant here: "Enter into the joy of your Lord,"[39] meaning you who have entered into his toil and sufferings.

---

those he had sent from Louvain to Coimbra (§366). He himself was about to leave Coimbra and wished to give them some parting gift; he writes of it as a "treasure" in the spiritual sense.

[34] 2 Cor. 12:14.

[35] Col. 2:3.

[36] The founders of religious orders and the great saints who are looked on as models for our imitation (§261).

[37] §357.

[38] 2 Cor. 8:9–15.

[39] Matt. 25:21.

▸ January 16

390 On the day of the five martyrs Berardo, Pietro, Acurzio, Adiuto, and Ottone of the Order of Minors,[40] I was present at divine services in the Church of the Holy Cross at Coimbra, where their bodies are buried. Here I was affected by a feeling of deep compassion for all those who are in manifest danger of damnation. Luther, the king of England, the Grand Turk, and some others came to my mind.[41]

391 I reflected on the goodness of God which allows such men and many other sinners, of whom I am the foremost, to live so long.[42]

I understood something which could easily be taken as a condemnation of myself and of others like me; for it is indeed possible not only that God grants these sinners time for repentance while he awaits their conversion, which in itself they can still effect by his gift, but also that he waits to see whether someone may wish to pray more for them or make efforts to convert them. He readily grants time to Suleiman the Turk[43] to see if any of us Christians might finally decide to help him before he dies.

We who have received the power of preaching and teaching should be very watchful lest many be lost through our fault and through our negligence. That God has entrusted many to us for instruction and admonishment about their salvation should make us afraid.

Everywhere many await us; let us then be in a hurry to make progress in all things and to be well prepared for them.

392 The blood of many martyrs summons us to those peoples among whom and for whose salvation they died. May it come about someday that some of our Society may have the opportunity and the heart to visit those Moroccans for whom these five martyrs offered themselves as the seed of salvation. They were the living words of God and of Christ; and so, when they could not find a land receptive to the words of the Gospel, they resolved to die there as good seed,[44] so that

---

[40] The Order of Friars Minor: Berardo of Carbio and companions are the Franciscan protomartyrs (*NCathEnc* 2:319; 9:933).

[41] See §25. Favre's charity reaches out to all. The king he mentions was Henry VIII of England. Lewis, an atheist converted to Anglicanism, has Henry in hell (C. S. 11).

[42] 1 Tim. 1:15.

[43] This was Suleiman I (1497–1566), tenth and mightiest Ottoman emperor, who reigned from 1520 to 1566. During his reign the Ottoman civilization and administration took their definitive form. For his personal dignity and brilliant court, the West gave him the title "the Magnificent." He was very much on the minds of European kings and princes in those days. Favre, then close to Morocco, was reflecting on the Arab world (§33 n. 65 above). See *NCathEnc* 13:783–784.

[44] John 12:49. At this time the whole of Portugal was in a fever of longing to

fruit, as yet ungathered, might someday be gathered in by some true laborers for Christ.

▸ *January 20*

393 On the day of the holy martyrs Fabian and Sebastian, there was very great flooding at Coimbra, destructive in many ways, not only to tender crops, but also to houses and furniture. That very day I said Mass for a deceased monk whom Martín de Santa Cruz had commended to me as a holy man.[45] I was given great devotion with regard to the deliverance of the souls in purgatory and with it a new perception and understanding especially about those who are detained there for very slight faults and are almost perfectly happy. For I was picturing to myself these souls, one by one, gradually entering a life of happiness and participating in beatitude. What I say must be understood as pertaining to accidental beatitude,[46] for essential beatitude is the total, simultaneous, and perfect possession of endless life, a state brought to completion by the aggregation of all goods.[47]

394 Here also I received great hope of the fine weather anxiously desired and sought in prayer for some days past. This feeling came after I had asked the Lord to deign to spare the poor people whose houses or goods of some other sort were being destroyed in that flood.[48] I kept asking him, however, to have pity on them as if all those goods belonged to people as pious and devout as that holy monk for whose soul I was celebrating Mass or as if everything belonged to the saints in heaven.

395 Here there came to mind certain desires of certain saints, and I felt that we should go to great pains to fulfill not only God's own purposes but also those that it is clear were from God in his saints. But I longed above all that we, the living, should take pains to fulfill each other's holy desires concerning the honor of God, the salvation of souls, and our own spiritual progress.

---

embark on a crusade—a fever which died down only with the death of Don Sebastian.

[45] Rector of the college at Coimbra (§369).

[46] Theologians of the later Middle Ages looked on accidental glory as the glory of the spirit reflected on the resurrected body. Favre's meaning here is that the blessed have already attained glory, but that glory is still capable of an increase. The distinction is by no means clear.

[47] The classical definitions of eternity and happiness formulated by Boethius, *De Consolatione* 3:2.

[48] §393. Although Favre prays for those who have suffered loss in the floods, his theology leads him to consider such natural calamities as punishment for sin (§57 n. 112; §230 n. 6; §386 above). See O'Leary, "Discernment," pp. 50–51.

396 After that, it happened that I was given a kind of holy daring to ask God to fulfill certain desires of mine—which came from him—concerning the restoration of Germany and the return of other peoples to the faith and to a life of perfect Christian discipline. May God himself grant the fulfillment of the pious desires he gives us, and may he bring to completion all the undertakings he conceives through his creatures.[49]

▸ January 21

397 On the day of the glorious virgin and martyr Agnes, I said Mass with the intention that God might deign to confer a special privilege on our Society. The privilege would consist of this: if only the sins committed by the present or future members of the order might not be laid to the charge of the Society itself! I refer, in the first place, to the sins committed before their entrance, then to all their other sins.

I made this petition because I felt a kind of holy fear lest the progress of the Society suffer by reason of the sins committed by each of us, either present or future members of the Society—and all the more so because many enter who have in many ways grievously offended God before entering.[50]

Then I prayed thus: "O good Jesus, do not impute our personal sins to this holy community. Let every attempt we may ever make against your honor, the salvation of our souls, and the salvation of our neighbor come to nothing. Do not, I pray you, O God, remember our many sins when we do something good and edifying. But if it seems good to you that we should undergo humiliations, bodily afflictions, or poverty as a punishment, spare us at least that punishment by scourging which is usually reserved for those wretched sinners who are abandoned to new sins and errors as a chastisement for the old.[51] Avert, O Lord God, from this, your young and dear family,[52] these punishments for sin."

---

[49] Through desires men conceive and plan great apostolic works, and God, from whom these desires come, is then the author of the works.

[50] During his short visit to Coimbra, Favre probably examined (as to suitability) and heard the confessions of a number who wished to enter the Society.

[51] Obduracy in sin. The punishment for this sin is the new sins it provokes.

[52] *Tua tenella familia* is an untranslatable expression referring to the Society.

These thoughts occurred to me because of my resolution to pray specially for some of Ours[53] (they are many) whose general confessions I had heard.[54]

---

[53] "Ours" (*nostri*) was the term used by the first companions of Ignatius to describe themselves.

[54] Many of the manuscripts, including H, end at this point. On the last page of manuscript H, the following has been added in a different hand: "There is a good deal missing up to and including the short part for the year 1546" (§442, §443) (*Multa desunt usque ad particulam anni 1546*).

EVORA

397a: With Araoz and another companion, Favre left Coimbra around January 20, 1545, reached Sardoal before midnight on January 23, and was in Évora with the court by February 2. The three covered a good part of the journey on foot, traveling sometimes by night; they had a mule which they mounted in turn.

▸ *February 2*

398   On the feast of the Purification, I felt a great and rather lively desire not to die before the things of God are properly arranged in my soul. I wished to see my soul in peace before it left my body;[1] to taste life, which is the Savior, before death;[2] to know the true light of life before I enter the darkness of death; to know the glory of Christ's Church and of our Society before I die. I wished also to be given grace not to let a day pass by without some notable fruit. For God gives us life to work out our salvation, and he assigns some good work for each day.

Stir up, therefore, in me, O God, not only those desires which ought to be fulfilled by the end of my life but also those you want accomplished daily. How happy the one who could tell what the Lord expects of him day by day![3]

▸ *February 3*

399   On the day of St. Blaise, one of the heads of the holy virgins which I had presented to Master Simão[4] for the Coimbra college was brought to Coimbra.[5] May Jesus grant that it be preserved there with honor and devotion until its own resurrection and that of all human bodies.

---

[1] A reference to the Gospel of the day (Luke 2:26). Favre's desire, however, has to do with the peace that comes from a purified soul.

[2] Another of the repeated references to death in these concluding pages of the *Memoriale*.

[3] A reference to obedience: Favre lived in its spirit, and this is a prayer for the gift of perfect obedience. See O'Leary, "Discernment," p. 128.

[4] Simão Rodrigues, one of the first companions of Ignatius whom Favre had known in Paris. At the time he was provincial of Portugal (§15).

[5] In a letter dated February 3, 1545, Favre wrote to the rector of Coimbra, Santa Cruz, to announce the coming arrival of Estrada with one of the heads of the Eleven Thousand Virgins in his baggage (*MonFabri*, p. 306).

291

▸ **February 20**

400 On the Friday after Ash Wednesday, I experienced a great desire that our Society should not lose anything by using the new Roman Breviary.[6]

I feared the usual consequences: that Ours might make ill use of the privilege by which they are not bound to recite numerous long offices aloud.[7] So I celebrated Mass for this intention, namely, that through the offices of working and of prayer of the heart,[8] we may fully compensate the living and the dead for our making less of the vocal office. This will be easy for those who love God and their neighbors; for, by preaching, hearing confessions, and personal exhortation together with mental prayer,[9] they can help both the living and the dead, making known to many of the faithful the needs of the dead and keeping their memory alive among themselves.

But if we do not see this, it will be preferable for us to be bound to a longer office and have less time available for other pious activities and prayers. In short, no one should waste time.

Let us help the living in all their needs, spiritual first, then corporal. Let us help the dead by engraving their needs deeply on our memo-

---

[6] This breviary *(Breviarium Sanctæ Crucis)* was the work of Cardinal Quiñonez, a Spaniard, and it was intended for the secular clergy, who were required to have special permission from the Holy See for its use. Jesuits, not being bound to office in choir, fulfilled those conditions, so we find Ignatius recommending it to Kessel in 1546. Francis Xavier favored it, and Canisius spread its use in Germany. Favre was more reserved. He must have regretted so much suppression: the number of hours was reduced, each hour having only three psalms; greater importance was given to Scripture; the structure was simplified; and the accounts of the saints' lives were much shortened. Favre's opinion may have been influenced by the bitter criticism to which Quiñonez was subjected in 1535 by the Sorbonne. But the breviary filled a need; it was reprinted more than a hundred times in thirty-two years. In 1551 it was suppressed by the Council of Trent.

[7] The old breviary used in choir by the monastic orders was longer, and there was added to it daily either the Office of the Virgin or the Office of the Dead (P. Batiffol, *Histoire du bréviaire romain* (Paris, 1911), p. 258). For "Ours" *(nostri)* see §397 n. 53 above.

[8] *Meditari ex corde:* The term *meditari* in the older monastic language meant prayers read either aloud or in a low voice. Here it means mental prayer or meditation. See *ConSJComm*, n. 8, p. 96; n. 1, p. 259.

[9] The main activities of Favre's pastoral ministry. By "personal exhortation" he means spiritual conversations with individuals or groups either outside the giving of the Exercises or during their course (§333 n. 234 above). The "meditations" or mental prayers may have been offered for "both the living and the dead" or, more likely, gave rise to those intercessory prayers of universal scope of which we so often find examples in the *Memoriale*.

February 21

401 On the Saturday after Ash Wednesday, immediately after the midday meal, I had withdrawn to recollect myself and to pray.[11] At the end of my prayer, I recalled the afflicted state of a person who had opened his heart to me. Then, as I began to go over in my mind the adversities and trials of all kinds endured by the majority of men for the sake of material gain, I was stricken with remorse and wept because I saw that my own life was free from any kind of adversity at all. For it seemed to me that others in the world are all undergoing tribulations of various kinds, while I am unaware of anyone's being against me. In truth, one is very much free from bodily and temporal trials when what one has and craves does not include the visible but only the eternal. But I grieved that I did not suffer more, at least for the invisible things.[12]

For just as worldly men suffer much and encounter many visible enemies in order to acquire, preserve, and increase their visible possessions, so those who are devoted to spiritual things should, in order to acquire, retain, and multiply them, have suffered many fierce assaults from their invisible enemies.

402 On the same day towards evening, as I was leaving the king's palace,[13] I found myself in the presence of a large group of mounted men drawn up to receive some general. This had attracted a huge crowd, as if for a great and splendid spectacle. I withdrew into a church nearby to escape the concourse and the tumult. While inside the church, I felt impelled by some curiosity to go out again and gaze at what I had just come inside to avoid. At that moment I looked up at a

---

[10] A reference to the convents where the first Jesuits preached and heard confessions. Such ministries helped to renew fervor in the recitation of the choral offices which the preachers themselves were not required to say. The offices said and sung in the convents were for the glory of God and the salvation of the neighbor.

[11] Favre, present at dinner with the court at Évora to answer theological difficulties, withdraws from the bustle and the chatter.

[12] A reflection on his experience with an afflicted person. This reminds him that most men endure suffering for temporal gain, while he himself is free from adversity. Considering his life of hardship, incessant labors, and frequent serious illness, one wonders what he means by "adversity." But he is considering an ideal, the imitation of Christ on the cross, and he sees how far short of it he falls (§139, §160, §290). See O'Leary, "Discernment," pp. 48–49.

[13] John III, king of Portugal.

crucifix and that impulse of curiosity ceased at once. With tears I have thanked my God for granting me the sight of his image, and I have sensed that the truly comforting spectacle is this: the memory that God almighty willed to take a body and to lay it aside in the sight of all the people, hanging between two robbers.[14]

403 Those who long to gaze on what is around them, let them gaze on this sight; let the insatiable appetites of the eyes, the ears, and the other senses be assuaged here. If you cannot yet penetrate deeply enough to find peace there, continue the quest; for one simple desire, one hard-won impulse of curiosity for that sight is better than the enjoyment offered to our eyes by all the other spectacles to be seen in the world. For if Mary has not been allowed to enter the holy sepulcher, let her not for this reason cease to stand outside the tomb and weep.[15]

▸ *February 24*

404 On the day of St. Matthew the Apostle, I presented two of the heads from the eleven thousand to the king and queen of Portugal. The king received the one I had from the Carthusians of Cologne; the queen, the one given me by the nuns of the convent of St. Maximinus.[16] I also presented them with two of the four large bones given me by the canons of St. Gereon—these bones had come from soldiers commanded by St. Gereon. To the prince of Portugal I gave one of the Society's bones which had come from the eleven thousand virgins.

May the Redeemer and Lord of all the saints grant them the grace of knowing how and desiring to conserve such relics as these and to arrange to have others conserve them in a fitting way until the day of the resurrection. May he grant them also the grace of being able to profit by the goodwill of these saints in heaven so that they will receive everywhere the favor of those spirits whose bodies they are going to venerate on earth.[17]

---

[14] An instructive example of discernment, which took place in a church. Favre had entered it to avoid a distracting spectacle and was at once tempted by curiosity to leave and gaze at the spectacle. This troubled him until he raised his eyes to the crucifix and became so filled with consolation that he instantly recognized the correctness of his decision to resist the impulse of curiosity. God had confirmed his decision. There was here no question of a choice between good and evil; he had reached a high degree of sanctity—it was a choice between the greater and lesser good. For a full analysis of the incident, see O'Leary, "Discernment," pp. 97–98.

[15] See John 20:11. The reference is to Mary Magdalen.

[16] §368.

[17] This passage, §404, is in Spanish except for the following: ". . . ut quorum corpora veneraturi sunt in terris, favorem spirituum eorum ubique consequantur." It is very likely a quotation but remains unidentified.

I told Their Highnesses that I personally could honor those relics in no better way than by entrusting them to their care. Their Highnesses then had me put them in a reliquary and put them in the queen's oratory.

▸ February 25

405 On the Wednesday after *Invocavit* [Sunday],[18] I said my customary litanies to obtain for myself and all my brethren a special and desirable benefit. For a new desire had arisen whereby I kept asking for the grace of rightly performing all those actions that I and others will have to give a special account of; namely, the ordering of our daily activities, the proper examination of our consciences, the recitation of the canonical hours, private confession[19] made with care and with tears, the celebration of Mass, the reception of Communion, the administration of the sacraments, the faithful explanation of God's word both in public and in private, and the holiness of all our dealings with men and women. These, then, are seven kinds of activity for the perfect accomplishment of which we must daily beg graces from God and from his saints. Therefore, I have directed to this end all the graces I am accustomed to seek during my litanies,[20] and on the day after the said Wednesday offered Mass for the same intention.

▸ March 18–19

406 On March 4, having at last obtained permission from the king of Portugal, the licentiate Araoz and I left Évora. We reached Salamanca on St. Gregory's day and entered Valladolid on March 18, the feast of St. Gabriel.

In that way, then, and by God's favor and guidance, was the order carried out which directed me to leave Cologne for Portugal with a view to my being sent on to Valladolid by the king. May God be blessed, who always and everywhere made the path of our long journey a happy one.

406a: John III, who had summoned Favre to Portugal, was with difficulty persuaded to allow him to leave with Antonio Araoz. Born in 1515, Araoz had become a doctor of theology at Salamanca, then went to join Ignatius in Rome. After a period in Naples, he journeyed to Spain with six scholastics who were to study in Coimbra (EppMixt 1:149). They reached Coimbra on

---

[18] The first Sunday of Lent. It was called after the first word *(invocavit)* of the introit or opening antiphon of the Mass, a versicle from Ps. 91 (90): 15–16.

[19] Confession made "to the ear" *(auricularis)*, that is, private or secret confession, as distinguished from public and general avowal of personal sin.

[20] §225.

April 8, 1544. Araoz then went off to the court of John III at Évora, where Favre found him in August 1544. They stayed at the court for a few days and were made welcome by two famous professors at the university who knew Favre well: the Dominican Francisco de Vitoria and the Franciscan Alonso de Castro (Astráin, Historia 1:242).

▸ March 20

407 On the vigil of St. Benedict, abbot, around nightfall before going to bed, I was given devotion accompanied with tears. I commended myself to God, to the Blessed Virgin, and to all the different orders of saints and begged them to grant me a favorable night. I prayed then that they might grant a peaceful night to the dead who are in purgatory and the same to all the living who are undergoing pain and hardship. For all those burdened with sins and for those in the act of sinning I begged heartfelt sorrow according to this text: "Every night I will wash my bed, I will water my couch with my tears."[21]

408 Moreover, when I heard some excessively merry and talkative people pouring out expressions of their dissoluteness in the adjoining rooms, I began to grieve that, for their part, they were preparing themselves so badly for their night's sleep and said this prayer: "We pray you, Lord, to visit these dwellings and all those inhabited by men; drive far from them all the snares of their enemies, visible and invisible. May your angels come and dwell in them to keep us and all others in peace, through Christ our Lord. Amen."[22]

408a: During this year 1545, exhausted by his many journeys and by his apostolic labors and suffering from constant temptations, Favre was tormented by the realization of his own weakness. At no other time did he make such frequent mention of his troubles (MonFabri, pp. 299, 313, 324, and so on). The following passage from a letter to Ignatius, dated April 15, is instructive: "Pray to Jesus for me, for I am in sore need. My greatest temptations at present are imaginary fears arising from a spirit of deception. . . . At other times, on the contrary, I feel a spirit of hope so abundant that it grows into an illusion and becomes a new temptation. In that way I live on between hope and fear because I am not yet founded upon that which never changes" (MonFabri, p. 324). He signs himself "the least of your sons" (hijo minimo de V.R.) (MonFabri, p. 325). During these last months of his life, prematurely worn out and worried as he so often was

---

[21] Ps. 6:7 in the Douay Version given here. The RSV (Ps. 6:6) reads better: "Every night I flood my bed with tears; I drench my couch with my weeping."

[22] The concluding prayer of the divine office still said during compline (§282, §293). Favre lengthens and changes it so as to include all men and begs protection for them against their enemies. An example of his tendency to amplify his prayer *(dilatare)* so as to embrace all those in any need.

about wasting the time still allowed him by God (no. 400), Favre in his weakness and helplessness reveals the soul of a child.

409 Sometimes we happen to take notice of benefits and favors that possibly come and can come to us; sometimes the opposite happens: we take notice of evils that only possibly threaten us. In the first state, we must beware of being overelated; in the second, let us not be overmuch cast down. Our good spirit knows how to make use of each of these two times as a remedy for the other: abundance to counter scarcity, scarcity to counter abundance. But the wicked spirit strives to turn each to our harm: abundance to pride and presumption, scarcity to faintheartedness and the discouragement of a good soul.[23]

410 On the day of St. Benedict, I applied my Mass especially for the benefit of the Society. I prayed to that holy patriarch Benedict to deign to protect and defend it as a loving and powerful father in Christ; to defend it against all the spirits of fornication, against all the spirits of this world, and against all spirits of wickedness and ill will;[24] and to protect it from all error, all culpable ignorance, and from sin of all kinds.

411 Honor, reverence, and esteem those who hold authority over you, especially superiors—and not only those who hold authority over you, but all those who surpass you in power, authority, knowledge, virtue, or age. Many can still be found who retain love and affection for their parents and superiors; many, too, who obey them and assist them in their needs; but there are few who honor them from the bottom of their hearts and have true respect for them. For your part, love all your neighbors and do good to them as far as you can. In particular, preserve for those in authority attitudes of reverence, honor, and respectful awe and other attitudes which rightly order the relation of inferiors to superiors; and likewise for your equals preserve the attitude of brotherly love, always showing consideration for them.

Lastly, to your inferiors be kind and gentle and easy of access like someone who loves that state, a seeker after the least and last place.

---

[23] Here the opposing spirits turn each other's activity to their own purposes; there is no mention of an intellectual element in the experiences described. See O'Leary, "Discernment," pp. 114–115 for a fuller treatment of the passage.

Paragraph §409 above is found twice in manuscript R (the second part of §155 and §409) and once only at §409 in the other manuscripts, except those ending at §397, which do not have it at §155 either. Textual criticism is very likely correct in assigning it to this position—a view which is confirmed by Favre's correspondence during that period; it deals with the same ideas.

[24] Eph. 6:12.

You will lead all people to lower themselves if you lower yourself to the last of men, who was Christ on the cross.[25]

---

[25] This passage, related in subject to §413 and §416 through §418, appears out of context. It is best placed here in the notes on obedience which were written about this period (*MonFabri*, pp. 284–287).

VALLADOLID

411a: On March 4, 1545, Favre and Araoz left Évora for Valladolid, where Prince Philip and his Portuguese wife had their court. The journey, including a stay overnight at Salamanca, took about fourteen days; the pair reached Valladolid on March 18, 1545. The prince and his wife being favorable to the Society, Araoz was allowed to preach to the court. Favre heard confessions, visited the sick, and gave personal spiritual direction. Both priests were hard put to find time for all who wanted to speak with them. Again, perhaps because of the new situation in which Favre found himself, his old diffidence and timidity began to revive, alternating, as he wrote to Ignatius, with moods of excessive confidence. He suffered as well from bouts of depression, from poor health, and again from his persistent fear of wasting time.

▸ *March 23 or 24*

412 On another occasion, when I arrived at the palace intending to listen to a sermon in the prince's chapel,[1] it happened that I was refused entry because I was unknown to the porter. So I remained there at the door for a while, remembering that I had often allowed various sinful thoughts and evil spirits to enter my soul while leaving Jesus with his words and his Spirit to knock and stand at the door.

I also reflected on how Christ had been so ill received everywhere in the world. And I prayed that it be granted the porter and me not to stand and wait for too long before the gates of paradise, undergoing purification. Many other thoughts, too, came to me in that place, causing me deep remorse.[2] So it happened that I came to love the porter all the more, he being the cause of my devotion.[3]

412a: The following undated passages, 413–419, which were written in the course of that year, have been brought together in this part of the Memoriale.

413 Then I wished fervently that none of the future members of our Society would ever be able to suffer any harm from suchlike or

---

[1] Prince Philip, regent of Spain at the time, and soon to become King Philip II of Spain.

[2] *Compunctio* is the word used.

[3] An example of discernment: a disagreeable experience leading to prayerful reflection, then to the identification of the source of Favre's feelings, and lastly to an understanding which is accompanied by an increase in devotion. See O'Leary, "Discernment," pp. 43–44 and 104–105.

299

greater refusals—I mean harm to their souls, as commonly happens to the proud and impatient.

Whoever wishes to fight in obedience to another's authority must submit all he is, all his actions, and his entire way of living to the good pleasure and judgment of his superior. He must measure himself according to the pattern set by him to whose judgment and instruction he has entrusted himself. Let it matter little to him that he pleases everyone or seems to be something if he does not please Jesus Christ our Lord, his judge and ruler.[4]

▸ **March 25**

414   On the day of the most holy Annunciation of the Virgin Mother of God, many thoughts came to me which led me to desire some good "annunciations," good news about my salvation. I longed for that day when I may be able to become more sure of life eternal. I judged that man happy who knows with some likelihood that he has found favor with God,[5] that God is with him, that he has been blessed among human beings, and that he does works acceptable to God. But wretched are they who care only whether they are in favor with some mortal man, whether he thinks well of them; who eagerly desire to know what they will receive from him and, finally, are overjoyed at hearing that their labors and offices or services are acceptable to their masters.[6]

415   Reflecting that Christ had become man on that day and that this event was the effective and real beginning of our salvation, I petitioned the Lord for the grace to begin effectively in action what up to now remains in the affections alone. Grant, O God, that my desires and affections begin now to be transformed into deeds and realities.

From eternity God destined Jesus Christ as the one to make expiation,[7] but before that day the Word did not become flesh. Today the Conceived of the Father became flesh;[8] may our conceptions, then, become blessed deeds and achievements or blessed fruit.[9]

---

[4] §224, §225, §292, §414.

[5] Luke 1:28–30, 42. No one is absolutely certain of his own salvation. His highest degree of certitude is moral certitude derived from those indirect signs which usually go with the state of grace. Favre uses phrases from the Angelus.

[6] The contrast between the service of Christ and service in the court is one of the themes of the *Memoriale;* at the time Favre was staying at the court of Philip in Valladolid. See §225.

[7] Expiation for sin. Rom. 3:25.

[8] John 1:14.

[9] Luke 1:42.

May God give us in each of the words and actions we employ in our work some new way of progress. Let us begin at once!

416 I had a wish to be reprimanded by everyone: whether above you or below you,[10] on your right or your left, and at any moment, whether you are joyful or sad, fervent or cold, and because of any imperfection or defect of yours, real or apparent. Nor should you set any limit for your admonitor; you should want him to observe the limit which can distress you most. This I would say, from reflecting on the fruit gained by the one admonished or corrected or reformed.[11]

417 A certain person[12] let me know that he would like to find in me this good quality: that I would admonish him as frankly as he admonished me. I prepared this response for him: Since our mutual admonitions have nothing to do with things that directly displease God but only with ways of speaking or conducting oneself or with other ways of dealing with people, it is difficult for me, who am a stranger in all respects,[13] to correct or reform in such matters those who do not make my ideas and viewpoint a rule for themselves.

It would be easy for me to say, "This is not to my taste or it displeases me or does not seem advisable." But the response will be that my judgment and my will are not a good rule, that it is better to be guided by the ways of their own country, and they will be more afraid of displeasing the many—as seems good to them—than me alone. So it will happen that I am impeded from being able or having the hardihood to admonish them.

It is otherwise with my subjects.[14] My will and my judgment are their rule in both good and indifferent matters, and they are disposed to submit themselves to their superior, however imperfect he may be, because it is their will to deny themselves in all things.

418 I myself acted in this way more than once when I was in Paris and Father Ignatius gave me some command. My customary response to him was that some courses of action which seemed good to him would not be tolerated in that country.[15]

---

[10] Favre addresses himself.

[11] The evangelical counsel of just severity to oneself. See Matt. 5 and 7; §288 n. 122 above.

[12] This person is unknown. In §418 he is identified as a friar.

[13] It is true that Favre was a stranger everywhere so that at this stage of his reflective process his intended reply shows prudence. He makes a distinction between the spiritual and the nonspiritual.

[14] *Inferiores:* his religious subjects whom he has no hesitation in admonishing.

[15] Students were forbidden to beg in the streets of Paris. Favre still tries to justify his refusal.

This, then, was the answer I intended to give the aforementioned friar, but in fact I never gave it. For I came to understand that it was nothing more than a temptation and that a spiritual infirmity underlay my words, but also something false.[16] I was given to understand that I am and have been weak in bearing admonitions. Those from superiors provoked me on too many occasions into objecting out of pride, scarcely humble and obedient as I was, whereas those from my inferiors or equals made me feel excessively discouraged.

May God grant me grace to keep to moderation and my own place in all things so that I become neither excessively disheartened by an inferior nor roused to indignation by a superior.

May God grant that I pay more attention to self-correction than to the manner and words of one who reprehends me.

419 He who does not have in himself or does not find any source of consolation is quickly overwhelmed by the burden of a critic. On the other hand, he who has or thinks he has a source of consolation in himself will speedily recover from criticism. It follows that you should be cautious when reprimanding those who are exceedingly dissatisfied with themselves, for they will be overly discouraged unless they are admonished tactfully, while those who are contented with themselves bear criticism more easily.

Therefore, you should treat the melancholic or the phlegmatic person in a different way from the choleric or the sanguine person.[17] But take care, for your part, not to show yourself either choleric, sanguine, phlegmatic, or melancholic; as the saying has it, "The wise will prevail over the stars."[18]

That comes about through the grace of our Lord Jesus Christ, who perfects natures, in himself, through himself, and of himself.

---

[16] At last he realizes the real reason for his hesitation: He was oversensitive to criticism from others and so was afraid of what the friar might say to him. For an analysis of this example of discernment (§417–§418), see O'Leary, "Discernment," pp. 98–99.

[17] Advice against harsh admonitions: Before admonishing get to know your subjects. Here Favre proposes the classical division of temperaments made by Galen. Based on the theory of the four humors, it held the field until nearly the end of the last century. The "you" is probably himself, but the passage may be part of an exhortation.

[18] The influence of the stars on the human temperament was looked on as all-important. It gave rise to various forms of determinism, widespread in Favre's day. The quotation is a stoic maxim: The wise man makes himself independent of the world by calming his passions. Once more Favre turns the old pagan idea into something Christian and acknowledges grace at work in the strength of the moral virtue of the wise man. See §134.

▸ *April 2*

420 On the day of the Lord's Supper, it struck me strongly that Christ had willed to leave to his apostles and then to all of us not only the example of all the good things he did through his physical body but also his body itself, the instrument through which he had done those things and in which he was about to suffer death. Oh, how wretched are we Christians if, having the instrument of God's divinity for food and drink, we have not become hardworking laborers!

▸ *April 3*

421 On Preparation Day,[19] when I had to hear [the confessions of] some young folk and very small children belonging to the household of a nobleman, a spiritual son of mine, certain proud thoughts came to me, and a spirit spoke to me inwardly: "You have not come here to minister to these small children, have you? Would it not be better to be where you could hear the confessions of some important people?" But when I had made a decision to spend my whole life—if it pleased God—doing nothing else but this kind of ministry, which is looked on as particularly contemptible and trivial by that spirit, there followed a great strengthening of the spirit of humility; and there was revealed to me better than ever the value of those works which, with a right intention, are devoted to little ones and those despised and rejected by the world.[20]

422 Here too let us set up stones[21] as signs not only of the good things hidden by God for little ones but also of the good things revealed to those who look after little ones and so become little ones themselves. For my part, it was my wish, and I considered it very worthwhile, forever to teach only the unschooled, the children, the country people, the poor, and the most forsaken.[22]

---

[19] Good Friday.

[20] Temptations to doubt the value of one's apostolate are all too common. Favre quickly recognizes the source of his temptation as evil; he deals with it by applying the Ignatian principle of *agere contra*—temptations should be met by their contraries. Consolation follows; here it is "a great strengthening *(confortatio)* of the spirit of humility." See O'Leary, "Discernment," pp. 44–45.

[21] A reference to the biblical accounts of Abraham or Jacob setting up stone altars as memorials where some divine manifestation had occurred. Gen. 26:25; 28:18; *DBibTheol,* pp. 582–583.

[22] Matt. 18:4–5. Ignatius regularly exercised a direct apostolate to ordinary folk. Such an apostolate is carried out today in a great variety of ways and circumstances.

Although the fruit often seems more abundant when we instruct the great ones of the world, God usually gives a greater blessing to the fruit that pertains to his little ones. For he who says "What you did to one of my least ones you did to me"[23] is certainly ready to esteem more highly the labor you have devoted to one utterly forsaken man than anything you will have done for the emperor.

Very dear brother, see to it that, just as a poor man is called someone left to God and Christ,[24] you consider him left to you as well, so that you may be his helper because he has no one else.[25]

423 On another occasion I became very sad and dejected to think that I was achieving nothing of note. Then I kept thinking I could not help being by far the least successful of all my contemporaries.[26] In truth, to be led to judge oneself so severely is by no means a drawback. However, the most merciful and compassionate God[27] and his Spirit, the consoler,[28] usually come to our aid even in such miseries. He who suffers thus should know, then, that God is admirable in that he is accustomed sometimes to add something of his own to the most trifling things and actions. Therefore, if one is very closely united to him, it will very likely happen that one's deeds done within that union will be more abundantly blessed by him from whom and in accord with whom the deeds are done. So do not wonder so much at what or how great is the accomplished work you see; wonder rather at the quality and magnitude of the power from which it proceeded. You should wish to be filled with grace and to do little things in a great way rather than not to grow interiorly and to do great things in a slackhanded way. The slightest actions done with a great blessing of grace are longer lasting and more fruitful than the greatest actions done with little grace.[29]

424 The words *"Popule meus . . ."* spoken to us as an appeal to adore the cross of Christ[30] touched me and penetrated me deeply. I kept

---

[23] Matt. 25:40 (DV).

[24] Both Mellinato (*MellConfess*, p. 430, n. 994) and de Certeau (*DeCertMem*, p. 416, n. 3) think that this passage may be part of a letter which found its way between the pages of the *Memoriale* and so came to be looked on as belonging to it.

[25] See Ps. 9:18.

[26] The first companions of Ignatius, the first generation of the Society.

[27] Ps. 86 (85): 15; Ps. 111 (110): 4; Ps. 112 (111): 4; and others.

[28] Favre uses the term *paracletus* from Greek. It is used in the Gospel and in the liturgy.

[29] §151–§154. Favre makes a typically extreme judgment about his lack of success in his work. But, as so often before, an appreciation of the value of small actions consoles him. It is the degree of union with God that matters. See O'Leary, "Discernment," pp. 49–50.

[30] "O my people, what have I done to thee?" The opening words of the

feeling more intensely than ever those reproaches of Christ, namely, that his vineyard has become exceedingly bitter to him; his people have deserted him and chosen Barabbas instead; they have tied to a pillar to be scourged the one who in times gone by had lighted their way by a pillar of fire; they have given him vinegar to drink who once gave them water from the rock to drink in the desert, and so on.

And I understood all these words as clearly aimed at me.[31]

▸ *April 5*

425 On the day of the Lord's Resurrection, I felt myself beginning to be elevated a little above myself towards Christ so that I desire and rejoice that the causes of all my consolations lie secure in him. Up to the present I have been either too elated or too dejected because of the good or the evil I was conscious of within me. If only I could see myself better in the future and measure my worth by the price of my redemption rather than by my labors and by my changing accidental states!

If only I could rise to the point of fearing my eternal ruin more because I have been ransomed by the precious blood of Christ than because my soul, as mine, is in danger of incurring the torments of hell and expulsion from the fellowship of those who praise God! If only I could understand from now on that my true gain consists in dying daily,[32] so that Christ may be for me living and life, salvation, peace, and joy!

426 Man hardly appreciates God's way of relating to him in all his works such as creation, redemption, and glorification. Hardly ever, or very rarely, does man notice this. And yet in human affairs there is scarcely anyone who does not see himself in all his accomplishments, that is, scarcely anyone who is not concerned about what view of him they give, what remembrance they provide, what regard they foster. Turn your eyes, then, toward him who keeps his eyes turned toward you in all his works, and stop wishing, in what you do, to catch the notice of men.

427 Now and in the future we shall experience that the charity of many is growing cold,[33] for there are very few who perform spiri-

---

reproaches *(improperia)* formerly sung at the Adoration of the Cross on Good Friday (Mic. 6:3–4).

[31] Favre's deeper awareness of Christ's reproaches was more than a scholarly understanding of the liturgical text. He applies his experience to his own life: "And I understood all these words as clearly aimed at me." See O'Leary, "Discernment," pp. 86–87.

[32] 1 Cor. 15:31; Rom. 8:15; Phil. 1:21; 3:7–8.

[33] Matt. 24:12.

tual works of mercy without recompense or who devote themselves to them in the way described by St. Paul when he says "Charity is kind, charity is patient. . . ."[34] The very ones in charge of charitable works are impatient and unkind; they have little faith or hope; they are unable to put up with inconvenience or suffer cheerfully the imperfections of their neighbors. So it happens that many men eliminate abuses in both ecclesiastical and civil administration, more from an intolerance born of a cold and bitter zeal for justice than from a warm zeal for charity itself. Charity should have the qualities enumerated by Paul; otherwise it grows cold.[35]

428 Once, when I was in a certain house, I remembered what I had heard some men had said in Portugal: that we should be afraid of certain persons.[36] So far we have not done so nor are we going to do so, for we know them to be, of all men, the most faithful and vigorous defenders of sound Catholic doctrine and the adversaries of all those who do not walk the path of truth in their teaching and thinking.

In this place, then, I felt great devotion in praying to the Lord never to allow any tempest not in accordance with his will to arise against our Society[37] from those men or any others at all. Here I kept wishing I had done the same thing in all the places, houses, palaces, towns, and regions where I have ever been; namely, that I had prayed that no hostility to us—or to any others who walk straight in the way of the Lord—may be able to arise, against God's will, in this and that place or people.

429 On another occasion, as I waited for a young man who had promised to come for confession and had twice disappointed me; when, I say, I had thus waited and was feeling distressed in spirit because I had already wasted, as I thought, six hours in the matter, I received great comfort from the Lord, for whose honor I was doing this.

I was then given this reason: If you are in the habit of spending hour after hour waiting at the doors of great noblemen and princes for the service of God and you do not resent it, knowing that a reward has been stored away for you, why do you feel more burdened when some other person, one of Christ's little ones, keeps you waiting? Will God

---

[34] 1 Cor. 13:4. Criticism of the German clergy.

[35] The history of many movements of reform in the Church, not deeply inspired by charity both in principle and in method, confirms Favre's diagnosis.

[36] It is clear from what follows that Favre refers to the Dominicans of the Inquisition. Ignatius had aroused their suspicion in Salamanca (*FN* 1:31). Then Melchior Cano found something to attack in the *Spiritual Exercises*. See *DeCertMem*, p. 419, n. 1.

[37] Favre means that God could will to test the Society by trials and that these trials could cause it to depart from the divine will.

give you less of a reward in this case than in that? How often do you make Jesus stand at your door? And yet you want him not to get discouraged, not to regret having waited; you want him not to be able to feel annoyed, not to be able to become impatient with you or bitter towards you. Be sure, then, to treat his little ones in the same way. Act yourself as you know he would act if his humanity were visibly and locally present in visible flesh.

Then there returned to me that devotion to each soul given me so often by the Lord, and with it there returned the resolve to suffer and labor for them not only in a universal or general way—which is less wearisome and more glorious—but also for each single soul, in that way imitating him who belongs wholly to each, who lived his entire life for each, and who suffered and died for each.[38]

▸ *April 16*

430 On April 16 I presented one of the heads of the eleven thousand virgins to Philip, prince of Spain, the son of Charles, emperor and king of all the Spanish territories. At the presentation my one great regret was that of being unable to offer two heads at the same time, as was my long-cherished hope, so that they might be preserved together by the prince and princess until one or the other of them should die.

May God grant me to see that day on which I may gaze upon those two heads enclosed in one reliquary; still more, may he grant that the prince himself and his wife the princess, through the intercession of the eleven thousand virgins, may be able to live in permanent peace, united by the bond of true charity and affection.[39]

▸ *April 30*

431 On the last day of April, the birthday of St. Catherine of Siena,[40] I celebrated Mass for the successful outcome of the so anxiously

---

[38] An example of discernment arising from reflection on an apostolic experience. Favre feels bitter because of the young man's discourtesy and lack of goodwill. His reflection on the way he has been treated leads him to compare his own reaction to the young man's insincerity and discourtesy with Christ's reaction to himself. The remedy is that he must learn patience, must learn to act as Christ does towards his little ones. By this kind of experience and by reflecting on it, Favre is continually purifying his intention and his attitude. Here, as always, he fixes his eyes on Christ his model, whose Spirit is at work within him. §412 n. 3; §413; §421 n. 20 above; O'Leary, "Discernment," pp. 46, 63–64, 104–105.

[39] Col. 3:14.

[40] It was the day of the saint's death. She had been canonized in 1461, so her feast was relatively recent.

awaited Council of Trent.[41] I found a special formulary for that intention in the rite of the church of Valladolid.[42] The petitions in it were that the Lord deign to provide for his Church through this council.

There came to my mind the needs of sinners, who will more easily be converted if the ministers of God's word and of the sacraments are reformed first; likewise the needs of all the afflicted, who will very much benefit when charity, now growing cold, recovers its vigor. There before me appeared the sick, for example, as if expecting assistance; and, on the other hand, the dead whose holy yearnings now come to naught appeared to me as if in exceeding torment at the thought that the heirs to their property and the ministers of the Church were not carrying out their duties in a fitting manner.

In this way many other benefits to be provided for by the council occurred to me so that I might desire them.

432 Another day, feeling very much downcast and depressed amid the pain and bitterness of my soul because of my lack of true fraternal charity and humility towards my critics, I lifted up my soul a little to God, and all this then seemed to be nothing at all. But also that one thing, namely, just lifting up my thoughts, seemed to me my best remedy on such occasions. For when thoughts are lifted up to higher things, none of the darts that can be hurled at the soul either wound or affect it in any way; for these trifles—call them railing, call them flailing—do not reach so far; I mean they do not rise all the way to the spirit thus lifted up in God, whose tent no flail comes near.[43]

Then raise up your mind without delay whenever some earthly thing—word or deed—influences your spirit, no matter whether it be toward human happiness or useless sadness.

Then I began to desire to enter more fully into the mystery of the Lord's Ascension, for as he ascends we are raised above all earthly things —now in spirit but eventually even in body and in accordance with our external senses.

---

[41] The opening of the Council, first arranged for March 15, 1545, then put off to May 3, did not finally take place until December 13 of that year.

[42] Probably a special Mass approved for the diocese of Valladolid. This passage gives evidence of Favre's constant preoccupation with deficiencies in the pastoral care of the German people (O'Leary, "Discernment," p. 104, n. 23).

[43] See Ps. 91 (90): 10. Again Favre finds consolation in raising his mind to God.

MADRID–GALAPAGAR

432a: *In May 1545, at the invitation of the cardinal of Toledo, Favre visited the infantas in Madrid. Then, accompanied by the cardinal, he went on to Galapagar, a big market town to the northeast of Madrid. They spent some days there, lodging in the presbytery attached to the benefice and the parish which had been made over to Pedro Ortíz in 1542 by Esteban Merino, then nuncio at Paris. Ortíz himself was with them in his presbytery. At Pentecost Favre returned to Valladolid.*

▸ *May 8*

433 On the day of the Apparition of St. Michael the Archangel, I arrived at Madrid to visit some noblemen and some friends in Christ. I had come from Valladolid, and during the journey I thought of many ways of instructing an old man who belonged to the group called *romeros*[1] in Spanish. I was also given an opportunity of consoling a greatly afflicted woman who had opened her whole soul to me. While staying in inns, I have always felt inspired to do good by instructing and encouraging people.

In the eyes of Christ and of his heavenly court, it is very good to leave in the inns and houses where we happen to stay some trace of good and holy behavior; for everywhere there is good to be done, everywhere there is something to be planted or harvested.[2] For we are indebted to all men[3] in every condition and in every place, just as we are looked after and strengthened everywhere by our most high Lord, whose fellow workers we are.[4]

434 I then acknowledged that I had often been negligent during the course of my numerous and varied journeys up to now—negligent above all in instructing or correcting, admonishing or consoling, those I happened to associate with or greet or merely see. For nothing should come into our sight or to our notice in vain, because our Lord Jesus Christ has permitted nothing to be without a purpose—not the sight of

---

[1] A *romero* was originally a pilgrim to Rome; the term was then extended to pilgrims in general. But because of abuses committed by some *romeros* during pilgrimages, the word began to take on a pejorative meaning.

[2] Favre comments on what a wandering apostle should be able to accomplish wherever he goes. These thoughts are the fruit of his many travels since 1539. See O'Leary, "Discernment," p. 47.

[3] Rom. 1:14.

[4] 1 Cor. 3:9. Favre's last sentence echoes St. Paul—a much-traveled apostle.

things, not the sound of any voice. But not without purpose, either, did he pass through certain places, rest his eyes on certain persons, and will to be now on land, now on the sea, at one time in a house, at another out of doors, at times among people, at other times by himself. His standing, his sitting, his walking, his eating, sleeping, and so forth were not without a purpose. For our part, let us waste no occasion of contact with anyone we pass or only lay our eyes on, all the more so, of course, if we have been prevailed upon to take a meal with them or lodge with them.[5]

435 Note here this effective remedy against carnal temptations, occasions of which are wont to arise among those who are obliged to lodge in inns and in houses of the laity where all kinds of men and women are to be found.[6] The greatest defense against such temptations is not only to say "Peace to this house" immediately on entering it and meeting whoever may be there but also to set about showing that one professes piety and truth, in order to edify. This will happen if you begin at once to say something edifying to those who will be conversing with you; for in this manner you will bar the way that leads to sins of impurity.

Some religious are conquered by this diabolical temptation, that is, they do not wish to reveal their profession,[7] with the result that those around them become more daring in the expression and the display of their impurity. These religious fear that the open manifestation of either their beliefs or their piety will prevent others from parading their corrupt ways.[8] As for yourself, take care that no one in your company or in

---

[5] During these last months Favre was constantly worried about the employment of his time, perhaps a presentiment that his life was drawing to an end. On March 2, 1545, he wrote to the community at Coimbra: "I earnestly beg you to pray for me to God because I do not know how to make use of precious time, and I am unable to find any time for doing good. Again I ask you, pray to God so that his Divine Majesty may grant me grace not to waste any time but rather to be able and willing to order all the moments of my life according to his holy will" (*MonFabri*, p. 313).

[6] There was much liberty, indeed license, in the German inns of the time. "In every inn there are three or four pretty young chambermaids. The hostess and her daughters and serving maids, although they do not allow themselves to be embraced as do the French chambermaids, nevertheless offer their hands for kissing to everyone, and in token of friendship allow themselves to be taken by the waist and hugged. They often invite themselves to drink with people, making use of great freedom in their language and their behavior" (A. de Béatis, *Voyage du Cardinal d'Aragón* [Paris, 1913], pp. 71–72).

[7] It is the way of the devil or the bad spirit to inspire this desire for secrecy and concealment (*SpEx*, [326]).

[8] One of the very rare examples of irony in Favre. He must have found such behavior in conflict with his idea of a vocation. Here one feels that he has been touched personally (*DeCertMem*, p. 424, n. 3).

your presence dares to spread abroad the sinful suggestions of his evil spirit.[9]

▸ May 14

436 On the feast of the Lord's Ascension, the saying of the apostle Paul came to my mind: "When I was a child, I spoke like a child, I reasoned like a child."[10] Then there came to me many desires for a spiritual ascent, namely, from boyhood to perfect manhood, from proneness to the basest feelings and tastes to conversation in heaven.[11] I prayed that whatever is transitory might even now be nothing to me and that I might prize and esteem more and more the things of eternity.

Then I wished to be less touched henceforth by what bodily eyes see and to be raised up through all the senses of my mind[12] so that spiritual things could effectually move and touch my spirit.

▸ May 23

437 One day when I was returning from Galapagar to Valladolid, there came to me the devotion of praying for each of the places I had to pass through on that journey. For each place I offered one Our Father and one Hail Mary while reflecting on the various needs that might exist there and also giving thanks and asking for whatever seemed necessary for each place. Then it was given me to extend this devotion to a more general good: I prayed for all the places where I myself or any other member of our Society had ever gone. In fact, I applied my Mass next day for that intention, and also that what we can in no way do may be made up for through the Savior, by the merits of his passion.

438 Once when I was duly reciting some of the canonical hours, I came upon that text of the psalmist where he says "Therefore will my people return here and full days shall be found in them."[13]

---

[9] This entry (§433, §434, §435) was considered so important by Peter Canisius that in January 1583 he quoted most of it in a letter to the general, Claudio Aquaviva, on the apostolate of the Society (*EppCan* 8:125–127).

[10] 1 Cor. 13:11.

[11] Phil. 3:20. The Douay Version of the phrase is given as being closer to the Vulgate, from which Favre always quoted. The Revised Standard Version has "commonwealth" instead of "conversation" *(conversatio);* in this context it has the meaning of "our real home."

[12] *Sensus mentis:* For the use of *sensus* see §257, §343, §345.

[13] Ps. 73 (72): 10 (DV). Favre prescinds from the context. According to the psalm, some Jews will return to the pleasures of the ungodly and share in their disbelief.

At these words I was given a feeling of deep sorrow because up to then I had not properly returned to divine things or properly employed any day or hour.

Would, O would that eventually my days may be found full of good deeds! Would that all idleness and all pointless activity may be removed from my life! Amen.[14]

> **438a:** *The rejoicing throughout Spain at the birth of a son on July 4 to Prince Philip, the emperor's heir, was changed to sorrow when the child's mother, Maria of Portugal, died four days later. At the end of the mourning period, towards the end of September, Philip moved to Madrid with the court, having instructed Favre and Araoz to transfer to that city.*

▸ July 8–12

439 On the vigil of the octave of the Visitation of the Blessed Virgin Mary, at a quarter past twelve, the princess Doña Maria, the king of Portugal's daughter, gave birth to a child. The next day I celebrated the Mass of the Visitation, commemorating the birth of Christ, the birth of the Virgin Mary, and the birth of St. John the Baptist. I had, in fact, made these three commemorations the day before also, desiring that through the help of these three births the newborn child might be blessed. I was granted rather great devotion about this matter.

But on July 12, at about four in the afternoon, the princess died. May her soul rest in holy peace.[15]

▸ September 14

440 On the day of the Exaltation of the Holy Cross, when I was on my way to celebrate Mass and a certain person addressed me in the street, asking me to be so kind as to hear his confession so that he could be cleansed, I told him I would willingly be Christ's broom for cleaning his conscience. Here, then, began in me this desire, to begin to be and be called Christ's broom.

Then I came to have various thoughts about that expression. I wished to be put in the same class as the brooms used for sweeping out houses, mainly because I remain wretched and dirty while cleaning others and because I collect all kinds of filth from the improvement

---

[14] §434.

[15] Though Favre had been with the court and often had conversations with the princess, he was not present at her deathbed (*MonFabri*, 334). The day after, he sent a long letter of sympathy and true Christian consolation to John II of Portugal, father of the young Princess Maria of Portugal (*MonFabri*, p. 333).

which, with Christ's cooperation, I effect in others in my capacity as servant. I saw too how quickly I become worn out like a broom. In spite of this I found much devotion in offering myself to Christ as his household broom for sweeping out spiritual dwellings.[16]

441 I wished too that our whole Society might be destined by God for this: that Christ, who has in his dwelling, the Church, so many illustrious instruments, might deign to begin cleaning out his dwelling in our time[17] and, for this purpose, make use of and shape us and all future members of the Society into the first, in a sense, and most menial implements, brooms, that is.

I offered the Mass of the Holy Cross for this, desiring that in heaven too I may deserve to be and to be called Christ's glorious broom —if I have first fulfilled the function of a lowly broom that I am unworthy of.

> **441a:** *In November 1545 Favre visited some towns near Madrid, then went to Toledo, where he spent ten days giving the Exercises. He was in Ocaña towards the end of December with the bereaved family of Cifuentes (majordomo to the infantas), who had died shortly before. Then he went on to Hyepes to join the nuncio, Poggio, returning to Madrid on January 13. There he wrote the entries 442 and 443 below, dated January 1546.*

▶ *January 20, 1546*

442 On the day of Sts. Fabian and Sebastian, when I was with a man in need of consolation, the only thing I could think of for the delight of his soul was this. All the spiritual trials of all men have their eye on, so to speak, and result from, an excessive fear of coming eventually to a condition like Christ's, or his Mother's, or the good thief's, or the disciple's. And what troubles them most is the fear of coming to the fate of Christ on the cross.

In such trials, of course, spiritual and temporal, he needed to bear in mind this distinction: Some fear for themselves lest they fall deservedly under the good thief's sentence; others fear for themselves lest they come, without deserving it, to a condition like Christ's; others fear that fate not for themselves but for their loved ones, and that is to fear the state of the most blessed Virgin Mother of God; still others fear for those who love them, and that is to fear the state of Christ's beloved disciple, who stood with the Mother before the cross of him who loved him.

---

[16] Matt. 12:44. The comparison seems somewhat forced, but it conveys Favre's ever present conviction of being an instrument in God's hands.

[17] The reform of the Church—a true and lasting inner reform—is one of Favre's constant concerns (§261, §262, §263, §264, §265).

Let these four persons, then, be brought before one's eyes: Christ hanging on the cross, the good thief fastened to the cross, the Blessed Virgin standing near the cross, and St. John the Evangelist.

On that day I celebrated the Mass of the feast, offering the sacrifice for this, that these holy martyrs may have at heart the trials and adversities of our whole Society.

443 During the first days of this new year, I have experienced a revival of my defects so that I am beginning to get to know them in a new way towards a new amendment.[18] I have felt especially that I need a new way of recollection of soul and that for this there is need for me to behave differently in external things so as to become more recollected and unified if I want to find and retain the Spirit of the Lord who sanctifies, corrects, and strengthens. Especially was I now seeing my need of more silence and more solitude.[19] I have also felt, during these days, through my experience of temptations my need of much grace to protect me against feelings of poverty[20] and against the temptations of various fears, needs, and deficiencies.[21]

443a: At this point the Memoriale *breaks off suddenly. Favre was to live only six months longer. He fell ill towards the end of February and was forced to remain in bed for about three weeks. His recovery was slow, and he had to some extent lost the use of his left hand. In spite of much pastoral activity in Spain, he could not get Germany out of his thoughts—especially Cologne (MonFabri, p. 397). In the meantime Ignatius, in a letter of February 17, 1546, pressed Ortíz to allow Favre to leave Spain for the Council of Trent—it had in fact opened there on December 13, 1545. Accordingly, he left Toledo on April 20, reached Valencia on the twenty-ninth, then made the short journey of two days to Gandía, where he saw the duke, Francis Borgia, and the Jesuit community. Returning to Valencia on May 3, Favre then journeyed on to Barcelona. On his arrival there on May 20, the tertian*

---

[18] A sentiment expressed by Favre again and again in the letters he wrote at the beginning of this year, for instance to the Fathers at Coimbra, January 13, 1546: "I should have experienced a real renewal . . . but I am in the same state this year as I was last year. I find myself no more ready to suffer and to serve than if there had been no other birth but one according to the flesh. . . . Pray for me that I may one day be able to say and write to you this good news: 'A child is born for us not only in Christ but also in me'" (*MonFabri,* p. 384); and in the same terms to Araoz (*MonFabri,* pp. 381–383).

[19] Unlike the preceding months during which Favre laid stress on going out of himself and on the requirements of the apostolate, he returns here to the need for interior recollection.

[20] Spiritual poverty.

[21] This final entry finds Favre still struggling against inner tensions, still indulging in anxious introspection, still only too well aware of his spiritual needs. So, on this doleful though by no means despairing note he ends or, rather, breaks off his *Memoriale.*

ague struck again almost at once, and by the time he was well enough to sail, the galleys had departed for Italy. However, he was able to take ship in Barcelona in early July and arrived at last in Rome on the seventeenth of that month. Towards the end of July he fell seriously ill with a fever that worsened daily. He knew that this illness was his last, made his preparation for death, and died happily on August 1, 1546.

Selected Letters And Instructions

Of Pierre Favre

• I •

To Ignatius of Loyola and Pietro Codazzo, on Ministries in Parma
Parma, September 1, 1540
MonFabri, 32–35 (*Epist.* 17)

This account of Favre's first apostolic mission shows the methods he followed in the pursuit of ecclesiastical reform.

The grace and love of Christ our Lord be always our protection and help.

Since I do not know whether I will have time to write you another letter from Parma, in this one I will give you a somewhat full account of the state in which I leave the harvest here. First of all, people were already making a practice of coming daily to the hospital here for confession and Communion. Regularly every Sunday, up to fifty persons, and often more, were receiving Communion with us. Among them are many laymen; this past Sunday I gave Communion to up to twenty; the others, more than thirty, were women, including some of the most prominent in Parma. There are many other parishes in the city in which the priests have accepted the excellent practice whereby anyone who wishes to do so is able to communicate anytime he desires.

Indeed, some of the parish priests are giving the Exercises to their subjects. We taught the Commandments right from the beginning when we came to Parma. Since then they have spread by way of the schoolmasters, some of whom have even given the initial Exercises to a number of their capable students. Likewise there are women who make it their business to go from house to house teaching the girls and other women who cannot go out freely. The first thing they give is always the Ten Commandments, the seven deadly sins, and then the material for a general confession. The results obtained by this method here inside Parma and outside it I neither know how nor am able to explain; neither am I able to say how much good has come in, both in the city and outside it, because of frequent confession. By now no one is considered anything in Parma who does not confess at least once a month. I was told a few days ago that in one town, on the past feast of our Lady in August, more than three hundred persons received Communion. The number and character of the priests brought back to a good life by way of the Exercises—all of them still persevering, some not backsliding, and some daily producing good results among other people—the canon [Jerónimo Doménech] will be able to tell you in part better than I could write. The sermons have also been a considerable factor in these results, beyond what can be known—and not only those preached by the two of us but also by three others who, after making the Exercises, have preached throughout the region, so that ten or twelve of the main towns in the Parmesan territory have been moved to a good life. I shall not repeat the fruits that have been achieved with little difficulty in Sissa, the residence of that Orlando who constantly hears confessions, gives exercises, teaches children, and preaches on every feast day, sometimes preaching in three or four villages on a given feast day. Since the Three Kings the lady of the castle has never failed to communicate weekly, together with many other persons. The lord of the same place, when it was learned that I was about to leave, sent for me to come there to hear his confession before my departure. A few days ago the Pallavicini in a town named Tabiano sent to ask that I come and teach them how to live a good life. A Lady Jacoba, a widow living alone, has an income of five hundred scudi, besides her dowry; she had decided that she would spend her entire estate and herself upon any pious work that I should direct her to. About five or six days ago, this Lady Jacoba, learning of my departure for Spain, went weeping to Lady Laura, the most prominent woman in the city and a relative of the Pope, tearfully pleading with her not to let me go but to write to the cardinal of Santa Fiora[1] to get the Pope to keep me in Parma. This she did, without my knowledge. I believe the city has also written to His Holiness with similar urgings that I not be allowed to leave here. You may be certain, no matter what happens, that I had no part in it. I beseech the divine Majesty to give us abundant grace so that the farther we are scattered physically the deeper we may strike spiritual roots by which we may be united for ever and ever. This will come about if we pray to the Lord's Spirit, which fills the entire world, always to guide us in conformity with his most holy will.

Don Diego [Laínez] and Master Francisco Estrada, and all the others here, are well.

Parma, September 1, 1540

On behalf of all these, yours in Christ,

PEDRO FABRO

---

[1] Guido Ascania Sforza, Pope Paul III's grandson.

• II •

Rules for the Sodality of Parma
Parma, September 7, 1540
MonFabri, 39–44 (*Epist.* 19)

Favre understood the importance of consolidating and spreading the results of his apostolic labors. In Parma he formed a confraternity of laypersons for this purpose, and composed for them the following rule of life.

Order and Help for Persevering in the True Christian and Spiritual Life

Dearest sons and brothers:

Since I must depart from Parma for Spain, I wanted to satisfy the excellent desire expressed by you and many other persons like you, who would not remain content with me unless I left them a remembrance, not of my person, but of the procedure they ought to follow in the way of God when they have no other instructor.

First, I would not have you mistakenly think that for your perseverance I would give you a different food from what I have given you hitherto. The philosopher would tell you the same: speaking of bodily food, he says that the same things which nourish a person also enable him to grow. Hence, you must stoutly believe that the spiritual exercises in which you have found nourishment for your spirit up to the present will still be necessary for you in the future, your essential food having been above all the heavenly bread on which the angels and all the saints always have been and always will be fed. This bread is far more important for your spiritual life than material bread is for your temporal life. Similarly for the other spiritual exercises: self-examination, confession, meditation, prayer, and the works of mercy.

You must be convinced that if by means of these exercises you have obtained some knowledge of yourselves and abnegation, some love of God and neighbor, it will be necessary in the future as well to continue steadily in these excellent practices with greater fervor of spirit. Your method and order for doing this daily should be as follows.

First, every evening, before going to sleep, kneel down and recall to your minds the four last things: death, judgment, hell, and paradise. Dwell on these for the space of three Our Fathers and three Hail Marys. Immediately thereafter, make an examination of your conscience, thinking first of the benefits received from the Lord God, and thanking him; and recognizing, on the other side, the sins you have committed that day, with sorrow and a firm resolution to confess them to your confessor at the regular time. This is called spiritual confession, when the person, acknowledging his sins in detail, accuses himself in the sight of God with contrition and the resolve to confess his sins orally at the proper time—a time which I want you to have in your thoughts and desires. This done, pray the Lord to give a good night to you and to all the other living, and some assuagement to the dead, saying for this three Our Fathers and three Hail Marys.

In the morning, before anything else, you will likewise say three Our Fathers and three Hail Marys so that he may protect you and all the other living from sinning throughout the day, and may give assuagement to the dead.

If you still have time, before the crucifix or at Mass listen to some word or think of some action of Christ in which to mirror yourselves and arouse yourselves to live well, not only that day but always and forever, grieving always for your sins and longing to live a better life. At the consecration or elevation of the sacred Host, you can begin to pray for remedies against your evils and for the graces that you stand in need of, such as courage, knowledge, peace, and so forth—and finally, as supreme grace, a hunger and thirst for justice. You may pray the true and very body of Christ to deign to come spiritually to your soul. Communicating spiritually in this way, stir up your desire for sacramental Communion, recalling the times when you communicated last and will do so next.

This spiritual Communion each day will be a powerful preparation for sacramental Communion, just as daily spiritual confession is a powerful preparation for making a good confession at the time agreed upon with your confessor. This is why I wish every Christian would inwardly adopt the practice, for every occasion when he will go to confession or Communion, so that he can better carry out this resolution, of saying each morning, "I will be going to confession and Communion on such-and-such a day"—even if it is still two months off. And so, spend half the time each morning dwelling upon your last Communion and the other half on the coming one. In this way you will show that you have reverence for Communion; otherwise, you risk never properly digesting and never having a perfect appetite for this food.

Never fail to go to confession and Communion at least once a week. Your other spiritual practices—prayer and meditation—which you perform daily, you should order to one or all of the following three effects: the honor of the Lord God and of his saints, your own salvation, and the salvation of your neighbors both living and dead. In this way, you will be growing daily through these devotions in some virtue that is needed for the better performance of your actions: humility, patience, prudence, and the like; you will grow in the knowledge and love of God; you will grow in love for your neighbor. Thus you will be able to stride forward on the way of salvation, ordering your spiritual life step by step.

As regards your bodily and temporal life, order your intentions and affections in such a way that your first aim in every corporal activity is the praise of God and the salvation of your own souls and of the souls in the bodies of those for whom you labor. See that it is God first of all who moves you to this labor—or to rest as well. In second place should be your own soul. After your own soul, you should labor for nothing more strenuously than for your neighbor's soul, either in your household or outside. In last place should come property and other things needed for your bodies. So take good care that there is no disorder in this matter. There will be none if you do not seek property beyond what is needed for your bodies, and if you desire for your bodies that condition which is best for your souls, and finally if you desire your souls to be conformed to God's will. It is from the last that you must begin; that is, you must first properly order your soul, and then seek the other things mentioned according as they help the soul more or less—not acting like those persons who first want to take care of their property and their bodies, thinking that they will then take proper care of their souls. Similarly as regards the neighbor, you should take care that, wherever possible, his soul is provided for before your own body; so that if there were one thing you could do either to defend yourself from bodily death or your neighbor from spiritual death, you should be readier to act against your neighbor's spiritual ill than your own bodily ill. If you preserve this order in your spiritual and temporal affairs, this would be the true remembrance that I would like to leave you now, asking you to pray as much as you can to the Lord God for me and for all my brothers in Christ.

Given at Parma, September 7, 1540

Your brother and spiritual father in Christ Jesus,

Don PIETRO FABRO

• III •

To the First Jesuit Scholastics at Paris, on Studies
Regensburg, May 12, 1541
MonFabri, 102–106 (*Epist.* 35)

To the first new recruits to follow in the footsteps of the original companions at the University of Paris Favre sent this set of reflections on his own experience and admonitions on how to combine their studies with spiritual progress.

May the grace and peace of Christ our Lord be always in our souls.

A letter from you in Paris, dated April 5, reached me on the third of this month. In it you give me matter for rendering thanks to God our Lord (if I can do no more) not only for your successful arrival but also for the good health of all the other brethren there which you report to me. May our redeemer Jesus Christ give all of you abundant grace so that you can bring your studies to the goal you have set before you, never unbending the bow of your intentions, in such a way that you may in the end rejoice in the Lord over the triumph you will gain if you do not let the spirit of learning quench the spirit of holy thought and feeling.

This wish of mine and of the whole Society will, under Christ's leadership, easily be achieved so long as you have as your review tutor the supreme master and ultimate imprinter of learning. This is the Holy Spirit, in whom whatever is known is known well, and without whom whoever knows anything does not yet know as he ought. Even the very words which Christ, our highest master, spoke with his own mouth require this tutor: "The Holy Spirit will remind you of all that I have said to you"; indeed it not only says that he will remind, but that he will first teach [John 14:26]. And so, if Christ our master, our light and peace, our way and our truth and our life, says we must have his Spirit not only for the feelings of the will and heart but likewise for the mind's knowing, how much more necessary will this be for other disciplines delivered by the mouth of lesser masters than Christ our Lord? You are already familiar with an example of what I am saying in St. Thomas: he not only strove to review his lectures in prayer, no matter what science or doctrine they were in, but also to go over them with his inward master before going to hear them from other teachers. In conclusion, what I beg of you in the Lord is that you always preview your lessons with this great tutor, and review them with him afterwards.

It gives me delight in the Lord that you have a great advantage over ourselves, or at least over me: even before you go to studies you already have a fixed goal towards which to direct them by the straight line of ordered intentions. Thus, already possessing the starting point upon which all forms of wisdom depend, so that you have entered your studies for his sake alone, and also possessing the truth of the means, you know just where you will end up when your studies are over. This cannot help enabling you to have peace and calm not only upon reaching the end of your studies but also (though in a different way) in the very midst of them—just as it was with calm and tranquillity that you came to start them.

The reason for this great benefit which you enjoy is that since you are striving straight forward through Christ, who is the *life* wherein you find your final perfect rest; and since you have already started off by the straight *way* which is Christ, it is inevitable that in the intermediary *truth* of the means also—that is, your studies—you should enjoy calm and repose, since you toil in him who is our very same mediator, the truth itself that came forth from the Father and returns to the Father by the straightest line.

And so you have grounds for thanking God our Lord; and so do we, even though, as I started to say, we never had the same opportunity to study in truth. We thought that letters would be sufficiently able to enlighten us about their starting point and end, as well as how they were the means. And so, not having first a true understanding of the starting point so as to begin well, nor of the true end in which to anchor our intentions, it was impossible for us to avoid confusion and anxiety regarding the means, since we did not know how to take as the truth of letters the good which they teach, but instead took the means for the end and the end for the means.

We had another great disadvantage (or at least I did): we had no idea that the cross deserved to have a place in either the starting point, the intermediary means, or the end. You, on the other hand, know that its most important place is in the intermediary means, where it is the presence of our mediator Jesus Christ. This is no small advantage that you have over us, to be at home with the cross. In addition, you have an understanding and sense of the way of proceeding of our Lord Jesus Christ, to whom we are so much in debt, some of us for his keeping them out of such a sea of obstacles and others for his rescuing them from it by his grace and mercy—not only so that they can redeem lost time but also so that they can learn more compendiously what they would never achieve by roundabout paths, namely, Jesus Christ crucified. Him we preach and propose for imitation in this life, not as reigning in this bodily life with glory and power, but in a way that can appear folly to the gentiles and those of this life: a scandal to the Jews, but to the good, the power of God and the wisdom of God.

I gave your letter to Cardinal Contarini, and, with his fatherly recollection of you, he insisted on reading it right away, even though he had at hand other business and papers, and he was delighted with it.

Regarding my own endeavors in this vineyard, which are beyond my abilities, I will write you nothing at present—nor do I think it really necessary since my letters to Rome will likely reach you.

The business of the faith is proceeding very doubtfully, so that we place our trust directly in God alone. What I mean is that the means being employed and discussed are, humanly judged, without value. But this much I do see clearly: the more futile prove to be the measures for restoring those who err in the faith, the more we see cases of persons possessing the faith who desire to "return to their former works," meaning, to a better life, lest their own candlesticks be taken from them [see Rev. 2:5].

If only we had great numbers of workers for this! If only we could reach the point where those who are so eager to build up the Catholic faith would also begin by their words and life to reconstruct and build up the fabric of morality—especially now, when mere learning is so ineffective against the heretics. With the world having reached such a state of unbelief, what is needed are arguments of deeds and of blood; otherwise things will only get worse and error will increase.

Words and arguments no longer suffice to convince the people here and heretics like them. So you would do well to urge the scholars in Paris to pursue the life-giving spirit of letters by means of a life that is visibly dedicated to Christ, if they are to win to the faith those who have fallen.

That is all for now. I beg you to give my greetings to everyone, particularly—after yourselves and Cáceres and Master Miona—to our teachers, de Gouvea, and anyone else you know who would be pleased to have my greetings.

May our Lord grant us to think and feel about him in the charity of God and the long-suffering of Christ.

Farewell.

Regensburg, May 12, 1541

Your dearest brother in Christ,

PEDRO FABRO

• IV •

Some Chapters on Faith and Morals
Regensburg, March–June, 1541
MonFabri, 119–125 (*Epist.* 40)

While in Germany in 1541, Favre and Bishop Wauchope gave the Spiritual Exercises to a number of secular and ecclesiastical notables. The following undated program of Christian life is almost certainly what they left with retreatants at the conclusion of their Exercises.

Some General Chapters on the End and on Individual Self-reformation

I. Taking for granted the principles of the faith according to the sound teaching of the Roman Catholic Church, the first thing that will help for the reformation of your previous life will be to go back over all the years of your prior life in bitterness of soul, making a general confession of all your sins to a suitable confessor. For from the terrible falls, shipwrecks, and other mortal lapses of your previous life, reviewed and wept over, you will learn cautions and procedures of great help for your future life. For no one can adequately pass to a good method of life and to knowledge and goodness unless he has before his eyes and deeply feels the many instances of disorder, ignorance, and malice in his previous life.

II. While it is extremely important that we be at all times engaged in examining our affections, thoughts, words, and deeds of every sort, so as to come to an accurate knowledge of our old and of our new man, I would nevertheless like to enjoin on you as a kind of law or commandment that you make this examination every night before going to bed. You must demand of yourself a strict account of the day. In the presence of your Judge who will one day appear, you must reprove, accuse, and convict yourself of what you have done wrong, and give thanks to God through Jesus Christ for what you have done or thought well. The form of this examination, which you should practice always and spend at least a quarter of an hour on, comprises the following five points. (1) You should give thanks to God for the benefits you have received on that day, recalling and going over them one by one. (2) You should ask God for grace to recognize and feel your sins committed that day. (3) You should turn to your own heart and demand a detailed accounting of your soul for your thoughts, words, and actions, noting those which seem deserving of reproof before God and his representative. (4) You should ask God's mercy on these sins of commission and omission. (5) You should resolve upon some good emendation of these sins and also upon mentioning in confession those which require the confessor's jurisdiction and judgment, such as all certain or doubtful mortal sins. At the end, say an Our Father and a Hail Mary for the remission of your sins.

III. Have a definite time for receiving the Holy Eucharist—at least weekly should you be a layman, if you desire to grow in the way of the knowledge of yourself and of Jesus Christ our Lord—or every two weeks. If this seems too hard for you because of your lack of devotion, at least do not go longer than a month. Mighty persons engaged in secular affairs and in handing down judgments need to receive this sacrament much more frequently than other people, and should be all the more urged so that, whatever else we ask of them, we at least obtain from them that they will receive Communion no fewer than six times a year: Easter, Pentecost, the Assumption, All Saints, Christmas, and the beginning of Lent. Whatever choice you make, be sure that you stick to your determination, so that you can make an effort to come with greater preparation from your daily preoccupations with work. Moreover, with regard to this Sacrament, any priest's devotion ought to be greater than that of the most devout layman.

IV. See that you have a booklet in the language that you know containing the whole of what Catholics call "Christian doctrine" or, as some term it, "children's catechism." This includes the twelve articles of faith, the Ten Commandments of the Decalogue, the four precepts of the Church (on celebrating feast days, hearing Mass on those days, the prescribed fasts, and confession and Communion), the deadly sins, the five senses of the body, the corporal and spiritual works of mercy, the three powers of the soul (understanding, will, and memory), the seven gifts of the Holy Spirit, the three theological virtues (faith, hope, and charity), the four so-called cardinal virtues, and the seven virtues opposed to the deadly sins. In addition to these it should also include whatever pertains to your own state of life, profession, rank, or office. Once you have got this booklet, be sure to have it read out to you frequently, especially until you have thoroughly memorized it, so that you will always have in mind the general boundaries and guidelines initially set forth for us as first principles of our believing and acting and upon which everything else is to be subsequently built.

V. Also draw up for yourself two other series of topics from which you will be able to derive numerous motives for spiritual devotion. One should consist of a brief, orderly sequence of the life of Christ, beginning with the Incarnation and going to his return to the Father, and so forth. You should draw up and organize another from the succession of the Litanies according to the practice of the Catholic Church, with a proper sequence of invocation, beginning with the Holy Trinity and proceeding to the virgins, widows, and persons who lived in continence, with several men and women saints being selected from each order. These three sequences—the one mentioned in the previous chapter and the two in this one—serve for the following. The first gives the topics which comprise the works we need to perform; the second rehearses the merits of Christ from which works chiefly draw their merit and consummation; and the third provides for the invocation of the saints so that everything may be applied to you more readily and effectively and bring you greater benefit through Christ by having a large number of intercessors. These sequences of topics will furnish you with plenty of matter for prayer and contemplation; but for these exercises you will have to set yourself a definite time in which you can force and compel yourself to the labor of asking, seeking, and knocking.

VI. There are certain universal principles conducing to perfection which you ought to commit to memory. They are these: Overcome yourself. Be your own opponent and enemy. Rein in your senses, even external. Dwell within yourself. Remember the four last things: death, judgment, hell, and paradise. Always hunger and thirst for justice by means of the desires of your thought and spiritual sentiments. Never be lukewarm but always hot or cold. Do not go, or even look, backwards. Advance and grow daily toward what lies ahead. Rejoice in the trials which are the lot of any person who undertakes God's service and a new life. Violently strive against the flesh, the world, and the evil inspirations of the spiritual tempter. Remember that if we wish anything from God we must ask, seek, and knock; that we must deny ourselves in our own judgment and senses, bear our own cross daily, follow Christ crucified, and so forth.

VII. In any spiritual exercise—whether contemplation, prayer, or other spiritual activity—for which you set aside a substantial amount of time, say a quarter hour or more, you should employ three aids. The first is that you look forward to the exercise ahead of time, thinking it through and performing it in anticipation. The second is that in the course of the exercise—say, your office—you should frequently stir up in yourself actual attentiveness of mind and affections; a help for this is to memorize the versicle "Father, in Jesus' name give me your Spirit." The third is that after completing the exercise you should always turn your mind back to it and reflect on how you comported yourself: if you did well, give thanks to God; if not, acknowledge your fault.

VIII. If these chapters open up the way to any progress for yourself, see that those under you, the members of your household, and your friends also get them. Not only this, but if there are any preachers you possess influence with, have them give exhortations on these points to the people. Your own having received them will not mean much unless you render them effective. A help for this will be to hang them all up on your bedroom wall.

IX. Steps must be taken in the first place to remove all abuses regarding food and drink, clothing, money, degrees of honors, dignities, and offices. This will be done by considering the purpose for which each of these was created and ordained. Then, from the proper use of indifferent things, it will be easy to avoid abuse of sacred things; for when one sees the end to which the goods of the Church were ordained for the holders of benefices or high offices, you will easily conclude that no one may hold several benefices if a single one suffices for a decent state of life in accordance with the fruit which he produces in God's Church. This, then, is what you must hold: The whole power of true reformation in these times lies in uprooting the lust of the flesh, the lust of the eyes, and the pride of life. Let us strive for purity of heart, poverty of spirit, and for the character of little children, and we will be threefold blessed.

X. If you do not know how to recognize your own faults, have recourse to true, faithful friends, and they will tell you. These are above all your own conscience and the angels of God. Get to know them, become familiar with them.

The grace, mercy, and peace, of Jesus Christ be with you.

PETRUS FABRI, humble servant of the Society of the Name of Jesus

Robert Wauchope, unworthy servant of our Lord Jesus Christ

• V •

To Alvaro Alfonso, on Fraternal Charity
Toledo, Spring 1542
MonFabri, 145–149 (*Epist.* 49)

Alvaro Alfonso, one of the two royal chaplains to whom Favre gave the Exercises in Speyer later in the spring (see below in his letter of April 27, 1542, pages 344–345), was planning to enter the Jesuit order. Favre depicts fraternal charity as the order's true foundation.

Copy of a Letter of Reverend Father Pierre Favre on Fraternal Charity, Found in an Old Book in the Verdun Novitiate

The grace and peace of our Lord and the communication of the Holy Spirit be with you always. Amen.

If, dear brother, you desire henceforth to be enrolled in the fellowship of the good and fittingly live your life with them in oneness of mind and heart, pooling all things together like the Apostles, it is more than anything else necessary that while carefully keeping the commandments of God and the Church, you become firmly convinced that you are like a limb of the Society, possessing neither a life nor any of life's functions that are its own, but only those which arise from the Society's heart and activities, even should these not fall within the scope of either the commandments of God and the Church or the nature of the priestly office.

Hence, you must conceive, by way of foundation, a powerful and unflagging desire for the Society's peace and union of hearts to be preserved and increased, not only by your own efforts but also by those of each and every man living in the Society; and you will (if need be) devote your own concern and efforts to their persevering and progressing in this humility and union of the members with the body. For this is no less important than for a man wishing to dedicate himself to physical accomplishments to be concerned to perfect his own body and sensory powers.

However, the enemy has often learned to his hurt how great a good is peace and union of hearts among those who in Christ bind themselves to each other as members of one body. And so he bends every effort and ingenuity to attack it, attempting, by spreading his tares, to overwhelm this fruitful seed and to pull up, scatter, and destroy those whom God has linked together.

To keep this holy resolution undamaged, then, it will be of great value to mark with care and faithfully commit to memory the following select points. With these weapons at the ready, you can break out of the enemy's ambushes and expel from your heart his perverse suggestions, in such a way that you will never be parted from this body, by a separation either physical or spiritual, but will instead, in truth of spirit, in agreement of judgment, and in conformedness of opinion, remain steadfastly in your original profession.

1. In the first place, then, you must realize and put into practice the content of this principle and maxim: that you should always will, defend, make the best case for, and advocate what your brother wills—struggling always against your own opinion and judgment and doing your brother's will instead.

2. Even though you seem to have quite reasonable cause to request or desire something, nevertheless, should your brother's wishes or reasons be otherwise, you must take care not to disagree with him or oppose him, not merely in word but even in thought. Even though you might consider your reasons for opposing him eminently just, tell yourself in reply that you have no just cause for so confidently assenting to your own judgment and so readily rejecting the other's view as wrong. Go on to reflect on how unjust of you it is to allow any animosity or indignation to arise within you for no prior reason and to turn aside from the peace, goodwill and loving inclination you once so well conceived toward your brother—a thing you should certainly value more highly than your own judgment and self-will, especially to the degree that no matter of faith or morals necessary for salvation is at stake.

3. Never pay attention to your brothers' faults (unless you happen to be responsible for their direction and correction). On the other hand, you should—whenever and as often as you please—examine with sharp eyes and imitate those virtues and behaviors of your brothers which most conform to the Rules.

4. Make steady efforts to go from virtue to virtue, so that the charity and goodwill you once embraced with so much warmth will never grow cold, but will be kept hot in spirit and grow greater every day. And the same should be observed with regard to the esteem and respect for others you once so sincerely formed: you must strive to preserve and increase it. For, given that your favorable judgment on others proceeded from deep and heartfelt humility, longsuffering, and charity, it is by these same practices, coupled with greater efforts at denying yourself, that it ought to be increased. For this purpose it is important to examine and investigate attentively not what virtue you possess which seems to

place you above others, but rather what fault of character you are most inclined towards which makes it clear that your place is below others. It is because we do the opposite, attending to our own virtues rather than our faults while looking at the bundle on the back of the man ahead of us, [that in us there] comes a swelling of arrogance, self-love, contempt, and low opinion of others.

5. Weigh with care what you perceive as excesses or aberrations in your brother; and when he is rated annoying or stupid or thoughtless not only by your own but by others' votes, examine this judgment with more than usual care and never follow the example of those who are led by a spirit of worldly wisdom. Ask yourself whether you may not have to be registered among those who form their opinions with eyes often darkened by the pitch of pride. I consider it therefore important that, the moment a feeling of disgust or indignation like this steals upon you, you should turn it not against your brother but against yourself, roundly accusing and indicting not your brother but yourself—for judging so rashly and harboring such rancor in your heart.

6. More generally, whenever this rancor in the heart begins to burgeon, cut it off at the roots and do not rest until you have pulled it out stem and all. The apostle Paul says, "Let the sun not go down on your anger," and "Let all bitterness be removed from your hearts" [Eph. 4:26, 31]. Do you want a sickle for this? Declare these feelings and imperfections without delay to someone experienced in uprooting them. With this sickle or instrument, if you apply it to the root, that is, to practice and action, you will rid your mind of the venomous growth of these feelings.

There is another way, harder but therefore all the nobler. It is, before you go to bed, frankly and humbly to declare these diseases and infirmities of your spirit not just to the physician but to the very brother against whom you harbor ill feelings. Thus you will not only reignite the quenched tinder of love with sparks of brotherly consolation and goodwill; you will also deal the proud enemy, who is vexed by the abasement entailed in such a reconciliation, a most degrading slap in the face.

7. Whenever any act or word on another's part displeases you or begets any estrangement of hearts, you should look at it carefully and ask whether what appears evil or disgraceful in your brother's exterior may not be present, even more evilly and disgracefully, in your own soul. From this, reflect above all on what a degraded mind and corrupted judgment you are operating with.

8. In general, reflect that the more keenly a man spies others' imperfections and vanities, the cheaper and viler he proves himself to be. Just as a man who raises his mind aloft to contemplate things of heaven and of God, by a kind of metamorphosis, as God imparts his taste and sweet-

ness to him, is transformed into a man of heaven and of God—in the same way, a man who is weighed down by his attachments and crawls on the ground seeing only his fellows' feet, namely, their attachments, is often himself seen to be aboil with a host of evil desires.

9. You must observe all these admonitions with exactness, along with whatever else leads to the practice and increase of this great good of brotherly concord. But you must above all take measures to make yourself pleasing to God and all the saints, full of goodwill toward your neighbor, docile to your superiors, and loving to your peers and inferiors. For this you must first of all be convinced that you have to wage war against yourself with no hope of truce, bridle the wicked desires of the flesh, rein in your outward senses, and wrestle against your own judgment and self-will. By "judgment" I mean not just that in which the spirit of sin or the will of the flesh, the world, and the devil are clearly descried, but also any area in which the will itself is not yet cut back to the quick. And since the will springs from nowhere but your own spirit, I call it your self-will. Therefore, be always equipped and armed; pursue this domestic enemy of yours; seize him until he gives out; strain every sinew to subdue yourself gloriously under your own feet; overcome yourself bravely; stoutly lock yourself up inside yourself. Secondly, bear yourself with your superiors in such a manner that, by sticking to the path they trace for you, you will constantly rise to ever more perfect degrees of self-abnegation.

• VI •

To Ignatius of Loyola, on Apostolic Activities in Speyer
Speyer, April 27, 1542
MonFabri, 162–166 (Epist. 53)

Sent in haste from Spain to assist the papal legate Cardinal Morone in Speyer, Favre was disappointed to discover upon arrival that the cardinal had already departed.

The sovereign grace, love, and peace of Christ our Lord be ever with us all.

I wrote last week pretty much what you will find in this letter, except that I then failed to make clear the great longing I necessarily have for your letters—the reason being so that I can learn what I ought to do. For you know the difference between being moved by oneself and being moved through holy obedience, which, in a word, is consummate counsel, true prudence, utter discretion, strength, and charity for whoever accepts it with perfect humility, patience, and joy.

Consequently, even I, being the kind of person in practical matters that I am and always have been, truly believe that if those who sent me to Germany had written to me that I should be in Speyer, or wherever the cardinal of Modena [Morone] was staying, on such and such a day under holy obedience, I would have managed and found a way to carry it out to the letter. But being told just to do what I could to get here, I was left so low in strength and faith that all I could find out how to manage or manage to find out was to arrive belatedly, as I did, and after the cardinal of Modena's departure from Speyer, on Saturday after the feast of the Resurrection—a piece of news that for me had more of the Passion than of the Resurrection to it. However, the letter written in Master Bobadilla's hand did me some good, saying what you will see in the copy of it. The truth is that he leaves me much freedom.

The bishop of Speyer has decided the following. The cardinal of Mainz having some five or six weeks ago sent a doctor to him as a special messenger with the request that the bishop of Speyer send me to his reverend lordship as soon as I arrived, he decided that he ought to write to him personally that I had arrived. Accordingly, he sent a personal messenger there to let him know that I had come. There has been no reply yet, so that I do not know the situation there as regards the cardinal of Mainz. Hence, I await developments on this score. I also await the decision promised me by the cardinal of Modena.

However, in the meantime I shall not fail to be active here in Speyer, especially inasmuch as I have these two lord chaplains of the royal princesses who have been in the Exercises for about a week, to my own and their considerable satisfaction. I cannot find strong enough words or comparisons to express half of what I find in them; our Lord's own hand has so clearly intervened that even before making their general confession, they have received the most evident gifts in its regard, of the sort that are most dearly desired and aimed at for the most perfect election.

Their ladyships the princesses,[2] the count of Cifuentes [Fernando de Silva], as well as Doña Leonor [Mascarenhas] and the rest of the saintly household, have given the chaplains leave to come and spend a year with us, or two if necessary, to get a thorough knowledge of the Spiritual Exercises and of our other instruments for the advancement of souls, so that they can then teach all of this to them when the ladies are unable to have ourselves or another of our Society there. This was their intention in giving this gracious leave, but I very much fear that things are being directed by a higher plan—even though this would not be against the household's intention, for it was also their desire that the

---

[2] Charles V's daughters, María and Juana.

chaplains should seek God our Lord as sincerely as they could in order to follow his holy will in all things, without concern for the created affections of such truly well-intentioned persons as these ladies are. If only all the women in the world were like them! But enough on this matter. I only wish to say in their regard that you should keep them in your prayers.

The vicar general has returned to the beginning of the Exercises with a view to making a general confession with me. Bishop Otto Truchsess likewise yesterday started them from the beginning, since the other time in Regensburg he only heard and wrote down the First Week. There is another doctor of canon and civil law who wants to make them; he met spontaneously with me to agree on an hour and a half of work. He still has not begun, nor would I be able to manage that much. The bishop of Speyer would be willing to give an hour a day for exercises if I could visit him in his castle a German league from here; but with all my other occupations I am not taking him up on it. So, thanks be to God, I have no lack of harvest to keep me busy.

Neither is there any lack of opposition and obloquy against ourselves. It is openly claimed and considered as a fact that we are fellows of the reformers brought with him by the cardinal of Modena. There is no doubt that he himself, and they even more, have stirred up in many persons a passionate agitation of evil spirits who wish them ill. What I mean is that when they spoke in terms of reformation and changing their lives, their interlocutors took it in the sense of their enemies, the evil spirits who rise up against good and holy inspirations. They also claim that since we three are divided up among three houses, we are obviously spies seeking out in different places the wicked secrets of the city and of the clergy so as to write to the Supreme Pontiff. But they are chiefly afraid of our stirring up the people against them by displaying a different way of living which readily wins over the consciences of the people and the approval of the commons.

It is true that Bishop Otto and a daily larger number of others are reassuring them about all this and consoling them with the statement that we have no intention of casting a supercilious reformer's eye upon them, but are ourselves the ones most anxious to improve and be reformed day by day, in conformity with the gifts of the sevenfold Holy Spirit.

For my own part, I rejoice in these criticisms, assigning the fault—and most of the punishment—to the devils rather than to the people here, who are not naturally malicious or inclined to take things ill—particularly the clergy here in Speyer, who without doubt fulfill their ecclesiastical duties better than any others in Germany. In the people too there is far greater devotion than elsewhere. It seems to be starting to increase once more. The principal preacher, in whose house I am staying, told me two days ago on the feast of St. Mark, when there was a general procession, that it had been twelve years since such devotion had been seen in the city. The devotion during the procession did seem considerable to me. Blessed be the Lord who does not forget his handiwork.

I shall say no more, beseeching his divine Majesty to give us the fullness of grace so that we may always and in every place know his most holy will and, once known, do it.

Speyer, April 27, 1542

Your least brother in Christ our Lord,

PEDRO FABRO

• VII •

To Diego Laínez, on Spiritual Graces Received
Speyer, August 30, 1542
MonFabri, 179–183 (Epist. 59)

Writing to Laínez at Venice, Favre responds to thanks for attentions he had given to Laínez's relatives in Spain, rejoices over Laínez's apostolic work in Venice, reports on his own health, and intimates the extraordinary graces he has been receiving while in Germany.

Dearest brother in Jesus Christ:

May the grace and peace of Christ our Lord be always in our souls, strengthening them and teaching them to recognize, perceive, and perform his holy will.

You could not believe, my brother in Christ our Lord, the special spirit that I received regarding your individual good the day that I was given the note from your hand written in Rome on June 1. For this alone I think I am more indebted to you than I would be capable of expressing.

As to what you say about your parents and blood kin in Almazán, believe that it was nothing in comparison with the love and desire which our Lord gave me, far greater—and purer than that of the old Adam—than it would have been if they had been my own parents according to the flesh. Accordingly, I consider myself deeply beholden to them for the humble and loving hearing and obedience which they gave me in whatever I was able to determine was needful or helpful to them for their spiritual welfare and the peace of their blessed souls. I shall never be able to forget them, till the next visit that we hope for.

I have already received a letter from Rome, dated this month of August, containing a copy of your reception in the city there [Venice]. In it I find matter for praising Christ our Lord, and I rejoice in him over your being called to that dominion. So also does the lord bishop of Caserta, presently apostolic nuncio to the King of the Romans, Girolamo Verallo, formerly apostolic legate to Venice, whom you know well. His lordship, desirous as always of the welfare of that region, in his response to a letter of mine wrote me the following paragraph among others:

"I am delighted that Master Laínez has been assigned to go to Venice. He is a person of discretion and of holy and learned life; and I trust in the Lord that he will produce great results, for he will find the matter in which he will be striving to produce them well disposed. For it will be easier for him to work in that portion of the vineyard of the Lord than for Your Lordship in the part assigned to you or to the Scottish doctor [Wauchope], Master Claude, or Bobadilla in their portions. The latter nevertheless toil on for Christ, particularly in Regensburg, which was more inclined to defection than to good edification." Thus far his reverend lordship.

Indeed, I have long desired that a member of the Society go there before worse dissolutions and errors occur. *[There follows a mutilated passage containing various greetings to be delivered and requests that Laínez say Masses]* . . . and another at the Incurables, remembering in particular to offer . . . at least once to God our Lord, asking that the divine favor enjoyed by those places be applied to me, and other graces. Likewise I wish that you would always keep in mind our needs here when you come across persons obedient and powerful in prayer, and the like. I do not imagine that you will easily be able to forget my personal needs, nor fail to remember the illnesses that I had in Parma—not only my illnesses but my deaths. Hence I ask that while forgetting what does not edify, you not forget me, giving thanks also to Christ our Lord, who through his infinite mercy has drawn so much well-being from my ills, far greater, certainly, than I will ever be able to acknowledge until I possess a heavenly mind and heart. Hence I can say with much truth that it was a blessed illness which in so many ways worked together unto me for good. Without it, as can happen, I would never have been able to recognize, find, or seek the remedies needed to recover from the bad condition I was in before falling ill. For you are quite aware that no one, otherwise in good condition, could have fallen into such an illness unless he was previously disturbed or inclined to this bad condition.

The bleedings made clear that the blood had long since been in a bad condition.

Might it please the Mother of God our Lord that I could give you an idea of how much good has entered my soul and remained there from the time I left you in Piacenza to the present day, in both knowledge and feeling as regards the things of God our Lord, of his Mother, of his holy angels, the holy souls in heaven and in purgatory, as well as regarding my own affairs: my highs and lows, my enterings into myself and goings out, the cleansing of body and soul and spirit and the purifying and disencumbering of the heart so as to receive the divine liquors and preserve and maintain them, while requesting for all this various graces, seeking them and knocking for them; likewise as regards the neighbor, our Lord granting methods and ways, truths and lives for knowing him and perceiving his goods and evils in Christ in order to love him, bear him up, suffer him and suffer with him, do and request favors for him, seek pardons and excuses for him, speaking well on his behalf before his divine Majesty and his saints.

In sum I say, brother mine, Master Laínez, that I will never be able to acknowledge—I do not say in deeds but not even in thought and simple apprehension—the favors which our Lord has done me and does me and is most ready to do me, binding up all my bruises, healing all my infirmities, and showing himself so propitious towards all my iniquities. To him be glory. Amen. May he be magnified and exalted above all things by way of all his creatures. Amen. And I too say Amen, and beg that you will render praise over this brother of yours, as I do over the whole Society.[3]

His lordship Otto Truchsess of Bavaria, presently apostolic nuncio sent here to give notification of the council, is returning to Rome and told me that he would be passing through those parts, and not without letting you know of his journey. And so I beg you to visit him and communicate with him the matters which you know are for his edification, for this is what his lordship himself desires. And be sure to write me individually through him, for his lordship will not fail to send me your letter.

I say nothing about ourselves, referring you to the reports which you can get from those in Rome. The two chaplains continue giving edification with their pilgrimages, which they make in pure mendicancy despite the times, men, heresies, and other such obstacles. And as I keep to my old style of embracing much and pressing little, I am making a little more progress, in faith and hope and longsuffering as the Lord gives, rather avoiding importunity and reproaches and rebuttals until I consolidate my position in this city. Enough of this.

May Christ our Lord be always for our continual favor and protection.

Speyer, August 30, 1542.

[PEDRO FABRO]

---

[3] The above two paragraphs were quoted by Laínez in the memoir of St. Ignatius which he wrote at Polanco's request. See *FN* 1:142–144.

• VIII •

To Ignatius of Loyola, on Apostolic Activities in Mainz
Mainz, November 7, 1542
MonFabri, 186–188 (*Epist.* 62)

In another account of his activities to Ignatius, Favre complains that he is constantly leaving places just when his efforts have begun to produce results.

May the grace and peace of Christ our Lord be always in our souls.

My last letter was in October. The bishop [of Speyer] had decided that I should lecture; the clergy were showing great goodwill, as were also the principal secular personages of the imperial camera as well as of the city; reconciliations of considerable importance had been brought about; and a great door was opened for reaping fruit. But I was being pressed to come by the cardinal of Mainz, and so, bidding farewell to Speyer as best I could along with my companions, I came here to Mainz. The cardinal, despite my making clear to him my lack of qualifications for so important a task, has decided that I should go with some of his scholars to the council. He said that I should prepare for this and that upon my return I will be able to lecture here in Mainz with his full spiritual and temporal backing.

Upon arriving here we entered upon some spiritual conversations and arrangements to give the Exercises. About four or five days ago I began with a respected cleric of the principal church, a man of excellent intentions and eager to make progress. He told me that our Lord had brought me here to Germany for his salvation. Likewise another cleric, engaged in the care of souls, promised Mosén Juan [de Aragón] to receive them from him. This very day I started giving them to a pair of bishops, each by himself. One is the suffragan and also preacher in the principal church [Michael Helding]; the other is the bishop-elect of Naumburg [Julius von Pflug], a noble and learned man. The good that I anticipate from these two bishops is greater than I ever deserved to see in this poor Germany.

God knows what I went through in Speyer, struggling against despair of any good for Germany and concluding towards the end with a highly favorable prospect. But now I see with all clarity that our Lord is keeping many souls for us here who are ready to receive our teaching. However, he is not allowing me to enjoy the fruit achieved until my return from the council. Our Lord knows the reasons why I do not deserve to stay in one place for any length of time but am always being taken away at the moment when the harvest begins to peak. So far I can clearly see that this has all been for the best, so that not for anything in this life would I wish that I had not left Rome for Parma, or Parma for Germany. Nor will I ever regret being called from Germany to Spain, much less being called back from Spain here to Speyer and from Speyer to Mainz.

I have decided to leave Mosén Juan studying here and to send Mosén Alvaro Alfonso to Louvain for greater convenience.

I conclude beseeching the sovereign Goodness to preserve us all on the road forward by the way of his most holy will.

Mainz, November 7, 1542

PEDRO FABRO

• IX •

Instructions for Those Going on Pilgrimage
Probably Cologne, Spring 1543
MHSI, *Epistolæ P. Hieronimi Nadal* 4:636–639

Favre probably gave these instructions for travelers to Alfonso Alvaro and Juan de Aragón, the two royal chaplains who entered the Society of Jesus, when he sent them on pilgrimage. The instructions were preserved among the writings of Jerónimo Nadal, S.J. They touch on a number of topics dear to Favre.

Father Favre, at Mainz, when he was asked for instructions for the pilgrimage[, wrote as follows]:

Some persons want to be delivered from their woes—poverty, hunger, toil, and the like—by turning immediately to creatures in order to find help in them. Others turn to creatures, but do it through God, asking him that they be helped by creatures and through them delivered from their woes, as with persons who in time of need pray thus to the Lord for deliverance: "Lord, give us bread; give us this or that; move this man or that man, and similar petitions." But there are others, walking more perfectly, whose desire is not to be delivered from their woes but to receive strength in the midst of them directly from the Lord. These persons ask him to grant them patience and courage, to take away their fear and similar emotions, so that they can bear their woes bravely. Their concern is for their interior woes; they care not for the outward ones and cast aside all worry about them, as Christ has taught us. At the same time they take care to guard against anything that smacks of tempting God.

Sometimes timidity and weakness of spirit can weaken our bodies. Conversely, robustness of mind can make our bodies robust. Hence, in our toils we ought to throw aside all fear, timidity, and so forth. The spirit will bear up our bodies.

When eating, drinking, and conversing with others, we ought to aim not at winning their approval but at edifying their consciences. There are some who pay regard to other people's characters and behave in such a way as to get their approval as affable and good-natured; these do not so truly edify others' consciences. Those who are concerned about their consciences, on the other hand, strive to live in such a way that they will always be pleasing both to God and to anyone who at all times could not but express approval of what is right and good.

Entering any city or town, we should call upon the angels, archangels, saints, and patrons of that city or town. We should greet them and call on them to assist us, just as we would in paying visits to men. We should converse with them and pray to them on behalf of the city or town placed in their charge. We should ask them to rule and guide it and on its behalf to beseech the Lord to move the hearts of its inhabitants to repentance and the like. We should also give thanks for the blessings that have been bestowed on those territories: the crops, the river, and so forth. As we consider how many enjoy these gifts and how few acknowledge them, we ought to render thanks in the name of all.

Seeing strangers on the road, even if they are soldiers or other men, we should not allow ourselves to have any suspicions against them. Our thought should be that they are good people, and we should pray for their good and should in a way unite ourselves to them with a bond of charity and love. Thus we will rid ourselves of fear, rash judgments, and the like. And if anything untoward does befall us, we should take it as coming not from man but from God; for nothing can happen to us apart from his will. Taking it in this spirit, as from the Lord's hand, we ought to bear it patiently and calmly.

Our words are of three kinds. They may represent our ideas, as when a person expounds in words some idea or insight he has had; these we could label "thought words." Again, some words serve to explain other words, as in the exegesis of Scripture and the like; these we could call "word words." Finally, some words recount things that we or others have done, to the praise of God; these we could call "deed words" or "action words." Now, while it is true that people generally take pleasure in the first and second kind of words, which nourish our minds, still, since what people want most is to act, they get more pleasure from the third kind and find them more useful for life, because through them they learn ways, methods, and procedures by which they can act.

Speaking of students, he [Favre] used to say that they should not take it ill to go back to learning the elements of Latin or basic logic, and the like. People would find it even harder to have to go back and learn how to speak their mother tongue, how to think at all and so forth; yet that is just what God did. He became a baby and over a period of time acquired a mother tongue and began to know and understand by what is termed experiential knowledge. More than that, he went so far back as to have his feet, hands, and other parts of his body grow larger little by little. Rightly seen, this is an amazing thing even in ourselves—how much more in God!

He used to say that in all of God's gifts we should consider three aspects: the gift itself, the one who gives it, and his motive in giving. This will bring us to have a high regard for each and every gift, as is the case in our dealings with human beings when these three elements are present. It is by not directing our minds to these three things that we often get a reputation for ingratitude, because we fail to value the gift as we ought.

He used to say that just as in any major or difficult undertaking we carefully plan out its execution beforehand, eager to perform it as perfectly as possible; and then after its execution look back with regret on any mistakes we have made, thinking, "Here or there I went wrong"—and similarly even with our conversations—in the same way we ought to plan out our prayer beforehand, saying, "I am going to make this prayer at such and such a time," filled with anticipatory eagerness to perform it with attention and devotion and to have it heard by God and so forth. And when it is over we should examine any faults we may have committed and rue our mistakes. In this way we will eventually reach the point of praying with fruit. He used to say it was amazing what care we take about things we are going to do or say, and how negligent we are in the matter of prayer, even though prayer is more important than anything else we say or do, however good. We go to prayer negligently and we leave it cold.

Simplicity and goodness should eventually get the upper hand over our natural way of thinking. That is to say, though on a natural level we might think it right to be angry or depressed over something, nevertheless goodness and simplicity ought to put up with it. Sometimes we are interiorly anguished; and though this spirit may speak what is true, reproving us for our many failures, nevertheless if it robs us of our tranquillity it is not the good spirit. The spirit of God is peaceful and gentle even in reproof.

• X •

To Gerhard Kalckbrenner, Prior of the Cologne Carthusians, on True Reform

Mainz, April 12, 1543
MonFabri, 194–200 (*Epist.* 66)

A deep friendship united Favre with the zealous Carthusian prior in Cologne, Gerhard Kalckbrenner (or Hammontanus). Together they labored for the interior renewal of the Church, which for Favre was the key to dealing with the threats posed by heresy.

Most esteemed and beloved Father in Jesus Christ:

May the grace of our Lord Jesus Christ and the peace which surpasses all understanding strengthen your heart and mind so that in all things you may know what is his good, pleasing, and perfect will.

Your Paternity's letter was delivered to me; though it was short, I had many grounds to welcome it with veneration. What I most rightly welcomed with joy was to see that I was remembered in Your Paternity's charity and love, not because I think or wish that this remembrance may bring me any advantage among human beings, but because I anticipate therefrom many good things through Your Paternity's prayers to God, to the Mother of God, and to the saints of his Spirit. And so, as earnestly as I can, I beseech Your Paternity to be mindful of me always (as I trust you will), so that having anticipated me in love you may not forsake me unto death. In return, as I am later in beginning, I shall always follow in reciprocating your love.

The second thing that I gathered with thanksgiving from Your Paternity's letter was the sense it gave me of how not only Your Paternity but those who resemble and imitate you have been stirred with an energetic spirit in Christ Jesus which has been quenched in so many others, and are being raised up while so many others are falling away. If only, Father and brother mine, if only the greater number of those who now sleep away amid enormous dangers sensed and realized this. If only the city of Cologne could assemble its every part and have ears to hear, and could hear the words being said to itself, "Do your former works, or I will come and take away your candlestick" [Rev. 2:5]. If only every person inside and outside the city could understand as being shouted to himself those other words of the Apocalypse, "If only you were hot or cold; but since you are lukewarm I shall vomit you out of my mouth" [Rev. 3:16]. But few lay any store by the candlestick, thinking they can have the candle without it. But the candle cannot last unless the golden candlestick does: there is no salvation outside the Church.

Many are giving thought to how they can be preserved from falling into the depths of this darkness. Mainz, Cologne, Speyer, Worms, and other cities who think they are still hot but are naked, lukewarm, and wretched in manifold ways—these cities and those like them would still prefer not to fall into the calamities wherein all too many other German cities are tossed about and drowning. And so all that we fear is becoming worse off than we are.

These are the evils which upset us somewhat but into which we have not yet plunged. But no one has any sense of the evils in which we have long been living. We want to avoid falling into what we are not yet, but have no contrition for the lukewarmness and death with which we long since made a pact. We fear becoming like those who have forfeited all peace, both at home and abroad; but meanwhile we have no shame over tarrying for so long in the same religious state in which those who fell were abiding shortly before their fall.

Why do we not reflect that those who fell had no firm footing? If we are on the same footing as they were, why do we not take thought not simply to avoid falling down but to leave this footing for higher and better ground?

And so since Christ calls us to be no longer "children of withdrawal unto perdition but of faith to the saving of the soul" [Heb. 10:39], let us ascend the mountain of the Lord [Isa. 2:3, Gen. 7:19] away from the waters, for this flood will overtop no mountain. Let us grow in length, breadth, and depth so that we may be built up into houses upon the rock, and not be afraid of these winds, these torrents, these rains.

Alas for us who sense this so little and are even less convinced of it.

What, I ask, would the heretics of this cold age do if they beheld a city determined to grow in teaching and putting into effect just one of the articles on which they chiefly dissent from us? If they were to see auricular confession now more highly esteemed than it has been—if they saw laypeople going to confession, being cleansed, and coming back the more joyful from their cleansing—they would lose their bold confidence in this regard. If they saw frequent Communion in the churches—some being strengthened and enlightened weekly, others every other week, and others on different days of the year—no one would dare agitate for the Zwinglian communion. Even should the watchdogs (God forbid) fail to keep these wolves out of so fervent a flock, the wolves themselves would quickly flee, for they are discomfited when they are laughed at or get no hearers—and what would they do if they were heard by no one and laughed at by everybody?

We should do the same with the other articles of faith: not just believe them, as heretofore, but begin to grow sincerely more devout in regard to them all—invoke the saints more often, show greater concern for the souls of the dead, celebrate Mass more fervently. I would go on like this about them all, except that in my haste I wish to avoid unnecessary wordiness. Why is it that our outward Christian symbols are being stripped from us if not because we ourselves have progressively rejected and despised them?

And so may Your Paternity continue in this holy and necessary ardor for helping the ignorant and erring [see Heb. 5:2]. For the time has come "for those who are approved to be made manifest" [1 Cor. 11:19]. You should exhort, strengthen, and stir up as many persons as you can who will themselves be capable of exhorting others. Be bold before God: it is his honor that is at stake, and he will therefore rebuff no one. Be bold before Christ, his only-begotten Son: the whole issue of the worship of his humanity is at stake. Be bold before the merciful Mother of all mercy and the other saints, whose memory is being subjected to destructive criticism. With such powerful patrons in your city, why do you all not return to your heart, O children of such tender charity? Indeed it is a sorrow to me that I personally should be thought helpful or necessary to any inhabitant of Cologne—not that I do not wish to be helpful to everyone, but that I indignantly reject such an evil as that Cologne should be wanting in any of those things which are available to everyone.

Search, reverend Father, search the city's nooks and crannies and you will find hidden treasures—treasures of sound teaching and piety. How grievous it is that there are so many people who are more afraid of reformation according to the faith to which they so tenaciously cling than they are of falling away from that faith. It is inevitable—indeed should long since have happened—that having made up their minds not to change for the better, they should change for the worse. They have no desire for the spirit or works according to their faith; rightly then do they receive a different faith and spirit that jibe with their works. What an amazing thing: People cannot—because they will not—change for the better or become more incorruptible in accord with sound doctrine, and so it is the Scriptures that are changed and corrupted in accord with carnal desires! But this is more than enough on the subject.

As for the pilgrimage [to Cologne] which Your Paternity urges upon me, I am at present in no position to say what I will be doing in the near future; I hope to be able to write you a definite answer in a few weeks. Meanwhile I shall take advantage of the company of Master Peter [Canisius], which brings me more enjoyment than I can possibly express. Blessings upon him who planted this well-grown tree; blessings upon those who in any way watered it—and I do not doubt that a share in this my blessing falls to Your Paternity, who in so many ways wrought upon this young man to be what he is and not to be like the young men of this world. It has truly made me an even greater lover of your city of Cologne to see that it was capable of nourishing such purity. I have no doubt that there lie hidden at this time other such young plants which are being prepared to summon many—and indeed that there are very many persons who can be converted according to the rules of Catholic life and become a source of strength to others. For Christ is glorified precisely by his setting aside from such a vast lump of infection a few vessels to be shaped and painted by his Spirit; the majesty of the craftsman will be shown in that what brings ruin to so many conspires to bring a small number of elect to the height of beauty.

Some withdraw from the monastic cloister and shun the habit; but there are others who are now returning to their cells more earnestly than before, and who do not fear the hairshirt. There are many who cannot be kept from blaspheming by any bands of faith; there will be others who are thereby confirmed in returning to silence, unwilling to sin even by idle words. The former multiply luxuries, foods, and other things of the flesh, quenching the Spirit; the latter multiply fasts, watchings, prayers, contemplations, weeping, and similar practices, as prescribed for those who have undergone discipline and been built upon Christ.

Courage, then, reverend Father; let your heart be strengthened. Plead with the Most High that he will use what is healthy to heal what is ill. And no longer think that you must first convert the worst and then those less badly off. It is better that those less badly off be changed for the good, and above all that anyone who is just by the grace of Christ, or even highly religious, should be justified even more and grow in the grace of the Lord. For how will the bad be changed into the good unless they see by example how easy it is for the good to become better? To come to a point, I would like to say in conclusion that Your Paternity owes much to Christ, who daily gives you food for your spiritual hunger and drink for your spiritual thirst. This is why I long to see Your Paternity—and if we cannot be consoled by sharing our bread, we will at least rejoice in sharing our hunger.

Here let me end, in Christ Jesus my Lord, in whom I bid Your Paternity once more farewell.

In haste.

Mainz, April 12, 1543

Your Paternity's servant and brother in Jesus Christ,

PETRUS FABER

• XI •

To Claude Périssin, Prior of the Reposoir Carthusians in Savoy, on Perfection
Mainz, May 28, 1543
MonFabri, 201–205 (Epist. 67)

This letter, the only document surviving from Favre in his native French, was written to encourage his kinsman in Savoy to continue striving for perfection.

Dear and beloved cousin and brother:

The grace of our Lord Jesus Christ and his sweet peace be with you, guard you, and save you, now and for ever and ever. Amen.

It is not two full months since I wrote you news of myself in detail, sending the letter directly to Lyons. I am sure that the letter already reached your hand before this one, and so consider it unnecessary to write any news. I am very anxious to hear about you, and it was mainly for that reason that I asked the present carrier to make a detour from his route to the Grande Chartreuse; he is supposed to return here as soon as he has delivered his messages. Thus you can write to me informally, without concern about correctness, and tell me all about how you are doing.

I strongly hope that your monastery is going from good to better and that all the religious entrusted to your protection are devout, so that our Lord will not have occasion to treat you as he has several of your neighbors, that is, by allowing the defection and decay that you see before your eyes.

I am great friends with your Carthusian brothers here in Mainz, where there are a number of religious with whom I occasionally retire, seeing their desire to grow spiritually; and they all esteem and listen to me as willingly as those of Reposoir would do; would to God I were as near to them.

Likewise, the prior of the Cologne Carthusians (who sent the present messenger) has written me recently, strongly asking and warmly urging me to visit Cologne, three days' journey from here. The need that prompts him to write is great and so I have decided to go there. The cardinal of Mainz is willing, so long as I return shortly.

I already find Germany filled with persons who are returning "to their former works," namely, to the imitation and teaching of their fathers. I begin to recognize that the heresies of this time are nothing but a lack of devotion, a lack of humility, patience, chastity, and charity. Hence, it is necessary to practice these virtues, earnestly begging the grace of him who is always available to those who pray for it and are willing to die in the effort.

Let us launch a battle against our mortal enemies; and when we succeed in wreaking vengeance on our self-will, let us take vengeance on our servants, that is, our flesh and outward senses.

If we find ourselves dissipated during the time of prayer by the distraction of vices, or vanity, or business, we should take care not to be so heedless in the face of temporal matters when engaged in our activities and conversations. When we find useless thoughts in our imaginations, let us immediately seek the roots from which these weeds spring. We shall easily find peace in church if we ceaselessly give battle to ourselves the whole time we are outside of church; we will quickly vanquish mortal sins if we will offer fierce battle and resistance against what we know are occasions of venial sin. We cannot find peace in our souls if we want to rest outside of ourselves.

Carefully examine your conscience, and every evening thank our Lord for the good you have received that day. Give yourself an exhortation or sermon with some good counsels for the future, once you have thoroughly scolded and upbraided yourself for the past. Then you can plan out the next day's work, looking forward to the periods and times of your bodily and spiritual activities. And when engaged in bodily exercises, strive as far as you can to keep in mind the time of your spiritual activities.

Item: Before saying your hours or Mass, take some quarters of an hour to prepare yourself inwardly, casting upwards some good desires and praying to our Lord and our Lady and his saints to help you to profit from it. For the greater is your desire to profit from it, the more our Lord will help you—even if he does not always seem to do so.

Likewise, after you finish your exercises, examine how you bore yourself, grieving that you profited so little.

Mere curiosity and vanities in your reading, with no spiritual profit, you ought to avoid, as well as any conversations which do not conduce to eternal peace.

If the fountains of tears are exhausted by too long a drought, pray our Lord that he will deign to rain them in your souls; and in the meantime do not forget to dig in the earth until you find water there.

I shall send you no news about here or about the Emperor or the general council, which is undoubtedly going ahead. These are matters alien to the accounting which you will have to render to our Lord according to your own spiritual profession and vocation, which consists in that "better part which cannot be taken from you" by enemies or by any other creature.

I am eager to know something about our sisters in Jesus Christ, the nuns at Melan[4]—whether or not the true spirit of life lives in them; and if it lives, whether or not it reigns; and if it reigns, whether or not it reigns in peace. I refer to the spirit of devotion, and then the spirit of consolation; and if they are consoled, I want to know what their consolation consists in, that is, whether it rests upon temporal things or upon spiritual ones, such as the words of our Lord and of his saints who have left such a plenitude of good instructions for us who have already left the world and occasions for pleasures of the flesh and vanities. Our Lord owes them the grace of understanding their vocation and the sweet sacrifice which they can offer to our Lord by being content and joyful in God's service as contained in their rules.

We must overcome ourselves; we must renounce ourselves and make war on ourselves. But all this is nothing when we compare it with the reward which is so nigh to us or consider the magnitude of the exchange we have made. For by leaving ourselves, we win God almighty, Father, Son, and blessed Holy Spirit; by leaving the world, we win the kingdom of heaven; and by vanquishing the evil spirits who seek our eternal destruction, we obtain the favor and good grace of all God's friends—the good angels and all the holy men and women in paradise.

And so we must take courage—and if we already have done so, take it again—so as to make a real start at yearning for all perfection. And then, like good farmers we must clear the stones from the field of our conscience so that we can sow and reap. I am convinced that there is still plenty of seed, and it is quite certain that our Lord, on his part, will not fail to give us a "good season," meaning a good spiritual winter for the grain to grow in the earth and a good spiritual summer for the crop to ripen. So be it. Amen.

I say no more except to ask you to pardon my writing you so informally and without order—the reason being that I do not have as much time as I would like to spend with you and to put in order for you a great book that would be more to your liking.

Meanwhile, pray to God for me and have all those under you do the same, for I do not forget you.

May Jesus be with you all.

At Mainz, from your cousin according to the flesh and your brother in Jesus Christ

Entirely yours,

PIERRE FAVRE
of the Society of Jesus Christ

---

[4] A convent of Carthusian nuns founded in 1292.

• XII •

To Gerhard Kalckbrenner, Prior of the Cologne Carthusians, a Letter of Spiritual Friendship
Mainz, June 14, 1543
MonFabri, 205–206 (Epist. 68)

A short letter which illustrates the role of friendship and personal contact in Favre's apostolate.

I have no words with which to respond briefly to the spirit of Your Paternity's letter. May Jesus Christ, who brings Your Paternity so low that there is truly nothing beneath you, deign to strengthen you in him who is all things in all.

If the Lord gives me some time free from my activities, I shall send Your Paternity something by way of response—although I know that I cannot really give any response by letter. For now, though, perhaps this would serve as a response of sorts—if there were anything in which I could be of actual service to you and your friends. Meanwhile, we must both strive to respond to the Spirit that so powerfully unites and inflames us mutually and who alone (from my side) can bring it about (as he does) that our converse is able to be more than merely mouth to mouth.

I was able to get to know the priors of Trier and Hildesheim only by way of ordinary external conversations; however, on a few occasions I did have a delightful meal with them, not merely of bodily foods but of holy conversations. If only they and I had been granted leisure to unfold to each other privately the depths of our hearts, as Your Paternity does in your letter. However, I did get this much profit from my visits with them, that they are going to aid me with their prayers, for which I give undying thanks to God, who deigns by so many ways and means to provide for the miseries of my soul.

And so I hope that Your Paternity will continue sharing with me many such advocates capable of relieving my spiritual poverty with their prayers. And may you also ever fare well in that welfare which is through and in Christ our Lord.

Your Paternity's fellow servant and brother in Jesus,

PETRUS FABER

Mainz, June 14, 1543

• XIII •

To Gerhard Kalckbrenner, Prior of the Cologne Carthusians, on Spiritual Difficulties in Midlife

Mainz, July 10, 1543
MonFabri, 208–213 (Epist. 70)

Particularly touching and intimate is this letter in which Favre joins the Carthusian prior in struggling with the stubborn limitations experienced midway on the spiritual journey.

Reverend and dear Father and Brother in Christ:

The grace and peace of our Lord Jesus Christ be with Your Paternity always.

From Your Paternity's entire letter and from nearly every sentence in it, I clearly see that there is no reply I could make which would satisfy your desires. If only I could hope to answer with deeds—for who could find a way to still that hunger of Your Paternity's, which only the divine Word can still, and he only in the glory of heaven? And who could slake that thirst which yearns towards all the waters of the divine Spirit? I refer to giving satisfaction through my ministry, inasmuch as Your Paternity says that you anticipate getting true instruction from me. Your Paternity should see and consider some way, so that we can share our riches and our indigence with each other, and then we can begin to discuss which of us should undertake the other's instruction. I will surely not be the one to go first; or rather, I will be convinced that Your Paternity needs less help than I and would make do with some briefer remedy and help than I would.

I hardly see what I can say for Your Paternity's consolation. I am sure you have long since grasped the rudiments of the spirit, so that in this respect about all I could try to do would be to make a student of rhetoric into one of grammar, or a student of logic into one of terms. But would this not be against Paul's words where he says, "Forgetting what lies behind, I strain toward what lies ahead" [Phil. 3:13]? Moreover, we see how hard it is for someone who has had a taste of higher gifts to come back afterwards to those he may have skipped over, and in which he should have long before sought greater perfection. Just as it happens in other disciplines that people advance by leaps, so in the path of the spirit it sometimes comes about that people make leaps—for example, when someone wishes for the light of life before he has been cleansed from the darkness of death; or when he wishes to experience the sweetness of life in his heart before he has received enlightenment in order to know the means thereto. It similarly happens that some persons are racked with desires for the purest affections in the spirit long before they have any wish to experience sufferings and mortifications in the body. All that I have been trying to get at here can be summed up if we say that many of us, indeed almost all of us, long far earlier and far more eagerly for our interior than for our exterior perfection.

I do not mean that our end, and the highest things, ought not to be our first concern. What I mean is that we tend to complain about our not yet experiencing the highest things instead of grieving that we are poorly equipped with the means thereto. The result is that we become impatient of the means by which one comes to die in our excessive haste to obtain the resurrection. We test the beating of our heart to see whether or not compunction is piercing it, and have not yet learned to endure the piercing of our body, or hardships or pains. We grieve at not resting in rest itself, and have still not reached the road which leads to that rest and must be sought in toil. We ask for many excellent things, and do not persevere in yearning for anything until we win it. And so we abandon this path and move on to the one that consists in seeking—and do not even persist all the way to the end of our seeking, that is, until we find at least some trace of what we seek. From here we move on to knocking at the door; and because we may have received some response in accord with the desires of our initial request, we now decide there is no more powerful means than sheer knocking, and that there is no way we can go forward unless the door is opened for us. Let this wisely be our only and abiding hunger and thirst, namely, that the door be opened to us, and in this way let us strive for divine realities and for them to penetrate us.

As a result the crusts of food or drink which are got by begging have no savor for us. As a result, those gifts which are casually trod underfoot, and which are found by seeking, are as nothing to the palate of our will—and yet we keep on asking and we keep on seeking, but as people who do not expect to receive anything by these measures, who do not believe that we can obtain anything by these means. We do it only so as to avoid self-reproach; we do it by way of keeping up an excellent practice; we do it to pass the time; we do it to avoid thoughts or some other ills; and indeed we do it well in many ways. But we fail to aim at the one thing we should be searching out in all this; namely, the very grace of thinking well, speaking well, acting well. By "well" I mean not first sweetly, and then clearly, and then strongly; but "well" in this sense: first strongly, second, clearly, third sweetly. In the first, we should not have flagged until all our natural bodily powers could be perfected, after once being repaired. In the second, we should willingly tarry for as long as it takes our minds to be in some measure repaired and perfected; for it is thereby that one reaches the restoration, calming, and quiet of the spirit's inward affections as well.

But what is the point of all this? The point, my Father, is to show that it is difficult for me—and possibly for Your Paternity—to be fitted under any art other than the Holy Spirit himself, who alone knows well our coming in and our going out, our going forward and our going back; who alone knows the mansions of our souls.

The case is perhaps different with persons who are just beginning the journey of the spirit and have not yet emerged from the bitterness of their sins—or even with persons who have not yet begun the journey. But for us poor sinners who are every day beginning, every day making progress, and every day getting some glimpse of our perfection, and have still not made a beginning but are constantly slipping backwards—who will prescribe some method for us? We have perhaps received much new wine, but the wineskins of our bodies and souls are still old. We have received many patches of new cloth, and have thus tried to repair our garments, which are of shabby cloth indeed. But who will hope to find enough patches of a size to make a complete garment? And even if by seeking they could be found, where is the tailor who will promise a decent-looking garment? We ought to have thrown away our old shabby garment first, and steadily sought another. We ought to have sought new wineskins and discarded the old ones before we received the wine. The danger is that in not seeking until now new vessels in which to transfer the wine, we may find our toil doubled. Similarly, in seeking a complete new garment we risk losing the patches that were already sewn onto our shabby garment. Well then, Your Paternity will say, must we abandon hope, we who every day behave wisely and foolishly, we who die and live without ever truly dying or ever truly beginning to live? Are we then worse off, you will say again, than the people who seem not yet ever to have begun dying or living? Certainly, I have not lost hope for us or for people like us (such as perhaps Master Daniel's father, the lord vicar). All I mean is that I have no art by which to repair these things which declare in how many ways they are deficient—indeed, it may even be that something needs to be added or taken away by that very light in which these deficiencies are seen. In this, however, I think Your Paternity can be more easily helped than I, because your complaint is only of nature and of duties which are lawful for nature—that is, hindrances arising from your bodily nature or some duty laid upon you in accordance with God's will. Would that my own hindrances consisted in this kind of necessities, so that I could justly pray, "From my necessities deliver me, O Lord" [Ps. 25:17].

With us, it is unnecessary things, it is vices, which hinder our spirit, not the spirit's body or the conditions laid upon it in its origin. Up till now, it is not original sin or the concupiscences it has left in me which torment me, for I still have the residue of my own acts—or at least habits—of mortal and venial sin which I have not yet expelled. I have not yet caught sight of my own natural state in which I was born, for I am still clad with the nature of sin and death which I got, not from Adam, but by the practice of my vices.

Would that I had by now returned to the goods and evils I had just after my baptism. Would that it were not my own actual sloth hindering my body and the executive power of my faculties, but rather some suffering or natural impairment given me by the Creator's will—and similarly with the other hindrances of my bodily or spiritual senses.

May Your Paternity pray for a man who has no obstacle to any kind of good deed, good thought, or good will outside his own spirit. Have pity for this man more than for yourself. But may you be strengthened in the Lord and in the power of Christ's humility. May you be consoled and refreshed, may you increase in joy and exultation; for you have no evil in which there is not true welfare, no trouble in which there is not solid peace, no hunger in which there is not solid food, no thirst which does not end at the fountains of the Savior. Grace will not fail Your Paternity, seeing you have begun, and wish to begin, so well. And if grace is not enough, God is yet kind and will grant you peace as well—peace, I say, at first in his cross and finally in his resurrection, through Jesus Christ our Lord. In him may Your Paternity fare well in every way, and forgive me for going on and saying in a plethora of words what could have been said in one; namely, that I long to be aided by Your Paternity as much as you hope to be aided by me—and that, no matter what I may have said, I have not lost hope for either of us. For he who is all things in everyone cannot fail to be present in many ways to me in and through Your Paternity, through Christ our Lord.

Yours in Jesus Christ glorified,
PETRUS FABER

• XIV •

To Cornelius Wischaven, on the Superiority of Hearing Confessions over Liturgical Singing
Cologne, January 24, 1544
MonFabri, 240–243 (*Epist.* 80)

Wischaven's employment was to sing the Gospels at numerous Masses, acting as a deacon. Favre urged him to transfer his energies to more directly spiritual work. Wischaven later became an outstanding Jesuit.

To Cornelius Wischaven

Dearest brother in Jesus Christ:

The grace and peace of the Lord Jesus Christ be always in our hearts.

Master Lambert[Duchâteau]'s letter will give you an account of our journey; from it you will learn that under God's protection and guidance we landed safe and sound at Cologne. So give thanks with us to the Most High, and also to all those friends of ours known to you there who prayed and interceded for us to Jesus our savior. At the same time, ask them not to cease praying for us: we need just as much spiritual assistance while physically secure in the city as we did when exposed to the danger of physical banditry en route, for in every place there are enemies of our souls and thieves who are out to steal and pillage our souls' goods.

Here I must perforce urge you to think over whether it would be a better thing for you to go back to your office of singing the Gospel in St. Peter's church, or to devote as much of your being as can belong to Christ to the activity of helping souls which you have begun. Of course my personal inclination would be for you to obey those who have been repeatedly begging you to resume your old office. In fact, through Mynheer van Heeze they have asked me to bid you do so if I have any influence on you. My reason and judgment, however, tell me only one thing: that we must be zealous for the better gifts [1 Cor. 12:31]. And you will be doing a greater good if you devote your whole self to strengthening souls gratis than if you withdraw half of yourself for the office which you resigned. I would think differently if you were unable to find any spiritual occupations. Those gentlemen have good and commendable arguments on their side; and even without arguments they might command our obedience, for you know how much we owe in Christ to the reverend dean, who is chiefly concerned with this matter. So I would have your personal inclination be the same as mine, but also have you do what reason urges. After all, they will continue their search and eventually find someone to perform the office as well as you.

Be steadfast, then, in pursuing whatever promises greater glory, gain, and advantage in Christ and for Christ. Do not look at what is merely permissible when you have before your eyes and hands something that with God is more than permissible. Never ask what God permits, but what he wants. Do not be one of those who, provided it does no harm to their consciences or to God's honor, wholly give themselves to doing everything they can for men's sake: they want to please men; they cling to temporal things so far as this is permissible and allowed. Instead, be one of those who wish to give themselves wholly to serving Christ in the measure of their knowledge and ability—those who resolve to please the Most High to the extent that the body and senses permit—just as the others long to serve flesh and blood with their body and senses to the extent that the Most High permits. No more. Farewell, dear Cornelius, and take strength in Christ Jesus our Lord.

Cologne, January 24, 1544

Your sincere brother and fellow servant in Christ,

PETRUS FABER

[A long postscript with greetings to various persons is here omitted.]

• XV •

To Cornelius Wischaven, on How to Hear Confessions
Cologne, late January 1544
MonFabri, 245–252 (*Epist.* 82)

The following is an extremely important document on how Favre conceived the crucial ministry of hearing confessions.

In questioning a penitent, the first thing is to find out whether his last confession was full and complete, so that in this confession he need only mention what has happened since then.

The confessor should also find out whether he made whatever satisfaction the previous confessor told him was needed, and whether he performed the penance imposed on him.

On the one hand, there is nothing wrong with letting a penitent whose conscience you have not yet come to know make his confession in his own way, following the usual procedure of going through the commandments, the deadly sins, the five senses, and so on. However, it would be more helpful and salutary to ask the sinner to start off by accusing himself of what he himself considers his worst sin. Almost everyone is conscious of being weighed down by one sin more than others; if the penitent is not, he should be instructed on the basis of what he confesses in his general confession. If he does name a specific sin, he should go on to give the times, places, and circumstances, stating particularly (so far as he can) how often he committed it and in how many ways. Then he should do the same for his second-worst sin, and so on. He should be helped with this and freed from any reticence arising from shame.

In questioning penitents about sins of the flesh, you should choose your words carefully, so that those with experience of the matter will understand but innocent persons will be unable to learn from your words what they had not learned by doing the thing.

In general, try to get the penitent to look into himself and state his own sins without fear and without any intimidation stemming from your words. However, you should not merely ask questions about the penitent's obligations under divine law and the precepts of the Church; you should also examine him carefully on his particular duties and the actions to which he is bound by his state of life.

With penitents who practice frequent confession and Communion and who are not in the state of mortal sin, you should recommend a detailed accounting so that they themselves can correct any faults they may have by way of action, speech, thought, or omission.

They should be especially urged to avoid tepidity; they should be led to more advanced and higher levels of the holy struggle and of Christian upbuilding. Even if they think they are securely fortified against their enemies' assaults, they should not think that this means they have completed the gospel tower which Christ tells us we should build.

The causes and occasions of their sins should be examined with a view to their removal; namely, conversations, places where they sin, and other factors which lead to the habit of sin. This is especially important with someone who has become enslaved to habitual sin.

It is especially important for boys and girls to root out self-abuse. They should be questioned about this, seriously but circumspectly. This vice has infected the whole world, particularly now with so many people having cut back or completely given up on frequent auricular confession.

It is also essential to examine them about their intentions in their state of life, their activities and pursuits, their associations, studies, conversations—their entire lives. They should be asked what their purpose is in living, in studying, in traveling, or begging, or amassing material goods. It will not be hard to discern the person's intentions and inclinations from the things that are on his mind.

He should be asked about matters of clothing, of affluence or poverty; about the instruction of his family members or other persons he is responsible for; about his administration of material goods; about how he uses his time, the hours of the day and of the night, and so forth.

If they confess any sin, they should be asked whether they have deeply repented of it; meanwhile they should be led to a sorrow arising from genuine acknowledgment of how they have gone astray.

Where anything involving satisfaction or retribution comes up, you must specifically deal with it and resolve it before going any further in case you mistrust your own memory. St. Gregory's *Pastoral Care* will be helpful for all these matters.

Afterwards care must be taken to establish the penitent solidly in all those good resolves which directly oppose his resolves when he was sinning or wanted to sin. Here effective exhortation is needed to ensure that the penitent does not retreat from a genuine and effective resolution to correct all the sins of which he acknowledges himself guilty.

Instead, it is important to introduce the penitent to a new and superior system of life. Once he has been shown a better way of living, together with guidelines for engaging in lawful and godly actions, he will become more courageous in holding fast to a course that is opposed to his sins. This said, it remains true that sometimes you simply cannot directly persuade a person to abandon a given sin and adopt the opposite course—for example, in the case of an enmity or a sinful liaison. In such cases, you should deflect the penitent's mind from this topic on which he is impervious to reason, and talk to him instead about other matters, such as death or God's gifts to him, or else urge him to praise God for having given him this or that grace. Once you have in this way led him higher towards fear or love of God, it will be easier for him to reject what before seemed so important to him: fleshly pleasure, honor, and the like.

You should get from him an express commitment to keep the precepts of the Church: hearing Mass every Sunday and feast day, fasting on the days designated by the Church, and so forth.

A penitent who confesses sinning against these commandments should be asked whether he has also sinned against faith by not believing that in the absence of a legitimate excuse these are mortal sins. He should be instructed until his mind adheres firmly to the truth, and then until he is firmly committed to effectively keeping the Church's precepts in the future.

In sum, you should endeavor to set the penitent straight on any matter where he has been going wrong. He should not leave you until he has reached a proper frame of mind regarding works of penance against his own sensuality, regarding the worship and honoring of God and the saints, and finally regarding his duties towards his neighbor.

He should be given specific instructions on prayer: what, when, and how. He should settle how often and on what days he will go to confession to a priest and receive sacramental Communion. He should be given definite guidelines for almsgiving.

It is indispensable that you teach your penitents how to apply their prayers and other good works. Many persons pray a lot and do many good things, but without an awareness of to whom and for whom or what they are praying.

You should teach them three sequences they can use for their prayers and meditations. First, they should know the Litanies for invoking God and the saints on their own and others' behalf, or for any need.

Secondly, you should teach them the chief mysteries of the life and passion of Jesus Christ our Lord, through which they can call upon the heavenly Father, the Son, the Holy Spirit, and all the saints. Third, they should be taught the elements of the catechism (the commandments of God, the precepts of the Church, the deadly sins and the contrary virtues), for these show them what they ought to believe and do, what they ought to detest, and what they ought to pray for. With these elements, it will be easy for them to formulate a variety of petitions for themselves and others, or give thanks, or ask mercy not only for the living but also for the dead, on whose behalf we can pray God to remit any punishment they still owe for offenses against the first commandment, the second commandment, and so on; or for any sin of pride which has not yet been effaced, and similarly of other sins; similarly with the senses, the works of mercy, the articles of faith, and so on; likewise the virtues which they made insufficient efforts to acquire when alive, and the like.

You should give your penances not just with a view to their making satisfaction for their previous life but also to their improving their lives in the future. As a penance you could give them something to memorize; for this, however, you need to leave sufficient time, prescribing that they learn the Ten Commandments or the articles of faith by such and such a day. Or you could direct them to visit churches to obtain indulgences, or hospitals and prisons to practice the works of mercy; or to make genuflections in various places before images of the mysteries of God or of his saints; or to hear Mass on weekdays. A given penitent might be told to furnish some poor person with clothes, or see to the adornment of some saint's relics in a church where they are not honored (with the permission, of course, of those responsible for them).

They should also be given methods for commemorating the events of the life and passion of Christ and the saints; this can be done using Our Fathers or Hail Marys.

In cases where we cannot impose the full and complete fast according to the custom of the Church, it would be proper if we tried to impose at least some abstinence, for instance, from cooked food at Friday supper one or more times, or the like, depending upon the person's constitution or situation. It would be good if the person abstained from even just a single dish, or at a single meal abstained from wine or a favorite food.

Besides obligatory penances, we can give others which the person could merit by observing but incur no guilt by omitting. We could give certain exercises of prayer or meditation for each day of the week. A person could be told, "Each night before going to bed and each morning before leaving your bedroom, say three Our Fathers for these three or four principal sins: in the morning, that you will not fall into the sin all that day, and in the evening that God will forgive any wrong you find you have fallen into, and will also preserve you throughout the night." Tell the person to do this, keeping in mind that he is to give you an account the following week, should you tell him to come back to you.

Above all, you need to seek the anointing of the Holy Spirit, which will be readily granted you if you ask for it earnestly. In hearing and handling confessions, you should always be meek and forbearing, preserving a spirit of gentleness, never giving admittance to the spirit of bitterness or any spirit of annoyance at a penitent's irritating behavior. You must never let this great and holy work become a source of annoyance to you, for we stand in the place of Christ, who bears the sin of the world. We must make sure that no sinner is ever made to feel bad in the very place where he came for the sole purpose of being examined, instructed, and judged by us, to whom he has come as the representatives of the gentle Christ. Let us avoid any Pharisaic superciliousness and a judgment which ends up alienating the person. So far as we can, we should never let a person leave us who would not willingly come back.

Sometimes it is necessary to be hard, but we should make sure that our parting is on good terms, except in cases where the person absolutely refuses to give up his sins. Such people may never be given absolution; for example, persons who live in concubinage, or practice usury, or refuse to pay debts they are capable of paying.

For frequent backsliders, the best help is frequent confession and Communion with the same priest.

Also: a method for examining themselves on the particular sins together with their occasions.

Also: some good works by way of mortification in the areas in which the temptations of the world arise. If sinners can be encouraged to do this, the devil realizes he is going to be resisted and will not attack them on the old ground so readily or so often. When they come back to confession, they should be closely reexamined on how they behaved since their last confession in regard to their particular sins and temptations; they should be encouraged to persevere by being shown the results that are ensuing. Even if their temptations seem on the rise, they should be encouraged to hope that they will eventually be freed from them altogether. Even if the most that is accomplished is that they do not fall into mortal sin, we should not get discouraged in our efforts with these penitents.

We should right away point out to people new ways of growing in virtue, but in the meantime consider it well worth our while if we can keep within the boundaries of God's way a person who had been outside it. Christ would still die for this alone, and he comes to our soul.

Why should we then be so demanding that we fail to realize that it is a great thing in God's eyes for a person even to come to frequent confession nowadays?

It is a fine thing to receive Holy Communion; it is finer if the person waits until you give your approval; this is a source of suffering to him and he reaps many other benefits he would lose if he did not go to confession. Charity is patient, is kind; it believes all things, hopes all things, suffers all things, endures all things. Charity never fails.

• XVI •

To Wendelina Van den Berg, on the Vocation of Her Stepson Peter Canisius
Cologne, February (?) 1544
MonFabri, 253–255 (*Epist.* 83)

Favre's greatest recruit to the Jesuit order was Peter Canisius of Nijmegen. In this letter we see the combination of charity and firmness with which he counters the indignation of Canisius's loving stepmother.

Very dear and honored lady in Christ the Lord:

You complain that Master Peter Canisius, who has hitherto always been the dearest of sons to you, has now turned altogether unnatural—and wholly, as you believe, through my doing. I, on the other hand, when I see this fine, virtuous young man so closely joined to me by the closest bond of spirit and love, and almost one with me in unity of mind and will, can only wish from my heart the best of everything for him, to the point where I also consider myself wholly under obligation to all of his relatives and kin. And by his kin I mean not solely those bound to him by the bond of Christian union and evangelical perfection, but also those who are his dear ones and relatives according to the flesh. This is why I earnestly and often supplicate and pour forth prayers to Almighty God for the soul of his father, lately departed in Christ, as well as for your own consolation and for your children and relatives.

"Is that so?" you will say; "then why have you called Master Peter away from us, when you knew how much counsel, assistance, and consolation we derived from his presence?" But I ask you, Christian lady, what would you do if you beheld on one side Jesus Christ desiring to take delight, enjoyment, and satisfaction in Master Peter's mind and spiritual progress, and on the other his dear ones and relatives according to the flesh longing by every means to glory in his fleshly presence and in his possession of fleeting and transitory goods? Certainly, if only you would admit me as an impartial judge in this case, there was nothing I could do better than desire to see him encouraged in his spiritual strivings, at the same time as I sought no advantage for myself through him and made sure that not one farthing of his estate should be converted to my use.

The whole issue, as I understand it, has to do with temporal goods. Few give any thought to the fate of Master Peter's soul, but many are gravely upset that the inheritance coming to him should be alienated. We grieve at one bit of soil being divided from another; we do not grieve at our own souls being withdrawn and torn away from their creator God, to cling to whom is supreme felicity. In any case, to my knowledge absolutely none of his temporal property has up to this point come into my possession—something I would rather die than see happen. God is faithful, and I trust that for his own glory he has made me also faithful in not even being able to contemplate seeking my own advantage in temporal things.

"Then why," you will say, "do you not prevent him from doing what you know will be extremely distressing to us all?" I do not know just how much he has withdrawn from the property in question. However, to speak my mind candidly, I cannot disapprove of what he has done. As I understand it, the property that you claim has been alienated was in fact devoted to religious and charitable purposes. Consequently, if we want to argue the matter, the property should not be thought of as having been alienated but rather restored to its true and rightful owner, God, to whom everything within the confines of this world belongs. And what actually is the crime here? You can be assured that the furnishings he took with him are with him and in his possession. Our little congregation has other ambitions; our Society covets other gains than that it should desire to heap up what will perish and be consumed in flames.

As to other reports that are spread about me, I deem them too foolish to be given credence by you—especially since I believe you to be persons who fear God and have learned to think only good of your neighbor. If they accuse me of being unknown and a foreigner, I confess it. I am a foreigner like all my ancestors—I am a foreigner on the territory of this province and I shall be a foreigner in every land to which God's goodness may lead me for as long as I live. My only effort and aspiration is that I might be a member of the household of God and fellow citizen of the saints.

• XVII •

To Francis Xavier, on Favre's Activities in Cologne
Cologne, May 10, 1544
MonFabri, 262–265 (Epist. 88)

To Xavier, in distant India, Favre wrote this matter-of-fact account of his work of preaching, hearing confessions, giving the Spiritual Exercises, andinterceding with the Emperor on behalf of the Catholic Church in Cologne. The letter helps dispel the erroneous impression sometimes given that Favre's only apostolate was individual spiritual direction.

May the grace and peace of Christ our Lord be always present and felt in our souls.

The last account I wrote you about my activities was at the end of January. Now I will summarize for you what has been happening since then. I shall do so under four headings. First, I would like to inform you that since returning from Brabant and seeing that I would have to stay some time here in Cologne, I began preaching in a school on Septuagesima Sunday and have continued doing so until now without a break on every Sunday or feast of any importance. I likewise preached on the Passion throughout Holy Week, except for one day, and throughout Easter Week, although the sermons on the Resurrection were not all in one place. My audience were mainly the university students, clerics, canons, some doctors of law, some licentiates in theology, some consuls of the city, the reverend archbishop of Lund, and other prominent persons who know Latin. The suffragan bishop and various other persons attended occasionally. I have been several times invited outside the school, in a chapter house (the second of the city) and in monasteries. I twice preached in a monastery of nuns, among whom, as I was told by their confessor, a licentiate in theology, there are some twenty or thirty who understand Latin.

Secondly, during this time I heard numerous students' confessions, occasioned by the sermons. Aided by Mosén Alvaro, I have had some ten or twelve who come regularly every Sunday, or at least every other week, and they regularly receive Communion. This has had a good effect, even upon certain secular persons and prominent ladies of the city who had been doing the same but, seeing it not much approved of, had begun to grow cool. In particular, a number of students whose faith had been corrupted have come to a genuine resurrection and acknowledgment of their errors. On Easter one of the city's consuls had himself and part of his family communicated by us in the principal parish of the city, where Mosén Alvaro and I said Mass and gave Communion to numerous laypersons, to the common folk's delight.

Thirdly, a young man, son of a prominent widow in the city, entered the Exercises; he made such progress that he did not stop until he had made a clear and specific determination to join our Society. He completed the Exercises in Holy Week. A cleric, who has long been a pastor outside the city, withdrew from all his occupations and came to spend ten or twelve days at our house, a period which he has now completed. He ended his general confession with me yesterday. He is a man of about fifty. I cannot find words or comparisons for the great and profound knowledge of Christ our Lord which he has received. He ceaselessly shows deep humility not only towards me but towards those who first told him about us, including Master Lambert [Duchâteau] and Mosén Alvaro. He praises God our Lord for the mercy done him by his divine Majesty in not letting him die before his soul had experienced what it did during the Exercises. His intention is to go ahead with them to the end. God knows whether I will be able to stay here that long or not. A dean, the second after that of the principal church, fell sick several days ago. After being visited by the reverend prior of the Carthusians, this man became very eager to have a visit from me, and so I went to his house. I have been there several times, and on other occasions have sent Master Peter Canisius. As a result, a true desire of conversion has been observed in him; he had been noted for his vanities and scandalous sins, being a prelate, a young man, and a doctor of civil and canon law. Yet he has decided to set aside all his business and dealings with people in order to withdraw for a few days to receive the Exercises, at least those of the First Week, and he is utterly resolved to give a good example of himself to the world in the future.

The soldier who was staying with Mosén Alvaro when I arrived has received the Exercises of the First Week and made his general confession. He is now working for us in the kitchen.

Fourthly, I shall mention a few miscellaneous items. A prominent lady in the city, a widow, is being strongly moved to enter religious life. She has asked my counsel. Even though all her acquaintances, learned doctors, and confessors advise her against it, she finds no peace with what the majority tell her, possessing strong interior inspirations of the good spirit to become a religious. Pray to God our Lord for her, for we are also obligated to her because of many good works she has done and is doing for us. There is likewise another lady who has put us under even greater obligation to pray for her because of the many measures she has taken for our corporal maintenance, even donating to us ornaments for an altar so we can say Mass. To these and some other laypersons who do not know Latin I have given talks through an interpreter. We also write letters to various places—Louvain, Liège, and elsewhere—where there is need for support or strengthening.

Upon his return from his native country, Master Peter Canisius brought along three young men to receive guidance in the service of Christ our Lord. They have come to me for confession, and two of them are already friars in the Carthusian house here. We have also rented a house where eight of us are now living, provided with all we need for our maintenance and expenses. From this you can gather how many good deeds are done for us by various persons here in the city who have been donating things to us entirely out of love for Christ our Lord: household equipment, cloth, beds, and other necessary items.

Of the good to the commonwealth being wrought by our Lord through the instrumentality of my collaboration with the university and clergy of Cologne in opposition to the heresies here, I say nothing because it is beyond my explaining. What I do know is what enormous trouble we take in writing to His Majesty's court. Were it not for what we have written, this city might have been lost by now. For this reason also I am somewhat more exposed to physical danger than anyone else here. May he who alone is the creator, redeemer, and glorifier of the whole world be praised and acknowledged in everything and for everything; may his grace and strength never be idle in us. Amen.

Cologne, May 10, 1544

Your brother in our Lord,

PEDRO FABRO

• XVIII •

Aids to Individual Self-Reformation

Probably Spring 1544
Revue d'Ascétique et Mystique 36 (1960): 346–349

According to its editor, Michel de Certeau, it was probably to the Cologne Carthusians, to whom he had also given a copy of the Exercises, that Favre gave these spiritual instructions as an aid to their work on behalf of spiritual reform. They are somewhat more demanding than the "Chapters" of 1541 (see above, pages 326–330).

The following points will be helpful for an individual person's self-reformation.

1. Taking for granted the faith transmitted to him by the sound teaching of the Roman Catholic Church, what will chiefly help him in beginning his life anew will be to make a careful review of his past life, year by year, and in bitterness of soul to make a general confession of all his sins. For this purpose he should make use of an excellent physician and advisor, to the extent that one can eventually be found. For the

more strongly he experiences remorse for his past errors, illusions, risks, unwittingnesses, frailties, and other similar evils of his previous life committed towards God, his soul, and his neighbor, the stronger a motivation he will be able to attain for leading a good life in the future.

2. Each night before going to bed, he should always reserve a half hour for exercising his spirit in interior matters. At a minimum, he should always include the following: he should regularly examine his conscience, in order to be able to reprove and accuse himself before God and correct his behavior for the following day. He should do this with a desire for steady growth on the path of good, by taking on additional internal, or even external, devotions by way of pious works or contemplations or prayers. If he cannot always be multiplying these because he is already making ample use of them, he should at least be sure to grow spiritually in the performance of those he has.

The examination itself can be made in the form and regular method indicated on the top of the second page of the Exercises: "How to Make the Daily Examen." After finishing the examination, he can plan out his spiritual and corporal good works for the following day.

3. Whether priest or layman, he should set himself a definite day for receiving Communion, and in all he does he ought to keep in mind that he is going to receive the Sacrament at such and such a time. If a priest, he should never let a week pass without communicating and offering the sacrifice of the Mass. Those unable to celebrate I also advise, with St. Augustine, to receive Communion every Sunday. A layman who went a month without receiving Communion I would hesitate to consider firmly resolved to persevere in the way of acquiring spiritual virtues. As to those who receive only on the principal holy days, I admit that they do more than the Catholic Church absolutely requires, but I could not at first blush make any other general judgment about them—except that they lack sufficient fear of falling into sin, since they so rarely have recourse to him who strengthens the weak, enlightens the ignorant, and gives our consciences security against evils. Anyone who deliberately refrains from Communion until Eastertide immediately declares himself guilty of being unaware of the value of Communion, or of having no wish for God's grace except for short periods. For I hardly think it possible that a person immersed in worldly affairs and in constant contact with sinners could persevere in walking along God's way in the strength of this divine food when received only once in a year. And what shall I say of those who do not receive even once a year? At Eastertide, when one of the two prisoners must be publicly set free, those who do not receive Communion clearly shout for all to hear, "Not this man, but Barabbas!"

4. Make sure the person has a little booklet written in a language he understands, containing in order all the commandments to which he is bound under mortal sin; namely, the Ten Commandments of the law, the five precepts of the Church, and in addition all the other duties of his profession, state of life, rank, office, and so on. Having this book, he should be careful to read it, or have it read to him, every day.

5. He should have some special daily exercises: some pious corporal or spiritual works of mercy and some others by way of contemplations. To be thoroughly provided with matter for these, it will help him to have (in addition to the points mentioned in the next paragraph) a brief and orderly sequence of Christ's life, death, resurrection, and present enthronement at the Father's right hand, from his incarnation all the way through to the end. Likewise, he should have another sequence for invoking the saints, beginning with Trinity of persons and continuing with the Mother of God, the angels, the precursors of Christ, the patriarchs, the apostles who followed Christ, the martyrs who suffered for him, the confessors who bore witness to him, the monks who sought out the desert in order to keep him always, the virgins who were continent for his sake, his widows, and so forth.

6. He should keep before his eyes a few general axioms and principles for the pursuit of perfection:

Overcome yourself.

Abide within yourself.

Remember the last things: death, judgment, hell, and paradise.

Always be hot or cold through fear or love; never be lukewarm, having neither of these.

Always hunger or thirst after justice, that is, strongly yearn for knowledge of divine things and for inward spiritual perceptions regarding Christ.

Ask, seek, and knock, in order to obtain all spiritual goods.

Do not consider human judgments against Christ's servants, but always have regard for their good consciences.

Rejoice when various trials befall us.

Deny yourself and bear your own cross daily.

Never look back, but always stride forward; for not to mount up is to fall back, not to advance is to retreat, and so forth.

• XIX •

To Guillaume Postel, on Persevering in the Humility of a Novice
Evora, December 3, 1544
MonFabri, 280–284 (*Epist.* 93)

Guillaume Postel was a brilliant and eccentric French humanist and orientalist who had known the first Jesuits at the University of Paris. He later spent some time as a Jesuit novice in Rome. There he bethought himself to write an enthusiastic letter to a fellow humanist, Nicolas Clénard, who, however, was five years dead at the time. The letter came to Favre's hands, and he wrote the following reply, obviously making an effort to match himself to Postel's temper.

Pierre Favre to his brother in Christ Guillaume Postel:

Greetings and all health which is in the name of Jesus.

We have seen the letter, dearest Guillaume, which you wrote on the seventh of the Calends of September to Nicolas Clénard. Blessed be God who has finally restored you not only to yourself but to all your friends. Towards Clénard you may indeed seem to have remained long asleep; but no wonder, seeing that by your own admission you have never until now been truly alive to yourself, nor to the citizens of heaven, nor to Christ. How could a man who was dead to all these have carried on frequent correspondence with even the dearest of mortals? Clénard would perhaps have found this excuse more convincing than the one you offer, that of distance and the lack of reliable messengers. At least I believe this is what he would say if he were able. However, he is far more certainly lacking in messengers than you are and far more certainly aware that "between you and him there is fixed a great abyss" [Luke 16:26]. Since you last heard of him, beloved Guillaume, he has lost his very hands; all power to write and answer letters has been taken from him. You, as one returning from the dead, shall be said to have arisen to render every good service to your friends; but he has now dwelt half a decade among the dead, not among us.

Men called to the same form of life—yet how differently now each hears the voice which called him! You claim you have let thirty-four years slip by without accomplishing, or even beginning, anything worthy of God. What would Clénard say to that? He would perhaps say that he died before ever having performed a single duty of a Christian man. Oh, if only this dead man were given paper, hand, and voice to reply word for word to your letter! Would he not confirm his Postel in the goodness and truth in which you now abide? Would he not praise your life-decision, your resolve, your vows? What would he think about your now hating the world and yourself? He would surely not disapprove of your bidding farewell to Ibn Sina and Ben Beithar,[5] having himself lost all employment of speech in the tongues of men. He would commend your counting as gain your holy conversation there, which passes over into the fellowship of holy spirits. For who truly knows how to value an entirely Christian life except one who dwells and converses with those above? Whether we suppose Clénard to be already in glory where we aspire to go, or to be tormented in the fires of purgatory because he did not hold to the path which lies open before us, he cannot but consider you blessed and happy in Christ and want to see you consolidated as firmly as possible in your resolve.

I do not present these things in Clénard's name as if you needed the advice or authority of the dead. You have the law; you have the prophets; you have Christ our Lord; you have the spirit of all wisdom and knowledge—anyone who does not hear these will not believe even if the dead should arise. My reason for making such mention of the departed Clénard was to let you know that your letter was capable not only of urging us who read it to go forward, but also of moving to tears or raising to greater glory the very dead to whom you unwittingly sent it.

And so, my beloved Guillaume in Christ, continue growing stronger in what we are told you have so happily begun. Hitherto your aim has been to make this beginning; from now on strain your eyes towards the goal of your labors. As long as you had not begun, you were immune to fears about the labors of perseverance; it would also be useless now to cajole you by telling you that even the best beginnings need to gain the crown which is bestowed only at the end. "End" has nearly the same connotation as "perfection." Go forward, then, to perfection in everything. Thus, if you have already left anything, leave it perfectly. If you have begun to close your eyes or ears or other senses upon a given thing, close them perfectly, never to reopen them upon it. If you have abased yourself in some matter, abase yourself in all. Let your patience also achieve a "perfect work" [James 1:4], so that you may spread wide in the Lord to the left as well as to the right, not only spreading wide in every way but also stretching out to every area of the holy acquirement of spiritual gifts.

Paul says that he forgets the things that are behind and stretches out only to what is before [Phil. 3:13]. We, however, have still not perfectly begun anything, and so must in a way stretch out to the things that are behind if our work is to attain its full perfection. For we still have to achieve that very oblivion, compunction, and detestation for what lies behind. We must grow in knowledge of sin, of vanity, of

---

[5] Favre writes Bembisina (= Avicenna) and Bembitarus, medieval Spanish Arabic writers on medicine, philosophy, and botany.

ourselves. We must form within ourselves scorn and contempt for temporal things. What you dismissed you must more thoroughly dismiss. For this is how there will eventually arise within us the vision, esteem, and comprehension of spiritual and heavenly things, the pursuit of virtue, and the love of God. We were extraordinarily pleased and delighted to hear that you seek the lowest things among your brothers, aiming at what is last and least, for this is surely great gain for you. Greatness of spirit does not consist in loving and embracing on our own great things—the great things of this world—but in stretching out to what is least. A mighty spirit is shown by love for the cross and for nothingness, not by love for power or greatness. So continue to exert yourself in what is least so that you may merit what is greatest in eternal life.

You know that in arithmetic a zero has no value; but you also know that it raises the value of the other digits when placed next to them. Moreover, the other digits, which have a value of their own, increase in value only as they are shunted to the side by others—and the further they are shunted aside, the more their value multiplies. Shall we not all rejoice, then, to know that you who have been added to our number acquire your worth and value through what is of lowest account in this life? Love to be named least by everyone if you wish to acquire for yourself a good name. Remain as long as you can in the last place. Seek out the humblest and most degrading services: you will thereby acquire the highest status in Christ crucified.

We all know that turnips, onions, and many similar products of the earth grow downward, concealing their bulk beneath the earth. We must imitate this in the beginning if we are to be truly rooted in Christ. He became obedient even to death on a cross, after first humbling himself even to the flesh with which he made himself one. If only we would all descend and become one with the lowliest services—or rather servants—in this life so as to grow in the humility to which we have consecrated ourselves. If only we would obey our superiors even to death on a cross. This might come about if—to use your words—we could banish "mine" and "thine" from our borders; and not only that, but if we could also truly banish "I" and "thou," so that Jesus Christ, our creator and redeemer, might reign in us and in others through us—he who reigns in himself with the Father and Holy Spirit, for ever and ever.

Evora, the third of the Nones of December, 1544

P[ETRUS] F[ABER]

• XX •

To the Jesuits of Coimbra, on Obedience
December 1544 (?)
MonFabri, 284–287 (Epist. 94)

In this instruction Favre inculcates a strict subordination of all our activities, however holy and apostolic, to the demands of religious obedience. He then urges sustained charity in the face of others' faults.

Father Master Favre, on Obedience

Obedience must be blind; that is, the truly obedient man must not wait on charity or reason or a sense of the fruitfulness of the work commanded him.

Likewise, when it does happen after all—by our Lord's grace and by dint of our obeying altogether blindly—that a way is opened up for us to know and sense the fruitfulness of what we were commanded, we must take care not to lose the spirit by which we originally inclined ourselves to obey, even if we should be subsequently recalled from our original command and given a contrary one. Thus, a man in obedience must never settle down to rest in any place or in any particular work subject to obedience, even if he experiences a holy and unmistakable spirit for it—not rest in it, I mean, in such a way that he loses his readiness for whatever obedience may enjoin.

Likewise, in a case where the will of the man obeying, informed by charity, desires to undertake something out of much zeal for the great fruit that is clearly to be seen in it, but where obedience commands another course in which no fruit at all can be seen—in such a case it will be good for the man to reflect that he did not take a vow to produce this particular fruit of charity, but a vow of obedience. He should consider that one does not take a vow to save souls following his own opinion, or even following the desires which our Lord may give him, but a vow to do what he is commanded by his superiors.

Likewise, it should be noted that sometimes our Lord, wishing to stretch us for greater good, may on the one hand impel our own will and judgment to consider a given thing good, while on the other hand actually intending that we do the opposite in conformity with the will of the one empowered to command which works should be carried out.

In conclusion, as we said above, obedience ought to be blind, and its execution and consideration must be viewed with eyes that are clear and untroubled by any sensual and worldly affections. We should take as our pattern and goal those words of great perfection which Christ our Lord spoke to us through his evangelist, "Whoever wishes to come after me must deny himself, take up his cross, and follow me" [Matt. 16:24].

That is, we must deny in ourselves all our own wishes and powers, all our own views, will, and judgment. We must instead submit ourselves entirely to the wishes, views, power, will, and judgment of our superiors. We must take up our own cross and not other people's crosses which may seem easier to us. We must do this with all humility and patience, ready to suffer whatever comes from the hand of our Lord. We must follow Jesus Christ with the cross of these labors, for from his hand we hope for their reward, as Scripture says: "If we suffer with him we shall reign with him" [2 Tim. 2:6]. We should not let ourselves be like many or even most men, who go burdened by crosses while following the world and its vanities, and whom at their day's end the same world, in repayment for the service rendered it by means of these crosses, will dispatch to other crosses—real and eternal ones.

It should likewise be noted how essential it is that people who are to live in a company or congregation with other persons should strive to preserve themselves in the good spirit with which they entered the company or congregation, and in the good opinion and conception which they initially had of everybody. And if it should ever happen that they lose that good spirit and the good opinion which they originally had of everyone, they should not rest or be easy until by prayer and other good works they recover that good spirit and opinion, and come to the view that the fault is in myself and not in my neighbors: they are what they have always been, perhaps better; it is I whose mind has changed—or, more accurately, worsened.

Likewise, if I should happen to notice some considerable fault in a member of the company or congregation, it should not make me lose the goodwill which I had up to that point, or allow any bitterness or passion towards him to enter my soul. Otherwise I will give occasion for great agitation in my conscience and disquiet of spirit. I should not even consider passing judgment on my brother—certainly not in conversation with others, but if possible not even in my thoughts. I should recall the words of Christ our Lord, "Man, who has made me judge between you?" [Luke 12:14]. Such people have superiors who are responsible for judging and correcting them. Let it be enough for me to be an impartial judge of my own faults: that will give me plenty of material for judging—and I should never grant myself a pardon for anything. As Seneca says, "Spare others, never yourself." Amen. Amen. Once more Amen.

• XXI •

To the Jesuits of Coimbra, on Friendship in the Lord
Evora, March 2, 1545
MonFabri, 310–314 (*Epist.* 103)

This letter of farewell to the Jesuit scholastics at Coimbra shows Favre's characteristic combination of human tenderness and austere supernaturalism.

The grace of our Lord Jesus Christ and the charity of the Holy Spirit be always in your hearts.

So far I have been unable to give you any definite information about our departure. The King, shortly after I returned here from my stay with you, granted permission to leave but then withdrew it. But, by the Lord's will, as I believe, we have at length overcome the obstacles and have wrung from him what he originally intended when he sent us, namely, that we might proceed to Spain. Pray, therefore, to him who is the life and salvation of all that he will be our companion on all our travels.

The day of our departure from the court here is not settled, but we have good hopes that it will be within the next seven days. Our business is urgent, and so, contrary to my hopes and both my own and your ardent desires, we will not be able to visit you on the way. I regret this intensely, and I suspect it will be a disappointment for your own love towards us. God knows how I would have wished to spend a few days there with you; he too knows what consolation and edification you anticipated from such a visit. But we must both acquiesce in seeing not our own but our Lord's will fulfilled.

And so I am now compelled to do by letter what I would more gladly have done by word of mouth, namely, write you a farewell that will win me a more secure place in your memory. For there is none of you, dearest brothers, who does not know how much I need the prayers of you all. I have no idea for how long I am bidding you farewell. It would perhaps be rash to say that I will again see each of the brothers among you before I die; and it would be a sign of excessive despair if I did not hope ever to be able to enjoy to satiety the company of many among you.

And so fare you well, and always serve Christ the Lord with gladness, for he is the source of all welfare. Let your whole concern be only this: to cling to no one but Jesus, who can never be taken away from you. The physical presence of mortals is sometimes good for us, but quite often an obstacle. And so we should grow used to the kind of company which is wholly of heaven. This passing company is beneficial if it leads us to what is eternal and never passes. The living voice touches and benefits us, but only so long as it turns us inward toward the interior voice that sounds in the heart.

I would say the same of the other senses, which make immediately present the differences among various things; they benefit us most when by their aid we are impelled towards the interior senses of spiritual realities. And we should cultivate these interior senses, my dearest brothers, all the more in the measure that the exterior ones cannot help us forward. And this is a gain indeed, especially for those persons whom Wisdom itself deigns to teach and to whom it is said, "Hearken and see, and incline your ear" [Ps. 45:11]. I have said all this in case there should be any who are overly grieved at having the presence of their friends withdrawn from them. If it was for the good of Christ's apostles that his physical presence should depart, although it was he who brought salvation to the world, will it not be necessary for us that whatever it is by which we are said to be present should depart—not just depart but even perish? Only one medium should remain between any of us: Christ, the mediator between God and men, who is all things in all. It is he that we should keep always present to us, and it is in him that each of us should look for himself and his brother. We should seek each other and mutually behold each other in our origin, our cause, our principle. If anyone wants me present, he should look at me in my price, that is to say, contemplate the price by which I was bought. He should look at the price in the "clefts of the rock" [Song 2:14]. If the one who is redeemed is not visible, then let the redeemer be present—present to the eyes, present to the ears, present in every other way.

So this is where I send you, dearest brothers, as I say fare you well: to the one whose saying farewell makes us fare well indeed, and whose making us fare well confers true welfare—him to whom I would also have prayers arise that your blessing might be of his dew and his fatness [see Gen. 27:28], for there is no other fullness in any creature of which you can all receive [see John 1:16]. May your smell be like that of the plentiful field which was blessed by the Lord Jesus [see Gen. 27:27]. (I here speak of the blessing which I know you want me chiefly to ask for you.)[6] May these blessings come upon you and overtake you. May you be blessed in the field of the Lord, and blessed among the citizens of the heavenly Jerusalem. Blessed be the fruit of your wombs, the fruit of your lips and works; blessed be the barns of your minds and blessed be your stores; blessed be your goings in to your own interior selves and your goings out. May your enemies fall down before your face; if they come out against you one way, may they flee before you

---

[6] What follows is a paraphrase of the blessing of Moses upon Israel in Deuteronomy 28.

seven ways. May the Lord send a blessing upon the storehouses of your three interior powers, and upon all the works of your hands. May he bless you in the institute to which you have bound yourselves, and may he raise you up as a holy congregation for himself. May the Lord open his excellent treasure, the heavens, that he may give your earth spiritual rain in due season. May the Lord and his kingdom be above you, so that your minds may be drawn upwards; may he be within you, so that you may be truly rooted in him; may he be as a firm foundation beneath you, so that you may always rely upon him; may he be at your right side, so that he will never let you swerve to pleasures or vanities; may he be at your left, so that you may never be broken by adversity; may he be behind you, so that through fear of him you will be recalled from any backsliding onwards to your perfection.

But let this be enough. May God do all this, whose spoken blessing effects the good it contains.

As for the questions you sent me, dearest brothers, I have not yet had time to reply to them. If only I had not wasted more hours than would have been required for the task! The fault is mine, then, and I beg you to pray on my behalf to God for it; I know that I badly waste good hours and fail to find hours for good works. And so I say once more: Pray the Lord that his divine Majesty will give me the grace not to waste time, but to have the ability and knowledge and desire to order every moment of my life in conformity to his holy will. I write this part in the vernacular because I want everyone of you, and those who come after you, to beg this grace for me from Christ our Lord, his mother, and all the saints; for my soul experiences no greater need than this.

And now I repeat my wretchedness a third time: help me, all of you, in all the ways I mentioned above and any other as well. Fare you well in Jesus Christ our Lord.

Evora, March 2, 1545

You most loving brother in Christ,

PETRUS FABRI

• XXII •

To King John III of Portugal, on the Death of His Daughter
Valladolid, July 13, 1545
MonFabri, 333–336 (*Epist.* 109)

To the early Society's most generous royal patron Favre wrote this fervent letter of consolation for the loss of the King's daughter Maria, consort of

Prince Philip of Spain, who died giving birth to Philip's ill-fated first son, Don Carlos.

Most high and puissant Lord:

May the grace and peace of Christ our Lord ever shield Your Highness's most serene heart and grant you the strength to drink this latest chalice which our eternal and almighty king, Jesus Christ, has prepared for Your Highness.

His divine Majesty knows what he does, and he himself says through the mouth of his apostle St. Paul that "for those who love God all things work together unto good" [Rom. 8:28]. And so we must be very attentive in order to know how to interpret in good part what comes purely from his hand, taking care not to fall under the sentence "Woe to those who call evil good and good evil, who call darkness light and light darkness" [Isa. 5:20]. Your Highness knows that the most bitter medicines are the most healthful; we must therefore believe that the greatest chastisements sent by Christ our glorifier are the clearest signs and most evident proofs of the secret and ineffable love with which he loves us and governs us. He wounds many with a single blow in order to heal many more. He kills in order to give life. He lets men fall into the depths so he can raise them up and place them very close to himself in heaven. Perhaps his divine Majesty appears severe with Your Highness, and even more with the tender heart of my lady in Jesus Christ, the Queen, beloved mother of her lamented daughter the princess (God rest her soul). But all this is nothing when we consider who it is who does this and when we consider the good that is being enjoyed by her whom we all mourn. If a loving and merciful Lord has willed now to consternate and dismay the whole world only that he might bring to joy and peace one so close to Your Highness, who will dare reproach him? And as he does this, will not Your Highness rejoice at seeing that the creator of the universe wishes to be served at his table by your sons and daughters? "If you loved me," she might well say, "you would rejoice, because I go to the Father [John 14:18]—who is not only greater than I but also greater than you, my parents."

Of her having passed to her heavenly Father there is no room for doubt or concern. May Jesus Christ grant the like grace to all of us who rightly bewail her—ourselves not least among them, since for her sake we came here summoned from distant parts—I from Germany and my companion the licentiate Araoz from the kingdom of Naples—and now are left here below deprived of the protection we enjoyed from her highness. I am unable to bear testimony as an eyewitness to the spirit with which her highness met her death; I have some regret in this regard, namely, that I had so little opportunity to visit her in her moment of need. But there are other witnesses more important and reliable than I who were astonished and deeply edified by the excellent preparations which her highness, providing for and almost foreseeing the dangers, had made before the time of childbirth. The father provincial of the Dominicans, a person deserving of no less praise than that of a saint, was constantly with her. From him and many other persons of like quality further details will be forthcoming on her highness's holy and precious death, and on how well she was prepared for the journey ordained for her by our Lord.

Your Highnesses should draw consolation from this, and no less from the assurance that her resolution had always been to live a good life. This, in my opinion, is a matter of considerable weight, given that nowadays there are other persons of high rank who make such resolutions on their last day in order to die well without ever before in their lives having made a firm determination to live as Christians. It was our Lord's will that her highness not die before experiencing what it was to be a mother, so that she might have more pity on her dear ones of both sexes who remain as orphans here below. Her goodness and meekness could not last amid the thorns of this false and empty world, and so Jesus Christ has chosen her for his company, ordaining that she first leave behind the blessed fruit of her womb.

I have said all this at considerable length, my most serene Lord in Jesus Christ, to show my wish that Your Highnesses, looking upwards, may not give way to flesh and blood beyond what is allowed by nature under the restraint of spiritual reason—for I realize that Your Highnesses will not be wanting in motives to give way to a reason that is purely human and according to the flesh. Blessed be the Lord who gives us reason which is above flesh, and gives us his Holy Spirit, the Paraclete, who is above all reason and without whom no one would ever be able to conform his mind to the will of our infinite God, just and merciful in all that he does and permits. May he deign in his boundless clemency to give Your Highnesses the grace of the ability, knowledge, and desire to raise your spirits towards the things which last forever. The things to which your hearts were in some measure bound go heavenward: your hearts must therefore wander after them. Our Lord does not wish Your Highnesses' treasures to become fixed on this earth lest your hearts be rooted in the earth. The object of our love goes before us, taking a form which we may love without danger, and so we must make no halt here.

Who could recount the tears shed here in the court and city of Valladolid—it would be an unending story and only increase Your Highnesses' sorrow. May Jesus Christ turn all this to the greater good of ourselves and of all those who had devoted such true love and loyalty to her highness. So loud were the cries here in the palace that it seemed as if all Spain lay dying and as if no consolation for anyone remained in this life.

Blessed be the upsetter of hearts, whose will it was to take from us so great a consolation—in his own good time although not in ours. May he be glorified for this and through this, whatever the pain to ourselves. Blessed be he for this by those who know him, however increasingly we see persons who do not know him or know his name of Jesus. May all things proceed as he pleases though all the world be left displeased. May her blessed soul rest in the glory of the saints despite those who anticipated glory through her exile thence. If the Lord chooses to glorify and console her at the price of our desolation and confusion, may everyone, including Your Highnesses, bless and praise him for doing so, for ever and ever. Amen.

Valladolid, July 13, 1545

Your Highnesses' servant and chaplain in Jesus Christ,

PEDRO FABRO

• XXIII •

To Martín Santacruz, Rector of the College of Coimbra, on Bearing Burdens Bravely

Madrid, January 13, 1546
MonFabri, 387–388 (*Epist.* 131)

A letter of encouragement to an overburdened superior.

Dearest brother:

In terms of relations between you and me, that is, of our deep mutual affection—stride constantly forward in all things; do not give way under your labors. And if hardships and the cross multiply and grow, you too must multiply and grow in Christ Jesus. Never ask to have your load lightened, only to have your strength increased. I certainly have an image and picture of the great load you bear, but our Lord gives me hope. In that hope is strength and whatever else you will need. Act manfully then, be of stout heart, and keep up your obedience to God. I say no more.

Your brother in the Lord,

PEDRO FABRI

• XXIV •

To Diego Laínez, on Dealing with Heretics
Madrid, March 7, 1546
MonFabri, 399–402 (*Epist.* 138)

From Trent, Laínez wrote to Favre asking advice on how to deal with the heretics of northern Europe. Favre's answer stresses the importance of personal relations and moral issues over theological argument. He does not suggest force as a means of restoring heretics to the faith.

Dearest brother in Jesus Christ:

May the grace and peace of our redeemer be always in our souls.

I never replied to the request you made in several letters that I send some guidelines for those who wish to save souls among the heretics and help their own. I may fairly claim your pardon, both because I lacked time to think about the matter and because there was no leisure here in the house. At present I might excuse myself by saying that my hand is not as strong as it ought to be—although the best excuse would be to acknowledge that nothing occurs to me that would be pertinent to your query.[7] However, I shall say a few things that have lately come to me.

1. Anyone wanting to help the heretics of this age must be careful to have great charity for them and to love them in truth, banishing from his soul all considerations which would tend to chill his esteem for them.

2. We need to win their goodwill, so that they will love us and accord us a good place in their hearts. This can be done by speaking familiarly with them about matters we both share in common and avoiding any debate in which one side tries to put down the other. We must establish communion in what unites us before doing so in what might evince differences of opinion.

3. Inasmuch as this sect of Lutherans are "children of withdrawal unto perdition" [Heb. 10:39] who lost the true attitude of heart before losing the true faith, we have to proceed with them from what helps toward the true attitude of heart to what helps toward true faith. It is just the opposite with the entrance of neophytes into the faith: the latter must first have their minds taught and corrected by means of the faith that comes from hearing, and then move on to the proper attitude of heart regarding moral teaching and works in accord with the faith they have received.

4. When undertaking to deal with a person not only of evil and corrupted doctrine but also of evil life, we must first find roundabout ways to dissuade and remove him from his vices before speaking to him

---

[7] Favre lost strength in one hand after his illness in March 1546.

about his errors of belief. Thus, I once had a man come and ask me to satisfy him regarding certain errors which he held, particularly regarding the marriage of priests. I shared my heart with him, and so he shared his own life with me: he was in a state of mortal sin, having lived for years in concubinage. Without getting into debates about matters of faith, I tried to get him to leave the life he was living. Once he had given up his sin and found himself free and able with the Lord's grace to live without the woman, his errors of faith collapsed without further mention, having resulted from his evil life.

5. Faced with the error regarding works which is almost universal among this sect, it is necessary to start from works and go on to faith. We must constantly speak to them about what will lead them to love good works. Thus, if someone asserts that the Church cannot impose an obligation under mortal sin to recite the office, hear Mass, or similar practices, we must exhort them so as to move their souls to the prayer and work in which hearing Mass consists. For the person had first lost his devotion for hearing Mass and reciting vocal prayers on a pattern or schedule, and then he lost his faith.

6. Careful note should be taken of what underlies their leaders' errors opposed to the precepts and ordinances of the Church and of the holy fathers: it is that they are so feeble when it comes to obedience and suffering that they think it impossible for them to keep the precepts and rules. Consequently, they need spiritual exhortation that will strengthen and encourage them, inspiring them with hope that with the Lord's grace they will be able to fulfill and suffer whatever may be commanded, and even more. I maintain that if by dint of teaching and fire of spirit someone could convince Luther to give up his possessions, submit himself in obedience to do what he was commanded, and resume the habit he abandoned, he would ipso facto cease to be a heretic, without further debate. Nevertheless, it would require spiritual power to enable him to do this; it would take much fire to bring him to the degree of humility, patience, and the other virtues which would be needed for anyone, as I said, to make such a change after so great a fall and subversion. Since it is difficult or impossible—apart from the finger of God—for such to take place in someone who has once been so subverted, it is not easy to have hope of these heretics' restoration.

7. A man who can speak with them on how to live well, on the virtues and on prayer, on death, judgment, hell, and the like—matters that lead even a pagan to amendment of life—will do them more good than another who is filled with theological authorities for confounding them.

8. In sum, these people need admonitions, exhortations, and the like, on morals, fear and love of God, and good works, to counter their weaknesses, want of devotion, dissipations, anxieties, and other evils;

the latter are not mainly or even originally a matter of the mind but of the hands and feet of the soul and body.

May Jesus Christ, the redeemer of all, provide for this with his Holy Spirit, because it is clear that his written word is not enough. I shall add no more for now, only asking you to remember that I write this out of obedience to the good spirit that prompts your request that I write you something on this topic. With more time I might well think of more to say, but I fear the above already contains it all.

Madrid, March 7, 1546

Your brother in the Lord,

PEDRO FABRO

• XXV •

To Peter Canisius, on Perseverance in Religious Vocation
Madrid, March 10, 1546
MonFabri, 409–412 (*Epist.* 139)

In the summer of 1545, Favre had written to Canisius from Cologne as follows: "Shortly after Pentecost, the lady widow of Master Johannes, who once was your hostess, . . . renounced the world, abandoned her children, forswore the comforts of life, and, following advice, began to profess the institute of St. Brigit. . . . The example of this noble and universally respected matron had an indescribable effect. I am commonly said to be behind the affair: the learned reproach me, the ordinary folk are amazed, the pious commend me, the worldly abuse me. I went two or three times to the monastery and took great pains to confirm her." Later, word reached Favre in Spain that the lady was having second thoughts, and at the end of a long letter to Canisius in Cologne he delivered himself of this "tract" (libellus), *as he himself calls it, on perseverance in religious vocation.*

. . . Master Johannes's lady, to whom I would be happier giving the title of Brigittine, is very much in my prayers and has been constantly since the time I left you. However, I am saddened to hear that she has been tempted to the point of turning backwards. God grant that those laying ambush to her soul and trying to prevent her going forward may not prevail. If only, if only I could now be granted just an hour with her! I have much to say to encourage and console her, if only she will turn her senses away from those who speak for her destruction. I urgently wish that if it will do any good, you visit her in my name and bring her my earnest greetings. With what can her enemies threaten her if she perseveres? Hardships perhaps, poverty, insults, humiliation, and the like—which make up the cross which we are told we ought to carry daily? Is not Christ clearly visible in these things? She should rather fear the threats coming to us from our own conscience, from our good angel, from truth itself: to have these as our enemies or disobey them is a harsh and unbearable torment. Oh, if the lady only knew what the Lord promises in return! If she knew what good things await her! She should recall her sins and the punishments stored up for sinners, that is, for those who have not done penance. She should recall the deeds and hardships of the life of Christ, of the blessed Virgin, and of all those whom we know by certain faith to have attained eternal life in heaven. She should also recall the sufferings that Christ endured for her and for everyone. Finally, she should recall and look with firm hope towards the glory that awaits her in heaven. If she finds living with her sisters difficult, she should know that she is earning the company of all the saints. If the bread she now eats is hard, she should know that in this way she will have the bread of angels. If she dislikes her lodgings in the monastery, she should take this as an occasion to contemplate and hope for her dwelling not made with hands, the house and city of the saints. I would say the same of enclosure, by which she will merit the freedom of the bodies of the saints; and of the labors imposed by obedience, which are the way to the everlasting dominion and rest promised by him who said, "Enter into the joy of your lord and be in charge of five cities" [Luke 19:19]. However, I am sure that none of these things can deflect a woman of her fervor and strength from the path she has once undertaken. For she had long since calculated the cost needed for this journey. She had resolved to renounce all that she possessed and, naked, to follow Christ naked. That is, she had calculated the cost needed for the battle and victory against our spiritual and fleshly enemies, and for the erection of the spiritual tower [Luke 14:28]. Even if it is the case, as she may now think, that she did not earlier calculate correctly the course she embarked upon, she is doing so now in her very struggles at abnegation of herself and of all things; and so she must not return to the world. To take back herself and what belongs to her would be simply to abandon altogether the calculation of the costs which she had begun, to lose what she had already accomplished, and to run the risk of coming to the day of accounting without ever resuming or completing the calculation. And if we never make this calculation, does it not follow that we shall win no victory over those enemies that strike terror in beginners and overwhelm the thoughtless? Does it not follow that the tower which we are eventually supposed to build will never see either the end or the beginning of its construction? This makes clearly evident the stupidity and ignorance of those who, for fear of not completing what they know has been excellently begun, abandon what they had started. What are they doing but refusing either to start on their own perfection or to complete it? Therefore let us not look or turn back once we have taken into our hands the holy plow. Let us not resume what by the Lord's grace we once vomited from our souls. If we find ourselves reacquiring a taste and a liking for what we once despised, spurned, and loathed, we ought not to think that our earlier taste or vision was faulty; we ought to return to our earlier sense and seek again the spirit by which we reached such a judgment upon things. If there is a change in our inner and outer senses regarding things which are still intrinsically worthless and nothing, we must constantly strive to bring our senses to that condition in which these things truly appear as worthless. Paul says, "Have this mind in you, which is also in Christ Jesus, who, being in the form of God, emptied himself, taking the form of a servant." We should each examine which form we are in, and should desire to have the form of a servant, to suffer and become obedient even to death on a cross [see Phil. 2:5–7]. Anyone who of himself does not have this Jesus ought to seek him from the one who gives all things; anyone who does have him ought to follow him. Many other thoughts are suggested to me by my longing for the welfare of the lady on behalf of whom I write this. However, should my wishes come too late, you will readily be able to ensure that I shall not have uselessly spouted this letter, or rather, tract, just as it came to me.

May Jesus Christ, who will come to judge every intention, strengthen your hearts in every good intention and your minds in every right and true knowledge. Amen.

Madrid, at the court of the prince of Spain, March 10, 1546

Your brother in Christ,

PETRUS FABER

• XXVI •

To Diego Laínez, on the Death of Laínez's Father
Rome, July 23, 1546
MonFabri, 434–437 (*Epist.* 147)

This is Favre's last surviving letter, dated just a week before his death. It informs Diego Laínez, then at the council in Trent with Claude Jay and Alfonso Salmerón, of his father's death, news of which Favre had received before leaving Spain for Rome. It is hard to escape the impression that Favre thought Laínez likely to be insufficiently sensitive to his family duties.

Dearest brother in Christ:

The grace and peace of our redeemer be always in our souls.

The secretary of the house[8] will report to the three of you on whatever you need to know, and so I will not encroach on his office—

---

[8] Bartolomeu Ferrão was secretary of the Society at the time.

although I know there would be plenty of personal matters to discuss with you and our brothers Masters Jay and Salmerón, which I will leave for when our Lord deigns to let us see each other in that unity in which those who are truly brethren in Christ may dwell together [see Ps. 133:1].

I do not know whether you have received word of the bodily death of your father according to the flesh. I learned of it through a letter from your sister Doña María. I sent her a reply to console those left behind in this life: your lady mother, your two sisters, and little Cristóbal. Be sure to write them yourself about this for their consolation—and do so all the more fully the further removed your own spirit is from being upset or inordinately disconsolate. To recommend his soul to you it will suffice for you to reflect upon what a son like yourself owes to a father such as yours (may he be in glory). I had the Masses said here by the fathers in the house, as well as earlier in Spain, writing, if I remember rightly, to Portugal, Valladolid, Alcalá, Valencia, and Barcelona, besides what I did while passing through various places where there are people who grieve at events of this sort, which are rightly a source of sorrow to the whole Society and to all who are close to it. But do not let this keep you from also fulfilling your own filial duty in this regard by writing to the dispersed brethren personally.

If you have not already heard of them, I must inform you also of the deaths of Father Hermes [Poën], who died in Valladolid shortly after my departure, and of the young Cornelius, who died while traveling from Portugal to Castile under obedience, so that you may show yourselves their brothers and do for them what you will want done for yourselves when you come to the same critical moment.

Our friend from Montserrat has written you, and I enclose his letter with this one.

Mosén Gou[9] is one of our many friends and supporters in Barcelona. He gave me a memorial from which you will see that a number of people in Barcelona are anxious to have a Carmelite friar "who is a son of the convent of the Barcelona Carmelites" and so forth. I enclose the memorial so that you may speak to the General of the order who is said to be there, so that his Paternity may do whatever he deems to be for the greater glory of Christ our Lord and other good purposes.

I have no other matters on which to extend myself. May our Lord extend and enlarge us in his holy love and knowledge, so that we may serve him to his pleasure and satisfaction "in holiness and justice before him all of our days" [Luke 1:75].

---

[9] Antonio Gou, who later entered the Society.

Give my greetings to the reverend Father Fray [Bartolomé Carranza de] Miranda, Dominican, to the Fathers Fray [Pedro de] Soto and Fray Alonso de Castro, to the very reverend Father Fray Ambrosio, and to Master Francisco de Herrera.

If you think that the cardinal of Santa Croce [Cervini] remembers me, please pay him my deepest respects. Tell him that I have been his faithful and eager chaplain since the time we first began to be so much in his reverend lordship's debt that we will never be able to repay him.

May the Holy Spirit and the mind of all the holy Fathers who took part in previous councils be with you and with all those who have any influence in the holy Council of Trent.

Rome, July 23, 1546

Your brother in the Lord,

PEDRO FABRO

• XXVII •

Teachings of Pierre Favre as Recorded by the Prior of the Cologne Carthusians, Gerhard Kalckbrenner

Archivum Historicum Societatis Iesu 8 (1939): 98–102

The following document serves both as an excellent summation of Favre's spiritual teaching and as a moving testimonial to the impact of his spiritual personality upon his close friend and collaborator in Cologne, Gerhard Kalckbrenner, to whom Favre addressed some of his most intimately personal letters.

On Love for Our Brother: A Memoir of Pierre Favre

Master Pierre says he has no wish to have zeal for the execution of God's justice, even if God were to empower him to bring punishment on evildoers, but only zeal for mercy. Thus, he is unwilling to dwell on others' faults and sins, but would rather offer excuses for them in his prayers and bring to God's attention any good he may have observed in the persons. Thus, he wants always to have a compassionate heart and feelings of mercy toward all, pleading with them in gentle words to amend their lives. And even if charity at times demands hard words of us, still we should never harbor in our hearts any indignation or hostility towards others. Whenever we do feel in ourselves such stirrings of indignation, we ought to hold off from rebuking the person until another time. Furthermore, we ought to use our imagination to transport into ourselves the miseries and sufferings of poor and unfortunate persons, so that we will show them compassion, long to help them all, and pray to God for them, seeing in them our fellow heirs and future lords. We should never welcome into ourselves evil thoughts about others, or let such thoughts find a way into us. We should turn them to good thoughts and to excuses on others' behalf, alleging to God in our prayers whatever about them is good (if there is any such left). Master Pierre said that in this way he had often had a great grace for praying on behalf of Luther, Melanchthon, and Bucer, wicked heretics though they are, asking for their conversion and salvation. This is how we ought to allege others' good works before the Lord: "Lord, though this man seems to fail in that matter, yet he still has such and such good things about him. Therefore, in your great mercy take pity on him, and restore to him the remaining good things that he lacks."

We must be always and everywhere seeking others' salvation, adjuring, instructing, urging, rebuking and giving wholesome warnings to those among whom we find ourselves. And, as much as we can, we should practice the corporal and spiritual works of charity and mercy.

We should urge laypeople to recollect and examine themselves at least once a day in the evening, taking note of the day's sins and asking pardon and grace; urging them also to go to confession and Communion every week or every other week. In this way, for several days before and after Holy Communion they will be more careful to beware of sin and of their evil tendencies, as they learn to recognize and confess these more clearly, things which they might otherwise never correct. They should also train their own families and other persons in these practices, drawing them to God so that they will do the same. They should be urged to visit hospitals, care for the sick, aid the poor, and devote themselves to other works of mercy. We ourselves must also perform corporal and spiritual works of mercy as much as we are able, as Master Pierre and his companions are constantly doing, so far as they can. It would be extremely good if preachers would frequently urge the people in this direction, namely, to undertake these works of mercy and to give generous donations and legacies to pious institutions for the help of the poor and the sick.

Master Pierre has a variety of methods for correcting and recalling the erring and sinful, gradually and patiently, according to their capacities, until he finally wins them for Christ. He never gives up; he says we should never abandon hope of anyone's reformation, no matter how wicked. But we should begin with small things, and gradually instruct people by word and example, lovingly putting up with their many shortcomings, until a full reformation is achieved. For the person's fall was also a gradual process, from lesser to more serious sins. We should also urge them to prayer, almsgiving, fasting and other pious works. Similar works should be urged upon those we want to bring to conversion, so that they can become capable of receiving greater graces. Whoever perseveres in this will overcome in the end.

Instruct laypeople to love and fear God above all things, and their neighbors as themselves. Explain to them the force of these commandments and the way to fulfil them. Get them to hear Mass devoutly, every day if possible, and to have a definite set of prayers to say, to recite the rosary of the Blessed Virgin, to honor their personal angel and some patron saints, and to be ready to die at any moment by preparing themselves to give their accounting to the supreme Judge who will examine and repay their deeds and merits. Get them to ponder often on Christ's passion and charity, and in honor of these to abstain from meat on Wednesday and to fast on Friday.

Towards the feast of the Ascension, Master Pierre urged people to say seven Our Fathers daily, so that on Pentecost Day they might receive the Holy Spirit.

The value of an indulgence is just what it says. But there are often in us hindrances which prevent our receiving the full effect of the indulgence; when, that is, we still have an attachment to remaining in some venial sin which has to be burned away in the fires of purgatory, and still have not repented or completely turned away from every sin, even venial, but still have a propensity toward certain venial offenses: frivolities, excesses, lying, and many other things. Our souls should be prepared by a total turning away from every sin and toward the virtues.

We should counter pusillanimity by always hoping for improvement and never despairing of anyone. And we should always exhort, strive, and labor with ardor, for pusillanimity makes a person downcast and lazy.

He spoke of the saints, and how we should invoke them with special devotion where their relics are. Similarly with the principal angel in charge of a city, the guardian angels of the individual persons, and the saints that lived there and taught the people by their words and example: these we ought to invoke on behalf of ourselves and of the inhabitants of that place. And we should give thanks to God for all the material and spiritual gifts he has bestowed on the people and the saints there, imploring pardon and grace for the people and offering ourselves to suffer injuries for their salvation if that could help them. In this way we can sometimes range about among creatures seizing hold of everything for God's praise and the salvation of souls. Nevertheless, when we and all our powers are interiorly united with God, that is a better thing.

Also, in time of sickness, we should thank God for the health enjoyed by each part of our body in the past, as well as for that of those parts which are still sound. And in time of want we should thank him for periods of abundance in the past when we failed to give him thanks.

For God bestows on us numberless goods which we fail to recognize, and so in time of suffering we should recall these one by one. And we should turn our minds away from the present pain, or at least strive amid our sufferings to be even more generous in resigning and attaching ourselves to him. You can also compare your pains with the passion of our Lord.

Note that God often lets carnal temptations and other disturbances befall a person when he grows sluggish and seems to be resting in his present good state and no longer making fervent efforts to go forward. In this way the person is shaken out of his idleness and tepidity of spirit. Sometimes, also, because of pride and other faults God humbles a person in this way and brings him to self-knowledge.

The gift of wisdom, which raises us up to the contemplation and savoring of heavenly and divine realities, directly extinguishes the spirit of fornication that strives to lead us away to the love of base things.

We should always precede our every work and effort with a pure intention and with devout prayer. We should offer our works to God for his praise, and then, with a great desire that they be for God's praise and others' salvation, carry them out with God and in God. Then they will be guided by God's special grace and are most meritorious.

We should persevere until death in every least detail of each and every rule and statute of our order, and never knowingly neglect one of them or withdraw ourselves from obedience to our superior's will in any matter whatsoever. Otherwise, we will, to our own condemnation, lose the inflow of God's grace which we receive from him as sons of obedience through our superiors; we will gradually fall from small to grave offenses, as has so often proved the case. For whoever withdraws himself from obedience to his superiors withdraws himself from the grace that God sends us through them, which is like the "ointment on the head, which flowed down onto the beard, the beard of Aaron, and down onto the hem of his robe" [Ps. 133:2]. Moreover, we should not, out of a desire to protect a place, yield an inch in order to curry favor with heretics, lest we give place to the devil.

We should frequently, both in prayer and at other times, gaze with the eyes of our mind on our Lord Jesus Christ, crowned with glory and honor amid the whole heavenly court and seated on the throne of majesty, guiding all events and personally beholding us and all our efforts. We should walk in his sight with great fear and reverence, invoking him with eyes humbly lifted heavenward and attending on him who is present to us everywhere.

The spirit of sadness, boredom, and bitterness is not the good spirit and does not come from God. It should therefore always be repulsed and another spirit sought from God. Temptations to gluttony, lust, and other vices can be easily overcome by contempt—by rejecting the thought of them instantly, refusing to let them into your mind, guarding your senses, and turning your mind energetically to worthwhile concerns and affairs. Never converse alone with a woman except in a public church or street, or in some part of a house where there are people present who can see you. In this way you will avoid ugly rumors and the temptations of the devil.

Never forget Master Pierre's constant work of exhortation, as he toils indefatigably to spur on and move both those who have turned away from God to become conscious of the devil's snares holding them captive to his will, and those who are good not to grow sluggish or stand still, but with a greatly yearning hunger and thirst to work for progress and to hasten eagerly towards higher things. Try to imitate this wonderful man, who was so afire with love for his brother's salvation that he was ready to spend himself for all, seemingly heedless of his own needs, paying no attention to the times for eating and sleeping when his brother's salvation demanded it. He nevertheless remained profoundly humble, concealing his own higher gifts and begging for the prayers of others, as though weak with the weak and imperfect, yet without ever letting slip any word or action that could be faulted. He said that it was our own lukewarmness, our irreverent reception of God's sacraments, and our corrupt lives and incorrigible shamelessness that caused all these heresies and the uprooting of all religion; God will begin to vomit us from his mouth unless we reform and return to our original fervor and strive to grow daily. Whatever progress we may have made seems to us no progress at all, for an extremely long road lies ahead, since we are still lacking in so many goods—things that we have not yet even asked God for.

To curb gluttony, do not worry or take thought about what you are to eat or drink. Rather, deliberately declare yourself willing and eager, for the sake of God's honor, to go hungry forever and never to eat or be filled again (or even to die of hunger like Lazarus in the Gospel, who perished from hunger just as the rich man did from overdrinking) if God should so desire or if you could continue serving God in the body while thus starving. In this way you will spurn all fleshly enticements and inclinations, so that you can cling fast to God and to divine things with a heart that is always free. "Blessed are you who hunger now," says the Lord, "for you will be filled."

You will find it easier to root out vices if you concentrate on the contrary virtues, loving and dwelling on these, rather than if you wrestle with the vices themselves. When the devil molests and assails you during prayer or some other duty and will not go away at a simple dismissal, then leave off the work and call aloud to Jesus with your whole strength until the devil retreats in confusion. Then resume what you had been doing. Do this as often as necessary, and he will be afraid to return. The devil is routed when he is strongly resisted, not when he is appeased or ignored. He is like a bad woman who is ruthless with a man who appeases her. Before every action, first say a prayer aimed at obtaining grace from God to perform the action well; for example, to pray well, speak well, act well, meditate or contemplate well—with a right intention of bringing glory to God and salvation to souls.

With all your strength, remain loyal and obedient to each of your superiors, reverencing them and occasionally renewing their love and prayers by conversation and correspondence, and having recourse to them in your doubts, so that you will be able continually to receive the flow of grace that comes from head to members, and to you as one of the members. Similarly, you should pray fervently for your own subjects, pleading for them and excusing them before God. Likewise, you should have toward everyone, whether good or evil, a universal heartfelt charity, giving them your compassion, congratulations, help, service, and prayers. In this way you will bountifully experience God's grace.

Always draw from whatever you see or hear some fruit or some occasion of compunction, prayer, praise, or imitation. If someone shows you reverence, repay him with a holy wish or a prayer on his behalf. If you see sinful men or women, or anyone else, say a few Our Fathers or pray for them mentally. When you tread the ground, fear hell lying beneath it; when you look at the heavens, sigh for the happiness that is there. You can find God in every creature, but concealed and hidden; you eat him in your food, drink him in your drink.

GLOSSARY OF THE MORE SIGNIFICANT PERSONS MENTIONED IN THIS VOLUME

AGRICOLA, RUDOLPHUS (1443–1485): Dutch scholar, painter, musician, opponent of scholasticism, and one of the founders of German humanism.

ALBERT OF BRANDENBURG (1490–1545): cardinal and Elector of the Holy Roman Empire, archbishop of Mainz; involved in the Indulgence Controversy that sparked the Reformation; later strong defender of Catholicism in his lands.

ALEXANDER VI (1431–1503): Rodrigo Borgia; pope (1492–1503); great-grandfather of St. Francis Borgia; patron of Raphael, Michelangelo, and Bramante.

ÁLVAREZ, BALTHAZAR, S.J. (1533–1580): early Jesuit writer on prayer; spiritual director of St. Teresa of Avila; assisted her in the reform of the Carmelites.

AQUAVIVA, CLAUDIO, S.J. (1543–1615): fifth general (1581–1615) of the Society of Jesus and, after Ignatius of Loyola, the most important general superior of the order; during his tenure the *Ratio studiorum* and the *Directory of the Exercises* were published; successfully surmounted crises both inside and outside the Society and saw its greatest expansion in numbers and influence.

AQUINAS, ST. THOMAS (1225–1274): Dominican friar; scholastic philosopher and theologian; known as the Angelic Doctor; author, among many other works, of *Summa theologiæ* and *Summa contra gentiles*.

ARAOZ, ANTONIO, S.J. (1516–1573): one of the earliest Jesuits; relative of Ignatius of Loyola; first provincial of Spain and then of Castile.

ARISTOTLE (384–322 B.C.): Greek philosopher, student of Plato, tutor of Alexander the Great; wrote numerous works, including *Nichomachean Ethics, Physics,* and *Metaphysics;* his philosophy became one of the bases of medieval Scholasticism.

BIEL, GABRIEL (ca. 1410–1495): German scholastic philosopher and theologian; expositor of nominalistic teaching of William of Ockham; his teachings would have an influence on the intellectual formation of the early Jesuits.

BOBADILLA, NICOLÁS DE, S.J. (1511–1590): born in Valencia, Spain; one of the first companions of Ignatius in Paris and one of the original Jesuits; chaplain in army of Charles V; wrote in defense of Trent.

BOETHIUS (ca. 475–525): Roman philosopher and statesman; by translating Aristotle into Latin, he helped bring Greek philosophy to the early Middle Ages.

BORGIA, ST. FRANCIS, S.J. (1510–1572): born in Gandía, Spain; one great-grandfather was Pope Alexander VI; another was King Ferdinand of Spain; entered Jesuits, 1548; ordained, 1550; elected third general of the Society, 1565; encouraged missionary work; canonized, 1671.

BOSCH, HIERONYMUS (ca. 1450–1516): Dutch painter of religious pictures, genre pieces, caricatures, representative of preternatural and gruesome subjects illustrative of his age.

BROËT, PASCHASE, S.J. (ca. 1500–1562): born in France; made the Spiritual Exercises under Favre and joined first companions in 1536; one of the first Jesuits; sent on first papal mission to help reform a monastery of Benedictine nuns in Siena, 1538; first provincial of France, 1555.

BUCER, MARTIN (1491–1551): German Protestant reformer; a Dominican who became a Protestant; worked towards reconciling the various reformers; shared many views with Calvin.

BUCHANAN, GEORGE (1507–1582): Scottish humanist and author; Latin poet; tutor to James VI; later became a Presbyterian leader.

CALVIN, JOHN (1509–1564): born in Noyon, France; theologian and convert to the tenets of the Protestant Reformation; established a theocratic government in Geneva; organized a body of doctrine known as Calvinism and presented it in one of the most influential Protestant works, the *Institutes of the Christian Religion*.

CAMPEGGIO, LORENZO (1472–1539): born in Milan; cardinal; taught law at the University of Bologna; entered the ecclesiastical state when he became a widower; papal representative at the diets of Nuremberg (1524) and Augsburg (1530); presiding judge at the divorce trial of Henry VIII and Catherine of Aragon.

CANISIUS, ST. PETER, S.J. (1521–1597): born in Nijmegen, Holland; met Favre in Germany and entered Jesuits in 1543; influential in reestablishing Roman Catholicism in parts of Germany and Poland; prepared an important catechism; canonized and declared a Doctor of the Church in 1925.

CARAFA, CARDINAL GIAN PIETRO (1476–1559): born in Italy; elected pope Paul IV (1555–1559); one of the founders of the Theatines in 1524; had a stormy relationship with St. Ignatius.

CERVINI, MARCELLO (1501-1555): Pope Marcellus II (1555) one of the presidents of the Council of Trent; greatly respected reformer; friend of early Jesuits; reigned as pope for only twenty-two days before falling ill and dying.

CHARLES V (1500-1558): born in Ghent, Flanders; son of Philip I of Spain; grandson of Ferdinand and Isabella; king of Spain, Holy Roman Emperor (1519-1556); friend and admirer of Francis Borgia; abdicated and retired to the monastery of Yuste in Spain, 1556.

CLEMENT VII (1478-1534): born Giulio de' Medici in Florence; pope (1523-34); entered Holy League with France against Charles V; suffered sack of Rome, 1527; made peace with Charles and crowned him emperor in 1530; refused to approve the annulment of the marriage of Henry VIII and Catherine of Aragon 1534.

COCHLAEUS, JOHANNES (JOHAN DOBENECK) (1479-1552): German priest and controversialist; ardent opponent of Luther and Reformation.

CODAZZO, PIETRO (1507-1549): Chamberlain at papal court; first (1539) Italian recruit to the Society of Jesus; instrumental in acquiring for the Society the church of Santa Maria della Strada and its adjacent house, which became the location of the Jesuit Curia and the church of the Gesù.

CODURE, JEAN, S.J. (ca.1508-1541): born in Seyne, France; one of the original Jesuits and the first of the ten companions to die.

COLONNA, VITTORIA (1492?-1547): renowned Italian author, many of whose poems are deeply religious; friend of Michelangelo and of Ignatius of Loyola.

CONTARINI, GASPARO (1483-1542): born in Venice; prominent layman and reform cardinal; excellent theologian; ambassador for Charles V; supported papacy's recognition of the Society of Jesus; worked toward the calling of a Church council.

DE CELANO, THOMAS (1190-1260): born in Italy; entered the Franciscans at the request of St. Francis; wrote the *Vita Prima* of St. Francis, 1229.

DOMÉNECH, JUAN JERÓNIMO, S.J. (1516-1592): born in Valencia; early Jesuit leader of first group of Jesuit students to Paris; preacher, founder of college at Valencia; held several administrative posts in the Society.

DOMINIC, ST. (1170-1221): born in Calaruega, Spain; canon at Osma, 1199; preached against the Albigensians, helped reform the Cistercians; founded the Order of Preachers (the Dominicans), 1216; canonized, 1234.

DUNS SCOTUS, JOHN (ca. 1266–1308): born in Scotland; Scholastic philosopher and theologian; Franciscan; known as the Subtle Doctor.

ECK, JOHANN (1486–1543): born in Swabia; Catholic theologian; most famous for his debate with Luther in 1518; author of many works, especially *Obelisci,* his reply to the ninety-five theses of Luther.

ERASMUS, DESIDERIUS (1466–1536): born in Rotterdam, Holland; ordained, 1492; most famous humanist of his time; classical and patristic scholar, first editor of Greek New Testament, opponent of Luther.

FARNESE, ALESSANDRO (1534–1589): cardinal; legate to Emperor Charles V; finishes building the Farnese Palace; great benefactor of the Society of Jesus, especially in the building of the Gesú. (There is another Alessandro Farnese, the uncle of the one just described, who became Pope Paul III.)

FAUSTUS, GEORG (JOHANN) (ca. 1480–1540): a historical figure whose colorful life inspired a variety of legends and tales; pretended to have the skills of necromancy, alchemy, and other black arts.

FRANCIS OF ASSISI, ST. (1181–1226): born in Assisi, Italy; spent part of his youth as a soldier and was taken prisoner 1202; a series of religious experiences caused him to reform his life; founded the Franciscans, 1209; canonized 1228.

GONÇALVES DA CÂMARA, LUIS, S.J. (1520–1575): early Portuguese Jesuit; at one time superior of the Roman house; it was to him that St. Ignatius of Loyola dictated his autobiographical memoirs; later tutor to the Portuguese prince, Don Sebastian.

GRANVELLE, ANTOINE PERRENOT DE (1517–1586): born in Ornans, Franche-Comté; advisor and diplomat for Emperor Charles V and his son Philip II of Spain; was Charles's representative at the beginning of the Council of Trent; cardinal, 1561.

GROOTE, GERHARD (1340–1384): born in Deventer, Netherlands; founder of Brothers of the Common Life and of a school of spirituality whose influence spread through Europe during the fifteenth century.

HERP, HENDRIK (ca. 1400–1478): born in Erp (Brabant possibly); Dutch mystic; entered Brethren of the Common Life but became a member of the Franciscans of the Strict Observance (1450); only a few of his many sermons were published during his lifetime; his *Mystical Theology* and *Mirror of Perfection* were widely circulated in Europe.

JAMES I (JAMES VI OF SCOTLAND) (1556–1625): born in Edinburgh; king of Scotland (1567) and of England (1603); son of Mary, Queen of Scots; very anti-Jesuit and proponent of divine right of kings; severity against Catholics engendered Gunpowder Plot.

JAY, CLAUDE, S.J. (1504–1552): one of the original Jesuits; friend of Pierre Favre; effective confessor; acclaimed professor at Ingolstadt; lobbied for education as the most important apostolate of the Society of Jesus in Germany.

JOHN III (1502–1557): king (1521–1557) of Portugal; great benefactor of Society of Jesus at home and in Portuguese territories abroad.

JOHN OF THE CROSS, ST. (1542–1591): born in Fontiveros, Spain; entered Carmelites, 1563; ordained, 1567; assisted St. Teresa in reforming the Carmelites (becoming the Discalced Carmelites); one of the greatest Christian mystics of all time; his writings, including *Ascent of Mount Carmel,* have become classics in spirituality and Christian mysticism.

KALCKBRENNER, GERHARD (ca. 1489–1566): born in Hammont in Limbourg; entered Cologne charterhouse, 1518; elected prior, 1536; champion of Catholicism versus Reformation; author of several works presenting Rhenish mysticism for the public; great friend of Pierre Favre.

LAÍNEZ, DIEGO, S.J. (1512–1565): born in Castile; a companion of Ignatius in Paris and one of the original Jesuits; indispensable theologian at Trent; elected second general of the Society 1558.

LEFÈVRE D'ÉTAPLES, JACQUES (ca. 1461–1536): born in Étaples, Picardy; Aristotelian humanist; patristic and biblical scholar; translated the New Testament into French; participated in the Circle of Meaux, an experiment intended to reform the diocesan clergy.

LOYOLA, ST. IGNATIUS, S.J. (1491–1556): born in Guipúzcoa, Spain; founder of the Society of Jesus (the Jesuits), 1540; author of *Spiritual Exercises;* elected first general of the Society, 1541.

LUDOLPH OF SAXONY (ca. 1295–1378): place of birth unknown; a Dominican and later a Carthusian; author of the extremely popular *Life of Christ,* which greatly affected St. Ignatius of Loyola at the time of his conversion.

LUTHER, MARTIN (1483–1546): born in Eisleben, Thuringia; initiator of Protestant Reformation; Augustinian friar; ordained a priest, 1507; his ninety-five theses of 1517 challenged the Catholic Church's teachings on salvation and indulgences; author of great German translation of the Bible.

MARSILIUS OF PADUA (ca. 1290?–1343): born in Padua, Italy; medieval political philosopher; his work, *Defensor Pacis,* was a juridical treatise against temporal power of the pope.

MELANCHTHON, PHILIPP (1497–1560): born in Bretten, Germany; German humanist, collaborator with Martin Luther and religious reformer, drafted Augsburg Confession; worked in vain toward reconciling Protestantism with Roman Catholicism.

MERCURIAN, EVERARD, S.J. (1514–1580): born in Marcour, Luxembourg; became a Jesuit in 1548; elected fourth general of the Society, 1573; first non-Spaniard to hold this post; completed "Summary of the Constitutions"; established Maronite and English Missions of the Society.

MORONE, GIOVANNI (1509–1580): born in Milan; reform cardinal and diplomat; president at the Council of Trent; with St. Ignatius helped found German College in Rome.

NADAL, JERÓNIMO, S.J. (1507–1580): native of Majorca; after theological studies in Paris and Avignon, entered Society at Rome in 1545; close collaborator of St. Ignatius and commissioned by him to present the draft of the Society's Constitutions to the Jesuits in Spain, Portugal, and Italy.

ORTIZ, PEDRO, DR. (dates uncertain): born in Toledo; theologian; at the request of Emperor Charles V, her nephew, defended Catherine of Aragon against the marriage annulment petition of Henry VIII; secretary for Pope Clement VII; advisor to Pope Paul III; earlier suspicious of Ignatius, he became great promoter of and friend to the Society of Jesus.

PAUL III (1468–1549): born Alessandro Farnese in Camino; elected pope, 1534; called the Council of Trent to its first session (1545–1547); approved several religious orders, including the Society of Jesus and the Ursulines; first Counter-Reformation pope.

PETER, LOMBARD (ca. 1095–1160): born in Novaro; one of the most famous of all medieval theologians; taught mostly in Paris; author of *Book of Sentences (Liber sententiarum)* which became a classic widely used and commented on by theologians for the next five hundred years.

PFLUG, JULIUS VON (1499–1564): born in Eyra, near Leipzig; bishop and theologian; a man of moderate views who was often asked to negotiate statements between Catholics and the Reformers; the last Catholic bishop of Naumburg.

PHILIP II (1527–1598): king of Spain and Naples (1556–98) and Portugal (1580). Ardent defender of Catholic faith against Protestants, Ruler in Spain's Golden Age.

PIUS IX (1792–1878): born Giovanni Maria Mastai Ferreti at Sinigaglia, Italy; elected pope, 1846; reputation at first as liberal; later very conservative ultramontane; proclaimed dogma of Immaculate Conception; convened Vatican Council I (1869–1870), at which papal infallibility was defined.

PLATO (ca. 427–347 B.C.): Greek philosopher; student of Socrates; teacher of Aristotle; founder of the Academy at Athens; author of dialogues, including *The Republic* and *The Apology;* later Platonism greatly influenced St. Augustine and subsequent medieval thinkers.

POLANCO, JUAN ALFONSO DE, S.J. (1516–1576): born in Burgos; secretary at the papal court; entered Society of Jesus in 1541; secretary and invaluable assistant to Ignatius; first biographer of Ignatius; historian of the early society in his *Chronicon;* his influence with Ignatius and on the early documents of the Society was highly important.

PUENTE, LUIS DE LA, S.J. (1554–1624): entered the Society in 1575; novice director, spiritual theologian who combined piety and scholarly precision in his writings, which became widespread and influential in the Society of Jesus.

REUCHLIN, JOHANN (1455–1522): born in Pforzheim, Germany; a German humanist and scholar of Hebrew; helped promote study of Hebrew in Germany; interested in the cabala.

RIBADENEIRA, PEDRO DE, S.J. (1526–1611): born in Toledo, Spain; became a Jesuit, 1540; held many leadership positions within the Society; author of first very popular biography of St. Ignatius.

RODRIGUES, SIMÂO, S.J. (1510–1579): among first companions of Ignatius in Paris and one of the original Jesuits; founder and provincial of Society in Portugal.

RUYSBROECK, BLESSED JOHN (1293–1381): born in Brabant; Roman Catholic mystic; Augustinian canon; author of *The Seven Steps of the Ladder of Spiritual Love;* his works are regarded as classics in both Christian mysticism and Middle Dutch literature.

SALES, ST. FRANCIS DE (1567–1622): born in Savoy; bishop of Geneva, 1602; one of the prominent leaders of the Counter-Reformation; famous as a confessor; his *Introduction to the Devout Life* a classic in spirituality; canonized, 1665; proclaimed Doctor of the Church, 1877.

SALMERÓN, ALONSO (1515–1585): Youngest companion of Ignatius in Paris and one of the original Jesuits; theologian, biblical commentator; preacher; first provincial of Naples; papal theologian at Council of Trent.

TETZEL, JOHANN (ca. 1465–1519); Dominican friar; German preacher of indulgences at beginning of Protestant Reformation.

TRUCHSESS VON WALDBURG, OTTO (1514–1573): born in Swabia; theologian; cardinal, 1544; initiated sweeping reforms as archbishop of

Augsburg; established a university and seminary at Dillingen; head of Roman Inquisition, 1555.

VITELLESCHI, MUZIO, S.J. (1563–1645): born in Rome; joined Jesuits, 1583; served as provincial at Rome and Naples; elected sixth general of the Society, 1615; extended missionary activities of the Society; established English Mission as a province.

WAUCHOPE, ROBERT (?–1551): archbishop of Armagh; teacher of early Jesuits at Paris; suggested sending Jesuits as papal legates to Ireland to survey situation (Broët and Salmerón went).

WIED, HERMANN VON (1477–1552): archbishop of Cologne and Elector of the Holy Roman Empire; originally hostile to Reformation, but gradually turned to Protestant cause; excommunicated and deposed in 1546, he died a Lutheran.

WISCHAVEN, CORNELIUS (1509–1559): first Flemish Jesuit, greatly influenced by Favre; even while a novice was director of one of earliest Jesuit houses with a written rule; called by Ignatius to Rome in 1547, became novice master in Rome and Messina.

WILLIAM OF OCKHAM (ca. 1285–1347): born in Surrey, England; English Scholastic philosopher; Franciscan; important contributor to development of formal logic; one of sources of Nominalism, as also of the Conciliar Movement of fourteenth and fifteenth centuries.

XAVIER, ST. FRANCIS, S.J. (1506–1552): born in Navarre, Spain; early companion of Ignatius and one of the original Jesuits; missioned to India and the Far East, 1541; one of the Church's greatest missionaries; first Jesuit to go to Japan; died off the coast of China; canonized, 1622.

ZWINGLI, ULRICH (HULDREICH) (1484–1531): born in the Toggenburg Valley of Switzerland; theologian and reformer; held that Scripture should be the only authority to guide the reform of the Church; maintained purely symbolic presence of Christ in the Eucharist against both Catholics and Lutherans; longtime pastor in Zurich, where he abolished celebration of Mass.

BIBLIOGRAPHY

I. Publications Containing Comprehensive Bibliographies

Lamalle, Edmond, S.J. See Georges Guitton, S.J., for Lamalle's bibliography on Favre: *L'âme du B. P. Favre*. Paris, 1934.

O'Leary, Brian, S.J. "The Discernment of Spirits in the *Memoriale* of Blessed Peter Favre." *The Way*. Supplement no. 35. London, 1979.

Plaza, C. G., S.J. *Contemplando en todo a Dios: Estudio ascético psicologico sobre el Memorial del Beato Pedro Fabro*. Madrid, 1943.

Read, W. J., S.J. *"The Industry in Prayer" of Blessed Peter Favre*. Rome, 1950.

II. Editions of the *Memoriale* in Order of Publication

Bouix, Marcel, S.J. *Memoriale Beati Petri Fabri*. Paris, 1873.

Fabri Monumenta. Vol. 48 of Monumenta Historica Societatis Iesu. Rome, 1972. It contains Favre's *Memoriale* on pp. 489–696. Original edition, Madrid, 1914.

Fouillot, Sébastien, S.J. "Memoriale Beati Petri Fabri." Collège Brugelette, Vals, 1853, 1858. Lithographed edition for private use.

III. Vernacular Versions of the *Memoriale*

Amadeo, J., S.J., and M. A. Fiorito, S.J., trans. and ed. *Beato P. Fabro, S.J., Memorial*. Buenos Aires. This Spanish version is a revision of the one prepared by J. M. Vélez, which was revised and published by J. M. March. Casulleras, Barcelona, 1922.

Boero, Giuseppe, S.J. *Vita del Pietro Fabro della Compagnia di Gesù, primero compagno di San Ignazio di Loyola*. Rome, 1873.

Bouix, Marcel, S.J. *Mémorial du B. Pierre le Fèvre*. Paris, 1874.

Coleridge, H. J., S.J. *The Life of the Blessed Peter Favre* from the Italian of Giuseppe Boero. Quarterly series, Volume 8. London, 1878. The second part of the volume contains an English translation of Boero's Italian version of the *Memoriale*.

Certeau, Michel de, S.J. *Bienheureux Pierre Favre: Mémorial*. Traduit et commenté par Michel de Certeau, S.J. Collection Christus, no. 4. Paris, 1960.

Mellinato, Giuseppe, S.J. *"Confessioni" di Pietro Favre (1506–1546), primo compagno di S. Ignazio*. Studio e traduzione di G. Mellinato. Ed. Pro Sanctitate. Rome, 1980.

Murphy, Edmond C., S.J., trans. The *Memoriale* in *The Spiritual Writings of Pierre Favre*. With Introduction and Commentary. St. Louis: The Institute of Jesuit Sources, 1996.

IV. Critical Restorations of Parts of the *Memoriale*

Dalmases, Cándido de, S.J., and Fernandez Zápico, S.J., eds. *Fontes narrativi de*

S. Ignatio de Loyola et de Societatis Iesu initiis, 1523–1556, vol. 66 of MHSI. Rome, 1943.

Iparraguirre, Ignacio, S.J. "Trozos selectos del *Memorial* del Beato Fabro: editados criticamente." *Manresa* 18 (1946): 373–376 (§289–§293); 19 (1947): 91–94 (§305–§307, §334–§345, §355).

V. Other Writings by Favre

Certeau, Michel de, S.J. "Un texte inédit du Bienheureux Pierre Favre." *Revue d'ascétique et de mystique* 38 (1960): 343–349.

Debuchy, P., S.J. "Une ancienne copie des Exercices." *Collection de la Bibliothèque des Exercices de Saint Ignace.* Brochures 52–53. Enghien, 1914.

"Faber Maguntiæ cum interrogaretur de instructione pro itinere." *Epistolæ Nadal* 4:636–639. Vol. 47 of MHSI. Madrid, 1905

Monumenta Ignatiana. *Exercitia spiritualia.* Vol. 19 of MHSI, pp. 206–207, 567–569, 579–623: "Textus B. Fabri." Madrid, 1919.

Pinard de la Boullaye, Henri, S.J. "Un nouveau texte du Bienheureux Pierre Lefèvre sur les Exercices de Saint Ignace." *Revue d'ascétique et de mystique* 22 (1946): 253–275.

Tacchi Venturi, Pietro, S.J. "Una lettera autògrafa del Beato Pietro Fabro." *Miscellanea Giovanni Mercati* 5 (1946): 427–431.

VI. Books and Articles on Favre

Bangert, William V., S.J. *To the Other Towns: A Life of Blessed Peter Favre, First Companion of St. Ignatius.* Westminster, Md, 1959.

Certeau, Michel de, S.J. *L'expérience du salut chez Pierre Favre.* Collection Christus, no. 5, pp. 75–92. Paris, 1958.

Creixell, Juan, S.J. "El Beato Fabro y la primera residencia jesuitica en España." *Manresa* 18 (1946): 317–328.

Dudon, Paul, S.J. "Sur une règle pour la communion fréquente donnée à Parme en 1540." *Recherches de Science Religieuse* 1 (1910): 172–179.

Galtier, P. "La confession et le renouveau chrétien." *Revue d'ascétique et de mystique* 30 (1949): 18–44.

Gardet, Clément, S.J. *Le Duc Charles III et le Père Favre.* Paris, 1934.

Guitton, Georges, S.J. *L'âme du bienheureux Pierre Favre.* Paris, 1934.

———. *Le bienheureux Pierre Favre, premier prêtre de la compagnie de Jésus.* Lyon, 1959.

Hansen, Joseph. *Die erste Niederlassung der Jesuiten in Köln, 1542–1547,* pp. 172–176. Beiträge zur Geschichte vornehmlich Kölns und der Rheinlande. Cologne, 1895.

Houben, Dr. A. "Faber en de Nederlanden." *Ons Geestelijk Erf,* 1955, pp. 125–163, 241–270, 337–357.

Iparraguirre, Ignacio, S.J. "Influjos en la Espiritualidad del Beato Pedro Fabro." *Revista de Espiritualidad* 5 (1946): 293–307.

———. "El concepto de vida espiritual, según el Beato Pedro Fabro." *Manresa* 18 (1946): 293–307.

———. "Carácter teologico y liturgico de la Espiritualidad del Beato Fabro." *Manresa* 19 (1947): 31–41.

Kettenmeyer, J. B. "Aufzeichnungen des Kölner Kartäuserpriors Kalckbrenner über den sel. Peter Faber." *Archivum Historicum Societatis Iesu* 8 (1939): 86–102.

Mellinato, Giuseppe, S.J. "Revisione testuale delle *Confessioni* di Pietro Favre." *Studia Patavina* 28 (1980): 565–583.

Orlandini, N. *Vita Petri Fabri.* Lyons, 1617.

———. *La Vie du R. P. Favre.* Bordeaux, 1618. A translation of the Latin original.

Plaza, C. G., S.J. *Contemplando en todo a Dios: Estudio ascético psicologico sobre el* Memorial *del Beato Pedro.* Madrid. 1943.

———. "La doctrina del Cuerpo Místico de Cristo, realidad viviente en la espiritualidad de Fabro." *Manresa* 17 (1946): 308–316.

Pochat-Baron, F. *A propos du bienheureux Pierre Favre, dit Lefèvre: Quelques notes sur sa paroisse natale et sur le lieu de ses premières études,* pp. 461–487. XVII Congrès des Sociétés savantes savoisiennes. Chambéry, 1906.

———. *Histoire de Thônes depuis les origines les plus lointaines, jusqu'à nos jours.* 2 vols. Annecy, 1925–26.

———. *Le bienheureux Père le Fèvre ou Pierre Favre.* Paris, 1931.

———. "Les paroisses de la vallée de Thônes, d'après les visites pastorales et autres pièces d'archives. Complément de l'histoire de Thônes." Mémoires et documents publiés par l'Académie salésienne. Bellay. no. 60 (1941).

Purcell, Mary. *The Quiet Companion: Peter Favre.* A Loyola Request Reprint, 1981. Chicago: Loyola University Press; original edition, Dublin: Gill & Macmillan, 1970.

Read, William J., S.J. *"The Industry in Prayer" of Blessed Peter Favre.* Rome, 1950.

Sola, Fr. de P., S.J. "La idea de Cristo en la Espiritualidad del Beato Fabro." *Manresa* 18 (1946): 329–341.

Sola, José, S.J. "El problema 'acción-contemplación' en el Beato Fabro." *Manresa* 18 (1946): 342–367.

———. "El Beato Fabro y los Ejercicios Espirituales de S. Ignacio." *Manresa* 19 (1947): 42–62.

VII. The works listed below are those referred to in the Introduction and the Text of the *Memoriale* with their footnotes. A few others found useful have been added.

Abad, Camillo M., S.J. *El venerable P. Luis de la Puente, S.J.: Sus libros y su doctrina espiritual.* Comillas (Santander): Universidad Pontificia, 1954.

———. *Vida y escritos del V. P. Luis de la Puente, S.J. (1554–1624).* Comillas (Santander): Universidad Pontificia, 1954.

Acta Sanctorum. Critical studies of the lives of the saints published by Jesuit scholars in Antwerp, Belgium, known as the Bollandists after their founder, Jean Bolland. They also edit the review *Analecta Bollandiana.*

Allen, P. S. *See* Erasmus.

Analecta Bollandiana. See *Acta Sanctorum.*

Astráin, Antonio, S.J. *Historia de la Compañía de Jesus en la Asistencia de España.* 7 vols. Madrid, 1902–1925.

Bangert, William J., S.J. *To the Other Towns: A Life of Blessed Peter Favre, First Companion of St. Ignatius.* Westminster Md., 1969.

Bataillon, Marcel. *Erasme et l'Espagne.* Paris, 1937.

Batiffol, Pierre. *Histoire du bréviaire romain.* 3rd ed. Paris, 1911.

Béatis, Antonio de. *Voyage du Cardinal d'Aragon (1517–1518).* Paris, 1913.

Biel, Gabriel. *Commentary on the* Sentences *of Peter Lombard.* 1501.

───. *Quæstiones de justificatione.* Ed. Carolus Feckes. Collection Opuscula et Textus. Series scholastica, fasc. 4. Münster, 1929.

Black, Christopher F. *Italian Confraternities in the Sixteenth Century.* Cambridge, 1989.

Bourilly, V. L., ed. *Journal d'un bourgeois de Paris sous le règne de François Ier (1515–1536).* Paris, 1910.

Braudel, Fernand. *The Mediterranean and the Mediterranean World in the Age of Philip II.* 2 vols. New York, 1976.

Braunsberger, Otto, S.J., ed. *Beati Petri Canisii Societatis Iesu epistulæ et acta.* 8 vols. Freiburg-im-Breisgau, 1896–1923.

Brodrick, James, S.J. *St. Peter Canisius.* New York, 1935; reprint ed. Chicago: Loyola University Press, 1962; original ed., London, 1935.

───. *The Origin of the Jesuits.* Garden City, 1960; original ed., London, 1940.

───. *The Progress of the Jesuits (1556–1579).* New York, 1947; original ed., London, 1946.

───. *St. Francis Xavier.* New York, 1953; original ed., London, 1952.

───. *St. Ignatius Loyola: The Pilgrim Years.* New York, 1956; original ed., London, 1956.

Buckley, Michael J., S.J. "The Structure of the Rules for Discernment." In *The Way of Ignatius of Loyola: Contemporary Approaches to the Spiritual Exercises,* 215–237. Ed. Philip Sheldrake. London and St. Louis, 1991.

Certeau, Michel de, S.J. "Le texte du *Mémorial* de Favre." *Revue d'ascétique et de mystique* 16 (1960): 89–101.

───, trans. *Bienheureux Pierre Favre:* Mémorial. With comments by the translator. Collection Christus, no. 4. Paris, 1960.

Chatellier, Louis. *The Europe of the Devout: The Catholic Reformation and the Formation of a New Society.* Cambridge, Mass., 1989.

Clancy, Thomas H., S.J. *An Introduction to Jesuit Life.* St. Louis: The Institute of Jesuit Sources, 1976.

───. *The Conversational Word of God.* St. Louis: The Institute of Jesuit Sources, 1978.

Copleston, Frederick. *History of Philosophy.* 9 vols. New York: Image Books Edition, 1963; original ed., London, 1946–1966.

Constitutiones et regulæ Societatis Iesu. Vols. 63–65 and 71 of MHSI. Critically edited texts of the *Constitutions* and *Rules* of the Society of Jesus, along with copious introductions and notes. Rome, 1934, 1936, 1938, 1948. Vol. I: *Monumenta Constitutionum previa.* Ed. A. Codina. Rome, 1934. Sources and records previous to the texts of the *Constitutions*, with historical introductions.

Dagens, Jean. *Bibliographie chronologique de la littérature de spiritualité et de ses sources (1501–1610)*. Paris, 1952.

Dainville, François de, S.J. *La géographie des humanistes*. Paris, 1940.

Dalmases, Cándido de, S.J. *Francis Borgia: Grandee of Spain, Jesuit, Saint*. St. Louis, 1991.

D'Arcy, Martin, S.J. *The Mind and Heart of Love*. London, 1945.

Dawson, Christopher. *The Dividing of Christendom*. London, 1971; original ed., New York, 1965.

Delumeau, Jean. *Sin and Fear: The Emergence of a Western Guilt Culture, 13th–18th Centuries*. Trans. Eric Nicholson. New York, 1990.

Denzinger, Henricus. *Enchiridion symbolorum definitionum et declarationum de rebus fidei et morum*. Ed. J. B. Umberg, S.J. 27th ed. Editorial Herder: Barcelona, 1951.

Dictionary of Biblical Theology. Ed. Xavier Léon-Dufour. London and Dublin, 1963.

Dictionary of the Bible. See McKenzie, John L.

Dictionary of the New Testament. Xavier Léon-Dufour. London, 1980.

Dictionnaire de Spiritualité: Ascétique et Mystique, Doctrine et Histoire. Paris, 1932-1995.

Directoria Exercitiorum Spiritualium, 1540–1599. Ed. Ignatio Iparraguirre, S.J. Book 2 of Monumenta Ignatiana, 2nd series. Vol. 76 of MHSI, 193–203. Rome, 1955.

Duforcq, Albert. *Etude sur les Gesta martyrum romains*. Paris, 1900.

Durlap, Adolf. "Demons." In *Sacramentum Mundi* 2:70–75.

Epistolæ P. Hieronymi Nadal. Vols. 13, 15, 21 in Monumenta Historica Societatis Iesu. Vols. 1–3: ed. F. Cervós, 1898–1905.

Epistolæ PP. Paschasii Broet . . . et Simonis Rodericii. Vol. 24 of MHSI. Madrid, 1903.

Epistolæ S. Francisci Xaverii. Ed. G. Schurhammer, S.J., and J. Wicki, S.J. Vols. 67 and 68 in MHSI. Rome, 1944–1945. An enlarged and improved edition of the Monumenta Xaveriana of 1899.

Erasmus, Desiderius. An edition of his works appeared in nine volumes at Basel in 1504. The standard edition is Le Clerc's (1703–1706), supplemented by that of W. K. Ferguson (The Hague, 1934). See also his *Opus epistolarum*. Ed. P. S. Allen and H. M. Allen. 11 vols. Oxford, 1906–1947.

Fabri Monumenta. Ed. F. Lirola. Vol. 48 of MHSI. Rome, 1972; original edition, Madrid, 1914. Letters and diary of Ignatius's companion, Pierre Favre.

Falconnet, Abbé Jean. *La Chartreuse du Reposoir, au diocése d'Annecy*. Montreuil-sur-Mer, 1895.

Farge, James K. *Orthodoxy and Reform in Early Reformation France: The Faculty of Theology of Paris, 1500–1543*. Leiden, 1985.

Flannery, Austin, O.P., ed. *Vatican Council II: The Conciliar and Post-Conciliar Documents*. Dublin, 1975.

Francis de Sales, Saint. *Introduction to the Devout Life*. Trans. Allan Ross. Lon-

don, 1934.
Ganss, George, S.J. "Endnotes on the Exercises." In his translation of *The Spiritual Exercises of Saint Ignatius.* St. Louis, 1992.

———, trans. *The Constitutions of the Society of Jesus* by Saint Ignatius of Loyola. With an Introduction and a Commentary by the translator. St. Louis: The Institute of Jesuit Sources, 1970.

Gelenius, Aegidius. *De admiranda sacra et civili magnitudine Coloniæ Claudiæ Agrippinensis Augustæ Urbium Urbis.* Cologne, 1645.

Gertrudis, St. *Insinuationes divinæ pietatis seu vita et revelationes. . . .* Cologne, 1536.

———. *Legatus divinæ pietatis: Accedunt ejusdem Exercitia spiritualia.* Paris, 1875.

———. *The Exercises of St. Gertrude.* Ed. and trans. by a Benedictine of Regina Laudis. Westminster, Md., 1960.

Gilmont, Jean-François. *Les Écrits spirituels des premiers Jésuites.* Rome, 1961.

Gleason, Elizabeth G. *Gasparo Contarini: Venice, Rome, and Reform.* Berkeley, 1993.

Goulet, Gerard. "Deux compagnons: Bienheureux Pierre Favre (1505–1546), saint Pierre Canisius (1521–1597). In *Cahiers de Spiritualité Ignatienne* 15 (1991): 5–29.

Guibert, Joseph de, S.J. *The Jesuits: Their Spiritual Doctrine and Practice: A Historical Study.* Trans. William J. Young, S.J. St. Louis: The Institute of Jesuit Sources, 1964.

Hallman, Barbara. *Italian Cardinals: Reform and the Church as Property.* Berkeley, 1985.

Harphius, Henricus. *See* Herp, Hendrik.

Herp, Hendrik, O.F.M. *Spieghel der Volcomenheit.* This contains the Introduction with Blomevenna's translation of the "Directorium contemplativorum." Ed. L. Verschueren. 2 vols. Antwerp, 1931.

Hughes, Philip. *History of the Church.* 3 vols. London, 1955. Vol. 3.

S. Ignatii . . . Epistolæ et Instructiones. Ed. M. Lecina, V. Agustí, F. Cervós, D. Restrepo. Vols. 22, 26, 28, 29, 31, 33, 34, 36, 37, 39, 40, 42 of MHSI. Madrid, 1903–1911. Vol. 1: The Letters and Instructions of St. Ignatius.

Jungmann, Joseph A., S.J. *The Mass of the Roman Rite: Its Origins and Development.* Trans. Francis A. Brunner, C.Ss.R. 2 vols. New York, 1951, 1955.

Knowles, David, and Dimitri Obolensky. *The Christian Centuries.* 5 vols. London and New York, 1969.

Lacouture, Jean. *The Jesuits: A Multibiography.* Washington, 1995.

Lainii Monumenta. Ed. E. Astudillo. Vols. 24–31 of MHSI. Madrid, 1912–1917. Letters of Ignatius's companion, Diego Laínez.

Lefranc, Abel. *La vie quotidienne au temps de la Renaissance.* Paris, 1958.

Léon-Dufour, Xavier, S.J. See *Dictionary of Biblical Theology* and *Dictionary of the New Testament.*

Lewis, C[live]. S. *Christian Reflections.* Fount Paperback. Glasgow, 1981.

———. *Screwtape Proposes a Toast.* Fontana Books. London and Glasgow, 1965.

Lubac, Henri de. *Corpus Mysticum.* Paris, 1944.

Ludolph the Carthusian. *Vita Christi Domini.* Venice, 1587.

Mâle, Emile. *L'art religieux du moyen âge en France.* Paris, 1922.

Martin, Dennis P. "Carthusians during the Reformation Era: 'Cartusia Nunquam Deformata, Reformari Resistens.'" *The Catholic Historical Review* 81, no. 1 (January 1995): 41–66.

McKenzie, John L. *Dictionary of the Bible.* London and Dublin, 1965.

Monumenta Historica Societatis Iesu. Madrid, 1894–1929; Rome, 1929– . Collection of the historical documents of the Society of Jesus in critically edited form. Abbreviated as MHSI.

Naz, R. *L'âme de la Savoie.* Chambéry, 1961.

New Catholic Encyclopedia. 15 vols. New York, 1967.

Nouvelle Revue Théologique. Louvain, 1950. Vol. 72: "Le divorce entre théologie et mystique."

Oberman, Heiko. *The Harvest of Medieval Theology: Gabriel Biel and Late Medieval Nominalism.* Cambridge, Mass., 1963.

———. *Luther: Man between God and the Devil.* New Haven, 1989.

O'Malley, John. *The First Jesuits. Cambridge, Mass., 1993.*

O'Sullivan, Michael J., S.J. "Trust Your Feelings but Use Your Head." *Studies in the Spirituality of Jesuits* 22, no. 4 (1990).

Ozment, Stephen E. *The Reformation in the Cities: The Appeal of Protestantism to Sixteenth-Century Germany and Switzerland.* New Haven, 1975.

Pastor, Ludwig F. von. *The History of the Popes from the Close of the Middle Ages.* Trans. Ralph E. Kerr and E. F. Peeler. 40 vols. St. Louis, 1891–1953; original edition, London, 1891. Vols. 5, 6, 10, 11.

Pedrizet, Paul. *Le Calendrier Parisien à la fin du moyen âge.* Paris, 1933.

Pérouse, G. *La Savoie d'autrefois.* Paris, 1960.

———. *Vieille Savoie.* 3 vols. Chambéry, 1937.

Peter Lombard. *Petri Lombardi Libri iv sententiarum.* Florence, 1916.

Petrus Lombardus. See Peter Lombard.

Poncelet, Alfred, S.J. *Histoire de la Compagnie de Jésus dans les Anciens Pays-Bas.* Part 1. Brussels, 1927.

Post, R. R. *The Modern Devotion: Confrontation with Reformation and Humanism.* Leiden, 1968.

Quicherat, J. *Histoire de Sante-Barbe: Collège, communauté, institution.* 3 vols. Paris, 1860–1864.

Rahner, Karl, S.J. "Angel." In *Sacramentum Mundi,* 1:27–35. New York, 1968.

———, "The Devil." In *Sacramentum Mundi* 2:70–75.

———. See *Sacramentum Mundi.*

———, ed. *The Teaching of the Catholic Church.* Trans. Geoffrey Stevens from the original, *Der Glaube der Kirche.* Cork, 1967.

Ravier, André, S.J. *St. Ignatius of Loyola and the Founding of the Society of Jesus.* Trans. Maura Daly. San Francisco, 1987.

Reiffenberg, F., S.J. *Historia Societatis Iesu ad Rhenum inferiorem.* Cologne, 1764.

Renaudet, A. *Préréforme et humanisme à Paris pendant les premières guerres d'Italie (1494–1517).* Paris, 1916.

———. *Humanisme et Renaissance.* Geneva, 1958.

Sacramentum Mundi: An Encyclopedia of Theology. Ed. Karl Rahner, S.J., with Cornelius Ernst, O.P., and Kevin Smith. 6 vols. New York and London, 1968.

Sandaeus, Maximilianus. *Pro theologia mystica clavis.* . . . Louvain, 1963; original ed., Cologne, 1640.

Schurhammer, Georg, S.J. *Francis Xavier: His Life and Times.* Trans. M. Joseph Costello, S.J. 4 vols. Rome, 1973. Vol. 1: *Europe.*

Schurhammer, Georg, S.J. and Joseph Wicki, S.J. *Epistolæ S. Francisci.* 2 vols. Rome, 1943–1944. For an English translation of this work, see M. Joseph Costelloe, S.J., trans. *The Letters and Instructions of Francis Xavier.* St. Louis, 1992.

Sheed, Frank J. *The Instructed Heart.* London, 1979.

Spiritual Exercises of St. Ignatius (text of the). Any edition bearing the marginal numbers of the Madrid critical edition of the *Exercises* in Monumenta Ignatiana. Monumenta Historica Societatis Iesu. Madrid, 1919.

Spitz, Lewis W. *The Religious Renaissance of the German Humanists.* Cambridge, Mass., 1963.

Thurot, Charles. *De l'organisation de l'enseignment dans l'Université de Paris au moyen âge.* Paris and Besançon, 1850; St. Louis, 1982.

Todd, John M. *Martin Luther.* London, 1964.

Toner, Jules J., S.J. *A Commentary on St. Ignatius' Rules for the Discernment of Spirits: A Guide to the Principles and Practice.* St. Louis, 1982.

Vatican Council II. *See* Flannery, Austin, O.P., above.

Villoslada, R., S.J. *La Universidad de Paris durante los estudios de Francisco de Vitoria, O.P., 1507–1522.* Rome, 1938.

Wulf, F., S.J., ed. *Ignatius of Loyola: His Personality and Spiritual Heritage.* St. Louis, 1977.

Young, William J., trans. *The "Spiritual Journal" of St. Ignatius Loyola.* Woodstock, Md., 1958.

INDEX TO THE *MEMORIALE*

Note: In the index below,

numbers **appearing alone** indicate the **boldface section numbers (§)** appearing before a paragraph or series of paragraphs in the text;

numbers followed by the letter *a* (for example, 203a) indicate the **linking passages** following those numbers, in this case the passage following §203. A linking passage is supplied by the translator to provide historical or other information on the text that follows or to supply a bridge between two sections separated by a lapse of time;

numbers followed by an *n.* (for example, 60 n. 121) indicate a **footnote** associated with those section numbers, in this case footnote 121 attached to §60;

numbers preceded by a *p.* (for example, p. 100) indicate **page numbers** in this volume, in this case page 100.

• A •

Aar (river), 24 n. 49
Abiba (companion of St. Stephen), 60 n. 121
Abraham
 Favre wishes to be servant to, 150
 reference to biblical accounts of, 422 n. 21
Abundius, 85 n. 161. *See also* Concordia
Achilleus, St., 182 n. 75
Aquaviva, Claudio (general of Jesuits), 435 n. 9
activity, apostolic. *See also* 141, 391, 415, 433
 care of the sick poor, 159
 confessions and the Exercises, 22
 the corporal works of mercy, 340–341 as an imitation of Christ, 361, 363 n. 1
 lack of success in, 423, 423 n. 29
 neglect of the neighbor, 434, 434 n. 5
 among ordinary people, 422, 422 n. 22
 the relation between prayer and, 126–129, 126 n. 255, 128 n. 263, 129 n. 261
 reward for good works, 290–292
 shortcomings in, 353–354
 wholehearted service of the neighbor, 323, 255, 304 n. 169
Acurzio, St., O.F.M. (martyr), 390

Adam (our first parent). *See also* 220, 293 n. 141
 Favre and the old Adam, 277, 278, 279
 Favre wishes to have been a servant, to 150
Adiuto, St., O.F.M. (martyr), 390
Africa, 28, 33
Agnes, St. (virgin and martyr), 232, 397
Agnillet, Antoine (parish priest of St. Jean-de-Sixt), baptizes Favre, 190 n. 100
Alban (Albanus), St. (martyr), feast of, 331, 331 n. 231
Albert of Brandenburg (cardinal and archbishop, elector of Mainz). *See also* 113a, 145 n. 2, 196, 196 n. 117
 allows Favre to leave for Cologne, 362a
 countermands his own order sending Favre to Trent, 203a
 Favre's criticism of, 205 n. 3
 his collection of relics, 215, 215 n. 16
 his pluralism, 203a
 orders Favre to lecture on Scriptures, 192 n. 106
 orders Favre to Trent, 145, 145 n. 2
 receives Favre, 203a
 and Tetzel, 203a
Alcalá, and Hozes, 17 n. 29
Alexandria, Favre prays for, 33, 33 n. 65

407

Alexis, St., 47
Alfonso, Alvaro. *See also* 368
    attends lectures at the Montanum with Canisius, 216 n. 17
    background, 32 n. 64
    in Cologne, 216
    joins Favre, 32, 32 n. 64, 179 n. 69, 233 n. 10
    leaves for Louvain, 179
    left in Cologne by Favre, 367
    meets Canisius, 299a
    pilgrimage to Trier, 101 n. 201
All Saints, octave of, 164, 166, 168
Aluminia (town), 179 n. 69
Amandus, St., 28
Amiens, 15 n. 27
Anacletus, St. (pope and martyr), 357
Andrew, St. (apostle), 183, 188
Angela da Foligno, Blessed, 342 n. 246
angels. *See also* 116, 117, 119, 142, 181, 191, 253, 315, 369
    conflict between good and bad 35, 175, 199, 250, 251, 252, 283, 311, 316
    invocation of guardian, 21, 28, 34, 118, 123, 200, 252, 260, 354
    nature of, 309, 310 n. 188, 311
    rebellion of, 293
Angels, feast of our Lady of, 56
Angera in Lombardy, 266 n. 71
Anne, St., 101
Annunciation, 42, 48, 51, 86, 97, 414–415
Antioch (city in Greece), Favre prays for, 33
Antioch, Patriarchate of, 33 n. 65
Antonia, Doña (of the household of the marchioness of Pescara), Favre prays for the soul of, 55
Antwerp, 90 n. 181, 362a, 363
Apollonia, St. (virgin and martyr), 244, 244 n. 25
Apostles, 46 n. 86, 101
Aragón, Juan de (João Aragonese). *See also* 233 n. 10
    background, 32 n. 64
    Favre prays for benefactors of, 76
    Favre prays for his pilgrimage to Cologne, 47
    his pilgrimage to Cologne, 47 n. 87, 49, 73, 73 n. 76 n. 152, 145
    joins Favre, 32
    leaves court to follow Favre, 179 n. 69
    returns from pilgrimage, 73
    sent to Portugal by Favre, 366

Araoz, Antonio
    background, 406a
    Favre leaves Coïmbra with, 397a
    his account of Ignatius and Favre, 12 n. 22
    leaves Évora with Favre, 406, 411a
    leaves for Valladolid with Favre, 411a
    preaches to the court, 411a
    receives letter from Favre, 443 n. 18
Archelaus (the tetrarch), 176
Arenthon, Sieur d', Favre stays with, 24 n. 42
Arians (heretics), 331, 331 n. 231
aridity, 128, 364, 371
Aristotle, 30 n. 60
Ascension, 20, 96, 98, 304, 305, 308, 436
Aschaffenburg
    Favre leaves Mainz for, 228a
    Favre visits Cardinal Albert of Mainz in, 203a, 204
    Favre with Stephen in, 252 n. 37
Asia, 28
Assumption and the Passion, 95, 98. *See also* 15, 85, 86, 87, 90, 97
Augustine, St., 107 n. 222, 109 n. 226, 161 n. 32, 355 n. 266, 357
Augustine, Brothers of St., 357
Augustine, nuns of the Order of St., 368 n. 11
Aureus (bishop of Mainz), 331 n. 231
authority
    honor for those who hold, 411
    submission to superiors, 413
Avales, Don Ferrante d' (marquis de Pescara), 55 n. 111
Avançon, Laurent de Saint-Marcel d' (bishop of Grenoble), ordains Favre deacon, 190 n. 100

• B •

Barbara, St., 188
Barcelona, Favre leaves for Rome from, 443a. *See also* 28, 32 n. 63
Bartholomeo, Canon Don, death of, 178
Bartholomew, St., 99, 368
Bassano, Claude Jay and Simâo Rodrigues in, 17
Beauvais (Dormans-Beauvais), Collège de, Xavier lectures in the, 14a
Bellay, Cardinal du (archbishop of Paris), ordains Favre priest, 190 n. 100
Benedict, St., O.S.B., 357, 407, 410

Berardo, St., O.F.M. (martyr), 390
Bernard, St., 92, 229 n. 1, 245 n. 31, 342 n. 246, 357
Bernardino of Siena, St., 229 n. 1
Bertrancourt (birthplace of Paschase Broët), 15 n. 27
Beyrouth, Pierre Farféni, titular bishop of, perhaps confirms Favre, 190 n. 100
Billick, Eberhard, O.Carm., 362a
Blaise, St., 399
Bobadilla, Nicolás de, 14a
Body of our Lord, feast of the, p. 60
Bonaventure, St., 342 n. 246
Bonn
  Favre in, 362a
  von Wied says Mass in German at, 362a
Book of Reformation, composed by Bucer and Melanchthon for von Wied, 362a
Bossuet, and comment on Bucer, 362a
Bourbon-Vendôme, Louis, Cardinal de, 102 n. 201
Breviary, the. See also 103, 116, 148, 235, 249, 250, 376, 405, 438
  for the better recital of, 37
  distractions during, 61, 61 n. 121, 122 n. 248, 135, 135 n. 274, 146
  Favre's fear about the shorter, 400, 400 n. 6, 400 n. 7
  grace to improve the saying of, 336
  greater attention to the words of, 172
  a meditation while saying, 118
  a special devotion and, 20, 20 n. 36
Bridget of Sweden, St., 256, 256 n. 51
Brigid, St. (abbess of Kildare, Ireland), 256 n. 51
Broët, Paschase, background, 15 n. 27. See also 15
Browiller, Arnold von, 362a
Bruckner, reformer, 362a
Bruno, St. (founder of the Carthusians), 28, 261
Bucer, Martin
  in Cologne, his plan for reformation, 362a
  Favre's wish for salvation of, 25 n. 52
  guides von Wied into heresy, 362a
  preaches in Cologne, 362a
Burgos (birthplace of Juan de Castro), 10 n. 19
Byzantium, Favre intends praying for, 33 n. 65

• C •

Caesarea (town in Palestine), 120 n. 241
Caesarius, St., 182
Caiaphas, 176
Calvin, John (reformer), 266 n. 77
Campo Verano, 85 n. 160
Canisius, St. Peter. See also 123 n. 250, 281a, 400 n. 6, 435 n. 9
  and Alvaro Alfonso, 216 n. 17
  background, 299a
  goes to Mainz and begins Exercises, 288a, 300 n. 156
  his election during the Exercises, 300, 300 n. 156
  makes vow to enter the Society, 299a, 309 n. 186
Cano, Melchior, O.P., and the Exercises, 428 n. 36
Cappadocia, 120 n. 241
Carafa, Gian Pietro (cardinal and later Pope Paul IV), feared by Ignatius, 20 n. 35
Carafa, Vincenzo (cardinal), gives faculties to companions, 15a
Carmelites, commemorate St. Roch in Paris, 90
Carolo, Stephen (Esteban) (novice from Speyer)
  accompanies Favre to Aschaffenburg, 203a
  background, 252 n. 37
  Favre responsible for support of, 233 n. 10
  good and bad angels and, 252, 252 n. 38
  his journey to Rome, 253 n. 42
Carthusian Order, 338
  Landsperg of the, 338, 338 n. 240
Carthusian rule, 261 n. 58
Carthusians, 367a. See also Kalckbrenner, Gerhard
  St. Bruno founder of, 261
  of Trier, 68 n. 136
Castro, Alonso de, O.F.M. (professor in University of Salamanca), 406a
Castro, Doctor Juan de. See also 190 n. 99
  background, 10 n. 19
  hears Favre's confession, 10
Catalonia, Favre preserved from brigands in, 32
Catherine of Aragón, 25 n. 52
Catherine, St., of Alexandria, 180
Catherine, St., of Siena, 342 n. 246, 368 n.

Catherine, St. *(continued)*
   11, 431
Catholic and Christian princes, Favre prays for peace between, 29
Catholic belief, 218, 265
Catholic Church, teaching of, 219. *See also* 221, 332
Catholic Doctors, 297
Catholic doctrine, 31
Catholic faith, defection of Germany from, 29, 44, 329. *See also* 44 n. 82, 204, 221
Catholic faithful, 350
Catholic leaders in Cologne, refute von Wied's reformation book, 361a
Catholic parish churches, 256
Catholic princes, 196 n. 117
Cerbonius, St., 147
Chair of St. Peter, feast of, 258
Châlon-sur-Mer, 193 n. 109
Chambéry, Shrine of Holy Shroud at, 47 n. 87
charity. *See also* faith; hope; 30, 37, 51, 54, 62, 71, 72, 96, 103, 120, 122, 136, 146, 160, 201, 203, 208, 265, 303, 305–306, 323
   in bearing with superiors, 39
   a contemporary lack of, 427, 427 n. 35
   destroyed by taking note of others' faults, 170
   an example of, 77
   Favre's first steps in fraternal, 11
   Favre's lack of fraternal charity, 432
   how to attain, 66–67, 67 n. 132
   infused at baptism, 221
   and its link with faith, 152–154
   and one's neighbor, 143, 151, 411, 143 n. 285
   and the saints, 198, 198 n. 119
   the welfare of seven cities, 33
   works of, 129
Charles II (duke of Savoy), 22 n. 41
Charles V (emperor)
   and Bonn, 363a
   favors von Wied's reform, 361a
   his policy of appeasement, 25 n. 52
   ruler of the Holy Roman Empire of Germany, 359, 359 n. 279
   unfavorable opinion of von Wied, 361a
   at war with Duke William of Cléves, 49 n. 91
   at war with Francis I of France, 15a, 230 n. 6

Chastity, vow and virtue of, 27, 35, 35 n. 71, 45
Château, Lambert du, 369 n. 9
Chlotar II (king of the Franks), 186 n. 84
Christian doctrine, 35
Christian Empire, 359
Christopher, St., church of, 281a, 289, 289 n. 126
Chromatius (prefect of Rome), 75 n. 149
Chrysanthus and Daria, SS., 148
Church, 266, 326, 398. *See also* 218 n. 21, 222 n. 30, 243, 256, 441
   critical position in Cologne of the, 361a. *See also* 398, 427 n. 35
   Doctors of the Catholic, 219, 377
   the hierarchical, 87
   interior worship in the, 266, 266 n. 77. *See also* 293 n. 141, 300 n. 156, 317 n. 206, 345 n. 249, 351 n. 257, 354 n. 264
   need for reform by minister of the hierarchical, 431
   religious orders in the, 265
Church of the Virgin of the Stairs (Maria ad Gradus) near Mainz, 196 n. 116
Cifuentes, Conde de, Fernando de Silva, 441a
Cinquecento, 262 n. 60
Circumcision, 204, 207, 365
Clare, St., 81
Clets (probable burial place of Velliard), 3 n. 12
Cletus (pope and martyr), 298, 298 n. 154
Cluses, and Velliard, 3 n. 12
Cochlaeus (Dobneneck), Johann, 20a
Codure, Jean. *See also* 15, 17 n. 29, 164 n. 37
   background, 15 n. 27
   makes Exercises under Favre, 15 n. 27
Coimbra. *See also* 388 n. 33, 390, 397a, 397 n. 50, 399, 406a
   difficulties in college at, 368a
   Favre's stay in college at, 382 n. 24
   Favre writes to community at, 434 n. 5, 443 n. 18
   flooding at, 393
Cologne
   Araoz, a pilgrim in, 73, 73 n. 144, 179 n. 69
   cathedral of, 216
   college of arts at, 367
   Counter-Reformation in, 361a
   and the doctrine of the Immaculate Con-

ception, 188 n. 96
and Favre, 222, 361a, 363, 367, 368, 377 n. 18, 406
Juan d'Aragón's pilgrimage to, 47 n. 86, 74 n. 146, 76 n. 151
Monita circa confessiones, written by Favre at, 333 n. 234
Cologne, Charterhouse of, parish priest of St. Christopher's enters the, 281a. *See also* Carthusians; Kalckbrenner, Gerhard; 338 n. 240, 367 n. 8, 368 n. 11, 404, 443a
Colonna, Vittoria (marchioness of Pescara), 55, 55 n. 110
Columba, St., parish church of, 368, 368 n. 11
Common Life *(vita communis),* Brethren of the, 98 n. 196
Compañia de Jésus, 14 n. 24
Compostella, 415
Concordia, St., and Irenaeus and Abundius, 85, 85 n. 160
Confessions, sacramental, 373, 397, 400, 405, 419
Conflict, spiritual, 35, 175, 199, 250, 251, 252, 283, 311, 316
consolation. *See also* 143, 146, 191, 241, 280–281, 304, 346
  and the Blessed Virgin, 89
  in Christ's generosity, 289
  from created things, 86
  in doing the will of God, 236, 236 n. 15
  during illness and with tears, 364
  in the knowledge of his redemption Favre finds, 425
  in the Lord, 197, 197 n. 118
  at Mass with tears, 92, 235, 257
  in a new kind of interior life, 280
  and prayer, 20, 20 n. 37, 21, 21 n. 40
  during prayer, 213
  should be founded on hope, 254, 254 n. 43, 254 n. 45
  and the shunning of some kinds of, 304, 304 n. 170, 304 n. 171
  and sorrow at not possessing it, 69
  to be sought only in God himself, 65, 65 n. 128
  in spiritual distress, 30, 30 n. 59, 35, 94
  after suffering, 355, 355 n. 265, 355 n. 266
  in the worth of small actions, 423, 423 n. 29
Constantinople, Favre prays for, 33, 33 n. 65
Contarini, Gasparo (cardinal)
  his objections to Ortiz, 19a, 20 n. 35
  papal legate to the Diet of Ratisbon, 19a
contemplation(s). *See also* meditation; prayer; 38, 68, 73, 95, 118, 128, 301, 306, 361
  on the body of Christ in the tomb, 271
  on each saint of the day, 182, 182 n. 77
  the Holy Spirit inspires new methods of, 22
  on the life of Christ, 175, 303
  a means for seeking God in the soul, 63
  the mixed life and, 126, 126 n. 256
  purely spiritual realities a subject for, 108
  on St. Michael the Archangel, 116
Conversini, Benedetto (governor of Rome), 15a
Coqueret, Collège de, Juan de Castro student in, 10 n. 19
cor. See heart
Cornelius. *See* Wischaven, Cornelius
Cornibus, Dr. Pierre de, O.F.M.
  background, 113 n. 228
  Favre prays for the soul of, 113
Corpus Christi, p. 60, 34, 322–324
Cosmas and Damien, SS., 114
Covenant, New, 207 n. 5, 358
Creator, the, 306, 344
Crockaert, Petrus, O.P., and de Cornibus, 113 n. 228
Cross, the Holy. *See also* 308, 390, 424, 440, 441
  and Favre's personal cross, 241, 241 n. 22, 241 n. 23, 277, 278, 279
  objects marked with the sign of, 130, 130 n. 263, 132, 132 n. 268, 133, 133 n. 270
  and the power of Christ, 211, 212
Cuvillon, Jean, background, 366, 366 n. 5
Cyriacus, Largus, Smaragdus (martyrs), 70

• D •

Dagobert I (king of Franks), 186 n. 84
Daniel, Master (Daniel Paeybroeck from Termonde), 366, 366 n. 6
  in charge of Jesuits in Louvain, 366 n. 7
Danube, the, 24 n. 49
David, Favre wishes to have been a servant to, 150, 150 n. 11
dead, the, 55, 257, 267, 373

Decius (emperor), 85 n. 160
Dels, Laurentius, in Louvain, 179 n. 69
demons. *See also* 250, 293, 315
   division caused by, 199, 199 n. 124
   interior torment caused by, 328, 328 n. 227, 328 n. 228
   the Holy Spirit protects against, 316, 316 n. 205
   power of the Cross against, 132
Denis, St., the Areopagite, 28, 136 n. 276
   and companions, 136
depression. *See* sadness *(tristitia)*
desires. *See also* p. 59, 3, 8, 56, 60, 78, 96, 136, 141, 163, 167, 190, 193, 196, 201, 202, 206, 214, 215, 216, 242, 261, 262, 265, 271, 282, 295, 315, 317, 319, 346, 348, 350, 361, 364, 365, 395, 398, 400, 405, 413, 415
   for actual poverty, 223 n. 10, 233, 233 n. 11, 234, 234 n. 13, 234 n. 14
   to become a spiritual adult, 436
   and the Blessed Eucharist, 142, 384
   a cause of distraction, 81, 81 n. 156, 81 n. 157
   that Christ be the sole cause of consolation, 425
   come from God, 139, 153, 155
   for devotion, 173, 173 n. 55
   for devotion leading directly to God, 54, 54 n. 108
   and faith, hope, and charity, 152–158, 152 n. 13, 153 n. 18, 153 n. 19, 155 n. 23
   for God's favor, 48
   for the good of Germany, 147, 396
   for good subjects, 39, 39 n. 78
   a hierarchy of, 63–67, 63 n. 125, 64 n. 126
   nature of, 63 n. 125
   not always effective, 160
   to preserve the same spirit all through a work, 52, 52 n. 100, 52 n. 101, 52 n. 102, 52 n. 105
   and the relation between prayer and action, 126–129, 126 n. 255, 126 n. 256, 128 n. 258
   for salvation, 414, 414 n. 5
   to serve wholeheartedly, 150, 150 n. 11, 151
   for spiritual understanding, 313, 313 n. 192, 314, 314 n. 201
desolation *(tristitia)* [sadness, melancholy, depression, etc.]. *See also* 65, 66, 69, 94, 125, 162, 191, 210, 284, 285, 299, 337, 360, 371, 409, 423, 432
   absence of devotion a form of, 64, 64 n. 126, 64 n. 127
   absence of interior motions a form of, 88, 88 n. 170, 88 n. 173
   aridity a form of, 209, 209 n. 8
   changing states from consolation to, 304, 304 n. 171, 304 n. 174
   to die to oneself a form of, 278
   Favre's imperfections a cause of, 12
   Favre's inability to accept his failings, a cause of, 241, 241 n. 22, 241 n. 23
   Favre's triple cross a cause of, 277
   Germany's apostasy a cause of, 329, 320 n. 229
   from a lack of spiritual progress, 294, 294 n. 142
   memory of imperfections a cause of, 101, 108 n. 219
   a mystical description of, 279, 279 n. 108, 279 n. 109
   remedies against, 110
   some advantages of, 268, 269
   suggestions for opposing, 259, 259 n. 57
   tactics when suffering from, 254
   uncharitable feelings and thoughts a form of, 143
Devotio moderna. *See* New Devotion
Devotion (many meanings, often synonymous with *consolatio*). *See also* 37, 93, 100, 151, 166, 168, 182, 241, 271, 282, 322, 325, 326, 336, 349, 350, 351, 354, 439
   absence of, 88, 101, 101 n. 199
   to the angels and saints, 28, 28 n. 54
   aroused by memory, 45, 95, 164
   and the Breviary, 29, 29 n. 57, 29 n. 58
   description of, 81, 81 n. 156, 81 n. 157, 337
   to the guardian angels, 35, 118
   link between faith and, 131, 131 n. 264
   during Mass, 80, 92, 94, 142, 164, 204, 235, 257, 273, 308
   practices of, 20, 20 n. 36, 22, 22 n. 43, 22 n. 44, 34, 106, 437
   a refuge from distractions, 135
   sacred things as objects, of 130–131, 130 n. 263, 133 n. 270
   that leads directly to God, 54, 54 n. 108, 65, 65 n. 128
   with tears, 92, 164, 235, 257, 407
Dijon, Charterhouse of. *See* Favre, Dom

Mamert
discernment of spirits. *See also* spirits; 11, 197, 202, 213, 226, 227, 229, 230, 258, 282, 297, 311, 410
during Canisius's retreat, 300, 300 n. 156, 301, 301 n. 157, 301 n. 158, 302, 302 n. 159, 302 n. 160
and desires, 63, 63 n. 125, 64, 64 n. 126
in desolation, 53, 54 n. 108
and devotion, 54, 54 n. 108
on fear of Germany's defection, 329, 329 n. 229
on the influence of the good spirit, 51, 51 n. 98, 52, 52 n. 100, 52 n. 101, 52 n. 102
on inner turmoil, 328, 328 n. 227, 328 n. 228
on the mixed life, 295, 295 n. 145
on a mystical experience, 188, 188 n. 92, 188 n. 93, 188 n. 95, 188 n. 96, 191, 191 n. 103, 191 n. 105
on obstacles to the conversion of souls, 259, 259 n. 57
on optimism and pessimism, 254, 254 n. 45
on opposing spirits, 409, 409 n. 23
on an outward show, 209, 209 n. 8
on a remedy against temptations, 435, 435 n. 7
on a state of soul, 229, 229 n. 3
on the spirit of optimism and of pessimism, 157, 158, 158 n. 27, 158 n. 28
on the value of good works, 85, 85 n. 162, 86, 87, 87 n. 168
discursus (discursos). *See* meditation
Dispersion of the Apostles, feast of, 46, 46 n. 85
distractions, 135, 188
Doctrine, Christian, 22, 35
Doménech, Jerónimo
background, 19 n. 32, 19 n. 33
in Louvain, 179 n. 69
vocation in Parma, 19
Dominic (Hélion), Carthusian of Trier, 68 n. 136
Dominic, St., O.P., 357
Dominicans of the Inquisition, 428 n. 36
Domitilla, cemetery of, 182 n. 75
Dormans-Beauvais, Collège de. *See* Beauvais
Dorothy, St., Favre prays for sufferers on the feast of, 242
Douai, John Faber from, 366 n. 6

• E •

Easter Monday, 277
Easter Sunday, 1, 17, 273, 282, 303, 425
Eck, Dr Johann (leading Catholic theologian), 19a
Ecumenism. *See also* 4, 9, 50, 327, 377
compassion for those outside the Church, 390–391, 390 n. 40, 391 n. 43.
good works and, 290–292, 290 n. 130
and love for heretics, 33, 33 n. 65
prayer for non-Catholics, 25, 25 n. 52
reformers and their faith, 218–222, 218 n. 20, 218 n. 21, 222 n. 30
true reform, 51, 51 n. 98
Eligius, St. (Eloi) (bishop of Noyon), 186, 186 n. 84, 188
Elizabeth, St., 37 n. 75, 380
Embrun, Diocese of, Jean Codure born in, 15 n. 27
Emerentiana, St., 235, 236
Engratia, St., of Saragossa, 28
Epiphany, 213, 217, 225, 226, 229, 369, 373, 379, 385
Erasmus, Desiderius, deposition of Ortiz against the errors of, 31 n. 62. *See also* 427 n. 35
Ercole II (duke), 55 n. 110
Estrada, his coming to Coimbra, 399 n. 5
Eucharist, the Blessed, and interior union, 104, 104 n. 209, 104 n. 210, 105, 105 n. 212. *See also* 114, 136, 352, 379–380, 420
effects of receiving, 345, 345 n. 249, 345 n. 251, 345 n. 252
on the external honor due to, 322–327, 322 n. 217, 322 n. 218, 324 n. 220, 326 n. 222, 326 n. 224, 336 n. 225, 327 n. 226
the lessening of veneration for, 92
the reception of, 223, 223 n. 31, 224
sacrament of, 147, 179
Eulalia, St., 28
Evaristus, St. (pope and martyr), 151
Eve, and the grace of faith, 220, 293 n. 141
Évora, and Favre
at the court of, 368a, 401 n. 11
Favre and Araoz leave, 406, 410a
Favre answers theological difficulties at, 401 n. 11
Favre arrives at Évora from Coimbra,

Évora, Favre arrives at *(continued)* 397a
Exaltation of the Holy Cross, 440

• F •

Faber, John, from Douai
  received into the Society, 366 n. 6
  sent to Cologne from Compostella, 366 n. 7
Faber, Peter, of Hall, 366, 366 n. 6, 366 n. 7
Fabian (martyr), 393
Fabian, St., 442
Faith, 118 n. 238. *See also* 29, 55, 58, 62, 74, 80, 86, 141, 153, 167, 230, 244, 265, 396
  accompanied by charity, 152
  an apprehension of God by, 318
  and the Blessed Eucharist, 326
  and Catholic baptism, 221
  and charity, 154
  and communication with angels and saints, 188
  and the creation of Lucifer, 293, 293 n. 141
  and the crucifix of Speyer, 130–133, 130 n. 263, 131 n. 264
  desires excite, 155, 155 n. 24
  different kinds of, 166, 116 n. 283
  the expression *fides ex auditu,* 103, 103 n. 207
  Favre and Laínez defend the Catholic, 81a
  Favre prays with deep feelings of, 30
  Germany's return to the Catholic, 44
  inspired by piety, 351, 351 n. 257
  and natural impossibilities, 152, 152 n. 13
  the process of losing Catholic, 218, 218 n. 20, 218 n. 21, 219, 219 n. 24
  resurrection of body an article of, 55
  reflections on two articles of, 272
  St. Paul's description of, 167, 167 n. 47
  thanksgiving for Catholic, 217
  the Trinity worthy of our faith, 317
  without works, 87, 87 n. 168
Farféni, Pierre, O.F.M. (titular bishop of Beyrouth), perhaps confirms Favre, 190 n. 100
Farnese, Constanza, daughter of Paul III, 18a
Fathers, the, of the Church, 203 n. 131, 293 n. 141
Fathers, founders of religious orders, 261, 388
Fathers *(patres),* patriarchs and prophets of the Old Testament, 59, 59 n. 119, 150, 150 n. 10
Favre, Dom Mamert, uncle of Favre and prior of Le Reposoir, 3 n. 11, 5a
Favre, Louis, and Marie Perissin, parents of Blessed Pierre, 1 n. 8
Favre, Blessed Pierre. *See also* consolation; desires; ecumenism; poverty
  accepts Wischaven as a novice, 365a
  again with the court at Évora, 397a
  in Aschaffenburg, 203a
  assisted by Ignatius, 8–12, 10 n. 19, 10 n. 20, 12 n. 22
  begins the *Memoriale,* p. 59 n. 1, p. 60, p. 60 n. 3, p. 60 n. 5, p. 60 n. 6
  childhood of, 1, 1 n. 7, 1 n. 8, 2, 2 n. 9
  at the college of Coimbra, 368a, 397, 397 n. 50
  with the court at Évora, 368a
  at the court of Prince Philip in Valladolid, 406, 411a
  dies in Rome, 443a
  founds Jesuit community in Cologne, 365a, 366, 366 n. 5, 366 n. 6, 366 n. 7, 367, 367 n. 9
  and Francis Xavier, 7
  gives Exercises to Canisius, 299a, 300, 300 n. 156
  goes to Worms with Ortiz, 19a, 20, 20 n. 35
  on his various lodgings, 286
  his vow of chastity at the age of twelve, 4, 35 n. 71
  and Ignatius, 8
  ill in Louvain, 362a
  imprisonment in France, 24, 24 n. 52
  and the Infantas' chaplains, 32, 32 n. 64
  journeys in Spain, 432a, 437, 437a, 441a
  leaves for Rome and the Council of Trent, 443a
  leaves Paris for Venice, 15a, 16
  letter to the prior of Le Reposoir, 332 n. 232
  letters to Canisius, 265 n. 70, 367a
  letters to Ignatius, 20a, 113a, 165 n. 40, 333 n. 234, 408a
  letters to the community at Coimbra, 434 n. 5, 443 n. 18

makes Exercises and is ordained, 13a, 14, 14 n. 24
other letters, 362a
pastoral success in Ratisbon, 22, 22 n. 41
to Portugal, 368
to Ratisbon by way of Speyer, 20a, 21
resolves to follow Ignatius, 13
returns to Cologne, 362a
to Rome and Parma, 18, 18a, 18 n. 31, 19, 19 n. 32, 19 n. 33
and Sainte-Barbe, 5a, 6
schooling of, 3–5, 3 n. 11, 3 n. 12, 3 n. 13
to Spain with Ortiz by way of Savoy, 24, 24 n. 48, 24 n. 49, 24 n. 50
to Speyer, 32, 32 n. 63
spiritual retreat in Vicenza, 17, 17 n. 29
summoned to Portugal, 362a
takes solemn vows, 23, 23 n. 46, 23 n. 47
transferred to Mainz and works there, 144a
visits Cologne and Bonn, 362a
and vows at Montmartre, 14a, 15, 15 n. 25, 15 n. 26, 15 n. 27, 15 n. 28, 15 n. 29
weak and in low spirits, 408a, 411a
works in Galapagar, Madrid, Ocaña, Toledo, 24 n. 52
fear of the Lord. *See also* 5, 9, 12, 48, 136, 162, 172, 329, 409, 425, 442
and Favre's parents, 2, 2 n. 9
fear and love, 203, 203 n. 131
fervor less good than, 173, 173 n. 55
and the Holy Spirit, 4, 4 n. 15
and Velliard, 3, 3 n. 12
Filippo (Philip) (prince of Spain, later to become King Philip II), 362a. *See also* 411a, 430, 438a
Filonardo, Ennio (cardinal, legate in Parma), 18a
Finding of the Holy Cross, 308
Flanders, Ignatius begs in, 7a
France, Favre says Mass for kingdom of, 102. *See also* 28, 32
Francis Borgia, duke, 443a
Francis I (king of France). *See also* 15a
allies himself with Suleiman I, 25 n. 52, 49 n. 91
takes dukedom of Savoy, 22 n. 41
Francis of Assisi, St., O.F.M., 123, 125. *See also* 57 n. 112, 342 n. 246, 357
Freud Sigmund, 104 n. 210

Friars Minor, Order of, the five martyrs of, 290, 390 n. 40

• G •

Gabriel, St. (archangel), 34 n. 67, 406
Galapagar, Favre works in, 24 n. 51, 432a. *See also* 24 n. 48, 437
Galen (Claudius Galenus) (Greek physician), 30 n. 60
and the theory of the four humors, 419 n. 17
Galilee, Herod Antipas tetrarch of, 176 n. 63
Gamaliel, companion of St. Stephen, 60 n. 120
Gandía, Favre sees Francis Borgia in, 443a
Ganss, George, on Compañia de Jésus, 14 n. 24
Gelderland, birthplace of Canisius, 299a
Emperor Charles V annexes, 49 n. 91
Gelenius, Aegidius, 368 n. 10
Geneva, Calvinist capital, 33 n. 65
Genevieve, St. (patroness of Paris), 28, 259
George, St. (martyr), 289
Gereon, St., canons of, 404
German Church, 329 n. 229. *See also* religion
Germany. *See also* 196 n. 117, 377 n. 18, 406a, 443a
and Favre, 31 n. 62, 32, 32 n. 64, 114, 215 n. 15, 225, 330 n. 230, 396
going over to heresy, 332
Jesuit foundations in, 367a
the total defection of, 329, 329 n. 229, 330 n. 230
Gerona, St. Narcissus at, 28
Gertrude, St., and her writings, 22 n. 45, 23. *See also* 122 n. 249, 342 n. 246
Gilbert, St. (confessor), 257
Giles, St., 112
God. *See also* 198, 353
his immensity, 161, 161 n. 32
his Trinity of persons, 245, 245 n. 28, 245 n. 29, 245 n. 30, 245 n. 31
through Christ Favre finds, 307, 307 n. 182, 307 n. 183, 311 n. 189
to know the will of, 346, 346 n. 252
the knowledge of, 295, 305, 305 n. 176, 305 n. 177, 306, 306 n. 178, 306 n. 179, 306 n. 180
the possession of persons in, 355, 355 n.

God, persons in *(continued)*
266
  the ugliness of the soul and, 344, 344 n. 248
  vision of, 337
Good Friday, 268, 421
Grand Bornand, Le, 3, 3 n. 11
Granvelle (imperial chancellor), and Favre, 362a
Gregorian Masses, 267 n. 78
Gregory, St., the Great (pope and doctor of the Church), 267, 267 n. 78. *See also* 368 n. 11
  feast of, 406
Grenoble, Favre confirmed by Jean-François, bishop of, 190 n. 100
Gropper, Dr. Johann (chancellor)
  chancellor in Cologne, 362a
  resists his archbishop, 362a
Grou, Jean Nicolas, S.J., 189 n. 98
Guadalupe, our Lady of, 28
  pilgrimage to the shrine of, 49
Guibert, Joseph de, S.J., quoted on tertianship, 17 n. 29

• **H** •

Halberstadt, Diocese of. *See* Albert of Brandenburg
Hall. *See* Faber, Peter, of Hall
heart *(cor)*. *See also* 68, 72, 104, 124, 135, 170, 189, 294, 298, 307, 362, 407
  and charity, 143, 143 n. 286, 143 n. 287
  and a higher form of prayer, 319, 319 n. 213, 319 n. 214, 320, 320 n. 215
  as an image of Unity in the Trinity, 45, 45 n. 83, 355, 355 n. 266
  and the interior perception of the divine words, 343, 343 n. 247
  and the knowledge of God, 109, 109 n. 221, 109 n. 223, 110, 110 n. 224
  and a new mystical grace, 188, 188 n. 93, 188 n. 94, 188 n. 95
  and spiritual rebirth, 194, 194 n. 112, 194 n. 113
  and union with God, 63, 63 n. 125, 64, 64 n. 126, 65, 65 n. 128, 66, 66 n. 129, 67
Heimbach, Peter von, 362a
Helding, Michael (auxiliary bishop of Mainz), makes the Exercises under Favre, 149 n. 4
Hélion, Dominic, O.Carth., 68 n. 136

Henry IV, Monsignor (bishop of Worms), 20a
Henry VIII, 25, 25 n. 52
  Favre's compassion for, 390–391, 390 n. 40
heretics, 151
Herll, Andreas, 267a
Herod Antipas (tetrarch of Galilee), 176, 176 n. 63
Herp (Harphius), Hendrik, O.F.M. *See also* 203 n. 132
  author of mystical theology, 110 n. 224
  and the word *intractio (intractus)* in the *Directorium* of, 188 n. 93, 229 n. 3
Hippolytus, St., 85
Holland, Peter Canisius from Gelderland in, 299a
Holy Cross, church of, Favre says Mass of the Holy Cross, 130, 308, 390
Holy Grail, the, legend of, 342 n. 246
Holy Innocents, 225, 225 n. 37
Holy Roman Emperor, 359, 359 n. 285
Holy Saturday, 272
Holy Spirit, the. *See also* 45, 75, 194, 287, 347
  all spirits in us ruled by, 253, 253 n. 41
  a comprehensive prayer to, 315, 315 n. 204
  control of other spirits to be sought from, 314, 314 n. 201
  external and internal worship, 266, 266 n. 76, 266 n. 77
  experience of desires in, 155
  the grace of perfection to be sought from, 246
  guidance from, 156, 156 n. 25
  help in misfortune from, 423
  hope for the indwelling of, 30
  how to find and retain, 443
  influence on the soul of, 89, 152
  love of God taught by, 203, 203 n. 129
  new methods of prayer received from, 22
  as one of the Persons of the Trinity, 245, 245 n. 29, 245 n. 30, 245 n. 31
  prayer for spiritual circumcision to, 207, 207 n. 5
  prayer for the indwelling of, 35
  prayer for the inspiration of, 103
  prayer to be taught by, 40
  prayers for Germans suggested by, 20, 20 n. 37
  protection against evil spirits to be

sought from, 316
sorrow for sin granted by, 299
total renewal to be sought from, 313, 313 n. 193
true reform comes from, 51 n. 98, 52
hope. *See also* 47, 123, 157, 158, 166, 286
  of angelic help with faith, 118
  of better service of Christ, 86
  of better superiors, 41, 41 n. 79
  of bodily health, 244
  and the Bull of the Jubilee, 230
  Catholic baptism with charity and, 221
  of exalted things with faith and charity, 155, 162 n. 34
  and faith deliver from spiritual distress, 30, 30 n. 59
  of forgiveness, 83
  founded on faith, 162, 162 n. 34
  of heaven, 59
  heretics seek reasons for faith and, 218, 218 n. 20, 218 n. 21
  for heretics with faith and charity, 33, 33 n. 65
  proper to a Christian, 254, 254 n. 43
  of a remedy for imperfections, 101, 101 n. 199
  for the restoration of the monasteries, 265
  of spiritual purification, 35, 35 n. 70, 35 n. 71
  veneration of the Blessed Sacrament in faith and hope, 326
  of working miracles through faith and charity, 152, 152 n. 13
Hozes, Diego de. *See also* 17 n. 29, 164 n. 37
  in Venice with Favre, 15a
humility. *See also* 262, 377, 421, 422, 429, 432, 440
  as lowly service, 150, 150 n. 11
  and service of Christ, 165
  synonymous with obedience, 39, 39 n. 77, 39 n. 72, 40–41, 41 n. 80, 42–43, 43 n. 81, 44, 45, 45 n. 83, 45 n. 84, 411, 413, 416–418
Hyepes, 441a
Hyginus St. (pope and martyr), 255, 255 n. 46

• I •

Ignatius (Iñigo) of Loyola, St. *See also* 10 n. 20, 15a, 20 n. 35, 39 n. 78, 47 n. 86, 48 n. 88, 61 n. 121, 121 n. 243,
126 n. 255, 128 n. 260, 225 n. 38, 234 n. 13, 268 n. 83, 422 n. 22, 423 n. 26
  assists Favre, 8, 9, 10
  and companions in Rome, 15a, 16–18
  general of the Society, 23, 23 n. 47
  and Favre, 4 n. 15, 12 n. 22
  and the Inquisition, 428 n. 36
  leaves Paris for Spain, 15a
  ordination in Venice, 15a
  and Ortiz, 20 n. 35
  and spiritual conversation, 333 n. 234
  at university, 7a, 10, 10 n. 19
  and vows on August 15, 14a, 15, 15 nn. 25–28
Ildefonsus, St., 28
Illiers, Milo d' (bishop of Luçon), ordains Favre deacon, 190 n. 100
Immaculate Conception, feast of, 20, 96, 97, 191, 192
imperfections. *See also* 11, 81, 83, 192, 231, 259, 269, 270
  Favre depressed because of his, 101
  and God's presence, 238, 238 n. 16
  makes too much of his, 258, 258 n. 55
  recollection a remedy against, 443, 443 n. 19
  unable to accept his, 241, 241 n. 22, 241 n. 23
Infanta of Portugal. *See* Maria, Doña
Iñigo (Ignatius), note on this form of Ignatius, 7a
Inquisition, and Dominicans of the, 428 n. 36
Irenaeus, 85, 85 n. 160
Isaiah, 193
Isidore, St., 28
Israel, 230 n. 6
Italy, state of religion in, 26, 30 n. 60, 443a
Infantas, daughters of Charles V, 32 n. 64, 179 n. 69. *See also* 432a, 441a
Ingelheim, Lower, Monsono buried in, 177

• J •

Jacques, Master (Jacques Faber), 366, 366 n. 6
Jacob, 422 n. 21
James of Compostella, St., pilgrimage to, 49
James, St., 28, 47, 53
Jay, Claude (Le Jay). *See also* 55 n. 110
  background, 15 n. 27

Jay, Claude *(continued)*
  co-founder of the Society and called Le Jay, 4 n. 14
  joins Companions, 15
  at La Roche with Favre under Velliard, 4 n. 15
Jean-François de Genève (bishop), confirms Favre, 190 n. 100
Jeremiah and circumcision, 207 n. 5
Jerome, St., regarded as patron of priests, 188 n. 238. *See also* 118, 375 n. 14
Jerusalem. *See also* 47 n. 87, 370, 374, 378 n. 20
  Favre prays for, 33
  Favre prays for Patriarchate of, 33 n. 65
  hope of pilgrimage gone, 15a
  pilgrimage to, 15, 15a
Jesus Christ. *See also* 20, 23, 26, 34, 35, 41, 46, 47, 53, 55, 62, 67, 72, 80, 91, 105, 110, 117, 140, 146, 147, 151, 160, 184, 191, 193, 201, 204, 205, 207, 213, 232, 235, 236, 239, 246, 247, 261, 262, 265, 266, 267, 312, 320, 322, 333, 356, 360, 434
  aspects of the Passion of, 95
  on the blood of, 342, 342 n. 246
  the blood shed on the Cross of, 120, 121 n. 243
  on the coming of, 379, 380, 383, 384
  communion with, 257
  external worship of, 266
  Favre as the broom of, 440–441
  Favre desires a secret visit from, 51
  fear of the Cross of, 442
  on finding, 182, 307, 307 n. 307 n. 183, 307 n. 184
  the Finding in the Temple of, 374, 378
  on the five wounds of, 361, 361 n. 289, 362
  the forbearance of, 115
  the generosity of, 255
  the glorified body of, 274, 275, 276
  the Good Friday reproaches of, 425
  the Holy Name of, 229, 229 n. 1
  the humanity of, 291, 369, 370
  the imitation of, 189, 189 n. 98
  the Incarnation of, 415
  the Infancy of, 227, 227 n. 42
  on knowing, 305, 306
  led by the Holy Spirit, 52
  the meekness of, 121
  merit rewarded by, 289, 289 n. 127
  the merits of, 149
  on mystical death through the Cross of, 279–281
  a new understanding of the Cross of, 268, 268 n. 79, 269
  obedience and, 381, 382, 413
  the parents of, 374–376, 382
  prayer against distractions to, 72, 72 n. 140, 72 n. 143
  prayers to, p. 59, 137, 147, 187, 397
  a reason for devotion to, 134
  a reason for the sufferings of, 77
  reflections on the Passion of, 270, 271, 272
  the resurrection of, 288, 288 n. 123, 288 n. 125
  salvation comes from, 228, 228 n. 44
  on seeking the Cross of, 211–212
  stages in the existence of, 96
  the tears of, 122, 122 n. 244, 122 n. 245
  two mysteries in the Infancy of, 43, 43 n. 80
  unity with, 264, 264 n. 64
  on the words of, 343, 343 n. 247
Jewish community, 205
Jews, Favre prays for, 151
Jodocus, St., 284
John (martyr), 336
John, St. (evangelist). *See also* 78, 199, 209, 340, 442
  before being Peter, Favre wishes to be, 198, 198 n. 122
  Favre on a mystical text from, 105 n. 214
  a text from, 379, 380
John, St., the Baptist, 20 n. 36. *See also* 22, 101, 269, 384, 439
  beheading of, 104
  example of penance, 332
  feast of, 19
  patron saint of Saint-Jean-Sixt, thus Favre's devotion to, 36 n. 72
John III (king of Portugal). *See also* 368a, 402, 402 n. 13
  asks for Favre, 362a
  Doña Maria, daughter of, 439, 439 n. 15
  reluctant to part with Favre, 406a
John IV of Hagen (archbishop of Trier), 20a
John XII (pope), feast of the Holy Trinity approved by, 317 n. 206
Jonas, the prophecy of, 158 n. 27
Jubilee
  bull of, granted by Paul III, mentioned

by Favre in a letter, 230, 230 n. 4
of Israelites, Favre inspired by the symbolic, 230
Judgment, Last, 385–387
justification, Favre's reflections on, 289, 289 n. 127, 290, 290 n. 130, 291, 291 n. 133, 292, 293 n. 135
Justin, St., 85
Justus (martyr), 28

• **K** •

Kalckbrenner, Gerhard (prior of the Cologne Carthusians). *See also* 25 n. 52
invites Favre to Cologne, 362a
receives letters from Favre, 263 n. 63, 356 n. 269
Kessel, Leonhard, S.J. *See also* Henry VIII
appointed rector in Cologne, 366 n. 7
Ignatius recommends new Roman Breviary (*Breviarium Sanctae Crucis*) to, 400 n. 6
and the *Memoriale*, 366
received into the Society, 353 n. 261
King of England, 25
Kings, the Three, 28, 43, 47, 49, 62, 66 n. 130, 73, 131, 213, 216, 227, 366, 369, 371. *See also* Magi; nominalism

• **L** •

La Peña, Juan de
background, 6a
among the masters remembered by Favre, 193 n. 110
Lady of August, Our, 15, 85
Lady of the Old Chapel, Our, 23
Lallemant, Louis, S.J., 189 n. 98
Lambert, Master (Lambert du Château), 338, 367 n. 9
Landsberg, Johann Justus
background, 338 n. 240
and the *Exercises* of Saint Gertrude, 22 n. 45
Favre prays for, 338
La Roche, and Favre. *See* Jay, Claude
Last Judgment, 169 n. 50
Laurence, St., 72, 74, 82
Law, Old, 266
Laínez, Diego
with Ignatius and Favre in Vicenza, 17
and Favre leave Rome for Parma, 18a
his family and Favre, 123 n. 250
takes vows in Montmartre, 14a, 15
Lazarus, 122

Le Reposoir, Charterhouse of
Dom Mamert Favre, prior of 5a
Favre gets advice from, 5a
Favre's letter in French to his cousin in, 206 n. 4
Le Villaret (Favre's birthplace), 3. *See also* 24 n. 49
Favre prays for, 33
part of the diocese of, 3
Lent, 241, 241 n. 20, 268
Leonhard, Father, 366. *See also* Kessel, Leonhard
Lewis, C[live]. S[taples]. quoted, 390 n. 41
Liège, birthplace of Lambert du Château, 367 n. 8
Limbo, 271 n. 89, 288 n. 124
Lille, Jean Cuvillon a native of, 366 n. 6
Lisieux, Collège de, or the Collège de Torcy, Claude Jay enrolls in, 15 n. 27
liturgy, 266, 266 n. 76, 266 n. 77
Loer, Dirk, edits *Exercises* of Saint Gertrude, 22 n. 45
Longinus, 120, 120 n. 241, 122, 144
Loreto, Shrine of our Lady of, 47 n. 87
Louis, St., 93, 102
Louis, St. (king of France), 94 n. 184
Louis, St., O.F.M. (bishop of Toulouse), 94 n. 184
Louvain. *See also* 11 n. 21, 21, 179, 179 n. 69, 366 n. 6, 366 n. 7, 368 n. 12, 368a
Antonio Strada and Francisco de Strada in, 179 n. 69
and Favre, 363 n. 1, 366
Favre's illness in, 362a, 363, 364a
Love of God. *See also* 54, 66, 170, 303
Christ offers himself as a sign of, 144
descends from God, 67, 67 n. 132
knowledge, leads to, 305–307
to be sought in all things, 153, 153 n. 306
love of neighbor. *See also* 76, 160, 277, 285, 287, 427, 431, 432, 433
and the corporal works of mercy, 340, 340 n. 243, 341
and Favre's prayer for his family, religious brethren and benefactors, 123, 123 n. 250, 348
genuine love of neighbor, 411
in helping the sick poor, 159
shown in prison, 24, 24 n. 50
in spite of his faults, 170
Loyola, Emiliano (Aemilian) de (nephew of Ignatius), 179 n. 69, 367, 367 n. 8

Lucia, St., 284
Lucifer, 293
Luçon, Favre ordained subdeacon by Monsignor Milo d'Illiers, bishop of, 190 n. 100
Ludolf the Carthusian, 98 n. 196, 120 n. 241
Luke, St. (evangelist), 387
Luther, Martin. *See also* 16, 25 n. 52
 and Gabriel Biel, 289 n. 127
 faith, good works, and justification, 87 n. 168, 289 n. 127, 290 n. 130
 Favre's compassion on, 390
 his theses on indulgences, 203a
Lutheran heresies, 332
Lutherans, 185 n. 83
 arrive in Cologne, 362a
Lyons, 24 n. 50, 32 n. 63
Lys, Collège de, Hermes Poen professor in, 366 n. 6

• **M** •

Madrid, and Favre, 24 n. 51, 432a, 433. *See also* 438a, 441a
Magdeburg, Archbishop of. *See* Albert of Brandenburg
Magi, venerated in Germany, 213 n. 14, 216, 216 n. 18, 227. *See also* Kings, the Three
Main, river, 203a
Mainz. *See also* 120, 196 n. 116, 281a, 289 n. 126, 308, 331, 331 n. 234, 347, 351a, 357, 361a, 366 n. 6
 bishop of. *See* Albert of Brandenburg
 doctrine of Immaculate Conception taught at, 188 n. 96
 and Favre, 113a, 144a, 159, 233 n. 10
 Peter Canisius in, 288a, 300, 300 n. 156
Malaga, Diego de Hozes, native of, 17 n. 29
man. *See also* 195, 345, 354, 383, 403
 his body an obstacle to some sins, 179, 179 n. 71
 his carnality, 107, 107 n. 218
 his changeable nature an advantage, 310
 his fear of suffering, 442
 his indifference to God's blessings, 426
 suffers for happiness in this life, 401
Marcellinus, St. (martyr and pope, bishop of Paris), 28. *See also* 298, 298 n. 154
Maria, Doña (Infanta of Portugal), 362a
 death of, 438a, 439

Mark, St. (evangelist), 294
Mark, St. (pope and confessor), 138
Martha, St. (virgin and martyr), 28, 55, 126
Martina, Blessed (virgin and martyr), 250
Martinianus (martyr), 361
Mary Magdalen, St. *See* 62, 101, 126, 403 n. 15
Mary, St., of the Portiuncula, 56
Mary, the Blessed Virgin (our Lady, etc.). *See also* p. 59, 23, 34, 40, 42, 43, 48, 49, 74, 80, 85, 88, 90, 93, 94, 101, 109, 113, 114, 123, 133, 135, 136, 142, 145, 164, 176, 182, 191, 192, 196, 225, 230, 231, 238, 303, 320, 379, 407, 439
 as advocate, 41, 45
 Christ in the womb of, 188, 191 n. 96
 deferred glory of, 360
 familiarity with the life and actions of, 110
 Favre commemorates the life of, 20
 Favre desires to be a servant to, 150
 Favre's reverence for purity of, 27
 the greatness of, 91, 91 n. 183, 95
 humility of, 39
 an image of, 208, 350
 and the Holy Spirit, 315
 and the mysteries of Christ's life, 86, 86 n. 165
 and the obedience of Jesus, 381
 the perfection of, 89
 reflections on the life of, 96–97
 sorrows and joys of Christ and, 98, 98 n. 196
Mascarenhas, Doña Leonora, 368
Mass, the. *See also* 34, 61, 68, 74, 78, 89, 112, 125, 140, 143, 160, 172, 183, 186, 204, 226, 227, 228, 243, 250, 254, 284, 289, 294, 308, 328, 331, 333, 357, 440, 442
 for Alvaro Alfonso, 179, 179 n. 69
 aridity caused by outward show during, 206
 to atone for negligence, 94
 on August 15 at Montmartre, 14a, 15
 for the bishop of Mainz and for Europe, 196
 and the Blessed Eucharist, 223
 for the city of Speyer, 130, 139
 at the communion of, 124, 142
 consolation without sensible devotion during, 273

desires during, 51, 201, 215–216
desolation during, 53
devotion with tears during, 92, 235, 257
distractions during, 81
for the efficacy of Favre's prayers, 22
for Favre himself, 246
Favre's first, 13a, 14
for Favre's parents, relatives, and fellow Jesuits, 123, 123 n. 250
Favre recalls his, 72
for Favre's spiritual renewal, 271
for fellow Jesuits and others, 99, 196, 229, 260, 261, 388, 397, 410, 441
for a French cardinal and for France, 102, 102 n. 201
the great value of, 80
a meditation during, 96
at the Memento of, 76, 113, 338, 175 n. 62
offered as a sacrifice and thanksgiving, 217
at the offertory of, 117
at the Our Father during, 74
for a Paris theologian, 113, 113 n. 228
for Pope Paul III, 255
a prayer to Jesus Christ during, 187
prayers for Germany during, 44
for priests, 190
for the souls in Purgatory, 70, 164
against the spirit of division, 199
spiritual trials during, 88, 197, 258
for the success of the Council of Trent, 431
thanksgiving for public disasters during, 57, 57 n. 112
a vow to refuse stipends, 26, 26 n. 53
Matthew, St. (apostle), 404
Maximilian, Master (Maximilian a Capella), 366, 366 n. 6
Maximin, St., of Trier, 28
Maximin, St., church and convent of (in Cologne), 368, 368 n. 11, 404
Medinaceli, Jacques d'Etaples, 24 n. 51
meditation. *See also* 43, 63, 110, 113, 125, 126, 134, 175, 342, 343, 364, 400
the *discursus* or meditative review of the mysteries, 22 n. 43, 30, 30 n. 61, 35, 35 n. 69, 42, 47, 68, 72, 74, 86
various methods of, 30, 30 n. 61
Medman, reformer, 362a
Melanchthon, Philip. *See also* Schmalkalden Articles
Favre prays for, 25, 25 n. 52
preaches in Cologne, 362a
Mellinato, Giuseppe, S.J., and history of the *Memoriale*, 422 n. 24. *See also* 88 n. 174, 107 n. 218, 170 n. 53, 244 n. 26
Memento of the Dead, 113
Merino, Esteban (nuncio at Paris), parish of Galapagar given to Ortiz by, 432a
Michael, St. (archangel), 34 n. 67, 116, 117, 178, 178 n. 68, 309, 433
Michael, St. (convent of, in Cologne), 368
Middle Ages, 96 n. 192
Mieussy (in Savoy), 15 n. 27
Monsono, Don Bartholomeo, 177, 177 n. 66, 178
Montaigu, Collège de, 7a
Montanum (college in Cologne), Alfonso Alvaro and Canisius at, 216 n. 17
Montfort, Count Jean de (Supreme Judge of the Imperial Court of Justice), 288 n. 119
Montfort, Countess de, Favre writes to, 288
Montmartre
  renewal of vows in, 136 n. 276
  vows in chapel of Our Lady of, 14a, 15
Montpellier, France, 266 n. 71
Montserrat, and Ignatius. *See* 24 n. 51
Montserrat, Our Lady of
  Favre's devotion to, 28
  pilgrimages to, 49
Morocco, 391 n. 43, 392
Morone, Giovanni (cardinal and papal nuncio)
  instructs Favre to visit Mainz, 144a, 362a
  and Favre, 144a, 362a
  nuncio to Germany in Speyer, p. 59
Moscow, 33 n. 65
Moses, 354
Mussbach, George (vicar-general to the bishop of Speyer), makes Exercises under Favre, 34 n. 66, 288 n. 120

• N •

Nadal, Jerónimo, and the active life of the Society, 126 n. 256
Nantua, Favre imprisoned in, 24 n. 50. *See also* 28
Naples, 406a
Narcissus, St., 28
Nativity of our Lord, 16, 86, 193

Navarre, Collège de, Xavier from, 6a
Nazareth, 375
Nereus, St. (martyr), 182 n. 75
New Covenant, 207 n. 5
New Devotion *(devotio moderna)*, and the pride of theologians, 113 n. 230, 377 n. 17
New Roman Breviary *(Breviarium Sanctae Crucis)*, 400 n. 6
New Testament, 207 n. 5, 266, 266 n. 76
Nicodemus, 60 n. 120
Nieder-Ingelheim, 177 n. 66, 177 n. 67
Nineveh, prophecy of Jonas about destruction of, 158 n. 28
Nuremberg, St. Sebald at, 28

• O •

Obedience. *See also* 381, 382, 413
　to the Catholic Church, 44, 44 n. 82
　leads to a reform of superiors, 37 n. 78, 41, 41 n. 80
　linked with the Trinity, 40, 41 n. 80, 45, 45 n. 83
　to unworthy superiors, 39, 39 n. 77, 39 n. 78
Ochino, Bernardino, O.F.M.Cap., apostatizes, 55 n. 110
Old Testament, 150 n. 10, 230, 230 n. 6, 266, 266 n. 76, 288 n. 124, 293 n. 140
O'Leary, Brian, S.J., 50 n. 95, 155 n. 23, 254 n. 45
Order of Minors (O.F.M.), 390
Orlandini, N., and the *Memoriale*, 12 n. 22
Orthodox Empire, 33 n. 65
Ortiz, Dr. Pedro (imperial ambassador, theologian). *See also* Contarini; 31 n. 62, 32 n. 63
　background, 19a
　and Favre, 24, 24 n. 48, 24 n. 50, 24 n. 51, 443a
　feared by Ignatius, 20 n. 35, 67 n. 134, 96 n. 194
Ottilia, St., 285
Ottone, O.F.M., martyr, 390
Oviedo, Andrés de, 179 n. 69
　a member of the Society, 366 n. 5
　sent to Portugal by Favre, 366

• P •

Padua 17
　Hozes dies in, 17 n. 29
Paeybroeck, Daniel, 366 n. 6, 366 n. 7
pagans, Favre prays for, 151
Palestine, pilgrimage to, 14a
papal bull, limiting number to be admitted to the community, 368a
Paris. *See also* 15 n. 27, 179 n. 69
　and Favre, 6–15
　companions' departure from, 15a, 16
Parma
　and Favre, 19
　Legation of, 18a
Passion Sunday, 269
Pastor (martyr), 28
Paternity, spiritual, 388–389
Paul III (pope)
　audience with Companions, granting permission for pilgrimage and ordination, 15a, 16, 17. *See also* 18a, 150, 230 n. 4, 255
　delays reform, 25 n. 52
　formally approves the Society, 18
　orders Favre to Speyer, p. 59
Paul Sergius, St., 28
Paul, St., 66 n. 131, 150 n. 10, 152 n. 13, 174, 179 n. 71, 194 n. 113, 202, 361, 388, 427, 433 n. 4, 436
Paul, St. (martyr), 336
Peña, Juan de la. *See* la Peña, Juan de
penance, sacrament of, 373, 397, 400, 405, 419
penitential practices, 129, 224, 230, 299, 373
Pentecost, 313, 328
Perissin, Dom Claude, O.Cart. (prior of Le Reposoir). *See also* Reposoir, Le
　advises Favre, 5a
　part of a letter quoted from Favre to, 332 n. 232
Perissin, Marie, Favre's mother, 1 n. 8
Perpignan, 32 n. 63
Pescara, Marchioness of. *See* Colonna, Vittoria
Peter and Paul, SS., feast of, 19, 342
Peter, St., 132, 150, 198, 198 n. 122, 201, 358, 358 n. 271, 380
Peter Lombard 13a, 245 n. 31, 271, 271 n. 90
Philip II of Flersheim (bishop of Speyer), 20a. *See also* 288 n. 120

Philip (Filippo) (regent of Spain), 438a.
  See also Maria, Doña
  becomes King Philip II of Spain, 412 n. 1
  Favre at his court, 414 n. 6
Picardy, Master Paschase Broët born in, 15 n. 28
Pietro, O.F.M. (martyr), 390
pilgrimage, as "experiment" (*prueba*), 47 n. 86
Pinosa, St., 28, 73
Pius V, St., 94 n. 186
Plantin of Antwerp, printing firm, 90 n. 180
Pochat-Baron, on Velliard's burial place, 3 n. 12
Poen, Hermes (canon from Renaix, professor in the Collège de Lys), 366, 366 n. 6
Poggio, John (nuncio, apostolic legate, cardinal), and Favre, 362a, 441a
Poghius, Thomas, 366 n. 6, 366 n. 7
Poland, 33 n. 65
Pontius Pilate, 272
poor, the, 159
pope, the, 23, 358
Porta Coeli, Charterhouse of (Valencia), 10 n. 19. *See also* Castro, Dr. Juan de
Porta Tiburtina, 85 n. 160
Portiuncula Indulgence, 57 n. 112
Portugal. *See also* 366 n. 7, 391 n. 43, 404, 406
  Favre commanded to leave Cologne for, 368
  Favre ordered back to Cologne from, 366
  Favre sets out for, 362a
  prince of, 404, 406
poverty. *See also* 46, 159, 240, 355, 369
  Favre vows to take no fee for his ministry, 26, 26 n. 53
  his desire for actual poverty, 233–234, 233 n. 10, 233 n. 11, 234 n. 13, 234 n. 14
  his prayer to the Holy Spirit for love of, 45
  his solemn vow of, 23, 23 n. 46, 23 n. 47, 356 n. 267
Praxedis, St., 51
prayer. *See also* meditation; contemplation; 58, 69, 76, 79, 84, 93, 104, 137, 141, 146, 155, 160, 168, 175–176, 179, 186, 188, 221, 226, 227, 228, 230, 239, 248, 256, 270, 271, 272, 285, 294, 309, 317, 318, 333, 347–348, 387, 415
  advice about, 37, 336, 337
  to the angels and saints, 28, 200, 282–283
  for the city of Speyer, 78
  for the dead, 55
  for the dean of Speyer, 34
  and the divine office, 29, 29 n. 58, 82
  an easier form of, 320, 320 n. 215
  Favre records graces given in, p. 60
  for the forgiveness of sins, 232, 235, 299
  a help against distractions in, 360
  for his fellow Jesuits, 46, 196, 261, 379, 394, 397, 400, 405, 407, 410, 428, 441
  for the Germans, 20, 44, 147
  for the gifts of the Holy Spirit, 315–316
  for the grace of purification, 30, 35, 89, 90, 187, 313, 356
  for the grace to serve Christ, 85, 225
  good works as preparation for, 126, 126 n. 255, 126 n. 256
  for heretics and all others, 25, 25 n. 52, 151, 159, 287, 354
  and the Holy Spirit, 212
  inspired by a journey, 21, 437
  lack of devotion in, 63
  the *Memoriale* opens with a, p. 59
  and the mixed life, 128, 128 n. 258, 341
  a mystical form of, 319, 319 n. 213, 319 n. 214
  during the night, 147, 151, 159
  for personal glorification, 275
  for priests, 190
  for a retentive memory, 140, 183
  and the *Spiritual Exercises,* 303
  for the souls in Purgatory, 70–71
  against temptations from evil spirits, 107, 328, 328 n. 227, 328 n. 228, 349
  of thanksgiving for calamities, 57, 57 n. 112
  of thanksgiving for health, 286
  for the uncharitable, 77
precursor of Christ our Lord, 39
Presentation of Mary, feast of, 27
Processus (martyr), 361
Protestant princes, 196 n. 117
Protestants, and frequent references to in the *Memoriale,* 202 n. 127, 219 n. 22, 222 n. 30, 279 n. 107, 322 n. 218
Prudence, 435
Pseudo Bonaventure, 120 n. 241

Pucci, Cardinal, grants permission for Companions' ordination, 15a
Purification of our Lady, the day of the, 237, 240

• Q •

Quiñonez, Cardinal, and the *Breviarium Sanctae Crucis*, 400 n. 6

• R •

Raphael, St. (archangel), 34 n. 67
Ratisbon (Regensburg)
  Charles III of Savoy at Diet of, 22 n. 41
  Diet of, 21
  Favre and Ortiz leave, 10 n. 19, 24
  Favre at Colloquy of, 113 n. 228
  Favre in, 22
  Favre takes solemn vows in, 23, 23 n. 46, 356 n. 267
  Favre works in, 24 n. 48
Reformation, the, 102 n. 202
Regensburg. *See* Ratisbon
Relics
  in Albert of Brandenburg's chapel at Aschaffenburg, 215, 215 n. 16
  Favre's aridity caused by a display of, 209, 209 n. 7, 209 n. 8
  Favre's uncritical attitude to, 368, 368 n. 10, 368 n. 11
Religion. *See* France, Germany
Remy, St., 8
Renaix, Hermes Poen of, 366 n. 6
Reposoir, Le, Charterhouse of. *See* Le Reposoir
Resurrection, the. *See also* 79, 113, 212, 274, 275, 276, 292, 360
  an article of the Creed on, 272
  and the beatification of souls, 288, 288 n. 124
  of the dead, 55
  Favre consoled on the day of, 273, 425
  and the Fourth Week of the Exercises, 303
  and the Most Holy Trinity, 82
  spiritual progress and, 110
Rhine, the, 177 n. 66, 308
Rhineland, Favre says Mass for the, 196
Ribadeneira, Pedro de, in Louvain, 179 n. 69
Roch, St., 90 n. 179, 266 n. 71. *See also* 47, 90, 266
Roche, La

Claude Jay at the school and succeeds Velliard as principal of, 15 n. 27, 267 n. 9
Velliard begins a school at, 3 n. 12
Velliard buried in, 3
Rodrigues, Simâo. *See also* 55 n. 110, 399
  frequently absent from Coimbra, 368a
  provincial of Portugal, 418 n. 15
  sends novices to Cologne, 366 n. 7
  and vows at Montmartre, 14a, 15
Roman Church, 31, 261, 265
Roman Curia, gossip spread about, by critics of the Church, 158 n. 27
Roman Martyrology, 255 n. 46
Romanus, St., 72
Rome. *See also* 19 n. 32, 32 n. 63, 75, 75 n. 148, 75 n. 149, 179, 252 n. 37, 267 n. 78
  Araoz joins Ignatius in, 406a
  bishop of, 358
  the Companions in, 15a
  Doménech in, 19 n. 32
  Favre and, 32 n. 63
  Favre dies in, 443a
  pilgrimages to, 47 n. 87
  religion of, 44
  romeros and 433, 433 n. 1
Russia, Favre intends to pray for, 33 n. 65
Ruysbroeck, Blessed Jan van (classical author of mystical theology), 110 n. 224

• S •

Sabbas, St., 188, 190
Sabina, St. (martyr), 11, 106
Sacrament, Blessed, 114
  lessening of devotion for, 92
sadness *(tristitia)*. *See* desolation
Saints (blessed), the. *See also* 34, 47, 48, 49, 82, 100, 109, 125, 143, 148, 175, 230, 241, 246, 267, 379, 404, 405
  celebrating through Christ the memory of, 235
  a celebration in heaven of all, 163
  communion of, 218
  and compensation in heaven for their negligence on earth, 119
  considerations suggested by images of, 215, 215 n. 15
  a desire to see the glorified bodies of, 60
  different functions on earth of, 247, 247 n. 33
  God to be found in, 110

the intercession of, p. 59
invocation of and prayer to, 21, 21 n.
  40, 28, 31, 51, 74, 101, 136, 147,
  167–168, 185, 200, 225, 232, 247,
  247 n. 33, 284, 407
meditation on the sufferings of, 50, 176
plan of a contemplation on, 182
praise of the Lord by the, 116, 118
a variety of petitions to, 244
veneration of the images and relics of,
  114, 331, 347
winning the favor of, 198, 198 n. 119
Sainte-Barbe, Collège de
  and Favre, 6a
  Claude Jay enters, 15 n. 27
  Favre and Francis Xavier enter, 6a
Salamanca, 428 n. 36. See also 406a
  Favre and Araoz stay overnight in, 411a
  Ignatius arouses the suspicion of the Dominicans of the Inquisition at, 428 n. 36.
Salmerón, Alonso
  ordained deacon in Venice, 15a
  and vows in Monmartre, 14a, 15
Samuel, 371 n. 7
Santa Cruz, Martin de (rector of Coimbra)
  Favre writes to, 399 n. 5
  his difficulties at Coimbra, 368a, 393
Santiago de Compostella, pilgrimages to,
  47 n. 87. See also Compostella
Saragossa, St. Engratia of, 28. See also
  24 n. 51
Sardoal, 397a
Sarmatia
  ancient name for Poland and Russia,
  33 n. 65
  Favre prays for, 33
Satan, 176. See also 128 n. 260
Saturninus, St., vigil of, 182, 183
Savoy
  Duke of (Charles III) chooses Favre as
  his personal confessor, 22
  Favre in, 164 n. 37
  Favre has interview with Duke of, 20a,
  22 n. 41
  Favre with relatives in, 24 n. 49
  Favre's devotion to the saints of, 28
Schmalkalden Articles, 104 n. 208
Scholastica, Blessed (virgin), 246
Scruples, teaching on, 6–14
Sebald, St., 28
Sebastian, Don, 392 n. 44
Sebastian, St., 75 n. 149, 393, 442

Sens, perhaps Louis de Bourbon, cardinal
  and archbishop of, 102 n. 201
Septuagesima Sunday, 231
Seraphia, St., 106
Seven Brothers of the Order of Minors, day
  of, 143
Seyne, Jean Codure born at, 15 n. 27
Sheba, 372
Shrovetide, 241, 241 n. 20
Sigüenza, birthplace of Peña, 6a
Silva, de Ferdinand (count of Cifuentes,
  majordomo to the Infantas and friend
  of Favre), 32 n. 64
Simon and Jude, SS. (apostles), 159, 160,
  162
sin(s). See also p. 59, 29, 71, 102, 147,
  224, 235, 262, 271, 302, 316, 407,
  410, 412
  calamities caused by, 230, 230 n. 6
  carnal and other, 107, 344
  charity a help against personal, 67
  committed at school, 5
  and death, 272
  and Doctor de Cornibus, 113
  Favre fears falling into fresh, 231
  Favre's tendency to, 270
  of families, 123
  and God's silence about Favre's, 299
  improperly confessed, 9
  and remission of punishment for Favre's,
  325, 325 n. 221
  and a request for confession, 440
  sadness caused by, 64
  of the Society, 397
  some imperfections are not, 81
  and the souls in Purgatory, 70
  state of original, 166
Sinners, 235, 242, 328, 373, 397, 407
Sissa, 19, 19 n. 33
Skodberg, Jörgen (bishop and exiled archbishop of Lund), 362a, 367a
Smet, Peter de. See Faber, Peter, of Hall
Snows, our Lady of the, 63
Society of Jesus. See also 123, 164, 367,
  392, 398, 400, 413, 437, 441, 442
  the apostolic vocation of, 255 n. 48
  combating Protestantism not sole work
  of, 33 n. 65
  confirmation of, 20, 20 n. 38
  destined for a union of contemplation
  and action, 126 n. 256
  Favre prays for, 196, 229, 261, 265, 397
  the Institute of, 356

Society of Jesus *(continued)*
  menial tasks performed by the early members of, 262 n. 60
  and obedience to the pope, 39 n. 78
Soleure, 32 n. 63
Sorbonne, 400 n. 6
Soto, de (confessor to the emperor), 362a
Sovereign Pontiff, 358
  Christ is represented by, 359
souls in purgatory. *See also* 31, 51, 92, 165, 166, 202, 338, 393, 400, 407, 431
  devotion to, 163, 164, 164 n. 36, 164 n. 38, 257
  and the resurrection of the dead, 55
  sufferings of, 71
Spain. *See also* 25 n. 52
  and Favre, 28, 24 n. 48, 179 n. 69
  hopes for a foundation in, 362a
Spech, Jacobus, 179 n. 69
Speyer. *See also* 34, 34 n. 66, 130, 139, 141, 147
  auxiliary bishop of, 288, 288 n. 120
  and Favre, p. 1, 20a
  Favre's regret at ending work in, 165 n. 40
  our Lady of, 87
  writes to Ignatius from, 113a
spirit(s). *See also* Holy Spirit; angels
  as a malign influence, 35, 35 n. 70, 176, 176 n. 64
  as a principle and guide of action, 194, 194 n. 112
  as principle of interior knowledge, 103, 103 n. 207
  definition of good, 101, 101 n. 199
  essential (principal), 89, 143, 143 n. 287
  occasional and personal, 88, 88 n. 174
  other meanings of, 52, 79, 82, 82 n. 158, 304, 304 n. 174, 329, 329 n. 229
  vital, animal, rational, 29 n. 60, 30, 313–314, 313 n. 191, 657, 659, 660, 661, 662, 663, 664, 665, 666
Spiritual Exercises of St. Ignatius. *See also* 34, 334, 364a, 441a
  Alvaro Alfonso makes the, 179 n. 69
  Canisius makes the, 300
  Castro changed by the, 10 n. 19
  Favre's exercitants and the, 24 n. 48
  fruit in Germany from the, 22
  idea of service in the, 150 n. 11
  Jay makes the, 24 n. 48
  made by Doménech in Parma, 19 n. 32

  petitions in the colloquies of the, 303
spiritual life, the
  and advice in trials, 432, 442
  apostolic labors, 353, 353 n. 259
  charity towards the living and the dead, 340–341, 340 n. 245
  discernment of spirits, 300–302, 300 n. 156, 301 n. 157, 301 n. 158, 302 n. 159, 302 n. 160
  doing penance for sin, 334–335
  dying to oneself, 277–281, 278 n. 105
  love of God and one's neighbor, 295–296, 295 n. 145
  and renewal of defects, 443
  service of God, 225, 225 n. 38
  spiritual circumcision, 207, 207 n. 5
  stages in, 378, 378 n. 21
  and suffering, 355, 355 n. 265
  and the sufferings of Christ, 361, 361 n. 289
  total transformation by the Holy Spirit, 313, 313 n. 193
  true and false consolation, 304, 304 n. 174
St. Jean-de-Sixt
  Favre baptized in, 190 n. 100
  La Roche a village in the parish of, 3 n. 13
St. John the Baptist patron saint of the parish of, 36 n. 72
St. Paul outside the Walls, Basilica of, solemn vows of Companions taken in, 24 n. 48
Stempel, O.P. (dean of Cologne theological faculty), helps Catholic resistance, 362a
Stephen, St. (pope and martyr), 141
Stephen, St. (protomartyr), 60 n. 120. *See also* 60, 198, 209
Strada, Antonio (de), in Louvain, 179 n. 69
Strada, Francisco de
  in Louvain, 179 n. 69
  sent to Portugal by Favre, 366
Suleiman I, (the Grand Turk). *See also* 25 n. 52, 49 n. 91, 391
  background, 391 n. 43
  Favre's compassion for, 390
Supreme Pontiff, vicar of Christ is, 359
Susanna, 75 n. 148
Susanna, St., 368 n. 11
Switzerland, and Favre, 24 n. 49, 32

• T •

tears
  because of an indifferent preparation for Communion, 197
  of Christ, 121, 122, 122 n. 245
  on Christmas night in the cathedral of Mainz, 193, 193 n. 111
  compassion for the dead with, 164, 257
  from devotion during night prayers, 407
  experience or knowledge with, 52, 52 n. 100
  from grief at the action of the bad spirit, 294
  at the harm done to the Church, 92
  during Mass and office on the feast of St. Emerentiana, 235
  at the sight of a crucifix, 402, 402 n. 13
  surprise at the absence of, 101
  at the thought of Christ's thorn-crowned head, 364
  at the thought of having so little to suffer, 401, 401 n. 12
  from an understanding of works of mercy, 340, 340 n. 245

Temple of Jerusalem, 374, 376, 378
  Christ's death and resurrection symbolized by the destruction and rebuilding of the, 268 n. 87
  the "return to the heart" corresponds to the ascent to the, 378 n. 21

temptations. *See also* 6, 27, 45, 143, 170, 179, 199, 254, 268–269, 283, 316, 402, 417–418
  advantages of, 296, 296 n. 147
  against chastity, 9, 30
  from the demons, 35, 35 n. 70, 35 n. 71
  to discouragement at Nantua, 24
  Favre becomes less accessible to, 191
  Favre's evil desires give rise to, 325, 325 n. 221
  against fraternal charity, 11
  to gluttony, 11
  a help against distractions, 188
  to idle and wicked thoughts, 69
  a need of grace experienced through, 443
  because of personal defects, 30, 64
  a remedy against carnal, 435
  against spiritual growth, 294
  spiritual realities are not remedies against, 54, 54 n. 108
  that cause divisions, 32

to vainglory, 10, 10 n. 20
why human nature is prone to, 309
Termonde (birthplace of Daniel Paeybroeck), 366 n. 6
Testament, New, worship of the, 266, 266 n. 76
Testament, Old, rites of the, 266
Tetzel, Johann, O.P., and indulgences, 203a
Theodosius (emperor), 331 n. 231
T(h)eonesto, St., 331 n. 231
Thomas Aquinas, St., his definition of corporeal spirits, 29 n. 60
Thomas (Poghius) (from Tournai), 366, 366 n. 6
Thônes, Favre's schooling in, 3 n. 11, 40
Tiburtius, St., 75, 75 n. 148, 75 n. 149
Toledo
  and Favre, 432a, 441a
  and Ortiz, 24 n. 51, 31 n. 62
Torcy, Collège de, and Claude Jay, 15 n. 27
Torquatus, 75
Toulouse, St. Louis (bishop of), 94 n. 184
Transfiguration, feast of the, 64
Trent
  Albert of Brandenburg countermands his order to Favre to go to, 203a
  Albert of Brandenburg orders Favre to, 145, 149 n. 6
  Favre offers Mass for the success of the, 431
  Ignatius presses Ortiz to allow Favre to go to the Council of, 443a
  the new Roman Breviary and the Council of, 400 n. 6
  the opening of the Council of, 431, 431 n. 4
Trier. *See also* 28
  Alvaro Alfonso's pilgrimage to, 101 n. 200
  Juan de Aragón's pilgrimage to Cologne and, 179 n. 69
  Monsignor John IV of Hagen (archbishop of), 20a
Trieste, Jean Codure and Diego de Hozes at, 17, 17 n. 29
Trinity, the Most Holy. *See also* obedience
  ascent in prayer to, 307
  the attributes of, 245, 245 n. 31
  the contemplation of, 109
  Favre commends himself to, 103
  Favre commends his faculties to, 183

Trinity, the Most Holy (continued)
  Favre links the Sunday offices, the Resurrection, and the, 82, 82 n. 159
  Favre's vows, faculties and, 45, 45 n. 83, 45 n. 84
  and harmony between Favre's faculties, 38
  a higher form of prayer on the feast of, 319, 319 n. 213, 319 n. 214, 320, 320 n. 215
  obedience and, 40, 41 n. 79
  our Lady's power with the Persons of, 192
  our Lady's service of, 91, 91 n. 183
  a prayer of adoration of, p. 59, 60 n. 3
  prayer to, for the soul of Doctor de Cornibus, 113
  prayer to the Persons of, 136, 160, 182, 182 n. 77, 198, 225
  present in the Blessed Eucharist, 352
  procession of Persons in, 315
  the relations between man and the, 318, 318 n. 208
  and renewal of Favre's being, 317, 317 n. 207
  spiritual progress and the feast of, 321
  as a worthy object of reason and faith, 317
Truchsess, Monsignor, later cardinal, 288 n. 119
Tullia, Doña, Favre prays for the soul of, 55
Turks, Favre prays for the, 151

• U •

Ursula, St., and companions. *See also* 49, 145
  false relics of, 368 n. 11
  Favre makes special thanksgiving to, 73
  honored in Germany, 28
  venerated in Cologne, 145 n. 1

• V •

Valdés, Alfonso de (secretary to the emperor), 55 n. 110
Valencia, Favre in, 443a
Valentine, St., 252
Valladolid
  diocese of, 431 n. 42
  Favre and Araoz arrive in, 496
  Favre and Araoz leave for, 411a
  Favre comes to Madrid from, 433
  Favre returns from Galapagar to, 437
  Favre returns to, 432a
  the rite of the Church of, 431
Val-Sainte, Charterhouse of, Dom Mamert Favre, prior of, 3 n. 11
Vatican II, 29 n. 57
  reference cited, 39 n. 78
Veilliard, Pierre (Swiss priest, Favre's schoolmaster). *See also* Jay, Claude; 165 n. 41, 190 n. 100, 190 n. 101, 353 n. 260
  background, 3 n. 12
  and Claude Jay, 14 n. 27
  Favre on, 3, 4
  remembered by Favre, 190 n. 100
  teaches Favre theology, 13a
Venice
  Alfonso Salmerón ordained deacon in, 15a
  and the Companions, 15a
  Companions ordained in, 15a
  Companions work in hospitals in, 16
Venlo, Treaty of, 49 n. 91
Verona, Bobadilla and Paschase (Broët) in, 17
Vicar of Christ, bishop of Rome as the, 358, 359
Vicenza, Favre, Ignatius, and Laínez in, 17
Villaret, Le. *See* Le Villaret
Virgil, quoted, 134, 134 n. 272
Virgin of the Stairs, the church of the, 196, 196 n. 116
Visitation, feast of, 19, 23, 39, 40, 42, 43, 45, 346, 354, 356, 439
Vita Communis. See Common Life, Brethren of the
Vitoria, Francisco de, O.P., 406a
Vittoria Colonna. *See* Colonna, Vittoria
Vogelsang, 338 n. 240

• W •

"White Ladies," convent of, in Cologne, 368
  Augustinian religious, 368 n. 11
Wied, Hermann von (cardinal-archbishop). *See also Book of Reformation*
  breaks promises, 362a
  plans reform, 362a
  says Mass in German, 362a
  a would-be reformer, 362a
William II, duke of Bavaria, 20a
Wischaven, Cornelius, background, 364a

Wischaven, Cornelius (nephew of the former), 366, 366 n. 7
Wittenberg in Saxony
  Favre prays for, 33, 31 n. 65
  Favre prays for the Lutheran capital of, 31 n. 65
  and Luther's theses on indulgences, 203a
Word of God, 135, 253, 343
world
  created, 318
  in negative sense, 69
  in neutral sense, 189
Worms. *See also* 19a
  collapse of Colloquy of, 20a
  Colloquy of, 15a, 20
  Favre against such colloquies while at, 20 n. 36

Favre departs from, 24 n. 48
worship, and earliest reformers, 266, 266 n. 77, 284, 347, 349–350, 352,

• X •

Xavier, Francis, St. *See also* 47 n. 86, 400 n. 6
  joins Ignatius, 14a, 15
  recommends Doménech in a letter to Favre, 19 n. 32
  retreat postponed, 14a, 15
  at Sainte-Barbe, 6a

• Z •

Zwingli, Huldreich, Swiss reformer, 16

INDEX TO THE INTRODUCTION, AND TO SELECTED LETTERS AND INSTRUCTIONS

Note: In the index below, numbers **appearing alone** indicate **page numbers** in this volume; numbers followed by an **n.** (for example, 375 n. 10) indicate **pages** and **footnotes** appearing on those pages, in this instance, footnote 10 on page 375.

• A •

Adam, Jean, 21 n. 47
Agricola, Rudolphus, 20
Alcalá, 31, 384
Alexander VI, Pope, 5 n. 10
Alfonso, Alvaro, 330, 340, 363, 364
Ambrosio, Fray, 385
angel(ology), 2, 42–48, 321, 329, 341, 349, 367, 382, 387
apostolate for souls, active, vs. chanting the Gospel, 354
    better serves the glory of God, 355
    Favre urges active apostolate, 355
Aragón, Juan de, 339, 340
Aristotle, 11
Avicenna, 369 n. 5

• B •

Barcelona, 384
Barthélemy, Jacques, 21
Bembisina, 369 n. 5
Bembitarus, 369 n. 5
Ben Beithar, 369
Benoit, Jean, O.P., 21, 21 n. 47
Biel, Gabriel, 15 n. 31
    and nominalism, 14, 21
Black Death, 6
Bobadilla, Nicolás, 27, 28, 334
Boethius (Roman statesman and philosopher), 20
Borgia, Francis, 54
Brandenburg, Albert of, 29
Brethren of the Common Life, 10
Broët, Paschase, 19
Bucer, 386
Buchanan, George, 12 n. 25

• C •

cabalism, 7 n. 13
Cáceres, 326
Calvin, John, 33
Campeggio, Cardinal, 7, 7 n. 14
Canisius, Peter, S.J., 345, 361, 362, 364, 365, 381
    and Favre, 30, 45, 48, 52
    his property devoted to religious purposes only, 362
    virtues of, 345
Canisius, Peter, S.J., vocation of, 361
    Favre's role in, 361
    Favre's unselfish interest in, 362
Carafa, Cardinal Gian Pietro, 19 n. 41
Carlos, Don, 376
Carolo, Esteban, 43
Castile, 384
Castro, Alonso de, 385
Celano, Thomas de, 35 n. 75
Certeau, Michel de, 50
Cervini, Cardinal, 385
Charles V, Emperor, 26
Christian Life Communities, 39 n. 86
Clénard, Nicolas, 368, 369
Cochlaeus (Dobnenek), Johann, 42
Codazzo, Pietro, 319
Codure, Jean, 19
Coimbra, 31, 371, 373, 378
    blessings upon scholastics at, 374, 375
    longing of scholastics for Favre, 373
    love for scholastics at, 373
Cologne, 30, 340, 343-345, 347, 350, 351, 354, 355, 356, 361, 365, 381, 385
consolation, Favre's, at the death of

431

consolation, Favre's *(continued)*
   King John III's daughter
     God brings good out of everything, 376
     virtues of the deceased, 376, 377
Constitutio of 1524, 7
Contarini, Cardinal, 28, 29, 37, 325
Cornibus, Pierre de, 21
Counter-Reformation
   in Bohemia, 5
   in France, 6
   in Germany, 6
   and relic hunting, 6
   and superstition, 6, 7

• D •

danses macabres, 34
Devotio moderna. See New Devotion
difficulties, spiritual, in midlife, 351, 353
   grace leads to advances, 354
   Holy Spirit the only guide, 353
   need for preparations before advancing, 352
   need for spiritual fundamentals, 352
   sloth impedes progress, 354
   vices impede progress, 354
discernment of spirits, 45
   rules for, 46
Doménech, Jerónimo, 25, 319
Duchâteau, Lambert, 355, 364

• E •

Eck, Johann, 37
Erasmus, Desiderius
   and Christian Antiquity, 13
   influence of, 13, 20
   recollections of University of Paris, 12
Estrada, Francisco, 320
Évora, 31, 368, 373
exorcism, 45

• F •

Farnese, Cardinal Alessandro, 28
Faustus, Dr. George (John), 35 n. 76
Favre, Dom Mamert, 10
Favre, Jean, 55
Favre, Pierre, S.J., 385-387, 389
   and the apostolate, 32, 38, 41
   best at giving the Exercises, 41
   and bad spirits, 44, 47
   consolation on the death of Maria, daughter of John III, 376-378
   death of, 31, 53, 55
   devotion to guardian angels, 43
   and discernment of spirits, 45, 47
   early influence of Ignatius upon, 17
   early life and traits, 9
   early ministry, 25, 26
   emotional characteristics of, 33
   and freedom of the will, 44
   his idea of reform, 13
   his letters and instructions, 51-53
   his principles for discernment, 46
   and ill health, 31
   and illuminism, 45
   knowledge of Protestantism, 39
   makes the thirty-day Exercises, 18
   ministry at Galapagar, 27
   ministry at Trent, 29
   parents of, 8
   as a pilgrim, 24, 31
   reputation as a saint, 32
   role of spirits in the world, 42
   at Sainte-Barbe, 10
   student of theology, 18
   subjective experiences, 23
   success at Cologne, 30
   superior of his companions, 19
   as a university student, 15, 19
   at Worms, 26
Favre, Pierre, S.J., apostolate of
   advisor of bishops, 339
   hindered by frequent transfer to different cities, 339
   hopes for a good spiritual crop, 349
   meager results of, 325
   methods followed during, 319
   need for prayers of others, 355, 373
   opposition from others, 335, 365
   practice of obedience to Ignatius therein, 334
   practice of obedience toward a cardinal, 334
   spiritual activities, 334, 339, 363
   Spiritual Exercises, 319, 335, 339, 364
   spiritual fruits of, 319, 336, 347-349
   vocational counseling, 364
Favre, Pierre, S.J., consolation offered

to King John III on death of his daughter, Maria
bitter medicine is best, 376
God brings good out of everything, 376
God's will be done, 377
personal sorrow of Favre, 376
raise one's spirits to higher thoughts, 377
reflections on the virtues of the deceased, 377
Favre, Pierre, S.J., methods employed for reformation
basic principles, 36
conciliation, 35
interior reform, 38
pastoral work, 39
rebuilding or restoration, 40
Ferrão, Bartolomeu, 383 n. 8
Francis Xavier, 11, 53
roommate of Favre, 15
fraternal charity, Favre's means toward, 330
acknowledging one's lack of virtue, 331
asking pardon of those harshly judged, 331
avoiding harsh judgment of others, 331
awareness of evil in one's own soul, 331
contemplatation of divine things, 333
distrust of one's own judgment, 331
ignoring faults of others, 331
peace and unity of hearts, 330
sacrifice of one's own will, 331
striving toward virtues, 332
union with the Society, 330
war against self-will, 333
friendship, Favre's aids toward spiritual, 373
Christ, mediator between God and man, 374
clinging to Jesus alone, 373
cultivation of interior senses, 374

• G •

Gonçalves da Camâra, Luis, 33 n. 72
Gou, Antonio, 384
Gouveia, Diogo de, 12, 21 n. 47, 326

Granvelle (imperial chancellor), 40 n. 90
Great Schism, 6
Gregory, St., 357
Groote, Gerhard, 10

• H •

Heeze, Mynheer van, 355
Helding, Michael, 29, 339
heretics, Favre's recommended manner of dealing with
charity to be used, 37, 379
cultivation of virtues leads to faith, 380
elimination of vices first, 379
emphasis on elements held in common, 37, 344, 379
exhortation of others to influence heretics, 345
need for exhortations toward better morals, 380
need for good example, 346
performance of good works leads toward faith, 380
practice of good overcomes errors, 344
proper attitude of heart in, 379
sinful practices led to loss of faith, 380
Herp (Harphius), Hendrik, O.F.M., 10, 30 n. 67
Herrera, Francisco de, 385
Hildesheim, 350

• I •

Ibn Sina, 369
Ignatius of Loyola, 54, 333, 339
and discernment of spirits, 45
as a university student, 16
Ile aux Vaches, sports at, 12
illuminism, 45
Imitation of Christ, 10 n. 21
India, 363
Infantas, Favre's ministry to the, 28
Inquisition
and Ignatius, 16, 19 n. 41
and the Exercises, 41 n. 95
suspicious of *Alumbrados,* 55

• J •

Jacoba, Lady, 320
Jay, Claude, 19, 27, 28, 383, 884

John III, king of Portugal, 375

• K •

Kalckbrenner, Gerhard, 30, 30 n. 67, 36, 38, 343, 343, 351, 385
  appreciation of his charity and goodness, 343
  common spiritual needs, 343
  esteem for his prayers, 343, 351
  spiritual friendship with, 350
Kessel, Leonhard, 48

• L •

La Peña, Juan de, tutor of Favre, 15, 20, 21
La Puente, Luis de, 48
labors, excessive, require courage, not relief, 378
Laínez, Diego, 24, 31, 41, 320, 379, 383
  death of his father, 383
  Favre's letters of consolation to relatives, 384
  Favre' sympathies, 384
  Masses offered, 384
  urged to write to his own relatives, 384
Laura, Lady, 320
Laurent, Thomas, 21 n. 47
Le Reposoir, monastery of, 10, 347
  signs of increasing perfection at, 347
Le Villaret. *See* Villaret, Le
Lefèvre d'Etaples, Jacques, 20 n. 45
Liège, 364
Louvain, 30, 364
Ludolph of Saxony, 10
Luther, Martin, 33, 386

• M •

Madrid, 27, 31, 378, 379, 381
Mainz, 29, 339, 340, 343, 344, 347, 351
Maria, daughter of King Juan III, 375
Marian congregations, 39
Mascarenhas, Doña Leonor, 334
Meaux, Circle of, 20
Melan, inquiries about sisters there, 349
Melanchthon, 386
Mellinato, Giuseppe, 51
Memoriale
  Favre's general spiritual progress traced in, 4
  function of dialogue in, 3
  history of the text, 48, 49
  literary structure of, 2
  purpose of, 2, 3
  as spiritual diary or spiritual biography, 1
Mercurian, Everard, 54
Miona, Master, 326
Miranda, Bartolomé Carranza de, 385
Montaigu, Collège de, 11, 20
Morone, Cardinal Giovanni, 27, 28, 333, 334

• N •

Nadal, Jerónimo, S.J., 340
Nantua, Favre's imprisonment at, 27
New Devotion *(Devotio moderna)*, 6, 10
New Way *(Via moderna)*, 14
Nijmegen, 361
nominalism
  doctrine of, 21, 22, 34
  and the New Way, 14
  voluntarist and extrinsecist, 23

• O •

obedience, Favre's aids toward attaining, 371
  avoidance of criticizing faults of others, 372
  imitation of Christ's obedience, 371
  openness to new commands, 371
  preserving blindness of, 371
  preserving earlier good motivations, 372
  willingness to sacrifice the better course, 372
Ocaña, 28, 31
Ockhamism, and Favre, 21
Orlandini, 48
Ortiz, Doctor Pedro, 19 n. 41, 25

• P •

Paris, 323
Parma, 25, 31, 41, 319, 321
pastoral care, 357
Peña, Juan de la. *See* La Peña, Juan de
penance, sacrament of, Favre's advice on its administration, 356

advice on prayer, 359
advice with intractable sins, 357
attitude toward material goods to be explored, 358
attitudes toward one's state of life to be explored, 357
caution regarding sins of the flesh, 357
dealing with backsliders, 360
dealing with temptations, 360
encouragment toward good resolutions, 358
gentleness with penitents, 360
kind of penances to assign, 359, 360
occasions of sins to be avoided, 357
performance of necessary restitution, 358
permission to receive Holy Communion, 361
possible sins against faith, 358
questions regarding penitent's obligations, 357
questions to be asked of penitent, 356
self-abuse to be warned against, 357
tepidity to be warned against, 357
perfection, pursuit of
earlier states of perfection to be forgotten, 370
value of humble service, 370
values of late-in-life conversion, 369
Périssin, Dom Claude, 10, 40, 347
Peter Lombard, 15
Philosophia Christi (Erasmus's), 13
Picart, François, 21
pilgrimage, F's instructions for those making a
careful planning and reflection needed, 342
concern for interior woes, 340
invocation of angels and saints during, 341
need to edify consciences of others, 341
patience with learning the basics, 342
regard for God's gifts, 342
robustness of mind needed, 340
simplicity and goodness needed, 342
thinking well of strangers during, 341
words to nourish the mind, 341
Poën, Hermes, 384
Portugal, 384
Postel, Guillaume, his communication with the dead, 368, 369
Pre-Reformation Europe, 5
Pflug, Julius von, 29, 29 n. 66, 339

• R •

Ratisbon (Regensburg), 26, 28, 37, 38, 323, 326
Regensburg. *See* Ratisbon
Reiffenberg, 48
Reposoir, monastery of. *See* Le Reposoir
Reuchlin, Johann, 7 n. 13
Ribadeneira, Pedro, 48
Rodrigues, Simâo, 32
Rome, 383
Ruysbroeck, 10

• S •

Sainte-Barbe, Collège de, 10
humanism at, 10, 12, 13
studies at, 12, 16
Saint-Jean-de-Sixt, 8
Sales, St Francis de, 55
Salmerón, Alfonso, 383, 384
Santacruz, Martín, 378
Savoy, 8, 27, 55, 347
Confraternity of the Holy Spirit in, 8
Le Villaret, 8, 9
Saint-Jean-de-Sixt, 8
Schmalkalden Articles, 37
Scotus, Duns, 14, 14 n. 30
self-reformation, Favre's means toward, 326
avoidance of vices, 329
daily examination of conscience, 327, 348, 365
exhorting others toward perfection, 329
general confession, 327
pious exercises, 367
preparation for Communion, 366
preparation for Mass, 348
preparation for prayer, 329, 348
regular reception of the Holy Eu-

self-reformation, the Eucharist *(continued)*
  charist, 327, 366
  review of past life, 366
  spiritual axioms, 367
  study of the catechism, 328, 367
  topics for prayer, 328
  topics for reflection, 329
Sentences of Peter Lombard, 15
Sforza, Guido Ascania, 320 n. 1
Silva, Fernando de, 334
Sissa, 320
sixteenth century
  and angelology, 42
  weakness of the Catholic side during, 37
sixteenth century, popular attitudes during
  fear of death, 34
  fear of the devil, 35
  invocation of the saints, 34
  skepticism, 34
Soto, Pedro de, 385
Speyer, 1, 26, 27, 38, 330, 333, 334, 346
spiritual life, Favre's methods to attain a true
  avoiding lukewarmness, 344
  avoiding vanities in reading matter, 348
  invoking power of the Spirit, 350
  looking toward the eternal reward, 349
  need for growth in, 344
  possessing an energetic spirit, 343
  prayers at Mass, 322
  prayers for spiritual devotion, 348
  regular confession and Communion, 322
  regular daily prayer, 321
  seeking God alone, 323
  spiritual Communion, 322
  spiritual exercises, 321
Standonck, Jan, 11, 20
studies of scholastics, Favre's advice regarding
  Christ the way and truth during, 324, 325
  goal to be pursued during, 324
  right intention during, 324
  the cross, intermediary means during, 325

• T •

Tabiano, 320
teachings, spiritual, of Favre, 385
  compassion for the miserable, 385
  desire for the reformation of others, 386
  drawing spiritual fruit from all experiences, 340
  encouragement to a good life, 386
  gratitude for health enjoyed, 387
  importance of strict obedience, 390
  love of the Blessed Virgin, saints, and angels, 387
  means to avoid temptations, 388
  need for pure intention, 388
  need for wisdom, 388
  obedience to the rule, 388
  recollection and use of sacraments, 388
  recollection of the Lord in glory, 386
  role of temptations, 388
  use of virtue to drive out vices, 389
  virtues of Favre as inspiration for our own lives, 389
  works of mercy, 386
  zeal for mercy, not justice, 385
Theatines, 19 n. 41
Thomas, St., 324
Thônes, 9
Toledo, 28, 330
Trent, Council of, 383
  Favre at the, 29
Trier, 350
Truchsess von Waldburg, Cardinal Otto, 28, 335

• U •

University of Paris, 11, 323, 368
  center of nominalism, 14
  daily life at, 12
  study of arts at, 11

• V •

Valencia, 384
Valladolid, 31, 375, 384
Van den Berg, Wendelina, 361
Vauvert, monastery at, 10
  influence upon Favre and companions, 18
Velliard, Pierre, 9, 16
Venice, Protestantism in, 33

Verdun, 330
Via antiqua, 14
Via moderna. See New Way
Villaret, Le, 8, 9
Vishaven, Cornelis. *See* Wischaven, Cornelius
Vitelleschi, Mutius, 56
vocation, religious, perseverance, in 381
  evil effects of failure to persevere, 381
  motives for perseverance in, 382
  temptations to abandon one's vocation not to be heeded, 383
von Wied, Hermann, 30

● **W** ●

waste of time, Favre's, 375
Wauchope, Robert, 21, 28, 326, 330
William of Ockham, 14
  and nominalism, 14
Wischaven, Cornelius, 45, 354, 356
workers, need for learned, in the apostolate, 326
Worms, 26, 37, 344
  center of Lutheranism, 26

● **X** ●

Xavier, Francis, 363

● **Z** ●

zero, function of, 370